Shakespeare in Canada:
'a world elsewhere'?

Edited by DIANA BRYDON and
IRENA R. MAKARYK

Shakespeare in Canada:
'a world elsewhere'?

UNIVERSITY OF TORONTO PRESS
Toronto Buffalo London

© University of Toronto Press Incorporated 2002
Toronto Buffalo London
Printed in Canada

ISBN 0-8020-3655-4

Printed on acid-free paper

National Library of Canada Cataloguing in Publication

Main entry under title:

Shakespeare in Canada : a world elsewhere / edited by
Diana Brydon and Irena R. Makaryk.

Includes bibliographical references and index.
ISBN 0-8020-3655-4

1. Shakespeare, William, 1564–1616 – Stage history – Canada.   2. Shakespeare
William, 1564–1616 – Appreciation – Canada.   3. Shakespeare William,
1564–1616 – Criticism and interpretation.   4. Shakespeare William,
1564–1616 – Adaptations.   5. Theater – Canada – History.   I. Brydon,
Diana   II. Makaryk, Irena R. (Irena Rima), 1951–

PR3109.C3S44 2002   822.3'3   C2002-901888-9

University of Toronto Press acknowledges the financial assistance to
its publishing program of the Canada Council for the Arts and the
Ontario Arts Council.

This book has been published with the help of a grant from the Humanities
and Social Sciences Federation of Canada, using funds provided by the
Social Sciences and Humanities Research Council of Canada.

University of Toronto Press acknowledges the financial support for
its publishing activities of the Government of Canada through the
Book Publishing Industry Development Program (BPIDP).

Contents

List of Illustrations ix

Preface xi
DIANA BRYDON AND IRENA R. MAKARYK

Introduction: Shakespeare in Canada: 'a world elsewhere'? 3
IRENA R. MAKARYK

Part One: Beginnings: Institutionalizing Shakespeare 43

1 Pioneer Shakespeare Culture: Reverend Henry Scadding and His Shakespeare Display at the 1892 Toronto Industrial Exhibition 47
HEATHER MURRAY

2 The Imperial Theme: The Shakespeare Society of Toronto, 1928–1969 66
KAREN BAMFORD

3 'A Stage for the Word': Shakespeare on CBC Radio, 1947–1955 92
MARTA STRAZNICKY

4 Stratford and the Aspirations for a Canadian National Theatre 108
MARGARET GROOME

Part Two: Shakespeare on Stage 137

5 Shakespeare *Canadiens* at the Stratford Festival 141
C.E. McGEE

6 A National *Hamlet*? Stratford's Legacy of Twentieth-Century Productions   159
JESSICA SCHAGERL

7 'Le Re-making' of le grand Will: Shakespeare in Francophone Quebec   174
LEANORE LIEBLEIN

8 Learning to Curse in Accurate Iambics: Shakespeare in Newfoundland   192
PETER AYERS

9 Liberal Shakespeare and Illiberal Critiques: Necessary Angel's *King Lear*   212
MICHAEL McKINNIE

Part Three: Critical Debates and Traditions   231

10 Continuity and Contradiction: University Actors Meet the Universal Bard   235
ANTHONY B. DAWSON

11 Canadian Bacon   255
PAUL YACHNIN and BRENT E. WHITTED

12 Canada, Negative Capability, and *Cymbeline*   274
ALEXANDER LEGGATT

13 Frye's Shakespeare, Frye's Canada   292
L.M. FINDLAY

Part Four: Reimagining Shakespeare   309

14 Nation and/as Adaptation: Shakespeare, Canada, and Authenticity   313
DANIEL FISCHLIN

15 Undead and Unsafe: Adapting Shakespeare (in Canada)   339
MARK FORTIER

16 Normand Chaurette's *Les Reines*: Shakespeare and the Modern in the Alchemical Oven   353
LOIS SHERLOW

17 Othello in Three Times   371
RIC KNOWLES

Afterword: Relocating Shakespeare, Redefining Canada   395
DIANA BRYDON

Appendix: Research Opportunities in Canadian Shakespeare   410
JESSICA SCHAGERL

References   417

List of Contributors   455

Index   461

Illustrations

Scene from the 1981 Stratford Festival production of *Coriolanus*   2

The Shakespeare Society of Toronto, 1962   68

Lucy Peacock in the Stratford Festival production of *As You Like It*   147

Cartoon from the Chicago *Sun-Times*   149

David Jansen and Graham Abbey in the Stratford Festival production of *Two Gentlemen of Verona*   152

The Upper Canada College Hockey Team, 1917   154

'The Pulpit and the Stage,' by John William Bengough   411

Preface

DIANA BRYDON and IRENA R. MAKARYK

The first book-length study of Shakespeare in Canada, this volume brings insights from a little-explored archive to contemporary debates about the cultural uses of Shakespeare and what it means to be Canadian. Although Canada boasts a long history of Shakespearean productions and reception, including adaptations, literary reworkings, and parodies, this is the first sustained attempt to investigate the history and reception of Shakespeare in Canada and to outline Canada's contributions to Shakespeare studies. In the international dialogue now developing between Shakespeare and postcolonial studies, Canada occupies an unusual but fascinating position. This study addresses the local uses of 'Shakespeare' in embodying cultural value and creating communal identities both under empire and after its dissolution.

The book has been organized to address a series of interrelated questions. Is there a distinctly Canadian Shakespeare? What is the status and function of Shakespeare in various locations within the nation: at Stratford, on CBC radio, in regional and university theatres, and in Canadian drama and popular culture? How have these functions changed over time? What is the contribution of Canadian scholarship to Shakespearean criticism? To what extent has Canadian Shakespeare scholarship been influenced by Canadian national concerns? Can we posit a specifically Canadian reading or production of Shakespeare? How can we theorize Canadian adaptations of Shakespeare? The aim throughout is to consider how Shakespeare – variously conceived as cultural icon, exemplary script, or infinitely adaptable medium for local self-expression – has been repositioned by the changing demands of different groups within the Canadian nation. The integrated essay collection, a critical mode that has played a major role in the development of feminist, cultural materialist, new historicist, nationalist, and internationalist work on Shakespeare since the 1980s, may be particularly effective, as Peter Erickson argues, in announcing 'new intellectual directions' and expressing 'collective action' ('Afterword' 251). We hope that it functions as such here.

Our structure is roughly chronological, moving from Heather Murray's account of 'pioneer' Shakespeare culture in the late nineteenth century to Ric Knowles's interpretation of Canadian adaptations of *Othello* in the last three decades of the twentieth century. We conclude with a brief appendix identifying resources for further research. *Shakespeare in Canada* is at once the result of extensive collaboration and the beginning, we hope, of new investigations.

The editors would like to thank the Shakespeare Association of America for providing the opportunity to develop the initial ideas for this manuscript in a seminar setting. We are grateful to all participants in that original seminar for their contributions to this endeavour.

Diana Brydon owes special thanks to the Social Sciences and Humanities Research Council of Canada for support during the writing of this book, and especially for the funding that enabled us to work closely with Barbara Bruce, research and editorial assistant on the project, in preparing the manuscript for publication. Both of us wish to acknowledge the stellar work that Barb has done in helping to bring this project to fruition. Barb has been a meticulous and indefatigable editor and support during this final year of preparations, a third pair of eyes, a perceptive reader, and an inspired source of suggestions for improvement throughout.

The authors are grateful to the anonymous readers for the University Press and the Aid to Scholarly Publications Programme of the Humanities and Social Sciences Federation of Canada for their careful readings and helpful advice. The book owes much to their generosity and imagination. Diana Brydon thanks the J.B. Smallman Research Fund, Faculty of Arts, the University of Western Ontario, for a further grant in aid of publication, and the research funds attached to the Robert and Ruth Lumsden Chair for further research support and funding the index. Dean Kathleen Okruhlik has been hugely supportive throughout this project. Special thanks are owed to Dorothy Hadfield for preparing the index. And, finally, we are grateful to our editor, Suzanne Rancourt, to our copy editor, Curtis Fahey, and to Barbara Porter and the other staff at the University of Toronto Press for their part in making our vision a reality at last.

Shakespeare in Canada

Scene from the 1981 Stratford Festival production of *Coriolanus* by William Shakespeare. Directed by Brian Bedford. Designed by Desmond Heeley with Len Cariou as Coriolanus and Mervyn Blake as Menenius. Courtesy of the Stratford Festival Archives. Photo by Robert C. Ragsdale.

Introduction: Shakespeare in Canada: 'a world elsewhere'?

IRENA R. MAKARYK

'Shakespeare is "the most important playwright in Canada."'
– Mavor Moore, 'A Theatre for Canada' 247

In a play not often produced on the Canadian stage, the patrician Roman warrior and would-be consul Caius Martius, surnamed Coriolanus, is banished as much for his pride and insolence as for his refusal to perform. In a wonderfully vituperative passage, Coriolanus stands at the city gates and snarls at the Romans who have banished him. Turning the tables, he banishes *them* with these words: 'Despising, / For you, the city, thus I turn my back; / There is a world elsewhere' (3.3.133–5).

Is Canada/Corioles such a 'world elsewhere' – a haven for the immigrant? Or, is it, as Coriolanus tragically discovered, the same as the Old World left behind? Dismissing the ingratitude of his fellow Romans, Coriolanus seeks a new world that will glorify his warrior skills but finds, instead, the same betrayal and, ultimately, death. Shakespeare's *Coriolanus* plays out the dynamic and interdependent relationships between received and new traditions and alliances, society and the individual, private and political loyalties, the 'here' and the 'elsewhere.'

Simultaneously alluding to difference and sameness, the phrase 'a world elsewhere' is an apt metaphor for the position of Shakespeare in Canada, a variant of Northrop Frye's now commonplace phrase, 'Where is here?' – the question of cultural coordinates. Is Canada the Corioles of immigrants fleeing from somewhere else? And if Canada is the 'elsewhere,' where, then, is the 'centre'? Is Britain the locus of tradition and value? New York? Paris? Kyiv? Beijing? Or, is the centre, in fact, really here: in St John's, Vancouver, Toronto, Winnipeg, Edmonton? Shakespeare or Chaurette? How and where do the worlds of theatre, literature, value, politics, and nation intersect? These are the questions raised and scrutinized in the chapters of this volume and studied through the prism of Shakespeare, the most translated and discussed of all writers and yet a playwright who remains deeply connected to Britishness.

Since the early nineteenth century, in many parts of Europe, east and west, and throughout the world, Shakespeare has been intimately bound up with issues of cultural nationalism and colonialism, of the centrality and possibility of the classics and their relationship to local culture. The late twentieth century has been preoccupied with notions of a 'universal' Shakespeare that has so easily, it seems, permeated a myriad of cultures. Postcolonial critique in particular has attacked the notion of a transcendent Shakespeare able to speak across centuries and across continents. At the same time, political theorists have begun to reassess concepts and typologies of nationalism. In the international dialogue now developing between Shakespeare and postcolonial studies, Canada occupies the unusual but fascinating position of a First World settler colony with a multicultural national community, a high standard of living, and the persistent remnants of what Australians term a 'cultural cringe.' Like other contemporary studies of Shakespeare, this volume is concerned with the local uses of 'Shakespeare' in embodying cultural value and creating communal identities both under empire and in current conditions of globalization.

In Canada, nation-building continues to be an ongoing process: thinking and rethinking the relationship between individual and community, past and present, concepts of centre and of periphery. Building a theatrical culture requires a similar task of reconsidering and reconceiving relationships: among actor, audience, and playwright; expectation, convention, and innovation. The first question that arises is the central issue of repertoire: what models, what sources should be used to imagine the nation? If a society in the process of transformation rejects the immediate past, then to what/whose past does it look for models? What, in themselves, do these models suggest? Omit? Express? And, finally, two related questions: what does this society want to become, and how will that becoming be reflected in or embraced by its cultural projects?

As long ago as 1964, Herbert Whittaker, the *Globe and Mail* drama critic, opined that, in a then recent edition of a reference book about Shakespeare, the entry on Canadian Shakespeare not only was exceedingly brief but also began in 1949, making no reference to its lengthy genealogy ('Shakespeare'). Nor has the situation much improved since. Not even most Canadians are aware that Shakespeare has had a long and complex history north of the 49th parallel. Often employed as a bulwark against other 'undesirable' traditions or cultures, Shakespeare has also served in many other capacities: as protector and symbol of high art, as morally edifying theatre, as an ally of solid British values, and as a tool of anglicization, among others. He has been the subject of mockery, parody, rewriting, and, at times, simple indifference. In the twenty-first century, these roles are complicated by Shakespeare's relocation in an increasingly globalized world in which culture is commodified and homogenized. Today, Shakespeare is a formidable cultural force whose influence seems to show increasing strength rather than signs of waning. But it was not always thus. His authority and centrality are assisted by the combined forces of his entrenchment in the canons of high and low culture, of the literary academy, and of the often more boisterous stage. Reinforced by adaptations, rewritings, and especially parodies, Shakespeare reigns supreme as one of Canada's pre-eminent playwrights. But how unique a creation is Shakespeare north of the 49th parallel? Is Canadian Shakespeare an imitation or mere variant of its Anglo-American cousins? What is the place of Shakespeare in Canadian culture? In the Canadian mythos? Can a Canadian Shakespeare be possible if Canadians cannot agree on what 'Canadian' is or what a 'nation' is? And why Shakespeare, anyway? Scholars from across Canada look at these complex, related questions.

The impetus for this book, the first on Shakespeare in Canada, arose specifically out of a response to the 'Nationalist and Intercultural Aspects of Shakespeare Reception' Seminar at the Shakespeare Association of America meeting in 1994. Some of the most interesting papers at that seminar focused on or alluded to Shakespeare in Canada and to theoretical issues of postcolonialism, translation, performance, and interculturalism. But, during that discussion, Canadian Shakespeare was often generalized or subsumed under other national categories. Both American and British Shakespeareans seemed either to ignore Canadian Shakespeare in its various manifestations or collapse it into other categories: Stratford, Ontario's productions, and Northrop Frye became American phenomena. Thus, the idea of a Canadian Shakespeare project was born the way so many other Canadian cultural and political projects have been, as an oppositional gesture.

Because no single scholar could address the range of Shakespearean cultural 'work' in Canada, Diana Brydon and Irena Makaryk gathered together a distinguished team of scholars at the first seminar on Shakespeare in Canada in 1998 at the Shakespeare Association of America annual meeting. Selected papers from this session were extensively revised and many others invited to form the present book. The authors demonstrate the cross-fertilizing excitement currently transforming two separate areas of English: Shakespearean studies, especially the growing subfield examining Shakespeare and national cultures; and Canadian dramatic, literary, and cultural studies. Like the editors themselves, the contributors work within, and sometimes across, these disciplinary divisions. They come together in this volume to address a series of interrelated questions. Rather than developing a single line of argument, the book creates a space – much like the ideal Canadian nation – where different voices and perspectives may be heard and a variety of methodologies engaged. Reflecting the current status of academic discourse, the dominant voices here are those of postcolonial critique, although historical, feminist, archetypal, and New Critical approaches may also be found.

In the hitherto absence of any full-length study of Shakespeare in Canada, the historical introduction that follows necessarily takes on more than what is usually expected of its genre, contextualizing the chapters of this volume in a narrative of Shakespeare's fortunes, good and ill, in the territory that is now called Canada. Opening up entirely new and little-explored material, much of it archival, this book presents a rich ground deserving of further exploration.

'What's past is prologue'

Canadian theatrical history became the subject of serious scholarly interest only after the Second World War. Jean Béraud, Herbert Whittaker, Murray Edwards, Leonard Doucette, Ann Saddlemyer, Richard Plant, Don Rubin, Eugene Benson, L.W. Conolly, and Anton Wagner, among many others, have shown that, before the arrival of the Europeans, many theatrical activities took place in 'Canada,' although the great richness and complexity of the ritual dramas of the Ojibwa, Iroquois, Kwakiutl, Plains, and other First Nations were, until recently, considered of little consequence and as having no subsequent influence on English or French theatre. For their part, both the 'founding' nations, the French and the English, seemed to have been impelled to astonish the natives not only with material goods and technological advances but also with their own performance art. In retrospect, these first productions uncannily seem to proffer a model for future theatricals: out-of-doors performances with courtly or high-art connections. As early as Sir Humphrey Gilbert's 1583 expedition to Newfoundland, 'theatrical activities' took place on board ship and in what is now St John's, Newfoundland. The French, too, wished to delight and amaze the 'Sauvages.' In 1606 the historian and minor poet Marc Lescarbot celebrated the return of Samuel de Champlain and Sieur de Poutrincourt to Port Royal with his *Théâtre de Neptune en la Nouvelle-France*, an aquatic pageant-verse drama celebrating Neptune, which included in its cast of characters four 'Indians' (played by Frenchmen), who, uttering a few Amerindian words, paid feudal obeisance to Poutrincourt. A visible celebration of French imperial power in the New World and an attempt to make a case to King Henri IV for more intensive colonization, this outdoor pageant, like that of Sir Humphrey, seems to be the atavistic theatrical model to which Canadians continually return, even in this new century: many Shakespeare productions are still played by the sea, in parks, and by rivers in festivals across Canada, simultaneously a tourist attraction and a celebration of the all-too-brief Canadian summer, much-longed-for holidays, and the Bard.

'Good wombs': Shakespearean Genealogies

Two significant roots, British soldiers and foreign touring companies, form the basis of Canadians' familiarity with Shakespeare. After the Conquest (1763), soldiers garrisoned to keep the peace between French and English and to protect the citizens against American invasion engaged in theatrical productions both to relieve the tedium of garrison life and as a gesture of good will towards the local community. The military troupes of Halifax, Quebec City, Montreal, Kingston, London, Toronto, St John's, and Saint John, along with the gentry-elite amateurs of those centres, naturally turned to a repertoire with which they were most familiar. Of necessity, not out of an impulse to authenticity, officers performed both men's and women's parts. At first, local women rarely joined the officers on stage. Thus, a performance of *The Merchant of Venice* on 9 March 1830 in Kingston may have been recorded because of the novelty of two women of 'visible timidity' appearing on stage. Probably the limited talents of the military prevented much Shakespeare, but the officers' efforts did lay the foundation for what turned out to be an enduring and surprisingly robust tradition of amateur productions.

The earliest recorded anecdotal references to Canadian Shakespeare productions in English date from the 1760s and establish two related patterns that were to recur over the next two centuries: one, the visit of foreign, especially English, professionals (some of whom settled in Canada), who took over from native amateurs; and two, their arrival by way of the United States. An American Company of Comedians arrived in Halifax in 1768 to play *Catherine and Petruchio*, Garrick's brief, farcical version of *The Taming of the Shrew*, sparking a hot debate about the morality of theatre-going. This first small group of eleven actors – four couples (the Moores, Allens, Pinkstons, and Bentleys) and Messers Bellair, Duncan, and Warsdale – had arrived from England in New York before the American Revolution, afterwards making their way to loyalist Canada by way of Albany. Founding the Company of Comedians, the first professional English theatre company to settle in the province of Quebec played mostly English eighteenth-century comedy and tragedy. The Montreal *Gazette* recorded the city's warm welcome – at least by its English residents.

One of Shakespeare's major drawbacks, the absence of overt moralizing – a general problem for eighteenth-century taste and aesthetics – was compounded in Canada by, on the English side, its double foundation of Puritanism, derived from Scotland and New England; and, on the French, by the Catholic objection to 'lewd' theatricals. Although Canada has no place in Jonas Barish's magisterial study of the anti-theatrical tradition, it might have provided an interesting addition because of its unusually concentrated passion for wholesomeness, decorum, and didacticism, a passion prominently displayed in the newspapers of the time. In the Maritimes, for example, 'Anti-Thespis' inveighed against 'Theatricus' in a psychomachia – a medieval type of play where vice and virtue battled over the fate of Everyman – involving the salvation of the local inhabitants. The *Nova Scotia Chronicle and Weekly Advertiser* (January 1770) proclaimed that 'a Christian cannot with a safer Conscience enter into the Play-House than into a Brothel' (Benson and Conolly 6). Two years earlier, the *Nova Scotia Gazette* had explicitly linked Shakespeare to the general degradation of the local Maritime community: morals, pocketbooks, women, and natural resources, all would suffer from the experience of viewing Shakespeare:

> It's no great Compliment to think,
> Our morals with our Cash must sink
> When Shakespeare comes to Town;

> Or that our Farms and Fisheries all,
> Our Merchandise too, great and small,
> And Women must come down. (qtd. in Bains 11)

This firmly fixed, passionate, sincere, but unsophisticated anti-theatrical attitude obviated the need for a public censor until 1913. Unlike in Britain, in Canada religious disapproval was usually enough to prevent or curtail 'unpleasant' or 'inappropriate' productions.

Eighteenth-century accounts of Shakespeare productions are both brief and scarce but suggest in their descriptions of the peregrinations of actor-managers that many of these small companies were special pioneers in their own right, travelling, as Moore, Allen, and Bentley seem to have done, throughout many of the colonies. Before Albany and New York, Moore's small troupe had played in Jamaica with exactly the same repertoire, thus suggesting that the American, Canadian, and Caribbean colonies were created from a shared urban theatrical heritage (and by the occlusion of a Native tradition). *Henry IV, Hamlet, Richard III, The Merchant of Venice, Othello,* and *Catherine and Petruchio* were all played in 'Canada' in the eighteenth century by a combination of amateur, professional, or visiting professional actors. As Yashdip Bains has shown, in the sixty-year period 1765–1826, 'Canadians' saw seventeen of Shakespeare's plays: ten in 1786, fourteen in 1808, nineteen in 1818 and 1819, and fifty in 1826, with *The Taming of the Shrew* remaining the most popular of all (Bains 199). But Shakespeare was not uniformly admired. Atlantic Canada, despite its early introduction to Shakespeare, was not very receptive to him, its inhabitants preferring farce. Saint John's *Daily Telegraph* satirized the taste of the local inhabitants by reprinting an article from the Washington *Star* in 1891 that admonishes Mr Shakespeare:

> Mr. Shakespeare should have had the opportunity of submitting his Romeo and Juliet to a modern manager, who says: 'What the public wants is fun, see?' He would then have had the pleasure of rewriting his drama somewhat in accordance to the above idea. Romeo has just executed a song and dance, in which the Montagues and Capulets joined, making a scene of hilarity that was alone worth the price of admission. Romeo begins a serenade, enter the most intelligent trained dog in the profession today. Juliet, who is one of the handsomest ladies on the burlesque stage, and incidentally a queen of song and exponent of terpsichorean art, tries to rescue him, but he catches his waist-band on a nail in the porch and is suspended in statu quo or thereabouts while the curtain goes down amidst the

thundering plaudits of a delighted throng. There is no doubt that Shakespeare missed a great deal by being born too soon. (qtd. in Smith 132)

'Unworthy scaffold': Playhouses and Players

The absence of audiences sympathetic to the theatre was compounded by the lack of facilities to produce Shakespeare. Indeed, the acceleration of Shakespearean productions came with the building of permanent playhouses. As Murray Edwards has shown, most early theatres were extensions of drinking parlours with the stage usually upstairs (19). Perhaps because of the parlour's effects, once the audience made its way up, it could not always be counted on either to respond sympathetically (or soberly) to the theatrical production or to suspend willingly its disbelief. Some of these theatres still survive, such as that in Wakefield, Quebec; but, although the stage remains intact, the rest of the tiny theatre is now, appropriately, an antique shop. Plays were also produced in hotels, ballrooms (the first recorded professional performance of *The Taming of the Shrew* took place in Frank's hotel ballroom in Toronto, 1826), and other venues, such as the Theatre Royal (more title than reality) established in 1870 by the First Ontario Rifles in Winnipeg at the rear of a store.

Although writing about a much later period, Samuel Marchbanks (Robertson Davies) wittily described the central importance of the physical stage for the performance of Shakespearean plays, as well as for the development of a Canadian drama as a whole, in a letter to one Apollo Fishhorn, a would-be Canadian playwright of the twentieth century:

> You want to be a Canadian playwright, and ask me for advice as to how to set about it. Well, Fishhorn, the first thing you had better acquaint yourself with is the physical conditions of the Canadian theatre. Every great drama, as you know, has been shaped by its playhouse. The Greek drama gained grandeur from its marble outdoor theatres; the Elizabethan drama was given fluidity by the extreme adaptability of the Elizabethan playhouse stage; the French classical drama took its formal tone from its exquisite, candle-lit theatres. You see what I mean.
>
> Now what is the Canadian playhouse? Nine times out of ten, Fishhorn, it is a school hall, smelling of chalk and kids, and decorated in the Early Concrete style. The stage is a small, raised room at one end. And I mean room. If you step into the wings suddenly you will fracture your nose against the

wall. There is no place for storing scenery, no place for the actors to dress, and the lighting is designed to warm the stage but not to illuminate it.

Write your plays, then, for such a stage. Do not demand any procession of elephants, or dances by the maidens of the Caliph's harem. Keep away from sunsets and storms at sea. Place as many scenes as you can in cellars and kindred spots. And don't have more than three characters on the stage at one time, or the weakest of them is sure to be nudged into the audience. Farewell, and good luck to you. ('Theatre' 192)

Throughout the nineteenth century, smaller communities continued to rely on their own unique theatrical structures. Henry Irving's secretary recorded the dismal circumstances in which Irving acted in Quebec City, which had long been superseded by Montreal as a theatrical venue: 'The theatre here would make you shriek. It is a cross between a chapel and a very small concert room and the stage is about half the size of that of St. George's Hall. The entrance is being washed now, but no amount of soap and water will repair the broken windows. The kind of people who play here as a rule are of the least intellectual order – we found two members of the preceding troupe on the stage – they were *two hens!*' (qtd. in Edwards 11).

We are grateful to Herbert Whittaker for information about such curiosities as the Queen's Arctic Theatre, where Commander G.H. Richards of Her Majesty's Navy, as manager and proprietor, led a company that came 'from the Pole itself to present to the nobility and gentry of North Cornwall a *corps dramatique* unequalled in this or any other country in the first act of the *Tragedy of Hamlet*' (1852). In this production, a Mr. W. McArthur played the roles of both Hamlet and Ophelia (Whittaker, 'Shakespeare' 79).

In larger centres, such as Montreal and Toronto, however, economic growth enabled the building of 'opera houses,' which were more receptive to Shakespeare and, especially, Shakespearean actors. Elaine Nardocchio counts 'at least' twenty-five theatres in Montreal between 1804 and 1898 (8), but their repertoire (which included some Shakespeare) was frequently shaped by Americans.

If Shakespeare was viewed with opprobrium in the Atlantic provinces, in central and eastern Canada he was frequently imagined as a barometer of propriety and some intellectual pretension. Regularized, moralized, and unambiguous, adapted Shakespeare was thus often used to open theatres and suggest their standing as something more than frivolous entertainment. In Halifax, the American Addison B. Price opened his Fairbanks Wharf Theatre with *Richard III* (1816), followed by *Othello, The Merchant of Venice, Macbeth, The Tempest,* and *Hamlet* (Bains 72). The first permanent theatre in Montreal, an upper-storey warehouse remodelled by the Edinburgh-born Mr Ormsby, produced *Catherine and Petruchio* (1805). Seth Prigmore, an English actor who had played in the United States, later took over Ormsby's theatre and also opened with the same play in 1808, followed by *The Tempest*. In 1825 the first season of tragedian-manager Frederick Brown's Theatre Royal in Montreal presented *Richard III, Hamlet, The Merchant of Venice, Coriolanus,* and *King Lear.* In Toronto, the new Grand Opera House was launched in 1880 with *Romeo and Juliet.*

While the performance space was undergoing change, the upper-parlour spirit did not always vanish as quickly; it seems to have continued to infuse at least some members of the audience with impatience and, occasionally, wit. In 1859 Barry Sullivan appeared in Montreal playing Richard III. When, in the last scene of the play, Sullivan delivered the famous lines, 'A horse, a horse! My kingdom for a horse!' a man suddenly shouted from the gallery, 'Would an ass do?' 'Yes,' retorted the angry actor, 'Come to the stage door' (Middleton, 'Theatre' 5). Something of this spirit of a 'Wild West' still lingered even after Confederation. In 1868 Charles Fechter arrived in Toronto to play various parts in *Hamlet.* When, in the opening scene, Bernardo twice queried, 'Who's there?' and, when no reply was heard, a voice from the balcony shouted, 'Darned if I know. Go on with the play' (Middleton, 'Theatre' 6).

By the late 1860s, the Canada First Movement, a political but also literary movement, encouraged the building of large theatres almost exclusively in urban centres like Toronto, Montreal, and Winnipeg, playhouses that, in turn, brought touring companies and star actors. Canadian stages welcomed, indeed invited and wooed, a plethora of stars, beginning with Edmund Kean in Quebec (1826), who was lionized when he played Richard III, then Shylock and Othello, and later King Lear. Kean claimed to have mesmerized a group of Huron in his hotel room by reciting Shakespearean speeches for them from his bed. Made their honorary chief, he was given the name of Alanienoudet. In the late twentieth century, this episode in Kean's life would serve as the basis for Marianne Ackerman and Robert Lepage's eponymous play.

Kean was followed by his son, Charles, and then by many other famous actors, among them William Charles Macready, Charles and Fanny Kemble, Charles Fechter, Sarah Bernhardt (nine appearances between 1880 and 1917, including in Winnipeg and Calgary), Ellen Terry, Henry Irving, Tomasso Salvini, Ernesto Rossi, Edwin Booth, Coquelin, and Helen Modjeska, most of whom played in Quebec. American Shakespearean actors also made their way north. These included Edwin Forrest, John Barrymore, and John Wilkes Booth, who last played in Montreal shortly before he assassinated Abraham Lincoln. Many of these actors also toured extensively elsewhere, some, like Bernhardt, going as far as St Petersburg, Russia. If we cannot speak of a globalization of culture in the nineteenth century, we can, at least, suggest that European and North American commercial theatrical trends were not as far apart as might be imagined.

This multicultural mix of touring stars – Italian, French, and Polish as much as English and American – helped create the theatrical canon in Canada. For them, Shakespeare was a wonderful star vehicle. But, if Shakespeare added lustre to the star, the star also added lustre to Shakespeare. Booth, Bernhardt, and Irving, rather than Hamlet, attracted audiences. Accordingly, plays were cut and reshaped to fit around star performers. The most frequently produced were those plays that easily accommodated themselves to the demands of star actors: *The Taming of the Shrew*, *Othello*, *Richard III*, and *Macbeth*. While much applauded, the reliance on foreign imported theatre reduced the need for an indigenous theatre and paved the way for British and American commercial exploitation and cultural dominance. It also entrenched Shakespeare in the theatrical repertoire, associating his name with the names of great actors.

Again, however, not everyone flocked to Shakespeare. Maritimers failed to fill the auditorium to see Junius Brutus Booth, preferring the circus to *Hamlet*, a situation that persisted until recently, as Leslie Yeo's autobiography, *A Thousand and One First Nights*, reveals. Despite the fact that Newfoundland is geographically the closest of Canada's provinces to England and, politically, has maintained the longest ties to it (not joining Confederation until 1949), it has been the most immune to Shakespeare, as Peter Ayers points out in his contribution to this book, 'Learning to Curse in Accurate Iambics: Shakespeare in Newfoundland.' Notwithstanding an interesting beginning – the demanding lead of *Richard III* (1841) played by fourteen-year-old Jean Davenport – Shakespeare has been ignored or parodied more than he has been staged there.

Dramatically accelerating in the late nineteenth century, visits of touring actors and companies in other parts of Canada contributed to the image of Canada as a receiver, not a creator, of culture. Canadians generally accepted the long-standing English-American axis as a 'natural condition' and no cause for complaint (Middleton, 'Theatre' 4). Indeed, Canada was so dependent upon American ties for its theatre, that, at times when the relationship between the two countries was strained, as it was during the War of 1812, there was very little or no English theatre in Canada. By the second decade of the twentieth century, this state of affairs was wholeheartedly embraced by J.E. Middleton, who wrote that 'there is no Canadian Drama. It is merely a branch of the American Theatre, and let it be said, a most profitable one' ('Theatre' 8).

The decades leading up to the First World War were full of Shakespearean productions. *Hamlet, Othello, The Merchant of Venice, Coriolanus*, and *As You Like It* were all presented in abridged form, *Richard III* in Colley Cibber's version, and *Romeo and Juliet* in David Garrick's version with its surprise ending. Theatre-goers were also treated to Davenant and Dryden's *The Tempest*, which provides a sister for Caliban, a sister for Miranda, and a man, Hippolito, who has never seen a woman; a *Macbeth* filled with choruses of witches and dancers; Nahum Tate's version of *King Lear*, with its happy ending; and *A Midsummer Night's Dream* with its splendid 'Amazons' – dancing girls. But, most popular of all with audiences, if not with critics, was Garrick's farcial two-act *Catherine and Petruchio*. Generally, Canadians' preferences closely replicated those of the English (see, for example, Marder 278–9).

By the turn of the century, touring companies had also found an audience at the universities. Ben Greet's English Players performed *As You Like It* and *Comedy of Errors* on the residence gardens of the University of Toronto. Outdoor productions of *A Midsummer Night's Dream* and *As You Like It* took place at the University of Western Ontario in 1904 (Plant 340, 342). The years 1912–14 were the heyday of 'the Road.' Raymond Massey recalled that Christmas 1913 in Toronto included productions of *Hamlet, Romeo and Juliet,* and *Macbeth* (21). Touring companies extended themselves as far as Winnipeg and sometimes Calgary, bringing *Macbeth, King Lear, The Merchant of Venice, Julius Caesar,* and *Hamlet*.

While welcoming foreign actors, Canada also produced its own talent. Hamilton-born Julia Arthur was among the most successful entertainers on the road, others being Margaret Anglin and Agnes Booth. Anglin, a daughter of the then speaker of the House of Commons who was literally born in the chamber, went to the United States, where she played Ophelia to James O'Neill's Hamlet; in Australia, she played Kate and Viola; and she pioneered what the Montreal *Star* theatre critic S. Morgan-

Powell called the 'new style of mounting and setting Shakespeare ... with its dependence on rhythm of line and of lighting subtleties,' emphasis on textual exactitude, and ensemble work (35). But Anglin and Franklin McLeay, who became the leading man in Sir Herbert Beerbohm Tree's company, were also early examples of the general practice of Canadians obtaining their professional training – and fame – elsewhere, causing critics like Bernard K. Sandwell (editor and theatre critic of *Saturday Night*) to complain in 1911 that 'Canada is the only nation in the world whose stage is controlled by aliens' ('Annexation' 18).

'Wider still and wider': Societies and Universities

Until the middle of the nineteenth century, the absence of bookstores and libraries made it unlikely that, except for a small group of the gentry and officers, few people could actually read Shakespeare. Indeed, in 1831, the Halifax *Monthly Magazine* asserted that for the majority of the population, Shakespeare was 'in reality but little known, though greatly spoken of' (qtd. in Bains 197). Playtexts were difficult to obtain, and amateur players, in quest of texts, were often reduced to placing hopeful advertisements in newspapers.

However, Shakespeare was being read and discussed in small circles or societies that sprang up in the 1830s and 1840s. Ladies' clubs admired Shakespeare for his creation of strong female characters. Gentlemen extolled his pioneer-like spirit, which seemed to encourage a break with old ties and approve the quest for new endeavours. In her chapter below, 'Pioneer Shakespeare Culture: Reverend Henry Scadding and His Shakespeare Display at the 1892 Toronto Industrial Exhibition,' Heather Murray examines the life and work of one of Canada's first cultural critics, Reverend Henry Scadding. For Scadding, Shakespeare was 'virtually a type of the colonist,' a representative of the 'Mother Country,' who embodied the 'beaver instinct' of Canada and was thus a 'symbol of the continual westward movement of culture and community.'

Flourishing throughout Canada, not only in larger towns like Hamilton, Toronto, London, Montreal, and Vancouver but also in unexpected places like Napanee, Ingersoll, Owen Sound, and Cape Breton, Shakespeare clubs fulfilled many purposes, including fostering debating and rhetorical skills. Some, such as that in London, claimed to encourage drama and to promote 'rational amusement' but, in fact, never produced a Shakespearean play. Others linked themselves with larger cultural and political projects: Anna (of *The King and I* fame) Harriette Leonowens (born Edwards) founded a Shakespeare Society in Halifax but also a book club, a woman's suffrage association, and the Victoria (later the Nova Scotia) School of Art and Design.

Later incarnations, such as the Shakespeare Society of Toronto, the focus of Karen Bamford's contribution to this volume – 'The Imperial Theme: The Shakespeare Society of Toronto, 1928–69' – were frequently dominated by women who organized social events, such as teas and annual dinners but were associated with and led by the (male) political, business, and academic elite. They celebrated Shakespeare's birthday; organized reading groups, competitive recitations, and public lectures; produced his plays; and proudly displayed their loyalty to the old empire. Under the presidency of G. Wilson Knight (1934–8), then professor of English at Trinity College, University of Toronto, the Society's productions reached new heights. Knight directed *Romeo and Juliet, Hamlet, Henry VIII, Othello, The Tempest,* and *1 Henry IV*, reverting to Shakespeare's 'original intentions,' that is, using minimalist staging and fluid scene changes and thus anticipating two significant features of the future Stratford Theatre Festival. The Shakespeare Society also staged productions at the Art Gallery of Ontario and the Toronto Central Library. In Montreal, the Shakespearean Society of the 1940s staged *Much Ado about Nothing, King Lear,* and *Romeo and Juliet.* In the cast were soon-to-be-notables such as Christopher Plummer, Leo Ciceri, and John Colicos. Focusing on simplicity of staging, speed, and narrative, like the Toronto and Queen's societies, the Montreal group also hoped to replicate the conditions of the Elizabethan stage.

In western Canada, a former head of the Toronto Conservatory's elocution department took up the 'mission' of 'preaching' Shakespeare by performing him 'at every chance' and 'with great success' (Robson 13). For Frederic Robson, writing in the *Canadian Magazine* in 1908, this was necessary, messianic work. Shakespeare was a mark of solid, natural intelligence – hearty fare for virtuous farmers. 'Of the people,' the Bard was opposed to the 'pampered' and effeminate urbanites. Robson observed that 'it may strike the reader as very strange that the greatest dramatic works ever written, those of William Shakespeare, which would seem to require a trained mind to fathom them, are scorned as uninteresting in the best educated centres of Ontario, while they are taken up with eagerness by the farmers of the West and the miners of the Canadian mountain towns' (12–13). Attacking the 'namby-pamby' townspeople for their desire for 'novelty,' Robson castigated them for their distance 'from rock bottom primitive virtues ... from simplicity of thought' (13). In this western view, then, Shakespeare, was healthier, simpler, moral fare: he was primitive yet bracing, good for one's moral fortitude. Robson explained Shakespeare's popularity in the prairies by suggesting that the inhabitants' independence of thought made the Bard congenial to them:

> Was it not that the quiet customed people of the prairies and mountain towns, with loves and hates unfettered by imitation of others or what others did or said or had ever done, felt that in *Hamlet*, for instance, was given them a lens whereby their eyes beheld the philosophy of their own lives? Would it not be accurate to say that the peasant, full-blooded and with good intelligence, might gain vastly more from Shakespeare than the prince of keener intellect, but more pampered tastes? That is why Shakespeare 'goes' in the west of Canada and the south and west of the United States while it falls flat in the middle districts; and these same middle districts of both countries generally claim a fair preponderance of discrimination and fair taste. (13)

By the mid-nineteenth century, a wider assimilation of Shakespeare came through the establishment of a provincial public education system, as Heather Murray's book *Working in English* suggests. Both at the newly created universities and outside them, in such institutions as the Margaret Eaton School of Literature and Expression (founded in 1907), Shakespearean excerpts (later plays) were often taught in conjunction with rhetorical studies in the freshman year. Students would also encounter Shakespeare in subsequent years as part of their study of Elizabethan literature. Eventually, Shakespeare migrated to the second-year level, where he became and remained the subject of separate course study. Mid-century, the first course on Shakespeare was offered by W.J. Alexander in Toronto on the comedies of Shakespeare, although some Shakespeare had already been taught by a historian, Sir Daniel Wilson, in the 1840s. By the 1860s, Canada led the way for the United States and Britain: Shakespeare became the keystone of the honours undergraduate program of McGill (Hubert 102), and soon of all other universities across Canada, where he was admired for his uplifting ideas and moral values.

Serious literary scholarship was slim, although public lectures on Shakespeare occurred with some frequency, including by the previously mentioned Reverend Henry Scadding, who gave the lecture 'Shakespeare the Seer' on the occasion of Shakespeare's birthday in 1864. Among early works about Shakespeare are Sir Daniel Wilson's *Caliban, the Missing Link* (1873), W.F. Osborne's *The Genius of Shakespeare and Other Essays* (1908), and A.W. Crawford's *Hamlet, an Ideal Prince* (1916). Studies of Shakespeare also include Canadian participation in the authorship issue. Paul Yachnin and Brent Whitted's witty piece in this volume, 'Canadian Bacon,' describes the historical background to the story of the one-hundred-year-old authorship issue in Canada, a milder yet more ironic variant of the British and American controversy.

International recognition for Canadian literary scholarship did not come until after the Second World War. One of the most prolific scholars, the British-born G. Wilson Knight, who taught at the University of Toronto for nearly a decade, published a series of important books on Shakespeare, the poet of 'royalism.' Among his best-known studies are *The Wheel of Fire* (1949), *The Imperial Theme* (1954), and *The Crown of Life* (1961). It was, however, the voluminous theoretical, interpretive, cultural, and editorial work of native-born Northrop Frye that gained wide acclaim for Canadian Shakespeare studies. Beginning with his *Anatomy of Criticism* (1957), the most influential book on genre of the twentieth century, Frye frequently used Shakespeare to work through his theories about literature. His *Fables of Identity* (1963), *A Natural Perspective* (1965), *Fools of Time* (1967), and numerous essays have made him a towering presence in Shakespearean and in Canadian cultural studies. In his chapter below, 'Frye's Shakespeare, Frye's Canada,' L.M. Findlay argues that Frye's preference for Shakespearean romance and comedy stems not only from his commitment to Christianity as a divine comedy but also from his commitment to Canada as a liberal democracy.

Other notable Canadian Shakespeareans followed, some of whom, like Frye, were critics and editors with connections to the University of Toronto: among them, Clifford Leech, F.D. Hoeniger, George Hibbard, Marion B. Smith, Sheldon P. Zitner, Alexander Leggatt, and many others. While edited and interpreted, Shakespeare was studied as poet rather than dramatist until the second half of the twentieth century. The shift was signalled by the creation of the first chair of drama in 1945, at the University of Saskatchewan (also the first such chair in the commonwealth); other departments of drama across Canada soon followed.

As elsewhere, so in Canada, the four hundredth anniversary of Shakespeare's birth brought forth a 'flood of words,' the consequences of which, McMaster University's B.W. Jackson observed, suggested that

'Shakespeare might once again die of a surfeit.' But 'happily ... Shakespeare survived the adulation' (Foreword vi). Writing in the same volume as Jackson, Herbert Whittaker proudly observed that Canada now had at Stratford a 'proper means for the celebration' of Shakespeare's genius. Using the language of the marketplace, he observed that Shakespeare's 'gift to the world's stages has multiplied in value' and brought together nations 'divided on all other matters' ('Shakespeare' 71).

'Imaginary puissance': Shakespeare, Amateurs, and a National Theatre

At the end of the nineteenth century, some of the first voices were heard expressing the need for an indigenous Canadian drama and a national theatre. The previously cited Frederic Robson, who found Shakespeare in the prairies so bracing, also argued that 'Shakespeare should have no monopoly of the theatre. No, let us breed more Shakespeares, and to do that the stage should be open to every playwright so long as his ideas are good and his purpose sound' (15). On the eve of the First World War, in an article entitled 'The Annexation of Our Stage,' Sandwell complained that Canadian arts were administered from foreign soil and the works sent to Canada were always about life among the leisured classes (19), a topic alien to the interests of many Canadians. Neither British nor American, Canadians, Sandwell argued, are 'evolutionaries': their life is separate but not apart from the old, yet also unrelated to the American political revolutionary experiment (19).

In the middle of the Great War, on 12 November 1916, the grandly named Canadian National Theatre opened in Ottawa at the Victoria Memorial Museum. Arthur Beverly Baxter exclaimed in *Maclean's Magazine* that 'this war has made the Canadian National Theatre not only possible but imperative' (38). Yet, expressions of the birth of a national consciousness – even if these meant not separation but equality with the British within the context of the empire – were still premature: the Drama League in charge had its headquarters in the United States and the English director/playwright/actor Harley Granville-Barker was called in to perform the opening ceremonies – a clear indication that Canadian sentiments about a national theatre had not yet found their practical or full realization, despite the growing strength of the amateur theatre.

Just as the visits of touring companies began to dwindle, amateur groups rushed to fill the void. Beginning with the officer class in the eighteenth century, amateur theatre continued to have elitist British associations. In 1907 the governor general, Earl Grey, initiated the Earl Grey Music and Dramatic Trophy Competition to encourage amateur groups. Around the same time, The Arts and Letters Club Players of Toronto was founded, and they, as well as the Masseys, became part of the impetus behind the creation of one of the most perfectly equipped little theatres in North America, Hart House Theatre at the University of Toronto (1919), which intended to be more of an 'art' than a university theatre. Although not opening the first season, Shakespeare was produced within the first three years: *Love's Labour's Lost* (a Canadian premiere) and *The Tempest*, with many of the sets produced and lighting problems solved by those quintessential Canadians, the Group of Seven's Arthur Lismer, Lawren Harris, A.Y. Jackson, and J.H. MacDonald. Also produced at Hart House was *Cymbeline*, a play discussed below by Alexander Leggatt in 'Canada, Negative Capability and *Cymbeline*.' In a genuinely new reading of the play, Leggatt argues that Shakespeare may be perceived as an honorary Canadian; there is something in his negative capability and internal variety that responds both to our political situation (in finding compromises and creative evasions) and to our cultural diversity.

Hart House was made available to students and to amateurs such as the Shakespeare Society of Toronto. Among the scholars associated with that group was, once again, G. Wilson Knight, as director and as actor – 'remembered for his Caliban' (Whittaker, 'Shakespeare' 81). By the late 1940s, university productions had 'uncovered' William Hutt, Charmion King, Eric House, Donald Davis, Ted Follows, and Kate Reid, among many others. In Edmonton, the Dramatic Society of the University of Alberta produced a number of Shakespeare plays, including a particularly successful modern-dress version of *The Taming of the Shrew* in 1938 (Stuart 150). At Queen's, W.S. Dyde created a Dramatic Club, which presented 'Evenings with Shakespeare': one act of his plays was performed every two weeks to club members. Similar work was carried out at Queen's by G.B. Harrison. In the 1930s and 1940s, the University of Manitoba's Dramatic Society produced *Hamlet*, *Macbeth*, and *Troilus and Cressida*.

In addition to university theatricals, the Little Theatre movement also included some Shakespeare in its repertoire. Beginning in Ottawa with the Ottawa Dramatic League (1913), by the 1930s, Little Theatres had multiplied throughout Canada. Regina produced *The Taming of the Shrew*, *A Midsummer Night's Dream*, and *Hamlet*; Winnipeg, *Macbeth* and

Romeo and Juliet; and Peterborough, *The Taming of the Shrew* (1949), a production starring Robertson and Brenda Davies. Davies would go on to use his experience with such amateur outdoor productions of Shakespeare as the basis for his novel *Tempest Tost* (1951).

With the end of empire and the beginning of the commonwealth, another landmark in political nationhood had been achieved. Coinciding with this development was, in the 1930s, the creation of the Dominion Drama Festival (DDF), the first truly national theatre, created by the governor general, the Earl of Bessborough, with representatives of drama groups from across Canada. For thirty years (except during the war), regional competitions were held annually in the spring, and finals took place in Ottawa. The DDF provided such impressive but foreign adjudicators as J.T. Grein and Harley Granville-Barker, who stimulated theatrical activity and raised standards. Among other works, scenes from Shakespeare were performed at such competitions. One of the memorable productions was *Hamlet* (1932) at the Ottawa Little Theatre, co-produced by the Montreal Repertory Theatre under the supervision and direct and active involvement of the governor general (who also planned the sets) and starring his son, the Viscount Duncannon. Duncannon, a Cambridge student, elicited an enthusiastic letter of praise from the prime minister himself, Mackenzie King: 'It was like drinking at a stream of living water to see and hear again one of Shakespeare's plays by real artists; after having been parched in the barren theatrical land of these times' (Whittaker, 'Shakespeare' 86). Although King's praises were probably overstated, they indicate his ardent desire to read into this production an augury of a 'new era' for Canadian theatre – a hope to be delayed for some decades yet.

During the Second World War, Shakespeare's birthday continued to be celebrated and his name used in war propaganda. As Karen Bamford points out in her chapter in this volume, 'The Imperial Theme: The Shakespeare Society of Toronto, 1928–1969,' Shakespeare was referred to as a 'national prophet' and one whose 'life-theme' was the great battle between St George and the Dragon. By the end of the 1940s, Canadians had had the opportunity to see Shakespeare in most parts of Canada or to read something about him. The time seemed ripe for English actor-manager Earle Grey and his actress-wife, Mary Godwin, to launch the First Canadian Shakespeare Festival at the University of Toronto's Trinity College quadrangle. On 2 July 1951, they planted a mulberry tree, purportedly a scion of the true Shakespearean root, in the quad. But this summer Shakespeare was only briefly successful. With the advent of the Stratford Festival, it began to unravel. By 1960, the Greys had gone home to England.

'This churlish knot': The State and the Stage

The government paid no attention to the performing arts until the 1920s, when the advent of radio made it necessary to do so. Setting a precedent for government intervention in cultural matters, the Aird Report (1929) led to the nationalization of radio stations as a bulwark against American influence and to the establishment of the Canadian Radio Broadcasting Corporation (CRBC, later the CBC). Between 1944 and 1955, the CBC presented over sixty radio adaptations of Shakespeare to help raise national cultural standards in the face of American commercialism. In '"A Stage for the Word": Shakespeare on CBC Radio, 1947–1955,' Marta Straznicky examines some of these productions, which put forward Shakespeare as a sign of cultural maturity, not of colonialism, and as a 'safe' author, preferable to native-born writers who dealt with more polemical social issues.

Of central importance to the development of radio drama as well as to Canadian theatre as a whole was the report of the Royal Commission on National Development in the Arts, Letters, and Sciences, better known as the Massey Commission (1949–51), to which so many of the chapters in this volume refer. An order-in-council summed up the report's thesis: 'That it is in the national interest to give encouragement to institutions which express national feeling, promote common understanding and add to the variety and richness of Canadian life, rural as well as urban' (Robertson xi). Robertson Davies's desire for a national theatre resulted in his contribution of a satirical dialogue to the commission's report in which the character of Lovewit complains, among other things, about Canadians' lack of opportunity to see Shakespearean drama 'in its proper form.' 'As far as the classics of the theatre are concerned, we are a nation of ignoramuses,' Lovewit avers ('Theatre: A Dialogue' 374).

While attacked for his elitism in many quarters, the co-chairman of the commission, Vincent Massey, later the governor general of Canada, was one of the most fervent and eloquent supporters of a Canadian theatre and a staunch believer in the social power of theatre. His quip, that it was 'almost as easy to be witty about the Canadian drama as about the Canadian navy. They each, at the moment, may seem to represent a well-meaning but rather insignificant effort to complete our national equipment – to suggest a pious aspiration rather than reality' ('Prospects' 53), was percipient and honest. Massey recognized that Canadian theatre was, in essence, only a province of New York but, unlike less clear-sighted cultural critics, Massey also found that the only visible counter to the Americans, British touring companies, were 'not unconnected to an all-British propaganda'; one mediocrity was substituted for another (53). Yet Massey also found that 'it is the struggle to discover a Canadian point of view that creates the artificial Canadianism that is an offence against honest art' (59). Canadianism, he argued, cannot be applied like a brush, in its externals, or in arbitrary rules. Sharing the view of many present-day theorists, Massey believed that Canada was a unit only in a political sense. There were, of necessity, several Canadas: its geography and different immigrant groups ensured that this was so. Despite Massey's own even-handedness, the Massey Report subsequently came under attack for laying the foundation of a colonial repertoire in the performing arts. It certainly was instrumental in creating the Canada Council and the Stratford Theatre Festival.

'Fair endeavours': Stratford, Ontario

While radio flourished in the 1940s, professional theatres grew, then waned. The first professional company after the war and one of the most successful, the New Play Society, was created by Dora Mavor Moore. She and her son, Mavor, would become two of the forceful and charismatic personalities connected with the creation of the Stratford Theatre Festival – undoubtedly the major event, the great leap into the unknown as Timothy Findley calls it ('Making') – in Canadian Shakespeareana. Spearheaded by local businessman Tom Patterson, who recruited British director Tyrone Guthrie, the Festival was to be a way of reviving Stratford's economy. The city administrators had, in fact, no knowledge of Shakespeare, as Patterson recalls. Mayor Dave Simpson's response to the project was, 'I don't know anything about Shakespeare, except that it's the name of a school on the east end of town. But if it's good for Stratford, then, I'm all for it' (Patterson and Gould 34). From these inauspicious beginnings, the Stratford Festival has grown to encompass three theatres with a total annual audience of approximately 650,000. It has produced all of Shakespeare's plays at least once and is now the largest classical theatre in North America. For some, however, it has become more tourist empire than national theatre. Margaret Groome's chapter, 'Stratford and the Aspirations for a Canadian

National Theatre,' examines the events leading up to the creation of the Festival, which marked the culmination of a nearly seventy-year desire for a national and professionalized theatre. Even though, as Groome points out, the Festival was founded by a British director and used British stars, it was hailed as the iconic achievement of Canadian cultural nationhood and has since became one of the 'mythologized moments' (to use William New's term) of Canadian cultural history.

Beginning as a tent affair, in 1957 the Festival moved to a permanent building with a thrust stage designed by Tanya Moiseiwitsch, which served as a model for many others, including the Crucible Theatre (Sheffield), the Chichester Festival Stage, and the Vivian Beaumont Theatre (Lincoln Center, New York). The 'reverse colonialism' of Stratford's influence was also, more rarely, experienced by its actors. Montreal-born Christopher Plummer recalled that, when he was a member of the Royal Shakespeare Company in 1961, he had obtained 'all the plum roles on the program ... "Richard III," "Benedict," "Henry II" in *Becket*! I ... a COLONIAL ... fresh from the crass New World, had come to take the wind out of their sails, beat 'em at their own game, show the Brits how to do what they do best! I was pretty cocky and insufferable, I tell ya!' (202).

In his 1950s, while proselytizing on behalf of the Festival, Tyrone Guthrie argued that the classics would give Canadian playwrights trained actors, a trained audience, and training ('Long' 211). He urged Canadians not to think in national terms, or of Shakespeare as an import. There is, argued Guthrie, no distinctly national way of doing anything (212). The inaugural production, *Richard III* with Alec Guinness (1953), was greeted with wild enthusiasm and set high standards of acting, directing, and production, but it was also regarded by some as initiating a three-decade tradition of dependency upon 'hired hands': British and American actors and directors, such as Michael Langham, Robin Phillips, Maggie Smith, Peter Ustinov, and Alan Bates.

Despite Guthrie's exhortation not to think in national terms, the early history of the Stratford Festival suggests that a Canadian style of Shakespeare production might be developed, if by that we mean an attentiveness to Canadian themes, issues, and realities. In 'Shakespeare *Canadiens* at the Stratford Festival,' C.E. McGee explores the possibilities and limitations of a distinctly Canadian way of producing Shakespeare by analysing Michael Langham's *Henry V*, with francophone actors playing the French (the playwright Gratien Gélinas played the French king) and anglophones the English, Richard Monette's pre-Conquest (1760) *As You Like It* (1990), and Richard Rose's 1913 *Two Gentlemen of Verona*

(1998). While Stratford has given the French-English question some attention, a First Nations Shakespeare has been a rarity. One exception is an Inuit-themed *King Lear* (1961–2) directed by Herbert Whittaker and performed by the Canadian Players, a travelling offshoot of the Stratford company.

Stratford's culturally authoritative position in Canada and in North America grew exponentially over the decades. Its success was followed on a smaller scale in the 1960s by a chain of professional theatres across Canada. With the growth of national feeling, especially after the 1967 centennial celebrations, government funding created new regional theatres, which also produced Shakespeare: the Manitoba Theatre Centre (Winnipeg), the St Lawrence Centre (Toronto), the Charlottetown Theatre, the Citadel (Edmonton), the National Arts Centre (Ottawa), and the Centaur Theatre (Montreal). Some of these have created riveting productions, such as the Citadel's *Richard III*, in which Brent Carver played 'the Duke of Darkness' as a completely handicapped royal, entering the stage on a motorized wheelchair (Dafoe, 'Duke'). In the past few years, co-productions between the Citadel and the National Arts Centre have resulted in some novel interpretations, including a feminist Desdemona (Megan Follows) in Michael Langham's *Othello* (1997), and a kind of 'corporate bitch' Kate in *The Taming of the Shrew* (directed by Denise Coffey,1997), whose 'true spirit' is released in the course of the play.

With the growth of Canadian nationalism during the 1970s, Shakespeare and Stratford came increasingly under attack from some quarters, since both were perceived as enshrining Canada's colonial dependence. Playwrights, still opining the cultural inferiority complex of their fellow Canadians, attacked Stratford for doing little to foster native Canadian playwrights or directors. Canadian nationalism was, however, complicated by the historical transformation of the theatre into a culture industry and by the sense that the world was in a post-nationalist, if not perhaps post-verbal, phase of development. Materialist critics attacked Stratford as a consumerist, philistine festival – a line of attack already initiated in the 1960s by the acerbic theatre critic of the Toronto *Star*, Nathan Cohen. Others, however, argued that the classics needed to be thoroughly assimilated before a native tradition could be created. The most articulate of such proponents, Robertson Davies, declared that, following the logic of 'the most blinkered nationalists' who rejected Shakespeare, we might as well similarly argue against classical music as 'museum' music (Foreword xv).

Such criticism has been exacerbated by Stratford's turn away from experimental productions and lesser-known plays in favour of musicals as well as by an increased Hollywood-like emphasis on costumes, props, and gimmicks. Already in 1959, Nathan Cohen's initial enthusiasm for the Festival dissipated as he complained that 'In effect Stratford was teaching an uncritical audience that Shakespeare's plays had no depth, but were just blueprints for pretty pyrotechnical exercises. The words were totally trivial, the characters mere wax figures, all to be juggled about at the director's caprice.' Cohen attacked Stratford for being the 'cultural equivalent of the Canadian National Exhibition grandstand show, an anti-artistic extravaganza ... dull in a new way' ('Theatre Today' 34). Similarly, the *New York Times* critic Brooks Atkinson, who praised the sets and costumes, critiqued Stratford for its 'overpowering externals' and 'shallow performance' (qtd. in Patterson and Gould 188). More recently, in calling for a reinvigorated Shakespeare, the *Globe and Mail* theatre critic Kate Taylor has tilted against the same windmills, attacking Stratford's 'Disney-like' productions that focus on spectacle and speed rather than plot and character or language. Taylor argues that, paradoxically, such an approach encourages the idea of an elitist Shakespeare, not accessible to the average spectator. Interestingly, such spectacular Shakespeare also hearkens back to nineteenth-century productions of adapted Shakespeare with lots of fine scenery, costumes, and star actors but with only a muted interest in the text ('Saving').

Thoughtful productions, such as Robin Phillips's *King John* (1993) or Marti Maraden's *The Merchant of Venice* (1996), have become increasingly rare and are found, for the most part, on the smaller stages of the Avon or Patterson theatres rather than on the large Festival stage. Douglas Rain as Shylock was a dignified, restrained yet also bitter, vindictive, and plausibly motivated businessman, operating in Italy in 1933, the year that Mussolini met Hitler. The production revealed the gilded, privileged world of Venice already launched on the path towards horror not by monsters but by its ordinary citizens, who were casually and thoughtlessly anti-Semitic. Rather than omitting the forced conversion speech at the end of the play, as did Michael Langham in his 1989 version of the play, Maraden boldly retained it, making the audience gasp in response. Whatever the response to the Stratford Festival, most critics and observers agreed that it was a timely endeavour and one which expressed 'a feeling,' as Sir Tyrone Guthrie noted with a touch of paternalism, that 'Canada has more to contribute to the wealth and health of the world than its material riches' (qtd. in Pettigrew and Portman 14–15).

'In th' marketplace': Summer Shakespeare

Beginning as it did under a tent and by a river, the Stratford Festival is linked to the most common way of presenting Shakespeare in Canada: in the summertime, under a tent or in the park. Almost every province of the country currently enjoys such a summer Shakespeare, as Canadians seem to prefer pairing their Shakespeare with a beautiful landscape – perhaps the result of long winters spent indoors; or, perhaps this is the theatrical equivalent of the theme so frequently encountered in Canadian fiction of the power and immensity, the sheer presence, of the land. Although we may count Sir Humphrey Gilbert's and Marc Lescarbot's productions as the first of Canadian summer theatre, the trend was seriously introduced in the 1880s and became a staple of Canadian life after the 1930s, particularly in 'cottage' country: the Muskokas in Ontario. Here, the so-called straw hat theatres produced the occasional Shakespeare within a general diet of light comic fare. Outdoor Shakespeare elsewhere is similarly usually unsubtle, although it may be visually and physically arresting. But there are exceptions. In the early 1950s, the Straw Hat Players (in Gravenhurst and Port Carling, Ontario) produced *A Midsummer Night's Dream*, a low-budget, modern-dress production, directed by John Blatchley, in which Oberon (David Gardner) appeared in a golden bathing suit and Bottom, dressed in shorts, was transformed into an ass by putting on a Second World War gas mask with ears. Since the budget did not permit fairies, Bottom mimed their presence. But production magic was there, nonetheless. A little girl of four or five claimed to have seen the fairies that Gardner mimed. The actor recalled, 'My mouth fell open. It was a moment of incandescent purity and it remains the one review that I will treasure forever.'

Straw hat theatre took longer to establish itself in the cities. One of the earliest of such outdoor urban Shakespeares was found at the top of Mount Royal in Montreal at Beaver Lake. The Open-Air Playhouse (where Christopher Plummer, among others, appeared) produced *The Taming of the Shrew* and *As You Like It* under the direction of Malcolm Morley, founder of the Canadian Repertory Theatre in Ottawa. Montreal's present-day open-air quasi-commercial version, the Repercussion Theatre, began by playing *A Midsummer Night's Dream* to eight hundred spectators at four performances but now annually welcomes nearly thirty thousand and also tours schools and various other venues in North America. Today, summer festivals include Shakespeare by the Sea (Halifax); Shakespeare by the Sea (Logy Bay, Newfoundland); the

Atlantic Theatre Festival (Wolfville, Nova Scotia); Repercussion Theatre (Montreal); Dream in High Park (Toronto); Assiniboine Theatre, Shakespeare in the Park (Winnipeg); Shakespeare on the Saskatchewan (Saskatoon); Bard-on-the-Beach (Vancouver); Rocking Horse Theatre (for children; Victoria); the Victoria Shakespeare Festival (Victoria); and the short-lived Ottawa Shakespeare Festival (Victoria Island, Ottawa). The last followed the time-worn trend of inviting British directors to start up a Canadian festival (Brigid Panet from the Royal National Theatre, who directed a successful *A Midsummer Night's Dream* under a tent, 1992). Much more successful and longer-lived is Ottawa's irreverent Company of Fools, founded in 1990 as a street theatre entertaining passers-by, and now a professional company.

In taking up the direction of *Twelfth Night* at the newly founded Atlantic Theatre Festival (1995), Michael Langham responded to questions about 'why stage Shakespeare's plays?': 'Because they can speak to us across centuries of universal human experiences. The dynamics of Orsino's self-indulgent mooning are easily recognizable to anyone who has seen a teen-ager sighing over a favourite song cued up on the CD player for the umpteenth time' (qtd. in Taylor, 'sprightly'). Langham's remarks suggest the current gulf between the literary and the theatrical worlds in their different response to Shakespeare, a gulf explored by Anthony B. Dawson in 'Collisions and Contradictions: Training University Actors to Meet the Universal Bard.' Dawson locates the crux of the tension between theatrical and scholarly (especially materialist) approaches to Shakespeare in the central issue of character and character-building.

Many of the summer festivals produce a similar canon of plays consisting of those that work well out of doors, especially *A Midsummer Night's Dream, As You Like It, The Tempest*, and *Twelfth Night*. The hallmark of these productions is enthusiastic rushing about, playing comedy for its outrageousness and slapstick, tragedy for its melodrama. Consistently billed in its promotional literature as 'accessible,' 'fun for children of all ages, 8 to 80,' and 'radical,' summer Shakespeare purports to 'blow the cobwebs off' the Bard.[1] However, this 'renovation' of Shakespeare seems to be confined to outdoor settings, contemporary references (especially to pop-culture icons), broad humour, and frenetic rhythms. Thus, for example, Shakespeare on the Saskatchewan (founded by Gordon McCall) produced a futurist Hamlet as a rock star in a post-nuclear world – in Chris Dafoe's witty phrase, Hamlet as 'The Road Worrier' (Dafoe, 'Stylish'); *A Midsummer Night's Dream* on a golf course; and *Romeo and Juliet* as a feud between French- and English-Canadian dirt farmers. Dream in High Park (Toronto) set *The Comedy of Errors* in a beach resort with a swimming pool, where mermaids cavorted Esther Williams–style. Winnipeg's Shakespeare in the Ruins presented a *Love's Labour's Lost* (2000) with computers, cellphones, and rap songs. In Halifax, Shakespeare by the Sea uses four kilometres of parkland and the eighteenth-century Martello Tower (built to defend the city from naval invasion) as its 'stage' and auditorium. In their trek up to 'Elsinore,' a small audience of sixty encounters the murder of the king, a funeral, sword fights, and Ophelia's body on the rocks. Halifax has also produced *A Midsummer Night's Dream*, with the Athenian lovers dressed in kilts of the province and Peter Quince as a recognizable Newfoundlander (1995), as well as *Comedy of Errors, Macbeth,* and *Titus Andronicus* (1999). The violence of *Titus* was deemed particularly suitable to outdoor, kinetic Shakespeare and promotional material advised that the stage manager, Marcel Boulet, had had seven years of military training, an allusion to the military precision of the whole operation.

The underlying message of most of these productions is that the plays are boring and therefore require gimmicks. The theatrical equivalent of pop-culture bestsellers – accessible, profitable, least differentiated – summer Shakespeare is a mass-market commodity aimed at the largest possible audience. Shaped, above all, by the 'universal' appeal of 'fun,' such Shakespeare hearkens back to the description of an 'ideal' *Romeo and Juliet* full of hilarity and physical action published in the St John's *Telegraph* in 1891 (cited above). Not surprisingly, too, while its externals of setting, props, or costumes might be original, such kinetically challenging, fast-paced productions differ little from their American counterparts. In fact, some festivals, such as the Manitoba Shakespeare in the Park, advertises this link: 'New York has it, Toronto has it, now Winnipeg has it' (qtd. in Engle, Londré, and Watermeier 385). Shakespeare, then, is fun, not taxing, and a mark of cosmopolitan, hip culture.

Yet these productions have their magical moments, too, especially when Canadian weather intercedes. British Columbia's Bard-on-the-Beach (founded in 1990) plays in a custom-made tent open to a 'glorious backdrop of city, sea, and mountains' (Engle, Londré, and Watermeier 384). Large casts and elaborate costuming as well as the wonderful natural setting make it a popular theatre. During a production of *A Midsummer Night's Dream* (1991), Oberon (Chris Humphreys) ran, as always, for his upstage right exit:

I had always used it [the exit] to launch myself, my arms and feathers flying, into the sky and drop out of sight onto a mattress a few feet below. Except this time, at the very moment I leapt, silhouetted against the stormy sky ... the entire horizon flashed white with sheet lightning! The audience gasped in almost eerie unison, as if they were fused by the vision. The actors were speechless. I rolled and ran for the tent ... God, the ultimate lighting director. That night the company played as if every speech was lightning-lit. Every weather reference was cherished. With uncanny timing, the storm wound down along with the play. It was truly magical. (309)

Alternative, Multicultural, and First Nations Shakespeare

Reinforcing the mobilization in the 1970s against British and American cultural influences was a groundswell of alternative theatres with their political and artistic revolt against large regional theatres, which represented the bulk of professional theatre in Canada and most of the dollars. Yet, surprisingly, alternative theatre (such as George Luscombe's Toronto Workshop Productions and Françoise Bread and Roland Laroche's Théâtre de l'Egrégore) has been receptive to a re-reading of the classics, including Shakespeare, and has often quickly blurred into the mainstream, as may be seen by the example of Robert Lepage, who quickly moved from alternative to mainstream commercial theatres and became an internationally acclaimed theatrical wizard; or Guy Sprung, who, in the 1980s, travelled to Moscow to direct *A Midsummer Night's Dream*. Protesting against the 'colonial' attitudes and traditions of British and French-born directors, against American imports, alternative Shakespeare has often been 'de-stabilized' or 'de-centred'; that is, contrary to the populist desire for entertainment found in summer Shakespeare, alternative versions staged a politically charged and serious Bard. Some, like Creation 2, launched productions deliberately to coincide with and subvert the mainstream Stratford Festival and its connections to high culture; thus, Creation 2 opened a *Richard III* at the same time as its larger competitor opened with that same play. Theatre Passe Muraille rehearsed but never actually produced a fascinating *Richard III*, in which an actress, draped over Richard, played his hump. Toronto's NDWT produced a well-received *Hamlet*, played alongside James Reaney's Donnelly trilogy, which provided the bread and butter for the company (Johnston, *Up* 245–6). The tension between alternative and commercial theatres was also apparent in the collective work *Shakespeare for Fun and Profit* (1977), which contrasted the simplicity of grass-roots theatre to the Stratford Festival's emphasis on spectacle, and in the Company of Fools (Ottawa), which performed 'the entire play of *Hamlet* ... in two minutes as a rap' ('Company' 2).

In 'Liberal Spectators and Illiberal Critiques: Necessary Angel's *King Lear*,' Michael McKinnie examines Richard Rose's productions of *King Lear*. Rose, an innovative director, has directed four versions of the play, most recently *Hysterica* (2000), which portrays Lear as an aging woman. McKinnie studies the issue of cross-casting and its role in transforming the on-stage relationship between the sex of the actor, the gendering of the character, the spectator, and the text within the specific political framework of conservative Premier Mike Harris's Ontario.

Despite the enormous influx of immigrants, multicultural Shakespeare, even in such diverse urban centres as Toronto, is still rare, as is aboriginal Shakespeare. Among these rarities is an adapted *Hamlet* (1999), staged by the Modern Times Stage Company at Toronto's Theatre Passe Muraille. Directed by Soheil Parsa, the play was set in the Orient, and the costumes were a mixture of kimonos, business suits, and Indian saris. The action was punctuated by gongs and the final duel between Hamlet and Laertes was reminiscent of a martial-arts contest. *The Tempest* has been particularly amenable to postcolonial stage interpretations, well before such interpretations became popular among scholars. The Tamahnous Theatre Workshop produced *The Tempest* at the Vancouver East Cultural Centre in 1974, directed by John Gray, in an experimental production in the tradition of Grotowski's 'poor theatre.' In 1992, in British Columbia, the Bard-on-the Beach festival staged *The Tempest* with a northwest Canadian theme, in which Ariel was played as Nanabush (an aboriginal trickster figure).

Other First Nations Shakespeare includes a Winnipeg group called Shakespeare in the Red, founded by Native actor Michael Lawrenchuk and British director Libby Mason in 1996. The group tours with predominantly Native productions of Shakespeare to theatres, schools, and community venues, and carries out workshops and other professional training for professional and semi-professional actors. They have experienced enthusiastic response from Native audiences to *To Thine Own Self Be True* (scenes from *King Lear, Hamlet, King John*, and sonnets 22, 25, 29, and 138, linked by a periodic return to the rehearsal scene of *A Midsummer Night's Dream*), accompanied by Native instrumental and vocal music.[2] Although such efforts have been attacked by cultural materialists as 'Uncle Tom-ism,' Shakespeare in the Red has countered by arguing both from an idealist, universalist position – Shakespeare belongs to everyone – but also from a practical perspective: professional aboriginal actors are under-represented in the classical theatre of Canada. This company offers them the training that may enable and encourage larger theatres to hire them and thus more frequently to consider non-traditional casting.

Distinct Shakespeare: Quebec

In Quebec, Shakespeare was neither part of the school curriculum nor part of the local professional acting companies. Shakespeare's lukewarm, if not negative, reception was the result of early uses of Shakespeare as a tool of assimilation. In the years preceding the construction of the Theatre Royal in Quebec, for example, Shakespeare figured in the campaign of English newspapers to anglicize francophones. Thus, the *Canadian Magazine* wrote in 1823:

> Were it possible, by means of a well-regulated English Theatre, to draw some of the French Canadians to the representation of some of [Shakespeare's] best pieces, the effects would doubtless be salutary, by tending to impart those feelings so much in unison with British hearts. To encourage this attendance, and to promote these beneficial consequences, I would recommend that considerable attention should be bestowed on procuring scenery appropriate and striking. This will not appear insignificant or frivolous. If we once reflect, that the first objects of Canadian imitation have been our dress and external behaviur ... Were the French Canadians drawn to our theatre, either by the love of novelty, or by the attraction of scenery and music, even though their knowledge of English were at first imperfect, they might there receive such a stimulus to improvement in our language, from the natural workings of curiosity, that they would soon participate in all those advantages arising from the Drama, which I have foretold to their fellow subjects. (qtd. in Doucette 80)

Despite such English assimilationist sentiments, some Shakespeare was produced in French in the early 1830s, interestingly, as the preferable alternative to imported melodrama and Parisian vaudeville. Introduced in Lower Canada (Quebec) by Firmin Prud'homme, a Parisian actor who claimed Talma as his mentor, Shakespeare was played in the eighteenth-century Ducis adaptations. Working with Les Amateurs Canadiens, Prud'homme staged the first production of *Hamlet* in Canada and also, later, *Othello*.

For the most part, Shakespeare's fortunes in Quebec waxed and waned with the political situation. While English Canada relied on touring companies, French Canada had to create its own indigenous theatre; as a result, *le grand Will* acquired widespread popularity only after the Second World War. Father Émile Legault, artistic director of Collège Saint-Laurent, founded Les Compagnons de Saint-Laurent, a religious theatre group in the mid-1930s, which went on to produce the classics, including some Shakespeare. Altogether, ten Shakespeare plays were produced in French between 1945 and 1965 (Gilbert). Among these was a pastoral *A Midsummer Night's Dream* produced by Pierre Dagenais's L'Équipe at Montreal's Hermitage Gardens (1945), where trees and rocks hid elves and fairies. Michel Garneau's *Macbeth*, translated into the French of early Quebec and 'perhaps the finest Shakespearian [*sic*] translation in the French-speaking world' (Lefebvre, 'Playwrighting' 65), was staged successfully in a tiny hall seating sixty. Monique Lepage and Jacques Létourneau founded the Théâtre-Club; their French director, Jan Doat, produced *Twelfth Night* in 1956, transforming the auditorium into a travelling theatre with a proscenium arch that moved towards the audience and included minimum portable sets and stylized costumes (Cotnoir 304). In the 1960s, the Nouvelle Compagnie Théâtrale presented major classics to student audiences. Little Shakespeare was produced between 1972 and 1986, when the separatist movement gained momentum. With the assassination of cabinet minister Pierre Laporte, the invocation of the War Measures Act (1970), and the first referendum on Quebec separation (1980), English authors like Shakespeare, but also classics as a whole, became unpalatable and were replaced by feminist, nationalist, and anti-Catholic plays.

Although *Hamlet* is the play most frequently evoked by other cultures (including English Canada, as Jessica Schagerl reveals in her chapter, 'A National *Hamlet*? Stratford's Legacy of Twentieth-Century Productions') to suggest the indecisive nature of nations or national identity, it was not frequently staged in Quebec, appearing first late in 1970 (Théâtre du Nouveau Monde), with a second production only in 1990. In '"Le Remaking" of le grand Will: Shakespeare in Francophone Quebec,' Leanore Lieblein explores the contexts and the contradictions inherent in the idea of creating a Quebecois local culture by way of a foreign text.

Robert Lepage has turned many times to Shakespeare in his explorations into multimedia, sexuality, and the act of creation itself. Lepage's love of image and technology has sharply divided critics between those who believe that his productions are perverse, leaden, humourless, and emotionally cold and those who find them brilliantly imaginative. *Elsinor/Elsineur*, variations on a theme of *Hamlet*, began with all of the roles, including those of Ophelia and Gertrude, played by Lepage himself, as a way to suggest Hamlet's isolated world, which depends more and more on his morbid imagination. For Lepage, '*Elsinore* is not a *real Hamlet* but rather a preliminary exploration of the meanderings of his thoughts and of his time – and perhaps, in a way, of mine.' Lepage's visually stunning productions include *A Midsummer Night's Dream* (1992), presented as a sexual nightmare staged in a massive mud-bath. (The audience in the first three rows was provided with plastic ponchos.) His *The Tempest/tempête* (1993) included an utterly uninhibited, anarchic Caliban, played by a woman, and an acrobatic Ariel, who, for over thirty minutes, was suspended from a lighting fixture over the stage.

Shakespeare often put in an appearance at the Théâtre du Rideau Vert founded in 1949 by Mercedes Palomino and Yvette Brind'Amour, and at the Théâtre du Nouveau Monde founded in 1951 by Georges Groulx, Jean Gascon, Jean-Louis Roux, and Guy Hoffman. At the latter, Martine Beaulne staged her *La Mégère apprivoisée* (*The Taming of the Shrew*, 1995), a study of theatre and the roles that the sexes play. It concluded with a new speech celebrating the equality of the sexes and featured a subversive Grumio attending Galileo's astronomy lectures. Other successful productions of Shakespeare include the provocative director Alexandre Hausvater's adapted *Lear* (1990), presented cabaret-style and employing a mortally ill actor in the title role. The effect was wrenching, as the character/actor progressively lost power, both political and physical. Montreal's Theatre 1774, generally dedicated to staging new plays and plays about women, reshaped and cut *Measure for Measure* (1993) by a third to focus on the issue of sexual harassment.

Shakespeare has also been a presence at the annual Festival de Théâtre des Amériques, where *Macbeth* and *The Tempest* have been performed. In one of the most inventive festivals, *Événement 38*, initiated by Yvan Bienvenue and Stephane F. Jacques of Théâtre Urbi et Orbi in Montreal (and later co-produced by Théâtre d'Aujourd'hui), all of Shakespeare's thirty-eight plays were rewritten into fifteen-minute segments by playwrights under the age of thirty-eight as a rebuke to theatre critics who bemoaned the absence of Quebecois 'Shakespeares.'[3] While now more than comfortable with Shakespeare, many Quebec playwrights, like their anglophone counterparts, still regard him as a commercial force taking away audience interest and public funds from native talent. Nonetheless, not hampered by a language shared with the

British and the Americans, francophones, unlike anglophones, are often more free to explore, deplore, and admire Shakespeare. In the best instances, it results in such rich poetic drama as that of Normand Chaurette's *Les Reines* (1991) (*The Queens*, 1992) and Jean-Pierre Ronfard's *Vie et mort du roi boiteux* (1981), as Lois Sherlow points out in her chapter, 'Normand Chaurette's *Les Reines*: Shakespeare and the Modern in the Alchemical Oven.'

'A gibing spirit': Imitation, Adaptation, and Parody

Canadian playwrights' concern that Shakespeare's prominence adversely affected the growth of a native theatre holds some truth, not only because his centrality in theatrical repertoires made it unnecessary to create new plays, but also because of the adverse influence his works exerted as models for dramatic writing during a time when, elsewhere, nationalism and cultural revival were flourishing. Indeed, Canada's political position as a dominion within a British empire is paralleled by the derivative nature of nineteenth-century Canadian drama. Pseudo-Elizabethan drama, like Charles Heavysege's *Saul* (1857) – praised and described as 'discerned and adopted' from 'Shakespeare's method' by the British critic Coventry Patmore (78) – and John Hutchinson Garnier's *Prince Pedro* (1877) are the most obvious examples of the failure to transplant the Shakespearean model into new soil.

If Shakespeare's influence impeded Canadian drama on one level, on another, it has been responsible for initiating the extremely fertile and distinct subgenres of Shakespearean parodies and serious adaptations, which have, from their inception, had a harder and a more pronounced politicized edge than similar efforts in the United States or the United Kingdom. It may, indeed, be here that we need to seek for a distinct Canadian Shakespeare. Certainly, it is not surprising that these genres constitute a subject of great interest in this volume. As a settler/invader colony founded on displacements, Canada has been well positioned to deal with revisions and rewritings of canonical works, for, as David Lloyd has argued in *Nationalism and Minor Literature*, in 'minor' literatures (the literature of a nationalist minority; in Lloyd's study, the Irish), there is an oppositional relationship to the canon. In Canada's case, a growing desire for equality with, not complete separation from, Britain marks its historical development (as well as French-English, aboriginal-settler, and American-Canadian tensions). Lloyd observes that the writers of 'minor' literatures make no claims in their work to representative status:

What is crucial to this definition of the minor status of their writings is their common perpetuation of non-identity in their writings ... neither narrative culminates in identification, racial, sexual, or social, that would stabilize identity ... If such minor narratives imply a critique of narratives of identity, they equally refuse to represent the attainment of the autonomous subjectivity that is the ultimate aim of the major narrative. This refusal in the domain of what is represented is replicated on the level of modes of representation, insofar as the minor text adopts writing strategies that are in some sense defined by their dependence on prior texts. (22)

For 'minor' literatures, parody – authorized transgression, dependent and yet opposed to an original – as well as translation and intertextuality are particularly appealing modes. Lloyd argues that the radical potential of minor writing, which emanates from the conjunction of political and ethical domains, overlaps with modernism and its crisis of canonicity. Linda Hutcheon, however, might argue that Canadian letters tend naturally towards the postmodern, if we accept her characterization of postmodernism as a recognition of the presence of the past, 'not a nostalgic return; it is a critical revisiting, an ironic dialogue with the past of both art and society, a recalling of a critically shared vocabulary' (*Poetics* 4). In Hutcheon's view, parody is the 'perfect' postmodern form, both incorporating and challenging that which it parodies (11). In refusing identity and representativeness, parody may, in some respects, indeed, be regarded as the mode best according with the Canadian myth of this country as a 'blank face' (M. Moore, 'Theatre' 238), a 'nobody' (Marshall McLuhan, 'Canada: The Borderline Case' 228), a country as a work-in-progress (thus, Jean Béraud: 'Canada, pays en devenir constant' 313) with multiple borderlines dependent upon negotiation and debate – a hearkening back to Sandwell's early-twentieth-century ideas about Canada as not separate but apart from Britain and yet definitely not American.

Simultaneously validating the (literary) past and subverting it, Canadians' penchant for parody/adaptation may usefully be seen in the Uruguayan critic Ángel Rama's terms as 'transculturation' – the process by which members of subordinate or colonized groups select and invent from materials transmitted by a dominant, usually imperial, culture. Rama's analysis is especially useful because it engages what is missed in some other postcolonial critiques: the energy and force of the cultural host, and its ability to select both what gets used in a culture and how it is used. Thus, while Heavysege's plays were an unsuccessful experiment in the development of Canadian drama, *Measure by Measure; or, the Coalition in Secret Session*, an anonymous 'biting and well-written farce' also written in pseudo-Shakespearean but mocking verse, satirizing the political manoeuvrings of the New Brunswick legislature in 1871 (Benson and Conolly 4–5), may, in retrospect, be regarded as 'mainstream' Canadian drama – if we categorize the hundreds of adaptations of Shakespeare as distinctly Canadian examples of what is 'mainstream': a text that simultaneously both embraces and rejects classical literary models, a text that is both here and elsewhere.

Both serious and satiric adaptations of Shakespeare are the subject of Daniel Fischlin's 'Nation and/as Adaptation: Shakespeare, Canada, Authenticity,' which examines the complexity of functions of the adaptations of Shakespeare and their troubling relationship to notions of Canadian national identity. From Charles Ebenezer Moyse's *Shakespere's [sic] Skull and Falstaff's Nose* (1889) to Rick Miller's *MacHomer: The Simpsons Do Macbeth* (1997), Fischlin re-examines issues of 'authentic' text and Canadian revisionings and shows how adaptations work on two fronts, both confirming a myth of authenticity and interrogating such a position through alternative readings. Mark Fortier, in 'Undead and Unsafe: Adapting Shakespeare (in Canada),' looks at the complex political and ethical negotiations required when Shakespeare is adapted. In 'Othello in Three Times,' Ric Knowles examines three Canadian rewritings of *Othello*: the regional and populist *Cruel Tears*, a country opera by Ken Mitchell and Humphrey and the Dump Trucks (1985); Anne-Marie Macdonald's feminist *Good Night Desdemona (Good Morning Juliet)* (1990); and Djanet Sears's interventionist *Harlem Duet* (1997), suggesting a changing relationship over three decades with Shakespeare and constructions of gender, race, ethnicity, and class in Canada.

Canadian fascination with revisionist versions of Shakespeare is indeed extensive and ranges from the serious to the outrageous in all genres and in both official languages: drama (John Herbert, Peter Eliot Weiss, Ken Gass, Judith Thompson, Margaret Clarke, Michael O'Brien, David Belke, Antonine Maillet, Norman Chaurette, Robert Gurik, Timothy Findley, Jean-Claude Germain, Jean-Pierre Ronfard, Michel Garneau, Tibor Egervari, Marco Micone, Jean-Frédéric Messier, John Sipes); fiction (Robertson Davies, Margaret Atwood, Carole Corbeil, Hubert Aquin, Sarah Murphy, Constance Beresford-Howe, Audrey Thomas, Leon Rooke); poetry (Elizabeth Brewster, Marjorie Pickthall, Suniti Namjoshi); music (Ted Dykstra, Loreena McKennitt); radio (Newfoundland Broadcasting Company, CBC); television (Wayne and

Shuster); pop/rock musicals (Cliff Jones); and political cartoons – by no means a complete list of either categories or authors.

'The bubble reputation': Multiplying Shakespeares

If Canadians were slow to acquire Shakespeare, they are now eager in their rush to possess him. Shakespeare is, at present, a profitable market commodity. While scholars may attempt to de-centre him in English departments across North America and England, the Bard is firmly entrenched in more than the narrow academic discipline of English studies. A presence, as we have seen, since the eighteenth century in theatricals, in satires and parodies, adaptations, and other rewritings, Shakespeare today is the property of both high and low culture, stage, classroom, text, intertext, and webtext. Thoroughly permeating all aspects of Canadian culture, Shakespeare is a ready-made, immediately recognizable source of meaning for any number of endeavours. Such multiplying Shakespeares increase the value of his ownership. Thus, the Ottawa *Citizen* announced on 5 October 1998 that a Canadian company, Shakespeare by the Sea, was 'first off the mark' in a 'worldwide race to perform Edward III,' possibly a 'lost' play by Shakespeare ('Halifax'). Taking the discovered text directly from the Internet, the Halifax troupe was satisfied in performing a play only available in excerpts. The rush for Shakespeare is even, at times, literal, as the *Globe and Mail* reported: 'In 1990, a Canadian living in Oxford set the speed record for reciting Hamlet's "To be or not to be" soliloquy. Sean Shannon completed it in 24 seconds. At this rate, the entire part could be recited in 17.9 minutes. Prairie winters are quite cold' (Kesterton).

While the activities of memorizing and academically centring Shakespeare have, generally, been in decline, there are also countervailing indications of revival. In Stratford, Ontario, Lois Burdett, a grade two teacher at Hamlet Elementary School, has, for the past two decades, been using Shakespeare to inform all aspects of the curriculum, from mathematics (how to order theatre tickets) to biology (a study of Shakespeare's plants). Burdett and Christine Coburn launched *Twelfth Night for Kids* (the play was rewritten in rhyming couplets), the first of a Shakespeare Can Be Fun! series. Other books on Shakespeare for children include Amanda Lewis and Tim Wynne-Jones's *Rosie Backstage* (1994). Shakespeare high school competitions are also making a comeback. The Shakespeare on the Platform Competition for high schools in the Ottawa-Carleton area, initiated by the English Speaking Union of

Canada (Ottawa Branch), and supported by the patronage of Tom Patterson (the founder of the Stratford Festival) and Christopher Plummer, has ambitions to launch not only a province-wide but also a national competition.

While part of the postmodern, postnational culture of the well-to-do consumer, Shakespeare remains, for others, a way of registering and reflecting what Walter Pater called the 'consummate moment,' the point when feeling and thought come together. Lest we think of Shakespeare as a kind of global conspiracy, we need to recall this 'Shakespeare effect' on the non-scholarly community, those who also help create canons and memorialize great writers. In a letter to the editor of the *Globe and Mail*, Manuel Cappel wrote about Shakespeare as solace and joy:

> In late June, 1990, I received a frantic phone call from my stepsister in California. My father, a recently retired nuclear physicist, had set sail in his 41-foot yacht from Cabo San Lucas in Mexico en route to Australia with only an inexperienced American kid of 20 aboard as crew. Two weeks or so out of port, Heinz (my father) had taken gravely ill and had died, leaving his terrified crew member a thousand miles from land in any direction with an old boat brim full of mechanical idiosyncrasies and worse, a corpse on board.
>
> Eric (the crew) followed the only sensible path available to him and buried Heinz at sea two days later. Subsequently he made his way to the Marquesas Islands in the South Pacific despite a lack of electronic navigation or self-steering gear. Once there, he phoned my stepsister Leslye and set the family-crisis machinery in motion.
>
> Someone from the family had to go down to Polynesia to relieve his emergency command of the vessel and to bring it to a U.S. jurisdiction for estate liquidation. To make a long story shorter, I departed Toronto for the Marquesas in July of 1990 with an experienced crew enlisted from my friends on the Toronto Islands here and succeeded in sailing the boat to Hawaii that summer ... It's been years since I have reflected on the exciting events of that summer. Then, just this past weekend, I was reading Warren Clements' Word Play column Don't Let the Bugbears Bite (Aug. 3) in which he quotes Ariel's song in *The Tempest*, full of alliterative imagery that only the Bard could write:
>
>> Full fathom five thy father lies;
>> Of his bones are coral made;
>> Those are pearls that were his eyes:

> Nothing of him that doth fade,
> But doth suffer a sea change
> Into something rich and strange.

> I can neither compose nor even imagine a more fitting and beautiful epitaph for my father than the above lines; all the more apt in that they address me directly, so to speak. This song, and Mr. Clements' article highlighting it, made my weekend. Shakespeare's plays are somewhat familiar to me and I recall reading *The Tempest* back in high school, but of course I had long forgotten any particulars and especially the above which will remain special to me. I thank you for this vignette. In the future I shall endeavour to read more Shakespeare!

Such responses raise the question, 'Why Shakespeare and not some other writer?' Does Cappel's study of Shakespeare in high school and his subsequently deeply felt response to his poetry confirm Shakespeare's universality or confirm the notion that Shakespeare's centrality in Canada depends solely upon his privileged position in the British, and by extension, the Canadian theatrical/literary/educational canon?

The question of Canadian Shakespeare, shaped by tensions between English and French, by its relations to the First Nations, to new immigrant groups, and to its elephantine neighbour to the south, is now locked into the global context of the World Wide Web. Numerous Canadian websites on theatre and theatre companies, Renaissance drama, and Shakespeare, as well as chat groups, contribute to the global reach of the Shakespeare industry. The image of the recently (May 2001) discovered portrait, the so-called Sanders portrait, purportedly of Shakespeare, in the family of a retired Ontario engineer was instantly transmitted across newspapers and Internet sites, giving rise to new speculation about the face of genius. Presciently, Marshall McLuhan declared in 1977 – well before the omnipresence of the Internet – that 'national unity now proves to be irrelevant under electric conditions which yet create an inclusive consciousness' (247). Rather than a nineteenth-century idea of national unity, a 'state of political ecumenism' dominates in Canada. This Canadian 'condition of low-profile and multiple borders' approaches, according to McLuhan, 'the ideal pattern of electronic living' (247). Strikingly similar to Julia Kristeva's transitional nation, which 'offers its identifying (therefore reassuring) space, as transitive and transitory (therefore open, uninhibiting, and creative), for the benefit of contemporary subjects: indomitable individuals, touchy citizens, and

Introduction 41

potential cosmopolitans' (42), Canada occupies multiple and transitional spaces where Shakespeare, elusive as always, shimmers.

Notes

1 From a promotional pamphlet for the 1997 Shakespeare by the Sea Festival, Point Pleasant Park, Halifax, Nova Scotia. The artistic director for the festival was Patrick Christopher.
2 Herb Weil, from the University of Manitoba, who has provided this information, wrote of the 'both jarring and beautiful' power of especially the passages on dispossession and alienation.
3 I am grateful to Patrick Leroux for this information on *Événement 38*. Leroux was one of the contributors to this festival of Shakespearean adaptations/transformations, being responsible for a well-received fifteen-minute *Cymbeline*.

PART ONE

Beginnings: Institutionalizing Shakespeare

In rethinking Canadian and Shakespearean studies, this book re-examines conventional wisdom about how notions of the nation, the literary, the traditional, and the cosmopolitan functioned in earlier periods. This section considers institutional placements of Shakespeare outside that of the university English department, in such differently constituted sites as the 1892 Toronto Industrial Exhibition (Heather Murray), the Shakespeare Society of Toronto (Karen Bamford), and CBC radio (Marta Straznicky). While the U.S.-based critic Bruce Robbins suggests, with a sense of discovery, that 'there is a growing consensus that cosmopolitanism sometimes works together with nationalism rather than in opposition to it' (92), such a recognition has long been a staple of Canadian understandings of the two terms, as articulated in novels such as Sara Jeannette Duncan's *The Imperialist* and historical studies such as Carl Berger's *The Sense of Power: Studies in the Idea of Canadian Imperialism, 1867–1914* and as elaborated in these opening chapters. Although it must be stressed that the term commonly used in the late nineteenth and early twentieth century for what we are terming a kind of cosmopolitanism was imperialism, which involved a different kind of cosmopolitanism than that advocated by Robbins at the end of the twentieth century, it is also important to recognize how such terms blend into each other, in sometimes discomforting ways. This section concludes with Margaret Groome's account of the aspirations for a Canadian national theatre and their ambivalent realization in the foundation of Canada's Stratford, an institution accorded further scrutiny in the opening chapters of Part Two.

1

Pioneer Shakespeare Culture: Reverend Henry Scadding and His Shakespeare Display at the 1892 Toronto Industrial Exhibition[1]

HEATHER MURRAY

'Shakespeare Virtually a Type of the Colonist'
— Henry Scadding, *Shakespeare, The Seer – The Interpreter* 22

The title of this piece – 'Pioneer Shakespeare Culture' – refers in several directions. It is the part-title of a pamphlet by the polymathic cleric, local historian, and bibliophile the Reverend Dr Henry Scadding, a busy and benevolent omnipresence of Victorian Toronto. This monograph was the printed catalogue of a collection of Shakespeareana assembled by Reverend Scadding and displayed during the Toronto Industrial Exhibition (the precursor of today's Canadian National Exhibition) during the 1892 fair. The display was the seventh in a series of (what would become) thirteen annual instalments of the 'Log Shanty Book-Shelf,' in which Scadding – who might well be honoured with the title of English Canada's first cultural critic – attempted to recreate the book collections of early York settlers, understand the role of reading in their daily lives, and map the literary terrain in which such reading occurred. The 'pioneer' of the title was often the exhibitor himself, who relied on both his collection and his memories in reconstruing the reading habits of the settlers. (Scadding was also a 'pioneer' in a second sense, as an early book collector, critic, and even scholar, contributing in a modest way to the new project of Shakespearean textual revision and emendation.) The 'book-shelves' were one feature of an annual assembly of historical 'relics' displayed in an old cabin which had been reconstructed on the exhibition grounds by the York Pioneers, a club of early settlers and their descendants who were determined to remind fair-goers of the pioneer roots – or, in Scadding's words, the 'germ' – of industrial modernity (Scadding, *Toronto's*).

At first glance, it is difficult to identify the role of 'Shakespeare' in such a Canadianizing project or to reconcile a specialized one hundred-item collection with a meagre home library of the early century. Thus, my purpose is to analyse the distinctive features of Scadding's interests in Shakespeare and to align the various vectors of the 'Log Shanty Book-Shelf' for 1892. Direct evidence of Scadding's intent for the exhibit, and of audience response to it, is scarce. Scadding's diaries ceased as his eyesight worsened in 1889; the early minutebook of the York Pioneers is long lost; and the catalogue of the display is oddly unlike others in the series in lacking a lengthy introduction.[2] Scadding did leave two interpretive clues, however. The first is his (not coincidental) placing of the Shakespeare display in 1892, the year that marked both the provincial centenary and the four-hundredth anniversary of Columbus's 'discovery.' (Of a more personal relevance, it was also the centenary of Scadding's father's first residency in Upper Canada.) The second clue is Henry Scadding's use of the term 'pioneer' to refer both to the early inhabitants of York and to cultural and intellectual figures from, or crucial to, the Renaissance and Reformation.[3] My method of work, then, is to move across a range of texts and documents and to read them into one another, a procedure that approximates Reverend Scadding's own in sermons and speeches and in his recreation of local history. For Scadding, authors like Shakespeare, Erasmus, and Horace were not simply read in Upper Canada; they could be read *into* Upper Canada. How Reverend Scadding read Shakespeare in, and into, late-nineteenth-century Toronto is the topic here.

Henry Scadding (1813–1901) proudly saw himself as a York pioneer. Indeed, his family could be classed among the earliest European settlers of the area.[4] His father had accompanied Lieutenant Governor John Graves Simcoe to Upper Canada in 1792. While John Scadding returned to Devon to be factor of the Simcoe family estates, he moved permanently to York in 1818, bringing his family three years later. The family settlement east of the Don River, near present-day Queen Street, would feature prominently in Henry Scadding's memoirs of early Toronto. When his father was killed by a falling tree in 1824, the bright and bookish Henry became the protégé of John Strachan, who arranged for him to be one of the first pupils at the newly established Upper Canada College. Scadding excelled in both scholarship and literary composition, and the prize books he received for these achievements – the Washington Irving biography of Seneca, for example, and an eight-volume octavo collection of Shakespeare's plays – influenced his literary tastes and laid the basis for his collection. These items would be prominently placed in the 'Log Shanty' displays of his later years.

Beginning in 1833, Scadding was sponsored by Elizabeth Posthuma Simcoe (the widow of John Graves Simcoe) for study at St John's College Cambridge, from which he graduated in 1837. (He later would receive a Cambridge MA and doctorates in divinity from Cambridge in 1852 and Oxford in 1867.) It was when working for a year at Sorel, as tutor to the sons of Sir John Colborne (the former lieutenant governor of Upper Canada), that Scadding had one of the formative experiences of his life, meeting the renowned art and Shakespeare critic Anna Jameson on her return journey to New York (a leg of her Canadian voyage not recorded in *Winter Studies and Summer Rambles*). The encounter was captured by Scadding in his later *Mrs. Jameson and the Collier Emendations.* He was charmed by her conversation, admired her nobility of mind, and would go on to amass a considerable collection of Jamesoniana including pictures, letters, and works, particularly prizing the New York edition of *Characteristics of Women* whose preface was penned during the winter of Jameson's Toronto residency and dated as such (Scadding, *Mrs. Jameson* 13).

Scadding was appointed to the staff of Upper Canada College and became its classics master in 1844, a position he would retain for almost twenty years. He also received priestly ordination and became incumbent of the new Church of the Holy Trinity in 1847; after serving the parish for almost thirty years, he was made canon of the cathedral church of St James. While ill health would plague Scadding all his life, an assistant assumed many of his parish duties, freeing him for the pursuits of the study and for civic involvement. His precarious state of health would remain always in an odd combination with his enthusiasm and optimism. In addition to the compendious *Toronto of Old* for which he is primarily known, Scadding was the author of scores of essays and monographs and innumerable published letters: opinions etymological, museological, philosophical, and theological flew from his pen. He was a founding member of the Toronto Athenaeum, of the Canadian Institute, and of the York Pioneers historical society (the latter two organizations remaining in existence today). This small, bespectacled, and bewhiskered cleric was everywhere in Toronto for a period of six decades: at dinners, concerts, convocations, exhibits, funerals, sermons, and meetings. (One wishes for a word other than *flâneur* to describe the man who *bobs* – rather than strolls – about the urban landscape and makes the city his own.) Neglected by later scholars (perhaps for the eclecticism, and seeming eccentricity, of his opinions), Reverend Scadding is thoroughly and fittingly inscribed into the fabric of his beloved Toronto.[5] His Trinity Square townhouse lies serenely in the shadow of the mammoth Eaton Centre; maps show the Scadding Court Community Centre, Scadding Avenue, and the Scadding Cabin; a copy of *Toronto of Old* is sealed in the time capsule at the base of the clocktower of Toronto's old City Hall.

Scadding left another important legacy in the form of the specialized collections amassed during his lifetime and deeded to institutions such as Upper Canada College, the Legislative Library, and the University of Toronto.[6] While there were some rare or curious items in his library (whose contours can be retrospectively traced by means of his will, the 'Log Shanty' catalogues, and institutional accession records), in general Scadding's was the library not of an antiquarian but of a scholar. In particular – to focus now on the items of Shakespeareana – Scadding's library evidences a man determined to follow, and to participate in, the developments in Shakespeare criticism and commentary as they unfolded over a period of almost seventy years.

While the collection may be, in Scadding's own words, 'pioneering' – in the literal sense of being started *by* a pioneer – as an amateur scholar and enthusiast Scadding was part of a widely developed Shakespeare culture in Upper Canada which can be traced to the pre-Rebellion years. The Toronto Shakspeare [*sic*] Club, a well established literary and debating club for young professional men, was flourishing as early as 1835. (Anna Jameson's husband, Robert Jameson, presided over the club on its reconstitution in 1836 as the Toronto Literary Club.) Dedicated Shakespeare societies would appear later in the century as far afield as Hamilton, London, Napanee, and Owen Sound (the latter two being women-only societies). Shakespeare was a staple of the less-specialized literary societies as well, such as the proto-suffragist Toronto Women's Literary Club (est. 1877), which used Shakespeare both to expand the general culture of its members and to explore themes of woman's character and capabilities, while the young African-Canadian women of the Frederic [*sic*] Douglass Self-Improvement Club of Amherstburg would begin their meetings with a recitation of Shakespearean quotations. Shakespeare study featured prominently in programs of self- and mutual instruction because it was popularly believed to provide an 'education in itself' for those with few study hours. Pronunciation, declamation, etymology, history, geography, politics, and 'classics,' to name only a few, could all be gained or gleaned from the study of Shakespearean scenes. Thus, Shakespeare remained a staple of the liberal arts 'curriculum' of the many Mechanics' Institutes initiated in the latter half of the century and was a cornerstone of the Chautauqua Literary and Scientific Circle correspondence courses followed by thousands of Ontario residents during the closing decades of the nineteenth century.[7] Shakespeare study also came to occupy a central position in the English curriculum of the provincial university, although not without controversy over the suitability of some plays for the newly admitted women arts undergraduates. Amateur scholarship flourished as well, with some 370 items of Shakespeare commentary appearing in Canadian cultural journals prior to 1900, according to the index of periodicals compiled by Thomas Vincent. In the years surrounding Scadding's 1892 display, the 'Baconian' controversy received especial attention; Canadian commentators appear to have judged the theory elitist and found it perfectly plausible that Shakespeare was a 'self-made' man (and mind), as many of them wished to be. Recalling the popularity of Shakespeare study in the nineteenth century, and the late-century framing of Shakespeare as a product of self-instruction and improvement, helps to reconstrue how a Shakespeare display might have seemed a suitable contribution to a provincial exposition. This context also allows us to contextualize Scadding's other work as a Shakespearean scholar. While he can be located within this amateur Shakespeare culture, Scadding can also be differentiated from it, both in the avidity of his enthusiasm and in the specificity of his concerns. Scadding contributed to the new enterprise of textual emendation, developed a theory of Shakespeare's relevance to contemporary times, and 'Canadianized' Shakespeare in a novel way.

Evidence of Scadding's interpretive endeavours appears somewhat cryptically in his catalogue *After Gleanings for the Log-Shanty Book Shelf of 1896*. Referring to his 1864 pamphlet *Shakespeare, the Seer – the Interpreter*, Scadding commented with his usual modesty on its favourable reception: 'This little production procured for me a place in Allibone's Index and also the friendly regards of several Shakespeare writers and students, e.g. J. Payne Collier, Halliwell-Phillips, Mr. and Mrs. Cowden Clarke, H.H. Furness, etc.' (*After Gleanings* 13).[8] Furness, the eminent American editor, had apparently promised to include Scadding's emendation to Sonnet 112 if a poetry Variorum should reach the press and regretted that Scadding's article 'Errata Recepta' had reached his attention too late to include the emendation of 'Runaway Eyes' in the new

Variorum *Romeo and Juliet*: 'It and you shall certainly receive due honour in the second edition' (Scadding, *After Gleanings* 13).

What were Scadding's emendations and were they eventually incorporated? In the compendious notes appended to *Shakespeare, the Seer – the Interpreter*, Scadding focuses on line 6 of Sonnet 112: for 'That my steel'd – sense or changes, right or wrong,' Scadding proposes 'That I am steel'd 'gainst censure, right or wrong' (Scadding, *Shakespeare* 31). While the full text of 'Errata Recepta' is no longer available, Scadding apparently refers to his *Romeo and Juliet* emendation in another context.[9] Noting the notoriously cryptic 'runnawayes eyes' in *Romeo and Juliet* (which remains to this day the most famous unresolved crux in the Shakespeare corpus [Holmer 97]), Scadding 'remember[s] once suggesting "Erinnys" for this "run-away"'s ... Erinnys to be taken to mean the civic discord reigning at the time in Verona' (Scadding, *Mrs. Jameson* 9). Despite Furness's courteous replies, Scadding's contributions do not appear in any printings of the Variorum *Romeo and Juliet*, nor in the Variorum *Sonnets*. 'Erinnys' was perhaps too wild an emendation to be included even among the twenty-nine pages of ingenious resolutions collated by Furness, and the Variorum *Sonnets* would not appear until long after the original editor's death.

Mrs. Jameson and the Collier Emendations (a monograph published in the same year as the Log Shanty display and excerpted in *The Week*) provides a more extensive meditation on textual emendation. This palimpsestic production presents Scadding's commentary on Anna Jameson's marginalia in her copy of J. Payne Collier's *Notes and Emendations to the Text of Shakespeare*, a work based in turn on the corrections and memoranda in a 1632 folio presumably found by Collier.[10] Scadding's principal concern is to follow the author of *Characteristics of Women* as she indicates through a system of keyed symbols her acceptance or rejection of Collier's emendations, and offers occasional suggestions of her own. Scadding concludes the volume by tracking the numerous variants on Shakespeare's own signature and makes a case for the orthographical correctness of 'Shakespeare.' While Scadding's contributions to the area of Shakespearean textual scholarship were modest, they did gain him some correspondence with leading scholars of the day, as witnessed by photographs of noted Shakespeareans, such as Mary Cowden Clarke and Charles Cowden Clarke, in his personal photograph album.[11] And he did, indeed, receive an entry in Allibone's *Critical Dictionary of English Literature*, the compiler even appending the comment 'Excellent' to the list of Scadding's publications (Allibone 2: 1943).

Scadding's scholarship is further characterized by his insistence that Shakespeare was of continuing relevance to the present day and that 'Honour to Shakespeare' could be an 'active living sentiment' (*Pioneer* 2). This concern had begun to preoccupy the cleric some thirty years before the exhibit of his Shakespeare 'Book-Shelf,' in his address to the St George's Society (which was, and remains, the oldest society in Toronto, and of which he was the chaplain). *Shakespeare, the Seer – the Interpreter*, delivered for the Shakespeare tercentenary, was published in 1864 and would be reissued in 1897. The introduction to the lengthy address was headed 'The Era of Shakespeare' and commences in this way:

> Why do the men of this generation turn back their thoughts so often to the generation of their fellow-men who lived some three or four hundred years ago? It is because that generation witnessed the commencement of a great crisis in human affairs, which affected deeply, in a variety of ways, our forefathers of *that* day, and their brother-men throughout all Europe; which has affected every generation of the descendants of these; which affects all Europe now; and through it touches ourselves and all other communities of men of these western continents. We all feel ourselves this day borne onward on one or another of the liftings in the great undulation of thought and new experience which then had its beginnings, and must be looked at in its origin, or it cannot be understood. (Scadding, *Shakespeare* 5)

Like other Shakespeare amateurs, Scadding saw the Bard as a repository of wise saws and modern instances, whose comments (whether on ethics, politics, or the condition of women) were resonant with issues of the day. An accomplished sermonist, he looked for ways to bridge old texts to modern times and could enliven a homily with topical allusions. But Scadding's sense of Shakespeare's modernity went further, as delineated in this quotation. Scadding saw Shakespeare as present at the initiation of the modern world, the time of the invention of printing, the translation of the Bible and works of antiquity, and the beginnings of global exploration and scientific discovery. Additionally, Shakespeare's works express the sense of living in a transformative time, shared by the denizens of the fast-paced years of the nineteenth century's end. That Scadding's sense of Shakespeare's contemporary presence is even more radical is signalled by the title of the talk: Scadding sees Shakespeare as having the abilities of a 'seer,' who can look both deeply into and beyond the constraints of his own time.

In deciphering this aspect of Scadding's argument, some connection can be made to the Shakespeare criticism of Daniel Wilson, the ethnologist, literary scholar, and University of Toronto president, whose death had occurred only the month before the opening of the Shakespeare Log Shanty display. In his *Caliban: The Missing Link* (1873), Wilson had analysed this character as a startling anticipation of the 'link' between animal and human hypothesized in recent anthropological and evolutionary theory: 'Only now, two centuries and a half after its production on the English stage, has it entered into the mind of the scientific naturalist to conceive of such a being as possible' (66). Shakespeare, in Wilson's analysis, is not only scientific but prescient: in *The Tempest* Shakespeare 'anticipates and satisfies the most startling problem of the nineteenth century' (192). What is, for Wilson, evidence of Shakespeare's ability to imagine beyond the boundaries of his day becomes in Scadding's speech evidence of Shakespeare's role in God's foreordination of events. Shakespeare's works, Scadding is hasty to add, are distinctly secular rather than sacred in their character; but it is precisely in this secular character that the poet's 'predestined, divinely-intended function' lies (*Shakespeare* 13). Shakespeare's life and work show how the human faculties can be both developed and harmonized; a 'seer' himself, he can teach his fellows to 'see.' Lest his vision, in its completion, appear too vast or too abstract, to his visionary powers Shakespeare adds the gift of interpretation, allowing him to be the teacher of his own works.

Scadding was characteristic of his time in following with interest the evolving disputes over Shakespeare's texts and canon; his belief in the continuing relevance of Shakespeare to the modern age was widely shared. His novelty emerges, however, in his 'Canadianizing' of Shakespeare, apparent in the collection, the cataloguing, and the staging of the 'Log Shanty Book-Shelf' for 1892 and in the catalogue's full-title: *Pioneer Shakespeare Culture in Canada: Collection of Shakesperian [sic] Literature, Begun at York, U.C. (Toronto), Circa, A.D. 1826, And added to occasionally from time to time down to the Centennial Year of the Province of Ontario, A.D. 1892, Being the Contents of The Log Shanty Book-Shelf for the Year 1892, Displayed in the Lodge of the Pioneer and Historical Society of the County of York, On the Grounds of the Industrial Exhibition of That Year, With an Introductory Note By the Rev. Dr. Scadding.*

Scadding Cabin, as it is now known, still stands on the Exhibition Grounds, shuttered for most of the year. Bounded by a split-rail fence, bordered by beds of homely nasturtiums, and shaded with lilacs and an aging chestnut tree, it is a quiet oasis from the roaring midway to the east, a contrast that must have been equally apparent to visitors to the bustling exhibition one hundred years ago. This eighteenth-century cabin, donated by a local farmer, was reassembled by the Pioneers in 1879 and originally bore a sign reading 'Governor Simcoe' in the belief that he had constructed the cabin to house staff or as a hunting lodge. With the death of Henry Scadding in 1901, it was named 'Scadding Cabin' after their honoured president. Ironically, it *was* 'Scadding Cabin' all along, a fact of which Scadding himself had long and in vain tried to convince his compatriots. Only in 1955 was it finally proven that this was the second of two cabins constructed by John Scadding in 1792 and sold by him with a parcel of land to the Smith family on his return to Canada in 1818 (Avigdor, 'Scadding Cabin' and 'John Scadding's'; T.A. Reed, 'Explanatory').

The 'Book-shelf,' according to an 1896 pamphlet describing the Pioneers' exhibit for that year, had become a 'distinctive feature' of the furnishings of the homestead cabin: 'The row of books so designated has in each year differed from the corresponding collection in preceding years, but in each case the collection on the shelf has been one that dated back for its commencement to the old pioneer days when literature was scarce and chance volumes of the most miscellaneous character were eagerly picked up whenever an occasion afforded.' (*Pioneers'* 3)

Scadding's especial contribution to the Pioneers' annual exhibit began in 1886, with the last occurring in 1898 (only three years before his death). Displays of books authored by or owned by early Torontonians, of early schoolbooks, of Devonshire literature and memorabilia, of early bibles, of early printing including incunabula, and of material by and on Erasmus preceded the Shakespeare exhibit. Collections of 'sententious' works, of literature pertaining to Horace, of early travel and exploration writing, of works of a miscellaneous character, of literature by or inspired by Seneca, and of scholarship on Native peoples provided the exhibits to follow. The displays appear to have been drawn almost entirely from the personal library of this renowned bibliophile. Catalogues were issued with all exhibits except the first, whose contents were retrospectively described in the catalogue for the next year; each catalogue contains detailed bibliographic descriptions of the items with (often rather idiosyncratic) comments about their provenance or significance. In almost all cases, a lengthy introduction prefaced the book-list, and the brevity of Scadding's prefatory remarks in the 1892 catalogue is an exception.

The 1892 Toronto fair had much to offer the thousands who flocked to its grounds for twelve days in September in search of awards, amusement, and education: displays of new inventions and labour-saving devices, agricultural competitions, 'Pawnee Bill's Wild West' show, and a grand spectacle and firework display titled 'Sardanapalus or the Fall of Nineveh' (*1892 Programme*). But the Pioneer exhibit seems to have been able to hold its own against these enticements. Rearrangements on the grounds meant that the cabin had emerged into greater visual prominence and was no longer occluded by the massive apparatus for the spectacle ('Now Let'); the Pioneers (by then the Pioneer and Historical Society) also gained publicity by holding their meeting in the opening days of the fair, before newspaper columns were monopolized by livestock judging and race results and reports of arrests for 'liquorous' disturbances. So solid a feature of the exhibition had the Pioneer cabin become that by 1895 the exhibition governors were contemplating the erection of a 'proper Museum' to house their displays since the cabin could not accommodate the 'many thousands of visitors' who wished to view the exhibit each year (*Industrial* 19).

The 1892 display, held in the building popularly known as the 'Simcoe Cabin,' made gestures both to the provincial centenary and to Columbus's voyage. Portraits and busts of early Toronto 'worthies' flanked a head of Columbus; sketches and maps of early Toronto and its harbour were juxtaposed with views of the monuments to Columbus at Genoa and Madrid; other engravings were intended to illustrate the times and voyages of Columbus (Scadding, *Pioneer* 3). A curious contribution was a map of the world with the eastern and western hemispheres reversed ('Another'). This was an interestingly early attempt to provide a non-'Eurocentric' world map; as Scadding noted in a one-page commentary in his catalogue for that year, the map could provide both context and scale for Columbus's 'discovery,' illustrating the relative brevity of his journey and the immensity of his geographic misconceptions. The map could have a further pedagogic benefit in highlighting the relationship of North America to the 'Orient' and in emphasizing North America's west coast – a further development of the 'westering' theme of both the exhibit and of Scadding's display.

Scadding's contribution to the 1892 Pioneer exhibit was a collection of one hundred items of Shakespeareana, a collection begun in 1826 (as announced in the catalogue title) and continued to the present day.[12] In his introductory note, Scadding contextualizes the origin of his collection in the reading culture of the day. Exposed first to the works of the Bard through the schoolbooks and collections of 'elegant extracts' then in favour and so important for forming the taste of the young, he delighted in being awarded a copy of the collected works as a prize for scholarly achievement. Next came 'the chance purchase of a small terra cotta bust on a low pillar-shaped pedestal' that helped to 'give definiteness to the poet's personality in the mind' (*Pioneer* 3). Scadding continued to acquire volumes both old and new, and he assumes that this represents the first collection of Shakespeareana to be assembled in (rather than imported to) York – thus the collection can be considered 'pioneering' in a double sense.

No evidence exists to indicate how the items were displayed in the cabin (were they labelled? Were plates or bindings given especial display?) or how they were used (could items be individually viewed or handled by the curious? Was someone on hand to answer questions? Were catalogues made available to visitors freely or for a fee?). That the items were categorized is suggested by the subdivisions in the catalogue, under the headings of Editions, Illustrative Works, Criticism, Fiction Relating to Shakespeare, and Biographies. The centrepiece of the show, judging from the care given to its description, was an 'exact reproduction by the photo-zincographic process' of the 1623 First Folio (*Pioneer* 5); this was lavishly bound and the page edgings gilded. A 1773 'Theobald' edition and 1776 'Johnson' edition also receive careful description; there were sixteen additional nineteenth-century editions or facsimile reprints. (One notable omission is editions issued by the New Shakspere [*sic*] Society, although critical works by affiliates of the society such as Furnivall and Dowden are included.) It is, at first, difficult to discern how Scadding differentiated 'Illustrative Works' from 'Criticism,' but the thirty-seven items categorized as 'Illustrative' appear to be those that would shed light on Shakespeare's background and processes of composition, including concordances, keys, analyses of Shakespeare's sources, and, in several cases, the source books themselves (Florio, Plautus, and Seneca, for example). Scadding's own *Shakespeare, the Seer – the Interpreter* and his friend the late (Sir) Daniel Wilson's *Caliban, the Missing Link* are among the works in this section. Under 'Criticism,' devoted more to questions of editing and interpretation, are to be found sixteen works, led by Anna Jameson's annotated copy of Collier's *Notes*; Scadding's commentary on Jameson's marginalia had appeared in *The Week* the February preceding the exhibit. (Jameson's own *Characteristics of Women* is not included in the display; a reason for this odd omission may be that other items of Jamesonia had appeared in earlier displays.) Scadding made his own position as a 'Stratfordian' clear by including several works on the Bacon-Shakespeare controversy among the eleven items of 'Fiction Relating to Shakespeare.' The final section of 'Biographies' contains some twenty works, although not all are biographies of the Bard strictly speaking: memorials, works on Shakespeare's life and times, and some studies of his contemporaries are included here. Overall, only a handful of editions predate the nineteenth century, and perhaps only the Florio *World of Words* and the Montaigne translation could be considered of real value even today.

This is the library of a working Shakespeare scholar, and it reflects the popular and critical trends of the century. Works of textual emendation and source scholarship are included, representing what one might call a first phase of Shakespeare scholarship. There are volumes devoted to illustrating the themes of Shakespeare's work, the integrity of his mind, and the unity of his life and work; such volumes represent a later direction often associated with, although not unique to, London's New Shakspere Society. There is even a selection of 'gift book' items such as sentimental volumes of Shakespeare quotations and picturesque Stratford views. The amateur student of Shakespeare, as well as the scholar, would have found much to recognize in this collection. But the Shakespeare exhibit is fully readable only within its double frame of the provincial centenary and the commemoration of the Columbus 'discovery'; one must imagine it surrounded by the maps, sketches, portraits, and busts with which the 'Book-Shelf' was juxtaposed.

The incorporation of a provincial industrial exhibition in 1879 presented opportunities swiftly seized by the York Pioneers. Involvement in the exhibition would raise the group's civic profile and allow them to contribute a historical dimension to an annual event devoted to progress and the wonders of the new. That the remains of the original French trading outpost, Fort Rouille, and the site of the disembarkation of American troops in 1813 were on the grounds now to be devoted to the exhibition lent additional impetus to their purpose. Unsuccessful in ensuring the preservation of ruins they believed to be the remnants of the fort, the Pioneers proposed instead the erection of a monument to this 'cradle spot' of trade and commerce, as Scadding had referred to the site in a letter to the mayor (qtd. in Walden 230).[13] Scadding's annual efforts to compile and catalogue his Log Shanty Book-Shelf often intersected with work on related preservationist projects. His 1887 diary shows him completing the annual catalogue (of the self-improving literature of a 'bookish' early settler) while supervising the inscription on the Fort Rouille obelisk, commenting on the commemorative poem Sarah Anne Curzon would deliver at the unveiling, and collecting the last of the overdue subscriptions for the monument. Revisions to the 1888 catalogue (on Devonshire memorabilia) were interrupted by the exciting discovery of skeletons during construction for that year's exhibition; Scadding promptly commenced visits to the excavation site, convinced that the burial ground of the fort had been uncovered.[14] In 1892 the Shakespeare exhibit was thoroughly intermixed with plans for the provincial centenary, which Scadding viewed as the centennial of 'The Establishment of the Representative System' (Scadding, *Centennial*).[15] At the Pioneers' meeting in the exhibition's opening days, a letter was read from the Honourable John Beverley Robinson, who conveyed the gratitude of Simcoe's English descendants for the group's efforts to honour their forefather ('Now Let'). The close of the exhibition marked the opening of the provincial parliament and the dedication of the Simcoe memorial site, a project on which the Pioneers had long laboured. (Reverend Scadding's speech closed the extensive program ['Parliaments'].) The Simcoe celebration was in turn closely related to the quadricentennial of the Columbus 'discovery'; in fact, Scadding had used the doubled anniversary to buttress his lobbying of the Legislative Assembly for the Simcoe memorial (Scadding, Letter). 'It goes without saying,' Scadding had advised the Pioneers, 'that we should all observe 1892 as a centennial occurring for the fourth time' (Scadding, *Address 1891*).

The Log Shanty Book-Shelf of 1892 thus has the effect of positioning 'Shakespeare' in relationship to 'pioneer' culture in ways additional to his popularity among readers of the early days. The first, and most obvious – and it is a point made explicitly by Scadding in his introduction to the catalogue – is that Shakespeare represents a 'Mother Country' whose ties to the newly settled nations are 'indissoluble' (Scadding, *Pioneer* 3). But the Old and New world connections are compounded by the circumstances of the Shakespeare display and by the series of 'frames' within which it would have been viewed – by the pictures, maps, and 'relics'; by the 'Simcoe Cabin'; by the provincial exhibition; by the centennial (and quadricentennial) commemorations; and by Toronto itself. In this complex context Shakespeare is, like Columbus, a 'pioneer' of the early days of the modern era, in which the known gives way to the unknown and the boundaries of the world expand, when a 'new' world is discovered but even the old becomes 'new.' He thus becomes, through a form of synecdochic substitution, a spirit of the commercial enterprise of which the industrial exhibition is a fruition. And while the literature of all the earlier 'Book-Shelf' displays had been framed to a degree by 'Simcoe,' given their location in the cabin of that name, on this particular occasion 'Shakespeare' and 'Simcoe' are placed in a relationship of adjacency in which the visitor is encouraged to contemplate their connections. 'Shakespeare Virtually a Type of the Colonist,' Scadding had determined in his 1864 tercentenary address, noting that Shakespeare was 'appreciated among the junior members of the family of nations' for exhibiting and embodying 'the BEAVER-INSTINCT,' a pioneering spirit common to both the Bard and the colonial settler (*Shakespeare* 22). 'Shakespeare,' like 'Simcoe,' becomes the symbol of the continual westward movement of culture and community (a movement that involves, but is not synonymous with, material progress) as well as the ways and means by which it is effected. Last, the triplet of Columbus, Shakespeare, and Simcoe encourages the moment of retrospection that was the explicit purpose of the York Pioneer displays. 'Our commemorations of the heroes of three and four hundred years ago,' Scadding had written in another context, 'are not only convenient *epochæ*, pausing-places from whence to review the past, and look forward hopefully to the future, but they assume likewise, in some instances, the declaration of principles – and protests ...' (Scadding, *Shakespeare* 9). 'Shakespeare,' then, functions as an illustration, an amplification, and a counterbalance of the values offered more generally by the exposition of 1892.

Lest the image of Shakespeare as a hewer of words and drawer of quatrains appear at odds with the prophetic genius envisaged elsewhere in Scadding's work, let me speculate on some further sinuous entanglements that ensue when we add the 'S' of 'Scadding' to 'Simcoe' and 'Shakespeare.' In two of the 'Book-Shelf' catalogues that would follow the Shakespeare display, Scadding would interweave in rather Proustian ways his reading experiences with incidents from his own life. These catalogues, written in the cleric's closing years, are more autobiographical than bibliographical in their impulse. The introduction to *Horace Canadianizing* of 1894 describes how he first became acquainted with the writings of the Latin poet when 'as yet a youthful inmate of a primitive Canadian pioneer homestead,' with the result that 'this primeval abode came to be associated in my mind curiously with numerous impressions derived from Horace' (3). And, conversely, 'to this day the language of the poet ... instantly receives colour and interpretation from one's boyish recollections' (3). What follows is an account in which Horace's writings and the events of the cleric's life are overlaid (a falling tree that spared the poet and one that took John Scadding's life), in which Horace is ascribed the rugged, rustic, earthy, energetic character of the early pioneer, and in which citations from Horace are found so applicable to the Canadian situation as to be woven into the 'warp and woof' of the new dominion (13). In a later catalogue, *Seneca's Prophecy and Its Fulfilment. A Memorial of A.D. 1897 and the Four Hundredth Anniversary of the First Sighting of the North-East Coast of North America, By John and Sebastian Cabot ...*, Scadding gives the account of his encounter with Seneca through the medium of Washington Irving's *Life of Columbus*, a work prefaced by a Senecan quotation in which the discovery of the New World is seemingly prophesized. As Scadding renders the passage, Oceanus will undo the bands which confine human enterprise and new spheres will be revealed. For Scadding, however, Seneca is a figure less of the first century than of the Renaissance, an influence on the Senecan playwrights and thus on Shakespeare himself. By a series of associations that are now more Joycean than Proustian, Seneca and Columbus become oddly collapsed, with the one motivating, and the one transporting, the other; Seneca's seemingly vatic pronouncement foretells the very presence of the boyhood Henry Scadding in his log shanty home.

In the absence of an elaborated introduction to the catalogue of the 1892 display, we cannot know in detail how Reverend Scadding would have related the works of Shakespeare to his own life (although we may assume, by the 1897 republication of *Shakespeare, the Seer – the Interpreter*, that he still adhered to the views of Shakespeare laid out some thirty years before). But we can locate Scadding's work as both a critic and a collector, and the 1892 display, within what one might call Scadding's 'theory' of reading. I have suggested at the opening of this essay that Henry Scadding might well be called English-speaking Canada's first cultural critic; analysis of his theory will help to substantiate that claim.

As will be clear from the specialized and occasionally idiosyncratic nature of the collections, in only a few cases was Scadding concerned to recreate an actual bookshelf of an early settler or to recapture a typical reading experience during (what historians of literacy now call) an 'intensive' reading culture.[16] But this does not necessarily mean that Scadding drifted away from the exhibits' original purpose, nor that he became concerned primarily with showcasing his own impressive collection. Rather, his intents were apparently more complex, and certainly multiple, as indicated by this excerpt from the 1894 catalogue, an introduction that gained a wider readership by being reprinted in the *Canadian Magazine* in that year:

> During the Toronto Industrial Exhibition, there has been displayed, now, for several years in succession, within the building known as the Pioneers' lodge, a collection of printed matter of a rather unique character, calculated to throw light on what we may term the incipient literatureism of western Canada. In addition to the early views, maps, plans, portraits and so forth adorning the interior of the lodge, a group of books has been set out in a separate compartment and distinguished by the homely title of the *Log Shanty Book Shelf*. In each successive year, the group has been a different one, but on each occasion the books have consisted of promiscuous gatherings likely only to be considered of importance during a primitive era in the history of a new country. (Scadding, 'Pioneer Literary' 18)[17]

Three primary points emerge from the above. The first is that Scadding is concerned less to recreate collections of the past than to delineate a state of (what he terms) 'incipent literatureism' or (what we might term) the literary field at a given moment (using 'literary' to indicate, as Scadding would have also employed the term, not *belles lettres* alone but a range of print production). The period on which Scadding concentrates roughly coincides with the pre-Rebellion years of his own boyhood. He characterizes book access and reading experience in this 'primitive era' as a combination of frequently repeated (and deeply personal) readings of familiar texts, with occasionally random (and often remarkably serendipitous) encounters with a broader range of materials. By using the term 'promiscuous' for the latter, Scadding indicates both the accidental nature of these encounters (given the scanty numbers and uneven distribution of print resources in the province) and the lack of discrimination of these early readers. For Scadding, 'promiscuous' is not a negative term: it connotes amateurism, enthusiasm, eclecticism, and the ability to make a reader's silk purse from a writer's sow's ear, to turn found textual objects to imaginative use. It characterizes his own experiences both as a reader and as a book collector.

The second point follows. Terms such as 'collection' and 'catalogue' may convey the impression that what Scadding valued primarily was heuristic order and good bibliographic housekeeping. In fact, it is the accidental (or seemingly accidental) nature of encounters in the literary field that most fascinates Scadding and that he uses the notes in his catalogues and essays to retrace. At times, reading the appended annotations to the bibliographic descriptions is like reading Borges *avant la lettre*, as we move – in the case of the Seneca collection, for example – from Scadding's fascination with the Senecan prophesy to Seneca's prescient interest in Cordoba (which would be the home of Cabot's royal patrons) and the amazing coincidence of the Seneca Indians and their 'stoic' natures. In many cases such uncanny collusions are – as the cleric is wont to explain – evidences of God's providence and preordination, of which even the wise writers of antiquity had occasional intuition. Scadding's 'theory' of reading is hermeneutic in both senses of the term. He is interested in the encounters of readers with texts, their journeys through them, the ways readers find themselves in the books they read, the parallels between texts and lives. For Scadding, the ideal reading is a *sortes* (in the sense of the *sortes Virgilianae*). But his concept of reading is additionally 'hermeneutic' in the sense of the biblical interpretive method in which Scadding himself was trained. Texts are read in terms of one another, as anticipations and fulfilments, types and antitypes. According to a phrenologist whom the cleric once consulted, along with the lobes of charity and of attachment to place, the prophetic faculty was his most developed (*Phrenological*).

A third point extends Scadding's hermeneutics to a historical theory. Scadding was interested in (what we might term) a cultural *relay*, in which texts, *topoi*, questions, and wisdom are passed from one historical epoch to another. This sense of the 'relay' is what, perhaps, best characterizes the 'Log Shanty Book-Shelf' project and lends the disparate exhibitions a coherence. Scadding is concerned to connect three eras: a 'classical' era (especially of the later Latin poets), the Renaissance (in particular the time of Elizabeth and of Shakespeare), and the 'primitive era in the history of a new country' ('Pioneer Literary' 18). In practice the three epochs are reduced to two: Scadding is concerned with the ancients primarily as they existed in (we might even say, were products of) the Renaissance: translated, cited, revered, and used. The parallelism Scadding wishes to establish is between a loosely 'Elizabethan' era and the society of Upper Canada and his own day, as was clearly indicated by the title of the 1892 Log Shanty display.

Scadding, then, describes a reading culture characterized by a deep intricacy of readerly lives and texts, by accidental reading encounters, and by redeployment for present purposes of materials from an earlier time. In other words, the reader is self-cultivating, adventurous, and an agent in the transplantation of cultures. For Reverend Scadding, to read – and to read Shakespeare – is to be a pioneer.

Notes

1 I would like to acknowledge library staff at the Archives of Ontario; the Baldwin Room, Toronto Reference Library; Thomas Fisher Rare Books Library, University of Toronto; the General Synod Library of the Anglican Church; and the Urban Affairs Library, Metro Hall, for patient retrieval of scattered Scadding items; and staff at the Church of the Holy Trinity, and the Toronto Historical Board, for other information. Special thanks to Linda Coban of the Canadian National Exhibition Archives, to David Galbraith for assistance with Shakespeare and rare book bibliography, and to Jill Levenson for advice on *Romeo and Juliet*.
2 Scadding's diaries for 1837–44 and 1866–89 along with other notebooks are in the Baldwin Room of the Toronto Reference Library. The York Pioneer and Historical Society Papers are in the Archives of Ontario, Toronto.
3 Thus, the Log Shanty Book-Shelves dealing with 'Pioneer Bibles' and 'Pioneer Typography' are devoted to early examples of European printing including incunables; 'Relics of a Pioneer Anti-Obscurantist' refers simultaneously to Erasmus and to Scadding himself.
4 In compiling this biographical sketch, I have relied in part on Edith G. Firth and Curtis Fahey's *Dictionary of Canadian Biography* entry and T.A. Reed's sketch of the Scadding family.
5 Scadding is also commemorated through the Scadding Award of Excellence of the Ontario Historical Society.
6 Scadding's will was probated 25 June 1901; an incomplete photocopy of the will is with the Scadding Papers in the Baldwin Room.
7 This material on literary societies comes from work by Heather Murray, published and forthcoming. The Toronto Shakespeare Club is described in 'Frozen Pen, Fiery Print'; the Toronto Women's Literary Club in 'Great Works and Good Works.' Other societies and the Chautauqua circles are discussed in '*Come, Bright Improvement!*'.
8 Writing a letter to Scadding on her own and her husband's behalf, Mary Cowden Clarke said that they were gratified by Scadding's appreciation of 'our Poet Idol's genius and worth' and praised the profundity and eloquence of some particular passages.
9 The printed version appears to be only a first instalment, since it is concluded by the words 'To be continued.' It appears, however, that Scadding sent the full text to his correspondents.
10 Scadding must have been aware of the controversy surrounding Collier's 'find' and the emendations, but for him the controversy lies in the fact that the emendations, 'if received, would oblige all preceding readers and stu-

dents of Shakespeare to alter their ideas' (*Mrs. Jameson* 3). He appears to have considered the folio authentic.

11 Henry Scadding's albums are in the Henry Scadding Papers, Thomas Fisher Rare Book Library, University of Toronto.
12 Unfortunately, there is no information either in the catalogue or elsewhere to indicate the order in which items were accessioned by Scadding.
13 Keith Walden's examination of the early exhibition contains an analysis of the efforts to commemorate Fort Rouille.
14 Diary entries 22 Aug. through 14 Sept. 1887; 27 Aug. through 11 Sept. 1888.
15 Indeed, the Pioneers appear to have been instrumental in the choice of 1892 (the centenary of the convening of the first parliament at Niagara) rather than 1891 (centenary of the division of the province into Lower and Upper Canada) as the official celebration date. Surely Scadding's personal ties to the Simcoe family, as much as Simcoe's innovations in governance, were responsible for this preference, as well as the coincidence of the provincial anniversary with that of Columbus's 'discovery.'
16 Most early inhabitants of Upper Canada would be characterized as 'intensive' readers; that is, their reading would be composed of repeated perusal of a limited number of almanacs, practical and agricultural manuals, religious materials, and perhaps a few favoured literary works, seasoned by newspaper, broadsheet, and sometimes magazine reading. In an extensive reading culture, the value of broad reading is stressed and mechanisms such as literary societies, libraries, and Mechanics' Institutes arise to meet this felt need.
17 By 'western Canada' Scadding, of course, refers to Canada West, the name for the province after 1841.

2

The Imperial Theme: The Shakespeare Society of Toronto, 1928–1969[1]

KAREN BAMFORD

His Honor To Address Shakespeare Society
Lt.-Gov. and Mrs. J. Keiller MacKay, attended by Mr. and Mrs. Donald Wright, will attend a meeting of the Shakespeare Society of Toronto in the United Empire Loyalist House tonight when the lieutenant-governor addresses the members on the subject of the Bard.
The president, Prof. J.W. Dodd, with Mrs. Dodd, will receive. Hostesses for the social hour following will include Mrs. Raymond Card, Elsie Keefer, and Mrs. E.L. Pequegnat. Prior to the meeting the officers, executive and honorary members will entertain the guests of honor at dinner in the Albany Club.
Planning to attend are Maj. and Mrs. James Annand, Lady Robinson, Canon and Mrs. R.P. Dann, Mr. and Mrs. W.G. Frisby, Mr. and Mrs. Raymond Card, Dr. and Mrs. Stanley K. Clark, Mr. and Mrs. Gordon Clarry, Mr. and Mrs. F.A. Dashwood, Mr. and Mrs. E.L. Pequegnat, Dean and Mrs. B.C. Diltz, Mr. and Mrs. John Griffin, Mr. and Mrs. W. Burnside, Elsie Keefer, Mrs. Norman A. McLean, Mrs. G.H. Milligan, Mr. and Mrs. Harvey B. Carlaw, Mr. and Mrs. Denis Critoph, Mr. and Mrs. M. O'Heany, Minnie Babe, R.L. Mudge, Vera Butcher, E. Blanche Potter and Mrs. J.C. Surgey.

– Toronto *Daily Star*, 5 Dec. 1962

A copy of the newspaper article quoted above appears in a scrapbook donated to the Archives of Ontario by Mrs Raymond Card.[2] Beside it is a clipping from the *Telegram*, in which reporter Rose Macdonald enthusiastically describes the event announced by the *Star*: 'It was a proud night for the Shakespeare Society of Toronto. Their patron, the Lieutenant Governor of Ontario, Hon. J. Keiller MacKay, addressed them on The

Bard. The Lieutenant Governor is an authority on Shakespeare – Burns too, but this was Shakespeare's night. Even those in the audience aware of their patron's enormous knowledge of Shakespeare's writing were newly amazed at his command of them. As a feat of memory alone this was stupendous.'

Below the clippings appears a snapshot of members of the Society at the summer home of Dr and Mrs Stanley K. Clark – 'The New Waygate,' Georgian Bay – dated 19 September 1962. Aging and dignified, most of the men wear suits and ties despite the casual setting, the women dresses or skirts and cardigans.

I begin with this page of the scrapbook because it illustrates several key aspects of the Shakespeare Society of Toronto (SST) in its later years. Most notably, the clippings highlight the Society's coveted affiliation with a political elite: an affiliation marked not only by the patronage of the lieutenant governor but also by the attendance of Mr and Mrs Donald Wright, son-in-law and daughter of the Rt Hon. Arthur Meighen (former prime minister of Canada and leader of the Conservative Party).[3] Representatives of other elite groups include academics (Professor Dodd, Ontario College of Education; Dean Diltz, Ontario Institute for Studies in Education), clergy (Canon Dann, Anglican Church of Canada), professionals and businessmen (Dr Stanley K. Clark, MD.; Raymond Card, member, Royal Architectural Institute of Canada; Mr F.A. Dashwood, barrister, solicitor, and notary public; Major Annand, former deputy head of the Crown Life Insurance Company), and even – improbably enough – titled gentry (Lady Robinson). The article in the *Star* is, in effect, a press release from the SST, designed to publicize these prestigious affiliations and to affirm the elite status of its members (especially those 'planning to attend'). The access to the Albany Club enjoyed by 'officers, executive and honorary members' of the SST similarly underlines their elite social status.

The other topographical marker in the notice, the United Empire Loyalist (UEL) House – at 30 Prince Arthur Avenue, a discreetly wealthy address – points to the predominantly British ethnicity of the SST members and associates: their celebration of Shakespeare was a celebration of their British heritage and, implicitly, an affirmation of their own cultural authority. The snapshot of the Executive and friends – twelve men and twenty women – visually represents the organization's gender composition and hierarchy. With symbolic propriety, it is a man who dominates the picture from its centre; flanked by demurely seated women (ankles crossed, hands folded), the central male sits confidently, his

Members of the executive and friends of the Shakespeare Society of Toronto, 1962, photographed at the summer home of Dr and Mrs Stanley K. Clark, Georgian Bay, Ontario. Archives of Ontario, MU 2663 F1149, File 25 'Scrapbook.'

head slightly cocked, his gaze challenging the camera. The photo also highlights the membership's advanced age in 1962: those pictured might be, on average, sixty-five. Although Major and Mrs James Annand are not in the photo, they did attend Keiller MacKay's lecture at the UEL house and, as honorary members of the SST, would have dined at the Albany Club with him. They were among the few original members of the SST at the event, and the occasion must have been a source of great satisfaction to Annand, who had long cherished the desire for the SST to enjoy the distinction conferred by patronage.[4] The *Telegram*'s glowing coverage of the event reflects not only the paper's conservative politics, but also its long and cordial relationship with the SST; for over twenty years the SST executive had cultivated Rose Macdonald, the theatre reviewer.[5] Thirty-four years after its founding in 1928,[6] the Shakespeare Society of Toronto seemed secure in the social prestige celebrated by this dinner at the Albany Club. Six years later, the Society dissolved.

The Shakespeare Society of Toronto was one of many dramatic societies that flourished in Canada during the first half of the century, the amateur groups commended diplomatically by the authors of the Massey Commission for doing 'remarkable work against remarkable odds, largely for their own private pleasure' (Canada, *Report* 193). Certainly the SST members did take pleasure in their work. According to its constitution, the Society aimed to 'study the works of William Shakespeare, produce his plays and those of his contemporaries and the music of the period, as well as to celebrate his birthday' (Constitution). Its purpose was thus to foster intellectual as well as theatrical endeavour, and the original vision, encompassing plays and music by Shakespeare's contemporaries, demonstrates an enthusiasm for English Renaissance culture broadly conceived. Its purpose was also, however, commemorative: from the beginning, the Society ritualized the celebration of Shakespeare's birthday. Although I have found no evidence that the SST ever produced a play by any Renaissance dramatist other than Shakespeare, in other respects it fulfilled its mandate faithfully. Through most of its forty years the Society organized annually a varied program of lectures, music, theatre, and – in a festive climax – a birthday celebration.

In any year, the Society would have roughly eight monthly meetings to which the public was invited for a small admission fee. Thus, for example, the schedule for 1945–6 included an opening 'Social' at the Heliconian Club; in November, a production of *The Merry Wives of Windsor* at the Northern Vocational School; in December, a 'Pageant Night' with scenes from *Romeo and Juliet, Henry VIII, Richard III,* and *Henry V*; in January, a lecture by Dr William Holman, 'Shakespeare's Knowledge of Medicine,' with scenes from *Romeo and Juliet*; in February, a lecture by Professor E.A. Dale on *Troilus and Cressida*, with scenes from *Hamlet* and *All's Well That Ends Well*; in February, a production of *As You Like It* at the commercial High School on Shaw Street; in March, a production of *Much Ado About Nothing*; and, on 23 April, the annual birthday celebration (President's Papers).

This program is unusual only in its inclusion of three full productions: more often in the 1940s the Society would mount one or two. It is typical, however, in the choice of comedies[7] and in the venues for these: although in the 1930s the SST regularly used Hart House Theatre, in subsequent years it played on diverse stages, in high schools, church halls, and community centres. The 1945–6 season is also typical in beginning with a social, at which guests probably enjoyed tea, piano and vocal music, and dramatic recitations. (Minutes of the executive meetings annually record plans for these socials, including the designation of those women who had 'consented to pour.') In other years, the social included a quiz, in which the audience was invited to identify quotations or costumed characters. The 1945–6 season is typical, too, in its inclusion of a 'Pageant Night.' In this context, 'pageant' seems to signify a series of discrete scenes. Easier to produce than a full play, the scenes allowed work to be shared more evenly and – crucially – allowed the participation of more female players.[8] The presentation of dramatic 'highlights' suggests a desire to appeal to a popular audience. It also suggests, however, the prevalent conception of Shakespeare as the master of human portraiture, according to which the meaning of a scene derives not from its relationship to a whole but rather from its skilful presentation of a universal human nature. One needs no more than a brief introduction to appreciate the representation of Lady Macbeth's ambition or the garrulousness of Juliet's Nurse.[9]

Finally, the 1945–6 season is typical in its inclusion of two lectures, one by a guest amateur (Dr William Holman of the 'Dept. of Pathology and Bacteriology') and one by a member who was also a literary scholar (Professor E.A. Dale). Dale, a professor of Latin at Trinity and University colleges, was one of a series of faculty who acted as intellectual arbiters for the SST. Two or three times a season, one of these academics would consent to address the members.[10] The title of Holman's talk, 'Shakespeare's Knowledge of Medicine,' illustrates the approach taken by many of the SST's speakers, who examine Shakespeare's relationship to something or someone primarily to demonstrate the playwright's genius. Thus, for example, in a 1948 lecture on Elizabethan 'Roman' plays, Dale examined Shakespeare in conjunction with Jonson and Massinger: 'Shakespeare is compared with rivals,' declared the *Telegram*, 'Prof. E.A. Dale assesses works of Jonson and Massinger but finds them in second rank.' The *Globe and Mail*'s caption is even more striking: 'Bard's tragedies perfect, Professor tells followers.'

For most of its history, women outnumbered men in the SST by roughly two to one. Especially in its early years, the Society frequently used the facilities of women's cultural groups, such as the Heliconian Club and the Women's Art Association.[11] Press coverage of the Society's events tended to appear on the women's pages of newspapers,[12] reflecting not simply the large role played by women in the SST but also the social perception of its activities as gendered female. Still largely excluded from the professional worlds of business and politics during this period, women were allowed to enter the public sphere as amateur guardians of culture.[13] Significantly, however, most of these women did not claim *authorship* of culture. Keepers of the shrine, they preserved and fostered the appreciation of culture created by men. Thus, under the eminently respectable cloak of Shakespearean devotion, the SST did offer its female members a limited measure of empowerment: they could appear on stage, direct scenes for the pageant nights, perform music, and participate in the decision-making process. (Women might have made up roughly 50 per cent of the executive in any year, occupying, of course, the lesser positions.) As women, they also assumed responsibility for stereotypical female tasks: pouring tea, taking minutes, writing letters, sewing costumes. Only rarely did they appear as lecturers, and then not on 'serious' subjects; only twice – to my knowledge – did a woman direct a full production.[14]

If the female members of the SST chafed at the restrictions of gender roles, the surviving documents do not reveal it. On the contrary, the 'ladies' appear to assent enthusiastically to the prescribed roles. When, in 1949, a committee of 'business men' failed to suggest any solution to the Society's chronic shortage of money, a women's committee was formed to assume the burden of fundraising. (Their efforts included the Society's first tea and bake sale.) In her report on the committee's first year, the convener, Elsie Keefer, modestly thanks 'the gentlemen of the Society for the consistent encouragement and appreciation [they] have given – the sometime[s] amused but always kindly counsel and ... very practical cooperation in our small beginnings' (Report 3). Her deferential conclusion similarly disclaims the significance of their work: 'The women's committee does not consider the pleasant social duties performed for the Society as other than first baby steps towards some sort of security – financial of course ... We wish to identify our unit more and more with the aims and objectives of a distinguished and educational Society' (3). Keefer subsequently became the first 'Lady Vice-President,' but she declared emphatically that a woman 'should never be eligible for the post of Chief Executive in the Shakespeare Society!' (Letter 1).

Because the SST was both amateur and predominantly female, its work – its cultural labour – is easy to ignore or dismiss.[15] We might agree with the writers of the Massey Report in characterizing the SST's activities as 'largely for their own private pleasure.' But this would be unjust. In the 1930s, in collaboration with G. Wilson Knight – Chancellor's Professor of English at Trinity College from 1931 to 1940 and president of the SST from 1934 to 1938 – the SST produced fine theatrical work, using a still innovative performance style of minimal scenery and fluid scene changes. As Knight later recalled, 'Toronto was in those years a vital centre of dramatic interest and ability; under amateur conditions, but enjoying the participation of ex-professionals and amateurs as good as any professional' (*Shakespeare's* 13). Raymond Mullens, reviewing the 1934 production of *Henry VIII*, congratulated the Shakespeare Society on 'a dramatic presentation of memorable beauty ... That an amateur company could give so big and so difficult a play with such sureness and beauty is something to marvel at' (10). When the production was revived six months later, Mullens declared:

> By its performances of 'Henry VIII' last season and this the Shakespeare Society of Toronto abundantly justified its existence ... Shakespeare has created a medium for the expression of the most poignant of emotion[s] – and because the players realize this and neither rant nor attitudize they appear to be consummate actors. A great star playing Wolsey would feel that he must indulge in all manner of vocal tricks to show how finished an actor he is; these Hart House players disdaining such tricks deliver their lines clearly, and the result is a great moment in the theatre. (22)

Reviewers called the Knight–SST 1937 production of *Antony and Cleopatra* 'an extraordinarily fine performance, impressively staged' (Macdonald, 'Acting') and the collaborative 1940 production of *Timon of Athens* 'one of the most remarkable feats in the annals of amateur dramatics' (Craig).

After Knight's move to Leeds in 1940, the theatrical quality of the SST's work appears to have declined. Reviews of its later productions are tepid. Nevertheless, the minutes of the executive meetings, especially during the 1940s, reveal the Society as part of a lively network of social and cultural organizations. It was invited several times to perform for other groups. In 1942 the Society performed for St Mark's Parkdale, for a women's group of the Church of St George the Martyr in John Street, and for the Women's Guild of St Simon's Church. In 1944 it performed for the Association of Speech of the Toronto and District Teachers' Association. Presumably, then, the performances of the SST gave pleasure to others, as well as themselves. They were also a source of philanthropic fundraising: the Society made frequent charitable donations.[16] Thus, on a local level, the SST made a significant contribution to the community.

As theatrical options widened after the war, invitations to the SST dwindled. The founding of the highly successful Earle Grey Shakespeare Festival in 1949 challenged the Society's primacy as a performer of Shakespeare, while the emergence of the professional Stratford Festival in 1953 wholly obscured the Society's efforts. After 1949, the Society limited its theatrical work almost exclusively to the performance of short scenes at its monthly meetings.

In her study of Canada's cultural formation before the Massey Report, Maria Tippett distinguishes between private and public amateur groups: the former, smaller group, with a limited or costly membership, engaged in exclusive cultural activities, while the latter, with an open or inexpensive membership, undertook to educate and cultivate the public (2–12). The SST belongs emphatically to the latter category. Membership fees were low ($2 initially, rising to $2.50 in the early 1950s), and the desire to recruit members is a constant theme in the minutes of the executive: they advertised through the daily papers, through the university, by phone, letter, leaflet, and bulletin. They even once considered financing a booth at the Canadian National Exhibition.[17] In spite of constant efforts, however, membership rarely rose much beyond 100. While officers of the Society do not often articulate their motives, their language frequently reflects a missionary zeal. Thus, in June 1944, 'Major Annand was granted full authority to produce "Merry Wives" for the Beaches Library Club, thereby giving us a foothold in the East End' (Minutebook). Several annual reports congratulate the members for bringing Shakespeare's works to a greater audience than ever. In 1950, under conditions of postwar economic stress, the new president, Walter G. Frisby, urged every member to help: 'We are all in for difficult times. The Shakespeare Society is not peculiar in facing the difficulty of surviving but it may, by acting wisely, by behaving with keenness of imagination, by possessing fortitude, assist in creating the new forms in which our intellectual, social, and moral achievements may be expressed' (Letter 1950). Four years later, he wrote to thank the Society for the gift of lifetime membership: 'Mrs. Frisby and I hope that pleasures may profitably continue in abundance and that experience may enrich all of us as we seek to contribute to the preservation of that which has been found refining and to the creation of that by which our civilization may continue in fruition, expressing itself in things cultural which will become inspiring to those privileged to succeed us' (Letter 1954).

Frisby's conception of culture as a source of refinement and inspiration, and of drama as the expression of 'moral' achievement, suggests the influence of Matthew Arnold.[18] Such a conception of culture was common among amateur groups in Canada during this period (Tippett 10–12) and informs the magisterial report of the Massey Commission.[19] The executive officers of the SST took the educational aspect of their work seriously: they understood themselves to be fostering High Culture – in fact, the highest culture.

As part of this goal, members of the Society organized reading groups, and one of these groups – led by Mrs Ruby Burnside – instituted in 1956 an 'Annual Dramatic Contest' in which individuals recited Shakespearean verse competitively. Members (five men and eleven women) contributed two dollars each to buy prizes (an engraved silver cup and a copy of Shakespeare's works). They also employed Leonard Crainford of the CBC as an adjudicator (Burnside 2–5). The second annual competition, advertised in the newspapers, attracted almost twice the number of entrants, who competed in two rounds.[20] Public interest in the contest grew steadily: by 1958, there were fifty-one competitors.[21] The publicity surrounding the initial competition makes it clear that the Burnside Reading Group saw itself as filling a role that should have been filled by the Canadian government. In presenting the trophy to the winner, the president, Raymond Card, 'deplored the fact that the federal government has done so little in the way of furthering the arts. If trophies, or some other recognition for achievement were offered by the government, Mr. Card said, many, many more persons would participate in the arts in order to gain that recognition' ('Beat'). Card's public comments align the SST with the many lobby groups that, in the years before and immediately after the Massey Report, were pressuring the federal government to support the arts.

The cultural zeal voiced by the SST's executive is closely connected with their construction of Shakespeare as an exemplar of Christian values. For them, propagating Shakespeare was akin to propagating the gospel; their cultural piety is inseparable from their religious piety. Although this was probably true of the SST from its inception – Wilson Knight's vision of Shakespeare is profoundly religious[22] – this emphasis becomes increasingly clear after 1950 when the names of clergymen begin to appear frequently in the minutes of the executive.[23] In 1955 the SST began the practice of collectively attending divine service at St Paul's Cathedral on 'Shakespeare Sunday,' following Shakespeare's birthday. Even laymen, like the lawyer Keiller MacKay and the physician Stanley K. Clark, chose religious themes for their lectures. Thus, when Keiller MacKay addressed the membership on the subject of 'Shakespeare and the Bible,' he represented Shakespeare as 'a diligent and devout reader of [the Bible's] unsearchable riches, which after germinating in his own soul, brought forth fruit – immortal fruit – to the glory of God and for the intellectual healing of the nations' (Speeches).

The philanthropic efforts of the Burnside Reading Group reflect the relative affluence of the SST membership as a whole. Although their class is difficult to define precisely, I assume that the members did not belong to the same small circle as the Masseys, since none of them ever wrote a cheque that would solve the Society's chronic economic troubles or establish a Shakespeare House for the Society's meetings. However, the addresses on the membership lists are primarily among the comfortable neighbourhoods around High Park, the Annex, Rosedale, and Mount Pleasant. To paraphrase B.K. Sandwell, if the members were not Masseys, neither were they the masses.[24] Most of them probably belonged to the Canadian 'middle-class' as described by John Porter: not the middle-majority, but the relatively small group who could afford a 'middle-class' lifestyle – a separate dwelling, a leisured wife/mother, a cottage, a university education (*Vertical* 125–32).[25] Income alone does not, of course, determine social class. Professionals such as university professors and the clergy might earn on average considerably less than doctors or lawyers but still enjoy the social prestige of an elite group. This was particularly true in Canada before 1960, when only a small percentage of the population attended university.[26] Thus, in 1948, two daily newspapers sent reporters to cover the pronouncements of Professor Ernest Dale on Shakespeare and his rivals. Like G.

Wilson Knight, R. Keith Hicks, and William Tindale – other intellectual leaders of the SST – Dale enjoyed not only the prestige of affiliation with the University of Toronto but the additional cultural authority conferred by an education at Oxford or Cambridge. As Porter argues, an 'important social mechanism for the co-ordination of elites ... is friendship, resulting from living together or having common experience of the same kind of social life' (*Vertical* 527). Voluntary organizations and social and cultural groups play an important role in connecting members of various elites – economic, political, intellectual. Members of the SST shared more than a love of Shakespeare; they also shared access to power in diverse ways: many of the executive sat on a variety of boards, committees, and councils.[27] Most of them also shared the most crucial factor in determining elite status in Canada at this time: British ethnicity. Outside Quebec, all Canadian elite groups during this period were drawn from a small section of what Porter calls 'the British charter group,' the section that 'continues in the educational stream through university and whose fathers are in middle level or higher occupations' (528).

From the perspective of a multicultural Canada, the ethnic homogeneity of the SST is striking. Even more striking, perhaps, is the extent to which ethnicity and patriotism (British, not Canadian – or, rather, British-Canadian) were explicitly celebrated in its veneration of Shakespeare. For the Society's members, as for Arthur Meighen, Shakespeare is associated with England and Englishness, with 'tradition,' with 'history,' with 'heritage.'[28] For G. Wilson Knight, Shakespeare was pre-eminently the prophet of England's imperial destiny. One of Knight's favourite texts in this regard was Cranmer's prophecy at the end of *Henry VIII*: 'Shakespeare's last word prophesies England's greatness; and England still labours to fulfil this inclusive, Shakespearean, destiny' (qtd. in *Shakespeare* 123).[29] While it would be unfair to assume that SST members generally shared Knight's fervent imperialism, the archival records suggest that many would have been sympathetic to it. At the Birthday Dinner on St George's Day, 23 April 1946, at which the Society presented a cheque for $50 to a representative of the British War Victims' Fund – the new president, Raymond Card, 'delighted the gathering with reminiscences of his early boyhood spent in Shakespeare's birth place' (Minutes: 1945–55). The following year, Card advertised the October meeting in terms that underlined the attractions of the executive's native – and, therefore, authoritative – ties with England:

On this evening, Major James Annand, the Founder, Past President, and our present Dramatic Director, will be welcomed back from his visit to England. MAJOR JAMES ANNAND will be our speaker – ENGLAND RE-VISITED – his subject. Major Annand's association with and knowledge of England, its plays and players – more especially Stratford-on-Avon and its Shakespearean connections, Coventry with its war-torn scars, and post-war England seen through his eyes, will be a pleasure for all to hear. (Plays)

Clearly 'England' was a drawing card; and not only England as the birthplace of Shakespeare, but England as the 'sceptered isle,' the seat of monarchs. Thus, in a 1948 executive meeting, Annand proposed presenting a program 'with a talk on Kings and Queens in History ... coming down to our present rulers, and ending the evening with a showing of the film, The Royal Wedding – making a charge of perhaps 75 cents and raising some funds for the Society' (Minutes: 1945–55). (Not surprisingly, *Henry VIII* seems to have been one of Annand's, as well as Knight's, favourite plays.)

The coronation of Elizabeth II in 1953 evoked an unprecedented testimony of devotion to the crown: the Reverend Emlyn Davies addressed the Birthday Dinner on the subject of 'The British Heritage'; Raymond Card composed a poem in honour of the occasion ('A thought for Coronation morning'), which he circulated to members in the June bulletin; and the membership secretary, Douglas Iliffe-Dean, concluded his annual report with a stirring call to action, linking the new Elizabethan age with a new ascendancy for Shakespeare: 'In this Coronation Year of Elizabeth the Second let us make Shakespeare the Shining Star of "Good Queen Beth" shine more gloriously than ever. Let William Shakespeare appear among us again as in the reign of Elizabeth the First – England's Crowning Glory – and from a further study of his writings draw faith and inspiration for the new Elizabethan age – an era which holds so many blessings and achievements for us all' (Reports).

Two years later, when the Reverend Cecil Swanson was invited to address the annual Birthday Dinner, he accepted in terms that make the Society's cult of Englishness explicit. 'I assume,' he wrote, 'that what is wanted is really a speech about England rather than about Shakespeare, although of course, I would not leave him out.' Presumably the executive concurred. According to the report in the *Telegram*, Swanson 'chose to speak on England rather than on her greatly distinguished son': 'Dr. Swanson's address, a choice arrangement of recollections by turns lively and grave, stressed the "historicity" of the English people, as exemplified at the Coronation itself. Descendants of figures named familiar [sic] in England's history and found in Shakespeare's historical plays move in the pageantry of the Queen's coronation' (Macdonald, 'Unveil').

Part of the Society's cult of their British heritage was its Twelfth Night Revels – an annual event from 1947 – in which costumed members acted the roles of Elizabeth I and her courtiers, watching dramatic presentations, joining in country dances and songs, and feasting on a banquet complete with a boar's head. Newspaper reports of the Revels delight in the recreation of Elizabeth's court ('Elizabethan England was revived last night' ['Old England']; 'Queen Bess Holds Court Again'). They also stress the participatory aspect of the event: 'Although some of the glittering and colourful period costumes worn at the revels were rented for the occasion, many of them were hand made by the wearers. About 50 persons participated in the various skits, choirs and dance groups. An equal number were spectators' ('Old England'). The Revels clearly suggest a powerful, collective fantasy of an idealized British past for which Shakespeare was a convenient symbol.

In the same season that the SST invented the tradition of Twelfth Night Revels, a pseudo-medieval crest appears on its stationary. It also began to associate itself more frequently with the United Empire Loyalists.[30] All three moves seem related to an earlier change in the Society's celebration of Shakespeare's birthday. In the first decade of the SST, the birthday celebrations seem to have comprised music, drama, and lecture in more or less equal parts. They were events one could attend casually and relatively cheaply.[31] Thus, in April 1933, in the Assembly Hall of the Public Library, over forty members of various Little Theatres presented scenes from *Henry VIII, Henry V*, and *A Midsummer Night's Dream*, instrumental groups and vocalists performed music by Purcell, and a guest lecturer compared Shakespeare and Shaw. Similarly, the 1940 birthday celebration, held in the galleries of the Women's Art Association, 'included a "Talk on Phrenology" by Mrs Rostance, singing, dancing, dramatic scenes, impersonations, a "Lucky Draw, Prizes, Refreshments, [and] Tea Cup Reading"' (Minutebook). The following year marked a definitive change, however: the celebration became a formal dinner. To attend one would have to buy a ticket in advance, at the cost of $1. On this evening, after toasts to the king, and Shakespeare, Robertson Davies addressed the company; a 'light programme' of music followed; and then guests were invited to retire to the reception room while the Society conducted its annual business meeting (including the election of the new executive).

The Birthday Dinners of 1941 and subsequent years strongly suggest the SST's emulation of the St George's Society. Founded in 1834, the St George's Society of Toronto was originally 'a patriotic and benevolent association, with the object of assisting Englishmen in Canada' ('St. George's Society'). From the beginning, however, it also served – in Porter's terms – to 'co-ordinate' (*Vertical* 526) Toronto's elites through an affiliation based on a privileged ethnicity, a bond celebrated annually with a church service at St James's Cathedral, a military parade, and an elaborate formal dinner on or near 23 April.[32] As well as roast beef, the traditional dinner featured ritual toasts to the monarch, to 'St. George and Merrie England,' the governor general, the lieutenant governor of Ontario, guests, and sister societies, and an address by an invited speaker. Toasts and speeches regularly celebrated race and empire.[33] They also, at least occasionally, used Shakespeare as an exemplar of the English. Thus, at the 1935 dinner, 'in memory of Shakespeare and other great Englishmen who served their country in their day and generation, two minutes' silence was observed during which time the "Last Post" and "Reveille" were sounded' ('World Peace'). Here the memory of Shakespeare is curiously linked in a kind of imperial cult with the memory of the war dead. A similar association appears in the *Telegram*'s notice of St George's Day in 1930: 'St. George's Day – the festival of England's patron saint. The day linked, wherever English literature has travelled, with the anniversary of Shakespeare's death. The day made forever glorious in the annals of British arms by the gallant exploits at Zeebrugge. The shout of "St. George and England!" comes down through the ages. As it echoes through the centuries to come, may each recurring festival of St. George find the little island kingdom an increasingly "Merrie England!"' ('St. George's Day'). During the Second World War, Toronto advertisers drew on the iconic power of both St George and Shakespeare to sell Victory Bonds.[34]

For G. Wilson Knight, the coincidence of Shakespeare's reputed birthday with the feast day of England's patron saint was 'natural enough' (*Shakespeare* 108). In his war propaganda, Knight stressed the link between Shakespeare, St George, and England:

We need expect no Messiah, but we might at this hour turn to Shakespeare, a national prophet if ever there was one, concerned deeply with the royal soul of England. That royalty has direct Christian and chivalric affinities. Shakespeare's life-work might be characterized as expanding through a series of great plays the one central legend of St. George and the Dragon. It would be well to face and accept our destiny in the names of both Shakespeare and St. George, the patron saint of our literature and nation. (*Shakespeare* 93-4)

He called his readers to a renewed apprehension of the significance of 'national symbolisms in crown, in patron emblems and in literature' ('St. George' 109).

Given the imperial associations of St George, it is not surprising that the SST should be drawn to his cult. Certainly, the SST's practice, from 1955, of attending church collectively on 'Shakespeare Sunday' suggests its increasing tendency to fashion itself on the model of the larger and more prestigious St George's Society. This imitative self-fashioning is nowhere more clear than in the Society's celebration of Shakespeare's birthday, however.[35] After 1941, an increasingly elaborate tradition accrued to the occasion, including the reading of 'greetings' from other Shakespearean institutions and individuals – not, of course, offered spontaneously, but solicited by the Society's secretary. The ritual nature of the proceedings was emphasized by the printing of souvenir programs, designed to lend prestige to the event. The program for the 1960 dinner lists: toasts to 'The Queen' and 'William Shakespeare'; the dinner menu;[36] the president's remarks; greetings from the director of the Shakespeare Memorial Theatre in Stratford-upon-Avon, from the director of the Stratford Festival, Ontario, from Professor G. Wilson Knight, and from the Vancouver Shakespeare Society; a personal greeting from 'our Patron,' the Honourable J. Keiller MacKay; a Toast to 'Our Guests' by Archdeacon Cecil Swanson and a reply by Judge Farqhuar J. MacRae; piano selections; the introduction of the speaker, by Leonard Crainford; an address by Herbert William Whittaker; 'Thanks,' by Earle Grey; and, finally, the singing of 'God Save the Queen' (Annual). In a specious attempt to make the ceremony coeval with the Society itself, the front cover of the program describes the dinner as the '32nd Annual.' On the back appears the date of the Society's creation, the identity of the founder and first president ('Major James Annand, C[anadian] D[rama] A[ward]'), and the names of all subsequent presidents with their dates of office, in a kind of royal or patriarchal succession. Like the claim that the dinner is the '32nd Annual,' this information implicitly claims for the SST the authority of age. It advertises the Society, engaged in the cultivation of a historical past, as itself a historical body.

If the Twelfth Night Revels celebrated an imagined Elizabethan past, allowing the participants to assume the identity of idealised aristocrats, the Birthday Dinner evolved into a celebration of the celebrants themselves. It became a self-congratulatory affirmation of their cultural authority. Arguably, the invented rituals of Birthday Dinner and Twelfth Night Revels served a compensatory function for the SST,[37] as the political, social, and cultural supremacy of the group represented by the Society's membership was increasingly contested both locally and nationally.

Shortly before the founding of the SST, Prime Minister Mackenzie King's assertion of Canadian autonomy in international affairs at the 1926 Imperial Conference signalled the end of the empire and the emergence of the commonwealth. British-Canadian loyalists branded such expressions of Canadian nationalism (associated with the Liberal Party) 'Separationism.' The late 1920s also saw mounting popular anxiety about 'aliens' – that is, not English-speaking – immigrants; or, in the words of a newspaper headline, the 'Swamping of Canada by non-Britishers.' At the local level, the notoriously conservative Toronto establishment was disturbed by fears of communism, which it associated with these 'alien' immigrants.[38] Loyalist organizations like the Orange Lodge and the Imperial Order of the Daughters of the Empire agitated to 'keep Canada British.'[39] Nationalist initiatives, such as the fruitless campaign to establish a Canadian flag, elicited fierce protests.[40] Speaking before the Empire Club in Toronto in 1929, Justice W.R. Riddell expounded the paradox of British-Canadian loyalism: 'What then, in fact, is a Canadian citizen? ... He is and must be a loyal British subject ... These, then, I conceive to be the two principles upon which the Canadian citizen governs his public conduct. First, a British subject I was born, a British subject I will die; and second, Canada is to be managed by as well as for Canadians with perfect loyalty to the Crown and perfect self-government' (qtd. in 'Canadian Citizen').

The challenge to British-Canadian hegemony came not only from 'alien' immigrants and Canadian nationalists but also from below the border. By the 1930s, the United States had eclipsed Britain as Canada's leading trade partner and source of foreign investment (Granatstein 364). At the same time, the widely perceived threat of American cultural dominance through mass media prompted loyalists to cling to 'the British connection.'[41]

At this juncture, Toronto's passion for 'Merrie England' – and England's incarnation in the figure of Shakespeare – probably emerged from a complex mixture of anti-modernist anxieties and imperialist identification. At the annual May Festival of the Eaton's Girls' Club in 1929, held on 'the beautiful and spacious grounds of Ardwold, the home of Lady Eaton,' a thousand spectators gathered to watch a pageant that featured – among other legendary and historical figures – Robin Hood and his Merry Men, Druids, King Arthur, Guinevere, Shakespeare, Anne Hathaway, King Henry VIII, and Catherine of Aragon ('Eaton'). The *Globe* account stresses the 'pomp and ceremony' of the occasion. While Lady Eaton dignified the revels of her Girls' Club with 'historical' May Day pageantry, Simpson's dignified its sale of home furnishing with an elaborate construct called Avon House: 'a two-storey residence on the fourth and fifth floors of the Store,' designed to recall one of the 'picturesque half-timber homes ... well known in Warwickshire, Gloucestershire, Sussex, Kent and the Shakespeare country round Avon district that inspired its name' (Simpson's). According to a newspaper account, titled 'Spirit of Merrie England Recreated in Home at Simpson's,' 'two inch bricks making the plinth and panels were brought from England, where they once formed part of old buildings of the Tudor period. The roofing tiles have weathered centuries of English rain, and the oak used throughout the building, as well as parts of the beams, half-timbers and windows, is genuinely old.' If these claims are true, Simpson's went to extraordinary expense to appropriate the cultural authority associated with a 'genuinely old' England and Shakespeare.[42]

Theatrical events gave added impetus to the cult of 'Merrie England' evident in Simpson's 'Avon House.' In early 1929 Hart House Touring Players were formed to take Shakespeare to secondary schools in the Toronto area, and the Stratford-upon-Avon Festival Company (forerunner of the Royal Shakespeare Company) performed eight Shakespeare plays in a two-week run at the Royal Alexandra (25 Feb.–9 March 1929). This was the Festival Company's first appearance in Toronto – indeed, the stop was part of its first transatlantic tour – and the city's cultural elite embraced the occasion. Lawrence Mason, drama and music critic for the *Globe*, devoted considerable space to both the tour and the Toronto run. The following month, in an article headed 'Shakespeare Week,' Mason exulted: 'It is gratifying to record the fact that Toronto has had two major Shakespearean presentations during this week of April 23, the 365th anniversary of the poet's birth, while London, Eng., has had none except those at the Old Vic, which go on all the time without regard to anniversaries, and New York has had none at all.' Mason's pride in Toronto's achievement is rooted in the perceived importance of Shakespeare's birthday as a commemorative occasion: as he implies, Toronto surpasses both London and New York – cultural capitals of the English-speaking world – in practical devotion to the memory of Shakespeare.

The Shakespeare Society of Toronto emerged in the atmosphere of colonial bardolatry suggested by Mason's remarks. Theatrically, it was born of the Little Theatre movement; culturally, it was at least in part a defensive response to the anxieties generated by Canada's emergence as an independent, modern, pluralist nation. By the early 1960s, the nostalgic British loyalism of the SST was becoming increasingly remote from political and social reality, both locally and nationally. Postwar immigration had radically changed the demography of Toronto.[43] At the same time, a native Canadian drama was developing. In April 1964, while the members of the SST were preparing to celebrate the 400th anniversary of Shakespeare's birth at the UEL House, with toasts, speeches, and the presentation of commemorative medals to past presidents, George Luscombe was establishing his Workshop Productions a few blocks away at the Colonnade on Bloor Street.[44] The social and political values represented by the SST survived in other places – in groups like the United Empire Loyalists and the St George's Society, in the boardrooms of Bay Street, and, not least, in Queen's Park and City Hall – but, nevertheless, in an era of insurgent Canadian nationalism and alternative theatre, the Shakespeare Society of Toronto had become an elderly anachronism. In 1965, despite the protests of British-Canadian loyalists, Canada finally acquired its own flag. With symbolic propriety, the SST expired in 1969, shortly after Trudeau's Liberal government committed Canada to a bilingual and multi-ethnic future.[45]

Notes

1 I would like to thank Susanne Marshall for her intelligent research assistance, Barbara Bruce for her patient editorial help, Heather McCallum for expert advice, and Henri Pilon for his help at the Trinity College Archives. I owe a special debt to Robert Cupido, who shared his knowledge of Canadian cultural history and commented on several drafts of this chapter.

2 Raymond Card was a founding member of the Shakespeare Society of Toronto, and twice served as its president. In addition to the scrapbook, the collection of papers relating to the Society (MU 2660–3) includes minutes of executive meetings, financial reports, and miscellaneous correspondence

and programs in twenty-four files. Records are relatively full between 1939 and 1955. Unless otherwise noted, references to archival material refer to this collection.

3 Donald Wright (1908–) had his own claim to elite status in the cultural arena, as a musician, composer, educator, and, latterly, philanthropist. He would have been known to the public in 1962 as the leader of the Don Wright Singers. His extensive entry in *The Canadian Who's Who* (1996) describes him as 'Freemason; Life Mem. ACTRA; Toronto Music Assn; Charter Mem., DFIB; Delta Upsilon; P. Conservative; Anglican' ('Wright').

4 Minutes of the executive meeting for February 1944 record Annand's opinion that 'it would increase the prestige and membership of the society if Patrons were procured' (Minutebook). However, it was not until 1958 that Keiller MacKay became their first officially designated patron (MacKay).

5 The executive sent Macdonald complimentary tickets to their functions, and, on one occasion, approved the purchase of a two-pound box of chocolates to express its appreciation of her reporting ('Minutes, 23 Dec. 1947').

6 The circumstances of the Society's birth are unclear. Documents of the SST from the 1940s and later claim that it 'was founded in 1928, by Major James Annand' (Birthday Dinner). The catalogue of the Archives of Ontario perpetuates this claim. However, I have found no evidence in the newspapers to substantiate it. On the contrary, a note in *The Curtain Call* records a dinner at a restaurant on 23 April 1931 for 'the formation of a Shakespeare Club, of which there is none in Toronto' ('Told'). Although this note names no founder of the club, Dora Mavor Moore may have organized the dinner: a folder labelled 'Toronto Shakespearean Society Founded by DMM Dec. 2, 1931,' among Dora Mavor Moore's Papers, contains a prospectus for 'The Shakespeare Society of Toronto,' beginning: 'The Shakespeare Society, the inaugural meeting of which was held in the Art Gallery on the second of December [1931], invites the membership of all who are interested in Shakespeare, whether for the dramatic, literary, musical or any other aspect of his work.' A pencilled annotation on the membership form attached identifies the address of the unnamed secretary as that of Dora Mavor Moore, and adds: 'Founded by DMM who got Major James Annand to be president – cf. Hart House Touring Players. Row with Mrs. Annand & DMM withdrew after this one show. Refer FWM for anecdote.' In February 1931 Dora Mavor Moore directed the Hart House Touring Players in a production of *Twelfth Night* for high schools in Toronto, Hamilton, and St Catharines ('Hart House' 5); James Annand was one of the players.

7 In partnership with G. Wilson Knight, the SST staged *Antony and Cleopatra* (1937), *Hamlet* (1938), *Romeo and Juliet* (1939), and *Timon of Athens* (1940).

Generally, however, it preferred comedies: *Merry Wives* and *Much Ado* were favorites. *Romeo and Juliet* was probably its most frequently performed tragedy.

8 During the war years, the gender imbalance became critical: in 1940 the ratio was roughly 4 to 1. Minutes of the executive for October 1940 and March 1942 reflect the need to cast more parts 'for the ladies.'

9 A 'Pageant Night' of February 1948 included *Romeo and Juliet* 2.5; *Hamlet* 3.4; *Taming of the Shrew* 3.1; *Macbeth* 1.5, 1.7, 2.1–2; and *The Merry Wives of Windsor* 2.1, with incidental music between scenes. Six of the eleven actors were women. The scenes from *Romeo and Juliet*, *Macbeth*, and *Merry Wives* performed on this evening appear to have been favorites.

10 Dale's involvement with the SST lasted from early in the 1930s – he was president in 1932–3 and again in 1942–3 – until his death in 1954. Other university faculty who played key roles in the SST included G. Wilson Knight, R. Keith Hicks, William Tindale, John Dodd and Bert Diltz. E.J. Pratt, Northrop Frye, Robertson Davies, Harold Wilson, and Clifford Leech appeared as guest speakers, but did not, apparently, become members.

11 Established in 1915, the Heliconian Club on Prince Arthur Avenue 'brought women writers, musicians, architects, and artists together for "social intercourse," which meant listening to lectures, readings, and music as well as viewing art exhibitions and theatrical performances' (Tippett 5–6). The Women's Art Association, also on Prince Arthur, was established in 1897 'to unite the few artists, craft workers and art lovers scattered through Canada into a voluntary educational movement for the preservation of the arts and crafts, and for the co-operation of the artists and workers' (National Council of Women 142).

12 For example, the notice in the Toronto *Daily Star* of the Society's birthday celebration in 1933 appears directly under the rubric 'Women's Activities' ('Birthday of Shakespeare').

13 See Tippett 103–4 for women's important role as patrons during this period. The National Council of Women's *Year Book* for 1928 reveals the wide range of social and cultural groups organized by women: see 144–78 for a list of local councils and affiliated societies. The National Council maintained standing committees on arts and letters as well as cinema and printed matter.

14 Josephine Anna Koenig directed *The Tempest* for the SST, 2 March 1938, at Academy Hall, Spadina Road ('Non-Professional'); and Winnifred Turnbull directed *Much Ado* in the Parish Hall of St Alban the Martyr, Howland Avenue, 28 March 1946 (President's Papers).

15 The clubwoman was the frequent target of anti-feminist humour in this period. See, for example, Gilbert Norwood's satirical article, 'Woman's

Clubs': 'What the poor creatures want is something to *do*, and instead of taking the simple way, which is to go home, throw all the electric gadgets out of the window and do some real work, they keep on inventing bogus causes to fuss about and become secretaries of and extort subscriptions for. But, when all is said, Causes run only neck-and-neck with Culture. Women can never be satiated by Browning Societies, Brontë Societies and those Dramatic Groups which crawl slowly over Shakespeare and that incessant *School for Scandal*, strewing the years with memories of polite but scanty audiences' (151). Coincidentally, Norwood, professor of classics at University College, addressed the Shakespeare Society on more than one occasion in the 1930s.

16 They clearly felt it incumbent on them to act philanthropically, especially during the war years. Thus, for example, in February 1941, Dale declared that 'it seemed rather invidious not to give a Major Prod[uction] in aid of some cause' (Minutes, 3 Feb. 1941), and, the following month, members of the SST performed a concert in aid of the British War Victims' Fund (Minutes, 3 March 1941). Minutes of April 1952 show a substantial donation to St Olave's Anglican Church.

17 In 1947, in a triumphalist mood, the executive members briefly considered changing the Society's name to 'The Shakespeare Society of Canada.' They decided against it – not because they felt they did not represent Canada as a whole, but because they did not have enough money to act on a sufficiently grand scale. They resolved to recruit more members and thus gain more funds (Minutes, 25 June 1947).

18 See especially *Culture and Anarchy*, where Arnold expounds his view of culture as 'a study of perfection, and of harmonious perfection, general perfection, and perfection which consists in becoming something rather than in having something, in an inward condition of the mind and spirit' (48).

19 'Culture,' the report declares, 'is that part of education which enriches the mind and refines the taste' (7). See also Malcolm Wallace's essay 'The Humanities,' submitted as a brief to the commission, and published in a companion volume, and Litt 99–101.

20 A handsomely printed program for the event claims 'the distinguished patronage of: the Honourable Dr. W.J. Dunlop [minister of education for Ontario, Conservative] and Mrs. Dunlop, the Honourable Mr. Justice J. Keiller MacKay and Mrs. MacKay, His Worship Mayor Nathan Phillips, QC and Mrs. Phillips, Archdeacon Cecil Swanson D.D. [rector of St Paul's Cathedral], and Mrs. Swanson, [and] Lady Robinson' (Second).

21 In February 1968, the thirteenth annual competition was cancelled owing to an insufficient number of entrants (Finding Aid).

22 See, for example, Knight's 1929 essay, 'Myth and Miracle,' reprinted in *The*

Crown of Life (9–31), and the various essays, written over forty years, gathered in *Shakespeare and Religion* (1967).

23 In a passage worthy of Oscar Wilde, the minutes for 2 April 1952 record that 'Head Table Guests [for the Birthday Dinner] were to include, Mr. and Mrs. Earle Grey, Rev, and Mrs. Sextus Stiles, Mrs. Salisbury Baker, Rev, and Mrs. Hudspeth' (Minutes, Executive Committee). In April 1953 Rev. Emlyn Davies, of Yorkminster Baptist Church, addressed the members at the annual banquet, and Rev. G.B. Phelan, of St Michael's College, spoke in February 1954. In April 1955 'Rev. Cecil Swanson, D.D., of St. Paul's Anglican Church, gave an exceedingly inspiring and helpful address' (Report of the General Secretary). Rev. Ramsay Armitage, D.D., principal of Wycliffe College and president of the Dickens Fellowship, spoke at the Birthday Dinner, April 1957, and Rev. Canon Guy Marshall spoke in April 1958 (Annual).

24 'On the Appointment of Governor-General Vincent Massey, 1952':

> Let the Old World, where rank's yet vital,
> Part those who have and have not title,
> Toronto has no social classes –
> Only the Masseys and the masses. (59)

25 In *The Vertical Mosaic*, Porter describes the difference between middle-class and middle-majority in Canadian society. He estimates that, in the mid-1950s, such a 'middle-class' lifestyle would have been available 'at the most [to] no more than 10 per cent of Canadian families' (132).

26 According to the *Census of Canada*, in 1961 only 4.9 per cent of males, aged 16–65, held a university degree (qtd. in J. Porter, *Vertical* 159, fig. 7).

27 See, for example, the entries in *The Canadian Who's Who* for Raymond Card (1973), Ernest Dale (1949–51), and Bert Diltz (1976).

28 One of Meighen's most popular speeches – delivered before Canadian Clubs across the country in 1935 and 1936 – was a tribute to Shakespeare entitled 'The Greatest Englishman of History.' Meighen represents Shakespeare as quintessentially English in his patriotism, respect for authority, tolerance, and good humour: 'He was English, too, in the reverence of his reaction to the profundities and mysteries of life ... And, just as surely, he was English in his practical commonsense view on the day to day problems of living ... if it be true, and it is, that what really makes a nation is a heritage of common memories, common exploits, common sufferings, then surely he is the peculiar and immortal pride of that great country, of whose children he is the all-expressive voice, in the book and volume of whose memories, achievements, traditions, he takes the noblest and the sovereign role' (290–1). A recording

of Meighen delivering the speech before the Toronto Canadian Club in February 1936 was subsequently made into a record album, and an anonymous admirer ordered a copy sent to every college and university library in Canada (Graham 3: 64). Keiller MacKay, patron of the SST, was an intimate friend of Meighen and for many years gave him an annual birthday dinner party (Graham 3: 184).

29 In his propaganda piece, *This Sceptred Isle*, a 'dramatisation of Shakespeare's call to Great Britain in time of war' (Program), Knight showed 'in splendidly delivered extracts' from Shakespeare's history plays how Britain's acquisition of empire had been largely involuntary and without any more than an heroic or more altruistic than merely selfish design [*sic*]; as from that characteristic English sense of social obligation that found constant expression in our protection of the weak against the strong throughout Britain's history, our unique sense of sportsmanship which other nations, who neither shared nor understood, derided' (from the anonymously written 'Shakespeare's Message').

30 The choice of the UEL House – instead of the Heliconian or the Public Library – as a site for the Society's meetings suggests a sense of affinity with the organization. Thus, in 1951, the executive unanimously approved a motion that the season's opening social would be held at UEL headquarters: 'Also that there would be no charge for the evenings entertainment, that the Society would rent the Hall and the Ladies Committee would be responsible for refreshments. Dr. Clark [the President] had 100 invitations printed to be sent to members of the United Empire Loyalist Toronto Branch to be present on that occasion, which he took care of personally' (Minutes, Executive Committee). Such lavish expenditure suggests a strong desire to woo the UEL membership. At least eight prominent members of the SST in the 1950s – Jessie Clark, Gordon Clarry, Ross Glassford, Norman Horn, Elsie Keefer, Mr and Mrs Richard Mudge, and Alan Playter – also belonged to the UEL. (Although UEL membership records are not open to the public, the secretary of the Ontario branch kindly confirmed the membership of these eight.)

31 Members usually paid nothing for admission to a social, pageant night or lecture; non-members were usually charged fifty cents. Everyone would need to purchase tickets for a full production of a play.

32 Although membership records for the St George's Society of Toronto are not open to the public, newspaper accounts of their dinners from the 1920s through the 1940s usually list numerous high-ranking politicians – such as the provincial premier and the mayor – senior clergy, army officers, and dignitaries from a wide range of professions and services. The report in the

Telegram of the 120th annual dinner simply declares that the 'visiting identities read like a Who's Who' ('Revive'). In 1964 a columnist in the *Telegram* dwelt on the business profile of the dinner guests and the Society's executive, which included Sir Ronald L. Pram, chairman of the Rhodesian Selection Trust Group, 'one of the world's biggest copper mining companies'; G. Alexander Phare, president of R.G. Smith, one of Toronto's oldest advertising companies; and, A.T. Hunt, 'chairman of Gestetner (Canada) Ltd. and a World War I captain in the Lancashire and Yorkshire regiment' (M. Porter). The St George's Society still flourishes in Toronto, though the annual dinner has become the Red Rose Ball. For the Society's declared aims and activities, see its website: www.stgeorges-society.on.ca.

33 See, for example, the account of the 1930 dinner, at which the 'toast to St. George and Merry England was proposed by Canon Cody [chairman of the Board of Governors, University of Toronto], who dwelt briefly on the virtues of the English race, and the large part they had played in the moulding of Canadian character.' Responding to the toast, Professor Gilbert E. Jackson, 'Toronto University, formerly of Cambridge, England ... said that the English race had ever been in the vanguard of progress and advancement of the welfare of humanity' ('Silence'). Twenty-three years later, Canon H.F.D. Woodcock, 'proposing the toast to Saint George and England ... said he could not see why people saw imperialism as the enemy of progress. "It never was, in the hands of the British Empire, which is always the protector of smaller nations and believes in fair play ... I am proud of the imperialism of [the] British Empire"' ('Revive').

34 A full-page advertisement for victory bonds in the *Telegram* shows a giant, athletic Saint George bestriding a battlefield, while fiercely determined allied soldiers attack the enemy (not pictured); the caption declares 'THE OLD-TIME SPIRIT of *St. George* still leads us to WIN!' Two days later, on 26 April, a more modest advertisement for the bonds in the *Telegram* followed a quotation from *Henry V* with an inspirational text: 'So said King Henry V of England on the eve of an invasion of the continent of Europe five centuries ago ... Today Shakespeare's words re-echo in our ears as we Canadians prepare to offer our wealth, our goods, our blood in a cause more honourable than Henry's.'

35 When Rev. Cecil Swanson accepted the invitation to address the SST at the Birthday Dinner in 1955, he observed that 'the date does not make much difference, although it occurs to me that the St. George's Society will be having a dinner and it would be well not to clash with them, for there will be many people who are members of both associations.' Entries in SST's Guest Book for 23 April 1956 begin with the legend: 'St. George for Merrie England';

and entries for the annual Birthday Dinners from 1959 to 1961 begin, 'William Shakespeare and St. George.'

36 Although roast turkey was served at the 1951 dinner, in subsequent years the Society eschewed such a North American dish and preferred the roast beef sanctioned by English tradition. By 1960, the SST's dinner menu, like that of the St George's Society, seems to have become a ritual: 'FRUIT COCKTAIL, CELERY, PICKLES, OLIVES, ROAST BEEF, GRAVY, HORSE RADISH, BAKED POTATOES, MIXED VEGETABLES, TOSSED SALAD, ASSORTED ROLLS AND BUTTER, FANCY CAKES, TARTS AND COOKIES, STRAWBERRY SUNDAE, COFFEE' (Annual).

37 For the compensatory function of modern invented rites, see Connerton 64.

38 Thus, for example, in 1930 it became illegal to make a public speech in any language but English; in 1931 a Toronto court ruled that under Canadian law communists could be sent to prison for up to twenty years. For information on the repression of free speech, see 'The Intellectual Capital of Canada,' and for F.R. Scott's comment on the anti-communist legislation, see 'Communists, Senators, and All That.' For a celebration of Toronto's (and Ontario's) loyalism, see Middleton, *Toronto's* 98–102.

39 See, for example, 'Grand Lodge plea for the retention of British ideals'; 'Keep Canada British Is Dominant Note at Ward 5 Dinner'; 'Empire's democracy lauded at Hamilton by Canon Shatford: British ideals discussed at [IODE] Provincial Chapter's annual meeting'; and the account of a 'missionary gathering' in Knox Church, Toronto: '"We have a great problem in Canada: is this country going to keep British or is it going to turn foreign?" demanded Rev. Mr. Hanna of Thornbury ... "British for all time," came from the assembly' ('Me Swear').

40 For the protest against the flag, see, for example, the editorial comment in the *Sentinel*, 9 June 1927, 'The flag issue again,' which begins, 'That near-bolshevist Canadian journal, the Ottawa Citizen, is determined to have "a distinctly Canadian flag," if such a thing is possible, which we very much doubt. Not having a strong sense of loyalty to the Empire, the Citizen is unable to understand the sentiments of the I. O. D. E., the S. O. E., and the Loyal Orange Association.' The intemperate rhetoric of the *Sentinel*, the organ of the Orange Lodge, would be comic if were not for the power the lodge wielded in centres such as Toronto, where the mayor and most of the city's officials were members.

41 Fear of American cultural dominance pervades the report of the Massey Commission. In *On Being a Canadian*, Vincent Massey makes clear his desire for stronger cultural ties with Britain as a defence against the American mass media. See also National Council of Women 65–6, 130–1, and Grant x–xi, 3–4, 31.

42 Paradoxically, the Tudor 'Avon House' was used to display furnishings that included, among other styles, those described as 'L'Art Moderne.' Thus, Shakespeare and 'Merrie England' were invoked to make the modern palatable to consumers.

43 Over half of the roughly 1.5 million immigrants to Canada between 1946 and 1961 went to Ontario (J. Porter, *Canadian* 73, Table C3), the great majority to settle in a rapidly expanding Toronto. Between 1958 and 1961, Italian immigrants outnumbered British (Richmond 4), and, by 1961, Italians constituted almost 8 per cent of Metropolitan Toronto's population (Iacovetta 210, Table 7). Given their predominance in the construction industry, Italians might claim literally to have built the new Toronto: see Iacovetta 57–64 for an occupational profile of the Italian immigrant community.

44 Herbert Whittaker's column in the *Globe* gives a sense of the theatrical excitement in 1964: 'This Friday marks something of a red letter day in Canadian theatre, only there are so many of them these days that it may not show up. On the same day the Crest completes its first cycle as a repertory theatre, down on Bloor Street a brand new and exciting theatre opens at the Colonnade, with a new version of a new play, written by a Canadian for one of the most inspired theatrical groups in the country' ('New Theatre').

45 The Official Languages Act of 1968 established French as equal with English at the federal level (Elliott 167). The 'merit point system' for ranking immigrants, introduced in 1968, initiated a trend of increasing immigration from the Caribbean and Asia. By the 1990s, 'non-white' immigrants constituted the largest groups arriving annually (Isajiw 85).

3

'A Stage for the Word': Shakespeare on CBC Radio, 1947–1955[1]

MARTA STRAZNICKY

The year 1953, when the Stratford Shakespeare Festival held its opening season, is a well-known milestone in the history of Canadian professional theatre, said to mark the advent of Shakespeare in Canada. As with most such points of origin, however, a prior history has been obscured by the rhetoric of arrivals, inaugurations, and beginnings surrounding the Stratford Festival. That history consists of broadcasts of professional productions of Shakespeare's plays on the trans-Canada radio network of the Canadian Broadcasting Corporation (CBC), a performance tradition extending back to the late 1920s when Jack Gillmore's CNRV Players produced the first radio versions of Shakespeare in North America and reaching its zenith with the internationally acclaimed adaptations broadcast on CBC's cultural program *Wednesday Night* in the early 1950s.[2] While the CBC has been duly credited with training many of the Canadian actors who worked at Stratford in the early seasons, the radio productions themselves have never figured in performance histories of Shakespeare in Canada. An account of those productions deserves to be told in its own terms – for what it can teach us about the role of Shakespeare in the CBC's educational and nationalist mandate, and for urging us to continue puzzling over the boundless performativity of Shakespeare's verse. But what is just as important, and perhaps unique, is that the radio adaptations bring into focus a branch of Canadian performance history in which Shakespeare is the domain of a public not easily stratified by class, education, or region.

The broadest context for understanding the genesis and nature of the Shakespeare adaptations of the 1940s and 1950s is the CBC's mandate as an educational broadcaster charged with building and preserving Canadian cultural interests. Under constant pressure to defend the legitimacy of such a mandate in a democratic state, and even more so the associated monopoly on network broadcasting it entailed, the CBC argued that a publicly funded and controlled network was the only way to guarantee the balanced programming that would reflect and enhance the full range of Canadian culture. Private, commercial broadcasters could serve only the undifferentiated 'mob,' their schedules of soap operas, quiz shows, and 'boogie-woogie' music catering slavishly to the 'lowest common denominator' whose mass was required to assure healthy profits.[3] In contrast, supporters of the CBC urged that the fundamental justification for public broadcasting was its unique ability to edify, to shape as well as to reflect taste, and thus to foster among Canadians an appreciation of that which is valued by civilized nations worldwide. Thus, for CBC supporters, radio programming could do more than fill an empty room with sound or provide a mindless way to pass the time; they believed that it could raise Canadian cultural standards above the crass commercialism that was beginning to dominate through the influence of American mass media. Although the interests and agendas of specific program directors and audience demands will also need to be considered, it is not difficult to see that Shakespeare fit nicely the CBC's self-image as a public educational broadcaster: a writer of unrivalled international status, a staple in Canadian schools, a figure who both permeates popular culture and is the subject of academic scholarship, Shakespeare was the ideal intersection of highbrow and lowbrow, of learning and leisure, of English culture and international stature that the CBC needed to fend off charges of elitism and nationalism. His plays also turned out to be superbly 'radiogenic.'

Adaptations of Shakespeare's plays would peak in the years 1944–55, with that period seeing the evolution of the form from half-hour 'readings' in individual plays for senior high school students to full-length productions on the CBC's premiere arts program, but Shakespeare was favoured broadcast material a good ten years earlier. The 'Shakespeare Cycle,' a series of eleven one-hour adaptations, was presented weekly from 9 October to 18 December 1938. The scripts had been prepared by Charles Warburton for NBC's *Radio Guild* several years earlier, and the lead roles were not always performed by Canadians, but an all-Canadian cast of over one hundred was hired for supporting roles and the production was handled by CBC staff. A feature in the CBC annual report for 1939 announces this as the 'most ambitious series of programs hitherto undertaken by the Corporation.' According to the report, which as ever is charged with justifying the expenditure of public funds, the chief value of the series was in presenting to the Canadian public the talents of leading Shakespearean actors and in employing a large number of supporting actors 'from various Canadian cities' (6). A five-year retrospective report issued in 1941 would additionally praise these productions for 'giving listeners – particularly young listeners of school age – a rare chance to hear Shakespeare's verse spoken as it ought to be' (*CBC Drama*). In the same pamphlet, the CBC defined itself as 'one of the inheritors of the great tradition of the British stage,' and furthermore as a 'public service' with 'special responsibilities'; the turn to Shakespeare was seen to be fully in accord with its own identity as a public, nationalist educator (*CBC Drama*).[4]

Although the educational benefit of the Shakespeare Cycle was only recognized *ex post facto*, the perception that Shakespeare was appropriate broadcast material for Canadian youth became the *raison d'être* for the first original Canadian adaptations of the plays. Aired in 1944 and 1945 as a series of half-hour programs appropriately called 'Readings from Shakespeare,' these adaptations consisted of the best-known speeches and scenes from plays that were in the high school curriculum: *The Merchant of Venice, Julius Caesar, Henry V, Hamlet, Macbeth, A Midsummer Night's Dream, Richard II,* and 'The Falstaff Scenes from *1 Henry IV.*' Except for *The Merchant of Venice* and *A Midsummer Night's Dream,* which were adapted by Andrew Allan, the texts for the series were prepared by Nora Alice Frick, then national script editor for the drama department. They were all produced by Allan, who had been appointed national supervisor of drama in 1943 and who would become the single most important figure in bringing Shakespeare to the Canadian listening public. Neither Frick nor Allan were satisfied that these versions of the plays were adequate for anything more than strictly educational broadcasts, bringing to young Canadian students oral renditions of the most famous passages from plays they were studying at school. And while they made no attempt to represent the complexity of the individual plays, their decision to render a small number of each play's poetic highlights in their entirety – rather than giving condensed selections from a larger number of passages – meant that the brief thirty-minute format managed to convey the principal intellectual and stylistic characteristics of the individual plays.

Nevertheless, carried as they were in a daytime slot on the *National School Broadcasts,* the 'Readings from Shakespeare' adaptations could have only a limited impact on the listening public. In contrast, the success of the earlier Shakespeare Cycle generated among Canadian listeners an unprecedented degree of interest in theatre, so much so that the CBC announced a National Radio Drama Contest, which it credits with stimulating a steady flow of plays to the drama department for several years afterwards (*CBC Drama*). By 1944, the year in which Allan launched CBC's celebrated *Stage* series, there was in Canada enough quality playwrighting to furnish original scripts for weekly half-hour productions. Although the aim of the series was initially to showcase Canadian talent, 'to establish in Canada, through the medium of Canada's national radio, a stage for the introduction of writers and actors to the Canadian audience' (*Statistics*), *Stage* would also become the first regular venue for non-scholastic broadcasts of Shakespeare's plays.

With full administrative, technical, and aesthetic control over *Stage*, Allan could ensure that the entire series was shaped by his view of broadcast drama as an intellectual, intensely verbal genre and by his commitment to programs that were educational 'in the truest sense' – 'in the sense that they are informative, that they stimulate the imagination, that they widen the horizons and understanding of the people' (Allan, 'Cheers' 2). In the first two seasons, Allan's vision was realized in a series of plays that set new technical and intellectual standards for broadcast drama in North America. The *Stage* plays were noted particularly for their controversial social themes, a facet that Allan would later associate with a specific historical moment: 'If many of our plays in the first year had what was called "social content," this was because the writers – in fact, all of us – were products of a Depression and a War. Ideas bred from those twin phenomena were inevitable, unless you put artificial curbs on them. And we had determined not to apply those curbs' (*Self-Portrait* 109). It was at first a well-calculated risk: what began as a 'coterie broadcast' became, over a mere two seasons, a program that was second in ratings only to Saturday night hockey, a winner of prizes at international radio competitions, and admired by the mainstream American press for its 'courageous and unafraid' content (Gould).[5] While Allan welcomed the critical recognition, his response to mass popularity was more ambivalent. Allan says he knew that 'we were in real danger' when *Stage* drew nearly as many listeners as *Hockey Night in Canada*: 'We had always had people arguing about us, which is healthy and useful because it draws attention to you. But then we got such a large audience that we cut right down through all types of people in the country and we became subject to the violent attacks of pressure groups' ('Andrew Allan Says' 6). Ironically, although Allan had been assured by senior administrators that the small audience for the experimental series would not jeopardize its longevity, the program's very success was what undermined its original aims (Allan, 'Stage' 2, 4).

By its third season, *Stage* was adapted to listeners' demands. The series was expanded to hour-long productions, Allan began to soft-pedal the social criticism in original plays and expanded the series to include adaptations from works of fiction and drama. It was at this point when the *Stage* series moved away from its commitment to specifically Canadian playwrighting and to 'living themes' that Shakespeare began to be broadcast (Allan, Letter).[6] In the first two seasons of the new format, Allan produced hour-long adaptations of *Romeo and Juliet, A Midsummer Night's Dream, Antony and Cleopatra,* and *Macbeth,* and over the next few years came *Love's Labour's Lost, 1* and *2 Henry IV* (each in two parts), and *Richard II* (originally broadcast on the *Wednesday Night* program, discussed below).[7]

The hour-long format meant that the *Stage* adaptations could represent more incident and character than could the half-hour 'Readings,' which of necessity emphasized a play's poetic qualities. The longer format also meant that the plays could be shaped to develop more than one issue. *Richard II* as adapted by Lister Sinclair for the hour-long format substantially differs from Nora Alice Frick's version in this regard. Frick opens the play with John of Gaunt's deathbed lament over the state of England, skips to 2.2 to show the queen 'lonely and disturbed,' and then moves to Richard's homage to his native soil upon returning from Ireland. The intervening political complications are conveyed in matter-of-fact fashion by the narrator, and this is the pattern for the remainder of the play. Frick's adaptation is thus designed to feature isolated scenes of heightened emotional and poetic intensity; the interest is more in personal loss than political condition, in literary more than dramatic qualities. Appropriately, she ends the play with the pathos of Richard's final lines, 'Mount, mount, my soul; thy seat is up on high, / Whilst my gross flesh sinks downward, here to die,' and elides altogether the hints of political and theological fallout of regicide present in Shakespeare's ending.

By contrast, Sinclair opens his adaptation with Bolingbroke's challenge to Mowbray. Not only does this restore a certain level of energy to the play, it sets the stage for power politics as much as personal tragedy. It also gives space from the beginning to Bolingbroke, who was effectively excluded from Frick's adaptation because none of the play's celebrated lines is spoken by him. Sinclair's Bolingbroke and the theme of resistance he embodies is certainly not as complex as in Shakespeare's play; the adaptation omits, for instance, Bolingbroke's calculated ambivalence concerning the deposition, his deft handling of the trial of Aumerle, and the very real threat of York opposition, preferring instead to portray his ascendance as an inevitable outcome of Richard's ill rule. Still, Bolingbroke's very presence serves to challenge Richard's legitimacy, a role that is reinforced with the interpolation of a triumphant 'Long live Henry, fourth of that name!' at the moment of Bolingbroke's crowning. Sinclair's Richard, however, is no less tragic for the presence of an opponent with just cause. In fact, the deposition is portrayed more as a single-handed coup than wide-scale revolt, so that Richard's dignity as a divinely ordained ruler continues to resonate even as Bolingbroke's treason is elided. The personal tragedy is also heightened with the inclusion of Richard's tearful parting from the queen and the complete rendition of his prison meditations (in the production typescript, these are cut after line forty-five to meet time constraints). To similar effect, the assault on Richard is made more intense by the murderers bellowing an interpolated 'Die Richard!' and the tragic irony of Exton's immediate remorse is carried through in the following musical theme, described as 'a solemn dead march.' The ending of Sinclair's adaptation has all the ambiguity of Shakespeare's – the promise of atonement seems a necessary if ultimately ineffectual measure. The additional half-hour broadcast time thus enabled Sinclair and Allan to present not just more of a play but more of a play's complexity; in this instance, balancing Richard's personal tragedy against political contingency gives dramatic scope to philosophical conflicts that Frick's adaptation conveyed only through the single, largely internal, perspective of the king.

This is not to say that the one-hour adaptations satisfied either producer or audience. In a comment heard on *Critically Speaking*, just prior to the *Stage* broadcast on 9 January 1949, Robert McDougall addressed the 'problem of compression' in the one-hour adaptations, citing in particular the loss of complexity and the futility of 'hewing and cutting' plays that 'are so well known and so reverently studied that every stroke of the cutting knife is certain to draw a shriek of pain from one quarter or another.' For the opposite reason, one listener criticized the one-hour format as a 'mistake' for a program purporting to reach an uneducated audience: 'Shakespearian plays to the average man who knows little of the plays gets little good from them, cut up, scenes left out and the greatest speeches with patches taken out of them, and the whole play made almost unintelligible' (Coulson). Even Allan himself felt that these adaptations were far from ideal, calling them in retrospect 'potted' versions and seeing them as timid and unadventurous compared with what was later accomplished on *Wednesday Night* (Untitled typescript).

But while Allan was dissatisfied with the technical aspect of the one-hour adaptations, he never saw the turn to Shakespeare and other classical drama as in any way compromising the *Stage* series. In fact, he believed that the standard of playwrighting in Canada could only improve if authors worked on the classics and was confident that Canadian talent would show to better advantage side by side with the best of international drama (Allan, 'Andrew Allan Talks').[8] Allan also felt that Shakespearean and other classical plays could enhance the broadly educational aim of the series, being as they were palatable to an audience whose 'post-war disillusion began to cast itself back in time, to look into other ages for keys to the maze into which we seemed to have blundered' (Allan, 'Stage' 2). Thus, although the Shakespeare adaptations were introduced to *Stage* as 'safe' broadcast material, as part of a strategy to reduce the series' emphasis on topical, controversial themes, they in effect served to reinforce the creative and intellectual standards that Allan had set. Perhaps most important, the Shakespearean plays heard on *Stage* reached a far broader and more varied audience than any of the earlier radio adaptations.

Allan was also the key figure behind the adaptations heard on *Wednesday Night*, the second of CBC's programs to feature Shakespearean drama. Launched in 1947, *Wednesday Night* was explicitly designed to target an elite audience and at the same time to expand the cultural function of radio broadcasting in Canada. The program featured a full evening of cultural material including music, opera, critical discussions, documentaries, and dramatic presentations. The first Shakespeare adaptations carried on the program were rebroadcasts of the hour-long productions originally heard on *Stage*. But the evening-long format of *Wednesday Night* was an opportunity to perform Shakespeare *in extenso* (Allan, Untitled typescript). Allan recalls that the move to performing the plays nearly complete and without celebrity actors was a venture that distinguished the CBC approach to Shakespeare. Unlike the Americans, who 'appear to need the excuse of presenting a star to justify Shakespeare, to render him (it seems) palatable to the public when it is felt he may be useful to prestige or the making of a gesture toward culture,' the Canadian approach evolved into something 'less timid,' using native talent, minimizing compression, and shunning the 'over-explaining, over-excusing, over-adorning by means of narration, sound, and music' that had encumbered the CBC's own earlier productions (Allan, Untitled typescript). Between 1948 and 1955, the year Allan retired as national supervisor of drama, *Wednesday Night* featured two-and-one-half-hour adaptations of *Julius Caesar, As You Like It, Hamlet, Twelfth Night, Macbeth, Othello, King Lear, Troilus and Cressida, Coriolanus, The Winter's Tale, The Tempest*, and, in 1953–4, Allan's 'favourite season,' the entire cycle of English history plays chronologically presented in seven monthly broadcasts (Allan, 'Exciting' 3).[9]

For the history plays in particular, the longer format and the decision to produce the plays in narrative sequence meant a substantial revision of dramatic interest. Although Sinclair's text of *Richard II* for the cycle broadcast was not a fresh arrangement, differing mainly in the addition of lines and scenes not used in the one-hour version, the material that was chosen for inclusion was meant to emphasize intellectual rather than political history. Allan explained the new perspective in a broadcast and accompanying essay published in the *CBC Times* just before the series began. Showing little interest in political issues such as 'the struggle for supremacy between King and Barons, the emergence of the Commons, the birth-pangs of nationalism,' issues that, Allan said, reflected preoccupations of modern historians more than Shakespeare and other Tudor writers, Allan and Sinclair emphasized the 'Tudor Myth': 'With the deposition of Richard II God's economy had been disturbed and nothing could be right again until that economy was restored' (Allan, 'Shakespeare' 2). To adjust *Richard II* to this scheme, Sinclair restored the advance references to events in *1 Henry IV* that had been cut when the play was performed singly, and he added passages denouncing the violation of Richard's legitimacy, those castigating Bolingbroke as a traitor and aggressor against God's law, and the many prophetic warnings of England's future miseries. Interestingly, within this broader philosophic context, Richard's personal tragedy becomes even more poignant. One might account for this simply by virtue of there being the opportunity to delineate a more gradual decline for Richard, but it also becomes apparent that Richard can fully emerge as a tragic figure only within the framework of the Tudor Myth. In the strictly secular setting of the one-hour adaptation, there is no rationale for seeing the deposition itself as a tragedy, with the result that whatever sympathy Richard may evoke is eclipsed by our sense that Bolingbroke's triumph is finally a necessary and desirable outcome.

Allan and Sinclair's fidelity to the Tudor Myth should not, however, be dismissed as a naive old historicist reading; Allan was well aware that in this version of events Shakespeare 'perpetuated' Henrician propaganda ('Shakespeare' 2). Nonetheless, he was convinced that Shakespeare shared with his contemporaries a *belief* in the meaning of history as the Tudor Myth represented it, and he saw it as his primary goal to 'enter the mind of Shakespeare and his audience and to present this entering to an audience of the 20th Century' (Allan, 'Sound' 2). In this, the CBC cycle was strikingly different from two earlier attempts to present a sequence of Shakespeare's history plays. In 1901 Frank Benson presented a series of six plays at the Memorial Theatre in Stratford-upon-Avon which is said to have 'chimed well with the national fervour and pride being expressed in England as a whole in the context of the Boer War' (Shewring 91).[10] Fifty years later, also at Stratford, Anthony Quayle directed the first tetralogy in commemoration of the Festival of Britain. The program insert for *Richard II* suggests that Shakespeare planned the tetralogy as 'one great play' which presents 'not only a living epic of England through the reigns of the three kings, but ... also a profound commentary on kingship' (Shewring 95). Andrew Allan covered the Festival for the CBC, and the idea of doing the entire cycle of English history plays must have taken shape that summer in Stratford (Allan, Internal memo). He felt, however, that Quayle's tetralogy did not go far enough in following 'the grand theme through to its conclusion in the other four plays' (Allan, 'Shakespeare's' 2), and he never approached the history plays as an English epic. When he turned to producing the entire cycle himself, he sidelined the English directors' emphasis on nationalism and politics in favour of replicating what Tillyard had called the 'Elizabethan world picture.' While it would be difficult to argue that Allan's decision not to politicize the history plays is a peculiarly Canadian phenomenon, certainly his appropriation of these plays for a Canadian cultural agenda without invoking concepts of nationalism – either to align Canada with England or to demarcate a distinct national identity – suggests the extent to which Shakespeare's theatre was for Allan and the CBC unproblematically part of Canada's cultural heritage. Judging by the praise for the *Wednesday Night* Shakespeare adaptations, CBC listeners agreed.

The history cycle of 1953–4, in addition to the *Hamlet* and *Twelfth Night* heard on *Wednesday Night*, were considered pivotal events in radio broadcasting; the series as a whole was valued for reviving listeners' love of Shakespeare, for making the plays available in communities without live theatre, and for the commanding articulation – in Canadian accents – of Shakespearean verse.[11] Much of this success is attributable to Allan's emphasis on language and the details of sound in broadcast drama, a legacy he himself traced back to the 'periods of greatest achievement' in English-speaking theatre ('Broadcast' 22). His was a 'stage for the word,' and the 'wonderful richness of words that the Shakespeare theatre had' was ideal for a medium of extreme verbal subtlety (Allan, 'Andrew Allan Says' 5, 6). Not surprisingly, Allan imposed extraordinary discipline on his actors. He directed by paraphrasing a line or speech, 'to explore or indicate its meaning by allusion,' and if this failed he would read out lines as he wanted them spoken (Frick, *Image* 33). He demanded perfection; actors who proved incapable of following his direction were quickly out of a job. Those who worked with Allan recall the trepidation with which they glanced up at the directing booth 'to see if he was pleased or displeased,' and some have even said that he diminished them as performers: 'He never accepted any kind of mistake ... he would not accept one single error ... He would not allow me as a performer to contribute anything other than what the writer wanted to say, so I became ... just a vehicle ... just an instrument, a voice, through which the writer was interpreted' (Frick, *Image* 29). Narration and music were used to enhance the effect where spoken words alone could not fully convey Allan's interpretation: narration to move listeners along in a sequence of historical events, to identify characters, and to explain references that would be unclear to a twentieth-century audience, and music more experimentally as an abstract reinforcement of a play's controlling ideas. Something of the rich aural texture of the productions can be gleaned from Allan's account of the leitmotifs used in the history cycle:

> Very little merely 'functional' music (*melodrame*) was employed. The *leitmotif* was used to suggest or introduce not merely persons but even ideas, more or less abstract. The theme, for example, which identified Richard II was introduced again and again in the subsequent plays to remind the listener not only of Richard but also of the idea of annointed kingship and the sin which had been committed and was in process of being expiated. The Bolingbroke theme became the theme of the House of Lancaster. The Yorkist theme, originally bold and heroic, became gradually distorted to represent Crookback Richard and the orgy of heedlessness which had come to possess the leaders of the realm. There was a *motif* which Mr. Agostini and I always referred to as 'Unhappy Realm,' and this was a little tune – moving, sad, and sometimes twisted – which served at proper moments to show the travail through which the whole body

politic must pass. Against this we had a theme which originally appeared with the unhappy Queen in *Richard II* when in the garden she hears the distastful [*sic*] but salutary lesson in horticulture from the philosophical gardener. This tune was the prettiest (I think) in the entire series: and it was used again and again to identify England's green and pleasant land, the indomitable toil of the countryman, the continuing values which go like a strain of health all through times of dis-ease [*sic*]. (Allan, Untitled typescript)

Music building on theme, narration used sparingly to set context, and flawless acting – these facets of Allan's productions reflect his extraordinary command of broadcast drama. But technical accomplishment alone could not have guaranteed the unqualified success of the Shakespeare adaptations. A further explanation is to be found in the fact that Allan's interpretive approach to Shakespeare was shared by the listening public. Allan was generally well read in the Shakespearean scholarship of his time, enough so that he could sift through competing approaches to settle on a theatrical and historical Shakespeare. In the broadcast talk he prepared as an introduction to the history cycle, he clarifies his position:

No pair of Kilkenny cats could oppose each other with less inclination to give quarter than an equal number of Shakespeare scholars. The editors, commentators, and the wrestlers with textual problems flourish among us, and of the printing of their disputes there is no end. Yet today the best of them have at least abandoned one position of their predecessors, that Shakespeare was for the reader and not for the playgoer. Today Shakespeare is back in the theatre, and the number of people who will pay to see him is very great. The risk which producer and player – beset by so much scholarship – must strive to avoid, is that of reducing Shakespeare's twentieth-century theatre to a parade of erudition, a museum of historical accuracy. The trick is to become enlivened without becoming enslaved. (Allan, Untitled typescript)

Underlying Allan's attempt to transpose Shakespeare to a contemporary Canadian context was the belief that Shakespeare could not speak to our time unless his own time was understood. To this end, all of Allan's productions were as historically authentic as he could make them. Shakespeare's text was treated with the greatest reverence, changes being permitted only to fit a play into the allotted time or to ensure clarity for a listening audience;[12] when accents were used they had to be from the right country, and obscure historical references were explained rather than modernized. And as we have seen, Allan put a great deal of emphasis on intellectual history, taking it as his responsibility to educate actors and audience alike. Rehearsals for historical plays would begin with a talk by Allan: 'He would discuss costumes of the period, the various figures who were important, the politics of the day and what was going on. And by the time you got up to the microphone to read this script you'd never seen before you were already transferred back into that period; you had all the background. It was an immense asset to any actor' (Frick, *Image* 23). As for Allan's audience, the approach clearly worked. Few of his listeners would have known that there were alternatives – Allan explicitly rejected psychoanalytic and new critical approaches – and, with the scarcity of Shakespearean theatre in Canada, there were precious few performances with which to compare the CBC adaptations.[13] But listeners overwhelmingly praised the broadcasts for 'enlivening' Shakespeare, and the long-standing relationship among the adaptations, educational authorities, and explicitly scholastic programs suggests that Allan's Shakespeare resembled the Shakespeare taught in public schools, though he was certainly more engaging and better spoken.[14]

The Shakespeare adaptations were so popular, in fact, that they were never targeted by critics who charged that *Wednesday Night* was unacceptably elitist. Although the CBC never disguised the fact that the program was designed to attract a self-consciously highbrow audience, many of whom were thought to have given up on radio, the terms used to announce the new mandate – 'a more advanced and challenging type of broadcasting ... for the more adult group of Canadian radio listeners' (*CBC Press*) – were frankly insulting to many in the regular audience. There was concern that 'serious' broadcasting would be pulled from other programs and concentrated on *Wednesday Night*, thus limiting it to listeners who had the leisure for an entire evening of radio, and the very legitimacy of a public broadcaster devoting so much time to a coterie audience was questioned.[15] Yet, among the many complaints about the 'unashamedly highbrow' *Wednesday Night*,[16] Shakespeare is never singled out as esoteric or irrelevant; in fact, one reviewer, Graham Allen, cites him as the kind of 'good solid fare' that will keep the program from falling into 'the pitfall of preciousness.' For Allen, while nothing can be gained by hearing experimental works such as Eliot's hopelessly over-intellectualized *Waste Land*, the 'old plays' of Shakespeare 'come to life' when spoken by professional actors and thus prime listeners to re-read with pleasure what once seemed 'dull and forbidding' (Allen).

The assumption that listeners who were alienated by the elitist programming of the *Wednesday Night* series were, nonetheless, likely to read Shakespeare indicates the extent to which Shakespeare was ingrained in mainstream Canadian culture at mid-century. Although Andrew Allan believed that part of his function as a radio producer was training the audience to understand and appreciate new artistic forms, his adaptations of Shakespeare were an easy sell.[17] Together with Allan's extraordinary professionalism and his non-experimental approach to the plays, the prior popularity of Shakespeare guaranteed success. Similarly, in the larger context of the CBC's mandate as a public broadcaster, charged with a broadly educational mission, Shakespeare was ideal: his plays were already palatable to a large cross-section of the audience, and broadcasting professional productions throughout the country, where most people had no access to live theatre, was obviously an enrichment of 'Canada's Artistic Nationhood' (W.E. Humphreys).[18]

But this conjunction of seemingly ideal conditions was relatively short-lived. In 1953 the CBC began broadcasting on television. The much greater expense of the new medium meant that program funds for radio were reduced and considerably less attention was given to the impact of radio programming. Also in 1953, of course, the Stratford Festival began its annual series of Shakespearean plays, and Allan's stable of radio actors, whose 'Tudor perceptions' he claims to have sharpened, proved ready to take their talents to the stage (Allan, *Self-Portrait* 123). Furthermore, after the Massey Commission tabled its report in 1951, the federal government began making grants for performing arts that enabled writers and technical staff to find work outside the CBC. One might regard these developments as key factors in the decline of Shakespearean plays on CBC radio, and certainly they all played an important role in the stimulation of new performance traditions that would eventually overshadow the radio plays (Fink and Jackson xiii). But equally important is Andrew Allan's own waning interest in his work as a producer of radio drama. By 1955, when he retired from his position as national supervisor of drama, Allan says that he felt his career had been fulfilled (Allan, *Self-Portrait* 124). The concurrent decline of Shakespeare productions on CBC radio (in the five years after Allan retired, only five Shakespeare plays were broadcast) indicates just how instrumental Allan himself was in bringing Shakespeare to the Canadian listening public. Without his influence, and without radio's near monopoly on professional performing arts in Canada, Shakespeare moved to other venues. No doubt many Canadians greeted that move with enthusiasm; but there were also those for whom a 'living' Shakespeare once again became inaccessible.

Notes

1. I wish to thank Penny Gay of Sydney University and the Australia and New Zealand Shakespeare Association for an early opportunity to present this research, and the staffs of the CBC Reference Library, the National Archives, and the CBC Radio D ama Archives at Concordia University for their invaluable assistance. This project was funded by the Social Sciences and Humanities Research Council of Canada through the Advisory Research Committee at Queen's University.
2. Broadcast and bibliographic information about the adaptations may be found in Howard Fink, *Canadian National Theatre on the Air: 1925–1961: CBC-CRBC-CNR Radio Drama in English. A Descriptive Bibliography and Union List*. Production typescripts of most of the adaptations are at the CBC Radio Drama Archives, Centre for Broadcasting Studies, Concordia University, and recordings are at the Moving Images and Sound Archives of the National Archives of Canada and in the CBC Program Archive in Toronto.
3. For a useful analysis of the debate between private and public interests in broadcasting at mid-century, see Litt.
4. *CBC Drama and Features* is one of a series of pamphlets describing the work of the CBC.
5. For a general account of the history of the series, see Goodwin.
6. 'Living themes' is Allan's phrase for topical content in the *Stage* plays.
7. *Romeo and Juliet, Antony and Cleopatra,* and *Macbeth* were adapted by Lister Sinclair; *A Midsummer Night's Dream* was adapted by Allan.
8. Not everybody agreed with Allan that working on adaptations was an encouragement to Canadian talent. Lister Sinclair, who adapted the vast majority of the Shakespeare plays Allan produced, felt that the change was detrimental to Canadian playwrights because they did the work only to earn money and consequently had less time to develop original drama (Frick, *Image* 79).
9. *1 and 2 Henry VI* were compressed into a single play, a task Allan has described as 'the biggest editing job I have ever undertaken' (Allan, 'Exciting' 3).
10. The six plays were *King John, Richard II, 2 Henry IV, Henry V, 2 Henry VI,* and *Richard III.*
11. A 'representative' selection of audience mail was compiled by Charles Jennings, general supervisor of programs, in October 1948. See 'Wednesday

Night—Audience.' One should bear in mind, however, that this folder is admittedly 'not the sum total of all mail received' (Jennings).

12 The only time Allan permitted himself a liberal hand in making alterations was in his compressed versions of *1 and 2 Henry VI*. According to a *CBC Times* article introducing the plays, Allan felt free to do so 'partly because large sections of the first two plays are not true Shakespeare, but Shakespeare doctored material from other writers. But whenever the real Shakespeare was in evidence (as in the Temple Gardens scene) the original was followed closely' (Allan, 'Exciting' 3).

13 Of new criticism, Allan has said, 'I know it is fashionable today to approach Shakespeare with the least possible reference to his social and historical context. I think this is wrong. Surely we cannot feel the weight of his words and images unless we have some idea what the weight of them was for the people who first heard and understood them, the audience for which he wrote' (Allan, 'Shakespeare' 10). For much the same reason, he rejected psychoanalytic interpretations: 'I have heard serious actors at important Shakespearean theatres discuss very strangely the relationship between Hamlet and his mother, or between Coriolanus and Aufidius. I am sure Shakespeare would be very surprised' ('Sound' 11).

14 Allan's earliest Shakespeare series, the 'Readings' discussed above, was planned and produced for the CBC's education department (*Julius Caesar, The Merchant of Venice, 1 Henry IV, Hamlet* [*CBC Annual* 1944 17]). The *Hamlet* from this series was expanded into six half-hour programs for CBC's *National School Broadcasts* in 1947. The play was introduced by G.B. Harrison of Queen's University and was intended 'for the benefit of high-school students studying English' (*CBC Annual* 1948 19). According to Pierre Berton, the *National School Broadcasts* 'standardized the Shakespearean plays studied in most provinces' (30). Revised versions of *Hamlet, Julius Caesar,* and *Macbeth* were broadcast on *Wednesday Night* in 1948, 1949, and 1950 respectively.

15 Most of these criticisms are found in press clippings rather than audience mail. See CBC Reference Library, file Wednesday Night. The CBC did, however, air a 'candid exchange of views' about *Wednesday Night* on 4 Feb. 1948. According to the press release, 'on that date, people from various walks of life, and from different parts of Canada will tell what they like or dislike about the CBC's Wednesday broadcast feature, and offer suggestions for improving it' (Wednesday Night). Listeners also took the opportunity to comment; the letters on file are overwhelmingly from *Wednesday Night*'s supporters.

16 Mavis Gallant uses the phrase to describe *Wednesday Night* fare and reports that 'many listeners find it too lofty, too dull, and too complicated' (7).

17 Interestingly, Allan compared his work in shaping audience taste with Shakespeare: 'You can often sneak things in which suggest what may happen tomorrow, what kind of things may become popular. I could cite Shakespeare on this. Most of Shakespeare's plays were written for popular consumption. In other words, there were demands he had to meet. You will find elements in there, and you will say, "Well, that's unworthy of Shakespeare." But he had to put them in, or he wouldn't have sold the plays, and he was a commercial writer. He happened also of course, to be a man of genius, so that in his plays, increasingly as time went by, things began to appear that were not demanded. And gradually these new things became more interesting to more people: and they wanted more of those things and they got them' ('Andrew Allan Says' 6)

18 A.H. Gillson, dean of arts and science at McGill University, deemed the *Wednesday Night* endeavour 'an event of the greatest significance to Canadian life, since it is a further indication that we are in the process of fast becoming an integrated Nation of no little promise and already considerable achievement.'

4

Stratford and the Aspirations for a Canadian National Theatre[1]

MARGARET GROOME

Canada, 2002. Shakespeare is ubiquitous – or at least Shakespeare in the form of that venerable Canadian institution, summer Shakespeare. Nearly a dozen such enterprises now struggle each summer against the vagaries of rough weather and mosquito swarms to bring the Bard to the nation.[2] The directors generally define their work either as in the 'tradition' of Canada's Stratford Festival or as something specifically distinct from that tradition. Fifty years after its founding, Canada's Stratford Festival still stands at the ideological centre for those who 'do' Shakespeare in Canada.[3] To analyse how Shakespeare and the Stratford Festival came to be invested with this authority is thus a crucial chapter in understanding the place of Shakespeare in Canada's national culture.

The postwar concern that Canada should quickly develop an internationally recognized national culture implied a pre-disposition to the inverse – that any Canadian cultural institution receiving international attention would immediately be acknowledged as a national icon. In the case of theatre, a strong impulse to professionalization was manifested in discussion of a 'national theatre.' A set of expectations concerning such an endeavour was widely circulated: a theatre company to lead the country, which would introduce the classics, particularly Shakespeare, to Canadians and would produce the 'best' scripts from other lands and peoples. It has been said that the Stratford Festival proved that Canadians were ready to support a 'first class' cultural institution. I would suggest that, on the contrary, the postwar discourse on theatre established a set of expectations regarding Canada's cultural needs and it was these expectations that a Shakespeare Festival seemed to answer. In doing so, the Stratford Shakespearean Festival became the longed-for national icon, as both cultural commodity and cultural authority.

The critique that follows proceeds from a cultural-materialist perspective and so is concerned with the terms in which Shakespeare's authority was circulated in Canada in the immediate postwar period, leading up to the founding of Canada's Stratford Festival in 1953. I begin with a discussion of the discourse on theatre and Shakespeare circulating in Canada after the Second World War and examine the mythologizing of Shakespeare as a 'civilizing instrument' in that discourse. This representation of Shakespeare as 'civilizing' exercised a formative influence in the process of defining and legitimizing the notion of a Canadian national theatre. I will show that, in spite of significant impulses towards a national theatre based on Canadian writing, this was overshadowed by a reverence for Shakespeare's works and the identification of Shakespeare as cultural authority. And so, for Canada, the plans for a Shakespeare Festival to be held in Stratford tapped into both a long-sought cultural respectability and desire for a national theatre. With the founding of the Stratford Festival, 'culture' and the idea of a national theatre became conflated with Shakespeare.

The relationship of the aspirations for a national theatre to nationalism was a vexed issue in both the prewar and postwar periods. Homi Bhabha's insight into the ways in which literature can both enforce and subvert relations between dominant and colonized cultures is suggestive in regard to the developing theatre scene in postwar Canada. I will show that a tension developed between nationalistic aspirations, on the one hand, and a reluctance to 'go too far' in loosening the ties to the British empire, on the other. This tension was manifested in theatrical discussions that stressed the importance of developing a national dramatic canon while simultaneously favouring the English model of theatre and making a decided turn to Shakespeare, as evidenced in the primacy ascribed to the Stratford Festival. It will be seen that the rhetoric regarding the founding and early years of the Festival provide a potent example of what Denis Salter has identified as the 'cultural and political orthodoxy' standing behind the idea of a theatrical canon – the belief 'that the theatre should be obliged to commit itself to the never-ending task of building a sense of national destiny' ('Idea' 71).[4]

It would be misleading to suggest that discussion of the need for a national theatre began only in the postwar period. In fact, the debate can be traced to the latter part of the nineteenth century when theatre critics began to focus on the need for distinctively *Canadian* plays. As early as the 1890s, it was argued that, in order to achieve a national dramatic canon, Canada needed a centralized national theatre.[5] This debate arose in response to the predominance of touring productions imported from Britain and the United States. Indeed, engagements in a large number of Canadian cities and towns had been a feature of American and British theatrical tours in the eighteenth and nineteenth centuries, presenting not just Shakespeare's works and other 'classics' but, notably, the work of contemporary American and British playwrights. 'Cultural independence' was thus a theme from the earliest days of national-theatre discussions, as was the suggestion that government subsidy would be necessary. Salter argues convincingly that these early advocates of a Canadian national theatre, such as critic B.K. Sandwell, regarded theatre as a form of High Culture, an idea borrowed from the English model of a national theatre ('Idea' 75–6). In the 1920s and 1930s, the English model continued to predominate, promoted preeminently by Vincent Massey, who would become governor general in 1952. This meant that, in addition to the conservative emphasis on theatre as High Culture, the importance of government subsidy and the need for a centralized national theatre, an actual edifice, were also stressed.[6]

I have taken the 'Ottawa Briefs' as a starting point for the postwar discourse on theatre. These were presented in June 1944 to the Reconstruction Committee of the House of Commons by representatives of sixteen national cultural organizations.[7] The Briefs asked the federal government for $10 million for grants-in-aid to assist in the construction of community centres, and for an annual budget of $1 per citizen to maintain these centres and provide them with libraries, theatres, and music, art, film, and educational services.

In July 1946 Herman Voaden discussed the Ottawa Briefs in an article with the suggestive title 'The Theatre in Canada: I. A National Theatre?' Voaden's discussion is a significant entry into the postwar discourse by virtue of his unique, wide-ranging contribution to Canadian theatre in the 1930s and 1940s – as a theoretician and essayist, as a teacher at Queen's University and the University of Toronto, as a leading administrator in several major arts organizations, and as an innovative playwright and director who experimented with expressionist drama. Voaden's voice thus commanded singular attention and respect in Canadian arts circles. Voaden concluded his 1946 article by noting: 'These protagonists of government support claim that if Canada is to become a world cultural power, as important in the arts as she is now in trade and industrial production, she must subsidize not only the radio and film, but the visual arts, music and the theatre as well. They maintain that only then will the theatre reach its true stature as a humane civilizing instrument, expressing and enriching the life of a young but potentially great nation' (391).

In this one paragraph, Voaden manages to coalesce several of the statements central to the postwar discourse on theatre in Canada: the yearning for Canada to become a 'world cultural power' such that its importance in the arts will match its economic progress; the need for government subsidy to attain this stature; and the humanist concept that theatre is a 'humane civilizing instrument' that enriches a nation. It would be misleading, however, to imply that the postwar discourse was organized around the proposal for government subsidy. I have identified a set of seven statements as dominating the postwar discourse on theatre, accessible in the essays of various figures writing about the Canadian theatre scene – figures such as John Coulter, Herbert Whittaker, Vincent Tovell, and Mavor Moore, in addition to Voaden.[8] The set of 'dominant' statements includes the three identified above, and, in addition, the desire for some form of 'national theatre,' the desire for an increase in the Canadian plays written and produced, the need to develop professional theatre companies, and the lack of facilities for theatre production. Voaden's humanist conception of theatre as a civilizing instrument is representative of the way theatre was portrayed at this time. The development of Canadian theatre was linked directly to the artistic education of the nation and this education was projected as exposure to and the preservation of the classics and 'universal' values. For example: 'Today drama still has a duty to perform. Priceless legacies of past ages are contained in old dramas. These can only be appreciated when they are frequently and worthily performed in the living theatre. It is essential therefore that theatrical practice co-operate with the vital principles of the human spirit. This will provide an outlet for the development of a national culture now and in the future' (Rowe-Sleeman 24). The 'classics' as the route to cultural respectability and the concept of a theatre that enriches by revealing 'universal' values were thus established as major discursive themes from the outset.

What is most significant about postwar statements linking Canadian theatre and the nation's cultural maturity is that, a full six years before the 1951 Massey Report, this maturity was associated with some form of national theatre. The notions of what this might be ranged from a set of institutions, national in spirit, to one centralized institution or a chain of decentralized, regional theatres. However the concept of a national theatre was expressed, it was inevitably associated with setting national 'standards' for theatrical production and, more nebulously, with standards of 'creative imagination.'

Postwar considerations of a national theatre were not restricted to articles in Canadian journals. During the spring of 1945, the drama committee of the Arts and Letters Club of Toronto, chaired by the English actor-director Earle Grey and with John Coulter as its driving spirit, sponsored a meeting of fifteen Toronto dramatic organizations to establish an Ontario council of a National Theatre Council and to promote a professional national theatre in Canada. The manifesto accompanying the invitation to this conference proposed that the 'fulcrum' for increased dramatic activity in Ontario would be a new, centrally located, modem theatre with its own costume and props workshop and, eventually, a theatre school; the similarities to the design of the Stratford Festival's permanent facilities need hardly be pointed out. A repertory of plays was to be performed by a resident company and then toured around the province and across the country. While the Ontario company was on tour, the Ontario theatre would be occupied by companies from the regions of the province and the rest of Canada. The manifesto also proclaimed the belief that new Canadian plays would be forthcoming with the building of an adequate Ontario facility.

There were a number of important themes in the manifesto's program. The idea of a 'national theatre' as a 'good thing,' a necessity, for a civilized country had not only been emphasized once again but had now also been acknowledged and sanctioned publicly by a set of organizations. The concept had thus attained the status of a principle on which a group of organizations were proposing to act. The manifesto similarly brought into focus what had previously existed only in embryo – the idea that a national-theatre scheme should involve a nation-wide sharing of theatrical activity. The assumption that the existence of a facility would in itself encourage Canadian writers reinforced an idea that had earlier appeared in the Ottawa Briefs. This concept of the importance of facilities would gain currency in the next few years and be accompanied by an emphasis on the external trappings of theatrical production. Eventually, however, the commitment to establish a national theatre waned among Ontario theatre organizations; by the third meeting, it was decided to discontinue the attempt to establish an Ontario theatre council.

Discussion of a national-theatre scheme also took place outside Ontario in the postwar years. In the western provinces, theatrical activity had actually increased during the war years, supported by departments of education or the extension departments of the universities of Manitoba, Saskatchewan, Alberta, and British Columbia and by grants from the Carnegie and Rockefeller foundations. On the basis of this activity, a Western Theatre Conference was formed and annual meetings held at Banff, beginning in the summer of 1944. At these meetings, attention was focused on ways to encourage playwrights, on the coordination and improvement of regional drama festivals, on the improvement of theatre facilities in schools and community centres, and on lobbying the federal and provincial governments to implement the proposals of the Ottawa Briefs (Voaden, 'Theatre Record' 185).[9] The 1945 conference also discussed the possibility of establishing a National Theatre Conference and National Theatre for Canada, but it took no immediate action. And so a structure actually existed in the western provinces that would have facilitated the establishment of the kind of national-theatre scheme projected by Coulter's group in Ontario. Yet the plans and ideas of the western groups enjoyed only a limited circulation beyond the Theatre Conference – they were not given the wider, national distribution accorded the plans of Ontario groups. It was, therefore, the Ontario plans that predominated in the postwar discourse on theatre in Canada; consequently, I have given greater weight to these.

As the plans to establish an Ontario Theatre Council were fading, Roly Young, the film columnist of the *Globe and Mail*, organized the Toronto Civic Theatre Association. This organization would reinforce several of the concerns already in circulation and would introduce one idea – 'entertainment value' – that would prove controversial but durable. Young's organization sought to establish a professional theatre in Toronto that would sponsor the writing of Canadian dramatic works (Voaden, 'Theatre Record' 186). To that end, it offered a substantial standing award for any Canadian play that was accepted for production. With the breakdown of the plans for an Ontario Council of a National Theatre, the Ontario theatre community looked to the Toronto Civic Theatre Association to become the Ontario seat of the national theatre, touring its productions across the country.

The objectives of the Civic Theatre Association tallied with those of 'Coulter's Council' on many points. As in the manifesto and working plan of Coulter's group, a major concern was to establish a large provincial centre of operation based in a modern, completely equipped facility. But the Civic Theatre Association's program differed from that of Coulter's Council in one major respect. In reporting on the public launching of the Civic Association in September 1945, Roly Young had commented: 'While this Civic Theatre is a cultural effort, it is not a highbrow one, and members were unanimous in agreeing that there would be no arty approach. Rather, the association aims to give entertainment value for every ticket sold, and the program has been chosen with an eye to its appeal to the theatre-going public' (qtd. in Voaden, 'Theatre Record' 186-7). The disavowal of 'art' and the declared intention to give 'entertainment value' top priority assumes that the theatre-going public is and should be concerned only with entertainment, not with art, and that the 'arty' cannot be entertaining. The false dichotomy between 'arty' and 'entertaining' productions is alarming, coming from a group representing the bulk of theatrical activity in Toronto at that time. The association was also expressing its assumption that a theatre need no policy other than to give the public something 'appealing' – the basic ethos of the commercial theatre to 'give the public what it wants.'

In the late 1940s, it was the nation's substantial amateur theatre activity, encouraged by the Dominion Drama Festival, that was the predominant theatrical force in the country. Indeed, amateur theatre productions had been a feature of the Canadian theatrical scene since the arrival of Europeans on Canada's shores. The DDF was begun in 1932, at the suggestion of the governor general, as an annual festival of amateur productions brought to a central location from communities across the country. The intention was to encourage a sense of shared purpose in the amateur theatrical movement and to provide these companies with an adjudicated showcase of their work and a forum for the exchange of ideas (Salter, 'Idea' 86). Even after a hiatus from 1939 to 1973, the Festival was recognized as a 'Canadian institution, perhaps the greatest artistic institution in the country' (Coulter 20). But it was unclear at this time how the DDF might fit into a scheme for a national theatre. In the early postwar days, some had envisioned the DDF 'spreading itself to become the national theatre of Canada with the special week of festival as only one ... of many activities' (Coulter 20). With the re-emergence of the DDF in 1947, it quickly became apparent that there could be no direct transition from the festival to a national theatre. And arguments that professional theatre must become established in Canada were being made with increasing frequency and vehemence. By 1947, it had become a common argument that at the core of a national theatre there must be professional theatre. The 1947 DDF finals provided a national forum for discussion of the need to develop professional theatre in Canada. Considerations of what 'professionalism' entailed were wide-ranging, encompassing views as disparate as the desire for no-risk, commercially successful theatre, on the one hand, and commitment to a certain 'quality' of production divorced from commercial success, on the other. The middle-ground between these two views was that professional theatre in Canada should be 'organized with as realistic an eye to finance and promotion as is the commercial theatre, though with other than commercial ends in view' (Coulter 20). This theme would have important ramifications for the Stratford Festival and the nature of its promotional activities. In turning a 'realistic eye to finance,' proponents of professional theatre increasingly recognized that this cause should receive government support.

The idea of government support for professional theatre was not the only theme on which there was general agreement. Those concerned with the concept of professional theatre, without exception, equated this with some notion of 'standards' or 'quality' of production. The most common idea of quality was that it be a 'superbly well done' production, not only well performed and directed but well executed at every level of production, including design, costumes, and props. The exceptional production standards established at Hart House Theatre at the University of Toronto were a major influence in this demand for a 'professional' quality of production. In the 1920s, the Hart House facility was one of the most up-to-date in North America, offering theatre directors a fine five-hundred-seat auditorium, with (then) elaborate lighting and effects and a professional staff of eight. Until the founding of the Stratford Festival, Hart House provided an ongoing model of professional technical standards, in contrast to the predominant Canadian practice of staging works in small, poorly equipped auditoria built to be 'multifunctional' rather than serve the specific needs of theatre. And so several theatre practitioners and critics looked to the advent of professional theatre in new facilities across the country to free Canadian theatre from small, inadequate stages and to provide large-scale productions – the terms 'lush' and 'spectacle' were even used. Throughout the 1950s and 1960s, the Stratford Festival's public-relations material would employ the terms 'quality,' 'lushness,' and 'spectacle' in describing the Festival's productions and the nature of their professionalism. It was then but a short step to the dangerous, automatic equation of quality *with* lushness and spectacle, an equation that would so predominate in Festival discourse that Nathan Cohen could observe, in a 1956 broadcast, 'We've been misled into the belief that decor is the thing in theatre' (*Views* 1 January 1956; qtd. in Edmonstone 235).[10]

In Ontario, the New Play Society attained the highest profile in the postwar period for its work as a professional theatre. And, of all the figures on the Canadian theatre scene, Dora Mavor Moore, founder-director of the New Play Society and one of the country's foremost actors and directors, had the most direct input into initial planning for the Stratford Festival. Moore would act as liaison between Tyrone Guthrie and Tom Patterson, founder of the Festival, and also between Guthrie and the Canadian theatrical community.

When the Second World War ended, there was no indigenous professional theatre in Toronto until the New Play Society was formed in 1946.[11] The major objective of Dora Mavor Moore in founding the New Play Society was 'to establish a living theatre in Canada on a professional but non-profit basis' (qtd. in Tepper 21). To this end, the Society sought to nurture Canadian talent, both playwrights and actors. In 1949 no less a critic than Nathan Cohen broadcast on a Toronto radio station that the New Play Society was leading the Canadian theatre scene, especially in its production of Canadian work: 'No other organization is doing so much to raise Canadian acting standards and to advance the cause of our national drama.' (*Across* 16 January 1951; qtd. in Edmonstone 121). Moore's work in founding and then leading this venture placed her at the centre of postwar theatre in Canada, a leading force in the nation's theatre community. Over a ten-year period, forty-seven of the Society's seventy-two productions were original Canadian scripts, thereby fulfilling Moore's dictum that 'no theatre could be fully Canadian, until it is the home of Canadian plays' (qtd. in Tepper 21). But Moore, significantly, also insisted that each season of Canadian plays be accompanied by a number of classics, considered to be her specialty as a director.

While there was certainly an increase in the number of theatres on the Canadian scene from the time the war ended until the founding of the Stratford Festival, and while a range of Canadian material was being produced in this period, most of the major concerns expressed in these years remained unaddressed in the actual theatre activity of the country. For example, it was felt that Canadian theatre still had no international profile and that the process of attracting international recognition had slowed to a near-halt after some promising efforts, lost in the glut of commercially oriented work, which replicated the 'hits' of other nations. These 'hits' were not sufficient to win the yearned-for artistic respectability. Government support was still being sought as the way to bring Canadian theatre into prominence. As the availability of 'commercial' theatre increased, so did demands for a humanist theatre, which would enrich and civilize the country. And no single institution, nor a system of theatres, had been deemed to warrant the label of the 'national theatre.' Indeed, it was felt that the increase in the number of theatres had been 'in the spirit of a boom-town mentality, and without that overriding sense of purpose and consistent artistic policy which is essential to the development of a meaningful national theatre' (Edmonstone 159). We have seen that the development of Canadian scripts was an integral part of discussions to organize the nation's dramatic groups into some form of national theatre, and individual theatre companies were also active in presenting new Canadian work. However, efforts to foster Canadian playwrighting would be undermined by the postwar emphasis on Shakespeare and the Massey Report's vehemence concerning the classics, and then eclipsed by the favouring of Shakespeare at the Stratford Festival. The cause would not be revived until the early 1970s.

Commentary on a 1932 production of *Hamlet*, staged jointly by the Ottawa Little Theatre and the Montreal Repertory Theatre under the supervision of the governor general, the Earl of Bessborough, is illustrative of the rhetorical emphasis that would be maintained in the postwar period (Whittaker, 'Shakespeare' 84): 'The MRTs *Hamlet* missed precisely this intellectual struggle ... There was little unity of action in this production and the entire stress was laid on the poetry of the dialogue, the colour of the decor, and the exterior action of the play. As a result one seemed to be witnessing not so much a production as a number of scenes' (qtd. in Whittaker, 'Shakespeare' 85).[12] The emphases recorded in this review are remarkably similar to what would later be stated in reviews of Stratford Festival productions, indicating that the production was dominated by the poetry, exterior action, and decor. The production was staged in both Ottawa and Montreal, given national coverage in the press, and hailed as fulfilling some of the aspirations for a national theatre. The effect of the widespread coverage of this production was to establish its approach to Shakespeare as pre-eminent in Canada until the work of the Earle Grey Festival in the early 1950s.

As part of the general proliferation of theatrical activity in Canada following the Second World War, several groups were formed for the express purpose of producing Shakespeare, such as Montreal's Shakespeare Society and Open-Air Playhouse and Toronto's Earle Grey Festival. The majority of these were directed either by someone brought in specially from England or by someone – Canadian or a transplanted Englishman – trained in England in the British rhetorical tradition.[13]

This was certainly true of Earle Grey, who founded (1949) and directed the Festival bearing his name. Grey's Festival was the most successful, ongoing venture in Shakespeare production in Canada prior to the Stratford Festival, and so its work occupied a central place in Shakespearean discourse until it was supplanted by the Stratford enterprise.

The artistic principle fundamental to Earle Grey was to produce the plays as they were done in Shakespeare's day. To Grey, this meant strictly according to the intentions of the author – he would take 'no liberties' (qtd. in 'Shakespeare Festivals' 10):[14]

> As far as possible twentieth-century notions would not be permitted. Stunts, fashionable slants, Freudian implications, and silly-clever ideas which are the bane of the contemporary Shakespeare theatre would be ruled out. Arrogant directors would not provide crutches to help the aged and halting playwright in his shamble to oblivion. The accumulation of varnish and the over-painting of centuries would be stripped off and the picture shown as Shakespeare's brush had left it. Our watchword would be 'Back to Shakespeare' ... our resolution would be to try and give our audience what *Shakespeare* had in mind when he wrote, and not some distortion or misconception based on modern ideas. (Grey, 'Shakespeare' 112)

The notion that the productions must try to recreate the intentions of the author and his acting company as manifested in an ideal production nearly four hundred years in the past, the association of any effort to relate the plays to one's own time as merely 'fashionable slants,' and the wholesale dismissal of 'modern ideas' were significant additions to the postwar discussions of theatre. Shakespeare's work was portrayed as a piece of Canada's heritage, with reverence due to Shakespeare as cultural authority – therefore, every effort must be made to preserve his work 'inviolate,' in the state it was first presented to the world. This is to treat Shakespeare's work as an antique, a commodity to be passed on in its original state, thereby promoting the idea that Shakespeare has little relevance to present problems but is to be enjoyed as revealing the wisdom and glory of a past age. The short history of the Earle Grey Festival concluded: 'In the intimate stillness of the quadrangle's quiet seclusion Shakespeare's noble lines pour forth, making a deep and lasting impression, transmuting the baser metal of a machine-made era into the golden enchantment of a glorious age' (Caillou). When Grey also stated that Shakespeare's plays would 'speak for themselves' and reveal an 'extraordinary timeless quality' (qtd. in Seeley), he offered a powerful statement of the essentialist position, which presupposes that Shakespeare's works are an unambiguous and direct source of the same wisdom for all persons and for all time.[15] This notion of rediscovering the 'real' Shakespeare is one that would be favoured in Stratford Festival discourse – first in relation to the technical experiment of staging the plays in a manner approximating the Elizabethan, and, in the late 1950s and early 1960s, in the emphasis given to the mistaken notion that authorial intention can somehow be captured in a theatre production.

In the four seasons prior to the founding of the Stratford Festival, the Earle Grey enterprise fostered a notion of Shakespearean production that would be perpetuated in many of its essentials at Stratford. Underlying the two festivals were the same assumptions concerning Shakespeare as cultural authority and Shakespearean production as a soothing entertainment, a form of commodity, through which one can escape from the 'outside world.' The Earle Grey Festival's emphasis on Shakespeare as cultural authority would be given powerful support with the release of the Massey Commission's Report in 1951.[16]

The Massey Report has generally been regarded as representing a central moment, 'a kind of watershed in Canadian attitudes to the arts' (Woodcock 11). The impulse behind the report was clearly that of 'fostering ... a national culture' and in this it was consonant with the postwar discourse on theatre (Cohen, Editorial; qtd. in Edmonstone 190). In summary, the Massey Report registered for the first time 'official' concern with the future of Canadian culture and proposed that this future lay in organized, professionalized, and institutionalized culture, with government funds to be committed to these ends. Moreover, the report was predisposed towards those institutions that might be able to play not just an artistic role in the nation but a cultural or political role as well – that is, those institutions that would further national pride by bringing international respect to Canada as a mature and cultured nation. The notion that the nation's 'cultural resources' are the foundation for Canada's life as a nation was the Massey Report's main theme: 'Canadian achievement in every field depends mainly on the quality of the Canadian mind and spirit. This quality is determined by ... the books they read, the pictures they see and the programmes they hear. These things, whether we call them arts and letters or use other words ... lie at the roots of our life as a nation' (Canada, *Report* 271). The essay on 'Theatre' in the Massey Report emphasized that, for a country to be civilized in the eyes of the world, it must have an active program of indigenous theatre, a national theatre that would act as a cultural resource for the entire nation. The report gave a notable emphasis to the idea of developing a theatre company that could lead the nation, arguing that there might come a time when a Canadian theatrical company will have unmistakably earned the right to be called a national theatre. By that time, it will have its traditions, its methods of work, its individual style, and its faithful and appreciative public (197). The report thus gave further weight to the need for professionalism in Canadian theatre, a need that had already emerged in postwar discussions: this national theatre company was to be the leading professional company in the country. However, the report failed to articulate what kind of professional theatre it envisioned for Canada; there was no indication of whether the commission was promoting theatre as a form of creative art or as a commercial enterprise; there were no direct considerations of the relationship of theatre to society, or of the specific kinds of scripts, including Canadian, that might be undertaken. The essay referred to the drama of fifth-century Athens and of Renaissance Italy as concentrating the full cultural resources of their societies, and it then stated, 'The drama has been in the past, and may be again, not only the most striking symbol of a nation's culture, but the central structure enshrining much that is finest in a nation's spiritual and artistic greatness' (193). The report thus proceeded from the humanist assumption that, at its best, drama is an ennobling art, and that there is no need to consider any other relationship that it may have to society. The commission also stated that the 'great heritage' of dramatic works is largely unknown to the people of Canada, implying that such works should be made available. The emphasis on the 'classics' is unmistakable, as is the downplaying of the possibilities for a vital Canadian drama. The report was clearly looking to a repertory whose reliability to move an audience had been established in another time and place.

This viewpoint was elaborated in a 'Special Study' prepared by Robertson Davies at the request of the Massey Commission and released as a companion to its report. Written in the form of a dialogue between two fictional characters, Davies's contribution was given powerful legitimation by its official status as a 'Special Study' for the commission. The satirical dialogue discussed at length the importance of the classics to theatre in Canada. And while the claim that the classics would amend the 'illiteracy' of Canadians was hyperbolic, the necessity of producing 'the classics' for Canada to be considered 'truly great' as a nation ran throughout the dialogue and was a crucial theme for Davies ('Theatre: A Dialogue' 373). Yet the only classics actually discussed in the 'Special

Study' were the works of Shakespeare. Davies emphasized that these must be experienced in performance, not simply read. One of the characters suggested that, if a group of Canadian schoolteachers professionally engaged in teaching Shakespeare were asked how many Shakespearean plays they had seen on stage, 'their answers would sadden your heart and chill your blood ... What can they know about Shakespearean drama if they have never experienced it in its proper form? Who attempts to explain the works of Beethoven if he has never heard an orchestra play them?' (373). It is important to note that this emphasis on Shakespeare likely played into an anglophilia, sometimes acknowledged and sometimes not, that Canadian communities with British roots felt in response to European postwar immigration. Moreover, these immigrants were themselves frequently coming from cultures in which Shakespeare's plays, performed in their own languages, played an important part in their nations' theatrical heritages. It is certainly possible that these two divergent elements complemented each other, establishing a context that facilitated the ready acceptance of Shakespeare's cultural authority (Makaryk). The Stratford Festival would emphasize Shakespeare's primacy as a cultural authority both to legitimize and to promote its activity. Davies's dialogue also gave great weight to the idea that theatre relies on a 'living tradition,' and identified this as 'a sense of the wonder and nearness of the great past.' (373). Davies thus provided a strong statement that Canadian theatre should look to Shakespearean production as the major tradition in which to root its work, and he cited England's Old Vic Theatre Company as a possible model for the kind of theatre needed in Canada. Understandable as this is, given that both Davies and his wife had worked at the Old Vic, the recommendation of the Old Vic was, in effect, yet another signal that Canada needed a major, possibly a national, theatre that could focus on the works of Shakespeare. At this time, the Old Vic was regarded as England's premiere classical theatre company, its foremost producer of Shakespeare's works, and the country's national theatre in all but name. The emphasis on the Old Vic as a model would be compounded when Tyrone Guthrie, the Old Vic's leading director in the 1940s, was hired as artistic director of the Stratford Festival.[17]

Davies's 'Special Study' lay the groundwork for the founders of the Stratford Festival, Tom Patterson and Tyrone Guthrie, to focus on Shakespeare as the basis for Canadian theatre. Moreover, Davies's emphasis on 'tradition' was combined with a summary dismissal of theatre as a social institution and of its works as social and political texts:

'Never forget those well-meaning enemies of art. They are the people who will not allow the theatre to be its own justification. The theatre is educational and recreative. But it is not so primarily. It's first of all an art, and it is as a form of art that it stands or falls. Let people get their hands on it who regard it as means of spreading some sort of education dear to themselves, or who think that it is a social medicine, and you will kill it as dead as a doornail' ('Theatre: A Dialogue' 385).

Davies's 'Special Study' thus helped entrench the idea that the most significant theatre for Canadians was the great, ennobling works received from the past. The informing concept for Davies and the Massey Commission is that which Alan Sinfield has identified in relation to the Royal Shakespeare Company as 'culturism' – 'the belief that a wider distribution of high culture through society is desirable' ('Royal' 164). The Massey Report and 'Special Study' demonstrated none of the passion concerning the need for Canadian plays that had marked the general postwar discourse on theatre, yet, they quickly became central documents in that debate. The essay on theatre in the Massey Report and the 'Special Study' – indeed, the entire Massey Report – not only expressed for the first time, official concern with the future of Canadian culture, they also interposed into the discourse the notion that this future lay in institutionalized culture and that government funds should be committed to this end. Moreover, the Massey Report articulated a specific predisposition towards institutions rather than individual artists, particularly those institutions that would further a sense of national pride and achievement by attracting respect to a mature and cultured Canadian nation. Plans to open a Shakespeare festival in Stratford seemed to meet this concern.

The genesis of the 'Stratford Idea' in the imagination of Tom Patterson is a story long since elevated to the status of Canadian folklore and accorded genial nods and smiles at the charming naivete of it all. This mythologizing began from the Festival's first days, with the filming of 'The Stratford Adventure' by the National Film Board in 1953 and the central place given Patterson's plans in Festival public relations. It continued with the publication in 1987 of his book *First Stage: The Making of the Stratford Festival.*

The narrative of the Stratford Festival usually relates how Tom Patterson had long felt that the idea was an 'absolute natural,' that it was the town's birthright: 'After all ... we had a city named Stratford, on a river named Avon. We had a beautiful park system. We had wards and schools with such names as Hamlet, Falstaff, Romeo and Juliet.' (*First Stage* 26).[18] Patterson's plan was thus irrevocably linked to the potency of the birthplace cult. When combined with those statements urging the production of the classics, especially Shakespeare, this identification laid the ground for the Stratford Festival to be labelled as the leader of the Canadian theatre scene before a single production had been staged. The narrative relates that Patterson returned from military service overseas determined, on the one hand, to enrich the lives of his hometown with a stimulating and well-respected arts enterprise and, on the other, to relieve the town's economic plight. In the postwar years, the town of Stratford was faced with the closing of the Canadian National Railway's repair yards, which had been at the core of the town's economy since the early years of the century. Patterson's avowed intention was to establish a festival that would do for the Canadian Stratford what the Shakespeare industry was doing for the economy of mother Stratford and Warwickshire. There was no discussion of the appropriateness of a Shakespeare festival in light of aspirations for developing Canadian drama. When no dissenting voices were heard – 'nobody can say that a Shakespearean Festival is a bad idea' – the plan to devote a festival to the works of Shakespeare gained force (qtd. in Pope 25). The absence of any clearly defined artistic objectives and the declared desire to emulate the success of Stratford-upon-Avon ensured that the desirability of immediate international attention, accompanied by economic success, would take root as central values in the initial planning of the festival.

Patterson's tenacity eventually led him to Tyrone Guthrie: 'Englishness' was quite literally being imported. A majority of commentators would now declare that the longed-for Messiah of Canadian theatre had been found, and it was but a short step for Guthrie's views to be treated as holy writ, the focus of the discourse on Shakespeare in Canada.[19] Guthrie arrived at Stratford with the desire to undertake a technical innovation in staging Shakespeare's works on an open stage. Publicity emphasized this idea as well as Guthrie's notion of using the text as 'raw material' around which one orchestrated a spectacle of effects and lavish costumes. In Guthrie's productions before coming to Stratford, 'spectacle' had been manifested in his elaborate choreography of crowd scenes, in lavish costuming, and in his repeated use of complicated stage business. Planning for a stage that would be deliberately austere, Guthrie proposed that 'luxury' be supplied by the costuming. Terms such as 'luxurious' occur with frequency in the Guthrie commentary. For example, Guthrie commented on what audiences want: 'For the price of their ticket they want not only the pleasure of the play; they want to feel that for a brief and glittering three hours they have bought, and therefore own, something largely, loudly, unashamedly luxurious' (*Life* 53). This would be accepted by the Festival's founding committee as a credo (Guthrie, 'Shakespeare at Stratford' 127–31),[20] recorded in such statements as 'Dr. Guthrie has a superb capacity to generate enthusiasm, and to brush away cobwebs' (Davies, 'Shakespeare' 21–2). In its early days, the Festival invested in an aesthetic of spectacle and effect. And in favouring such visual lushness, the Festival made implicit its view that this was simply the nature of things (J. Berger 109).

It has always been emphasized that Guthrie was a tradition-breaker. More to the point was the unmistakable emphasis on the idea that the technical innovation of the open stage would be a progressive, even experimental, enterprise by which to advance Shakespearean production. This point was made as much by those reviewing the Festival's plans (and later its productions) as by those within the Festival. It quickly became a staple of the Stratford discourse, as basic to the Festival as the specific conventions of staging that would come to be associated with the design of the stage.

In its very first season, the Stratford Festival would be lauded as proof that Canada had attained a maturity in cultural matters to match its achievements in the economic sphere. The continued affirmation of this idea over the Festival's initial three seasons would reinforce the authority of the aesthetic identified in commentaries on the Festival's work. Moreover, this was the first step in positioning the Festival as a producer of Shakespeare, the nation's foremost cultural commodity. In this light, the conception of theatre and of culture on which the Festival was founded, and the aesthetic favoured in its initial seasons, possess a significance outside their immediate impact on those attending the Festival. In promoting the Festival's aesthetic of spectacle and effect to the entire nation, the Festival discourse registered this aesthetic as the predominant, authoritative notion of theatre for Canada in these years. I would suggest that the ascendancy of spectacle in the early years had wider implications than those signalled by such terms as 'costume drama' and 'pageantry.' Nor should we simply accept that one can account for this aesthetic as something necessary to attract an audience seeking to put wartime austerity behind it (Guthrie's reasoning). I believe that it is of paramount importance to try to understand the *effect* of such an aesthetic and the way technical matters of production dominated Festival discourse, since, as David Margolies reminds us, there is 'no "pure cultural excellence"; even aesthetic principles relate to social and class values' (243). None of the reviewing community discussed the implications of the Festival's reliance on an aesthetic of spectacle and effect and none suggested that the Guthrie variant of 'spectacle' frequently meant that the transgressive potential of the Shakespearean text (that is, the potential of both performance texts and dramatic texts to play a role in political and social transformation) was subverted by the physical and technical elements of the performance text.

In its first three seasons the Festival would be hailed as an enterprise of national significance, proof that Canada had come of age in cultural matters: the triumph of the first season was emphasized repeatedly, establishing the Shakespeare Festival as the answer to the quest for cultural respectability. The times were propitious for a large-scale arts enterprise to be promoted as a significant national achievement, and for that enterprise to be appropriated as a product to be 'consumed' by the entire country, as a means of sharing in that achievement. With each successful Festival season, the discourse articulated the same aesthetic of spectacle and effect. And with the achievement of three successful seasons, a formidable vision of theatre would be conveyed to the Festival's larger constituency – the entire nation. This aesthetic taught the nation that Shakespearean production entails the predominance of facile effects. The Festival discourse thus implied that the audience knew little about Shakespeare, that it needed to be educated concerning his significance and shown that his work was 'likable.'[21] In these initial years, the Festival failed to give any indication that theatre might function as a commentator on the social situation, that theatre and culture possess the capability to resist society.[22]

The Festival's 'Charter' is a key document in this regard and the closest the early Festival would come to a declaration of its objectives.[23] Its first stated objective was 'to promote interest in, and the study of, the arts generally and literature, drama and music in particular.' This was directly associated with the notion of humanist education, education as appreciation of the works of the past. The Charter's second objective was 'to advance knowledge and appreciation of and stimulate interest in Shakespearean culture and tradition by theatrical performances and otherwise.' The implication was that the lessons the Festival would offer were fundamental to a civilized society, that productions of Shakespeare's work were something to admire and 'visit' as one does a museum, something separate from one's day-to-day life. Equally striking was the inference that it was Shakespeare who would somehow introduce Canada to its 'own' cultural traditions. The Charter did not identify the Festival merely as a national leader in the arts; it claimed that the Festival was qualified and positioned to be a major factor in the cultural education of the nation. Above all, the Charter viewed Shakespeare as the foundation for the advancement of theatre in the nation and implied that it was both natural and right that the Stratford Festival, as the producer of Shakespeare, be the centre and focus for Canadian culture.

Before the Festival opened, fundraising material identified the Festival as the focal point of the nation's culture in its scale, boldness, and innovations:

> We are writing to you as one who has already shown a concrete interest in the cultural and spiritual growth of Canada ... As you will realize, this is a project of national significance and one which will require the support of interested citizens right across Canada ... you might be interested in the developments ... which ... demonstrate ... the importance of the project to the development of theatre in Canada.
>
> This undertaking is much too large to be the responsibility of any one community or group. (Showalter 6 April 1953)[24]

Another piece of promotional literature emphasized the Festival's importance not only to the development of theatre but for all of Canadian culture: 'The strength of the cast, the unique stage, but above all, the daring nature of the venture have already created interest ... However the true value of the Festival centres around the opportunity it affords of creating a focal point for Canadian culture in keeping with our economic and industrial growth' (Showalter 5 May 1953).

Just as the Charter viewed Shakespeare as standing at the centre of Western culture, so Guthrie commented frequently on the necessity for Canada to produce Shakespeare as the appropriate way to introduce Canadians to their cultural traditions. Guthrie even went so far as to suggest that a distinctive Canadian theatre would emerge *only* out of a study of Shakespeare and other classics, that a distinctive national style of production, writing, and criticism, as well as acting, would develop only by 'evolving a distinctively Canadian comment on the classics' ('First' 28). And so both the postwar discussions and the emerging Festival discourse repeatedly proposed that Shakespearean 'tradition' and 'conventions' inherited from the past be respected, thereby affirming Shakespeare as cultural authority. For example, in the 1953 souvenir program for the first season, an ad for the John Hancock Insurance Company congratulated the Festival for introducing the glories of the past to the present: 'Congratulations to Stratford, Ontario for bringing to the heart and imagination of the world, a cultural treasure.' The implicit theme was the notion of enhancing Shakespeare as cultural authority, of creating the 'right atmosphere' for the proper 'appreciation' of that authority. The increasing strength of this theme positioned the Festival as *the* organization to lead Canadian theatre, the appropriate model and authority for theatre production in the country.

After the first season, it would be proposed that the Festival's work should be extended by establishing 'true facsimiles' elsewhere in Canada – by those trained in the 'home theatre.' A corps of theatre workers was to be trained in those methods that had made the Stratford Festival so 'effective': 'In short, a tradition must be established' (Davies, 'Future' 5). The Festival's values and practices were thus to provide not just the model for theatre production in Canada but the basis for a national theatre tradition, a tradition described as 'a sympathetic yet discriminating knowledge of the past, as ration for a well-planned voyage into the future' (Davies, 'Future' 5). Indeed, this was one of the main themes elaborated in Robertson Davies's discussion of the 'Future of the Festival' in the 1954 souvenir program. The Stratford Festival was thus positioned to act as the model for theatre in Canada, and its discourse would take root as the dominant one in the country.

Less than a month after the very first 'first night' (11 July 1953), a number of Canadian articles went further, evaluating the Stratford Festival as an enterprise of historic importance, the nation's long-hoped-for triumph on the international arts scene – one that pointed the way for Canada to be a significant voice in cultural matters. A previously incipient statement began to appear in a more powerful form: the Festival was of historic importance not only to Canada but wherever theatre was taken seriously. A number of themes coalesced in the statement that the Festival had revolutionized theatre worldwide: 'This country now finds itself in the forefront of a development of the theatrical art which has its roots deep in what is best in the classic theatre, and which sweeps aside much of the accumulation of rubbish which has cluttered the theatre' (Davies, 'Through' 8). A direct connection was drawn by writers such as Robertson Davies between the design of the Festival theatre and the best of classical theatre. This design was identified as the 'theatre of the future,' an 'artistic bombshell' exploding 'just at the time when Canadian theatre is most ready for a break with the dead past and a leap into the future' (Davies, 'Through' 8). In its 1953 program, the Festival was identified as an experiment 'enabling the plays to be staged in the convention for which they were written.' The article also expressed the hope that the Festival stage would achieve universal popularity and become 'the blueprint for Shakespearean and perhaps other classical production' (C. Clarke, 'Stratford Festival'). In the reviews and articles concerning the Festival's opening, this claim was widely applauded and affirmed as the Festival's major achievement – 'the audience for the first time in many of their lives, saw Shakespeare produced as it should be produced' (Patterson, 'Festival' 2). The Festival was simultaneously portrayed as in direct descent from the best of the classical tradition and as a progressive enterprise. These themes were adopted as a staple of Festival publicity and disseminated to the nation.

But what is of greatest import about the claims of international significance was the conflating of references to Shakespeare and the Festival with references to the country. More than identifying the Festival as the beginning of a truly national theatre, the discourse portrayed the Festival as a symbol of what the nation could accomplish in the arts (Davies, 'Through' 8; House 60–5). The Festival and Shakespeare were heralded as fulfilling much of what had been looked for in the postwar theatre scene and so were seen as national resources. In the course of the first three Festival seasons, this view would become increasingly explicit, and in the years 1956–9 the appropriation of the Festival and Shakespeare in the cause of Canada's cultural respectability evolved into an article of faith. For example, before the 1956 season opened, the Stratford Festival was said to have achieved the status of a national institution and the authoritative voice in Canadian cultural matters, a claim substantiated with the announcement that the Festival would take a production of *Tamburlaine the Great* to Broadway and represent Canada at the Edinburgh Festival with a production of *Henry V* in which director Michael Langham cast French-Canadian actors to portray the French court. Langham's declared intention was to point to the compromise in the last act between the French and English as one that might be relevant to the Canadian situation – the first Shakespeare production at the Festival to comment directly, however distantly, on Canadian society. The production was especially significant for helping to solidify the Festival's image as the theatre to represent the nation. Indeed, Langham commented in 1968 that he felt it had simply been common sense to use the French-Canadian actors since their involvement 'could help realize some of the national identity which Stratford was instinctively beginning to seek' (7). Yet, in spite of the Festival's 'seeking out' of a national identity, Canadian plays were not produced at the Festival until its eighth season, 1960. The two short plays produced in that year were winners in a competition sponsored by the *Globe and Mail*, but they were given scant attention in reviews of the 1960 season. The 1960s would see the sporadic production of Canadian plays, one each in 1961, 1966, 1968, and 1969. It was not until the early 1970s that Canadian works became a consistent feature of the Festival season – a full twenty years after its founding. With the tenure of Englishman Robin Phillips as artistic director, from 1975 to the end of the 1980 season, the production of Canadian works became sporadic.[25] Indeed, at a Toronto press conference on 29 October 1979, Phillips stated, 'That will be our emblem for the decade ... Stratford in the 1980s will be exploring and exploiting its internationalism' (qtd. in Pettigrew and Portman 2: 171).

In both the Broadway and Edinburgh tours of the mid-1950s, the Festival was conflated with the nation but the assertion was elaborated: the Festival's fame had become the nation's fame, and the Festival was billed as the artistic voice of the country, sent out to the 'corners of Christendom' to speak of the nation's attainment of a 'civilized, sensitive and adult' state (L. Roberts). With these tours, the Festival would also be identified as the arbiter of Canadian cultural standards and the country's pre-eminent cultural showpiece, a commodity to be cherished by the entire nation. But it was in the Festival's campaign for a permanent theatre, beginning in the fall of 1955, that we find the most decided shift in emphasis: not only was the Festival promoted as vital to Canadian culture and theatre, it was now declared to be *the* institution at the centre of Canadian cultural life.

In the campaign booklet *An Appeal to Pride*, the Shakespearean Festival is clearly identified as both cultural authority and commodity. All Canadians were asked to share in the project, since the Festival had proven itself as a theatre and as a demonstration of the maturity and spirit of the nation's people ('Canadians no longer accept undigested the standards of taste set elsewhere. They have placed their own criterion of excellence on the world stage'). The campaign was thus grounded in the powerful idea that, just as the Festival was leading the nation, so would its supporters be the nation's cultural leaders, that the Festival's future was directly related to their 'good name.' The emergent theme was that the Festival belongs to the nation. In the closing words of *An Appeal to Pride*, the descriptions of the Festival as commodity and cultural authority were fully interlocking: 'The Festival has won the approval of Canadians. This approval is a natural thing. When Canadians watch the Stratford stage, they see the reflection of their own deepened perception and judgment. It is their own growth ... the growth of their country ... which is mirrored in the performance before them.' Other campaign brochures reiterated these statements, identifying the Festival's value as an educational enterprise in the cultural sphere in general and not just in relation to drama and theatre.[26] One brochure, *The Need for a Permanent Theatre at Stratford*, proposed that a corporation supporting the Festival would find itself and its products endowed with the Festival's well-known 'success and quality': Stratford was represented as a commodity conferring quality and success by association, the theatrical variant of a Gucci label. With the campaign for a permanent theatre, the discourse began to articulate a consistent statement that the Festival was a cultural force standing alongside the very best cultural institutions in the world. It was therefore only natural for the Festival to be Canada's cultural representative around the world, its authoritative cultural voice and supplier of the nation's cultural respectability.

I would suggest that Alan Sinfield's proposition that 'Shakespeare' is one of the places where English society works out its understanding of itself was also true for Canada in the period leading up to the founding of the Stratford Festival and on through the 1950s and 1960s (Sinfield, 'Reproductions' 130–1). Indeed, the authority attached to Shakespeare in the English-speaking cultural tradition was compounded in the case of Canada's Stratford Festival, since it provided the basis on which to claim cultural maturity and respectability. By the time of the Festival's first season, the notion that had come to dominate in the discourse on theatre in Canada was that of cultural deference to the cultural authority of William Shakespeare and to the institutions through which his work could be appropriated – which for Canada was the Stratford Festival. This positioning would enable the Stratford Festival discourse to delimit the boundaries of what was permissible as the 'Canadian Shakespeare' in the 1950s and 1960s.[27]

Notes

1 I would like to thank the McConnell Foundation of Montreal for financial support of much of this research, undertaken for my unpublished PhD dis-

sertation, 'Canada's Stratford Festival 1953–67: Hegemony, Commodity, Institution.' I am currently revising the dissertation for publication. Some aspects of the argument and a few of the examples also appear in my article 'Affirmative Shakespeare at Canada's Stratford Festival.'

2 Across the nation, there are at least twelve theatre companies or festivals (amateur and professional) that operate in the summer months producing Shakespeare's works exclusively or predominantly. Most of these work in outdoor sites ranging from hillside amphitheatres to an ocean-side cliff. These include: MUN Drama, St John's; Dick's Kids, St John's; the Atlantic Theatre Festival, Wolfville, N.S.; Repercussion Theatre, Montreal; Toronto Free Theatre ('The Dream in High Park') and Skylight Theatre, Toronto; Another Shakespeare, Ottawa; Shakespeare in the Park, the Winnipeg Shakespeare Company, and Shakespeare in the Ruins, Winnipeg; Shakespeare on the Saskatchewan, Saskatoon; the Bard on the Beach, Vancouver; the Nanaimo Festival, Nanaimo, B.C.

3 This chapter accepts the general assumptions of those who analyse the institutional mediation of Shakespeare, including the assumption that neither Shakespeare nor institutional practice stand outside historical and social determination. Therefore, the critique of institutional practice cannot proceed on the basis that there is some other real or natural Shakespeare that is the normative standard for evaluating the institution. In this regard, see Bristol, *Shakespeare's*. Also see Dollimore and Sinfield, 'Cultural Materialism' on the point that Shakespeare's work is continuously reconstructed through various diverse institutions functioning in specific contexts.

4 Indeed, Richard Paul Knowles has proposed that the Stratford Festival may be seen as a site to explore 'contesting versions of Canadian nationalism' ('Nationalist' 26).

5 In his article 'National Theatre/National Obsession,' Alan Filewod states, 'Since the 1890s theatre critics in Canada have wrestled with what appeared to be a simple problem: if we have a Canadian nation, then a Canadian drama must be one of its proofs; therefore we must have a national theatre to advance the national drama' (5). Denis Salter also discusses how the push for 'a distinctively Canadian kind of national theatre begins as early as the nineteenth century' ('Idea' 71).

6 Alan Filewod and Denis Salter have both given accounts of the long debate concerning a national theatre. Both establish that, from the 1890s to 1939, there was a clear bias towards English culture, and, in 'The Idea of a National Theatre,' Salter comments on the 'faith in Shakespeare as a canonical writer' (80). This article is also extremely helpful for its discussion of the desire, often expressed before the Second World War, for the development

of Canadian plays (87). Indeed, Salter's article is insightful regarding the ways in which the very idea of a 'national theatre' was largely unrecognized as problematic: 'There were few dissenting voices asking if the ideology of nationalism, or at least of this kind of programmatic nationalism, should be rigorously contested as an instance of political and artistic tyranny' (85). Filewod argues that the impetus to establish a national theatre 'was initially proposed as a means of recuperating Canadian theatre from American cultural expansion' ('National' 5). Although Filewod is not as vehement as Salter that a national theatre was potentially detrimental, he does note that the 'proposed solutions to this American influence may seem in retrospect to be regressive' ('National' 6). It is Salter who makes the important observation that those concerned with the idea of a Canadian national theatre in the years preceding the Second World War, including John Martin-Harvey, Harley Granville-Barker, and Vincent Massey, promoted the English model of a national theatre and managed 'to embed a set of reactionary cultural values' in the discourse ('Idea' 79). These included favouring Shakespeare for his expression of 'so-called universal, transhistorical values' (79). Richard Paul Knowles's article 'From Nationalist to Multinational: The Stratford Festival, Free Trade and the Discourses of Intercultural Tourism' is also extremely suggestive in its argument that the Festival's founding was 'discursively constructed as the founding of a Shakespearean National Theatre in Canada after the British (imperialist) model, in which Shakespeare was used to serve the interests of cultural colonization by a dominant ... elite' (26).

7 The House of Commons Special Committee on Reconstruction and Re-establishment, also known as the Turgeon Committee since it was chaired by James Grey Turgeon, was established in 1942 'to study and report under the general problems of reconstruction and re-establishment which may arise at the termination of the present war' (qtd. in Tippett 171). See Canada, *Minutes*. According to Maria Tippett, the sixteen organizations had been prompted to submit their 'Brief' to the Turgeon Committee by Dorise Nielsen, the Labour Progressive MP for North Battleford. She was herself a member of the Turgeon Committee (231). By 1946, these organizations had constituted themselves as the Canadian Arts Council. In 1950 there were eighteen member organizations in the Arts Council: the Royal Academy of Arts, the Royal Architecture Institute of Canada, the Canadian Authors' Association, La Société des Écrivains Canadiens, the Federation of Canadian Artists, the Canadian Music Council, the Dominion Drama Festival, the Canadian Handicrafts Guild, the Canadian Guild of Potters, the Canadian Group of Painters, the Canadian Society of Painters in Water Colour, the Canadian Society of Painter-Etchers and Engravers, the Sculptor's Society of

Canada, the Canadian Society of Graphic Arts, the Canadian Society of Landscape Architects and Town Planners, the Arts and Letters Club, Manitoba Arts Council, and the Canadian Ballet Festival Association.

8 Originally from Ireland, John Coulter became a major Canadian playwright, best known for his trilogy of plays on Louis Riel. He also wrote overview articles on the state of Canadian theatre which appeared regularly in such major Canadian publications as *Saturday Night*. Herbert Whittaker was a director and the leading theatre critic at the Montreal *Gazette* (1944–9) and then at Toronto's *Globe and Mail* (1949–75). Vincent Tovell was a theatre critic whose reviews appeared in such major academic journals as the *University of Toronto Quarterly*. Mavor Moore, the son of Dora Mavor Moore, was a playwright, actor, director, and journalist/critic, moving with ease among these various roles.

9 Voaden provides a useful summary of theatre events in the western provinces but does not examine the ideas informing these events in any detail. Other reports on theatre in the west similarly concentrate on events. See also Alan Skinner 25–8.

10 Nathan Cohen, Canada's best-known and internationally respected theatre critic in the 1950s and 1960s, made a singular contribution to the Festival's discourse. Cohen praised the Festival in its first season but thereafter was strongly critical in his reviews of productions and overview articles on the Festival. As early as the second season (1954), he commented that the Festival seemed to be tainted 'by an opportunism that could very well be its undoing' (*Views* 11 July 1954 and 24 July 1955; qtd. in Edmonstone 226, 229). See also Cohen 'Theatre Today: English Canada' and 'Stratford after Fifteen Years.' By the mid-1960s, Cohen was more vehement, commenting that the Festival had evolved 'into an arts promotion enterprise, a glossy merchandising of culture in the mass media sense – that is, serious in its pretensions and superficial in its essences' ('Stratford So Far' 7). While other reviewers expressed dissatisfaction with *elements* of specific productions, such as casting choices, Cohen was unique in his general dissatisfaction with the Festival year after year. More significantly, Cohen stood alone in the 1950s and early 1960s in questioning the standard, unexamined view of the Festival's cultural authority as a 'good thing.'

11 John Holden's Actors Colony Theatre was active as early as the mid-1930s and was the first Canadian professional company in the Toronto area, but the New Play Society was the first to include Canadian work.

12 Thomas Archer of the Montreal *Gazette*, writing in *Saturday Night* and quoted in Whittaker's 'Shakespeare in Canada.'

13 A notable exception was Theodor Komisarjevsky, who came from England to

direct a modern-dress production of *Cymbeline* at Montreal's Open-Air Playhouse. More conventional were the same group's productions of *The Taming of the Shrew* and *As You Like It,* under the direction of Malcolm Morley. At Toronto's New Play Society, Dora Mavor Moore brought her background with the Old Vic to the direction of several Shakespearean productions, including *Macbeth.*

14 The 'Shakespeare Festivals' article was quoting from 'Whither Now?' – the final article in Caillou, Walter, and Chappell.

15 The intention to present 'soothing entertainment' may well be *explained* as a reaction to the horrors of the Second World War. However, even though we may now be able to establish and understand this context, this does not mean that we can dismiss the cumulative effect established by such discursive statements concerning the significance of theatre and Shakespeare to Canadian lives. I am concerned in this chapter to analyse the implications of certain ideas established by the discourse rather than to explain the origins of its constituent elements. These effects are the major focus of my PhD dissertation, 'Canada's Stratford Festival 1953–67: Hegemony, Commodity, Institution,' and of my article 'Affirmative Shakespeare at Canada's Stratford Festival.' In the article I argue that a materialist critique of the Stratford Festival discourse reveals that the preferred reading inscribed therein is consistent with the ideology of the 'culture industry,' as that term is understood by the Frankfurt School. According to the Frankfurt School formulation, in the ideology of the culture industry, 'the autonomy of works of art has been eliminated such that they function as commodities in which the capacity for critique has been abrogated' (Groome, 'Affirmative' 140). This same perspective is central to my understanding of the production of Shakespeare's works prior to the founding of the Stratford Festival.

16 In all subsequent references the more commonly used title, the Massey Report, will be used to refer to the *Report: Royal Commission on National Development in the Arts, Letters and Sciences, 1949–1951.*

17 This favouring of the Old Vic would continue even when the Festival was well under way. In 1957 Michael Langham, the English director who succeeded Guthrie as artistic director in 1956, commented that he had a vision of the Festival becoming 'as potent a theatrical label as the Old Vic' (qtd. in Lee).

18 See also Patterson, Interview 45, Pilditch 242–7, and Reaney 112–13.

19 The most central of the articles about Guthrie, appearing shortly after the opening of the Festival, include Davies, 'The Director' and 'The Genius of Dr. Guthrie'; Moon, 'Why Guthrie Outdraws Shakespeare' and 'A Towering Figure'; and Edinborough, 'Large Life with High Jinks.' See also C. Clarke, 'Stratford Ontario (Canada)'; Cohen, 'Tyrone Guthrie: A Minority Report';

A Canadian National Theatre   135

Davies, 'Through Ritual to Romance'; McVicar, 'From Little Acorns ... Stratford's Shakespearean Festival'; L. Roberts, *A Report from Stratford*; and Scheff, 'Shakespeare Arrives in Canada.'

20 See also the following items by Guthrie: 'The Development of Live Drama in Canada'; 'First Shakespeare Festival at Stratford, Ontario'; 'A Long View of the Stratford Festival'; 'Problems of the Next Stratford Festival'; and 'Shakespeare Finds a New Stratford.'

21 In 1959 Nathan Cohen made a similar, though more pessimistic, suggestion based on his *viewing* of the Festival's work rather than on an extended critique of the Festival discourse. Cohen stated, 'In effect Stratford was teaching an uncritical audience that Shakespeare's plays had no depth, but were just blueprints for pretty pyrotechnical exercises. The words were totally trivial, the characters mere wax figures, all to be juggled about at the director's caprice' ('Theatre Today' 34). I would suggest that it was the *Festival discourse* that played the pre-eminent role in constructing 'Shakespeare' for the nation.

22 I develop this argument in much greater detail in my PhD dissertation, 'Canada's Stratford Festival 1953–67: Hegemony, Commodity, Institution' and in my essay 'Affirmative Shakespeare at Canada's Stratford Festival.'

23 Each year the Charter was quoted in the pamphlet prepared by the Festival for widespread, free distribution: *The Stratford Festival Story*. This was an annual publication, and each issue covered the history of the Festival from 1953 to the date of issue. In the early years, the Charter was also quoted in various articles about the Festival. For example, see McVicar.

24 The fundraising letters were sent out with the signature of Dr Harrison Showalter, the president of the Festival Foundation at the time.

25 Following is a list of the Canadian work produced at the Stratford Festival between 1953 and 1976. This is based on records in the Festival Archives and also draws on the compilation of productions made in Appendix I of Pettigrew and Portman's *Stratford: The First Thirty Years*: 1960 – two Canadian plays from the *Globe and Mail* Stratford Festival Competition: *The Teacher* by John Gray, and *Blind Man's Buff* by Alfred Euringer; 1961 – *The Canvas Barricade*, a 'contemporary Canadian comedy' by Donald Lamont Jack; 1966 – *The Last of the Tsars* by Michael Bawtree; 1968 – *Colours in the Dark* by James Reaney; 1969 – *The Satyricon* by Tom Hendry; 1970 – *The Sun Never Sets*, a one-man show devised by Patrick Crean; 1972 – *La Guerre, Yes Sir!* by Roch Carrier, *Mark* by Betty Jane Wylie, and *G.K.C.*, a one-man show based on writings of Chesterton by Tony van Bridge; 1973 – *The Collected Works of Billy the Kid* by Michael Ondaatje, and *Inook and the Sun* by Henry Beissel; 1974 – *Walsh* by Sharon Pollock, and *Ready Steady Go* by Sandra Jones; 1975 – *Fellowship* by Michael

Tait, and *Oscar Remembered*, a one-man show on Oscar Wilde compiled and performed by Maxim Mazumdar; 1976 – *Eve* by Larry Fineberg. It can be seen from this list several works written by Canadians were not actually set in Canada.

26 For example, *The Need for a Permanent Theatre at Stratford* and *Six Dividends in Perpetuity: Why You Should Invest in a Great Canadian Enterprise, the Stratford Permanent Theatre Fund.*

27 Alan Sinfield, in an article on the Royal Shakespeare company, comments that 'a major role of theatre criticism is to police the boundaries of the permissible' ('Royal' 176). For further discussion of the concept of the 'permissible,' see Crowley 145.

PART TWO

Shakespeare on Stage

Part One concludes its examination of Canadian Shakespearean institutions with the establishment of the Stratford Festival. The opening chapters of Part Two (by C.E. McGee and Jessica Schagerl) look more closely at Stratford's productions and its legacy, as prelude to a more thorough consideration of the theatre as a particularly important institutional site for understanding Shakespeare in Canada. Part Two ranges from mainstream through to alternative stagings of Shakespeare in different parts of the country, paying particular attention to Quebec (Leanore Lieblein), Newfoundland (Peter Ayers), and downtown Toronto (Michael McKinnie). This section, the book's lengthiest, explores Helen Gilbert and Joanne Tompkins's assertion that 'the ideological weight of Shakespeare's legacy is nowhere felt more strongly than in the theatre, where his work is still widely seen as the measure of all dramatic art, and the ultimate test for the would-be actor or director, the mark of audience sophistication, and the uncontested sign of "Culture" itself' (20). Elaborating on the implications of such pressures, Denis Salter notes, in 'Acting Shakespeare in Postcolonial Space,' that 'Stratford raises the recurrent postcolonial question about place: where is – and therefore what is – the Stratford stage?' and its corollary, 'what kind of Shakespearean acting will seem natural here?' (121–2). Attentive to the many different places that constitute 'Canada' and the interpretive communities (including directors, actors, reviewers, and audiences) that produce, receive, and make meaning out of Shakespeare in these different contexts, this section considers production history, audience interaction, and theatre-reviewing culture collectively to deepen our understanding of theatre culture and its constitution of the 'natural' in Canada.

5

Shakespeare *Canadiens* at the Stratford Festival

C.E. McGEE

In the aftermath of the opening season of the Stratford Festival in 1953, Tyrone Guthrie was still justifying the Stratford project, still trying to secure its future, by arguing that productions of Shakespeare's plays were indispensable for the development of Canadian theatre as such. 'Any distinctive national style,' he asserted, 'whether of acting, producing, writing or criticising plays will be founded on the study of the classics. It will only be, in my view, by evolving a distinctively Canadian comment on the classics that any satisfactory native dramatic style will be achieved. Such comment will occur not only in criticism but in performance, since all performance is equally a comment upon, as well as a re-creation of, the work performed' ('First' 28).[1] That Guthrie, the founding artistic director of the Festival, took up the topic of a Canadian style of performing Shakespeare was understandable, since a rhetoric of Canadian nationalism had been deployed from the very outset of the Stratford Festival project in order to obtain the moral, political, and financial support necessary for the undertaking. Nationalism, stirred by the engagement of Canadians on the battlefields of Europe, found expression after the war in the development of cultural policies and arts institutions that were supposed to shape Canada's identity so as to guard against foreign threats. Guthrie played upon the temper of those times, both in portraying classical drama as the challenge that Canadian professionals had to take up for there to be any hope of 'a distinctive style of Canadian theatre' ('First' 28) and in representing the founding of a Shakespearean festival in Stratford, Ontario, as a national rite of passage from adolescence to adulthood, from an inarticulate yawp to intelligent, even eloquent, speech: 'In its new self-awareness Canada is suddenly conscious of this lopsidedness in its own development. There is a great desire to talk in tones that are less feeble and tentative and to talk sense. Therefore an occasion like this Festival, which provides an opportunity for some tens of thousands of Canadians to participate in a dignified and adult form of artistic expression, is timely and is welcome' (Guthrie, 'Is Canada' 27).

In response to Stratford's first season, critics celebrated the Festival in similar terms, not as the successful realization of a business venture to buttress the economy of the town, as Tom Patterson conceived of the project, but as a breakthrough for the nation. The local Chamber of Commerce shared Patterson's goals, of course, but supported the Festival in more grandiose terms as 'a focal point in the dramatic and cultural life of Canada.'[2] Newspapers from Vancouver Island to Prince Edward Island re-broadcast the Stratford Festival's press releases describing the opening on 13 July 1953 as, modestly, 'Canada's most ambitious theatrical venture' or as, more effusively, 'one of the world's dramatic events of the year.'[3] Other critics, eye-witnesses of the event, concurred. Herbert Whittaker, for instance, writing for the *Globe and Mail*, described opening night as 'the most exciting night in the history of the Canadian theatre' (*Whittaker's* 36). Transported by the excitement of that night, CBC Radio critic Nathan Cohen described the occasion as 'a cultural event of the greatest magnitude for Canadians' and 'a milestone in our theatrical history' (qtd. in Edmonstone 214–15).[4] No wonder, given the insistence on the national significance of the Stratford Festival, that Guthrie himself entertained the possibility of producing Shakespeare's plays 'in a distinctively Canadian way' ('Long' 166).

Within a year, however, Guthrie's confidence that a 'Canadian' production of a classical work might be brought to the stage – or at least his readiness to assure Canadian bureaucrats and potential sponsors that such a possibility existed – had waned. Reflecting on the topic in the light of Stratford's second season, he mused, 'I don't know how far it may be possible to interpret a classical play in a distinctively Canadian way' ('Long' 166). Testing out possible grounds for such a production, he noted the distinctive traits of Canadian actors: their freshness of outlook, their reliance on life experience in developing character, and their reluctance to improvise freely (172). These qualities, however, which he observed in rehearsals and set in contrast to the traits of British members of the company, were not strong enough to determine the character of the final product on stage. He also speculated that Canadian habits of speech might Canadianize a show, but he specified only a few peculiar forms of pronunciation, and these he represented as examples of 'bad speaking' (186) of which the Canadian actors were not guilty. 'No one could mistake them for Englishmen,' he wrote, 'yet they avoid the more rasping mannerisms and slovenliness of much current Canadian speech' (185). Ultimately Guthrie withdrew from the argument, suggesting that the effort to stage Shakespeare in a Canadian way was a retrograde step, a step away from the modern age in which 'all geographical and ethnological differences are being ironed out' (167), a step back into nineteenth-century ideas of nationality and nationalism. Canada was, in Guthrie's view, too vast and too diverse a country to produce 'a single, distinctive national type' (167).

The possibility of performing classical works, including Shakespeare, in a Canadian way also engaged the imagination of Nathan Cohen. He responded to the last year of Guthrie's work as artistic director at Stratford in the terms Guthrie himself had introduced: 'The point, if you like, is that there is no such thing as a Canadian style of doing Shakespeare, and won't be for a long time' (Cohen, 'Theatre Notes' 425).[5] Cohen argued that there could be no Canadian style at Stratford as long as what he called 'the Guthrie style' predominated there (424). A Canadian style required Canadian actors not only with talent, but also with training, and, as far as Cohen was concerned, Tyrone Guthrie had nothing to teach them: 'As long as they look right, and move well, he is satisfied' (424). The Guthrie style, disdainful as it was of 'the language and spirit of any text,' favoured melodramatic and farcical elements, pageantry and spectacle, 'mob scenes' and 'mighty images' (424–5). According to Cohen, Guthrie made himself the star of whatever play he directed, so that the Canadian actors in the Stratford company remained 'far from ready for the great classical roles' (425). As a result, Guthrie's work betrayed the possibilities of 'the important thing about Stratford ... what distinguishes it from all the other Shakespearean Festivals,' that is, its thrust stage, 'a stage merciless to mediocrity' (425).

Both Cohen and Guthrie reached similarly inauspicious conclusions about the possibility of doing Shakespeare in a Canadian way. Yet their engagement with the topic did suggest an array of aspects of productions that might mark them as distinctively Canadian: casting and acting, through which a Canadian personality would manifest itself;[6] peculiarities of pronunciation and rhythms of speech; a stage, unique among Shakespearean festivals (in the early 1950s at least); a certain geography; and, if not a 'national type,' then an identifiable ethnic diversity. Ironically, the last two of these items – the two that Guthrie judged to be passé in the modern world – were to provide the basis for Stratford Festival attempts to Canadianize Shakespearean plays.

In these respects, Festival productions followed the precedents of early modern drama that featured 'Canadians.' In November 1606, for instance, Sieur de Poutrincourt, master of Port Royal in Acadia, returned to the colony where he was greeted by a series of shows on water. One of these featured four 'Indians' ('sauvages') of the region who affirmed the supremacy of the king of France and presented Poutrincourt, the king's representative, with 'un quartier d'Ellam ou Orignac,' 'des peaux de Castors,' 'des Matachiaz, c'est à dire, echarpes, & brasselets' and the promise of some fish not yet caught (Fournier 47–9). Similarly, in 1635, Aurelian Townshend included a 'man of Canada' as the leader of an antimasque procession of two Egyptians from Memphis, three pantaloons from Bergamo, and four Spaniards. As he entered into the presence of Queen Henrietta Maria and her ladies, he provided a glimpse of the land and its native people:

> From Canada, both rough and rude,
> Come I, with bare and nimble feet,
> Those Amazonian maids to greet
> Which conquered them that us subdued.
>
> (Townshend 636)

These entertainments suggest, first, the possibility of Canadianizing a production by using the geography and architecture of the country: the harbour and fort of Port Royal served as the backdrop for the pageants of welcome because they were the real destination of Poutrincourt. Second, what marks the shows as recognizably Canadian, as it did for their first European audiences, is the inclusion of members of the country's First Nations, represented as obeisant peoples, who offer their conquerors samples of the produce and products of the local economy. Finally, what constitutes European culture in Canada is the rivalry between the king of France and the king of England, or, later, that between French Canadians and English Canadians. The means used to identify Canada and Canadians in these early modern shows recur in much later Stratford Festival productions. Twice have they drawn on the Canadian social fabric in casting shows, and twice have they set the plays in a recognizably Canadian ambience – in every case, with surprising and contradictory results.

In casting his production of *Henry V* in 1956, Michael Langham drew on the 'two solitudes' of Canadian society, on the tense co-existence of French and English in the country. With Christopher Plummer playing the lead and several Stratford regulars as the English nobility, Langham hired Québécois actors to play the French roles. To capitalize on this collaboration at a time when ticket sales were lagging behind those of previous years, Langham promoted the production as a manifestation of English-French cooperation.[7] He sustained this theme within the show too, by bringing the production to a culmination in which the two peoples gathered together in happiness and harmony. Contemporary critics overlooked the obvious problem presented by the story of *Henry V* – whatever harmony occurred did so as a result of the defeat of arrogant, bungling Frenchmen by a band of heroic English soldiers. One reason for this oversight was Tanya Moiseiwitsch's design, celebrated by Whittaker as 'a wonderful job of Plantagenetizing' (*Whittaker's* 60). Safely decked out in medieval attire, the characters and their stories were not readily applied to Canadian social conditions, but the artistic collaboration remained significant. Casting intended to serve Shakespeare's play resulted in a production that served the theatrical ambitions of both the acting companies involved: 'The Quebec press wrote of Canada's "national theatre," expressing pride in what actors from Le Théâtre du Nouveau Monde had accomplished' (Pettigrew and Portman 1: 121).

Langham also hoped to Canadianize the 1960 production of *Romeo and Juliet* in the same way. He imagined, but never brought to completion, a production in which the tension between French and English in Canada would inform the family feud that divides Capulets from Montagues; the former were to be francophone, the latter anglophone. In 1968 Director Douglas Campbell took a step towards the realization of Langham's idea when he cast the French-Canadian actress Louise Marleau as Juliet. But Campbell immediately backed away from Langham's concept by casting a young American actor, Christopher Walken, as Romeo. Working with the American designer Carolyn Parker, Campbell 'dressed the people in what appeared to be late eighteenth-century Ruritanian costume' (Edinborough, 'Stratford' 383), thereby removing the production safely beyond the range of any resonance it might have had through its design with Canadian social conditions. Judging the casting of Marleau as Juliet to be a 'disaster' because her accent made her speeches incomprehensible, Edinborough concluded that 'even to prove a politico-cultural Canadian point, one cannot assume that all English Canadians know *Romeo and Juliet* so well that Juliet's speeches do not have to be understood' (383–4).[8]

In both these cases, productions drew on Canada's two founding nations in the casting but obscured the relevance to Canadian culture with the costumes and decor. Do productions clearly set in a Canadian ambience fare any better? Is it any more effective to use identifiable features of Canada to communicate Shakespeare, or aspects of Shakespeare to interpret Canada? Again, there have been, so far, only two Stratford Festival productions that have made the attempt: Richard Monette's *As You Like It* (1990) and Richard Rose's *Two Gentlemen of Verona* (1998).

Monette's *As You Like It* made use of both the physical and the human geography of Canada. A huge metallic tree with brightly lit red, orange, and golden leaves dominated the stage. At the outset of the production, aboriginals, voyageurs, peasants, and gentry entered singing the Québécois folk song, 'Un Canadien errant,' and at the end the ensemble celebrated happily with step dancing to the music of fiddles and spoons. Designer Debra Hanson unfurled blue banners bearing the fleur-de-lis to announce that this was New France and made the stage eighteenth century by including, as one reviewer noted, 'everything but the trading post store ... a birchbark canoe, moccasins, head-dresses, blankets, snowshoes, toques, sashes, bows and arrows' (Brown). The wardrobe bible makes clear the care Hanson took with details: a wheelbarrow contained 'Mac apples' and root vegetables (carrots and turnips); picnic platters had venison, grapes, maize, and not just fish, but 'white fish'; and Touchstone presented Audrey with '19 black-eyed Susans.' Like an emblematic character in an Elizabethan pageant, William epitomized life in forests of eighteenth-century New France: besides a musket, two pistols, and a knife, he carried two pheasants on his belt, two salmon on a string, a rabbit on another cord, and snowshoes across his back. Sound-effects amplified this scene, as audiences heard, besides the strains of some of Quebec's most popular folk songs,[9] the sounds of a horse fly, a loon, a bullfrog, cicadas, crickets, goats, and a flock of Canada geese flying south. Costumes, properties, music, and sound-effects combined to create the setting specified by Richard Monette in his director's notes: the environs of Quebec City and l'Île d'Orléans in the late fall of 1758, a year or so before the English defeated the French in the Battle of the Plains of Abraham.

Although quite precise about the fictive time and place of the action, Monette shed little light on the reasons for his choice. He coyly restricted his explanation to saying that he found the Plains of Abraham reminiscent of the Forest of Arden. Presumably it was the natural beauty

Lucy Peacock as Rosalind in the Stratford Festival production of *As You Like It*, directed by Richard Monette, designed by Debra Hanson, at the Festival Theatre, 1990. Courtesy of the Stratford Festival Archives. Photo by David Cooper.

of the place, now a national park, that made it seem an appropriate correlative to the pastoral world of *As You Like It.* Why 1758? The year before the battle that still informs antagonism between the English and French in Canada may have been chosen in order to capture the pastoral world of the play, especially if that period was presented with some nostalgia for a vision of prelapsarian Canada. Monette, however, did not suggest even these general, generic ways of accounting for the setting of the production.

Critics' opinions filled the vacuum created by the director's reticence. Christopher Potter, having contrasted the 'gonzo atmosphere' of Monette's *As You Like It* to Robin Phillips's 'Amish' production of the same play in 1987, a production in which the stylization threw into relief often overlooked dimensions of the text (see Dawson, 'Impasse' 324–7), concluded that there was 'scant contemplation' in Monette's Canadian concept.[10] Some reviewers, disagreeing with Potter, attributed more deliberation to Monette; they implied that he had thought through the value of eighteenth-century New France as a setting and chose it because it would provide a spectacular design. 'The Quebec concept is primarily for color,' wrote Wilder Penfield. 'What matters is that it has inspired an experience as pleasing to the eye as to the ear.' Many other critics concurred: John Laycock ('Showbiz, not politics [assuming they are separated] is Monette's true sourcebook'); Stewart Brown ('Too much should not be read into this Quebec setting ...'); Audrey Ashley ('The maple syrup is, as the Bard himself might have said, laid on with a trowel. Never mind. It's all done, I presume, in a spirit of fun ...'); and, Nancy Sheppard, who was, ironically, the most dismissive of all even in her high praise for the show ('Although the play is set in and around Quebec City in the mid-1700s, time and location have no real significance. It's theatre at its best'). In all these reviews, as in Monette's own simplistic explanation for the setting of *As You Like It*, there is an acknowledgment that the production engages with the Canadian scene but also a denial of the significance of that engagement.

But the Canadian scene was not insignificant; it was significantly temporary. While the ambience of those roughing it in the bush was thoroughly Canadianized, the elegant costumes, such as those for Rosalind before and after her trip to Arden wood (see p. 147), would have suited any European dukedom in the eighteenth century. Ultimately the audience, like most of the characters, was to leave Canada behind and return to the city and to civilization, where imported fashions from the mother country govern taste. Once out of the backwoods, Monette's *As*

Cartoon juxtaposed in the Chicago *Sun-Times* (7 July 1990) with a review of the Stratford Festival production of *As You Like It*, a review claiming that 'for one brief sweet moment, a spectator forgets the nasty controversies that punctuate the tedium of everyday lives.' Courtesy of Brian Duffy, *The Des Moines Register*.

You Like It became English costume drama displaying the high style of the colonizing peoples.

Canadian history, however, overtook the production and created a context that politicized the reception of it. Interviewed shortly before the production opened, Monette explained that the concept of his *As You Like It* had been decided long before the Meech Lake Accord and the political debates it provoked. He went on to note that the times had complicated what he intended: 'With Meech Lake having reared its head, I fear it [*As You Like It*] will look like a great political message, which it is not intended to. It's interesting that you create something, put it out to the world and the world bring its own life to it and you cannot deny that' (qtd. in Bono). What Monette feared did not come to pass. Patrons did not derive some political message from the production, but it did elicit reactions that conjoined it to the political debates of 1990. David William reported that 'within the same twenty-four hours ... one person going out had said, "This production will separate Canada forever," whereas another had said, "This production will succeed where the Meech Lake Accord has failed"' (5). Canadian reviewers of the show were unanimous in commenting on the potential relevance of the production to political conditions in Canada. Unlike most American critics (see p. 149 for a notable exception) who interpreted the tree arching over the stage as symbolic of harvest time, identified the aboriginal characters as 'North American,'[11] and guessed that maybe the production might have some political relevance (as Terry Doran, a *Buffalo News* critic, put it, 'It's a wonder Quebec separatism isn't snuck in'), Canadian reviewers to a person identified the tree as a maple and discussed the resonance of this production with current events, even if they went on to downplay the significance of that resonance. One critic, Robert Reid of the *Kitchener-Waterloo Record*, wished for a production with a stronger political point. Although he judged the production to be marred by 'crippling superficiality,' Reid thought that Monette's decision to set the action in Quebec in 1758 was 'inspired'; but he wanted more – he wanted an image that might shape the nation in the future:

> While his instincts were right not to wring a political message from a play about the various aspects of love, he missed a marvellous opportunity by not setting the story in post-Conquest Quebec.
>
> Had the banished Duke Senior been made English rather than Quebecois, for example, the wedding between his daughter Rosalind and Orlando de Boys could have become a powerful symbol to the rest of the country of marriage between two founding cultures.

Reviews of Monette's *As You Like It* made it clear that the production was read by Canadian critics as a distinctively Canadian production relevant to the politics of the day.

Just the opposite was true of Richard Rose's *Two Gentlemen of Verona*, which he set in Canada and England in 1913 so as to give the production a political edge. Such political relevance has been a standard feature of Richard Rose's work at the Stratford Festival. In the production of *The Taming of the Shrew*, which he directed on the Festival Theatre stage in 1997, he moved the characters from the Old World to the New World in the 1960s, from the rural Italy of Petruchio's house to New York's little Italy where the Minola family lived. As a result, the production represented the United States of America as the land of bilk and money. The very last image was that of Katherina and Petruchio, side by side on a bed on the upper stage, throwing into the air the cash won through his wagers and her dutiful performance. Calling attention to its anti-Americanism, some of the American scholars attending the Waterloo Conference on Elizabethan Theatre took the production to be *typically* Canadian. Their interpretation should not be dismissed as typically American. If ever there was a *Shrew* that invited development in Canadian terms, this was the one, since Toronto was in the 1960s (the period in which the production was set) the second largest 'Italian' city in the world, and it had, and has, a skyline that is as recognizable to most patrons of the Stratford Festival as that of New York. Richard Rose, however, decided to open the show with the lighting up of the cityscape of New York so that the crass materialism that he found in the play (and in the New World) could be safely seen as something that exists south of the 49th parallel. Even the use of the accent of the Bronx, an accent not unknown to Stratford audiences, reinforced Canadian stereotypes of the American scene. Paradoxically, non-Canadian stylization Canadianized this production.

In the case of Rose's 1998 *Two Gentlemen of Verona*, however, some eleventh-hour decisions downplayed the political point so that all but a few critics missed it or ignored it. The production began with a full blackout in the Festival Theatre during which audiences heard the sounds of skates cutting into ice, then a shot which pinged off a goalpost, and the cheering of a crowd. The lights came on with the flash of a camera and the winning side posing for a team photo. Valentine emerged from this group as the star player and the hero of the day. In Rose's reading of the play, a reading radically at odds with that of many critics,[12] Valentine was more mature, accomplished, and clever than Proteus, who tiptoed precariously across the ice sporting his school beanie, scarf, and blazer; even

David Jansen as Proteus and Graham Abbey as Valentine in the Stratford Festival production of *Two Gentlemen of Verona*, directed by Richard Rose, costumes designed by Charlotte Dean, at the Festival Theatre, 1998. Courtesy of the Stratford Festival Archives. Photo by Cylla von Tiedemann.

his ring and cuff links, neither visible to the audience, bore the school crest (see p. 152). Instead of being a cunning traitor to his beloved, his friend, and his friend's lady-love, this Proteus was a nerd who had to be hoodwinked into maturity. When he threatened to rape Silvia in the finale, her impatient 'O heaven!' (5.4.59) dismissed the threat as if it were utterly ridiculous.[13] Julia's through-line paralleled Proteus's, in that Lucetta, despite her talk of reason and restraint, was understood to be encouraging Julia into adult relationships. As a romantic comedy, this *Two Gentlemen of Verona* became a story of the maturation of callow youths – and youths more callow for being Canadian, colonial innocents abroad in need of experience available in a more sophisticated culture. Rose emphasized this process by revising the time scheme of the story. He changed Valentine's reference to a sixteen-month sojourn in Milan (4.1.21) to 'seven months' so as to keep the action to one year beginning in April and proceeding through the outdoor activities of summer, to falling leaves at the end of 2.5, snow in Act 4, and spring again in the finale. Rose's time scheme set forth a single year of change culminating in the promising new life of spring.

For the critics, this production was identifiably Canadian because of the hockey. Valentine wore a typical early-twentieth-century uniform, like that of the first Upper Canada College hockey team (see p. 154), and his camaraderie with his team-mates provided a clear instance of the male bonding that the play establishes at the outset. In this production, however, hockey was also part of a narrower scene, that of a private boys' school. Elizabeth Copeman, assistant stage manager for the show, made the connection to Upper Canada College specifically in a note on the music for the opening scene: '*Music*: ucc-ish [Upper Canada College-ish] song and cheer.' Here hockey is part of a Canadian upper-class milieu, which Rose developed further in 1.3 by making Antonio and Panthino owners of a pulp and paper mill, suggested on stage by the delivery of logs, a paper-wheel image, and the high-pitched sounds of a saw. For 2.2 and 2.3, the stage represented the docks of some Canadian port from which Proteus, nattily attired just for travel, and his man, Launce, set off from Canada for the English court. Richard Rose's *Two Gentlemen* began in Canada, but in the upper echelons of Canadian society. Could the production do otherwise? – probably not, given a story that requires that the central characters have an entrée into aristocratic circles at court.

Proteus fit in nicely there in Rose's production, donning as occasion required a linen or silk cutaway suit, fencing gear, a smoking jacket, or

The Upper Canada College Hockey Team of 1917, a source for Charlotte Dean's costume designs for Valentine and his teammates in the Stratford Festival production of *Two Gentlemen of Verona* (1998). Courtesy of the Upper Canada College Archives. Photo by Farmer Bros. Ltd.

the ascot, jodhpurs, and bowler hat for hunting. He and Valentine moved effortlessly from their privileged position in the colonies into the world of the leisured class of England: outdoors they painted and sketched, hunted and went horseback riding; indoors, they whiled away the time, as the list of properties for 2.4 indicates, with products from colonial pulp and paper mills – newspapers, notepaper, sketching pads, playing cards, origami, paper dolls, paper airplanes – and the occasional glass of champagne. Elizabeth Copeman made explicit the mood Rose hoped to establish: 'When music ends [at the end of 2.1],' she noted in her production file, 'we feel the silence/stagnation of the court,' adding, 'this is more important for the next court scene [that is, 2.4].' The cumulative effect of the court scenes was to suggest that this privileged class might welcome a little war in Europe if only to relieve the boredom, and naive young men from the colonies would answer the clarion call, as the school song they sang at the outset promised. Put bluntly,

Richard Rose's *Two Gentlemen of Verona* offered, or was to offer, insight into the causes of the First World War and the consequences for such naive, rich young men from far-off regions of the British empire, like Canada.

The production was to be one in which the dark cloud of war hung over the happy ending. There were reminders of war throughout: the school song, the wings of the school crest, the toy airplanes with which the Duke and Sir Thurio played, and the sound of a zeppelin from which flyers announcing Valentine's banishment were dropped just before the interval. Until a week before the show opened, it was to end with the entrance of Lord Kitchener, in uniform, bringing the Duke a copy of the newspaper announcing the assassination of the Archduke in Sarajevo. While the family photo was taken in celebration of the love of the young couples, now properly paired off, the sounds of artillery were to be heard in the background. However much the young characters had matured in love and friendship, they still had no inkling that what was in store for them was the war to end all wars and the loss of innocence with a vengeance. David Jansen, who played Proteus, understood the implications of the concept to which the cast had committed themselves during rehearsals: 'Contextualizing the experiences of the characters in a pre-World War I situation, and seeing them go off to war ... there would be a very strong sense of futility. Such an ending would have negated everything they had learned in the course of the play' (7). Preview audiences prompted Richard Rose to change the ending, to make it less problematic. Having described the ending in which Proteus and Valentine were led off in separate directions to war, Jansen observed that

> audiences wouldn't allow it. They fought against it ... given the kind of circular nature of the staging – the opening image of the play is of a group photo and the penultimate image of the play is, again, a group photo – that signified to them a kind of 'wrapping up' of the action and that's when they wanted to applaud and they did. Richard at first bumped up the sound levels of the battle and I think, though I don't want to put words in his mouth, I think he finally realized that he was fighting against a momentum that he had himself created and that audiences were really responding to. (6)

With only four productions that have made use of aspects of the Canadian scene, the Stratford Festival provides too small and too diverse a sample for generalizations. In Michael Langham's *Henry V* and Douglas

Campbell's *Romeo and Juliet*, what Canadian casting gives with one hand, antique costumes and decor take away with the other. Similarly, the historical moment of performance of Richard Monette's *As You Like It* gave its pastoral, nostalgic, spectacular Canadian ambience of 1758 an unexpected relevance to Canadian politics in 1990. If historical circumstances made this production more Canadian than it must have been through rehearsals, a stubbornly romantic play and an audience that knew its own mind scuttled Richard Rose's effort to historicize, Canadianize, and problematize *Two Gentlemen of Verona*. For the Stratford Festival, Canada remains largely 'a world elsewhere,' a world scarcely discovered but, when explored, full of surprises and contradictions.

Notes

1 I am indebted to Richard Paul Knowles, 'From Nationalist to Multinational: The Stratford Festival, Free Trade, and the Discourses of Intercultural Tourism,' throughout the introduction of this chapter, and throughout the entire piece to Lisa Brant and Jane Edmonds, archivists of the Stratford Festival, for their generous assistance with the materials in their care. Thanks also to Kate Jacobs of the Stratford Public Library, Juris Zommers of the Hamilton Public Library, Anne Joslin Slater of the Buffalo and Erie County Historical Society, Rita Burza of the Windsor Public Library, Marcella Zorn of the Ann Arbor District Library, Sharon Shipley of the National Library of Canada, and Susan Wells of the St Thomas Public Library for their help documenting reviews quoted in this chapter.
2 This phrase formed part of a motion by Alf Bell, in response to Tyrone Guthrie's report to the Chamber of Commerce and the Citizens' Committee, a report recommending the foundation of the Stratford Festival; Pettigrew and Portman quote an excerpt from the motion made at the meeting of 21 July 1952 (1: 37).
3 These phrases are ubiquitous in the press clippings of opening night; see The Stratford Festival Archives, Vol. 1a (268), ff. 57v–92v.
4 These assessments of the Festival occurred in broadcasts on 19 July and 9 August 1953 respectively, the scripts for which form part of the Cohen Archives, now in the care of the National Archives of Canada in Ottawa.
5 Cohen's critique of Guthrie first aired on *CJBC Views the Shows* on 24 July 1955; quotations from this script are from the version published in the *Queen's Quarterly*, listed below.
6 The immanence of something Canadian in the acting seems to me to be a

mystification. Normally, audiences have to be educated as to the nationality of the actors in order to see their Canadianness through their roles. The advance publicity for the 1954 Stratford season certainly functioned in this way, noting again and again that Frances Hyland, though trained in England, was born and raised in Saskatchewan; the clippings in the Stratford Festival Archives, vol. 2 (10 Jan.–30 June 1954), ff. 16–25, document this story. Just as audiences of 1954 were encouraged to see a Canadian *actor* through the roles she played that year, so were those of 1992 invited to see through Megan Porter Follows's Juliet one of the most famous of Canadian *characters*, Anne Shirley, heroine of *Anne of Green Gables*. Both advance notices and certain features of the production itself enforced the connection between Follows's Juliet and her award-winning role in the CBC/PBS films of *Anne of Green Gables* and *Anne of Avonlea*. 'Particularly in her rendition of "Gallop apace,"' wrote Kenneth Steele, 'I saw not an impatient Juliet but a rapturous Anne Shirley reciting a favorite poem, like "The Lady of Shallott"' (16).

7 See Knowles, who judges Langham's production to be 'perhaps the most cynical attempt to exploit the rhetoric of national unity' ('From' 24), and Moira Day, 'Shakespeare on the Saskatchewan 1985–1990: "The Stratford of the West" (NOT),' for an alternative assessment of Langham's production and its rhetorical context.

8 Langham's concept for *Romeo and Juliet* would be given sustained consideration at Stratford, but not until 1990 and not on one of the Festival's permanent stages. In the summer of that year, *Romeo & Juliette*, directed by Robert Lepage and Gordon McCall, was presented in a tent in Upper Queen's park, adjacent to the Festival Theatre. In this production, the Montagues were played by actors from western Canada and directed by McCall in Saskatchewan, while the Québécois actors playing the Capulets were directed in Quebec City by Lepage. The two groups of actors came together for only three or four rehearsals before the show opened as part of the Shakespeare on the Saskatchewan Festival. The set for this production, as mounted in Saskatoon and later in Stratford, featured a strip of asphalt as the Trans-Canada Highway. The Capulets, in soliloquy and among themselves, spoke only French. The Montagues retained, for the most part, the elegant English of Shakespeare's script. While *Romeo & Juliette* brought French Canadians and English Canadians together in a successful theatrical collaboration, the reception of the show revealed other fissures, such as that between western Canada and central Canada and that between older members of the Stratford Festival acting company and younger ones. See especially McCall and Day.

9 Among the materials related to this production in the Stratford Festival

Archives are photocopies of several French-Canadian folk songs. Culled from at least four different songbooks, this group of songs reveals that popularity was the principle governing the selection of pieces for the production. Many contain such marginal annotations 'always popular' and 'very well known' and others with explanatory notes have the details about the currency of the song underscored. Although the pictures that accompany some scores probably had no direct influence on the design of the production, they do illustrate its romanticized portrayal of New France, one in which canoes co-exist with fine European fashions.

10 Given the Mennonite communities in southwestern Ontario, this production of *As You Like It* in 1987 had local relevance. I have not added it to the list of Stratford's Canadianized productions of Shakespeare because such religious groups are obviously not distinctively Canadian.

11 David Gardner's Inuit *King Lear* (1961) provides a striking parallel. Gardner portrayed Lear as an Inuit chieftan in order 'to find a primitive society that was Canadian' (Garebian 151–2) The setting was recognized as such by Canadian audiences, but when Canadian Players toured the United States with the production, some American audience members made it their own. As Keith Garebian told the story of the tour, 'Yankee colonialism grated on the company. At a party, someone remarked, "We're absolutely fascinated that you would set the play in Alaska." The actors all looked at one another as if to say, "Jesus Christ! Here we are Canadian Players who have worked hard to find a primitive Canadian context, and in the States, it's "our Alaska"' (151–2 and 157).

12 One of the surprising aspects of some of the reviews of Rose's production was that the reviewers' summaries of the story ignored Rose's interpretation and represented Valentine as one of Shakespeare's many less than brilliant young men and Proteus as a treacherous cad; see, for instance, Greenberg, Portman, and Suczek.

13 Richard Rose based his production on the Freeman Folio text of *The Two Gentlemen of Verona* and used the New Cambridge edition as a back-up.

6

A National *Hamlet*? Stratford's Legacy of Twentieth-Century Productions

JESSICA SCHAGERL

Is a great Canadian Hamlet important? No, not really for anyone else, but for Canadians it is crucial because in achieving it we are set free from the kind of inferiority complex that has plagued us for far too long.
– John Fraser of the *Globe and Mail*, writing about the 1976 production of *Hamlet* (qtd. in Pettigrew and Portman 2: 81)

Considered by most critics and actors to be a masterpiece – if not *the* masterpiece – of English drama, *Hamlet* remains the most prominent inheritance of cultural and political colonialism for theatre companies in many nations, and, as theatre historians and Shakespearean scholars alike have frequently documented, it has helped to define their cultural and political identity (see, for example, Kennedy, *Foreign*; and Kishi, Pringle, and Wells). In English-speaking North America, however, *Hamlet* is rarely political; instead, many of the political scenes (especially the Fortinbras plot) are often omitted from the playtext in order to maintain a focus on the tragic events of Hamlet as an individual (Kennedy, 'Introduction' 4). The play has been performed in Canada since the nineteenth century, at first especially by travelling productions, and its increasing popularity in the latter half of the twentieth century is evinced by its central position in the Stratford Festival's repertoire.[1] The repeated production of *Hamlet* in Canada, particularly in large theatres like the Stratford Festival's, seemingly remains necessary for the achievement of cultural capital even within the postcolonial and postmodern Canadian context, to paraphrase John Fraser from the epigraph above.

'Not surprisingly,' argue Helen Gilbert and Joanne Tompkins in *Postcolonial Drama: Theory, Practice, Politics*, 'the ideological weight of Shakespeare's legacy is nowhere felt more strongly than in the theatre, where his work is still widely seen as the measure of all dramatic art, the ultimate test for a would-be actor or director, the mark of audience sophistication, and the uncontested sign of "Culture" itself' (20; see also Foakes [passim]). Generally, though, *Hamlet* is not the play to which critics turn to assess the theatre's postcolonial engagement with Shakespeare; in Canada and elsewhere, this role is most often played by *The Tempest*.[2] The articulation of interracial, intercultural, and interreligious encounters in *The Tempest*, but also in *Othello* and *The Merchant of Venice*, might seem to place them more neatly into postcolonial discourses of race and cross-cultural encounter than *Hamlet*. Recent critics, however, have successfully drawn on *Hamlet* as a lens through which the colonial encounter can be examined; perhaps Ania Loomba's idea of *Hamlet*'s potential, as performed in Mizoram, as functioning as 'both as a display and a displacement of resistance' ('*Hamlet*' 226), may partially explain why successive artistic directors and producers of the Stratford Festival return to *Hamlet* more than any other play. *Hamlet* thus plays a formative role in the encounter between Shakespeare and Canada, especially when, to paraphrase Loomba, we gaze at Canada through *Hamlet* ('*Hamlet*' 235).

Hamlet retains an imaginative hold on the Canadian theatre, its performers, and audiences. At the Stratford Festival alone, the different interpretations offered in 1991 and 1994 were equal to the combined number in the 1970s and 1980s. In addition, Shakespeare festivals across the country have showcased the tragedy in modern interpretations: in a one-hundred-year old military tower in Halifax harbour; as grunge at Shakespeare on the Saskatchewan; backing onto English Bay in Vancouver; on university campuses; and in various smaller fringe theatres throughout the country. *Hamlet* gained wider popular appeal in North America, not only from the usual Shakespearean festival venues presenting the play, but also from the Franco Zeffirelli 1990 film, starring Mel Gibson, and Kenneth Branagh's 1996 version. Branagh, as well as other movie stars such as Kevin Kline and Daniel Day-Lewis, have also acted the role in major stage productions. The tendency to search for stars to lead in the most famous of Shakespearean tragedies is also apparent in Canada: Keanu Reeves drew record crowds in Lewis Baumander's 1995 Manitoba Theatre Centre's production, and Paul Gross (of the CTV television series *Due South*) played Hamlet at Stratford in 2000. Yet, for all of this seeming diversity (of location, costuming, directorial vision, and star quality), the discourses surrounding *Hamlet* largely remain those of universality.

For David William, director of the 1991 Stratford production and the Festival's artistic director, the play's popularity was no coincidence, and it had more to do with contemporary anxieties than star-power: 'I think that in society, in times which are fairly critical, like now, we do tend to find in great classical works, a kind of voice, a pillar, a reflection of our problems. At those times you do find certain plays recur because they contain so many echoes, resonances that still work and are still with us now' (qtd. in Cowan). Stratford's audience was further cued to the significance of *Hamlet* by Neil Ingram, an actor from the Young Company, whose observations appeared next to William's 'Message from the Artistic Director' in the 1991 program. Writing about the necessity of the Stratford Festival to combat Canadian 'cultural malaise,' Ingram underlined William's conception of *Hamlet* and also suggested the importance of the play for Canadian culture: 'I cannot think of anything better for a nation wracked with self-doubt than seeing its national production of *Hamlet*.' Ingram and William speak to the play's contemporaneity, but the production of *Hamlet* at Stratford is much more than 'a reflection of our problems': variously produced since 1953 to show the Canadian achievement of British High Culture, Stratford productions of *Hamlet* in the 1990s suggest an increasingly complex engagement with the drama (an engagement that, as Andreas Bertoldi speculates in a different context, may encompass the tension between the universalizing tendency of psychoanalysis and 'any socio-political analysis of a specific colonial dynamics' [240]).

In the summer of 1957, Michael Langham directed Canada's first domestic, professionally acted *Hamlet*, which opened the permanent Stratford Festival Theatre designed by Tanya Moiseiwitsch and Tyrone Guthrie. Aware that expectations ran high, Guthrie and Langham wanted to display a program worthy of the new theatre. Critics were quick to notice that 'no Shakespearean theatre could aim higher than to baptise itself with *Hamlet*' (Edinborough, 'Canada's' 511–12). Montreal actor Christopher Plummer in the title role and Douglas Campbell as Claudius led a cast that included Joy Lafleur as Gertrude, William Hutt as Polonius, and a pregnant Frances Nyland as Ophelia; but the 1957 *Hamlet* was widely condemned by most leading critics for its uneven performances and onstage miscues (Pettigrew and Portman 1: 133). Part of the problem may have stemmed from Langham who, according to the review in *Shakespeare Quarterly*, 'seemed so determined not to be daunted by the problems which the production of this intensely difficult play raises, that he ignored them,' instead sweeping through the plot without much concentration on individual motives (Edinborough, 'Canada's' 513).[3] Although the role of Hamlet demands an exceptionally wide spectrum of behaviour, Christopher Plummer seemed to play each scene separately: he 'started off as a gangling, insolent youth, became more manly when speaking with Horatio,' was overtaken by fear when he met the Ghost, acted 'berserk' with his mother in the closet scene, yet was 'quietly authoritative with the players and gravediggers' (513). Claudius was a master manipulator, described as 'cruel, calculating, calm and collected'; Gertrude, in contrast, was called 'a sinuous flippant creature' (513). Frances Nyland's Ophelia 'stole the play from Hamlet' ('a severe criticism of the direction' [514] and one that speaks to the power of Ophelia's role) and, in doing so, shifted the emphasis away from the final scene to her own death. On the whole, local critics and interested observers conceded, *Twelfth Night* was by far the superior production (512–13).

Twelve years later, the 1969 Stratford Festival stressed the history and tradition of *Hamlet* in performance by publishing inset photos of other famous Hamlets (none Canadian) in the souvenir program, among them, Sarah Bernhardt (1899), Sir John Gielgud (1929), Sir Laurence Olivier (1948), and Sir Michael Redgrave (1950).[4] Directed by John Hirsch, the production cast Kenneth Walsh as Hamlet, Leo Ciceri as Claudius, Angela Wood as Gertrude, and Anne Anglin as Ophelia. Hirsch's *Hamlet*, called 'diffuse and meaningless' and 'mindless, self-indulgent,' was a populist *Hamlet* not concerned with the court, leaving aside the politics of power to portray Hamlet as an ordinary man (Edinborough, 'Director's' 444). Hirsch conceived his *Hamlet* as 'democratic': the spare stage and vaguely modern drab brown and gray costumes illustrated his interest in undermining the values of the court by focusing on the actors and the text (444). Walsh was criticized for being an inexperienced Shakespearean actor, speaking his verse without reflection and not fulfilling the role of the complex character (Pettigrew and Portman 2: 10). The production had a good individual performance by Leo Ciceri as a 'regal' Claudius, but, as critic Arnold Edinborough noted, 'when Claudius becomes so imperious as to be noble, the business with the poisoned rapier becomes unbelievable' and the rest of the production thus untenable ('Director's' 443–4). Hirsch's 1969 *Hamlet*, though it played to 93 per cent capacity – a testament to its commercial appeal – was also deemed an artistic failure by critics (Pettigrew and Portman 2: 9–10). In 1969 it was *Measure for Measure* – not *Hamlet* – that was heralded as 'a dramatic spectacle of immense significance: a deeply moral play seriously concerned with the very moral issues with which our day is confronted' (Edinborough, 'Director's' 446).

In 1976 co-directors Robin Phillips and William Hutt conceived an innovative production in which Nicholas Pennell and Richard Monette alternated the title role to both critical and popular success. The novelty worked because Monette and Pennell were vastly different: Monette was the more vulnerable, with more emotional intensity and 'more frenetic and desperate,' whereas Pennell 'was not precariously balanced, was less dangerously volatile,' and stayed more in control (Berners Jackson 198). These alternating performances of Hamlet in a production with few other changes 'had the effect of clarifying the relationship of Hamlet to his environment, of making us look again to the structure of the play for the source of our feelings about Hamlet,' and implied that the circumstances of the play remained unaltered by the actions of the main protagonist (198). Hamlet's black attire was adopted by most of the court, and, although Ophelia protested by wearing a pretty flowered dress, in the mad scenes her bright colours gave way to the all-encompassing black worn by the other characters, creating an atmosphere that suggested conformity to a mundane and oppressive existence (199). The stage likewise remained bare (except for a few props that were carried on when needed) and allowed the audience to appreciate the physical presence of the actors (198). Michael Liscinsky acted the part of Claudius as a 'heavy fleshed sensualist in his prime whose unattractive joviality was an attempt to conceal his hardness'; he drove Gertrude (Patricia Bentley-Fisher and Pat Galloway, also alternating) to drink (199). Marti Maraden as Ophelia appeared 'with her arms bound to a yoke' and was 'woman-handled rather roughly by a wardress-like female' (199), a directorial decision with unclear significance for the audience and one that many critics considered 'gratuitous cruelty' (Pettigrew and Portman 2: 82).

By 1986, *Hamlet* was turned over to Stratford's Young Company. To little critical praise, Brent Carver played Hamlet in both John Wood's *Rosencrantz and Guildenstern Are Dead* and John Neville's *Hamlet*, a production that 'was almost always better when its hero was offstage' (Weil, 'Shakespeare' 239). The cross-casting continued with James Blendick (Claudius), Elizabeth Shepherd (Gertrude), Lucy Peacock (Ophelia), Richard Curnock (Polonius), Lorne Kennedy (Horatio), and William Dunlop and Keith Dinicol (Rosencrantz and Guildenstern). The Shakespearean production suffered in comparison to its partner play, since the actors of the Young Company were more at ease with the twentieth-century drama (239). Here again, the directorial vision was circumspect. One critic, Herbert S. Weil, Jr, decried the play for its 'incidental ideas, [and] little coherent interpretation' and noted that 'one rarely feels confident that one knows what the director is after' ('Shakespeare' 239).

With no strong tradition of successful professional *Hamlets* produced at Stratford, these early attempts are distinguished by continued problems of interpretation and cohesiveness. The production that seemed to work best – that of 1976 – was still marred by legitimate concerns over directorial vision and conception. The Stratford Festival and the play's directors were often quick to play up the history and traditional mystique of *Hamlet*, but these first Canadian productions were not works brilliantly embodied or imaginatively conceived. Although Canada experienced political and social controversies while these plays were being conceived and performed, political discourses had not become all-pervasive or all-encompassing. *Hamlet*, which might have gained potency from such discourses (as it has elsewhere, particularly in eastern Europe and, closer still, Quebec), linking notions of cultural independence with political sovereignty, seemed a play without Canadian roots, belying its long and sustained history of interpretation throughout English-speaking Canada. These Stratford Festival readings of *Hamlet*, examined through the critical lens of postcolonial theory, offer much to re-view (to borrow Leanore Lieblein's phrasing ['Theatre' 168–9]); but, for present purposes, the 1991 and 1994 Stratford productions of *Hamlet* bear more extended review. In 1991 the more overtly political production proposed an imperialistic, confident realm with a deliberate political slant; in 1994, changed political circumstances, combined with a radical cutting of the text, created a production that accurately reflected many Canadians' preference for psychological and sexual interpretations, and distaste for the political.

David William's *Hamlet* opened the Stratford Festival's thirty-ninth season in 1991 with Colm Feore as Hamlet, Leon Pownall as Claudius, Patricia Collins as Gertrude, and Sidonie Boll as Ophelia. The production was set in nineteenth-century Europe, and the costumes effectively conveyed an aura of wealth and prestige that masked the corruption of the court. David William's decision to forego elaborate staging (except for the spectacular dumb show in Elizabethan costume for 'The Mousetrap') meant that the production foregrounded the text, rather than props and stage-effects. In his second year as artistic director, William made few cuts while using a collation of the First Quarto (1603), Second

Quarto (1604), and First Folio (1623). Though it was called 'admirably clear' and 'accessible' by reviewers (Ashley, 'Feore' 1; Chapman, '*Hamlet*'), the few line changes to the playtext meant that William's 1991 *Hamlet* ran approximately three hours and forty-five minutes.[5] The production's length necessitated an interval; however, most reviewers found the placement of the intermission inappropriate, coming as it did just before Hamlet's 'Now might I do it' speech when he stood with sword raised ready to kill Claudius (3.3) (Ashley, 'Feore' 1; J. Craig 89).

Colm Feore wanted audiences to perceive the duality of his Hamlet. In an interview with the Toronto *Star*, he revealed some of his questions in preparation for the role: 'Can I begin to pretend to be as intelligent, sensitive and generous as he is?' Later, he noted that 'there is a feminine side to him [Hamlet] that is very intuitive, intelligent and sensitive that has to reconcile itself with the active, decisive hard side' (V. Wagner, 'Stratford's'). Despite Feore's intended emphasis on Hamlet's sensitivity, newspaper critics felt that Feore played Hamlet as an insolent, active young man who became consumed with avenging his father (Ashley, 'Feore' 10). Feore's physicality was displayed in novel ways: by twisting his limbs around a chair, balancing on the upper level of the tiered set while taunting Polonius, quickly confronting Claudius after 'The Mousetrap,' and dancing exuberantly on the upper platform rail (Brady 241; J. Craig 89). The audience was meant to understand that this Hamlet was capable of action but was feeling a range of conflicting emotions because of his father's desire for posthumous revenge. He showed distaste for his mother's actions by flinching when Gertrude touched him (Ashley, 'Feore' 1); correspondingly, Gertrude 'crumpled' when reproached by Hamlet in the closet scene (J. Craig 89), then acknowledged Hamlet's fears about the sexual corruption of the court by refusing to reciprocate when Claudius embraced her (Brady 239). Reviewers noted that, although Hamlet was concerned with his mother's 'o'er hasty' marriage – as demonstrated when he thrust a locket containing a picture of Claudius into her bosom in the closet scene – neither Gertrude nor Claudius seemed motivated by sexual pleasure (239). Instead, Patricia Collins played the role of Gertude as a 'sumptuously clothed and coiffed mannequin,' motivated by comfort and social position, while the authoritative Claudius was determined to maintain and consolidate his power (239).

Among the supporting characters, there was uniform praise for Mervyn Blake's Gravedigger, who was made into a 'genuine character, a rustic philosopher whose humour provides a breath of freshness amid the fetid air of the Danish court' (Ashley, 'Feore' 10). Conversely, the technically embellished voice of the Ghost irked most reviewers who noted its resemblance to the evil spirit in the film *The Exorcist* (Brady 239; J. Craig 90), and, although this rightly could have been associated with the postmodern alienation of technology and subjectivity, one critic went so far as to call it 'communication by cellular phone from Purgatory' (J. Craig 90). Horatio (Wayne Best), Laertes (Bradley C. Ruby), and Rosencrantz and Guildenstern (Paul Miller and Tim McDonald) were contemporaries of Hamlet, suggesting a clear generational divide within the court (J. Craig 89). An exciting duel between Hamlet and Laertes concluded the action, summarizing, however briefly, the struggle for control (Ashley, 'Feore' 10).

Set in a deliberately romanticized yet imperialist Victorian era designed by Debra Hanson, this *Hamlet* emphasized the opulence of the elite and court, their pomp and circumstance but also corruption. The costumes, especially Claudius's leopard-skin hunting cloak and Gertrude's lavish dresses worn with diamond tiaras, intimated 'the reigning monarch's successful entrenchment of themselves in Elsinore as well as the scale of their heavy-handed revel' (J. Craig 89). Louis Applebaum's music and Harry Frehner's lighting strongly emphasized the gallantry represented at court, with 'ceremonial music befitting royal occasions' (Ashley, 'Feore' 1). Most of the other military figures, including Polonius (Edward Atienza), were dressed in scarlet uniforms; Rosencrantz and Guildenstern appeared in coordinated green- and mustard-coloured suits, while the ladies-in-waiting wore riding habits, all reinforcing the luxuriousness and leisure of this Danish court (Sidnell 154). The acquisition and consolidation of power and material wealth was a continuing theme through the 1991 production and, in fact, points not only to Stratford's obsession with spectacle but also to both the politics of the Stratford Festival and national politics (see especially Knowles, 'Shakespeare, 1993').

The extravagance of the production was celebrated in the program for the Stratford Festival's 1991 season, replete with images of luxury for a production sponsored by the Bank of Montreal. As Kathleen E. McLuskie has pointed out in the context of a Young Vic company production of *Timon of Athens* of the same year, 'Shakespeare is expensive to produce but even when the plays enact a social critique, the name of the bard can be satisfyingly linked with Royal Insurance, or Hewlett Packard' (88), or, as in the case of the Stratford Festival's 1991 season, the Bank of Montreal, Union Gas, and IBM. The politics of Claudius's power were fully revealed when, as Hamlet was being sent off to England after the death of Polonius, torturers in the service of the court led away a nameless prisoner, who evidently had recently been flogged (J. Craig 90). Political stability in this Denmark meant complete and utter compliance with the government's wishes. There was no question about the fate that would have befallen Hamlet: capital punishment was an effective deterrent against a questioning of those in power. An authoritarian regime marked by conspicuous consumption on the one hand, and obsession with power on the other, careened toward disaster – a vision of imperial Europe before the First World War. Or was it?

Denis Salter suggests that 'a favoured postcolonial strategy of resistance has been to update and resituate the Shakespearean text,' with 'the underlying assumption of these kinds of resitings [being] that the Shakespearean text will be forced to relinquish some of its prescriptive authority, that it will become more accessible, like a fetishized consumer product, to audiences conditioned by the values of late capitalism' ('Acting' 127). In this production, however, it was not the location of the play or its updated look that was the best example of the production's attempt at postcolonial engagement. Rather, Ophelia's role and the inclusion of the Fortinbras plot demonstrated a postcolonial concern with the motifs of political stability and the disaster of imperialist, authoritarian regimes.

The coming disorder of the kingdom was foreshadowed by Ophelia's veiled sexual behaviour and gestures and her subsequent self-fragmentation. Likewise, personal and political echoes resonated in her mad speech, and disjointed allusions made pointed reference to the sexual corruption and failure of society. Ostensibly, Ophelia was a distraction from the governance of the realm and the politics of the main plot – a young girl consumed by pressures beyond her comprehension and control – but her incoherence demonstrated the failure of the court to maintain its hierarchy and order, which in turn suggested an overall loss of power and validity. Even before the entire court collapsed in the final scene, Ophelia's death symbolized the end of the dynastic succession, leaving only Gertrude to say, 'I hoped thou shouldst have been my Hamlet's wife' (5.1.244). The effectiveness of Ophelia's mad discourse lay in the way the particularized image of Ophelia pining for her lost world – her father, Hamlet, society in general – could be transferred to the more general, yet local, concern with the fragility and possible disintegration of Canada. If, as in Robert Gurik's play *Hamlet, prince du Québec*, Hamlet represents Quebec, and Horatio represents René Lévesque, then Ophelia, not her father, signifies Canada; rather than Quebec (Hamlet) dispatching Canada (which implies a degree of agency, however misguided), Ophelia's madness and death underscored the nation's own fragile psyche and the (as-yet-unrealized) potential for self-destruction.

Although the 1991 Stratford production was set in nineteenth-century Europe during a time of rising nationalism, build-up of arms, growing unease, and political-religious turmoil (Cowan 48), the inclusion of the Fortinbras ending reinforced the idea that political stability could be established, even if dynastic succession could not. All was not lost: consensus and compromise, best signified by Horatio's emphasis on speaking with Fortinbras in his final two speeches, could still be achieved with Fortinbras as the ruler of Denmark. In this sense, Fortinbras was a much-wished-for figure of stability and compromise – a relief – not an intruding foreigner who might signal the devastation of a culture, as one might have presumed. Yet the splendour of the production did not necessitate the audience taking away a distinctly 'Canadian' – if there is such a single concept – interpretation of the action. Here, Stratford's tendency to opulent costuming here is of a piece with a general trend; hence, it was possible to come away from the production without any political interpretation and simply delight in its beauty.

While the 1991 production emphazised a political reading of the play, the 1994 eschewed all politics for psychological and sexual readings, a *Hamlet* focused on individual action, to the expedient ends of the play's co-director, Richard Monette. Monette had taken over the artistic direction of the Festival when ticket sales had seriously declined, and his aim, therefore, included wooing back theatre audiences and appealing to the large percentage of Americans who neither knew nor cared about Canadian politics. The 1994 season's *Hamlet* was directed by both Monette, who has acted in over forty productions at Stratford (including as Hamlet in 1976), and William Hutt (co-director in 1976), who also played the Ghost of Hamlet's father in this production. It was performed not on the main Festival stage but in the smaller Tom Patterson Theatre, a long, converted-for-theatre-use indoor court. Debra Hanson's design was simple and devoid of large props. Two large candelabra and a reddish wood and wrought-iron table-set were the only large props for most of the play; an 'abstract metallic sculpture' was onstage for the prayer scene.[6] The 'general austerity on stage' (Kirchhoff, 'Hamlet') was contrasted with 'vivid, theatrical lighting' by Kevin Fraser, especially during 'The Mousetrap'; 'slanting light across some scenes' suggested 'cross-purposes' (Coursen 65). Hanson provided an eclectic collection of costumes: Gertrude (Janet Wright) wore a red gown; Claudius (Peter Donaldson), a modern grey military uniform with a red sash edged in black; and Polonius (Douglas Rain), a turtleneck beneath his suit (Liston 95). Most of the other costumes were contemporary, in a spectrum of greys, blacks, and earth tones, although the play-within-the-play was richly costumed in order to stress its theatricality (Kirchhoff, 'Hamlet'). The design and the costumes worked together to create an atmosphere of casual formality – 'Gap' Shakespeare – infusing a vaguely twentieth-century *Hamlet* with twentieth-century themes of sexuality and psychology.

Stephen Ouimette as Hamlet was praised for his good stage presence, dramatic range, and verbal dexterity (Kirchhoff, 'Hamlet'). Reviewing Monette's 1994 Stratford production, H.J. Kirchhoff of Toronto's *Globe and Mail* liked 'the tighter focus on Prince Hamlet himself, and on the tragic events in Elsinore.'[7] Hamlet was physically rough several times in the production, especially to both Gertrude and Ophelia, suggesting undertones of sexual violence. He ripped the locket containing Claudius's picture from the necklace of Gertrude and 'rammed it into her belly (or possibly lower)' (Liston 96). As a result, Gertrude let Claudius walk off the stage by himself before dropping the locket on a table and exiting separately, prompting a continued distancing of the two until the end of the production (Liston 96). Similarly, in the nunnery scene, Hamlet responded with physical anger to Ophelia, attacking her for Gertrude's betrayal. His tirade against face-painting carried a too obvious significance because Sabrina Grdevich's Ophelia was heavily made-up (Liston 96; Coursen 63). Claudius, as played by Peter Donaldson, had 'plain spoken strength and emotion,' while Douglas Rain as Polonius was 'unusually humourous,' appearing to appreciate Hamlet's attempts at humour even when they were directed at him (Kirchhoff, 'Hamlet').

The reception of the supporting characters was marked by diversity of critical opinion. Appearing in a white military uniform, William Hutt's Ghost suggested the supernatural with a monotone voice; he also doubled as a comical First Gravedigger (Liston 95; Kirchhoff, 'Hamlet'). Sabrina Grdevich's Ophelia played the mad scene 'in an annoyingly shrill voice' (Kirchhoff, 'Hamlet'). John Stead choreographed a quick final duel between Hamlet and Laertes (Antonio Cimolino) – fought with swords instead of the modern pistols seen earlier in the production – and Claudius and Laertes wrestled briefly before succumbing to death

(Liston 96). In the final scene, Horatio (Tom McCamus) took over Fortinbras's lines giving Hamlet a proper burial, then held the crown of Denmark aloft, suggesting either that he would assume the kingship or that the country would continue even without its royal family (Coursen 62; Liston 95).

The script for the 1994 production was substantially edited from the First Quarto, Second Quarto, and First Folio. Monette moved Hamlet's 'To be or not to be' speech from its Second Quarto/First Folio position before the nunnery scene to the preceding scene. The result was that Hamlet's philosophizing occurred while Polonius was still on stage, although in shadow; Hamlet's 'Fare you well, my lord' at the end thus seemed directed at Polonius (Liston 95; H.R. Coursen writes that Polonius says the line [64]). Occasionally, as Coursen has astutely pointed out, Monette's cuts posed some dramaturgical problems. For example, Hamlet killed Polonius with the dagger that was to have been used for killing Claudius in the prayer scene; he had it in hand, thus contradicting Gertrude's line telling Claudius that Hamlet 'whip[ped] out his rapier' (4.1.10). Elsewhere, although there was no dumb show, Ophelia still asked, 'What means this, my lord?' and 'Hamlet's "miching mallecho" made no sense at all' (examples are from H.R. Coursen 62).

Monette's most extensive and important changes involved, as reported, 'all the business about international politics' (Liston 95; Kirchhoff, 'Hamlet'): the characters Francisco, the English ambassadors, Voltemand, Cornelius, the Norwegian captain, and Fortinbras were cut, along with Horatio's account of the long-standing conflict between Denmark and Norway and Hamlet's encounter with Fortinbras. The loss of this subplot from the play, combined with the other cuts including Ophelia's funeral, meant that Monette's 1994 *Hamlet* ran about 165 minutes, in comparison to the almost four-hour version of David William. Although some critics preferred this abridgment (H.J. Kirchhoff, for example), others felt that the speed of the delivery, combined with the substantial transpositions, meant 'the incessant bustle often tended to rob proceedings of its essential drama, negating the cleverness of lighting, stage movement, neutral costuming, minimal props and menacing music' (Chapman, 'Ouimette's').

The elimination of Fortinbras's role in *Hamlet* heightened a psychological rather than a political interpretation. Monette's 1994 decision to excise the obvious political message afforded by Fortinbras proved to be a manifestation of the general absence of political discourses, which perhaps reflected the (Canadian) audience's weariness with constitutional affairs (see Thomas). The decision to eschew an overtly political ending may have paralleled the popular displeasure with politicians and 'top-down,' elite-inspired political solutions such as the Meech Lake Accord. The fact that the elite of Hamlet's Denmark was destroyed and that there was no saviour in sight suggested, on the surface, that political stability remained elusive.

While reflecting some of the popular political scepticism and plain lack of interest in politics, the 1994 production moved towards a more familiar 'Hollywood-ized' interpretation, one perhaps calculated to appeal both to the large percentage of American tourists in the audience and to film viewers who may have seen the recent films of Branagh or of Zefferelli. In Monette's version, inspired by its psychological, character-centred predecessors, Ophelia likewise became more centrally important. The movement away from stage convention (through an independent and sexually charged Ophelia instead of a passive character) diminished Ophelia's role in the political discourse at the same time as it reacted against the dominant traditions inherited from the British stage. Traditionally, emblematic and symbolic stereotypes of female madness and madwomen informed the performance conventions of Ophelia. These sharply defined and clearly gendered conventions included a white dress, wild flowers, dishevelled hair, and 'distracted' speech, accompanied by sexual imagery and gestures, all of which ended with suicide by drowning.[8] Reviewers noted that Sabrina Grdevich as the 1994 Ophelia 'seemed somewhat lost with the illuminating visions of cadence and speech that the text provides' (Chapman, 'Ouimette's'); in other words, her performance did not follow the multiple implications of the text but rather foregrounded her sexuality at the expense of all other insights into the social and political problems of the realm.

In Monette's production, Ophelia's going to the court meant entering a brothel and becoming a prostitute. Verbally, Ophelia had already prostituted herself by helping her father and Claudius and by lying to Hamlet. In Monette's version, the verbal prostitution foreshadowed her physically acting the part of a whore. One reviewer politely described part of her mad scene: '[Ophelia] inspected the place where Claudius's trouser legs joined. ... Ophelia had her revenge, forcing the king to respond to her, to look on as she invaded her skirt with her hand on "By Cock"' (Coursen 64).[9] The movement away from a conventional portrayal of Ophelia suggests a redefinition that might be interpreted as significant from a postcolonial standpoint; however, Ophelia's redefinition was ironically accomplished by adopting the American theatrical and cinematic traditions of sexual defiance, abrasiveness, and cynicism, what Denis Salter has called the 'ontological security of personal psychology ... privileged in late industrial societies like the U.S. whose postcolonialism has been deliberately hidden beneath its status as a superpower' ('Acting' 128).

A more daring, sexual, confrontational, but also more cynical interpretation of Ophelia than ever before, Grdevich's performance suggested not only the audience's distaste for the political but also Stratford's preoccupation with adopting American cinematic modes to ensure financial success. Monette was, after all, mirroring the recent film tradition of sexuality initiated by Olivier and subsequently reinterpreted by Zeffirelli and many others. By the use of flashback, Zeffirelli especially suggested a sexual relationship between Hamlet and Ophelia, played by Helena Bonham-Carter. Recalling these fresh and – owing to American cultural dominance – widely available cultural images, Monette's *Hamlet* stressed not only political but sexual cynicism as well.

This above account of mainstream ways of representing Hamlet reveals that Stratford productions have, ultimately and disappointingly, been imitative, echoing first British and then American theatrical models rather than developing the (once crucial) idea of a Canadian Hamlet. Rather than a politically charged drama, we have (perhaps refreshingly, we might wish to admit, with a certain distaste still for constitutional wrangling and referendum fatigue) a *Hamlet* that is more spectacle than social commentary. Firmly located in the fashions and tastes – stage and cinema – of their own times, these Stratford productions share a limited engagement with postcolonial textual and performative possibilities: rather than take a unique or firm stand, English-Canadian directors at Stratford seem content to bypass a Hamlet that would confront issues of our own nation-building and identity.

Notes

1 See Somerset, items 20 (1957); 168, 170, 192 (1969 Stratford production and tour); 313, 314 (1976 production and tour); and 529 (1986). All information about the productions comes from the annual Stratford Festival Programs, housed in the National Library of Canada.
2 See, for example, Brydon, 'Sister Letters' and her Afterword in this volume. Scholarship about *The Tempest* and (post-)colonialism is substantial. For a range of critical opinions, see P. Brown and Brotton.

3 The description of the 1957 production, including all quotations, comes from Edinborough, 'Canada's' 513–14.
4 Interestingly, the only other inset photos are of Ellen Terry and Mrs Patrick Campbell as Ophelia. See the 1969 Stratford Festival Program.
5 Among the lines cut were the discussion of 'little eyases' (the Player Queen – Kate Hennig – was female), the speech about Priam and Hecuba, and Hamlet's banter with Osric. See J. Craig 89.
6 'After Claudius's futile attempt to pray and Hamlet's decision not to kill him at that time, Hamlet hit the sculpture with his knife, alerting – whether deliberately or not – the King to his presence' (Liston 95).
7 'Richard Monette made several good decisions in directing the Stratford Festival's *Hamlet*, none better than cutting out all the business about international politics' (Kirchhoff, 'Hamlet').
8 Owen E. Brady's review for *Theatre Journal* does not even mention Ophelia's portrayal. The Romantic image of Ophelia 'feeling too much' and 'passionately driven to madness' dominated portrayals for one hundred and fifty years (until around 1948). John Everett Millais's famous nineteenth-century painting is only the most obvious example of such an interpretation, sexuality and feminine madness being closely linked in the portrayals of the period. See Charney and Charney, Lyons, E. Showalter, M.F. Wilson, Ronk, and Neely.
9 William T. Liston in his review for *Cahiers Elisabethains* was more explicit: 'During her mad scene, she attempted fellatio on Claudius, and also mimed masturbation' (96).

7
'Le Re-making' of le grand Will: Shakespeare in Francophone Quebec[1]

LEANORE LIEBLEIN

It has been claimed that the appropriation of Shakespeare in Quebec has been one means of articulating the nature of the Québécois theatrical institution.[2] However, the definition of the theatrical institution in Quebec continues to be challenged by subsequent appropriations of Shakespeare. Although it is usual to look at a Shakespearean appropriation in terms of its distance from a source text, I suggest that theatrical appropriations, because they are destined for performance, also need to be looked at in relation to their distance from the many con-texts – including other productions and adaptations – that are part of their creation. They are, after all, performed within a community that has a history, including a history of prior performances, and address themselves to an audience whose experience of its own theatre-going contributes to its reception of new work. In this chapter I argue that, in Quebec, Shakespearean appropriation participates not only in a dialogue (quarrel?) with Shakespeare but also in a conversation with its theatrical milieu. Thus, I suggest that over time the function of Shakespearean appropriation in francophone Quebec has changed. What may once have been a response to Shakespeare and all that Shakespeare implied has become as well a response to other Québécois Shakespeares.

At issue is the question of what, in the face of the discourse of a universalized Shakespeare, constitutes a *Québécois* Shakespeare. Whose Shakespeare can be taken to be Québécois? Or, to paraphrase Susan Bennett in *Performing Nostalgia*, in whose voice is a text performed or taken to be performed (22)? To the extent that the plays of Shakespeare were believed to embody a universal human nature, a Shakespearean Other could be said to speak for a Québécois Self. But by the 1970s, Québécois Shakespearean appropriations had begun to deform and repudiate the Shakespearean Other. Shakespeare was made to speak with a Québécois voice, which, it was implied, represented a Québécois 'nation' with a shared language, history, culture, and experience of oppression. Subsequent decades, however, have seen Shakespearean revisions of this Québécois voice. More recent Québécois Shakespeares have implicitly addressed their predecessors and in so doing have implied another – less monolithic – Québécois voice.[3] In the first two parts of this chapter, I explore the emergence of a Québécois voice in Shakespearean adaptation; in the third part, I examine its contestation and revision.

Passing the Shakespeare Test[4]

It was only after the Second World War, with the proliferation of professional theatre companies, that professional performance of Shakespeare in French in Quebec became relatively commonplace. Gilbert David in his *théâtrographie* enumerates eleven productions between 1945 and 1970 and thirty-eight during the equivalent time period between 1971 and 1996. Shakespeare in francophone Quebec has become an increasingly visible part of each season's programming.

From the beginning, francophone Shakespeare in Quebec was a response to what Québécois theatre had been – and had not been. The first permanent professional theatre companies in francophone Quebec, founded around the time of the Second World War as an alternative to touring productions from abroad and the prevalence of burlesque, vaudeville, and melodrama at home, made the performance of the classics of world theatre including Shakespeare an important part of their mandate. Thus, to take a few examples, L'Équipe (1942–8), under the direction of Pierre Dagenais, presented an outdoor production of *Un Songe d'une nuit d'été* (*A Midsummer Night's Dream*) in 1945; Les Compagnons de Saint-Laurent (1937–52, turned professional in 1948) presented *Le Soir des rois* (*Twelfth Night*) in 1946 and *Roméo et Juliette* in 1950; and the Théâtre-Club (1953–64) staged another *Twelfth Night* (as *La Nuit des rois*) in 1956. The two companies of the postwar period that have survived to the present day were a bit slower off the mark, but the Théâtre du Nouveau Monde (TNM, founded 1951) presented *Richard II* in 1962, and the Théâtre du Rideau Vert (founded 1948) presented *Le Songe d'une nuit d'été* in 1965. Since then, both companies have continued to produce Shakespeare with increasing frequency.[5]

The model for Shakespeare production, of course, came from abroad, an unavoidable result, in the first instance, of Quebec's colonial relationship to both France (especially in the area of language, culture, and education) and England (especially in the area of economics, government, and politics). More concretely, however, most of the first generation of theatre practitioners producing Shakespeare were indebted to European models for their training. For example, many had worked as members of the Compagnons de Saint-Laurent under Father Émile Legault, for whom Jacques Copeau and his disciples had been both models and mentors. Other directors were European in their origins or education: Robert Speaight (*Roméo et Juliette*, 1950) was British, Jan Doat (*La Nuit des rois*, 1956) was French, and Paul Hébert (*La Mégère apprivoisée* [*The Taming of the Shrew*] 1956) had resided in London and studied at the Old Vic School under the French Michel Saint-Denis, who was subsequently to found the National Theatre School of Canada. Thus, in producing Shakespeare, Québécois theatre was demonstrating (with a bit of help from abroad) its capacity to participate in a European tradition.

For audiences, the performance of Shakespeare in Quebec in French prior to 1968 was proof of the maturity of the Québécois theatrical institution, not only in its ability to engage the classics of world theatre, but also in its ability to compete with other theatrical institutions. A review of a 1953 television production of *La Mégère apprivoisée*, for example, is haunted by the question of how we stack up:

> Le monsieur qui s'installe devant un appareil de télévision sait très bien qu'il n'est pas à l'*Old Vic*, pas non plus au *Nouveau-Monde*. Et celui qui comparait la *Mégère* de CBFT aux spectacles de théâtre qu'on nous transmet de Toronto ou des Etats-Unis, celui-là concluait que le travail de l'équipe montréalaise, dimanche soir, se classait d'emblée au-dessus de la moyenne. (Pelletier)

> The gentleman who sits down in front of a television set knows perfectly well that he is not at the *Old Vic*, not even at the *Nouveau-Monde*. And this viewer, who Sunday evening compared the *Shrew* of CBFT to theatre productions broadcast from Toronto or the United States, concluded that the work of the Montreal team ranked without question above the average.

The measure of success in this review is the ability to match or exceed what has been deemed successful elsewhere. 'Elsewhere' in 1953 might be London, England, across the border in the United States, across a provincial border in Toronto, or down the street at the TNM. The new kid on the block is measured against previous productions which implicitly embody a standard to be met.

That such productions might not constitute an appropriate measure and that local conditions might generate different local Shakespeares is not entertained. Nor is it a possibility that can be entertained so long as there is only one Shakespeare: the genius whose work transcends time and space and embodies a universal human nature is one for whom there is, by extension, only one (universal) voice. It is this that also explains the ease with which translations made exclusively in France – indeed, made even in the nineteenth century and earlier – could be unapologetically and unself-consciously (though not unproblematically) used. In principle, any translation that claimed to be 'faithful' to the letter or to the spirit of Shakespeare could do. In practice, as Charles Bolster has amply documented, such translations were found in performance, especially by the actors, to be far from satisfactory. However, it was only in 1968 that Jean-Louis Roux, with his translation of *Twelfth Night*, produced the first Shakespearean translation made in Quebec to be performed by a professional company. Even then, however, though it was made in Quebec, it was not made into Québécois: 'I did not translate *Twelfth Night* in "French-Canadian," or "North-American" French – I translated it in *French*' (Bolster 108). To this day, such prominent Quebec translators of Shakespeare as Roux and novelist-playwright Antonine Maillet continue to insist that their primary objective is 'fidelity' to Shakespeare.[6]

Productions prior to 1968 (and certainly many thereafter as well) tended to participate in the universalizing discourse of *le grand Will*. (The phrase itself, for example, appears in Gérard Pelletier's review of the *La Mégère apprivoisée* cited above.) At the same time, even these early Shakespearean productions were aware of themselves and their audience as a community with a shared experience and a freedom to foreground that experience. One example may be seen in the one-hour version of the *Shrew* adapted for radio broadcast in 1951 by André Audet. It is littered with references that could make sense only to a Québécois audience. For example, the director of the acting troupe within the Christopher Sly frame who is given the name of Gaskun is played by Jean Gascon, who also plays Petruchio. The name Gaskun, as well as allusions to other local people, places, and plays, could resonate only with audiences to whom Jean Gascon, a founding director of the TNM, also known to listeners from his performances with the Compagnons de Saint-Laurent, would have been familiar (Bolster 51–3).

Indeed, the discourse of Shakespearean universality can be seen to pull in two directions. On the one hand, it naturalizes all in its path to a Eurocentric humanistic ideology that homogenizes and effaces difference. In this perspective, to pass the Shakespeare test is to turn away from local history and tradition, to value the Other-defined transcendent over the contingent, and to produce a Shakespeare that can hold its head up to Shakespeares in Ontario, the United States, and even England. On the other hand, the discourse of Shakespearean universality facilitates, even authorizes, local allusion, because, after all (it is said), we are all the same and Shakespeare speaks similarly in all times and places. At its most facile, the assertion of local provenance can amount to displaying a bottle of a locally produced beer in a tavern scene. At its most subversive, it can mean riding in roughshod indifference over the Shakespearean text since, presumably, everyone knows what it means anyway.

This paradoxical combination of reverence and cavalier high-handedness was displayed in the landmark 1946 production of *Le Soir des rois* by the Compagnons de Saint-Laurent. On the one hand, the production was imagined within the tradition of high modernist Shakespeare, whose roots went back to productions of the play by Harley Granville-Barker in London in 1912 and Jacques Copeau in Paris in 1914. On the other hand, as is clear from the documentation and reception of the production, Shakespeare was an excuse for staging the groundbreaking set and costume designs of Quebec painter Alfred Pellan. It is reported that Pellan, who did not have time to read the script, created his designs on the basis of a potted summary of the play presented to him by actor Jean Gascon. While the program and reviews of the production suggest that its reading of the play was quite conventional, the results were received as original and stunning. Nevertheless, everyone agreed that the Compagnons had staged not Shakespeare, but Pellan. Though the desire to stage *le grand Will* was motivated by familiarity with a tradition of a high modernist Shakespeare, in the absence of a continuous Québécois tradition of Shakespeare performance, it turned into the celebration of the world-famous Québécois artist who had returned from Paris to Quebec because of the outbreak of the Second World War. The result was a Shakespearean production of uncharacteristic freedom and originality (Lieblein and Neilson 400–8; Sherlow 191–3).

This paradoxical Québécois relation to Shakespeare in the post–Second World War period is epitomized in the phrase *le grand Will*, which, as we have seen, appeared in the 1953 review of *La Mégère apprivoisée* and continues to be used, especially by journalists and critics, to this day. According to a colleague in the Société Française Shakespeare, the phrase is not common in France (Dorval), nor have I, to my recollection, come across its equivalent in English. The appellation presupposes Shakespeare's greatness. But it also cuts him down to size, and by presuming acquaintance with Shakespeare on a first-name basis, it further suggests familiarity, even intimacy. However, the intimacy is with a universal Shakespeare who is capacious enough to accommodate and survive local allusions and artistic visions. It is still through his voice that the plays speak.

Shakespeare, Prince of Quebec

Shakespeare production in francophone Quebec in the period following 1945 may have taken liberties with the Shakespearean text, but it did so, as has much Shakespeare production in Quebec since, in the name of Shakespeare. By 1967, the centenary year of Canadian Confederation, however, the authority accorded British (or surrogate English-Canadian) and French cultural values had increasingly been challenged, and there was much reason to resist the cultural authority of a Shakespeare or of made-in-France translations of Shakespeare.[7] Because of its communal and collective nature, theatre was an important site for demonstrating this resistance. In the years leading up to the first referendum on Quebec sovereignty in 1980, an emerging national dramaturgy was directly linked in the discourse of the period to the question of nationhood. The implicit assumption was that there was – could be – a Québécois voice, embodied in a Québécois language, a Québécois culture, and a Québécois nation. As playwright Claude Levac wrote in 1969:

> Quand les dramaturges québecois [*sic*] auront trouvé une armature, une structure théâtrale qui nous soit propre, à l'égal de notre épine dorsale collective, nous aurons non seulement une dramaturgie authentique et nôtre, mais aussi un pays. (Loranger and Levac 16)

> When Quebec playwrights will have found an armature, a theatrical structure that is our very own and the equal of our collective dorsal spine, we will not only have found an authentic dramaturgy which is our own, but also a country.

In consequence, it became important to throw off those theatrical structures that were 'not our own.' The result was a series of plays performed by new young companies in alternative performance sites that specifically set out to mark their space of difference from the institutional theatres committed to the western European dramatic heritage and the theatrical canon which they promoted. A play like the *Cid maghané* in 1967 by Réjean Ducharme set out, as the use of the Québécois colloquialism *maghané* suggests, to 'wreck' Corneille (Brisset 148–59).[8] Another, *Les Enfants de Chénier dans un autre grand spectacle d'adieu* (1969) (*The Children of Chénier in Another Big Spectacle of Farewell*),[9] used the metaphor of a boxing match to bring Euripides and Shakespeare, as well as Claudel, Corneille, Marivaux, Molière, and Racine, among others, into the ring. In a fight to the finish against the Champions of France, victorious Local Amateurs not only distanced themselves from the *grand répertoire* but literally defeated it (Godin and Mailhot 134).

One of the instruments marking this space of difference was language. The year 1968, in which Roux translated *Twelfth Night* into what he asserted to be a placeless French, was also the year in which Éloi de Grandmont used the dialect of working-class east-end Montreal known as *joual* for Shaw's cockney in *Pygmalion*, and the year that Michel Tremblay brought *joual* to the stage in *Les Belles-soeurs* (Brisset 33–4). Annie Brisset has argued that it was through a process of appropriation and deformation of canonical texts by the imposition upon them of an explicitly Québécois language that a Québécois dramaturgy was forged. The Québécois language was used to take possession of canonical authors, not by translating them but by deracinating them.

Shakespeare occupied an ambiguous place in the dramaturgy of this period. Robert Gurik's *Hamlet, prince du Québec* (1968) was a first step in rethinking the Québécois relationship to Shakespeare. Francophone productions of Shakespeare between 1945 and Gurik's play had consisted almost exclusively of the romantic comedies: three productions of *Twelfth Night*, two of *A Midsummer Night's Dream*, two of *Shrew*, and one each of *The Merchant of Venice*, *Romeo and Juliet*, and *Richard II*. In Gurik's hands, Shakespeare became not romantic, but political, and the production of his play showed not that Quebec artists could do Shakespeare but that they could undo it. *Hamlet, prince du Québec* is marked by its *ir*reverence towards Shakespeare and Shakespearean performance.

For Gurik, Shakespeare's play became a grid onto which he mapped an allegory of Québécois politics in 1967. Hamlet, of course, was Quebec itself, 'with all of its hesitations, with its thirst for action and liberty, constrained by one hundred years of inaction' (Gurik 6).[10] King

Claudius represented 'l'Anglophonie,' which implied not only the economic force of English-speaking Canada (and the English-speaking world in general) as well as the power of the federal government over Quebec but also, historically, the defeat of the French by the British on the Plains of Abraham. The queen stood for the church and its unholy alliance with Ottawa. Prime Minister Lester B. Pearson was Polonius, the courtier-Canadian in the service of British interests; his son, Laertes, was Pierre Elliott Trudeau, at the time Pearson's minister of justice who was to succeed him as a strongly federalist prime minister. Hamlet's friend Horatio was the pro-independence party leader René Lévesque, who would eventually become Quebec's separatist premier, and 'le Spectre paternel,' the ghost of Hamlet's father, was French President Charles de Gaulle, whose controversial 'Vive le Québec libre' from the steps of Montreal's City Hall had electrified some and outraged others.

To the extent that Shakespeare's play could be appropriated to reflect the political situation of Quebec, Shakespeare was confirmed as a universal (and prophetic) playwright. But to the extent that the cultural authority of Shakespeare was appropriated to authorize a rebellion against the imposition on Quebec of English language and culture, *Hamlet, prince du Québec* was subversive. Gurik followed the details of the Shakespearean plot, and indeed enjoyment of his play was enhanced by a spectator's familiarity with *Hamlet*. But his play simultaneously displaced the Shakespearean text, refusing, among other things, its historical, geographical, and metaphysical traditions and affiliations in order to embrace the Québécois community and agenda.

Shakespeare was used to stage the history of Quebec and its people. But the Quebec Gurik staged was the product of a particular political vision at a particular historical moment. Hamlet became the voice of a Quebec whose legitimate aspiration was national sovereignty – 'Être ou ne pas être libre' ('To be or not to be free'). Though, like the gravediggers who represented two generations, people might disagree on specific ends or means, there was no question that they shared the same history of oppression and exploitation and the same desire for liberation. Thus, the Québécois voice with which Shakespeare was made to speak represented a vision of a homogeneous Quebec for which national sovereignty was a shared objective.

For all its deletions and alterations, Gurik's *Hamlet, prince du Québec* stayed devilishly close to the Shakespearean text. Other playwrights of the same period used other strategies as they set out to demolish Shakespeare more aggressively. Jean-Claude Germain's *Rodéo et Juliette* in 1970, for example, invoked Shakespeare in its title in order to make him practically disappear. Jean-Pierre Ronfard's carnivalized *Lear* in 1977 offered a scatological fantasy that dethroned not only Lear but Shakespeare and 'legitimate' theatre as well. Although the playwrights differed in their level of optimism and the specific content of their political visions, what these plays had in common, in addition to the violence done to Shakespeare, was their assumption of the possibility of a coherent Québécois voice rooted in a Québécois language and culture.

That assumption is perhaps best exemplified in Michel Garneau's *Macbeth*, 'traduit en Québécois,' in 1978. By calling his *Macbeth* a translation, Garneau insisted on its distance from the 'français' into which Shakespeare had, to date, been performed in Quebec.[11] In addition, by translating Shakespeare into 'Québécois' in 1978, two years before the anticipated referendum on Quebec sovereignty, he affirmed that Quebec had a language of its own that was worthy of even *le grand Will*.[12] Unlike Gurik, Germain, and Ronfard, Garneau did not dethrone Shakespeare by explicitly rewriting his plays. Rather, he chose to enthrone Québécois by, ironically, making it the voice of Shakespeare. But since language is inseparable from culture, the implicit result was a Shakespeare – and a Macbeth – who had become Québécois.

Like the plays of Germain and Ronfard, Garneau's signalled its distance from what Shakespeare in Western culture (institutionalized in Canada in the Stratford Festival) had become by using a language that was specifically not associated with High Culture. Further, Annie Brisset has shown how Garneau's choice of words transformed Macbeth's Scotland into the New France of Québécois history and refigured the struggle to overthrow the tyrant Macbeth as a struggle for the national liberation of 'not' pauv' pays' ('our poor country') (193–257). Garneau's translation, for which he coined the word *tradaptation*, is in constant struggle, not only with Shakespeare, but also with other translations of Shakespeare. As Denis Salter has written, 'Garneau's twofold project of translation *and* adaptation is a sustained exercise in linguistic preservation of a kind peculiar to minority cultures struggling for autonomy on many different front(ier)s at once' ('Between' 63).

All of these Shakespeares, and others like them, were performed by alternative theatre groups in fringe spaces. They resisted the Shakespeare of the 'institutional' (which is to say heavily subsidized) theatres, the Shakespeare of the *grand répertoire* whose association with a colonial European tradition was experienced as coercive. And they assumed the possibility of a Québécois voice, one that could speak for a language, a culture, and indeed a nation.

'Le Re-making' of *Le Grand Will*

It is within the theatrical history and institutional context that I have been describing that I wish to focus now on Shakespearean adaptation in 1990s Quebec.[13] Once again the work of adaptation has made a space for a new Shakespearean voice, this time one that is neither monolithically universal nor monolithically Québécois. It is a voice that has made itself heard by defining its difference from other Québécois Shakespeares, and it is a voice that is articulated as much in its reception as in its performance.

Though the theatrical institution in Quebec has changed enormously in the interval between the 1970s and the 1990s, the Shakespearean presence has, if anything, been consolidated. To take the example of the two largest and oldest institutional theatres in Montreal, between 1990 and 1999 there were at the Théâtre du Rideau Vert productions of *Twelfth Night* (1993), *The Tempest* (1997) and *Hamlet* (1999), and at the Théâtre du Nouveau Monde productions of *Hamlet* (1990), *King Lear* (1992), *The Merchant of Venice* (1993), *The Taming of the Shrew* (1995), and *Romeo and Juliet* (1999). In addition to the plays discussed above, it is productions like these that form the background within which the adaptations I discuss below take on significance.

I would like to begin with *Le Making of de* Macbeth, created by Pigeons International in 1996.[14] Unlike Michel Garneau's 1978 *Macbeth*, *Le Making* does not render Shakespeare's play into Québécois. Nor is there any evident allusion to Garneau's translation. Shakespeare's *Macbeth* is, in fact, rehearsed in English by *Le Making*'s bilingual cast. Nevertheless, by the time *Le Making* was produced, Garneau's version of the play had become legendary in Quebec, and since 1978 it had become the translation of choice for *Macbeth* productions, though significantly the play had been avoided by the institutional theatres in Montreal.[15] In addition, along with Garneau's translations of *Coriolanus* and *The Tempest*, it had been part of the recent experience of many theatre-going Montrealers. The Robert Lepage production of all three Garneau translations, in what was called a *Cycle Shakespeare* and promoted as a journey into the history of the Québécois language, had toured internationally and had been featured at the Montréal Festival de Théâtre des Amériques in 1993. In fact, Pigeons International's original plans to work on *Macbeth* had been postponed when the Lepage/Garneau cycle was announced (David, 'Le dernier-né').

It is hard not to see in the bare-breasted amazon strength of *Le Making*'s Lady Macbeth an inverted citation of the vulnerable body of a nude Lady Macbeth in the Lepage production. Similarly, the 'radio interviews,' in which at various times members of the cast of *Le Making* approach a microphone that drops down from the flies to describe their own experiences and interpretations of their participation in the production, evoke the broadcast journalism frame of Lepage's production of the Garneau *Coriolanus* in the same cycle. But, more important, it is the language of *Le Making of de* Macbeth that comments on the Garneau translation and its predecessors. In *Le Making*, the language of Shakespeare constantly bumps up against the linguistic urgencies and realities not of 1978 but of the 1990s in Quebec: the movement back and forth between two languages, the accents of francophone actors rehearsing in English, the awkward attempt of Richard to produce a poem in English iambic pentameter, the Italian-accented French of the *concierge* Angelo, who, contrary to stereotyped expectations, has played Shakespeare in his youth. Even the title, with its stumbling redundancy that doubles back on itself and suggests a speech impediment, foregrounds the schizoid nature of bilingualism. The language of *Le Making* is not the Québécois language that in 1978 was an essential tool in the building of a culture and a nation. Nor, on the other hand, does it offer an image of the bilingualism-as-institutional-fact mandated by the federal Official Languages Act of 1969, which declared English and French to be the national languages and required that all services be made available in both. Rather, it is the de facto experience of many Québécois whose native language, like that of Pigeons's founding artistic director Paula de Vasconcelos, may be neither English nor French in an officially francophone milieu.

However uncertain, bleak, or optimistic the Shakespeares of Gurik, Ronfard, and Garneau in the 1970s may have been, they all implied a Quebec that had a coherent cultural, and possibly national, identity. *Le Making of de* Macbeth insists on the multiplicity of voices and accents and experiences, and even the multiplicity of performance traditions, that are part of doing theatre in 1990s Quebec. *Le Making of de* Macbeth in fact consists of multiple *Macbeths* and multiple citations of other theatrical practices, among them the overacted theatre school version that Henri brings to his audition and an interpolated marionette version of the play narrated in Québécois-accented French. There are allusions to theatre for children, dance theatre, and multimedia installation and performance art, all of them important modes of performance in 1990s Quebec.

Le Making displays in multiple ways the difficulty of arriving at a consensual reading of Shakespeare. The controversy surrounding other productions of the decade suggests that *Le Making* was not alone in having fractured the unified Québécois voice of the 1970s Shakespearean adaptations and the universalized Shakespeare that has persisted, especially and most often, in the institutional theatres. In the fall of 1993, for example, *Le Marchand de Venise* (*The Merchant of Venice*) at the TNM found itself head to head[16] with Le Marchand de Venise *de Shakespeare à Auschwitz* (*Shakespeare's* Merchant of Venice *at Auschwitz*), written by Tibor Egervari and produced by the Théâtre Distinct of Ottawa,[17] a few blocks away at the Salle Gesù which had, in fact, hosted a number of Shakespeare productions between 1946 and 1976 (David, 'Shakespeare').

Journalists and critics had a field day juxtaposing the two productions. A promotional piece by theatre critic Robert Lévesque in *Le Devoir* asked, 'Assistera-t-on à une guerre des deux Shylock?' ('Will we be witnessing a war of two Shylocks?') ('La semaine').[18] Similarly, a two-article feature spread in the Saturday *Gazette* emphasized, if not the competition, the dialogue that the 'counter-play' was expected to produce (Donnelly, 'Hath' E1).

The TNM production insisted that 'the human side of the character' transcended ethnicity and religion. 'I see him as a victim,' said Gaston Lepage, who played Shylock. 'Before judging an action that seems cruel, you have to look at everything that was done to this man. They steal his daughter. They steal his money and his business. They steal his honor. At a certain point, when you have a means of vengeance that's legal, you revenge yourself, with the law' (qtd. in Donnelly, 'Hath' E1). However, the possibly tongue-in-cheek allusion of Pat Donnelly, in whose *Gazette* article Lepage is quoted, to the separatist premier of Quebec serves as a reminder that a sense of victimization and vengeance can never be divorced from an ideological context: 'Hearing these guys talk, the rich cruel Venetians sound suspiciously like *les Anglais*, with Shylock as a misunderstood Lucien Bouchard' ('Hath' E1).

Egervari's voice in his play is a direct reply to the TNM position. In his foreword to the typescript, the author makes clear the impossibility of separating Shakespeare's play from the history of its performance and interpretation. He situates himself as a Jew and a Shoah survivor as well as a man of the theatre with a need to understand, by experiencing them, the theatrical consequences of a 'truly evil' Shylock. 'To accomplish this,' he writes, 'I had to adopt the point of view of a true anti-semite' (*Shakespeare's* 2).[19] Hence, in Egervari's play, Shakespeare's Shylock, Tubal, and Jessica are played by an SS officer, his assistant, and an Aryan actress brought in for the part. The remaining roles are assigned to Jewish and gypsy prisoners. The rehearsal of Shakespeare's lines occupies a major chunk of Egervari's text, and their easy appropriation in a Nazi context exposes the effortlessness with which they can be made to collaborate with a fascist perspective. As Egervari points out, *The Merchant of Venice* was the most popular of Shakespeare's plays in Nazi Germany, with some fifty productions between 1934 and 1939 (Groberman E8; Habicht 116).

The staging of *Le Marchand de Venise de Shakespeare à Auschwitz* was certainly not meant to imply anti-Semitism on the part of the TNM. It was meant, however, to question the supposed ideological neutrality of humanistic productions like that of the TNM *Le Marchand de Venise*, and to create a space on the Quebec stage for a francophone Shakespeare that did not deny its historical rootedness (even though those roots may not have been in the Plains of Abraham) and pretend to neutrality.

Controversy also erupted the following season when in the spring of 1995 the TNM itself presented, as its fourth Shakespeare since 1990, what it called in its publicity an 'adaptation' of *La Mégère apprivoisée* (the title usually given to *The Taming of the Shrew*) by the playwright Marco Micone. Micone's version, to which he gave the title *La Mégère de Padova, d'après* La Mégère apprivoisée *de William Shakespeare* (*The Shrew of Padua, based on William Shakespeare's* The Taming of the Shrew),[20] was, on the whole, a loose translation of Shakespeare's play, with a number of cuts, alternations, transpositions, and additions. However, as the allusion to Padua in his title suggests, he made of the Italian context of Shakespeare's play an important intertext. Thus, he added lines in Italian and enlarged the role of the servants, scripting for them numerous comments on master-servant relations. He also provided Grumio with an extended scientific discourse, including references to the plague, the Copernican universe, and the lectures of Galileo, which would have been taking place in Padua at the time. Even more controversially, he altered Petruchio's lines at the end of the play to command Katerina *not* to come, and she replied by coming in order to disobey him. Finally, the role of Petruchio was taken by Christopher Sly and Katherina was analogized to the Page of the Sly frame. At the end of the play, Petruchio became Sly again, and the two exited quarrelling joyfully about the sun and the moon, to return at Kate's request to the country.

Most recent productions of *Shrew* gesture towards equality of the sexes as a precondition for domestic harmony, and that certainly had been true in the case of productions in Quebec. The implications of the Micone ending, however, are much more uncomfortable, in that it does not exclude or marginalize Sly and reincorporate the couple into the play's society. The lovers cross class lines, and Sly becomes the protagonist in a text that has foregrounded the oppressiveness of master-servant relations and given to the servant Grumio an independent mind and scientific curiosity.

Some critics, needless to say, objected in the name of Shakespeare and especially lamented the lost 'macho' qualities of the play (the side of the play that was 'très gars' ['very guy'] and 'sauvage' ['savage,' 'rough,' 'wild']) (Boulanger; R. Lévesque, 'La gentille'). But the most focused resentment was against Micone's cultural otherness: 'Micone était à l'aise, dans son registre et sa culture, en traduisant le gentil Goldoni. En adaptant le féroce Shakespeare il passe à côté des choses, il est dépassé par le génie d'attaque du plus brillant écrivain du théâtre universel' ('Micone was at ease, in his [linguistic] register and his culture, when translating the gentle [*gentil*] Goldoni. In adapting the ferocious [*féroce*] Shakespeare he misses the point, he is outstripped by the genius of attack [*génie d'attaque*] of the most brilliant writer of the universal theatre') (R. Lévesque, 'La gentille').[21] However, Micone, who objects to the homogenizing tendency of Quebec culture, has made clear that the historical and multicultural specificity of his text, which in his version of *La Mégère* made audible the play's marginalized voices – of servants, of women, of Italians – was deliberate: 'En tant qu'immigrant, j'ai voulu insister sur l'héterogenéité de cette culture' ('As an immigrant I wanted to insist on the heterogeneity of this culture') (Telephone).[22]

The 1998–9 season saw remarkable adaptations by two other – this time Russian – immigrants. *Le Songe d'une nuit d'été*, directed by Oleg Kisseliov, and *Hamlet*, directed by Alexandre Marine, were also deliberately disruptive.[23] Although they were different from one another, both productions were semiotically rich and provocative. They had in common their small playing spaces, reduced casts, relatively low budgets, heavily edited and rewritten scripts, physicalized performance, expressionistic lighting, eclectic mix of period, costume, and musical styles, and some actors whose native accents were evident through the French in which they performed. They were experienced by reviewers and spectators as alternatives to other recent productions of the same play in the institutional theatres and often explicitly compared to them.

Even more than Micone's *Shrew*, Kisseliov's *Dream* at the Théâtre Espace la Veillée gave voice to the dispossessed. In it the mechanicals displaced Theseus and Hippolyta (who disappeared) as the motor of the play, Peter Quince became the author/dreamer of Shakespeare's *Dream*, and the dilemma of the four lovers did not become part of the play until well into the production. The *Hamlet* of Théâtre Deuxième Réalité in the same season also offered a substantially stripped down version of Shakespeare's play. It lasted less than two hours, was played by only seven actors, and employed a set consisting only of four small tables on wheels. Its Hamlet was an anti-hero, many of whose soliloquies were cut.

Both productions were seen in explicit contrast to other productions of the same play. Kisseliov's *Songe* brought to mind two productions by Robert Lepage, one at the TNM ten years earlier, from which it was seen to be 'light years' away (Blais), and one three years earlier at the Théâtre du Trident in Quebec City. His decentring of the main plot and his focus on the subterranean and earthy were contrasted with Lepage's emphasis in his staging on the vertical and aerial in 1988 and on the aquatic in 1995 (Choquette; S. Lévesque, Interview; Pilon). Marine's production and Vitaly Makarov in the role of Hamlet explicitly refused the interiority that had characterized the Théâtre du Rideau Vert *Hamlet* just a few months earlier.

Both productions offered brutal, not beautiful, Shakespeare, implicitly resisting what Shakespeare in the institutional theatres had become. Their aggressiveness was expressed in the lighting schemes which often made one squint to see, in the physical risks taken by the actors in their movements, in the derisive treatment of clichés of romantic love, and the in-your-face music ranging from opera to jazz. What one critic wrote about Kisseliov's *Songe* applied to Marine's *Hamlet* as well: 'The most interesting thing about *Le Songe* is its refreshing contrast with the polished sameness of so much French theatre in Montreal. It takes the immigrant's dare' (Donnelly, 'Absurd'). As a special issue of *Cahiers de théâtre Jeu* on the recent 'Décennie russe' ('Russian decade') in Montreal made clear, directors like Kisseliov and Marine have been changing the face of Quebec theatre (Vaïs 83).

To return to the opening question, in whose voice is the Shakespearean text in Quebec performed? As the above examples show, Shakespeare in Quebec has been contested terrain. Shakespeare has been

Shakespeare in Francophone Quebec 189

appropriated as the ground on which a succession of Québécois voices have been in dialogue with one another, voices through which they have articulated themselves and through which the theatrical institution has continued to evolve and change. Whether, as in the 1970s, the Québécois voice tended to presume the possibility of a monolithic language, culture, and nation, or, as in the 1990s, it tended to contest such a possibility, it has refused to be silenced by the universal humanistic voice attributed to *le grand Will.*

Notes

1 An earlier, and considerably shorter, version of this chapter was presented to the Shakespeare Association of America in April 2000. The research for this chapter has been supported by the Fonds pour la Formation de Chercheurs et l'Aide à la Recherche (FCAR) of the ministry of Education of the government of Quebec. I wish to thank colleagues and graduate students of the McGill Shakespeare in Performance Research Team, and especially Professor Patrick Neilson and research assistant Matthew Bergbusch.
2 This argument has been most fully developed by Brisset.
3 How a production is received and 'read' depends on what it is able to communicate, but what it communicates depends on the ability of an audience to read its signs. This is not to suggest that a non-Québécois audience cannot 'read' or enjoy a Québécois Shakespeare or that Québécois Shakespeare, especially in our increasingly global artistic economy, does not participate in a historical and artistic moment that may be larger than its local context. It is to suggest, however, that within the local artistic economy productions may implicitly speak to one another and engage in a dialogue about the nature of the theatrical enterprise within their community of origin.
4 This term was coined by Catherine Graham.
5 Theatrographical information on all stage productions of Shakespeare until 1998 including, where available, dates, theatre company, venue, director, and translator can be found in David, 'Shakespeare.' Productions since 1998 and others not included in David's *théâtrographie*, such as adaptations, I have listed accordingly in the References.
6 Maillet and Roux reiterated this assertion at a roundtable discussion on the 1999 Théâtre du Rideau Vert production of *Hamlet*, for which Maillet did the translation. See also Roux 40.
7 Cf. Bélair 66: '[Il faut] faire en sorte que la culture québécoise ne soit plus considérée comme une sorte de sous-produit de la culture française mais

bien comme une culture authentique' ('[We must] ensure that Québécois culture is no longer thought of as a spin-off of French culture but in fact as an authentic culture in its own right').

8 Thanks to Geneviève Lortie for suggesting this translation of the word.
9 Chénier was a 'patriote' of the 1837–8 Rebellion.
10 My translation. What follows is a paraphrase of Gurik's description of his characters.
11 In addition to Roux's translation of *Twelfth Night* in 1968, the 1970s also saw performances of Shakespeare in Québécois translations of *Hamlet* in 1970 and *Julius Caesar* in 1972, also by Jean-Louis Roux for production at the Théâtre du Nouveau Monde.
12 As Andrès and Lefèbvre wrote at the time, 'Tout comme Shakespeare donnait par son travail un statut poétique à une langue qui n'en avait pas encore, Garneau désire prouver la richesse du langage Québécois et le mettre sur un pied d'égalité avec les autres langues' ('Just as Shakespeare, through his work, gave poetic status to a language that did not yet have it, Garneau wishes to demonstrate the richness of the Quebec language and place it on equal footing with other languages') (84). Garneau's Québécois is an invented language, but one rooted in the dialects and linguistic usages of past and present Quebec.
13 In Shakespearean terms, the decade of the 1980s in Quebec is bracketed at one end by the massive six-part, fifteen-hour *Vie et mort du roi boiteux* (*Life and Death of the Limping King*) by Jean-Pierre Ronfard and the Nouveau Théâtre Expérimental in 1981–2 and, at the other end, by the *Printemps Shakespeare* (*Shakespearean Spring*) of 1988, which saw huge – and hugely impressive – productions of *A Midsummer Night's Dream*, the second tetralogy, and *The Tempest*. By the end of the decade, Quebec had begun to export its theatre to the world, and, in order to do so, had found a theatrical language and a theatrical voice that transcended the issues of Québécois nationhood. However, as I have argued elsewhere, the productions of the Shakespearean Spring transcended local politics and desires by once again claiming for Shakespeare (and themselves) a transcendental, universal voice ('Theatre').
14 I am grateful to Pigeons International for having generously provided a video, typescript, and other documentation of this production.
15 According to David's *théâtrographie*, Macbeth has been performed five times since 1978: by the Théâtre du Trident in Quebec City (1983), by the Théâtre Haut Parleur (later Ô Parleur) in Montreal (1991), by the National Arts Centre in Ottawa (1991–2), at the Festival du Théâtre des Amériques in Montreal (1993), and by Les Têtes Heureuses in Chicoutimi (also 1993). Only the last of these productions did not use the Garneau translation.

16 *Le Marchand de Venise* ran 5–30 October 1993. However, its official opening (press night) was on 7 October. Le Marchand de Venise *de Shakespeare à Auschwitz* was performed in French on 7, 8, 14, and 15 October and in English on 9, 16, and 17 October 1993.
17 Egervari, who lives in Hull, Quebec, originally created the play in 1977 with students at the University of Ottawa, where he is a professor. However, it was only in 1993 that it made its way into professional production for the first time. I am grateful to the author for having provided typescripts of both the French and English versions of the play.
18 Lévesque noted that, according to a press release, Théâtre Distinct's decision to perform in Montreal was a direct response to the decision of the TNM to stage the play. There had, however, been an earlier attempt to bring the play to Montreal (Groberman E8).
19 For the sake of convenience, I am quoting from the English version, translated by Annick Léger.
20 Marketing concerns prevailed, and the more recognizably 'Shakespearean' title was retained. My thanks to Marco Micone for having provided a typescript, and to the TNM for having made available a videotape of the production.
21 I have deliberately chosen to translate this passage literally (and hence awkwardly) in order to retain the etymological force of the words used in French. The reference to Goldoni is an allusion to a well received earlier TNM production of *La Locandiera* which, like *La Mégère*, was directed by Martine Beaulne in a translation by Marco Micone.
22 Micone elaborates on the position from which he translates in S. Lévesque, 'Traduire' passim. For a fuller discussion of this production, see Lieblein, 'Taming,' and Knowles, 'Focus.'
23 I am grateful to the Théâtre de la Veillée and Brenda Lamb of the Théâtre Deuxième Réalité for having provided video and other documentation of these productions.

Learning to Curse in Accurate Iambics: Shakespeare in Newfoundland[1]

PETER AYERS

> 'There is,' said the non-Canadian playwright in whose festive honour (in Stratford, Ontario) the largest single share of Canadian public funds is annually consecrated, 'a tide in the affairs of men ...' The history of the Newfoundland theatre has had much more to do with the tide of socio-economic affairs than with the arrival of any stork from Drury Lane.
> – Chris Brookes, *A Public Nuisance: A History of the Mummers Troupe* 12

The history of Shakespeare in Newfoundland is defined by a variety of paradoxes, most of them associated with the island's colonial and post-colonial history. Chris Brookes, writing from the perspective of his own alternative to 'that non-Canadian playwright' (12), namely, the documentary agitprop of the Mummers Troupe, offers an ironic demonization of the cultural imperialism represented by the funding of the Stratford Festival. It is one that opens a variety of useful perspectives for considering the topic, of which the most obvious is the cultural-materialist/new historicist preoccupation with the hegemonic status bestowed upon the Bard.

It is a context that seems particularly useful in considering the matter of Shakespeare in Newfoundland. The geographical isolation of Newfoundland ensured that the island remained culturally attached to Britain long after the rest of North America had developed its own distinctive models. Politically, the case is even more extreme; Newfoundland enjoyed an ostentatiously protracted colonial status, indeed establishing a postcolonial first of sorts by rejecting representative government in 1933 in favour of direct rule through London, in the form of the Commission of Government that held power from 1933 to confederation with Canada in 1949.[2]

The distinctive demographic patterns of settlement, of which the dominant element was the profusion of scattered outports dotted about the coast, linked to each other and to the world beyond only by sea, largely precluded the development of conventional theatrical activity for most of the island; in its place grew up such seasonal festivities as 'mummering' and the community entertainments known as 'concerts.'[3] Conventional theatre, by contrast, became associated almost exclusively with the mercantile, social, and political centre of Newfoundland life, St John's, with offshoots in those few larger towns that had grown up around mining or logging, such as Gander, Grand Falls, and Corner Brook. Such places, the residences of the, in Newfoundland writer Chris Brookes's words, 'stuffed-shirt culture-vultures' (15) who valued theatre for the social receptions and cast parties associated with it, naturally looked abroad for their models, with London and New York being the most obvious centres of influence.

For most of the last four hundred years, consequently, conventional theatrical activity in Newfoundland has suffered from a profound cultural disassociation from the community at large; it has been unknown over the greater part of the island, and, where it has existed, it has been shaped by demographic and cultural forces that have generated material that has been almost entirely imported and consequently unrelated in any obvious way to the lives of those who have watched it.

Shakespearean productions in Newfoundland began somewhat implausibly with an 1841 production of *Richard III* in which a fourteen-year-old girl, Jean Davenport, 'the fair child of genius' as *The Newfoundlander* described her (qtd. in O'Neill 78), played the title role. The second woman to appear on the stage in Newfoundland, she effectively opened the stage for women, and, during her two weeks in St John's she further demonstrated her range by playing both Juliet and Sir Peter Teazle (O'Neill 78). Miss Davenport's tour established a pattern for visiting companies, if not for cross-dressing, that was to endure for the next one hundred years. Shortly after her departure, a professional repertory company arrived from Halifax for a season; it was sufficiently successful to lead them to return for the next three years. Thereafter, St John's became a regular stop for touring companies; its geographical position made it a natural jumping-off point both for American companies moving westwards into Canada and for British companies covering the eastern seaboard. It was, in Paul O'Neill's words, 'a golden age of professional theatre in Newfoundland' (80), one that was to last till the Great Fire of 1892.

It was also a golden age for amateur theatre, which became more socially respectable to the same degree that it provided a useful outlet for the cultural energies of an increasingly prosperous middle class; a variety of small companies, which provided a rich and varied array of theatrical offerings, sprang up throughout the city. It was not a golden age for Shakespearean production, however; after the triumph of *Richard III*, there is no evidence of a Shakespearean performance until 1900. The gap of fifty-nine years is, on the surface at least, something of a surprise, given the ideological factors that one might suppose to have been conducive to celebrations of the imperial Bard.

Yet the surprise is short-lived in light of the economic factors governing both touring professionals and local amateurs, then as now. Neither can afford to wager much on the possibility that High Art will bring in either crowds or cash. The former, to survive, are obliged to get the best return on the minimum of investment, which, in practical terms, means the fewer actors the better. The latter, forced only to cover costs, are nevertheless driven to please as many of their supporters as possible to obtain both the audience and the unpaid help upon which such companies depend; in practice, this means a repertoire filled with the contemporary and the popular. Shakespeare does not fulfil either set of conditions. The institutionalizing of Shakespeare in the last half of the century as the touchstone of both imperial and domestic values and verities, so extensively chronicled by the cultural materialists, does not, in short, translate into a rush towards Newfoundland productions.

In such a context, the surprise is that touring companies managed to do Shakespeare at all. In 1900 the Lyceum Players performed *The Merchant of Venice*, in a period where a list of contemporary amateur performances consists of *Captain Kid, The Sleeping Beauty, The Yellow Dwarf, Dr. Jekyll and Mr. Hyde, A Study in Scarlet, By Force of Impulse, The Man of Gold, Under the Gaslight, Mavourneen, A Sprig of Shamrock, A Woman's Honour, Colleen Bawn, Killarney, The Irish Alderman, The Eagles' Nest, The Marriage of Kitty, The Creole, The Arm of the Law, Under Western Skies, The Littlest Girl, Brothers, Snow-bound, The Days of '98, True Irish Hearts,* and *Where Breakers Roar.* The Glossop-Harris Company, which toured in 1926 and 1929, brought with it *Twelfth Night, Antony and Cleopatra, Henry VIII, The Merchant of Venice, Macbeth, Julius Caesar, Hamlet,* and *Romeo and Juliet.* The last is specified as being only the balcony scene, so it is possible that the others were likewise abbreviated versions intended to serve as only part of the bill, accompanied by their more conventional offerings (Whiteway 8).

Shakespearean records after 1929 are thin, perhaps because many have not yet been found, but more plausibly because visits from touring companies dwindled with the Depression and then ceased altogether with the war. Amateur theatre, always strong in St John's, was by contrast going from strength to strength. Shakespeare, however, did not fit well into the sort of amateur theatre agenda that emerged under such conditions; the plays performed tended to be heavily oriented towards the West End or Broadway and showed a distinct taste for light comedy, Irish classics, and large musicals. The focus shifted after the Dominion Drama Festival instituted an all-Canadian competition in 1967, but not in favour of Shakespeare. Indeed, there are no records of any Shakespearean productions by any of the established amateur groups.

Shakespeare does make a brief reappearance, however, in 1951 and 1952, with the arrival of the last major touring company to make Newfoundland a base, the London Theatre Company. The company itself is of considerable interest; it grew out of a visit in 1947 of the Alexandra Players, formed from members of the Alexandra Repertory Theatre in Birmingham.[4] The tour lost money, but one member of the company, Leslie Yeo, saw further possibilities and created a company of his own, the London Theatre Company, to do the same thing more efficiently. The first visit was in 1951, with the intent being not to tour as such but to settle in St John's for twenty-six weeks, from October to April. In subsequent years, the stay was gradually shortened, as the company attempted to expand its base by touring the mainland. It came annually from 1951 to 1957; not only was it the last touring company to come on a regular basis, but it was the only more-or-less residential professional theatre Newfoundland was to see until the 1970s.

For the reasons suggested above, the range of the company's offerings was limited by economic considerations. Only two of the 106 productions it mounted were Shakespearean: *The Taming of the Shrew* in 1951 and *The Merchant of Venice* the following year. Both were successful but stretched the resources of the company too far and required local volunteers. While perhaps not 'community theatre' in any sense that Chris Brookes would acknowledge, the London Theatre Company did indeed make a profound impact on the community in a variety of ways. For many, it was the first exposure to first-rate professional theatre on a regular basis, one that is still fondly remembered more than forty years later, not least because it has not been duplicated in quality or quantity since. In another context, the impact was more direct: about a quarter of those involved chose to stay in either Newfoundland or mainland Canada.[5]

Two reasons for the collapse of what had been to that point a strongly supported institution have been provided by those involved, one of which has some bearing on the subject of this chapter. The first, less relevant, is the advent of television in Newfoundland in that year: the novelty was evidently such that people clustered in each others' houses to watch the test-pattern rather than go out to the theatre. The second is more interesting, namely, the unrelenting hostility of a particular paper, the *Evening Telegram*, and its reviewer, Sylvia Wigh, who had briefly served as an assistant stage manager to the company in 1951 before being let go. By 1957, her comments were sufficiently vitriolic to lead Yeo to request that the *Evening Telegram* cease reviewing at all.

What seems to have been fundamentally wrong was that the London Theatre Company was gradually changing the theatrical landscape in ways that did not please all. In St John's, the amateur theatre was (and to some extent still is) a small, isolated, and inevitably incestuous world: one day's reviewer is the next-day's director or the day-before's leading actor; everyone knows everyone, and interlopers are generally unwelcome. Sylvia Wigh herself ran the Theatre Arts Guild with an iron hand, choosing the plays, casting them, and directing them. The repertoire of the amateur theatres was not so different from that of the London Theatre Company; the overt hostility of the reviews would seem to be closely related to the struggle for cultural dominance.

The matter is of interest in a variety of contexts. While St John's was blessed with a variety of different reviewers, Wigh was undoubtedly the most influential. Her reviews reflect decided opinions on what might be considered appropriate material for Newfoundland audiences; anything more adventurous than the usual fare of the amateur repertoire was treated with hostile condescension.

Shakespeare, after an absence from St John's of a decade, again enters into this story with the Memorial University Drama Society (MUDS) determined to mark its move into the Little Theatre with a lavish 1961 production of *Macbeth*, with a cast of fifty, including some of the city's finest actors (professional and amateur), costumes from Malabar's, and no expense spared. The reviews were uneven; Wigh praised the lavishness of the production but went on to comment that 'it is not surprising that we should discover many weaknesses among a cast of 50 amateur actors, many of whom had never been on stage before.' She then noted 'the poor tonal quality of the individual actors' before going on to praise virtually all of the principals. Others took the same line. Alison Feder, then a member of the Memorial English department, likewise criticized the verse-speaking of the production, and lamented the lack of voice training, before listing the honourable exceptions, which turned out to be virtually every major actor in the play. What, in the end, she names as her particular grievance was the verse delivery of the Weird Sisters.

The general sense conveyed by these reviews is that Shakespeare is somehow not appropriate in St John's. One revealing moment occurred in a 1967 television interview with a high school teacher who was directing a production of *Julius Caesar*. Wigh wanted to know if the text had been 'translated,' since clearly the local Calibans would be incapable of understanding it as written. In such a context, the neglect of Shakespeare is not as surprising as it might first appear.[6]

Other factors were also at play, however, that resulted in Shakespeare assuming more prominence both in the theatre and in the cultural politics of Newfoundland; in the later 1960s, Shakespeare began at last to assume the role, in however peripheral a fashion, assigned him by new historicists/cultural materialists. The centennial celebrations of 1967 profoundly changed the face of theatre in Newfoundland, and in ways that both directly and indirectly have some bearing on the topic at hand; a Stratford Festival touring production of *Twelfth Night*, for example, arrived in St John's to bring a taste of the centre to the margins. The theatrical landscape changed in a more material sense as well. In many provinces, cultural centres were built to mark the event, and Joey Smallwood, first premier of Newfoundland after confederation with Canada in 1949, was never one to be left behind. Determined that Newfoundland would do no less, he had a series of such centres built across the island and, in so doing, transformed the theatrical world in generally unforeseen ways. The process had no master plan and was informed by no precise sense of what exactly these buildings were for, or for whom.[7] They raised, as a consequence, a variety of questions, many of which still remain unanswered thirty years later.

The Arts and Culture Centre of St John's was the flagship of the five built, and it was there that the questions were most intense. Would a professional company be created to fill the space, a 'Theatre Newfoundland' that might correspond to, for instance, 'Theatre New Brunswick'? Would there be at least a resident amateur company, the St John Players, for example? Would there be an artistic director to oversee theatrical policy? In the event, none of these things happened. Control over the centres was vested in the figure of the director of cultural affairs, a newly created post. The man chosen was John Perlin, scion of one of the old merchant families, with strong links to the amateur theatre, strong links to Britain, and decided views on the future direction of theatre in Newfoundland.

Perlin's basic policy was to offer entertainment, of any sort, to be provided by whoever would pay the rent; as he was fond of observing, Shakespeare was, after all, an entertainer. Thus, the Arts and Culture centres were host to everything from Raveen the Magician to ethnic cultural displays.[8] However, the taste of the public was to be raised if possible by exposure to High Culture, and, in 1970, what might be called local institutional Shakespeare appears for the first time in the almost four hundred years of Newfoundland theatre. In that year, Perlin produced *Hamlet*, the first of three Shakespearean productions that would appear at yearly intervals; *1 Henry IV* followed in 1971 and *The Merchant of Venice* in 1972. They were intended partly to appeal to and attract high school and university students studying them in the classroom, but also to provide an appropriate venue for classic drama of the highest artistic respectability, evidently with the thought of creating an audience fit for them. All three were directed by Michael Cook, dramatist, director, critic, actor, and professor of English at Memorial University. His productions were, in general, well received, and audiences were fair to middling,[9] but the scheme died.[10]

The high point of institutional Shakespeare coincides, ironically enough, with another series of related events that set out to undermine the very foundations upon which Perlin was trying to erect his monument to cultural authority. In 1972 Chris Brookes founded the Mummers Troupe, with the intent of wresting drama out of the hands of the stuffed shirts, the bureaucrats, the supporters of the status quo, and the middle-class supporters of the Dominion Drama Festival with their middle-class drama, in order to give it back to the 'real' Newfoundlanders by showing them their lives as they were (at least from a Marxist perspective) and the forces that controlled them, thus giving them the political awareness needed to change them. It was in this context that Brookes looked to mummering, rather than Shakespeare, for his inspiration: 'It is in The Bay, not in St. John's, where the real essence of Newfoundland culture lies' (10). His intent was perhaps no less paternalistic than Perlin's, but the means were different: Brookes wanted to create a company that could react swiftly to issues of local community interest, and 'get there quickly and roll up its sleeves, providing a community mirror in which residents could get a clearer look at their needs and problems' (10). Around the same time, Codco emerged, equally anti-establishment, though with a decidedly different agenda: one focused on improvisational comic satire rather than politics.[11]

Shakespeare, evidently, had no place in the alternative theatre as it emerged in Newfoundland: indeed, his status as an instrument of cultural and ideological domination embodied for the young radicals all that was wrong with the old theatre, now to be dismantled by the new. Unfortunately, there was not much Shakespeare to be dismantled, but there were the high-profile DDF competitions, almost as good a target, and in 1971 Brookes had already commenced his assault with the Gorilla Theatre group, which protested against the subregional festival held in the Arts and Culture Centre by posting signs in the washrooms stating that 'competition kills theatre ... theatre is dead,' handing out ballot forms for the best-dressed audience member, and committing other such subversive acts (McKim).[12]

It is of some interest that the alternative theatre that emerged was also the first professional theatre Newfoundland had known since the disbanding of the London Theatre Company. It did not, however, pay its own way: it increasingly relied instead upon the Canada Council and other government agencies.[13] Out of this situation arise a number of ironies, some of them directly connected to the topic of this chapter. In 1976 Donna Butt and Rick Boland left the Mummers to set up Community Stage Theatre, and in 1978 Donna and David Ross founded Rising Tide. In the meantime, Andy Jones and others, seeking to wrest control of the Mummers' St John's base, the Longshoremen's Protective Union (LSPU) Hall, from the established clique, formed the Resource Foundation for the Arts, which would become the Resource Centre for the Arts. (The Mummers eventually disbanded in 1982.) Both Rising Tide and the Resource Centre for the Arts, in their own fashion, remained committed to the same pattern of community-based, socially engaged, collective dramatic creation that Chris Brookes had instituted, but they also had to consider their audiences and their funding and eventually turned to conventional scripted plays as one means of maintaining both.

Thus it is that Shakespeare is recalled, under improbable circumstances, from the wilderness. The *annus mirabilis* is 1982, from the perspective of this chapter at least, though few involved would have guessed it.[14] In that year, the Resource Centre for the Arts staged a *Newfoundland Tempest* that attracted an enormous amount of attention, and that, in certain respects, expanded the possibilities of Shakespeare in Newfoundland in ways that would be, over the years, explored in many different contexts. The intent was to use Newfoundland as the site where Old World meets New; the director, Stephen Bush, noted that Shakespeare might well have known of John Guy's settlement at Cupids in 1610 and been excited by the dramatic possibilities it opened up. The production was steeped in Newfoundland culture: local accents were used, on the grounds that they were closer to Elizabethan English than either standard English or North American dialects; a prominent local band, Figgy Duff, provided the music; and audience members were dragged up on stage to join in a jig. Prospero was played by Andy Jones, by this time a major theatrical figure outside Newfoundland as well as in.

Bush's premise, that Prospero might well have drifted up on the shores of Newfoundland, attracted much critical mirth, but the production itself was taken very seriously, and with little of the condescension customarily reserved for Shakespeare (although Marilyn Dufett did feel obliged to begin her review with the comment, 'Reading *The Tempest* is heavy going. I rediscovered this fact several snowy nights ago, again struggling to come to grips with "Willie the Shake" [high school nickname for the Bard]'). No fewer than eight reviewers discussed it in the press and on the CBC; astonishingly enough, even Ray Conlogue in the *Globe and Mail* gave it some coverage.

Disappointingly enough, the production did not seem to work as planned. The critical responses were surprisingly uniform in their judgments: the accents were too varied, the verse-speaking too erratic, and the performances disappointing. Andy Jones himself was held to have done less than justice to Prospero. Nevertheless, there was no gloating over the spectacle of a bold experiment gone wrong; for the first time, it would seem, there was a general sense that there was a much better reason for doing Shakespeare than merely paying lip-service to High Culture.

Another, rather less well-noticed, production took place in 1982 that is also part of this new age in Shakespearean production. Wendi Smallwood, grandniece of Joey and then an undergraduate at Memorial, enlisted the services of two faculty members, Gordon Jones and Allan Hall, and those of a local high school teacher, Morris Hodder, to direct a series of scenes from various plays. The production, somewhat whimsically entitled *Much Ado about a Midsummer's Shrew*, had unforeseen and rather less whimsical consequences: the experience persuaded Jones to go on to direct thirteen full-length productions of Shakespeare in the summers following, and, in the process, turn them into something of a St John's institution, with excellent houses and increasing numbers of interested student actors. It was the beginning of a new role for Shakespeare in St John's and Newfoundland, one that has had enormous ramifications.

In 1984, perhaps caught up in the momentum, a subgroup of Resource Centre actors led by Michael Wade formed the Newfoundland Shakespeare Company, which did a series of productions over five years. Rising Tide followed suit, in 1986 and 1987 mounting productions of *Midsummer Night's Dream* and *Romeo and Juliet*. It was, it would seem, a golden age for Shakespearean production, with at least three every year, all quite different, to gratify every taste. The reality was somewhat different: the nuggets were rather less prominent than the dross, and the mines seemed frequently salted. The range, however, provides many and illuminating contrasts and, perhaps more important, raises a variety of questions concerning the motives for choosing Shakespeare in the first instance, the values embodied in the productions, and their comparative success in pleasing audiences.

To turn first to the professional productions: these were on the whole disasters – ill-conceived and worse executed. Rising Tide's effort seem to have been little more than an attempt to get school audiences and to demonstrate the company's mainstream appeal in order to keep its funding. A concern with doing justice to, exploring, or challenging the works in question was clearly not a significant part of the plan. A superficial topicality was aimed at, as, for example, in a St John's setting for *Romeo and Juliet*, but it was not thought through. No attempt to fix issues of class and social status in a Newfoundland context was made. The lovers themselves were reduced to randy adolescents with deep mouths and long tongues. Accurate iambics did not get a look in. Egos were clearly more central than texts: *Romeo and Juliet* was rejigged to make the Nurse (played by Donna Butt) the central figure of the tomb scene. Rising Tide's heart was clearly not in these productions, and poor houses for *Romeo and Juliet* did not help. Shakespearean production ceased for some considerable period, resuming only in 1992 in collaboration with the director of Sir Wilfred Grenfell College's bachelor of fine arts theatre arts program, Ken Livingstone.

A far more extreme example of professional but inept Shakespearean production was provided from 1984 to 1988 by the Newfoundland Shakespeare Company. Productions of *Hamlet*, *Richard III*, *King Lear*, *Timon of Athens*, *Macbeth*, and *The Winter's Tale* appeared in succession, all directed by Michael Wade, and, with the exception of *Timon of Athens*, all starring him in the lead. Despite the fact that Wade had at his disposal some of the best actors in St John's, these were perhaps the worst productions in the collective theatre memory of the city. John Holmes, for many years a sympathetic and compassionate theatre critic for the *Evening Telegram*, who could always be counted on to do a brief plot synopsis rather than speak ill of a struggling company, described the production of *A Midsummer Night's Dream* as 'pitiful and fraudulent,' and concluded, 'I am astonished that such experienced and clever artists as Greg Thomey, Andy Jones, Leon Sobiesky and Charles Thomlinson could have allowed themselves to be associated with such a tawdry, worthless presentation.' His review of *Richard III* in 1985 has achieved a near-legendary status: 'I went to the LSPU Hall Wednesday to see *Richard III*. I left at the first intermission. It continues until Saturday.'

The rationale offered by Wade in his promotional material (presumably used to get the Canada Council and Newfoundland and Labrador Arts Council grants which paid for these productions) is of some relevance to the larger concerns of this chapter. He suggested that the Newfoundland Shakespeare Company was called into being by the felt need for Shakespearean production in Newfoundland, hitherto sadly lacking. He further suggested that part of the problem was the inability of audiences to respond to such material when done seriously, and that the Newfoundland Shakespeare Company was in the process of creating audiences for professional theatre. Again, the spectre of Shakespeare transformed into a touchstone of cultural values is raised. As it happens, however, Wade's claims are eminently disputable, and the evidence would seem to suggest that Wade was more interested in institutionalizing himself than Shakespeare. Gordon Jones, reviewing *Timon of Athens* for CBC Radio, perhaps summed up the issue most adequately. Quoting from the promotional material concerning the effort to create an audience for professional theatre, Jones commented, 'I beg to differ. What the Newfoundland Shakespeare Company needs to do is to develop a professional theatre for audiences. It still has some way to go to achieve that goal.' A similar point was made by John Gushue in a review of *Hamlet* two years earlier, simply entitled '*Hamlet* really icky.'

Jones's fourteen productions with the Memorial University Drama Society (by now called MUN Drama) from 1982 to 1997 offer a significant contrast to those of the professional companies. As they emerged over this period, they made no pretense of being professional, but they did strive to be good amateur theatre. Using a young cast, cutting texts liberally, and concentrating on clarity and coherence rather than iambics, Jones established a model of successful student drama that generated a large and loyal following and, not incidentally, made lots of money, or at least enough to ensure that another production could be mounted the following year. This seems a reasonably important point, one that will become increasingly relevant in the years to follow. Jones's Shakespeare seems in this context counter-institutional, at least in the academic sense, a body of material produced not because it interrogated conventional cultural verities, whether aesthetic, ideological, or otherwise, or to win competitions, but because significant numbers of people wanted to do it, and equally significant numbers of people were willing to pay to see good drama competently done. Jones was blessed in having at hand a large number of students with real talent and with little opportunity to display or develop it through the existing amateur or professional companies. Not surprising, the reviews were consistently good, with the exception of one by Michael Wade on CBC Radio. Presumably getting his own back, he observed of Jones's *Twelfth Night* that the most serious shortcoming was the flawed direction, 'which showed little knowledge of the theatre and less knowledge of Shakespeare. The actors and crew worked wonders in overcoming this handicap, but in future the director should stay in the classroom and leave the theatre to professionals.' History provides its own dry commentary on the relevance of his review.

During the same period, a productive and creative relationship was developed between MUN Drama and the theatre-specialization program that was established within the English department in 1985. This, designed to offer a training in the elements of practical theatre, became a springboard for a large number of talented people to find a way into theatre, through teaching or administration, going on to the National Theatre school, or setting up independent productions or companies on their own. Many of them honed their skills in Jones's summer Shakespeare as well. Although the theatre-specialization program did not itself produce Shakespeare, it did a number of productions of Renaissance drama, including *Bartholomew Fair*, *The Alchemist*, *The Knight of the Burning Pestle*, *The Duchess of Malfi*, and a staged reading of *The Spanish Tragedy*.

In such a context, a 1992 Rising Tide co-production of *Hamlet*, in collaboration with the first graduating theatre class of the fine arts program recently established at Sir Wilfred Grenville College, offers an interesting, if cruel, contrast. This was institutional Shakespeare with a vengeance, the most celebrated of his plays produced in the capital's Arts and Culture Centre with an enormous budget, under the auspices of two of the institutions which, by the nature of their work, might reasonably be said to have privileged access to the material. In the event, it was a disaster in almost every respect, an embarrassment to the professionals and would-be professionals who collaborated in it and to the institutions responsible for it. Peter Gard, reviewing for the *Newfoundland Herald*, commented wryly, 'There is, admittedly, a good deal of pleasure to be had in seeing a truly frightful attempt at a famous play. The stories you get to tell afterwards usually cover the price of admission. Jim Davis as Hamlet managed to out-vacuum Mel Gibson, a feat I thought impossible.' The only reason for doing it at all, clearly, was the prestige attached to the name of the play; apparently, neither director nor actors cared whether the play might actually work, or why it might be worth doing at all.

The pattern of summer Shakespeare instituted by Jones, however, went on from strength to strength. In 1994 a group of students associated with the theatre-specialization program formed a new company and used for their first production the generic label 'Shakespeare by the Sea.' It was a open-air production of *The Tempest* on the cliffs of Logy Bay, which stretches out into Conception Bay, which itself stretches out into the north Atlantic. It was a demanding site, and a demanding production, which had to compete with a variety of distractions, among them the scenery itself, the whales, the blackflies, and weather that was either good or, more commonly, bad. As with all such productions, it put a premium on voice production and made subtlety problematic. Despite such distractions, it was a strong production and proved successful among both critics and audiences. The following year brought *Lear*, and the next, *Macbeth*. Perhaps because of the necessity of forceful and sustained articulation, the iambics were remarkably good in all these productions.

In the summer of 1997, possibly lured by the prospect of a tourist bonanza generated by the celebrations surrounding the five hundredth anniversary of Cabot's presumed landfall in Newfoundland, the organizers made the extraordinarily ambitious step of going professional, paying performers and production staff and turning it from a one-production affair into a festival. Thus, there was a repeat of *Macbeth* at Logy Bay, an open-air production of *Hamlet* in downtown St John's, and a variety of Shakespearean spin-offs, among them *Rosencrantz and Guildenstern Are Dead*, *I Hate Hamlet*, and *Willful Pursuits*. By necessity, the festival was partially dependent upon grants and, even with grants, was not a financial success; however, the creation of a body of mixed professional, semi-professional, and amateur theatre practitioners, working together on a variety of Shakespearean productions because they believed such plays could be made to work on one level or another, for people who paid to come because they, too, believed the same, marked an interesting development in the history of Shakespearean production in Newfoundland and one that has had important consequences.

These productions raise some interesting questions about the nature of summer Shakespeare generally, and outdoor Shakespeare more particularly, some of which were put explicitly by Kate Taylor in a 1998 review of the Halifax Shakespeare by the Sea Festival (a festival begun the same year as that in Newfoundland but unrelated to it; the Newfoundland one, not surprisingly, goes unnoticed by Taylor) in the *Globe and Mail*. She observes that outdoor Shakespeare, being a 'populist and popular project,' may well make the plays 'highly accessible and fun to watch,' but it does not plumb their depths or reveal enduring insights. It makes Shakespeare 'popular,' she concludes, but not 'relevant.' The generalization in its own right seems hard to sustain. In order to be accessible and popular, any production, indoor or out, Shakespearean or otherwise, must needs to be competent and to offer more than picturesque scenery; in such a context, it might be objected that relevance is in the eye of the beholder. Bad outdoor Shakespeare by the same token is neither popular nor accessible. The point is evident in the interesting contrast provided in 1996, once again, by the collaboration of Rising Tide Theatre and the director of the Sir Wilfred Grenfell theatre program. This time, it was *The Tempest*, presented as part of the Summer on the Bight festival in the town of Trinity, well away from St John's and, more important, most of its reviewers.[15] While enlivened with some good performances and striking touches, not least among them a scantily clad Ariel in bondage gear, it was susceptible to the reservations expressed by Kate Taylor towards summer Shakespeare more generally: duly picturesque in setting, it was pedestrian in conception and execution. Its only function seems to have been to provide a light break from the usual Newfoundland fare of the festival.

More recent Newfoundland productions illustrate the same point in different ways. In 1998 Rising Tide again offered a Shakespearean diversion at the Summer on the Bight festival, this time *Macbeth*. The setting, the base of a lighthouse on the tip of a long peninsula jutting out into the bay, was magnificent. Some of the individual moments were splendid: a single piper provided both atmosphere and, occasionally, an intensity out of all proportion to the source. Unfortunately, the piper was the high point of the production: it was more generally dismal, with Macbeth himself being the most dismal aspect of it. The murmurs among the audience as they headed back to the car park echoed those of the frustrated guests at the banquet: they did not suggest popularity, far less accessibility. Relevance, like iambics, went by the board.

Shakespeare by the Sea's 1998 production of the predictable *A Midsummer Night Dream* in the predictable park, in a predictably conservative fashion, with lots of predictably romantic fairies, would not seem at first sight likely to offer any exceptions to Taylor's generalization, but it did. A strong cast, with the lovers and fairies particularly outstanding, created a production that neither did, nor was intended to, lead to any fundamental questions about the play, or what it was really trying to do; however, it was a pleasure to watch and offered as many enduring insights, and as much relevance, as should be reasonably expected of any solid production. It was also, not coincidentally, popular and accessible. Gordon Jones's review justly concludes that the production 'blazes no new trails, but it offers a spirited excursion along charted pathways of the enchanted forest.'

The *Macbeth* and *A Midsummer Night's Dream* discussed above were both orthodox productions; both, however, can be set against two other productions of the same plays which were far from orthodox and which might suggest that Taylor's generalizations are not fundamentally viable. While it is doubtless regrettable that these two plays should so dominate Shakespearean production here and elsewhere, they were sufficiently diverse to make the experience of comparison and contrast interesting in its own right.

Ken Campbell's *MakBed* at the LSPU Hall, in one sense at least, hearkens back to an earlier period in Newfoundland theatre history, being an English touring production. Like the very first such recorded performance of Shakespeare in Newfoundland, that of the *Richard III* earlier discussed, it was all that current academic orthodoxy would have Shakespearean production be: it broke new ground outrageously and with zest. More specifically, it was a pidgin-English adaptation/translation of the play, one employing no more than two hundred words. The setting and the particular variety of pidgin employed, that of the Republic of Vanuatu, formerly known as the New Hebrides, provided a postcolonial alternative universe where Western values, and in particular Christianity, have been done away with, and life had been restored to the honest integrity of warrior days, and where real men eat each other while decked out in costumes created out of the detritus of Western civilization. The ostensible point of the production was to make the case for pidgin as a world language; as with many other aspects of the production, though, this seems less postcolonial theory than postmodern jokiness, one given emphasis by the comic business provided by a number of local street musicians and entertainers. There were no iambics, and not much relevance either.

The most interesting production of the season, and indeed for many years, was neither indoors nor outdoors but underground. Jillian Keilly, who has established her credentials as a radical director in many contexts, including an ambitious cross-dressed *Julius Caesar* in 1995, created an astonishing tour de force with a production of *A Midsummer Night's Dream* in an abandoned mine shaft on Bell Island, a twenty-five-minute drive and a further ten-minute ferry ride from St John's. The intent was obviously and conspicuously serious: to make the magic world of the play itself serious, which means, in the context of the production, variously amazing, unbelievable, scary, and wonderful.

The choice of the mine shaft was based on the complete darkness that it offered. Keilly made much use of black light for the supernatural world: characters appeared and disappeared instantly by simply turning around so that their fluorescent markings were visible or invisible. Comparison with Peter Brook's celebrated, and vastly influential, 1971 production of *A Midsummer Night's Dream* is instructive. Brook used the circus as a vehicle to suggest and explore the play's magic; impressive as the results generally were, the device did not, to me at least, justify the hyperbolic praise showered upon the production. Brook's actors were in their circus guise competent but far from magical; they did no more than any reasonably fit person could have learned to do with intensive practice, and the mechanisms were transparent. Keilly's production worked with simpler mechanisms, perhaps, but they were astonishingly effective.

Keilly's *A Midsummer Night's Dream* offered, among other pleasures, the opportunity to reflect upon many of the commonplaces that now tend to dominate discussion of Shakespearean production. Chief among these is the assumption, suggested by Taylor and articulated more forcefully in many academic discussions of the plays, that the relevance of Shakespeare generally, and Shakespearean production more specifically, must be defined exclusively in terms of transgression, that is, of interrogation of the text and its ideological assumptions. Only thus can a Shakespeare production be said to be doing useful cultural work. Regrettably, it is not clear that useful cultural work necessarily serves a useful purpose. Certainly, Ken Campbell's *MakBed* pushed the envelopes, crossed the boundaries, and transgressed like crazy. It was also trivial, a thin joke that ultimately failed to amuse. Keilly's *Dream* offered no such radical pleasures but did provide something more important: it made the experience of the play seem like the very first time and very magical indeed.

Given the extraordinarily unstable history of Shakespearean production in Newfoundland over the last four hundred years, it would be unwise to draw too many sweeping conclusions concerning the phenomenon. Newfoundland, as so often, is here again a rule unto itself. There is no Culture Industry, and most certainly no 'Big-Time Shakespeare,' as Michael Bristol calls it. What is more interesting is the fact that for the first four hundred years of its history the island had little, or more often no, Shakespeare at all; in the last two decades, however, it has been awash in another extreme, that of Small-Time Shakespeare. The results have been destabilizing. Put to the test, the traditional professional companies have often proved less adequate, and less highly trained, than amateurs; High Culture has often become low farce; and the institutional values that are conventionally alleged to cling to the Shakespearean canon, and Shakespearean production, have been most certainly honoured more in the breach than in the observance.

In certain respects, there is nothing peculiarly distinctive to Newfoundland in this situation, but what is distinctive is the role Shakespeare has played in the emergence of a new cultural landscape, one with important implications in the larger context of persistent poverty, high unemployment, and a frighteningly high level of out-migration. In 1993 Peter Gard, having praised handsomely Jones's production of *As You Like It* went on to conclude with depressing prescience: 'I have mixed feelings about the success of *As You Like It*. What has happened to our thriving professional community? What will happen to these skilled actors in the near future? You can only do so many high-school tours and so much unpaid acting and then what?' The answer was, in a sense, self-generated. Through Jones's Summer Shakespeare, Shakespeare by the Sea, and the independent companies that have sprung up around them, some degree of hope for survival has been offered to the highly talented people of whom Gard speaks, who could have found no niche, and certainly no income, in either the old professional or amateur companies. Many have indeed left the province, but many have stayed. Shakespeare has been central in the process: it was through Shakespearean productions that Jillian Keilly gained the experience, and established the background, for a larger theatrical career that won her in 1998 the John Hirsch Award as most promising emerging director.

Discussing Shakespeare more generally in relation to the culture industry, Michael Bristol concludes on an uncharacteristically lyrical note, citing Mikhail Bahktin: 'Like any product of the culture industry, Shakespeare as a commodity is more often than not trivial and inconsequential. Even in the most vitiated and meretricious productions, however, the semantic potential of Shakespeare's plays can "break through" to a "more intense and fuller life." The possibility of breaking through is what makes Shakespeare essential. Shakespeare is a vital continuation of the past; his work can force even the culture industry to express something beyond crying all the way to the bank' (*Big-Time* 117). Of the recent productions discussed in the pages above, certainly more than a few have been meretricious and vitiated, though none has led anyone to run crying to the bank except to beg for an overdraft. Collectively, however, they have 'broken through' to a degree that is both a wonder and a pleasure. It would be agreeable to think that this phenomenon will last and develop, but, whether it does or not, it has accomplished much already, not least in demonstrating that Shakespeare has an existence outside academic discourse.[16] It has established above all that people will produce, or pay to see produced, good Shakespearean productions of whatever nature, even at the cost of some economic risk or physical discomfort, not because they have been conditioned to believe that they ought to, or because of the cocktail parties that ensue, but because it gives them pleasure and perhaps some illumination into their lives. Having done so, they will go on to produce, or see, other productions, that will do the same. Even Chris Brookes, I suspect, could not wish it otherwise, iambics and all.

Notes

1 The title of this paper alludes as well to two other notable islanders forced to wrestle with the crisis of cultural identity and values, namely, Derek Walcott and Caliban. The former resolved to learn how 'to suffer in accurate iambics' (Walcott); by contrast, the latter learned chiefly how to curse. Much of this chapter is based upon material in the Centre for Newfoundland Studies at Memorial University, and I am indebted to all the librarians there. I am even more indebted to Denyse Lynde and Gail Weir, of the Department of

English and the University Library respectively, who are in the process of retrieving as much as possible of the vanishing theatre history of Newfoundland as part of the STAGE Project (SSHRC Theatre Archives Grant Enterprise).
2 For an excellent account of the process, see Hope-Simpson.
3 For a brief discussion of the concert, see Ches Skinner.
4 The company arose out of the fact that the actress-daughter of Sir Eric Bowring, one of the great St John's merchants, had recently married the director of the Alexandra company, and he wanted to show her off in her home town. Alec McCowen was a juvenile lead in this tour. See Yeo 82–3.
5 Thus, Leslie Yeo, the founder, went on to become the first artistic director of the Shaw Festival; John Holmes stayed to join the CBC and became a fixture of St John's theatre as critic, actor, and co-founder of the Theatre Arts Club. Other members of the company who stayed include Joseph Shaw, Gillie and Moya Fenwick, Norman Walsh, Denny Spence, Barbara Byrne, Hilary Vernon, and Gladys Richards.
6 I am indebted to my colleague Dr Annette Staveley, who was the teacher in question, for this story.
7 A well-known anecdote concerns the establishment of the Corner Brook Arts and Culture Centre: after a political dinner in that city, Smallwood announced that two prominent businessmen at the table, Art Lundrigan and Sir Christopher Chancellor, had agreed to put up $300,000 apiece; it was the first they had heard of it, but, in the end, they found it advisable to keep quiet and pay up.
8 Perlin's views extended to what 'entertainment' ought to be; he reserved to himself the right to bring in shows from outside Newfoundland, rather than encourage those varieties of local talent of which he disapproved.
9 Attendance varied from 63 per cent to 40 per cent, which, for a theatre the size of the Arts and Culture Centre, seating over a thousand, is more than respectable.
10 Thereafter, 'institutional' Shakespeare largely disappeared from the Arts and Culture Centre, although in 1983 and 1988 Perlin brought in the London Shakespeare Group to perform *Twelfth Night* and *Much Ado.*
11 Interestingly enough, yet a third company also emerged: the Newfoundland Travelling Theatre, led by Dudley Cox. Like Brookes, Cox took theatre around the island but was primarily interested in light comedy, with the occasional foray into Newfoundland drama.
12 It is not without irony that the show Brookes interrupted was Cook's *Colour the Flesh the Colour of Dust,* since Cook is one of the few dramatists that Brookes somewhat grudgingly acknowledges as a contributor to the development of an indigenous drama (36).

13 In the last year of the London Theatre Company, Yeo was offered one of the first Canada Council grants, but refused it: 'I didn't want subsidies sitting on the seats; I wanted bums' (265).

14 The focus of this chapter has inevitably been upon St John's, since Shakespeare has not been strongly represented outside of the city. It is worth noting, however, that *Macbeth* was produced in the first year of the Stephenville Festival, 1979, and *Hamlet* in 1980. Thereafter there seem to have been no further productions, although in 1983 the festival did tour scenes from Shakespeare extensively to schools throughout the region. It should also be noted that the festival at Trinity, Summer on the Bight, has done annual productions of Shakespeare since 1996.

15 Gordon Jones did review the repeat of *The Tempest* in 1997 and *The Winter's Tale* in 1999. There have been no other reviews of note.

16 In 1999 three more notable Shakespearean productions took place that suggest that an optimistic view of the phenomenon may not be out of place; certainly none of them was subject to Taylor's strictures. *The Winter's Tale* was performed throughout the town and on the beach at Trinity, this time directed by Richard Rose; a matriarchal version of *Much Ado* by Patricia Bromley was done at the old gun emplacement at Cape Spear; and the most recent was a Mafioso version of *Richard III* by Shakespeare by the Sea at the LSPU Hall. Regrettably, I saw only the last. The first two were by repute interesting, if flawed; the last was certainly entertaining, though perhaps too consciously clever for its own good. Whatever else they were, however, they were not quick-fix High Culture sops for the masses. The following year was almost as rich, with a traditional but intense *Love's Labour's Lost* in Bowring Park, and a Second World War version of *Julius Caesar* at Cape Spear. Both were well received, and neither was 'lite.'

9

Liberal Shakespeare and Illiberal Critiques: Necessary Angel's *King Lear*

MICHAEL McKINNIE

Necessary Angel Theatre, one of Toronto's more prominent and long-lived small theatre companies, produced *The Tragedie of King Lear* at the Canadian Stage Company's Berkeley Street Theatre Upstairs in Toronto in the spring of 1995. The most conspicuous feature of Necessary Angel's *King Lear* was that it was partially cross-cast. Director Richard Rose cast Janet Wright as Lear; the roles of Kent, Edmund, and Albany were also performed by women; and Goneril was played by a man.[1] There have been other cross-cast *King Lears*, including Mabou Mines's well-known New York City production in 1990 and Canadian performance artist Beau Coleman's solo 'Queen' Lear at the University of Alberta in 1995.[2] But only Necessary Angel's *King Lear* claimed that its casting was made on the basis of merit and invited the media and audiences to view it as the central issue of the production.

That Necessary Angel should perform *King Lear* in Toronto in 1995 has particular resonances given the production history of both Shakespeare and the play in international and Canadian contexts. Susan Bennett argues that *King Lear* occupies a distinct position within the Shakespearean production canon in Western theatre at the present historical moment. On the one hand, *King Lear* is 'an (if not *the*) example of a great play' which 'should (even if it does not always) make great theatre' (46). On the other hand, *King Lear* has been subject to a number of high-profile 'radical' interpretations and adaptations throughout Western theatre that 'occupy a tense yet sometimes generative relation to their Ur-text' (48). Bennett suggests that this proliferation of *King Lears* is illuminating because, in their constant revision of textual and staging assumptions, they offer models of how the supposedly transhistorical 'greatest play' of the 'greatest playwright' encounters the immediate and local 'performative present of multivalent theatrical signification' (78). *King Lear* has become a key site where the tension between a universalist cultural conservation and an immanent cultural subversion is performed in contemporary Western theatre practice.

Richard Paul Knowles analyses the ways in which the Stratford Festival in general, and *King Lear* in particular, manifested this tension within the context of Canadian theatre practice. Knowles argues that, at its creation in the 1950s, the Stratford Festival was envisaged as a way through which Canadians would demonstrate their full participation in humanist and imperial culture, for which Shakespeare was the standard-bearer. He points out that performing Shakespeare has historically been associated in Canada with a postcolonial aspiration to cultural maturity and performing *King Lear*, 'constructed as [Shakespeare's] greatest play,' has been marked as the best way to demonstrate the achievement of that maturity since the Stratford Festival's 'great' production of 1964 ('From Nationalist' 20). Furthermore, the centrality of Stratford in the production history of Shakespeare in Canada in general, and *King Lear* in particular, has tended not only to universalize but also to nationalize the significance of the play's production. Knowles argues that the repeated attempts by the Stratford Festival to position itself, from the 1950s until the 1980s, as Canada's de facto, if not statutory, national theatre extended a discourse (reaching back to the late nineteenth century) in which the production of, or aspiration to produce, Shakespeare links universal and national values.

Knowles also suggests, however, that as the Stratford Festival increasingly accommodated economic multinationalism in the late 1980s and 1990s (and produced Shakespeare's work less and less), 'his plays at the same time became the site of various anti-hegemonic attempts at (re)appropriation outside the Festival' ('From Nationalist' 35).[3] A range of 'particularist' productions (35) were staged throughout Canada, including Skylight Theatre's aboriginal *Tempest* on the Queen Charlotte Islands (1987, 1990) and Theatre Columbus's clown *Twelfth Night* in Toronto (1990).[4] Significantly, these productions did not seek to use Shakespeare to reclaim the space for a national drama evacuated by the Stratford Festival. Knowles argues that, unlike a national Shakespeare that relied on the texts as semantically and culturally secure artefacts, this group of particularist work simultaneously undermined the authority of the Canadian nation-state and the Ur-Shakespeare with which it had been associated. This historical moment, then, marked a new, less nationalist, and more oppositional dialectic of Shakespeare production in Canada: instead of a universalist Shakespeare complementing national cultural aspiration, universalist Shakespeare's main counterpart was a group of more fractious and local competitors.

Necessary Angel's *King Lear* straddles, and then explodes, the tensions that Bennett and Knowles identify: between the conservationist and the radical, and between universalist, humanist ideology and the particular 'shifting site[s]' of signification that constituted the political and cultural economies of theatre practice in Toronto and Ontario in 1995 (Knowles, 'From Nationalist' 35). When Necessary Angel performed *King Lear*, it increased its cultural capital, implying that it had matured as a company and that, even though it was small in size, it had achieved the stature necessary to engage the 'greatest' work of the 'greatest' playwright. That it set aside three years to work on *King Lear* in a variety of ways, a commitment it has never made to any other existing text, only amplified the company's investment in the play. The production's cross-casting was promoted as a way to support this investment, where bringing liberal, meritorious labour practices to a theatrical mode of production – casting 'the best person for the job,' regardless of the sex of the actor or the gender of the character – would be recognized as a commensurate response to the greatness of *King Lear*.

But this assumption overlooked two things. The first was that the province of Ontario was in the middle of a fierce battle over new provincial employment-equity legislation. Much of the debate centred on how merit would or would not be abandoned as a rationale for hiring, and the media frequently expressed alarm that women and people of colour would gain advancement in spite of being unqualified for a given job. Casting women as male characters, which Richard Rose thought illustrated a commitment to merit, instead appeared to reviewers of the production as a type of employment equity and, therefore, an attack on both merit and a universalist Shakespeare. The production assumed that its meritorious casting would be judged solely within the particular history of a theatrical economy, and not the political economy beyond the walls of the theatre.

The second was that, once spectators took their seats in the auditorium and the lights went up, they were presented with a contradictory *mise en scène*. The production's pictorial stage and the actors' naturalist acting approach implied that the production would literally make visible what Rose believed to be the play's central theme: an ascent from barbarism to humanism. But the periodic dissonance between the cross-casting and the text, and the production's repeated foreclosure of the privileges usually accorded to sight within the modern theatre auditorium, meant that the apprehension of this humanist teleology was often frustrated. Necessary Angel's *King Lear* proved that a reconciliation of a universalist and particularist Shakespeare was impossible in Toronto in 1995. The production demonstrated that the theatre auditorium is not an autonomous space through which liberal ideals can be confidently pursued, but rather a site of contest where Shakespeare becomes the medium through which theatrical and non-theatrical economies of value compete. This contest meant that, instead of confirming a universalist understanding of Shakespeare, Necessary Angel's *King Lear* resulted in a particular, if unintended, critique of theatrical liberalism in Toronto.

Establishing a Liberal Theatre Economy

When I refer to theatrical liberalism I mean three things: a sense that the contemporary subject has ascended to a more fully 'human' and, therefore, ontologically transparent state; a sense that this ascent is achieved through merit; and a sense that the purpose of theatre in general, and Shakespeare specifically, is to secure a sense of civilization by representing (indeed, mirroring) this liberal-humanist teleology back to the subject. Necessary Angel explicitly framed its *King Lear* as a project concerned with the civilization of the human subject. In terms of characterization, dramaturgy, and scenography, it repeatedly insisted to audiences that its concern was how 'probably the greatest of Shakespeare's plays,' as Janet Wright put it (qtd. in V. Wagner, 'No Gender'), traced and secured a liberal-humanist subjectivity and 'civilization' (Necessary Angel).

It is in this discourse that Necessary Angel's justification for cross-casting is located. Director Richard Rose argued that 'traditional' casting, which matches the gender of the character with the sex of the actor, was based on arbitrary conventions that did not apply in the 1990s. To subvert these naturalized conventions, Rose suggested a form of 'non-traditional' casting in which actors would be selected for their roles on the basis of merit. He claimed to have chosen 'the best actor, male or female, for the part' (Necessary Angel). He also argued somewhat contradictorily that, while cross-casting may imply that Necessary Angel's *King Lear* was 'an exploration of gender' (Necessary Angel), the production's success would be measured according to its ability to make the audience forget gender: 'I'm quite confident that if we stay true to the story, those gender issues won't be an issue' (V. Wagner, 'No Gender').

In their pre-production features on *King Lear*, Toronto's newspapers reproduced Rose's representation almost unquestioningly. Vit Wagner, a theatre writer for Toronto's largest circulation daily, the Toronto *Star*, opened his feature with the question, 'When it comes to Shakespearean performance, is it possible that the best man for the job might well be a woman? And vice versa?' ('No Gender'). John Coulbourn, the theatre critic for the Toronto *Sun*, the city's daily tabloid, quoted unquestioningly Rose's statement about 'the best actor, male or female, for the part,' though he did not acknowledge that these words came not in response to a question but were taken verbatim from a Necessary Angel media release ('Fit'). Chris Winsor of the weekly newspaper *eye* accepted that Rose had 'cast whomever he felt was best suited for the role,' regardless of gender, and added approvingly, 'Now there's an idea.' *NOW*, the city's larger weekly arts-and-politics newspaper, confirmed Necessary Angel's representation by focusing on 'acting rather than gender' (Lawless, 'Necessary').

In making a claim for its cross-casting on the basis of merit, Necessary Angel made a liberal claim about the division and organization of theatrical labour. The issue of individual merit is at the heart of liberal debates about equality of opportunity: the coordination of, access to, and suitability for work in a capitalist labour market. The stakes of these debates are high. 'After all,' notes one group of labour analysts, 'the process of selection and allocation of individuals in labour organisations implies the distribution of career possibilities, and consequently, of life chances ... whether one likes it or not' (Glastra et al. 164). Liberal philosopher James Fishkin defines the merit principle as a belief that 'there should be widespread procedural fairness in the evaluation of qualifications for positions' (22). Fishkin, following John Rawls, claims that the 'process of selection and allocation of individuals in labour organizations' is necessarily circumscribed by moderate scarcity, and the goal of liberalism should be to ensure 'fair competition among individuals for unequal positions in society' (19). Merit is one way to grapple with the 'issue of assignment' when it comes to allocating work when there may not be enough work to go around (45). For egalitarian (or 'left') liberals like Rawls, this is an issue of distributive justice; for economic neo-liberals like economist Milton Friedman or Ontario Premier Mike Harris, individual merit is one of the cornerstones of unfettered free markets. Common to both strands, however, is an anxiety about merit itself, and a desire that a set of individual attributes manifest themselves as labour talents or skills to be evaluated independently of so-called native characteristics like sex, race, or ethnicity (Fishkin 28).[5]

Necessary Angel framed its cross-casting as a way to bring procedural fairness to a competitive theatrical labour market. Procedurally, Richard Rose's casting gave an actor like Janet Wright access to a substantively and qualitatively different part than 'traditional' casting would normally allow her. The reason she accepted the role of Lear was, she said, 'because [as a woman] you don't get those kind of parts in Shakespeare. You're always playing the support' (Coulbourn, 'Fit'). In a liberal sense, this is bringing fairness to a theatrical labour market. Wright's individual skills were believed to be equal to the demands of the role, and Rose's cross-casting eliminated arbitrary barriers of work assignment that prevented the full application of those talents (Lawless, 'Necessary'). Wright's sex was a 'native characteristic' that should not have foreclosed the deployment of her skills as an actor.

Richard Rose and the cast's acceptance of a meritorious rationale for casting conditioned certain conceptions of characterization. Knowles calls these 'psychophysical and linear conceptions of character, motivation, and action' that are 'culturally privileged and deeply inscribed in [contemporary] theatrical discourse' ('Shakespeare, 1993' 215). In practice, the production understood characterization as a naturalist process, whereby an actor seeks to collapse the ontological distance between herself and a character in order to suppress the markers of acting and for the character to be apprehended as a 'real person.' The ontological merger of actor and character is, as W.B. Worthen points out, a central ideal of naturalistic acting technique: 'At its most extreme, it requires the performers to refrain from acting, to become identical with and thereby transparent to "character"' (*Modern*, 55–6). Worthen argues:

> Realistic acting erases itself from view, renders the actor the vehicle of a fully coherent 'character' already present in the dramatic text. The actor's performance is rendered theatrically invisible, and aesthetically palatable, through a thoroughgoing identification between the conventions of 'acting' and the manifest codes of social enactment ... This attitude is evident, too, in popular responses to the theater, which often betray this deeply idealized conception of dramatic performance. When the *Times* critic A.B. Walkley asks 'What is the very quintessence of acting but the effort to bring about the complete identity' between actor and character, he inscribes in that identity a typical hierarchy of value: 'If the actor *is* the part, so that you

fail to distinguish one from the other, then he has achieved what he set out to do and he deserves all the praise he gets.' (*Modern* 19)

A supposedly objective set of performance skills therefore favoured naturalist performance training and encouraged the audience to engage the performances on the liberal-humanist terms inscribed in that training. The corollary to this understanding for Necessary Angel's *King Lear* was a desire to elide the possibilities of gender being performative in the interest of making that 'real person' a metaphor for a universal humanity. '[W]hat [an actor] might bring to the role,' Rose said, is independent of 'the gender of the actor' (V. Wagner, 'No Gender').

The goal of performance for the Necessary Angel company was posited as the ability to fuse successfully what Richard Rose called the 'personal identity' of the actor with that of the character (V. Wagner, 'No Gender'). A recurring ideal of Necessary Angel's *King Lear* was that a kind of individualist, humanist metaphysics would allow the actor to subsume himself or herself completely to the character, rendering actor and character indistinguishable and indivisible. The risk was that gender might prevent this ontological assimilation by reminding an audience of the distance between actor and character. The company frequently spoke of ontological assimilation being the best way to resolve away the 'gender issues' in the text (V. Wagner, 'No Gender'). Rose stated: 'Once you start doing the work of telling the story, playing the intentions, understanding the needs of the characters, the issue of male/female slips away' (V. Wagner, 'No Gender'). Diana Belshaw, who played Kent in both the workshop and full productions, said, 'This time, I realized I don't have to play a man – I *am* a man. The play has such a strong emotional throughline that it doesn't matter what gender you are' (Lawless, 'Necessary'). Janet Wright asserted, 'If I meet you and you say you're Janet Wright ... I'm gonna think ... [an expressive shrug] ... but if we start talking and you *are* Janet Wright, that's a different thing"' (Coulbourn, 'Fit'). David Jansen, who played Goneril, argued that when a male actor plays a female character 'the approach doesn't really change. You're looking for intentions, scanning text, searching for clues. Once you strip away the surface, in terms of say, anger, you see the same things. You discover the similarities between gender, as opposed to the differences' (Winsor). When the male actor submerged himself in the character, he read gender as the realm of the same, not of difference.

Perhaps this way of approaching characterization can be traced to the fact that Necessary Angel situated its production as a 'natural' evolution from an 'arbitrary' point of departure. Since the 1995 production followed the previous year's workshop, it necessarily responded to the workshop's staging approach. Unlike the full production, the workshop was completely cross-cast, resulting in little emphasis on meritocracy and a much stronger emphasis on characterization as the explicit performance of gender. Belshaw claimed, 'In the workshop we were much more aware of gender, because it *was* the issue' (Lawless, 'Necessary'). Instead of playing a 'human being,' the actors had to figure out what it might mean to play a man or a woman and then demonstrate their choices. Although he did not approve of those choices, one reviewer's description points to the way those choices could not be assimilated into naturalist characterization: 'The women playing men: all growly, square-shouldered, chest out, swagger. The men playing women: effeminate, falsetto' (Winsor).

Rose decided, however, that this reversal was just as arbitrary as the traditional casting that he was trying to undermine. In a press release, he encouraged the media to read the full production as beyond gender politics, hiving off the 'sexual identity' of the actor, by which Rose meant the actor's gender, from 'personal identity,' which connoted a set of individual performance skills and ability to assume a character seamlessly. He offered meritorious casting as the means to resolve away any tension between characterization and gender: 'Last year I was intrigued to see how an actor of the opposite gender would inform and affect a role, but I discovered that casting the characters unilaterally with members of the opposite sex was just as arbitrary as "traditional" casting. The sexual identity of the actor was far less important than their personal identity. How will the story be affected if I simply choose the best actor, male or female, for the part?' (Necessary Angel). When covering the 1995 *King Lear*, the media picked up Rose's mode of contrasting the workshop and the full production, quoting Rose's description of the workshop's casting as 'arbitrary' (V. Wagner, 'No Gender'), using the description 'arbitrary' uncited (Lawless, 'Necessary'), or framing the workshop's full casting reversal as an imposed abstraction on the text: what Winsor referred to disparagingly as 'the Big Idea' (31). The response to arbitrariness, then, was meritorious casting, which naturalized the full production by supposedly de-gendering it.

The production also conformed to the modern notion that the 'issue' of Shakespeare's plays is characterization itself. Dramaturgically, then, the plot of *King Lear* was conceived as the narrative structuring of the lead character's personal transformation into a liberal-humanist subject. Elinor Fuchs locates this reading of Shakespeare in emerging modern conceptions of liberal subjectivity: 'From the eighteenth century on, theorists looked almost exclusively to Shakespeare as they began to advance a standard inwardness for character and, as a parallel development, began to revise the Aristotelian assimilation of character to plot ... to link character, actor, and spectator in a mutual play of subjectivity (intended here in its allied senses of consciousness of self and spiritual inwardness)' (25). Necessary Angel read Lear's 'journey' as a progression toward a humanism that, ultimately, was not tragic but epiphanic (Necessary Angel). Lear's death was envisioned as a display of contrition, love, and knowledge gained by turning inward, a final abandonment of regal artifice in favour of becoming simply a 'human being.' Albany's comment that Lear 'knowes not what he sayes, and vaine is it / That we present us to him' (Rose and Kugler 116) marked Lear's death as the completion of a journey of humanist self-consciousness.[6] Lear's inability to engage the other characters in the scene was a sign of an inward revelation about his personal identity, and his comment 'Ill [*sic*] see that straight' marked this recognition (116). Edgar's final admonition that 'The weight of this sad time we must obey, / Speake what we feele, not what we ought to say' implied that Lear had brought a new transparent identity into being, one that did not observe convention but rather 'was who it was' (117). The actor who played Edgar did not direct this speech to any particular character onstage, but instead turned it downstage as a general address, including the audience each time he said 'we.' The final scene framed the play as the story of Lear clearing a space for a transparent liberal-humanist subjectivity by inaugurating the terms on which civilized society would be built, and asked the audience to sanction this reading.

Furthermore, the production's *mise en scène* emphasized visual and ideological transparency, encouraging a spectatorial position from which nothing would be obscured; the spectator would have a plain view. The theatre building itself emphasized transparency: with its wood beams stripped bare and brick walls exposed, the interior of the Berkeley Street Theatre revealed itself completely to the arriving spectator. The dominant visual element of *King Lear* – its set – extended this emphasis on a plain view further. The production reversed the standard physical configuration of the Theatre Upstairs. Instead of the audience being seated on risers parallel to, and looking down on, the stage, the audience was seated on what would normally be the stage floor, looking up at the risers that were now the playing space. A large black frame, like the frame of a painting or the border around a movie screen, divided the audience and the stage, and a series of door-sized frames containing windows of various sizes defined playing spaces within the larger border. This produced a spectatorial position that strongly emphasized the visual and pictorial. A white scrim drawn across a smaller frame was positioned at the back of the stage, and risers stretched across the width of the playing area and progressed up towards the back frame. A platform attached to the lower border of the frame functioned as a banquet table in the opening scene and, later, the cliff and part of the heath. The set used the two-dimensional pictorial techniques of painting to give the impression of greater depth. The smaller frame upstage, enclosed by the larger frame downstage, gave an illusion of distance, and the risers enhanced this perception: by progressing from the downstage frame to the upstage frame, the risers appeared to stretch into the horizon, and, because they extended horizontally across the playing space, they encouraged actors to move laterally across the stage so as not to throw the visual field out of scale. The *mise en scène* was composed with the understanding that audience members were, first and foremost, viewers.

Though *King Lear*'s set was not, strictly speaking, a proscenium arch, its introduction into a black-box theatre space effectively installed the same relationship between audience and stage that a proscenium does; if anything, the fact that its borders stretched nearly the entire height and width of the small theatre framed viewing even more insistently than a proscenium. For Worthen, this type of scenographic framing 'not only circumscribes a dramatic world, it establishes the characteristic relation between actor, role, and eavesdropping audience through which its meanings are realized' (*Modern* 17). The pictorial stage divides the world of the stage from the world of the audience, implying that the two do not, and should not meet, placing the spectator in the role of individual, detached, impartial observer and transforming character into something that is behind the frame, on full display, and coherently apprehended (18).

Visual plenitude marks the ability to read bodies as an index of who people are, and to reproduce the way things are: in effect, to gain and fix ontological and social knowledge for the purposes of both regulation and reassurance. Necessary Angel's *King Lear* did not rely on the realistic reproduction of various locales in the play; that would likely be impossible. But the production did, at least initially, offer the promise of visual plenitude to the spectator. If the first encouragement was the building and the second was the set, the third incentive was the staging of the opening of the play. When the performance commenced, the audience was presented with Kent, Gloucester, and Edmund in full light. When Lear and the others assembled for the division of the kingdom, they sat at a banquet table stretched horizontally across the bottom of the frame, with Lear in the middle of a long side of the table. The composition of the stage picture mimicked da Vinci's 'Last Supper' and revealed how the viewing privileges of the audience were factored into the blocking of the scene. Although audience members might expect Lear to be sitting at the head of the table, for them to recognize his power in the pictorial stage he must be placed in the centre of their view, which was the middle of a long side of the table. Lear's daughters were placed accordingly at his side, political power progressing out from the king. The opening scene, staged with the characters facing front and in full light, gave the audience a complete view: the opening scene was about the unmediated visual apprehension of a political structure. The characters were displayed and framed so that the audience had a total view, and, implicitly, total knowledge of the world of the play.

If the final scene of the production attempted to interpellate a liberal spectator by embracing the audience, then the staging of the beginning of the play confirmed the audience's civility through negation. Richard Rose described *King Lear* as narrating 'what we need to live in order to survive in a natural state versus a civilized state' (V. Wagner, 'No Gender'). The social formation represented at the opening of the play, dominated by a king costumed in crudely stitched animal skins and furs and a court grotesquely gnawing meat off bones, asked to be understood as barely above barbarism. The liberal spectator was intended to apprehend an atavistic world onstage and comprehend that what was on full display *did not* include him or her. Through affirmation and negation, the *mise en scène* flattered the spectator by positioning the audience as modern, impartial, omniscient, and civilized.

Disrupting a Liberal Theatre Economy

A theatre event may repeatedly insist on its liberalism, but that does not necessarily mean that it does so convincingly. In fact, Necessary Angel's *King Lear* is an illuminating test case of the way in which the unfolding of a theatre event – what happens in the three and a half hours *King Lear* takes to transpire – can split those economies of labour and theatre apart, and make untenable the liberal Shakespeare that the production intended to confirm. By the time Edgar turned to the audience and said, 'Speake what we feele, not what we ought to say,' his line could not register as inclusive because the production had already undermined the liberal spectator for whom it was intended.

Through cross-casting, Necessary Angel's *King Lear* demonstrated the impossibility of changing who plays a role without throwing into relief a range of theatrical conventions that were assumed and preferred to be transparent. Many of these conventions centred on a correspondence between an actor's body and a role, and so the production's emphasis on vision and visibility meant that actors' bodies became visual indices of the violation of these conventions. Cross-casting destabilized a naturalized sexual division of theatrical labour and used actors' bodies to illuminate the criteria, latent and manifest, employed in assigning performance labour within a mode of theatrical production.

The most visible of these debates is over what is commonly known as 'non-traditional' casting. 'Traditional' casting is a modern theatrical practice. It uses the sex of an actor as the first criterion of suitability for playing a role: between actor and role, sex should correspond (though the necessity of race correspondence has never been as strictly observed in Western theatre – witness generations of white actors playing Othello). The assumption of correspondence, is, of course, somewhat leaky in practice. The practice of casting women in women's parts, as it were, postdates Shakespeare, and women actors have played leading male roles as star turns, such as with Sarah Bernhardt's famous performances of Hamlet or Charlotte Cushman's Romeo. Insofar as Shakespeare is part of Western theatrical 'tradition,' the 'traditional' way of casting Shakespeare was unknown in the playwright's time and has never been completely entrenched since. Nonetheless, 'traditional' casting is the dominant and often expected casting convention in twentieth-century Western (particularly anglo–North American) productions of Shakespeare.

The difficulty, however, is that a revision of theatrical casting conventions in the name of liberalism does not necessarily mean that an audience will make the same conceptual shift simply by entering the theatre. The 1995 production of *King Lear* took place in the midst of a furious public debate over employment equity that was going on in the province of Ontario at the time. Ontario elected its first New Democratic Party provincial government in 1990, and this nominally social-democratic administration was committed to introducing equity legislation requiring employers to diversify their workforces. Bill 79 was passed in 1994 at a time of severe economic recession and amidst widespread acrimony. The controversy over this legislation only deepened the following year, at the same time as Necessary Angel's production: 'Although Bill 79 was opposed from the outset, in the spring of 1995 criticism erupt[ed] with great intensity ... In the heated discussions, notions from the US debates such as reverse discrimination and 'fixed quota' resurfaced. The financial consequences of the policy were denounced and opponents claimed that the policy had stimulated the hiring of unqualified personnel' (Glastra et al. 167). Carole Ann Reed argues that 'massive layoffs and downsizing were making the population in Ontario feel pessimistic, economically besieged, worried about their future and unsympathetic to those who they saw as getting "special" rights and privileged access to any jobs that might come up' (47). The case against employment equity was usually made on the basis of merit and suggested that gender and race would be used to trump individual talent and threaten Ontario's wealth. The *Globe and Mail*, the conservative national broadsheet, went so far as to suggest that unemployed Ontarians should 'ferret out an ancestor who claimed native roots or a history on an African slave ship. Or they might consider inventing such a relative' (qtd. in Canadian Press).[7]

Many reviewers of *King Lear* pointed out sceptically that Richard Rose's casting allowed women actors the opportunity to play roles that they would not otherwise, and Geoff Chapman, writing in the Toronto *Star*, made the link to the political struggle over employment equity explicit. Chapman stated, 'This is all well and good for women actors who rarely get a crack at these particular big roles' but that this 'production seems to be merely another manifestation of employment equity, for the cross-casting adds nothing to this classic journey of mind and spirit' ('Cross-casting'). Chapman's comment reveals that Necessary Angel's *King Lear* invoked a non-theatrical labour economy through performance but was unable to prevent that labour economy from being used to evaluate the production. Within a theatrical labour economy, Richard Rose's claim that he was casting on the basis of merit was logical if open to dispute. The 'traditional' method of assigning work within the theatre labour market never assumed that all parts were open to competition through merit; in fact, 'traditional' casting's sexual division of labour explicitly foreclosed this possibility in the name of social mimesis. One could argue that abandoning 'arbitrary' conventions brought illiberal casting into line with wider work-assignment practices that were believed to be based on merit. Within a broader labour economy, however, Rose's casting seemed to bolster an attack on both liberal labour ideals and a humanist Shakespeare, appearing as a Trojan horse of employment equity when read within the context of the broader Ontario labour economy.[8] Employment equity challenged a naturalized division of labour by dismantling dearly held liberal notions of individual skill, opportunity, and competition; in violating its own naturalized division of labour, Necessary Angel was seen as doing exactly the same thing and undermining a 'classic journey of mind and spirit' in the process. The company's claim that it was casting on the basis of merit had no way of being accommodated.

Cross-casting also referenced and then violated a particularly significant type of naturalist correspondence: physiological verisimilitude. In *Naturalism in the Theatre*, Émile Zola argues that 'the great naturalistic evolution, which comes down directly from the fifteenth century to ours, has everything to do with the gradual substitution of physiological man for metaphysical man' (367). If the major concern of the theatre should become the liberal bourgeois subject – what Zola called the 'natural man' in 'the tangible world' – this would require a new emphasis on the body's transparent apprehension by the audience (367). Zola's call for 'detailed reproduction' was not simply limited to costumes and scenery but extended to the bodies of the actors onstage (369). Under naturalism, characters that were 'true to life' (369) would be realized only when the audience no longer had to try and ignore the fact that 'Queen Dido was a boy' with a 'budding beard' (367). When reviewer John Bemrose used a range of physiological qualities – hair, facial features, and depth of voice – to evaluate the quality of acting in Necessary Angel's *King Lear*, he made manifest the perniciousness of naturalist expectations of physiological verisimilitude, and the extent of the production's violation of those expectations: by pronouncing this violation an 'emasculation' and using the language of impotence, Bemrose also illustrated, on theatrical and symbolic levels, how the absence of such physiological detail can provoke a phallic anxiety in the male reviewer.

In addition, the bodies of the actors produced a corporeal and textual dissonance that removed the possibility of using *King Lear* to reveal humanist ontology transparently. In any cross-cast production of *King Lear*, there are going to be 'epiphanies,' as Diana Belshaw put it, or moments in which the text reminds the audience of the physiological gap between actor and character (Lawless, 'Necessary'). These epiphanies began to unravel the harmony between characterization and dramaturgy. Certain moments in the text reminded the audience of the gendered friction between actor and character and began to pry apart Necessary Angel's conception of the production and the play in provocative ways: for example, Lear's statement to Albany in 1.4 drew attention to the doubly feminized body of actor and character:

> Ile tell thee:
> Life and death, I am asham'd
> That thou hast power to shake my manhood thus,
> That these hot teares, which breake from me perforce
> Should make thee worth them   (Rose and Kugler 32)

When Janet Wright, as Lear, uttered the admonition 'Oh how this Mother swels up toward my heart! / Histerica passio, down thou climbing sorrow' (50), she demonstrated the validity of Coppélia Kahn's argument: 'Lear's very insistence on paternal power, in fact, belies its shakiness ... Women and the needs and traits associated with them are supposed to stay in their element, as Lear says, "below" – denigrated, silenced, denied. In this patriarchal world, masculine identity depends on repressing the vulnerability, dependency, and capacity for feeling which are called "feminine"' (35–6). Other moments where the crosscasting provoked the text into revealing complex, and often unexpected, links between gender and power were when Lear cursed Goneril (David Jansen) with

> Heare Nature, heare deere Goddesse, heare:
> Suspend thy purpose, if thou did'st intend
> To make this Creature fruitfull:
> Into her Wombe convey sterility,
> Drie up in her the Organs of increase,
> And from her derogate body, never spring
> A Babe to honor her   (Rose and Kugler 30)

and when Goneril sent Edmund (Maggie Huculak) back to Cornwall with 'This kisse' (Rose and Kugler 82). The presence of an 'other' actor drew attention not to the text's humanism but to its repeated linkage and anxious exercise of patriarchal and political power.

These kinds of epiphanies are, however, inevitable in any cross-cast *King Lear*. But Necessary Angel's *King Lear* was particularly provocative because of the ways in which its pictorial *mise en scène* offered, and then denied, its initial promise of visual plenitude. While emphasizing looking, the *mise en scène* progressively undermined the privileges of sight. Recall that the inaugural banquet scene presented a complete portrait; from this scene on, though, the production repeatedly foreclosed the possibility of the audience gaining such a coherent picture again. First, stage lighting became progressively dimmer and more selective in what it revealed. One became aware of having to look harder to see less as the show proceeded. The door-like frames were frequently placed between the audience and the characters, and, because these frames contained windows of different sizes, the bodies of the actors were often cut off or partially obscured. While framing was initially the pictorial mechanism that defined an open field of vision, here it defined a field of obscurity. The body of the actor and character was fractured and its reassuring visual totality denied.

Second, Charlotte Dean's costumes emphasized androgyny. Many of the characters were dressed in black cassocks, which frustrated any physiological correspondence between the body of the actor and the gender of the character. Rather than de-gendering the character, the costuming meant that spectators simply could not read the body of the actor as the primary site of gender production and characterization.

Third, the outer frame – the one closest to the audience – was not always inviolable. When Lear and Gloucester sat together on the heath in 4.5, Janet Wright and John Gilbert's feet dangled over the bottom edge of the frame. The effect was unnerving. Suddenly the outer frame, whose presence had largely been forgotten until this point, came back into view. One was reminded that, even in the pictorial stage, the field of vision is not detached and objective; it is, in fact, staged, and the spectator is complicit in that staging.

Fourth, and finally, David Jansen's performance as Goneril became a spectacle for male reviewers in ways that women actors playing male roles did not. In several reviews, Jansen's performance was equated disparagingly with that of a drag queen (Bemrose; Chapman, 'Crosscasting'; Coulbourn, 'Her'). I disagree with this normativity of this assessment, and its validity apart from this is somewhat ambiguous; Jansen's performance was one of the more successful in the production because, in spite of his naturalist statements about characterization, his performance resided in the gendered space between himself and the character. But it is interesting that these reviewers immediately assumed that Jansen's performance was parodic (there was nothing about his performance, for example, that could be described as camp). This is due, in part, to the fact that Jansen was the only male actor playing a female role. Because several women actors played male roles, their casting was normalized to a degree, while Jansen's could not help but appear anomalous. More significantly, Jansen was visually *unnatural* to reviewers: his was not only a man's body in women's dress, his was clearly a man's body in a woman's character. This spectacle was heightened in 4.2 when the scene opened with Oswald (Steve Cumyn) assisting Goneril in finishing her dressing. From a heterosexual spectatorial position, one literally saw too much. The act of dressing gave a brief glimpse of the male actor's body and provided visual evidence of the division between actor and character. Moreover, the scene provoked heterosexual anxiety because, for a split second, one saw two men in an erotic display. It was impossible, as Lear put it later, to 'see that straight' (5.3.116). Reviewer John Bemrose's description of Necessary Angel's *King Lear* as an emasculation is indeed an accurate description, but he locates the effect in the wrong place: it was not the text that was emasculated, but the spectator. The production promised that the visual would equal objective and complete knowledge, then denied or exploited this. One saw and knew either too little or too much. The pictorial stage, which was supposed to represent the world transparently and reassure the audience, revealed the spectator as mystificatory and mystified.

Conclusion

Necessary Angel's *King Lear* attempted to add a third combination to Knowles's genealogy of Shakespeare in Canada: consensus Shakespeare. If an alliance between a universalist Shakespeare and a national Shakespeare has been giving way in recent years to an opposition between a universalist Shakespeare and an anti-hegemonic particularist Shakespeare, Necessary Angel's *King Lear* sought to arrest this split and paper over the tension between universalist and particularist Shakespeares. Since realizing the 'greatness' of Shakespeare by appealing to a national, unifying Shakespeare was no longer imaginable in 1995, the company conceived of a Shakespeare that would confidently address its Toronto audience by tying together those points where liberal theatrical and labour economies seemed to concur. The production suggested that, if nothing else, the value of merit was widely agreed upon in society at large and that a meritorious approach to *King Lear* would consolidate both audience and text. In performance, however, this consensus proved impossible. Necessary Angel's *King Lear* was a paradigmatic, if inadvertent, example of performed immanent critique: by advocating, and then pushing theatrical liberalism to its logical limits, the production undermined the naturalized and naturalist assumptions sustaining its approach to characterization, dramaturgy, and scenography. In the process, it provoked a question that it ultimately could not answer: if a consensus Shakespeare was no longer tenable by the time the show was over, what kind of illiberal Shakespeare is possible? Like Necessary Angel, I cannot claim to know the answer, but beginning to provide an adequate response to the question would appear to involve Shakespearean productions in Canada paying far closer attention not only to the gendered economies in which their performances reside but to their local political economies as well.

Notes

1 I must declare an interest: I worked at Necessary Angel in 1995 and 1996 and did a dramaturgical apprenticeship on this production of *King Lear*.
2 In director Lee Breuer's staging for Mabou Mines, Lear became a matriarch presiding over a dysfunctional family of sons in the 1950s' American South. Unlike Richard Rose, Breuer reversed the gender of many of the characters. See Solomon for an analysis of this production, and Dobson for an analysis of Beau Coleman's interpretation. Susan Bennett also discusses a number of revisions and adaptations of *King Lear* in *Performing Nostalgia*.
3 Knowles observes that 'by 1993, only 3 productions of a total of 10 were of Shakespeare (versus a high of 7 of 13 in 1979)' ('From Nationalist' 35).
4 Knowles includes Necessary Angel's *King Lear* in his list of particularist Shakespeares, but it is significant that the production he cites is the 1994 workshop rather than the 1995 full production (which would not have occurred by the time the article was written). The full production explicitly disavowed the complete cross-casting of the workshop in the interest of a more universal and humanist appeal.
5 The inability to categorize class is indicative of these classifications' shakiness, but they are deployed nonetheless.
6 All quotations from *The Tragedie of King Lear* are taken from the unpublished production script, edited from the Folio 1623 and Quarto 1608 by Richard Rose and D.D. Kugler, with notes by Skip Shand. This text contains no line numbers, and so I have cited by page.

7 After Mike Harris's Progressive Conservatives defeated the New Democrat government in the summer of 1995, one of their first legislative acts was to repeal the employment equity law as a 'return to merit.'
8 That the production appeared as a Trojan horse of employment equity only applied insofar as cross-casting extended to sex and gender. All the actors in the production were white, so this was not a target for critics. There was, however, an anxiety around all of the markers that would be used under employment-equity legislation, so a panic over gender and a panic over race were often conflated.

PART THREE

Critical Debates and Traditions

The disputes, implicit and explicit, revealed in the productions that are analysed in Part Two are differently configured and expanded in Part Three, which is devoted to surveying some of the critical debates and traditions in which the study of Shakespeare in Canada participates. Anthony B. Dawson examines the assumptions behind the training of university actors through work with Shakespeare and the tensions between these and the academic debates currently animating Shakespeare studies. In keeping with the book's interest in interrogating the various constructions of Shakespeare as author and text put into play by differences between the popular and the academic traditions of Shakespearean reception, Paul Yachnin and Bruce Whitted explore Canadian contributions to the authorship question. This section concludes with two chapters that set up an implicit dialogue between two dimensions of the Frygian legacy in constructing understandings of Shakespeare and of Canada. Alexander Leggatt and L.M. Findlay explore different avenues suggested by the Canadian and Shakespearean criticism of Northrop Frye, therefore presenting radically different views of the possibilities for theorizing literature within and against the nation. Yet there may also be a sense in which nation as negative capability and national will are complementary rather than opposite poles of this construction. Certainly each essay takes national investments in Shakespearean scholarship and criticism with the utmost seriousness. This section as a whole further demonstrates that there is no single tradition of Shakespearean critique in Canada, but rather that Shakespeare, as author, shorthand for the playtext, and cultural icon, has been mobilized, and may be reconfigured, in a variety of sometimes conflicting ways.

10

Continuity and Contradiction: University Actors Meet the Universal Bard

ANTHONY B. DAWSON

In 1991 the University of British Columbia (UBC) theatre department mounted two productions of Shakespeare on its main stage. In many ways, the two shows stood in vivid contrast with each other. The first, *Hamlet*, was a highly conceptual production, designed as a futuristic, postmodern exposé of the utter inescapability of naked power. The set was an electronic fortress dotted with TV screens and linked with cellular phones, the characters were flattened into dolls and pawns, and the text was pasted together in unprecedented ways – spliced to bits of *Rosencrantz and Guildenstern Are Dead* and sections from the movie *The Legend*. The production of *Romeo and Juliet*, on the other hand, was relatively 'straight,' using a more or less uncut text, with most of the emphasis placed on telling the story and getting the actors to understand what they were doing. One event emphasized directorial concept – the overall look and meaning of the production – while the other underplayed 'vision' and focused on the process the actors might or could undergo in doing the show.

There were, however, some ways in which the two productions were of a piece. Most obviously, both were 'Canadian.' One of the issues here is precisely what that might mean in the context of producing Shakespeare. Could it mean (one hesitates to ask) that the tendency to obscure their Canadianness was very much in evidence? Certainly each of these productions was more or less 'international' in style, though in different modes; neither responded to the exigencies of the local in any very discernible way. This is a likely result of doing Shakespeare in English-speaking Canada, where the weight of British tradition and the influence of internationally renowned directors inevitably make a mark. But it invites further investigation, just because the tension between the international and the local is an example of the kind of contradiction I am interested in exploring in this chapter. The *Hamlet* production was 'international,' in the sense that it was heavily influenced by the conceptual style of many German and eastern European productions of Shakespeare in the 1970s and 1980s (and earlier).[1] The *Romeo and Juliet*, directed by Neil Freeman, an influential acting teacher in Canada with British roots (both personal and, more important, in terms of his perspective on Shakespeare), seemed to be situated somewhere between American and English Shakespeare: less obviously focused on 'method' than most American productions would be, and more focused on text, but, nevertheless, distinctly North American in voice, design, and overall 'feel.' If 'Canadian' meant anything in those seasons in the early 1990s, it meant eclectic, open to a range of influences. But it also seemed to involve a turning away from, or a lack of direct concern with, the local – there was nothing distinctly Canadian or regional about either production.

Related to the submergence of the local in the international, and more directly to my point in this chapter, is the nature of actor training as it is typically practised at Canadian universities and theatre schools. While such training brings to bear a wide variety of techniques – movement, voice, scene analysis, even combat – the emphasis tends to be on connecting theatrical representation to universal meanings, especially in the construction of character. Since universal human meanings have come under a dark cloud of suspicion in literary and cultural studies, and yet seem very much alive in theatrical circles, it seems worth investigating the contradictions in play and their potential fruitfulness. In essence, I am interested here in a particular historical/cultural moment, the early 1990s at UBC in Vancouver; but I want to read that moment in relation to a larger history, looking back as far as Shakespeare's own period and place and forward to the present in Canada as a whole.

I had the opportunity to speak at some length with a number of the young actors-in-training (along with a few designers and directors) who were involved in the two productions I have mentioned,[2] and I will begin by presenting the results of our discussions, in order to investigate the assumptions and implicit understandings that often go into the translating of Shakespearean texts into stage representations – in Canada and elsewhere. Indeed, the present chapter, like the object of its investigations, is caught in the tension between the universal and the particular. The discussions took place at UBC in 1992, although similar (but not identical) ones could have taken place in a variety of Canadian universities and colleges over the last couple of decades.[3] I welcomed the opportunity to speak with student actors, since part of my purpose was, and is, to examine the implications of Canadian theatrical training as it seeks to negotiate the universal/local opposition, and no single author looms as large as the stubbornly local, and at the same time expansively universal, Bard.[4]

In the interviews, my method was to pose a series of similar questions to each of the young actors, questions that covered the specifics of their roles, their relations to other characters, their view of their task as actors in relation to the role of the director, their sense of how to deal with the multiplicity of meanings that a Shakespearean text might be said to elicit, and their ideas about the appropriateness of certain standard strategies of character development (such as the 'through line') to Shakespeare. I enquired, too, about their awareness of any underlying assumptions concerning Shakespearean 'meaning' and how to bring it out, and I asked them to articulate their views of the overall concept (if any) guiding the shows they took part in, their understanding of the ideological assumptions of the text in its historical context, their feelings about venue and audience expectation, and their general understanding of Shakespeare as a cultural phenomenon. I did not, however, administer a questionnaire or move through the questions in the same way with every interview. Instead, I followed what seemed like the natural bent of the conversation in the hopes of uncovering bits of subtext which, as in the Stanislavskian approach to character, might lead me to interesting insights. I make no claims, therefore, to the putative accuracy of social science. Rather, what I adduce as evidence is partial and anecdotal. For all that, however, my findings may be considered roughly representative and, I think, can open up questions about theatre training and Shakespeare that go well beyond the confines of one department at one university.

The best way into an analysis of the sort I want to carry out is to think about *character* and the utterly pervasive force that the term and the concept have today in actors' training and work.[5] It stands as an unquestioned truth that what the actor does is create character. Recent cultural and literary theory, on the other hand, has not made much room for character. It tends to see subjectivity as troubled and riddled, regarding the notion of the interiorized self as suspect – a construct deployed within a given cultural regime as a means of maintaining and/or mystifying certain structures of power. If actors tend to view the Shakespearean text as the basis for an investigation of character, materialist critics tend to see that same text as ideologically invested in, and complicit with, the very idea of selfhood as we now understand it. They consider it naive to harbour a notion of self as something independent of discourse, as stable and real. For actors in training, on the other hand, such a destabilized view of selfhood would seem to cut against the fundamentals of what they see as their art.

That the approach to character and text taken by the young actors I spoke with *is* representative might be illustrated by some comments of Michael Mawson, appointed principal of the Stratford Ontario Festival Conservatory for Classical Theatre Training in 1999: his aim in training his actors is, he says, to 'investigate the ingredients that lie behind the text' (qtd. in Cushman, 'Shakespeare'). While not fully accepting the method idea of subtext, Mawson believes, according to Robert Cushman, that an actor has to 'be a particular character with a particular story to arrive at those lines, and it is this level of subtext – what he defines as "why you are saying this" – that Mawson finds essential' ('Shakespeare'). This is getting close to what I see as a Canadian/eclectic way of seeing the relation between text and character, and I want to investigate that line of thinking further in what follows.

One of the most common assumptions about approaching a role made by the young actors with whom I spoke is that their characters are on a 'journey.' This is a metaphor that kept coming up over and over, and one that is familiar to almost anyone who has worked in the theatre. It remains a paramount assumption and has close links to important transhistorical humanistic values. In a recent interview, noted Irish actor Stephen Rea had this to say about his role in *The Crying Game*: 'The emotional journey in *The Crying Game* is that Fergus realizes that you can love anyone ... by the end of the movie he knows, and we all feel it, that you can love anyone – race, gender, nationality are all meaningless' ('Irish'). It would be hard to find a materialist critic who would agree with that last statement. And yet such views not only have currency in today's theatres, they need, I believe, to be taken seriously.

Like Rea, my young actor-interviewees think it is both possible and desirable to find a series of moves that, taken together, form a more or less archetypal pattern, one that tells a recognizable and applicable story. Related to this is a deep-seated understanding of character as stable and coherent, of identity as something complex but ultimately unitary and knowable. This is the (unstated) theory with which actors are typically taught to work, and it goes with another key assumption – that the 'text' is the 'source.' The text holds the secret of the journey, the traces of the figure that the actor seeks to *find* or *build*, to cite two common, though significantly different, metaphors. Actors invoke the text in their efforts to see their characters as moving from one place to another. They look for the 'arc' or 'through-line' that will provide coherence and stability. But the differences between *finding* and *building* a character point to a question about this coherence: is what is sought (the essence of the character) already there and, hence, simply to be discovered, or does it have to be constructed out of clues and potentially contradictory traces?

Out of this dilemma (does one find or build?) arises a conflict between opposing conceptions of character and meaning – unitary and relatively stable versus multilevelled and radically destabilized. The actor who played Hamlet at UBC spoke of 'tunnelling' in a single direction, recognizing that this meant cutting out a lot but insisting at the same time on the need to be 'specific' (another influential term in acting theory today). He seemed to conceive of 'specific' and 'multilevelled' as opposites. Playing a specific motivation meant playing one thing hard, and, in the words of the UBC Romeo, finding the 'impulse-reality' underneath it. Specificity comes from the text and is a result of 'Stanislavsky motivation meet[ing] Shakespearean expression' (in the formulation of 'Romeo'). From such views, we may derive the following principles (among others): the textual meanings may be, and often are, multilevelled, even contradictory; the specific motivation or meaning must be sought in the text and played, even if this means reducing or eliminating the acknowledged multiplicity; the specific must at the same time be typical enough to be recognized as widely applicable, even universal; hence, the text may be said to contain this universal meaning, despite the fact that contradictory or opposite meanings may equally be derived from the same text.

Let me try to make this more precise, if also more paradoxical, by means of an example. I want to reproduce part of the conversation I had with the actors who played Juliet and Romeo, among the most thoughtful of the young actors I spoke to. 'Romeo' in particular was able to articulate what both saw as the relations among text, subtext, and universal or transhistorical meaning. I asked him and 'Juliet' about how they might deal with the problem for a modern audience of responding to true love that is couched in such highly ornate language (we had been talking about the lovers' first meeting and their shared sonnet, with its self-consciously witty word-play and love rhetoric). Here is Romeo's answer:

Because the impulses and the emotions are so timeless, and one of the things that makes ... Shakespeare ... work on such a gut level is [that] as long as you, the actor, understand the impulse first and foremost and can translate it in a way that the audience can understand – the impulse that is finding expression in this language, the basic impulse ... [then the audience will get it]. It's almost like we could act that scene non-verbally of Romeo's advance –

AD. But it would be very different, wouldn't it?

Romeo. It would be different, but I think you can find an impulse-reality underneath it, where you could write exactly the same scene in contemporary language or non-verbally – it's just that the impulse in that particular style finds expression that way and ... it's tough to codify it ... but with the purity of that impulse, you can make an audience buy that language ... when they see it coming almost as a tactic involved with the impulse ...

AD. A tactic on the playwright's part?

Romeo. On the part of the characters – you see the characters using that language to accomplish their objectives ['Juliet' in the background: 'Yeah.'] ... I love you, I am wooing you, and this is the technique that I employ to do it ['Juliet': 'This is the way that I do it.'], which is not the technique that we employ now, but if I can see the same impulse that is underneath ... [General discussion of how training encourages them to ask ...] especially with something like Shakespeare, why does your character use that language that way, not what was the playwright doing, but what – it's like Stanislavsky meets that 'elocution' ... Stanislavsky motivation meets Shakespearean expression ... I have to tie this particular beautiful poetry ... into a psychological motivation ... you know, that inner life of the character, so that ... [references here to John Barton's *Playing Shakespeare*] you bring to the language a feeling that you're coining it ... it sounds more like it comes from the impulse, because I am trying so hard to convey this emotion to you, this feeling to you and –

Juliet. These are the words that I choose to use at that time –

This sometimes eloquent struggle to articulate the relations among language, feeling, and character no doubt sounds familiar, at least to theatre practitioners. And that is one reason I am citing it. Its familiarity can obscure its potential interest as a sign of the cultural weight that ideas about selfhood carry and how the theatre works to produce, and reproduce, them. In this discussion, what is most in evidence is that certain emotions are timeless, that the inner life of the character is what the actor seeks to project, that this inner life expresses itself through 'objectives,' and that the text is both the *source* and the *product* of these objectives. At the same time, paradoxically, the actual words of the text are not strictly necessary to a transmission or communication of what the actor has come to understand from his/her study of the text. The understanding exists independently of the words. Thus, the text is both indispensable and, at the same time, oddly redundant. When the text is referred to over and over again as the source, one sometimes forgets to ask, what is it the source of? The above dialogue would suggest that many Canadian student actors are trained to see it as the source mainly of the subtext (in Mawson's terms, 'why you are saying this' [qtd. in Cushman, 'Shakespeare']), or what 'Romeo' refers to as the 'impulse-reality.' The actor's job is to bring that 'reality' to the surface; in that way the audience can be made to 'buy' the language – that is, accept it as credible. What we are left with, then, is a notion of subtext as universal, text as historically and culturally determined, with the result that the differences between Shakespeare's culture and our own are elided in favour of an underlying identity of impulses.

While there seems here to be a contradiction between theory and practice (that is, an awareness of the local in theory and appeal to the universal as a basis for practice), we would be wrong, I believe, to adopt the view that such ways of thinking are entirely confused, still less a deliberate obfuscation. I would argue, on the contrary, that it is worth taking the transhistorical assumptions seriously. After all, passion has hardly disappeared from modern life (despite the neo-puritanism of a certain brand of materialist critique). Most of us can recognize and empathize with the heat of Romeo and Juliet's passionate and precisely modulated exchange. It is important not to get caught up in an overly rigid binary – transhistorical is not the same thing as ahistorical. Persons existed in 1600 as they do now. Historically speaking, notions of interiorized personhood were an important aspect of what made the Elizabethan theatre effective with audiences.[6] It is important, therefore, to see the sometimes inchoate attempts to formulate ideas about interiorized character as part of a long tradition going back to Burbage and running through David Garrick, Henry Irving, and John Gielgud to the present at Stratford or Niagara-on-the-Lake.[7] Appeals to naturalness and truth to life have been a major criterion in Western acting at least since the Renaissance. This does not erase the local or historically specific. In the case of *Romeo and Juliet*, the poetry is part of that specificity, and it raises the temperature rather than casting a chill. But there, of course, is the rub. The language does make a difference; it has historical and local meanings that should not be overlooked.

This raises a general difficulty. Theatre training seems to be flying in the face of what historicist and materialist theory has been at pains to impress upon us over the last generation: that meanings are constructed and contingent; that notions of selfhood, and even feelings, have a history; and that the desire to 'speak with the dead,' however well motivated, is bound to be frustrated. Materialist theory has been famously distrustful of idealist and essentialist conceptions of selfhood, seeing them, and the transhistorical meanings they carry, as mystifications that obscure the differences between one historical period and another and naturalize the power relations of bourgeois culture. Ideas about universal truths or unchanging human nature are viewed with suspicion, as are the texts that have been used to support claims about such truths. Shakespeare's performance-texts are now typically read in terms of the cultural work they are said to have done in the past and are doing in the present.[8] Thus, theatrical reproduction is understood, as it is by W.B. Worthen, for example, as a crucial site where the questionable (because complicit) 'authority' of Shakespeare is disseminated in contemporary culture.

Actors, on the other hand, whether Stephen Rea, the students I spoke with at UBC, or Royal Shakespeare Company (RSC) veterans speaking from the pages of such books as Carol Rutter's *Clamorous Voices* or the *Players of Shakespeare* series, usually seem uninterested in the potentially contradictory ideological situation of the work they do. They remain either unaware of, or resistant to, the idea put about by some cultural analysts, that their reproductions of Shakespeare support a particular deployment of power relations, one that they would no doubt deplore if they were conscious of their complicity. (They are, of course, interested in the effects of their work, in *production*, we might say, if not *reproduction*.) Indeed, theatre practitioners are often committed to a subversive or oppositional account of what they do: the women in *Clamorous Voices*, for example, frequently describe their feminist interpretations, performed sometimes in spite of directorial objection or even tyranny. In doing so, however, they just as frequently locate their oppositional stance *in the text* – that is, they ground it in textual (Shakespearean) authority. For them, Shakespeare can be liberating, and their appeal to his work is often couched in broadly humanist terms (such, too, is the case with directors like Peter Brook, Ariane Mnouchkine, and scores of theatre practitioners working in, and against, totalitarian regimes).[9] From a materialist standpoint, such humanistic appeals are theoretically naive – they fail to take into account the power relations that such reproductions of 'Shakespeare' support. From an actor's point of view, on the other hand, a materialist analysis might be regarded as not only wrong but useless – it could even tend to undermine her practice altogether. She might, for example, develop an understanding of Isabella (in *Measure for Measure*) in contemporary 'feminist' terms chiefly because it can ground a pragmatic approach to bringing off a strong *personal* effect (in both senses: the impact of the character as person, and the personal stake of the actor). In other words, talk about Shakespeare as a repository of liberal (the word, let us remember, derives from the Latin for *free*) humanist values can be a way both to build the individuality of one's character and to take a politically progressive position. Moreover, to do so is to participate in a tradition, one that has played a major role in places as diverse as Soviet-dominated eastern Europe, India, or South Africa.

One can grant, of course, that Shakespeare's cultural authority, as understood by astute critics like Worthen, is not always progressive and is disseminated through the theatre. I am interested, however, in the ironic disjunction between how theatre practitioners frequently describe their work and how that work is read by what Harry Berger calls 'slit-eyed analysts' (*Imaginary* xiv).[10] One of my purposes is to open up a dialogue between what might seem to be incompatible positions, or at least to maintain the different views in dialectical tension.

While materialist critics are committed to seeing the Shakespearean text historically, the modern-day producer generally is not – or at least not in the same way. Actors and directors want to speak to today's audiences, and this hope typically leads to looking for what is common between 'Shakespeare' and ourselves, rather than to an emphasis on the historically and culturally specific. This is not to say that actors and directors eschew historical 'research.' They often spend time and energy sifting through historical accounts for ways of bringing the past to the present. But their interest is in reducing, or even erasing, the differences between past and present, whereas historicist criticism, especially that influenced by Foucault et al. is committed to underlining those differences, even to the extent of declaring an absolute incommensurability between then and now.

How does the producer go about 'gaining Shakespeare's effects,' to use Granville-Barker's phrase?[11] Are these effects always the same? Is it possible to seek in the text for those elements that one might assume to have affected Elizabethan audiences, and transfer them into modern terms without disturbing their essential nature? If it is possible, is it desirable? Peter Brook emphasizes the problem of 'serving the author.' For him, that is the hardest job of all: 'If what you want is for the play to be heard, then you must conjure its sound from it' (43). There is clearly a possibility of contradiction here, of which Brook seems aware – the text in its historical context is silent; it must be played like an instrument in order to make it harmonious to modern ears. The potential falsification is balanced by an appeal to universal, or at least transhistorical, values – the hope is that a music will emerge that is equivalent to, though not identical with, what was heard originally. It would be easy enough to criticize such an attitude as a mystification,[12] but I want for the moment to give it full credence. The notion of universal applicability is widely current in today's theatre, despite the incursions of postmodernism – not only in training programs, as my discussion with the student actors reveals, but in playbills, director's notes, grant applications, and just about every other form of para-theatrical activity, as well as in the thrust of most Shakespeare productions.[13]

One way of viewing these universalist assumptions is to regard them as a sign of a mostly submerged theory about human behaviour and psychology, one that can support, if only in an inchoate or unarticulated way, a certain kind of practice. While such theory is not directly confronted, it is still of course there and plays its part. I would suggest that the double demand of Shakespearean production, to be 'true' to the text and to speak forcefully to one's audience, can be most easily accommodated by a resort to a universalism that sees transhistorical truths in the historicized text and regards the human journey as the basis of the theatre's affective power. Paradoxically, however, the most powerful effects can often arise out of the particular and local. This suggests a need to extend and articulate the theory, to ask why an appeal to broadly 'human' values should be necessary at all. One answer takes us around to Worthen's position: that Shakespeare's cultural authority confers value on one's practice. Another might be to link the local and transhistorical in a dialectical way – that is, to see the particular as compatible with, as well as antithetical to, the 'universal.' The universal, in such a formulation, should not be seen as obliterating all difference but as defining a kind of encounter; this does not mean giving up on the concept of humanity, but seeing it in terms of a dialectical relationship between local and international, particular and general, historically specific and transhistorical/traditional.[14]

Earlier, I discussed the way that the text functions in relation to actorly objectives and subtext. At UBC, and elsewhere in Canada, the text has another, paradoxical life as a product of specific historical practices – in other words, it is conceived in terms quite strikingly different from the way it is deployed to find or build character. Neil Freeman, the director of the UBC *Romeo and Juliet*, leans heavily on the early texts, especially the First Folio, for his work with actors, inducing them to examine the material facts of the printed text for breathing patterns and interpretive clues that supposedly mirror the acting techniques and ways with rhetoric adopted by members of Shakespeare's original company. He bases his strategy on a number of assertions about the differences between the 'ancient' (that is, early modern) and 'modern' (edited) texts; for example, the latter are 'based on grammar' while neither the 'hand-written texts ... nor the Quartos and Folios, were based on grammar but on rhetoric.' Freeman defines *rhetoric* as 'a verbal form of arranging logic and argument in a pleasing and entertaining fashion so as to win ... debates' (i). He claims that 'grammar was not yet a science' and that, when in the eighteenth century the texts were re-edited, 'rhetoric was (inadvertently) removed from the plays simply by repunctuating the texts' according to newly invented 'grammatical knowledge' (i). Despite the historical doubtfulness of these claims, Freeman has gained prominence as an acting teacher, workshop leader, and expert on Shakespeare's text. His views of the text are, in fact, influencing a whole generation of Canadian actors.[15] The very concreteness of his approach is part of its appeal – a colon means X, a capital letter means Y – especially to actors who are looking for something 'specific' to hold on to.[16] And the appeal of his method is enhanced by the apparently scholarly attention to the Folio; it *looks* like bibliographical learning and hence confers a certain cachet.[17]

If actors approach this historicized text in order to find their characters, they have to perform a double operation: first, notice the text's historical difference and, second, assume, as an authenticating sign of that difference, that a certain transhistorical sameness is inherent in it. Only the true historical text yields the human truth: 'The old texts, thanks to their rhetorical theatrical base, provide the essential elements of living, breathing, reacting humanity' (Freeman ii).[18] Or again: 'Thanks to their rhetorical base, the sentence structure of the first scripts clearly illustrates the stepping-stones of the human argument and self-discovery. And because of their lack of grammar, at those incredible moments when the theatrical human condition becomes irrational, unlike the modern texts trapped in their grammatical necessity, the early theatrical scripts demonstrate irrational sentence and punctuation structures'[19] (ii). These passages evince a paradigmatic form of the contradiction between the assertion of the historically and culturally specific and the assumption of essential, universal, human 'truth.' If the universal truth is 'in' the text, how could it be obscured by the mere contingencies marked by historical changes in conventions of punctuation? While the historical claims may be there mainly to bolster what is really a simple strategy, to get actors to look for eternal verities in the text,[20] it might be more fruitful to see them as an attempt to register historical difference without giving up the appeal to common humanity. The difficulty of linking Shakespeare's effects (local, particular, culturally circumscribed) to modern meanings is, once again, in evidence, this time in a textual version.

While it is true that there are unexamined theoretical problems associated with Freeman's practice, and these problems are analogous to some of the contradictions sketched earlier in relation to the construction and playing of character, at the same time it is also true that his position is consistent with a long tradition of locating power in Shakespeare's text. It is clear that Freeman wants to historicize the text in some ways, by insisting on its difference from modern texts. So the UBC students whom I interviewed, like many students since, were being taught at one level to historicize, but the goal, nevertheless, was/is to bridge the gap between past and present. Historical difference is produced in order to be elided. That is, the very act of historicization is part of a strategy to deny its necessity, to replace it with a universalist construct; but, also present, by implication anyway, is an awareness of the power of the local and particular, its 'truth.' This links to a contradictory attitude towards the relations between the early texts and the production of meaning. In my discussion with Freeman, he spoke of the 'human journey' implicit in Shakespeare's plays and characters. His view is archetypal and Jungian in some ways. He also told me that he does not regard the text as a 'stable object,' although one would not gather that from his writing; the text, he suggests, 'only works when it is spoken in this space, by this actor' (Interview). One can infer, then, that the text is a construct, and it is something radically indeterminate. This seems to rest uneasily with what he has said elsewhere. The students, for their part, have derived from their training the view that the early texts are stable and fixed, yielding emotional truths. They regard the historical *materiality* of the printed text, as described in Freeman's *Introduction to the Folio Scripts*, as foundational, even though the words (Romeo and Juliet's sonnet, for example) need to be anchored in essential human truth for a modern audience to 'buy' them. There would seem to be room here, then, for the kind of dialectical 'encounter' mentioned earlier between local and universal, one that we in Canada might be especially well placed to facilitate. It would require awareness of the constructed and indeterminate nature of texts like the Folio, rather than a fetishization of them, together with a painstaking sense of how the 'universal' may indeed be produced through such a local encounter.

While the actors search for the through-line or human journey for their characters, they also bring to bear another principle, one that emerged in several of the actors' comments and in my talk with Freeman. That is the idea that the 'quality' of a particular scene, rather than a strictly conceived sense of character, will determine the acting of it. Character is both primary and subordinate, both deeply embedded in the text and constructed out of frankly interpretive strategies. In my discussion with 'Romeo,' he spoke not only of the importance of Stanislavskian motivation, designed to give the poetry specificity and thus prevent it from being mere recitation, but also of a different possibility – of letting the language work on him, 'knock' him around. He quoted Freeman's dictum: 'If you just play objectives, you'll flatten the language.' This cuts against the American Method's appropriation of Stanislavsky and seems to derive more from British style and approach. It spells out a notion of the language as doing other things besides conveying impulses or revealing subtext. But as far as I could see, the two views stand in uneasy and untheorized relation with each other (is this, perhaps, typically Canadian?!).

Whether we are talking of text or character, then, we are confronted with a pervasive split between stability and indeterminacy. The deeply held belief that character is unitary, knowable, and stable is set in opposition to the awkward sense that 'character' is unpredictable, unknowable, perhaps even illusory. So, too, at the level of the text, 'what Shakespeare wrote' is viewed as a source of eternal truths while also being regarded as a construct. Some of the students were aware of the possible contradictions implied by this doubleness as it applies to character, but much less so in relation to the given text. They did not see the early texts as themselves problematic, as constructed or intersected by patterns of authority and authorship. If they were taught this, they would be in a better position to ground their sense of the universal in the historically specific.

As I suggested earlier, the co-existence of what seem like contradictions, or untheorized dichotomies, may be explained in terms of the dominance of the idea of practice in theatrical work. One inescapable thing about theatrical production is its pragmatism, its need to make do with what is available. This is the very thing that produces the anti-intellectualism one so frequently encounters in the theatre – its impatience with theory and prevailing distrust of anything that does not obviously 'work.' It is this that makes critics like Harry Berger reciprocally impatient.

Berger has developed a theory of how Shakespeare favours reading over play-going, text over performance ('Text'). For Berger, performance is limited by its concern with isolated characters and their stories, embodied by the charismatic presence of the actual actor. Presence, he claims, highlights the 'world' of the play over what he calls the 'community,' but what materialist critics might call the cultural discourses that inform the text (*Imaginary* 152). The latter are, for Berger, more accessible to reading because reading allows for an erasure of the boundaries erected by actorly presence and insistence on character. In this view, character becomes the crucial stumbling block to an understanding of the ideological and cultural forces at work in a given play. As a corollary, Berger might conclude, although he does not draw his argument in this direction, actors work on the text, just like critics, but, if they direct their interest solely or primarily towards character, then they cannot provide us with complex and contradictory meanings, only with charisma. Berger, like many materialist critics, wants to downplay the pleasures associated with recognition of, or identification with, character in order to highlight complexity of meaning – hermeneutic suspicion extends (and this comes as no surprise) even to enjoyment. His view is Brechtian in some ways – he sees audience identification with actor/character as detrimental to wider understanding. Recent performance critics (for example, Barbara Hodgdon, Susan Bennett, Ric Knowles) have taken a parallel, though somewhat different line; emphasizing reproduction over production, they have sought to fold the emotional effects of theatre, the ways in which it moves audiences, into their analyses, showing the ideological dimensions of even the most immediate experiences inside theatres. A brilliant reading, such as Hodgdon's unravelling of the multifarious implications of twentieth-century *Shrew*s, may nevertheless refuse the very effects the actors, and perhaps the text (at least the text as it is interpreted in and through the performance), seem to be seeking,[21] just as materialist hermeneutics frequently refuses to take at face value what would seem to be the text's manifest aim.

While it is true that theatrical pleasure, frequently tied to character and subjectivity, is itself ideologically fraught, and true also that Shakespeare's authority is far from absolute, to assent to the affective power of Shakespearean characters, even at times their liberatory power,[22] is hardly a bad thing. Indeed, it seems to me a necessary thing. In other words, maybe theatre people, despite their hermeneutic naiveté, are on to something. After all, they have a long ethical history to back them up, and they have developed a set of practices that, in many times and places, has been aimed against oppression. While Berger is no doubt right to insist that there are other meanings around besides those invoked by a certain style of performance, and indeed other pleasures too, it seems to me crucial to attend to the ethical tradition of acting, rooted as it is in what some would dismiss as essentialist notions of character and selfhood.

Hence I do not see any value in abandoning the search for conveying meaningful and interesting *persons* to an audience, at least not in regard to the production of Shakespeare – for him, the person is a key element of theatrical pleasure.[23] Nevertheless, training actors to recognize contingency, to understand textual and psychological indeterminacy as a way of encountering some of the fixed strategies of Stanislavskian methodology, could open them up to new ways of approaching character, new meanings, new pleasures. It should be possible to develop a multifaceted kind of production, built on both a more complex actorly awareness of cultural positioning and a more precisely historicized conception of text and personhood, one that nevertheless can deliver a sense of rooted universality. Directorial 'concept' frequently aims at bridging the historical gap, perhaps by linking strategies of mystification in our own world to analogous strategies in the cultural and historical world from which the text emerged. But this, too, can lead to contradiction and even, it may be argued, ethical failure.

The UBC *Hamlet* provides an interesting example. Directed by Gordon McCall, a maverick Canadian director with an experimental and iconoclastic bent, the production was designed to be, in McCall's words, 'hammer and chisel' Shakespeare. The concept, insofar as the students could explain it (some of them confessed to never quite getting it), derived from ideas about the Ceaucescu regime in Romania and generally emphasized the inescapability of power, its pervasiveness and corruption. The idea was to fragment the text, using electronic multiplication and distortion – the 'To be or not to be' speech was delivered via a bank of flickering TV sets in which the image of the speaker was shifted and recombined in multiple ways.[24] Power was utterly oppressive, and Big Brother had the advantage of the video camera and the cellular phone.

The concept was not really that original, but I raise it here in order to highlight the difficulties of the isolated deconstructive gesture. I asked the students involved with this production two questions about their relations to their roles and to the director, and I got the same answers from all of them. First, there was no attempt to change the style of acting or the strategies for 'finding' the character in the text, although some such change might reasonably be expected to go along with the subversive thrust of the concept. In other words, the students were expected, more or less on their own since the technical aspects of the production took up so much of the director's time and energy, to find their characters' through-lines, 'arcs,' or 'journeys' in the traditional ways. There was no attempt to find an alternative style of playing that might match the iconoclasm of the production – a Brechtian approach, perhaps, where the traps of traditional actorly representation might have been exposed and linked to the other power traps the production sought so overtly to underscore. Second, the deconstruction of power relations that the production worked to achieve did not extend to the actual structure of authority as it was manifested during the rehearsal process. That is, the director exercised his power in traditional ways, so that he ended up reproducing the very structure in his relation to the actors that his production was designed to critique in the society at large.

In general in this production, the actors' work was subordinate to the overall concept, so that specific textual analysis was much less prominent in rehearsal than in *Romeo and Juliet*. Most of the actors expressed disappointment with this, which is not surprising given their training with Freeman. In the event, they fell back on what they had learned elsewhere (several of them spoke of being trained to be 'director proof') and tried to 'build' a character on their own. Naturally, they relied on the 'text' as the 'source,' but the obviously constructed nature of the 'text' for this production confused them. When the actor playing Hamlet brought a copy of the Folio text to rehearsal, McCall's response (as the actor reported it) was both dismissive and, in the context of UBC, amusingly refreshing: 'Throw that shit away!'

Without adopting quite such an extreme position, we might want at least to pause over the advantages of not obviously flushing away the text, whether early or modern, but of aiming some suitably deconstructive arrows at its authority – thereby recognizing its nature as a construction, and hence not originary in any absolute way. This is a well-established practice in textual theory and bibliography these days, and some of the work being done in that field might be usefully transferred to theatrical training. We might want also to question the absolute primacy of character in training actors, and the reliance of character on subtext. When an actor speaks of 'building' a character, we could take the metaphor seriously and represent that process as a self-conscious one, a process of construction that does not seek to convey absolute 'human truth' but a certain perspective possible at a given time and place (also, I would emphasize, a type of 'human truth'). So, too, we could try to develop in young actors a sense of their positioning as subjects, and hence produce the possibility of their placing themselves, as interpreters, in a self-aware position. If we were to do this kind of work, theatre training might more closely resemble literary training in the ways that it would highlight the cultural situating of the interpreter. But, at the same time, we need to pay attention to the ethical tradition associated with character and the kind of universalism supported by that tradition. While the Canadian context is not the only one where such a dialectical approach might be grounded, it seems a suitable one – not least because of our placement between two historical empires, our immigrant alertness to the interplay between local and international, and our particular brand of liberal-democratic culture. Certainly, let me end by insisting, it would be folly to give up on the representation of recognizable persons by living, present actors, a strategy that can make the Shakespearean theatre not only pleasurable and illuminating but politically engaged and, I would argue, *liberal*, in the fullest sense.

Notes

1 In Hansgunther Heyme's startling production of *Hamlet* in Cologne in 1979, for example, everything was mediated electronically via a video camera and an array of monitors, while the main character was split in two: an actor wan-

dering fitfully around the stage almost speechless, and the director in the auditorium declaiming the Schlegel translation over the sound system (see Hortmann 275–9); Alexandru Tocilescu's production of 1989 in Bucharest (which played in London in 1990) provides another example: it stressed terror and interrogation (Stříbrný 134–5).

2 I would like to thank all the actors, technical staff, and directors who shared their thoughts with me, especially Kerry Davidson, Neil Freeman, Mara Gottler, Barry Levy, Mike O'Donnell, Laara Sadiq, Tom Scholte, Troy Skog, Lisa Waines, and Edel Walsh. Thanks, too, to Peter Loeffler for helping with the organization of the interviews.

3 There are, of course, alternative approaches to training actors; the most influential are those that favour the body first and foremost, as practised by people such as Judith Koltai and, in Quebec, Jacques Lessard (the situation in francophone Canada is very different and outside my purview). For accounts of their work, see Koltai and Beauchamp. However, my focus here is on what for better or worse might be called the 'mainstream.'

4 The original version of this chapter was written for a Shakespeare Association seminar. Since my views have changed somewhat, the present version offers an altered argument and quite a different focus from the original, but much of what I said then is still relevant today. Though the paper remained unpublished, it circulated as part of a thought-provoking conversation that has led to some stimulating analysis. Richard Knowles and W.B. Worthen, among others, have expanded the investigation into actor training with their analyses of the ideological content of voice work (Knowles, 'Shakespeare, Voice') and character formation (Worthen, *Shakespeare* 99–125).

5 This is a point developed at greater length by Worthen (*Shakespeare* 99–125), who cites the original version of this chapter.

6 For the best and fullest discussion of interiority in the period, see Maus; see also Dawson and Yachnin for opposing analyses of the role and construction of personhood on the early modern stage. In the first chapter of that book, I cite, among others, Nashe's description of the powerful effect of the actor bringing the character of Talbot to life (the spectators, 'in the tragedian that represents [Talbot's] person, imagine they behold him fresh bleeding' [14–15]), and discuss the well-known account of a young actor moving his audience with his depiction of Desdemona (19–20).

7 Garrick, for example, was always praised for his naturalness; he said of the great actor that he 'will always realize the feelings of his character and be transported beyond himself' (qtd. in Donohue 220).

8 See, for example, Knowles, 'Shakespeare, 1993,' and Hodgdon, 'Katherina' and 'Looking.'

9 I have developed this point at more length in an essay on 'international Shakespeare' to appear in the forthcoming *Cambridge Companion to Shakespeare on Stage*, edited by Stanley Wells and Sarah Stanton.
10 Berger is caricaturing how performance critics view their more suspicious colleagues.
11 'Gain Shakespeare's effects by Shakespeare's means when you can ... But gain Shakespeare's effects; and it is your business to discern them' (xl).
12 As Richard Knowles does; see 'Shakespeare, Voice' 95–6.
13 I speak here chiefly of mainstream theatre, and its university-based cousins; but even avant-garde productions of Shakespeare often rely on such general appeals.
14 Aleida Assmann (98–100) develops this idea of a redefined universalism, using Hofmannsthal's metaphor of erotic 'encounter' in which separateness is allowed full weight (as opposed to 'embrace' which collapses difference into unity).
15 Formerly at York University in Toronto, Freeman has been at the University of British Columbia for over ten years; he has given workshops all over Canada, and his views and methods have become widely disseminated and practised.
16 W.B. Worthen neatly demonstrates the reversibility of Freeman's 'evidence' and hence brings out the arbitrariness of the meanings Freeman adduces, despite the claims to Shakespearean authenticity (*Shakespeare* 124).
17 However, textual scholars have wholeheartedly rejected the kinds of claims he makes, since they stress the complexity of the transmission process that his approach, for the most part, leaves out of consideration.
18 It is not clear from this why 'rhetoric' is seen as more 'human' than grammar; both are, after all, human constructs.
19 One has to ask here what exactly 'irrational' sentence (or punctuation) structure is (and is 'sentence structure' itself not a grammatical term?); 'irrational' according to what criteria? Are the implicit criteria for determining irrationality not developed from eighteenth-century rationalism and the theories of grammar that flowed from it?
20 My guess is that, if and when this works, it does so because of the unfamiliarity of the text being looked at and the consequent need for actors to attend more closely to the words on the page than they are used to doing with 'modern' texts.
21 I am thinking here of the Fairbanks/Pickford and Burton/Taylor movies and the gaps between what they apparently thought they were doing and what Hodgdon shows them to be doing.
22 The history of production of *Hamlet* in Russia and the Soviet Union is a case

in point. See Dawson, *Hamlet* 184–9, 234–8, and Stříbrný 26–8, 44–9, 83–5, and passim.
23 See chapter 1, 'Performance and Participation,' in Dawson and Yachnin for a full discussion of the importance of the person for Elizabethan acting and performance.
24 Compare the Heyme production mentioned in n.1.

11

Canadian Bacon

PAUL YACHNIN and BRENT E. WHITTED

In his authoritative discussion of the Shakespeare authorship controversy from its inception in 1856 to 1991, the American scholar Samuel Schoenbaum touches on the activities of anti-Stratfordians in the United States, England, France, Germany, Italy, Holland, and India; he mentions not a single Canadian (385–451). We have found many of them, on both – or all three sides – of the question: adherents of Francis Bacon, Shakespeare, and, more recently, Edward de Vere, Earl of Oxford. The controversy in Canada is well over a hundred years old and is still going strong today.[1] We will discuss two turn-of-the-century Baconians, Richard Bucke and Samuel Baylis, and we will glance briefly at the more recent activity of a small but productive group of amateur scholars devoted to Oxford's cause, especially Elizabeth Appleton of Toronto and Nina Green of Kelowna, British Columbia. Their work reaches a mostly self-selected readership, but their scepticism about Shakespeare's authorship of the plays chimes with a broader feeling of doubt about the Bard, which seems to be in the air everywhere one goes. All professional Shakespeareans will have heard this familiar question on numerous occasions from their students as well as from interlocutors encountered casually on airplanes and elsewhere – did the man named Shakespeare *really* write the plays?[2]

In this chapter, we will delineate the Canadian history that constitutes the background to this question, not to mention the fact that the story of the Canadian authorship controversy adds a previously unnoticed historical dimension to recent works of fiction and drama like Leon Rooke's *Shakespeare's Dog* and Ann-Marie MacDonald's *Goodnight Desdemona (Good Morning Juliet)*, both of which share a strong interest in questions about artistic agency and the relationship between art and social power. Overall, we are going to tell something about a story that has not yet been told. Moreover, as we will suggest, the general character of the material we are studying seems to bear on the character of the nation, especially insofar as 'Canadian Bacon' tends to be milder and somewhat more ironic than other kinds.

The most important early figure in the authorship controversy was the American Delia Bacon (1811–59; no relation to Sir Francis).[3] The daughter of a failed pioneer and missionary, educated at Catherine Beecher's school in Hartford, Connecticut, she went on to become a writer of both fiction and anti-Shakespearean polemic and to attract the sympathy and support of a number of eminent men of letters – notably, Ralph Waldo Emerson, whom she converted to anti-Stratfordianism, and Nathaniel Hawthorne, who paid for the publication of her 675-page book, *The Philosophy of the Plays of Shakspere* [sic] *Unfolded* (1857), which followed her 1856 essay on the topic in *Putnam's Monthly*. She was passionate almost to madness against Shakespeare. Driven by the belief that she had discovered the previously undetected 'true' meaning of the plays, she declared that the drama contained a hidden political and philosophical wisdom that could have issued only from an aristocratic mind. And animated by a snobbism unwarranted by her own social background, not to mention her citizenship in a great democracy and trading nation, she railed against Shakespeare's low birth, village education, and degrading work in the commercial theatre: 'this old showman and hawker of plays ... this old lackey' ('William' 9); 'a stupid, ignorant, illiterate, third-rate play-actor' (19).

In the period leading up to the publication of her attacks on Shakespeare, Bacon created a small sensation on the American lecture stage, and then, in 1853, she sailed to England, with a letter of introduction from Emerson to Thomas Carlyle. While amused by her, Carlyle in turn offered to recommend her to the librarian at the British Museum; however, she preferred the life of her imagination to the rigours of the archive. Like Constance Ledbelly, the protagonist of *Goodnight Desdemona*, she was drawn to the gravesite of her ghostly father – to Bacon's sepulchre in St Alban's and subsequently to Holy Trinity Church in Stratford where she spent part of a night trying to hoist Shakespeare's gravestone. This terrible comedy in the Stratford church was of a piece with her mission to unearth the proof of Bacon's authorship of Shakespeare's drama – the trove of documentary evidence that she believed lay buried with the bones of the 'old showman and hawker of plays.'

Her career established a pattern for the many anti-Stratfordians who followed her, an example in which perhaps five main characteristics can be identified. First is the conviction that the text contains a veiled global meaning, complete with indicators about the identity of the author – a level of meaning intended to remain secret until brought to light by a brilliant and original interpretive intelligence. Many of her followers, of course, developed this intuition about the 'true' meaning of Shakespeare into a dizzying range of cryptographic analyses of the First Folio (and other contemporary works), which deploy complex and unsound mathematical models in order to demonstrate that the plays were not composed by Shakespeare. Second is the voluble contempt for Shakespeare himself, especially for his 'baseness' and commercialism. Third is the powerful model of the quest, which ruled many who followed in Delia Bacon's footsteps to Stratford, and which is charged with the desire for buried treasure (usually supposed to be Bacon's manuscripts). Connected to this is the appeal of the sacred place where the sacred hoard is to be unearthed. Indeed, a number of Americans who came after her also travelled to England and sought to excavate a variety of English sites in their quest for documentary evidence (see Schoenbaum 413–19). A number became unbalanced or came to realize a pre-existing imbalance. Fourth is the apparent compulsion to write at great length against Shakespeare's authorship. Delia Bacon's book is just under 700 pages; later books are even longer: *The Great Cryptogram*, by the American politician and visionary Ignatius Donnelly, runs to 998 pages in two weighty volumes. The final, and overarching, characteristic is the sense of election and mission that animated everything Delia Bacon undertook, from her special insight into the plays themselves to her ability to convert normally rational persons such as Emerson to her determination to prosecute a crusade both in print and across the haunted geography of the English countryside.

This sense of haunted mission is of a piece with her highly recursive and reiterative prose style, where phrases and parentheses exfoliate abundantly within almost every paragraph. Here is one passage chosen at random (it is typical also in that its historical assumption about the initial reputation of Shakespeare's works is unfounded):

> And the impression which these works produced, even in their first imperfect mode of exhibition, was already so profound and extraordinary, as to give to all the circumstances of their attributed origin a blaze of notoriety, tending to enhance this positive force in the tradition. Propounded as a

fact, not as a theory, its very boldness – its startling improbability – was made at once to contribute to its strength ... The wonderful origin of these works was, from the first, the predominant point in the impression they made – the predominant marvel in those marvels, around which all the new wonders, that the later criticism evolved, still continued to arrange themselves. ('William' 3)

It is worth speculating briefly about what drew Delia Bacon to this argument, to which she devoted her life, and especially what it was about the controversy that caused so many others to take up the torch during the latter half of the nineteenth century and the early part of the twentieth. Bacon herself was ambitious to move in the circles of the cultural elite, but she was also independent minded and evidently wanted to stand out from the members of the elite. She was pleased to be introduced to Carlyle, and to drink tea with him and with James Spedding, the great editor of Bacon's works, but she stalwartly defied them when they dissented from her views – and she cannot have been entirely surprised that they *did* dissent. The structure of the argument suited perfectly her divided desire, since it allowed her to embrace the orthodox elite's admiration of Shakespeare's works – the holy of holies of Western literary culture – and yet to challenge the orthodox view of this literature on other grounds.

Beyond Delia Bacon's particular motivations, the argument likely appealed to so many in America because it provided them with a way of working through America's relationship with its founding culture, of recovering aspects of Englishness jettisoned by the young republic and yet also asserting core American values, including resistance to English High Culture. Indeed, American anti-Stratfordianism is based on a recuperation of aristocratic and elite cultural values coupled with an attack on bourgeois commercialism – all this motivated, ironically enough, by an earnest, angry, demotic defiance of elites and traditions.[4] In a striking way, furthermore, the furore over the authorship of Shakespeare's plays connected with the class and culture war going on in the nineteenth-century American theatre, where populist 'American' versions of Shakespeare's plays competed against elite domestic and English versions, and where differences between acting styles or the nationality of the star could lead to actual civil disturbances, such as the Aster Place riot in 1849, where populist anger against 'aristocratic' audiences and highbrow acting styles of Shakespeare resulted in a large-scale, violent protest and the shooting deaths of twenty-two workingmen by the New York City militia (Levine 63–5).

The early Canadian apostles who took up Delia Bacon's mission did so in another key. Overall, the Canadians did not confront (and re-appropriate) English High Culture directly but rather found themselves between the cultural traditions of the Old World and the social and artistic energy and manifest destiny of the United States. Not that the Canadians were without passion. One of these, Richard Maurice Bucke (1837–1902), was an extraordinary man.[5] (As we will see, his contribution to the authorship controversy is illustrative of the 'in-betweenness' of the Canadian position.) Having come in his infancy to rural Upper Canada from England with his parents, Bucke as a young man travelled in the frontier territories of the United States; hiring on to work on a westbound wagon train, he fought the Shoshone Indians, prospected for gold on the Carson River, and lost a foot to frostbite in the Rockies. He returned to Canada in 1858 to complete a medical degree at McGill University, after which he pursued literary and philosophical studies in London and Paris for several years. Even in Europe, however, he was haunted by the rugged beauty and freedom of the American frontier. In 1863 he wrote in his diary,

> I was wholey [sic] carried away by it [Charles Kingsley's novel, *Westward, Ho!*], far from the dim east and north once more westward to the most divine land of America, fairly wallowing in the glorious sunshine & rich vegetation of the south and west, the wild grandeur of the western wilderness that I know so well! but must never, never more see except in such visions – Ye mighty scenes of mountains, river, forest, and lovely valley how ye passed before me, almost turning my brain with indescrible [sic] feelings of longings, regret, exultation & despair, – to think to have seen such & never more to see, a cripple, a wreck – (*Richard* 23)

Fortunately, he recovered from this mood of despair and pursued a highly successful career in Sarnia and London, Ontario, as a physician, scientist of nervous and mental diseases (he was president of both the British Medical Association [psychological section] and the American Medico-Psychological Association), and advocate for the humane treatment of the insane. His work as a scientist, moreover, did not prevent him from following his literary and 'metaphysical' interests. Indeed, in addition to his scientific publications, Bucke wrote a number of philosophical-metaphysical works, including *Man's Moral Nature* (1879) and *Cosmic Consciousness* (1901).

His thinking on these matters was galvanized by Walt Whitman's *Leaves of Grass* (Whitman was another eminent sceptic about Shakespeare [see Whitman, 'What Lurks']). Bucke was so moved by Whitman's vision that he visited him in 1877, after which the two men became close friends and spent time together in Canada and New Jersey. Bucke published an important early study of *Leaves of Grass*, helped to prolong Whitman's life when he became ill, was a pallbearer at his funeral, and became one of his literary executors. Indeed, Bucke thought of Whitman more as the progenitor of a new religion than as the author of a body of innovative poetry (*Richard* 19–41). In his 1883 study of Whitman, he spoke of how his first meeting with the poet transformed his life (he wrote of himself in the third person):

> he did not realize anything peculiar while with him, but shortly after leaving a state of mental exaltation set in, which he could only describe by comparing to slight intoxication by champagne, or to falling in love! And this exultation, he said, lasted at least six weeks in a clearly marked degree, so that, for at least that length of time, he was plainly different from his ordinary self. Neither, he said, did it then or since pass away, though it ceased to be felt as something new and strange, but became a permanent element in his life, a strong and living force (as he described it), making for purity and happiness. I may add that this person's whole life has been changed by that contact (no doubt the previous reading of *Leaves of Grass* also), his temper, character, entire spiritual being, outer life, conversation, etc., elevated and purified in an extraordinary degree. (*Walt Whitman* 50)

Bucke was certainly aware of what he called Whitman's 'American equipment' and powerful vision of 'the future glories of American civilization' (135, 154). The central argument of the book, however, is about the universality of Whitman's poetic and spiritual gift to humankind. While, of course, Whitman's celebration of himself and of America never shrinks from claims to universal applicability, it seems nevertheless to have been Bucke's intention to scrub the poetry clean of its American ethos, including the Americanism of its language, to 'denationalize' it and restate its vision in terms of 'cosmic consciousness.' 'There is nothing,' Bucke says, 'of which humanity has experience that it does not touch upon more or less directly ... *Leaves of Grass* belongs to a religious era not yet reached, of which it is the revealer and herald' (182–3). About *Leaves of Grass* itself, he says: 'It is modern, fresh, universal, spontaneous, not following forms, taking its own form, perfectly free and unconstrained, common as the commonest things, yet its meaning inexhaustible by the greatest intellect, full of life itself, and capable of entering into and nourishing other lives ... always young, pure, delicate and beautiful to those who have hearts and eyes to feel and see ...' (156).

In the midst of his very full life, at the centre of which was his relationship with Whitman and his poetry, Bucke found time to take part in the Shakespeare authorship controversy. Like many men of letters of his time, Bucke – almost as a matter of course – was a staunch Baconian. He was well acquainted with the literature of the controversy; in the first of his two anti-Stratfordian essays, he listed and commented on the most significant longer works, which he had evidently read, including the volumes by Bacon and Donnelly (see 'Bacon's Cipher'; a catalogue is on page 273 of the article).[6] But his own contribution to the debate was brief and measured, with none of the derision for 'the old showman and hawker' characteristic of American Baconians, and little of their interpretive and cryptographic compulsiveness. Although he was certainly a truth-seeker on a lifetime quest of discovery and a man with a lively spirit of adventure, Bucke offered for the most part only a well-organized digest of the standard Baconian arguments as well as the discovery, which he attributed to 'Dr. Platt, of Lakewood, New Jersey,' of the true significance of the Latin word-play in *Love's Labour's Lost* ('Shakespeare' 376). Not surprisingly, it tended to confirm that Bacon was the author of Shakespeare's plays.

It is only at the end of this essay, in his peroration on Bacon's gift to humankind, that Bucke's prose rises to the prophetic tones of a Delia Bacon or an Ignatius Donnelly. The *Canadian* nature of Bucke's anti-Stratfordianism becomes clearer in light of what could be called his metaphysics of history as well as his belief in the formative role of certain great individuals, both of which aspects of his thinking emerge at the end of his essay. In Bucke's view, Francis Bacon was a world-historical figure, whose true importance and salvific influence would be realized only once his authorship of Shakespeare's plays was established as fact:

> And through the revelation of the true meaning of these [that is, *The Sonnets*] and of the plays, the intellectual world will pass into an experience comparable to a fresh created and divine sunrise. More than all, a new and most majestic figure will appear before the eye of the world – Francis Bacon! ... This man, restored to his full proportions, will step for the first time upon the stage of the world and will become the friend, the teacher – yes, even the saviour of thousands. For we shall see him as he lived, and lives, and his life will pass into the life of each one of us who is worthy. And

this, perhaps the greatest intellectual force, the most potent individuality that our planet has produced, will become and continue a deathless source of the purest and most exalted inspiration. ('Shakespeare' 378)

If we reflect on the fact that the terms of Bucke's praise of Bacon are identical to those applied to Whitman – and indeed to the landscape of the freewheeling American west – then we can understand that, not only is it the case that Bucke tends to think in highly romantic terms about great men, but also that the figure of Bacon serves to strengthen Bucke's project of denationalizing the destiny-laden energy of the United States itself. This attempt to transfer the inspirational force of American society and art to a leading figure of the English Renaissance perhaps helps explain why Bucke placed his publications about the authorship controversy only in Canadian and British magazines.

This negotiation between American and English influences, which motivated Bucke's representation of Bacon as American and Whitmanesque, characterizes the work of another Canadian Baconian of the period. In 1907 Samuel Mathewson Baylis, an official in the federal Department of Agriculture, was moved to pen the following 'cipher-sonnet' (it appeared first in Baylis's book, *At the Sign of the Beaver* [1907] and was reprinted in a paper he read before the St James Literary Society in Montreal on 17 February 1910):

> Fearsome the shadow of yon awful curse
> Uprears its threat'ning finger o'er the stones
> Where troop awed pilgrim throngs above dry bones
> Whisp'ring a name false-carven lines inherse –
> Poet's light blade, catch-coin to deck lean purse.
> The yard, all wondering, the magic owns,
> And clapper-claws the lack-shame daw, enthrones
> Him bard who struts and mouthes Want's bartered verse.
> Fame, perjured blazon, usances, and lands,
> And gentle sepulchre for base-born clay,
> O'erweigh the witness of the unsigned pact
> 'Twixt needy wit and nimble greed's demands.
> Mimes the vain actor night's slow hours away –
> Time calls for 'Author' in the curtain-act!   (*'Shake-Speare'* 21)

Baylis's poetry reproduces the overwrought style of Delia Bacon's prose, her prejudice against the 'vain actor' reduced by 'Want' to the trade in verse, and her crusading attitude against the shameless, base-born 'daw' whose grave is flocked by the superstitious and ignorant. In addition, Baylis was a devoted amateur scholar of the controversy. Appended to his St James's paper is an eight-page bibliography, many items marked to indicate that they are 'in the library of the writer.' Yet, while his library was replete with volumes of misinformation, Baylis's attitude is markedly different from that of Delia Bacon and many of her American followers. He demurs from hunting through the 1623 Folio for encrypted evidence of the 'true' author. He writes a brief essay rather than a thousand-page book. (Neither he nor Bucke attempted to excavate Shakespeare's gravesite.) On the whole, the Canadian seems far less passionate or irrational; indeed, the *playfulness* of his Baconianism is clear from the cipher-sonnet quoted above, which spells out '(FRANCIS BACON), Baron (V)erulam and Viscount St. (A)lbans' when one reads the first letter of the first foot of line one, the first of the second foot of the second line, and so on. This element of fun is evident also in Baylis's sonnet in honour of Delia Bacon (when read from the bottom, the initial capitals spell 'MISS DELIA BACON'):

> Not as the Maid defied the banner'd power
> Of furious England ravishing her France
> Comes she, with bravery of sword and lance.
> All-weakly armed, fond Idol-cult's high tower
> Breasting, she fronts Opioniatry's fell shower,
> And cruel stab of lip-curled arrogance,
> In fearless quest. Ah! Daughter of Mischance,
> Lost, all! – Friends, Reputation, Life's full flower!
> E'en as the Maid, by ruthless bigot Time
> Despitely used, enshrined in after days.
> So, owning Poesy's golden lamp defiled,
> Song's laurels shameless worn by buskin'd mime,
> Imperial leaflet shorn from mummer's bays
> May 'Shake-Speare's' England yield New England's child!
> ('Shake-Speare' 24)

The association of Delia Bacon with the Maid of France seems almost inevitable, and it would no doubt work in an American context as well, since the identification of the advocate of the truest English literature with the liberator of France from the English yoke expresses the ambivalent attitude that a colonial culture typically feels towards its founding nation. Baylis's poem, however, is part of an exercise in cultural triangulation rather than binary opposition. His nation is not the 'New England' brought forth out of England by dint of Delia Bacon's 'fearless quest' and tragic suffering. He is absent from the struggle, on the sidelines – a position suggested by the negative assertion with which the poem begins, which causes an interpretive hiatus until lines four and five, and by the overall elegiac tone, which signals that there is no longer any fray to join. This triangulation, which places the Canadian in the position of an observer, is continued in the history of the controversy recounted by Baylis, where he opposes English effeteness to American energy and industry:

> The first serious attack was ... made by Delia Bacon in her scintillating article ... and by William H. Smith, in a letter to Lord Ellesmere, later in the same year, the one by implication, and the other directly, attributing the authorship to Lord Bacon, and both to the horror and indignation of affronted orthodoxy. The Englishman, after having amplified his letter into a little book and shot his bolt, promptly retired from the fray, complacently leaving Time and the disputants to settle the matter. The brilliant American woman elaborated her theories into a large work ... ('Shake-Speare' 13–14)

The example of these two turn-of-the-century Baconians suggests that in Canada the Shakespeare authorship question (on both sides of the issue) was a pastime for gentlemen – doctors, government officials, and the many other professionals and clerics who made up the membership of the St James Literary Society or the Shakespeare Club of Montreal.[7] This kind of recreation – with its formal dinners and amateur scholarly jousting – nevertheless was involved in something like the development of a Canadian identity.[8] More recent participants, almost all of whom are partisans of the Earl of Oxford, have shifted the tone of the work and the field of its operation – roughly speaking, from a political to an institutional sphere. The publications of modern Canadian anti-Stratfordians remain characteristically compact, but they are oriented (in a love/hate relationship) towards the institutional culture of the university rather than situated between the national cultures of the United States and England. Oxfordians are as vexed about the academy as their predecessor Baconians were about the world of elite literary culture. Like Delia Bacon before them, modern Oxfordians seek recognition and acceptance by the establishment; and, also like Bacon, they are inclined to denounce the members and instruments of that establishment (in their case, these include the Shakespeare Association of America, the *Shakespeare Quarterly*, and university-based Shakespeareans in general), all of which they see involved in a massive conspiracy to keep hidden the true author and true meaning of Shakespeare's plays. Of course, the nature of the establishment in question has changed in radical ways: modern Shakespeare studies tend to be highly professionalized and therefore remain insulated from society at large, whereas literary amateurs such as Bucke or even Baylis would have had much in common with the professional scholars of their day, and indeed Bucke was able to publish what was recognized as legitimate literary biography.

Neither Elizabeth Appleton nor Nina Green has full-fledged academic credentials, neither has a university appointment, and neither publishes in recognized academic journals or through regular academic presses.[9] This exclusion from the professional field of Shakespeare studies, however, does not prevent them from writing seriously and soberly; indeed, it seems to compel a dry academic prose, filled with arcane historical facts and speculative claims, an unintended and unfunny parody of the historical–literary scholarship of a previous generation. Only in the concluding sentence of the concluding paragraph of her *Edward de Vere and the War of Words* does Appleton conjure something of the passion of Delia Bacon's prose; the rest of the paragraph, and the rest of the book, is uniformly respectable and unexcited, especially with its emphasis on the importance of coming to logical conclusions on the basis of carefully examined evidence:

> It may therefore now be seen that once the cover names which have protected Oxford's identity for so long have been penetrated, a vast body of new evidence has been brought to light. Gabriel Harvey and Thomas Nashe appear to believe that the combatant Oxford was that hidden genius we know under the name of William Shakespeare. They have now provided us with important new evidence about Oxford. With their help, we can examine the war of words further in depth to discover whether the Stratford Shakespeare or Nashe's 'Gentle Master William,' the attacked Oxford, was that genius who was the Soul, the Singularity and the Miracle of his Age. (*Edward* 51)

Overall, such dispassionate argumentation seems worlds away from Delia Bacon's flights of praise and condemnation. Indeed, modern Oxfordians are more likely to be found prosecuting their argument in a modern research facility like the British Library than haunting the graves of St Alban's or Holy Trinity Church, Stratford.[10] They resemble Delia Bacon only in that they challenge the exclusivity of an elite group (to some degree, of course, they also seek to be included in the group). Their views remain steadfastly on the margins, hardly noticed by the academy except when magazines such as the *Atlantic Monthly* (October 1991) or public TV invite well-known Shakespeareans to take part in a staged debate. In the field of popular culture – with the *Atlantic Monthly* and PBS lying at the upper end of the field – anti-Stratfordianism is now clustered with 'New Age' trivialities like the belief in the power of the pyramids or anxiety over the epidemic of alien abduction. This assimilation into a pop marketplace of intellectual trifles is ironic enough, especially given the snobbism and earnestness of the Oxfordian movement, but most important is the fact that the crusade against Shakespeare has lost its force as an instrument in the formation of national culture.

The intellectual and literary energy that characterized Bucke and Baylis, having fled from modern anti-Stratfordianism, is now to be found in writers like Leon Rooke and Ann-Marie MacDonald, both of whose work continues the project of developing a Canadian cultural identity in terms of Shakespeare and the question of authorship.[11] Rooke's and MacDonald's works seem unencumbered by the need to work out a peculiarly Canadian place between England and the United States. They are, therefore, free to challenge and adapt Shakespeare, and they contribute to the formation of a national culture by assimilating his cultural authority into their own political and artistic vision. In Rooke's Governor General's Award–winning novel, *Shakespeare's Dog* (1983), the dog, Hooker, narrates the events leading up to his master's departure to London to make his fortune in the budding professional theatre. While the novel is not directly concerned with the authorship controversy, its dog's-eye description of the lower-order social and family context of Shakespearean creativity answers the generations of Baconians and Oxfordians who have taken Shakespeare's 'baseness' as an argument in itself against his authorship of great literature. 'The stooge,' Hooker says. 'He'd been up there all day, minting rhyme, scratching dandruff from his empty head' (8).

Rooke's novel asserts High Art's embeddedness in the rich soil of common life (including the life of dogs), not to mention its formative association with the pleasures of the body. Not that he advances an idea of art as entirely at ease with domestic life. Shakespeare struggles to escape from his impoverished family and the bemired town of Stratford, mostly because of his dreams of social advancement, especially his fantasies about the court. Anne Hathaway upbraids him for refusing to change diapers (12) or get 'meaningful employment': 'But nay, you're all lit up by prince and princess, king and queen, you don't care snit about the real world!' (13). But the courtly fantasies that motivate him are themselves far from being refined; indeed, Shakespeare's own doggy imagination carnivalizes the Petrarchan adoration of the Virgin Queen, the traditional centrepiece of anti-Stratfordian Elizabethanism:

> Queen E. shall stop over [at New Place], as she did at Leicester's when I was a modest, giggling boy. She called the Earl her Sweet Robin then. I shall be her Sweet William. Oh a clown can make her laugh, but it will take Sweet William to keep curl in her hair. Stick with me, Hooker, and we'll go visiting her. I'll take you inside her Great Hall and behind it into the Great Chamber, and from it into the Presence Chamber, and if you don't piddle the tiles I'll take you into her Privy Chamber where you can plunge your nose between her great white thighs – if, that is, there's room for us both. (145–6)

Whereas Delia Bacon and her American followers defied the traditions of elite literary culture and also reclaimed the metaphysics of aristocratic blood, which Americans had renounced in the revolutionary period, Rooke revises the conventional figure of Shakespeare in order to assert the everyday, socially and sexually rooted nature of literary creativity. The earthiness of the novel's content and style is of a piece with the spirit of populist protest against elite Shakespeare, a sentiment that led to the Aster Place riot of 1849 or (to choose a less violent and more Canadian example) a populism that motivated the provocative, multicultural London production of *A Midsummer Night's Dream* by Québécois director Robert Lepage (see Hodgdon, 'Looking').

MacDonald's *Goodnight Desdemona (Good Morning Juliet)*, winner of the Governor General's Award for Drama in 1990, participates more directly in the tradition of the authorship controversy in Canada. Indeed, it is both a satire of anti-Stratfordianism and a serious examination of the relationship between authorship on one side and personal, sexual, and national identity on the other. Constance Ledbelly, the protagonist of the play and a latter-day Delia Bacon, even practises anti-Stratfordian cryptography: 'If you take the second letter of the eighteenth word of every second scene in "Othello," and cross reference them with the corresponding letters in "Romeo and Juliet," it says: "I dare not name the source of this txt'" (23). Of course, the play itself is not Baconian, or, rather, it is complexly Baconian and anti-Baconian. That is, it mocks the foolishness of anti-Stratfordian interpretive practices and assumptions. Constance explains the lack of an *e* in *txt* by speculating, groundlessly, on the printing history of the Folio (24). She also believes that she is about to discover the secret global meaning of Shakespeare, a breakthrough that, she hopes, will transform the world: 'Whoever cracks the Gustav code will be right up there with Darwin ...' (23). (It is difficult not to agree with the otherwise loathsome Professor Claude Night when he warns Constance against 'Traipsing after the Holy Grail' [22].) On the other hand, the play in general seems to believe that Shakespeare does have a hidden global meaning and that this secret meaning is potentially transformative, depending on the reader's intellectual and spiritual capacity. That is the point of the inscription on the 'Gustav Manuscript' (the mysterious text supposed to hold the key to the true significance and authorship of Shakespeare):

> You who possess the eyes to see
> this strange and wondrous alchemy,
> where words transform to vision'ry,
> where one plus two makes one, not three;
> open this book if you agree
> to be illusion's refugee,
> and of return no guarantee –
> unless you find your true identity.
> And discover who the Author be. (27–8)

Indeed, once we take into account its emphasis on self-help and gender, the play's evident faith in the linkage among powerful literary texts, revelations about authorship, and personal self-discovery puts it in a direct line with Bucke's belief in the millenarian impact of the announcement of Bacon's authorship of Shakespeare, which, he said, would cause, 'the intellectual world [to] pass into an experience comparable to a fresh created and divine sunrise. More than all, a new and most majestic figure will appear before the eye of the world – Francis Bacon! ... his life will pass into the life of each one of us who is worthy.'

The difference between Bucke and MacDonald includes not only the latter's irony, individualism, and feminism but also her emphasis on an oppositional relationship between Canada and its founding culture rather than the triangulated situation of Canada imagined by turn-of-the-century Baconians. At first, Constance is a consummate figure of Canadian in-betweenness, appearing on stage singing the bright-eyed American tune 'Young at Heart,' carrying a Complete Works of Shakespeare, and also sporting 'a bright red woolen toque with a pom-pom at the end,' a marker of nationality that she absent-mindedly wears throughout the first scene (14).[12] However, the American element (including the can of Coors Lite in Scene One) soon disappears from the play, leaving a set of parallel oppositions – woman against man, assistant professor against full professor,[13] 'low' Canadian speech against 'high' English, lowbrow against highbrow culture, comedy against tragedy, and Constance as the author of Shakespeare's plays against Shakespeare himself. The authorship and meaning of Shakespeare's plays is the ground upon which these binaries are articulated and fought over. The play concludes with an inversion of conventional hierarchies, especially with the triumph of the feminine and comic over the masculine and tragic. Constance discovers the true meaning of the Gustav Manuscript (named for another ghostly father in the play – Carl *Gustav* Jung) as well as the true authorship and significance of Shakespearean tragedy, which, of course, turns out to involve uncovering Shakespeare's perverse plagiarism of what were feminine, life-affirming comedies in their first incarnation.

In the play, the toqued Canadian Constance (facing an academic posting in Regina) is set against the smooth, 'perfectly groomed and brogued' Professor Claude Night, complete with his 'Oxford accent' and his impending appointment at Oxford University. Night's polite and ironic phrasing is contrasted with Constance's straightforwardly conversational style; his command of standard English allows him to mock her speech in ways suggestive of cultural, class, institutional, and gender domination – a hierarchical relationship that the play will eventually undo:

Professor. Your fascination with mystery borders on the vulgar, I'm afraid.
Constance. I can't help it. I'm a fallen Catholic. It's left with me with a streak of 'whodunit.'
Professor. Well who did dun it? What became of this mysterious source material? (24)

Much of the fun of the play depends upon a more general contrast between Shakespeare's highbrow language and Constance's middlebrow Canadian speech. This stylistic contest, of course, is also a clash of values, since tragic language embodies an idea of inflexible commitment to heroic self-assertion and black-and-white kinds of judgments about people and situations, whereas Constance's language is self-deprecating and remains open to a range of views about life. When a smitten, bisexual Romeo woos a transvestite Constance by the poetic strains of 'Liebestod,' Constance answers in the prose of everyday life:

> *Romeo.* Boy, what love can do, that dares love attempt.
> Therefore my kinsmen are no stop to me.
> *Constance.* They are to me! I'm not a hero, I'm just a school teacher.
>
> (63–4)

Even when Constance's speech falls into (a rough version of) iambic pentameter, her vocabulary and speech rhythms still collide meaningfully with those of Shakespeare's characters:

> I wish I were more like Desdemona.
> Next to her I'm just a little wimp.
> A rodent. Road-kill. Furry tragedy
> all squashed and steaming on the 401
> with 'Michelin' stamped all over me. ... (49)

While the play carries on a critique of highbrow language and the tragic values it embodies, the ending produces a rich mix of Canadian prose and quasi-Shakespearean poetry (here Constance is upbraiding Desdemona and Juliet for their suicidal commitment to love):

> *Constance.* I've had it with all the tragic tunnel vision around here. You have no idea what – life is a hell of a lot more complicated than you think! Life – real life – is a big mess. ...
> *Desdemona.* Nay, thou speakst wise.
> *Juliet.* Aye, fools were never wise.
> *Desdemona.* Could any fool reveal, how we were wont to err?
> *Juliet.* Or get us to concede, what we will gladly swear?
> *Constance.* What's that?
> *Desdemona.* To live by questions, not by their solution.
> *Juliet.* To trade our certainties, for thy confusion.
> *Constance.* Do you really mean that?

[*Juliet and Desdemona nod, 'Yes.'*]
Ghost. [under the stage] Swear. Swear.
Desdemona and Juliet. We swear.
Constance. Then I was right about your plays. They were comedies after all, not tragedies. (85)

This happy inclusion of a style of expression representative of the founding culture into a renewed community dominated by the sound and good sense of middlebrow Canadian prose is of a piece with the recuperation of Shakespeare, who manages to travel between the high and low poles of the play's cultural and ideological territory, so that he emerges as both Constance's antagonist and the guiding figure of her self-discovery. Indeed, the ending of the play is the fulfillment of Delia Bacon's dream of discovering the lost Baconian manuscripts. In a setting that is at once the Capulet family monument, the place of Hamlet's meeting with his father's ghost, and Shakespeare's gravesite in Holy Trinity Church, Stratford, Constance at last receives the documentary proof of authorship:

Constance. That's me. I'm the Author!
[*A golden hand rises up through the surface of the slab upon which Constance lay. The hand holds a scrolled Manuscript page. Constance takes the page and unscrolls it.*]
It says ...
'For those who have eyes to see:
Take care – for what you see, just might be thee.' (86)

The *golden* hand of the dead father (not to mention the gold pen that is Constance's souvenir of her encounter with Shakespeare) is a transvalued remnant of the class hatred of nineteenth-century Baconianism, which saw Shakespeare as base metal in comparison with the twenty-four-caret refinement of the aristocracy. More important than the range of prejudices that have motivated anti-Stratfordianism, however, are the ways in which the Shakespeare authorship question has been taken up as a positive, postcolonial register of gender, class, and cultural self-authorship. Canadian Bacon, thus, is more than a fascinating part of the broader history of the authorship question; it has been and continues to be an important instance of the use of Shakespeare as an instrument of the formation of national identity.

Notes

1 We use the word *controversy* advisedly. What started as a controversy in the middle of the nineteenth century has now become a one-sided attempt on the part of anti-Stratfordians to gain the attention of professional scholars. Exceptions to this state of affairs happen only when some institution (like the American Supreme Court) or some magazine (such as *Harper's*) spark or organize a formal debate.
2 We are so certain about Shakespeare's authorship that we will not engage with the anti-Stratfordian arguments, which seem to us without substance. We refer the sceptical reader to the concise and convincing essay by Jonathan Bate, 'Golden Lads and Chimney-Sweepers.'
3 Information about Delia Bacon derives from Schoenbaum 385–94; Hopkins; and T. Bacon.
4 Mark Twain's attack on Shakespeare's claim to his works exemplifies in a comic register how support for an Elizabethan courtier could work to express populist aspirations against hierarchical power and traditional wisdom. See Twain, esp. 4–19.
5 Information about Richard Bucke derives from Roberts and Tunnell 75–7; Coyne; and Bucke, *Richard*.
6 Note that substantially the same argument about the secret meaning of Shakespeare's epitaph had also been made by the Ontario resident, Hugh Black, in a New York magazine in 1887. See Black, 'Bacon's Claim.'
7 According to Fred C. Newman in his book *The First Fifty Years: A Brief History of the St. James Literary Society*, the Society, which was founded in 1899 and met at Montreal's stately Windsor Hotel, included many lawyers, ministers of the church, and other high-ranking members of Montreal society. The Shakespeare Club, which dated back to the middle of the nineteenth century and also met at the Windsor, had the governor general as its patron. See *Laws of the Shakspeare [sic] Club*.
8 To be sure, this identity was exclusive rather than inclusive – oriented equally towards the United States and England, as well as being white, male, anglophone, and upper class.
9 See Elizabeth Appleton, *Edward* and *Supplementary*. Nina Green is the editor, publisher, and principal contributor to the *Edward de Vere Newsletter*, vols. 1–67 (1989–94), and more recently an editor of the web-based anti-Stratfordian journal, *Spear Shaker Review*.
10 Appleton thanks 'the officials and the staff of the British Museum for their courtesy and helpfulness' (*Edward* viii).

11 Also see Jeffrey Holmes. Note that Leon Rooke was born in North Carolina in 1934 but has lived in Canada since 1969.
12 Note that MacDonald identifies 'Young at Heart' by its first line, 'Fairy tales can come true.'
13 MacDonald seems to mean something like 'research assistant' or 'sessional instructor' by the designation 'Assistant Professor.'

12

Canada, Negative Capability, and *Cymbeline*

ALEXANDER LEGGATT

Since no one now lives in Elizabethan England, Shakespeare is always read through foreign eyes. No single culture can claim a privileged understanding overall, but readers from a variety of places can find aspects of Shakespeare to which their cultures give them special access. Thus, Camille Paglia is unshocked by Cleopatra's verbal and physical violence, since 'as an Italian, I have little problem reconciling violence with culture' and Cleopatra's 'sadistic images' remind her of the way her 'immigrant relatives' used to talk: 'May you be eaten by a cat!'; 'May your eyes be torn out'; 'May they sew up your anus' (217–18). Martin Orkin can read *The Tempest* as a politically charged, resistant text in the context of contemporary South Africa. For Evgenia Pancheva, 'the 1992 *Much Ado About Nothing* is a play about Bulgaria's fear of manipulation. Things can't just happen in this country – they are always stage-managed' (247).[1]

Can a Canadian reader join in? There are joke possibilities, of course: we understand the complaints about taxation in *Henry VIII* through the GST; as users of Canada Post, we recognize the problem of undelivered mail in *Romeo and Juliet*. But the fact that, as a Canadian Shakespeare critic, I have instinctively begun with jokes betrays a certain Canadian diffidence. A critic in South Africa or eastern Europe has strongly defined, urgent political problems to identify with, matters quite literally of life and death. But in a country known (rightly or wrongly) for its blandness – a country notoriously unresponsive to Northrop Frye's question, where is here? – from what position does one read? Sitting down; but what else?

What follows is deliberately personal, drawing on experience and general knowledge to create a rough working sense of Canada as an entity. I was born in Trafalgar Township, Ontario, and I live in a community that, though recently swallowed up by the amalgamated City of Toronto, is still informally known as East York. The place names that mark my life are an English naval victory in the Napoleonic Wars and a city in the north of England. The map of the area that surrounds me is marked by names like London, Stratford, Waterloo, Kitchener, and Chatham. The coins in my pocket bear images of the queen. I live, in another words, in a country that was created by the British empire, and in which the language of everyday life still marks that fact. I am writing this essay in English.

Canadian history, as I was taught it in school, is a series of moments of coming of age, as Canada became increasingly independent of the mother country, not by violent revolution but by a series of legal changes. Yet some of our transitional moments have been touched by violence: the capture of Vimy Ridge by Canadian soldiers in 1917 was a rite of passage of a traditional kind – young men proving themselves in war. It has a legendary position in the story of Canada's development, but it was also an achievement in a European war, to which Canada was committed by her membership in the British empire.

As one empire recedes, another advances. A check of television listings or magazine racks will confirm the pervasiveness of the American cultural empire in Canadian everyday life. So, some would say, will a check of papers at academic conferences, where the material may be Canadian but the critical modes are those that prevail at the Modern Language Association of America. The jokes that try to keep some sense of Canadian identity going – a Canadian is an American who has government health insurance and does not own a handgun – are desperate attempts to patrol the southern border, and the one I have just repeated characteristically concedes far more than it asserts. As I write, the idea that Canada should give up its own currency and simply use the American dollar is under serious consideration.

What is left? Attempts to define Canadian identity in the popular press fix most often on multiculturalism. The Toronto *Star* for Canada Day 1998 featured a symbolic drawing in which the flags of many nations were joined together in a single swaying ribbon. Indignant readers demanded to know what had happened to the Canadian flag, and the *Star* made amends on Canada Day 1999 with a photograph of children from a local school, standing in a circle, taken from below with a fisheye lens and holding in the centre of the picture a large Canadian flag. But the emphasis of the previous year's edition remained: the children themselves represented what the caption called 'a city that is being enriched by growing ethnic and cultural diversity.' I recall a visitor from England, returning from a walk downtown, declaring with keen delight that he had just seen 'all the nations of the earth,' and, if I am asked to say what I enjoy about living in Toronto, that is where my answer usually begins.

Beyond the cities, the wilderness. Another coming of age for Canada was the development of what purported to be a distinctive style of painting in the work of the Group of Seven: rock, water, trees, wind, and (for the most part) no people, no sign of human habitation. The Canadian imagination responded then, and responds still, to the notion of an empty landscape. Though it has been lived in for thousands of years, Canada does not feel so obviously lived in as many European countries do; and (judging by the stories I read in school), if there is a characteristic Canadian way to die, it is far from shelter, in a snowstorm.

Where, then, is the place from which Canadians speak? Pockets of society that speak multiple languages and bear the marks of cultures that came from elsewhere, the cultures of empire-builders and immigrants, and around them a wilderness? Is that a position? And what of the obvious factors I have omitted? To name only three: the people who were here first and who do not think of themselves as immigrants; Quebec, the province that insists on only one language; and the fact that Toronto is not the only city in Canada. (My sense of multiculturalism as a defining Canadian characteristic may appear to some other Canadians as typically Torontocentric.) I have subjected the reader to these commonplaces, and to the commonplace reservations about them, because they all bear on what I want to suggest about reading Shakespeare in Canada. If Canada speaks with different voices, so does Shakespeare; if, in the words of the English critic Jonathan Bate, Shakespeare's nation 'has been many nations and can potentially be every nation' ('Shakespearean' 115), the same may be true of Canada. The most positive view of the ongoing Canadian experiment is that, if we can gather 'all the nations of the earth' into a workable society, we can provide a new model for nationhood to counter the demand for ethnic purity that has become in practice one of the most sinister forces in the contemporary world. The greatest fear is that the strains of diversity will tear us apart.

In this situation the enemy is decisiveness: a stern line against Quebec's aspirations, a stern line in favour of them, a stern line against immigration. No more compromise; let us settle this matter once and for all. Perhaps we should revive the memory of Mackenzie King, not for his contacts with the spirit world or his devotion to his mother and his dog, but for his genius in refusing decisions, the very quality whose influence on Canada F.R. Scott found baleful:

> We had no shape
> Because he never took sides,
> And no sides
> Because he never allowed them to take shape. ('W.L.M.K.' 27)

'Conscription if necessary but not necessarily conscription' was King's characteristic way of dealing with the irreconcilable demands of opposing voices. But Canada survived him, and may have survived because of him. In the repatriation of the constitution (without Quebec's signature) and in the Meech Lake and Charlottetown constitutional agreements (which provoked nothing but disagreement), his successors have attempted to be decisive. Whether the country will survive these attempts is still unclear.

There is a classic defence of indecisiveness in art: John Keats's description of the quality that 'went to form a Man of Achievement, especially in Literature, and which Shakespeare possessed so enormously – I mean *Negative Capability*, that is, when a man is capable of being in uncertainties, mysteries, doubts, without any irritable reaching after fact and reason' (81). Keats describes a writer open to different views, different voices, a writer who would rather hold to uncertainty than kill it by moving to a firm conclusion. If this is a valid kind of literary genius, it may be a valid kind of political genius as well. Keats's term, Robert Weimann has suggested, 'may be translated into the authorisation of difference and diversity' (200), and in the Canadian context those are politically loaded words.

With all this in mind, I have chosen *Cymbeline* for an experiment in the Canadian reading of Shakespeare, encouraged by Samuel Johnson's attack on it for, among other things, 'the confusion of the names and manners of different times' (235). Johnson complains of a temporal multiculturalism, as different historical periods seem to be present simultaneously. Listed in the Folio as the last of the tragedies, relisted now in the recently invented category of Final Romances, and having some claim to be a chronicle play like *King Lear*, *Cymbeline* also practises a kind of generic multiculturalism. In its political aspect, it deals with nationhood not as a given (we live here, this is our country) but as a matter of negotiation and redefinition.² From a European perspective, James R. Siemon has recently seen the play as 'an early modern encounter with factors of transnational community and group fragmentation resembling those now occupying postmodern speculation' (296). I would like to apply a self-consciously Canadian perspective, drawing on the position (positions?) roughly outlined above. The discussion falls under three headings, whose Canadian resonance should be obvious: empire, wilderness, identity.

As Canada is marked by the language of the British empire, Britain in *Cymbeline* is marked by the language of Rome. Belarius's claim that his body is 'marked / With Roman swords' (3.3.56–7)[3] is symbolic of a more pervasive marking.[4] Hiding in Wales, Belarius, Guiderius, and Arviragus take names with British or Celtic resonance: Morgan, Polydore, and Cadwal. But their true names have a Latin ring, suggesting what may be called the Grey Owl effect: they belong to the empire, and their attempt to go native is a fake. The religion of Rome, and the gods of Rome, mark the characters' language throughout. Waking beside a headless corpse she thinks is her husband's, Innogen surveys his body in a blazon that evokes the Roman gods: 'His foot Mercurial, his Martial thigh, / The brawns of Hercules'; she misses only 'his Jovial face' (4.2.311–13). His body is marked not with Roman swords but with Roman images. A British captain greets a crucial move in the Britons' defeat of the Roman army, 'Great Jupiter be praised, Lucius is taken' (5.3.84).

Jupiter is the play's all-powerful god, taking the role played by Diana in *Pericles* and Apollo in *The Winter's Tale*. Appearing in a vision, Posthumus's dead parents rebuke the god for not playing his role as protector of their son:

> Whose father then – as men report
> Thou orphans' father art –
> Thou shouldst have been, and shielded him
> From this earth-vexing smart.   (5.3.133–6)

In reply, Jupiter, while declaring that Posthumus's life has unfolded under his influence – 'Our Jovial star reigned at his birth, and in / Our temple was he married' (5.3.199–200) – and promising that his future course will be happy, sounds not like a benevolent father figure but like a remote, angry power whose workings are not to be questioned:

> No more you petty spirits of region low
> Offend our hearing. Hush! How dare you ghosts
> Accuse the thunderer, whose bolt, you know,
> Sky-planted, batters all rebelling coasts? (5.3.187–90)

Paternal in his care for his charges, but not to be questioned and having a brisk, violent way with rebellion, Jupiter shows the two faces not just of divinity but of imperialism.

If there is a native British mythology, we catch only glimpses of it. There are stray references to fairies (2.2.9, 3.6.41). In Wales, we glimpse beliefs and practices that speak with a non-Roman voice. Belarius and the princes begin the day with what sounds like a ritual formula from a nature-religion: 'Hail, heaven!' (3.3.8–9). Though the effect is partly dictated by the demands of the story, it seems to be the British practice to leave corpses exposed on the earth – taking care, for a reason never specified, to lay the head to the east (4.2.256) – while the Roman practice is to bury them (4.2.388–400). All of this suggests pre-Roman beliefs, driven to the margins of the characters' consciousness and the geographical margins of the island, losing in the process whatever proper names they had. Only the Roman gods have names.

The British characters, as it were, dream in Roman. Posthumus literally does, in his vision of Jupiter. Innogen wakes from a drugged sleep to the dream-like horror of the headless corpse, whose parts she names in Roman language, and whose missing 'Jovial' face leads to the terrible cry, 'Murder in heaven!' (4.2.313). Earlier, in her bedchamber, she reads the tale of the rape of Philomel and falls asleep just at the point where Philomel (in Giacomo's creepy euphemism) 'gave up' (2.2.46). As she does so, Giacomo emerges from the trunk, a nightmare of sexual invasion come true. The Roman story becomes her dream, and Giacomo is its reality. He comes bringing another Roman story with him:

> Our Tarquin thus
> Did softly press the rushes ere he wakened
> The chastity he wounded. (2.2.12–14)

Our Tarquin; he enters her chamber not just for his own private purpose but as the representative of his people. From 2.2 through 2.4, Giacomo's attack on Innogen is juxtaposed with Rome's impending attack on Britain, and his later participation in the Roman defeat seems to him a punishment:

> I have belied a lady,
> The princess of this country, and the air on't
> Revengingly enfeebles me. (5.2.2–4)

It is not always healthy to be an imperialist; the land you conquer can avenge itself by sickness.

The Lucrece story (which, like the wager-plot, begins with men boasting of their women) dominates this section of the play. But there are side-glances to other Roman stories that suggest other ways Giacomo's relationship with Innogen could go. The hangings in the chamber include Cleopatra's meeting with Antony at Cydnus (2.4.70–1): a visiting Roman meets a friendly welcome from a foreign princess, who is sexually available. But 'the chimneypiece' is 'Chaste Dian bathing' (2.4.81–2), suggesting the story of Actaeon and the punishment of a voyeurism more innocent than Giacomo's. Through all the ironic play of mythological language, one thing remains constant: the Roman, entering the bedchamber of a British princess, is culturally at home. He recognizes all the stories, which come from his world. The sexual and military invasions of Britain may fail, but the cultural invasion has succeeded.

In the British resistance to Rome over the issue of paying tribute, there is a stirring cause – no taxation without representation – and what some modern readers may see as historical inevitability. Sooner or later the imperial powers fold their flags and depart, leaving the natives in charge. But for a Canadian it is not so simple: the part of the population that can truly claim to be native is very small, and a genuine withdrawal of invaders and immigrants would mean that most of us would have to leave. (The case for doing this is summed up by a bumper sticker I saw on a reservation: 'Canada. Love it or give it back.') A withdrawal of the American economic and cultural empire would mean that many of us would lose our jobs. The decisiveness of freedom fighters in other parts of the world is stirring to contemplate, but in us the spirit of Mackenzie King is strong.

In *Cymbeline*, British resistance to Rome is equivocal, and it has been that way as far back as the play's vision goes. Posthumus's father, Sicilius, fought the Romans; but the Roman Philario, in whose house the banished Posthumus finds refuge, is an old friend of Sicilius (1.1.98–100). Philario reports, 'His father and I were soldiers together, to whom I have been often bound for no less than my life' (1.4.23–4). Were they enemies who showed each other courtesy, or were they sometimes on the same side? Judging by Belarius's complaint that he fell from Cymbeline's favour through a false report that he was collaborating with the Romans (3.3.66–8), the episode the play shows is not Cymbeline's first conflict with Rome. Yet, in conversation with the Roman ambassador, Caius Lucius, the British king relaxes and starts to reminisce:

> Thou art welcome, Caius.
> Thy Caesar knighted me; my youth I spent
> Much under him; of him I gathered honour,
> Which he to seek of me again perforce
> Behoves me keep at utterance. (3.1.67–71)

The sudden obscurity of his language may indicate his discomfort at the turn events have taken: you taught me honour, and my profit on it is, I know how to fight you. The clear, relaxed voice of the first part of the speech is the voice of a Rhodes scholar who will always be grateful to Oxford.

In the present, Cymbeline and Caius Lucius are careful to distinguish between their mutual esteem at the personal level and the conflict that history has forced on them. For Cymbeline, Lucius is

> A worthy fellow,
> Albeit he comes on angry purpose now;
> But that's no fault of his. (2.3.53–5)

Lucius speaks in his official voice, then drops it for his personal one:

> War and confusion
> In Caesar's name pronounce I 'gainst thee. Look
> For fury not to be resisted. Thus defied,
> I thank thee for myself. (3.1.64–7)

This is not the sort of conflict in which natives and imperialists demonize each other in order to work up the necessary rage or fear. Here, people on both sides know each other too well for that.

In his strongest, most principled and idealistic defiance of Rome, Cymbeline speaks in a voice that is calm and reasonable, with only a touch of justifiable anger:

282 Alexander Leggatt

> You must know,
> Till the injurious Romans did extort
> This tribute from us we were free. Caesar's ambition,
> Which swelled so much that it did almost stretch
> The sides o'th' world, against all colour here
> Did put the yoke upon's, which to shake off
> Becomes a warlike people, whom we reckon
> Ourselves to be. We do say then to Caesar
> Our ancestor was that Mulmutius which
> Ordained our laws, whose use the sword of Caesar
> Hath too much mangled ...   (3.1.45–55)

He speaks for freedom, law, national pride. He does not shout slogans; he argues and explains.

The trouble is, he goes on explaining, and the more he explains, the more uncertain and defensive he sounds. The Pannonians and Dalmatians have risen against Rome, 'a precedent / Which not to read would show the Britons cold' (3.1.72–3). His declaration that the Britons are a warlike people slides into an apologetic claim that he is being led from below:

> Our subjects, sir,
> Will not endure his yoke, and for ourself
> To show less sovereignty than they must needs
> Appear unkinglike.   (3.5.4–7)

We begin increasingly to detect the unspoken message: this was not my idea. The fiery speeches of defiance come from the Queen and Cloten, and Cymbeline will eventually blame his refusal of tribute on 'our wicked queen' (5.4.464). When the Romans land, the Queen and Cloten are out of action, and Cymbeline seems at a loss without them: 'Now for the counsel of my son and queen! / I am amazed with matter' (4.3.27–8). His chief accomplishment in the battle is to be taken prisoner. In short, he is hardly a decisive centre for British resistance to Rome: too much of his personal life, and his sense of himself, is invested in the imperial power he is trying to defy.

It is left to the Queen and Cloten to beat the drums and wave the flags, and they do it in grand style. Describing Roman ships broken on the British coast, the Queen stirs (for the first audience) memories of the Armada, and, in a style reminiscent of *Henry V*, she urges Cymbeline

Canada, Negative Capability, and *Cymbeline* 283

to recall his heroic ancestors (3.1.16–22). Cloten gets off one of his best lines in the national cause:

> Britain's a world
> By itself, and we will nothing pay
> For wearing our own noses.   (3.1.12–14)

Giving this role to the play's villains has caused some critical bewilderment; but a Canadian reader (we are less given to flag-waving than our southern neighbours) may be better placed than most to understand it.[5]

Cloten's speech combines independence with insularity. Innogen is capable of thinking beyond Britain, willing to leave it if necessary, willing to imagine a world elsewhere:

> Hath Britain all the sun that shines? Day, night,
> Are they not but in Britain? I'th' world's volume
> Our Britain seems as of it but not in't,
> In a great pool a swan's nest. Prithee think
> There's livers out of Britain.   (3.4.137–41)

Her island will always be special for her, a place like no other. But she can leave. Though Britain and Rome are on a war footing, Pisanio advises her, without apology, to take service with Lucius (3.4.173–4); and, several plot developments later, that is just what she does.

The war has other ramifications, however. That Canada matured through two European wars is an old commonplace of our history. Even so, in *Cymbeline*, war is presented as a rite of passage through which a young man finds himself. Posthumus's father, Sicilius, was given a surname, Leonatus, because of his achievements in battle (1.1.28–33). For the exiled princes, war is a rite of passage for which they long desperately: they participate imaginatively in Belarius's war stories (3.3.87–98) and, as the sounds of war surround them, Arvigarus bursts out, 'What thing is't that I never / Did see man die' (4.4.35–6). Belarius sees where they are heading: 'The time seems long, their blood thinks scorn / Till it fly out and show them princes born' (4.4.53–4). The battle, in which, joined with Posthumus and Belarius, they take the role of common soldiers, face impossible odds, and turn the tide, is their Vimy Ridge.

But how decisive is the play's handling of this theme? Chagrined at the poor reward for his own service, Belarius, in his lectures to the young men, lists war, along with city usury and the arts of the court, among the evils of society:

> the toil o'th' war,
> A pain that only seems to seek out danger
> I'th' name of fame and honour, which dies i'th' search
> And hath as oft a sland'rous epitaph
> As record of fair act ...   (3.3.49–53)

Belarius's first response to the Roman invasion is to hide out and have nothing to do with it. Eventually he joins in, his old keenness revived; but the critical voice may not be completely silenced in the general excitement. And we have to notice that, while victory shows the princes' true mettle, it seems to coarsen Cymbeline. His determination to kill his prisoners is not the game as played between gentlemen, and Lucius rebukes him:

> Had it gone with us,
> We should not, when the blood was cool, have threatened
> Our prisoners with the sword.   (5.4.76–8)

He has his own threat to utter: 'Augustus lives to think on't' (5.4.82). At last they are decisive with each other, and the courtesies of their earlier scenes fall away; but, in the process, something of civilization is lost. War as a path to national achievement and self-definition is presented in a way that can stir excitement, but we should notice the misgivings, the opposing voices (conscription if necessary but not necessarily conscription), the play's final refusal to take sides.

The princes emerge from Wales, which is presented here not as a society in its own right but as a wilderness. Cymbeline's instruction that Lucius be escorted 'Till he have crossed the river Severn' (3.5.17) suggests that west of that river he has no authority. But Wales is as empty of people as it suited the first empire-builders to imagine Canada was. The only characters we see there are three British exiles, camping out. Innogen asks directions of two beggars, who seem to know the country no better than she does (3.6.8–11). Calling into the cave, she is clearly unsure what level of civilization, if any, to expect:

> Ho! Who's here?
> If anything that's civil, speak; if savage,
> Take or lend.   (3.6.22–4)

In fact, there is no society, no community, and, when Innogen offers the cave-dwellers money, she is rebuffed (3.6.52–4).

The only town is the seaport of Milford Haven, whose significance is shifting and ambiguous. Emrys Jones's classic article associated it with Henry Tudor's invasion to save England from Richard III; thinking to meet Posthumus there, Innogen celebrates it as a blessed place (3.2.58–61). But it is Posthumus's idea that at Milford Haven Pisanio should kill her; it is at Milford Haven that Cloten plans to kill Posthumus and rape Innogen; and Milford Haven is picked as the rendezvous point for the Roman invasion.[6] In the end, the general convergence on Milford Haven is like the general convergence on Dover in *King Lear*: everyone is going there, but no one seems to get there. Innogen complains to Pisanio, 'Thou told'st me when we came from horse the place / Was near at hand' (3.4.1–2), and, though she glimpses it once, it disappears as she approaches:

> Milford,
> When from the mountain-top Pisanio showed thee,
> Thou wast within a ken. O Jove, I think
> Foundations fly the wretched ...   (3.6.4–7)

A place without society, without maps, where the chief tourist activity is getting lost, whose one town vanishes like Brigadoon, and where the only natives we see are not real natives – the Wales of *Cymbeline* has no answer to the question, where is here?

For Belarius, as for Duke Senior in *As You Like It*, the wilderness is a place from which he can moralize about the evils of society. But the princes, who have known only the wilderness, lack the experience to do even this, and they complain of the emptiness of their lives. Guiderius calls his life 'A cell of ignorance,' and Arviragus declares, 'We have seen nothing. / We are beastly' (3.3.33, 39–40). In old age they will have (unlike Belarius) no history, nothing to talk about (3.3.35–6). (Another Canadian theme emerges, one that residents of other former colonies will recognize: we will never amount to anything so long as we stay here.) In the wilderness they do not even know their true names, and do not know that they do not know. Frye's question – where is here? – easily shifts into another, who are we? If identity depends in part on where we are, and if we imagine where we are as an empty space, what is our identity? Behind the usual mistaken-identity conventions of romance (disguises, lost children) lies a deeper sense of identity as shifty and finally unreal,[7] a sense that names, faces, and histories are inscribed on a space that is finally a blank.

Who is the Queen? Where did she come from? She has no proper name, and we have no way of locating her social origins. Cloten has a proper name, but his fussy insistence on his rank suggests not a real gentleman but a social climber, anxious and defensive about his status (2.1). Parentage may help to confer identity, but the Second Lord, Cloten's resident heckler, wonders 'That such a crafty devil as is his mother / Should yield the world this ass' (2.1.49–50). And who, if anyone, was his father? Our last glimpse of him is a headless body, in someone else's clothes, his identity erased. Innogen, thinking the corpse is Posthumus, finds her own identity wiped clean by her husband's death: 'I am nothing; or if not, / Nothing to be were better' (4.2.368–9). The feeling is brief, but the fear it touches on is basic.

The identity problem centres on Posthumus.[8] The First Gentleman's account of him begins, 'I cannot delve him to the root' (1.1.28), and, while Cloten is dislocated from his mother by their difference in character, Posthumus is dislocated from his parents in a more literal way. His name marks him with the fact that his father died before he was born, and his mother died giving birth to him. Her ghost complains that she never saw his face (5.3.129–30). He was born into a hostile world: 'That from me was Posthumus ripped, / Came crying 'mongst his foes' (5.3.139–40). This initial alienation continues in adulthood: Cymbeline gave him his name, and Innogen's choice of him as a husband guarantees his worth (1.1.40–1, 50–4); however, for marrying Innogen, Cymbeline banishes him from Britain, exiling him from the people who defined him.

The mix of British and Roman loyalties we see in Cymbeline works in Posthumus as a mix of national identities, an internal multiculturalism like that of a so-called hyphenated Canadian (Italian-Canadian, Ukrainian-Canadian, and so on). Though self-consciously British in his foreign exile, he is associated with Jupiter in small touches that anticipate the vision scene: Innogen says of her marriage, 'I chose an eagle' (1.1.140), and Giacomo declares, 'He sits 'mongst men like a descended god' (1.6.169). A Roman oath has surprising power to make him credit Giacomo's lies: 'Hark you, he swears, by Jupiter he swears' (2.4.122). In the vision itself, Jupiter claims to guide Posthumus's life. Yet Rome is not truly his place: when he leaves his island his reputation shrinks. (Another Canadian theme: the local fame that fails to travel.) In Britain, the First Gentleman bestows extravagant praise on Posthumus (1.1), but, for Giacomo and the nameless Frenchman, he is nothing special: 'I could then have looked on him without the help of admiration' (1.4.3–4); 'I have seen him in France. We had very many there could behold the sun with as firm eyes as he' (1.4.10–11). Giacomo's report that in Italy he has forgotten his marriage 'and himself' (1.6.113) and its later resurfacing in Innogen's belief that 'Some Roman courtesan' (3.4.123) has corrupted him are deceptions that have an underlying truth. Putting Innogen on the table as his stake in the boasting contest and the wager plot, and believing Giacomo's false report, Posthumus has indeed 'forgot Britain' (1.6.113) and emptied his own nature to the point where a headless body can stand in for him.

Posthumus's shifting identity becomes literal when he returns to Britain as a Roman soldier, then switches to British dress, helps defeat the army with which he came, and resumes his Roman guise in order to be taken prisoner and executed. Through all of this he has one consistent aim:

>   so I'll die
> For thee, O Innogen, even for whom my life
> Is every breath a death ...   (5.1.25–7)

In sleep, Posthumus catches a glimpse of his lost family, his father and two brothers, but the vision is as fleeting as Innogen's glimpse of Milford Haven:

> They went hence as soon as they were born;
> And so I am awake. Poor wretches that depend
> On greatness' favour dream as I have done,
> Wake and find nothing.   (5.3.220–3)

Yet he is not quite left with nothing: the riddling tablet placed on his breast, which he finds when he wakes, crosses the border from dream into reality with the promise that both Posthumus and Britain will be restored 'Whenas a lion's whelp shall, to himself unknown, without seeking find, and be embraced by a piece of tender air' (5.3.232–4). Salvation will come not through decisive action or self-assertion, but when will and identity are suspended, and a man who does not know himself will find without seeking. Posthumus's response to this prophecy is a continued longing for death, the ultimate suspension of will and identity, and the British jailer is so impressed with what he thinks is Roman stoicism that he utters a plea for international unity: 'I would we were all of one mind, and one mind good' (5.3.295–6). Posthumus's resignation, and the jailer's vision of the healing of a broken world, take us into the play's extraordinary final scene.

Pisanio, who has done so much plot-contriving in the earlier scenes, has already given up and declared, 'Fortune brings in some boats that are not steered' (4.3.46). As the finale unfolds, he shows a similar resignation when he recognizes Innogen: 'Since she is living, let the time run on / To good or bad' (5.4.127–8). The finale itself is an intricate tour de force in which confusions are cleared up, lost identities are recovered, and characters return from apparent death. However, it is driven not so much by the decisive wills of the characters as by their openness to events as they unfold, and it is shot through with images of surrender: as Pisanio gives up any effort to control the plot, Giacomo surrenders his claim to have won the wager and gives back his winnings; Posthumus surrenders his claim of revenge; and, Cymbeline, moved by this example, reverses his intention to kill his prisoners:

> *Giacomo.* (*kneeling*) Take that life, beseech you,
> Which I so often owe; but your ring first,
> And here the bracelet of the truest princess
> That ever swore her faith.
> *Posthumus.* (*raising him*)   Kneel not to me.
> The power that I have on you is to spare you,
> The malice towards you to forgive you. Live,
> And deal with others better.
> *Cymbeline.*   Nobly doomed!
> We'll learn our freeness of a son-in-law.
> Pardon's the word to all.   (5.4.415–22)

This general surrender of claims leads to the most striking of all, Cymbeline's declaration,

> Although the victor, we submit to Caesar
> And to the Roman empire, promising
> To pay our wonted tribute ...   (5.4.461–3)

The British victory, which has provided so much of the narrative drive in the final scenes, appears to vanish. The Roman soothsayer has already, in a vision, seen his own national symbol disappear:

> I saw Jove's bird, the Roman eagle, winged
> From the spongy south to this part of the west,
> There vanished in the sunbeams ... (4.2.348–50)

At first, he reads this as a sign of Roman victory; later, he reads it as a sign of Roman-British unity:

> [this] foreshowed our princely eagle,
> Th'imperial Caesar, should again unite
> His favour with the radiant Cymbeline,
> Which shines here in the west. (5.4.474–7)

He never takes the most natural reading, that Roman power will dissolve in the face of British splendour. But, putting his vision together with Cymbeline's submission, we see that the condition of Roman-British unity, 'all of one mind,' is mutual surrender. It is fitting that in this final scene we cannot tell where we are: Wales or Britain, near London (there is a British prison, and the Queen's death seems to have taken place nearby), or near Milford Haven. As national claims vanish, so does the geography on which such claims are based.

Cymbeline's final command celebrates this new unity in a symbolic form that has a modern resonance:

> Let
> A Roman and a British ensign wave
> Friendly together ... (5.4.480–2)

The red ensign that did duty as the Canadian flag, before the present flag was adopted, combined the Union Jack with the Canadian coat of arms. In the federalist rally in Montreal that preceded the second Quebec referendum, people painted their faces with the maple leaf on one side and the fleur-de-lis on the other. At crossing points on the longest undefended border in the world, a Canadian and an American flag wave (more or less) friendly together.

Claims are surrendered on both sides, and we are all of one mind. But to end on that note would be un-Canadian. Too assertive. In Thomas King's short story 'Borders,' the narrator's mother, asked her citizenship at a border crossing into the United States, replies 'Blackfoot.' Ordered back to the Canadian border, she gives the same answer. The result is a protracted bureaucratic standoff in which the family is suspended between border points, unable to move in either direction. Finally they are free to go, and free to return, and the story ends: 'I watched the border through the rear window until all you could see were the tops of the flagpoles and the blue water tower, and then they rolled over a hill and disappeared' (145). In the story, the vanishing flags of two recently invented nations accompany the re-emergence of an older nation. But the image may resonate, as powerful images do, beyond its immediate purpose. In the present context, it matters most that the Canadian flag disappears, like Milford Haven, like the Roman eagle. There is a hope here for a sense of community that will transcend the claims of conventional nationality, dispensing with old symbols to create a neutral space in which different voices can speak freely, as in the multivocal space of a Shakespeare play. But, just as the surrender of claims that allows harmony is always close to the surrender that is mere surrender, so there is also the fear that neutrality will collapse into emptiness, that the place from which we are speaking will vanish, that our voices will no longer be ours and will have nothing of our own to say.

Notes

1 Pancheva's immediate reference is to a contemporary production, but there are implications for critical reading as well.
2 The seminar on *Cymbeline* at the 26th Annual Meeting of the Shakespeare Association of America (at the Renaissance Cleveland Hotel, Cleveland, 1998), chaired by Jodi Mikalachki, included a number of papers on questions of national identity. These included papers by Ronald Boling, Elizabeth French, Megan S. Lloyd, Martin Orkin, Avraham Oz, and Terry Reilly. I found my thinking for this paper stimulated by all of them, and by the general discussion in our meeting.
3 All references to *Cymbeline* are to the Oxford edition, edited by Roger Warren (Oxford: Oxford UP, 1998), which means adopting two Oxford innovations about which I am dubious: 'Innogen' for Imogen and 'Giacomo' for Iachimo. This has been useful to me as a small gesture towards defamiliarizing the text, but to some it may appear a typical example of Canadian passiveness in accepting guidance from abroad.
4 As Jodi Mikalachki puts it, it is 'as though his body were a literalization of the Roman writing of ancient British history' (106).
5 On the principle that a people may be best understood through its jokes, a story from the Cold War may help. An American, a Russian, and a Canadian

arrive at the Pearly Gates. St Peter asks each in turn how he got there. The American replies, 'I died defending freedom and democracy against the menace of international communism.' The Russian replies, 'I died defending the freedom of the workers against the forces of capitalist imperialism.' The Canadian replies, 'These two brought me.'

6 In his (untitled) paper for the Cleveland seminar, Ronald Boling produced evidence of long-standing English anxiety about Milford Haven as a likely point for enemy invasion.

7 Although it is not so literally a recognition-token as the mole on Guiderius's neck (5.4.364–9), the mole on Innogen's body is still key evidence of Giacomo's 'knowledge' of her, and it shifts as he describes it from on her breast to under it (2.2.37–8, 2.4.134–5).

8 Heather McAfee's paper on the search for origins in *Cymbeline*, presented in my graduate seminar on Shakespearean comedy, has helped my thinking about this character.

13

Frye's Shakespeare, Frye's Canada

L.M. FINDLAY

As the reconditioned engines of millennial federalism kick into life, some familiar Canadian questions take on a special urgency. What *is* Canada on the threshold of the new millennium? What *will* it become after crossing this threshold? What role will culture, particularly literary culture, have in fashioning a fresh national and international identity or set of identities for this country? Where, one might ask, is Northrop Frye when we need him? Well, his example as a public intellectual using his influence to direct public policy and debate is still with us, and we can look to events like the Toronto symposium *Reflections on the Public Good* (7 November 1998), featuring six of Canada's most prominent public intellectuals, as working with Frye's legacy. But one can learn more from Frye about the connections between personal and national identity formation and literary imagination than is readily available in his more public forays and record of service on bodies like the Canadian Radio-television and Telecommunications Commission. And I propose to use some of his writings on Shakespeare to elucidate his thinking about Canada's colonial and postcolonial relation to Great Britain, and hence to the exacting gift of the English language and the enriching and encumbering effects of English literary, scholarly, and political traditions in Canadian contexts. Frye's Shakespeare, sometimes by design and sometimes inadvertently, can help us understand Canada as a set of proto-canonical dramatic productions – predominantly comic and romantic – whose staging and interpretation remain in consoling as well as cautionary senses a *popular* activity. While I would rather liken Canada to a history play than to a comedy or romance, I have to admire and continue to learn from the ways in which a literary scholar applies his specialized knowledge to a broader range of social and political issues, connecting the apparent timelessness of Shakespeare's art to some of the distinctive contingencies of Canada in the twentieth century.

This chapter is organized into three main parts. In the first of these, I examine Frye's work on Shakespeare as instrumental in his own scholarly self-fashioning and in his reading of the nation as history, myth, and poetic genre. As a leading theorist and exegete, Frye demonstrates the power of theory to frame, indeed claim, the canon, and helps prepare the way for later waves of theory that for at least two decades seemed to ignore or undervalue casually his groundbreaking and widely influential formulations and interpretations. Yet Frye's Shakespeare is about politics as well as mythopoetics and is in part a coming to terms with the political realities of his own time and place. This accommodation is most often oblique yet predictive of the line he will take in his later writings on explicitly Canadian and contemporary themes. In the second part of the chapter, I will pursue continuities and compatibilities from the reading of Shakespeare's politics to Frye's own, and show how this leads to symptomatic unfairness in his discussion of French Quebec, Canada's aboriginal peoples, and Canadian Marxists. In the third and final part of the chapter, I speak more explicitly and consciously from my own version of the here and now in Canada today, and against the liberalism Frye uses Shakespeare to promote.

Like Shakespeare, Frye cannot be left to the guardianship of liberal humanists. I prefer to return him to the terrain neither he nor Shakespeare has ever vacated nor ever fully can: namely, the terrain of ideological struggle where aesthetics and politics are variously and adversarially interrelated. In so doing, I do not seek to diminish (even if I could) his importance to literary studies in general and Shakespearean scholarship in particular. (As Alexander Leggatt, for instance, has shown in his fine recent study of comedy [75, 94–6, 146], Frye's ideas attract their share of anti-formalist animus, but they are still influential, particularly in the areas of comedy and romance, and are more likely to be modified than mutilated or dismissed.) I wish to rethink the nature of Frye's importance and offer a more radicalizing version of him than the one promoted by so many of the contributors to *The Legacy of Northrop Frye* (1994) and intensified in *Rereading Frye* (1999).

Frye's Shakespeare

Frye's writings on Shakespeare are voluminous and their continuing presence in Shakespeare studies substantial and complex. They helped make him a world figure and a Canadian icon whose work by 1987 had already generated Robert D. Denham's 449-page *Annotated Bibliography of Primary and Secondary Sources*, to be followed two years later by the John Ayre biography, in which a former Victoria College student and journalist brings out most effectively the extent of Frye's fame and the power of his Canadian presence. Far from pretending to deal comprehensively or definitively with that fame and presence, I now offer a reading of Frye's reading of the Bard attuned to topics and elements especially connectable to his understanding and portrayal of Canada.

From his early experience of Shakespeare through the uniquely negative filter of Pelham Edgar's class for undergraduates at Victoria College (*Northrop Frye in Conversation* 47), through his Oxford reprise of *the* English curriculum and Emmanuel College essays on theological topics, Frye showed a strong and increasingly distinctive sense of Shakespeare's qualities (as recorded, for example, in *Collected Works* 1.435; 2.532, 603, 738; 3.58, 107, 336). In the pivotal essay on 'The Function of Criticism at the Present Time' (1949), he is already using the Bard to clarify the theories that will dominate the *Anatomy of Criticism*. It is significant that this essay is reprinted in a volume dedicated to Canadian identity (see Ross) as well as revised for the 'Polemical Introduction' to the *Anatomy* in 1957. Canada and the canon are interconnected parts of Frye's intellectual maturation, and they come together in interesting ways when he is intent on advocating a criticism that is autonomous, systematic, and capable of progressing beyond a state of 'naive induction' (*Anatomy* 15):

> There is as yet no way of distinguishing what is genuine criticism, and therefore progresses toward making the whole of literature intelligible, from what belongs only to the history of taste, and therefore follows the vacillations of fashionable prejudice. I give an example of the difference between the two which amounts to a head-on collision. In one of his curious, brilliant, scatter-brained footnotes to *Munera Pulveris*, John Ruskin says:
>
>> Of Shakespeare's names I will afterwards speak at more length; they are curiously – often barbarously – mixed out of various traditions and languages. Three of the clearest in meaning have been already noticed. Desdemona – 'dusdaimonia' [miserable fortune] – is also plain enough. Othello is, I believe, 'the careful'; all the calamity of the tragedy arising from the single flaw and error in his magnificently collected strength. Ophelia, 'serviceableness,' the true lost wife of Hamlet, is marked as having a Greek name by that of her brother

Laertes; and its signification is once exquisitely alluded to in that brother's last word of her, where her gentle preciousness is opposed to the uselessness of the churlish clergy:
– 'A *ministering* angel shall my sister be, when thou liest howling.'
On this passage Matthew Arnold comments as follows:
Now, really, what a piece of extravagance all that is! I will not say that the meaning of Shakespeare's names (I put aside the question as to the correctness of Mr. Ruskin's etymologies) has no effect at all, may be entirely lost sight of; but to give it that degree of prominence is to throw the reins to one's whim, to forget all moderation and proportion, to lose the balance of one's mind altogether. It is to show in one's criticism, to the highest excess, the note of provinciality.
Now, whether Ruskin is right or wrong, he is attempting genuine criticism. He is trying to interpret Shakespeare in terms of a conceptual framework which belongs to the critic alone, and yet relates itself to the plays alone. Arnold is perfectly right in feeling that this is not the sort of material that the public critic can directly use. But he does not seem even to suspect the existence of a systematic criticism as distinct from the history of taste. Here it is Arnold who is the provincial. Ruskin has learned his trade from the great iconological tradition which comes down through Classical and Biblical scholarship into Dante and Spenser, both of whom he had studied carefully, and which is incorporated in the mediaeval cathedrals he had pored over in such detail. Arnold is assuming, as a universal law of nature, certain 'plain sense' critical axioms which were hardly heard of before Dryden's time and which can assuredly not survive the age of Freud and Jung and Frazer and Cassirer. (9–10)

Frye employs history in order to devalue the particular version of it associated with connoisseurship, not so as to impugn history as such. In a self-consciously polemical text he features a 'head-on collision' in order to illustrate a distinction fundamental to his own project. The juxtaposition of Ruskin and Arnold on the theme of Shakespeare leaves neither Victorian sage undamaged. Frye, only too aware of the power of Canadian Arnoldianism (see, for example, Murray, *Working* 68, 73–5), aligns himself with Ruskin as a gifted but erratic precursor of himself, a precursor too unsystematic to activate an Oedipal reaction in him but strong enough to reveal the weaknesses of Frye's real competition. The two solitudes of 'the critic alone' and 'the plays alone' are brought together in a way that exposes Arnold to the very charge he levels against Ruskin. Frye ignores the callousness of Arnold's mention of mental imbalance in connection with a man already well known for his proneness to such breakdowns, and Frye ignores, too, the political implications of Arnold's 'moderation' and 'proportion.' He latches instead onto the notion of provincialism, and does so, one suspects, because it resonates strongly with his own continuing insecurities as a Canadian intellectual on the international stage. By crediting Ruskin with putting Shakespeare in an appropriate conceptual framework, Frye entitles himself to moderate the claims of Arnoldian classicism and displace a pagan Greek *architektonike* with a mediaeval Gothic one that celebrates the very iconological knowledge most recuperable by Ruskin and by himself. With the backing of this kind of 'tradition' and its distinguished adherents, Frye feels confident in prophesying the end of Arnoldian provincialism and the rise of 'genuine criticism.' Not surprisingly, critical 'provincialism[s]' come off much worse in the *Anatomy* (62, etc.) than Frye's own multimodal practice.

Frye's Shakespeare in the *Anatomy* creates a comprehensive, five-phase schema ('stages in the life of a redeemed society' [185]) within which his later work on the Bard will complicate and more fully vivify his readings of particular passages and plays. The discussion of comedy is fairly traditional and hence firmly connected to socio-political issues. Like so many other writers on this topic, Frye emphasizes the power of convention and the achievement of social integration despite a volatile intergenerational politics. *All's Well*, for instance, is a 'problem' and exception that proves a strong rule in favour of youthfully driven love matches rather than arranged marriages, and the general movement 'from law to liberty,' to the 'green world' (180–2) and back again. This movement supplements and renews social structures by accessing ritual and dream and that which is desirable but not necessarily achievable. Individual comedic iterations are situated by Frye within a larger pattern culminating in works that are 'more subtle and complex' than the early comedies but also 'more archaic and primitive' – as in the doubling of the 'materials' of *The Winter's Tale* and *Pericles* as 'both far-fetched and inevitably right' (184). The more powerful revealing of the 'inner forms of drama' signals an arrival both at drama's 'bedrock' and at 'the still center of the order of words' (117). An apparently implausible mix of progression and regression marks the passage into anagogy, where 'nature becomes, not the container, but the thing contained ... This is not reality, but it is the conceivable or imaginative limit of desire, which is infinite, eternal, and hence apocalyptic' (119). Frye knows full well that 'anagogy' is a difficult term, and in the glossary at the end of the *Anatomy* he explains it as 'relating to literature as a total order of words' (365). He uses this term to induce ongoing effort in his readers, to affirm the bonds between theology and literature and the interconnectedness of centre and structure, and to underscore continuities from the Middle Ages through the Renaissance to the modern world. He finds anagogy best defined in Dante and some of its most compelling exemplifications in Shakespeare. This double source of a four-part schema (literal, symbolic, allegorical, and anagogic) in religious faith and literary imagination is more to Frye's liking than the theories of polysemous meaning offered by modern symbolic logic or semantics, because it attests to the closeness of literary and religious canons and to the legitimacy of literature looking to itself to account for the literary. This gaze is both centripetal and dependent, compromising literary authority and autonomy only within the context of faith. Anagogy is difficult to get straight and keep straight, but it is at work in all words with spiritual power, including the 'more uninhibited utterances of poets themselves' (122).

Comic revelation may allow for the alarming possibility of 'an omnipotent human society,' but only in the escape from 'any actual civilization or set of moral values' into the fully logocentric realm beyond '*mimesis logou* [and within] the Logos, the shaping word which is both reason ... and *praxis*' (120). Anagogic criticism accordingly sees literature as autonomous but not reclusive, allowing in its anagogic efforts the 'radical form of metaphor, "A is B," to come into its own' while confirming that 'poets are happier as servants of religion than of politics, because the transcendental and apocalyptic perspective of religion comes as a tremendous emancipation of the imaginative mind' (124–5). Neither the critic nor the poet can achieve the cosmic singularity of anagogic man, or fully incorporate nature in culture, and that leaves us with tensions and discrepancies in the world of lived experience where 'the autonomy of culture, which may be provisionally defined as the total body of imaginative hypothesis in a society and its tradition,' must be defended. To do just this is 'the social task of the "intellectual" in the modern world; if so, to defend [culture's] subordination to a total synthesis of any kind, religious or political, would be the authentic form of the *trahison des clercs*' (127). Frye appeals to the authority and value of a totality inaccessible except through anagogy (and apostrophe), and he depends on this conditional access as a shield against the totalitarian exploitation of ideas of wholeness and unity which has occurred only too often in history. Such dependence is an act of intellectual responsibility and residual, non-sectarian faith. Social redemption in this world requires the autonomous imagination, and that autonomy reproduces itself by exceeding or opposing dominant orthodoxies.

The idea of comedy as articulating relations between the primordial and the political, an activity much in evidence in recent scholarly work on resurgent nationalisms in eastern Europe (Stepan 232), is given further play by Frye in the Bampton lectures at Columbia University in 1963. These lectures explore the '*development* of Shakespearean comedy and romance' from 'a middle distance' where these plays seem like a 'number of *simultaneous* chess games played by a master who wins them all' (Frye, *Natural* xxii; emphasis added to bring out the tensions between the synchronic and the diachronic, including mythic schemata and history, here and elsewhere in Frye). Frye chooses to talk about comedy because that is where his time has most recently been spent, but he refuses to confine himself to specialist details of chronology or textual cruces. Once again, he defines himself by difference from Arnold, this time on the grounds that Arnoldian 'high seriousness,' even when expanded by modern scholars into a defence of literary realism, still tends to devalue what matters more to 'an Odyssean critic ... attracted to comedy and romance' (*Natural* 2). The intellectual outsider as generalist builds on the conventionality of the popular – in this case detective fiction – in order to refigure Shakespeare as scholarly in his own non-Jonsonian way, working with great accuracy within the apparent permissiveness of 'oral tradition' and functioning 'like Bach, as a scholar of the ear' (22). Accordingly, a play like *Pericles* need not be worked over until one fully separates the 'unmistakeable' poetry of the final three acts from the 'undistinguished bumble' of the opening two (38). This play is structurally sound even if stylistically inconsistent, and that is because Shakespeare 'had no principles of anything except dramatic structure' (39). This claim prompts an immediate question: 'Why, then, is there so determined an effort to make him an incompetent thinker as well as a great poet?' (39). Frye answers his own question by returning to the Arnoldian/Odyssean distinction he started with, and we begin to realize that he is talking once again about his own refusal to entrap the imagination within the entanglements of the 'real' and other ideological constructs. Frye is defending work that is 'conventional, popular, and primitive' (72) and hence outside the illiberal loop of High Culture and 'high seriousness.' Such work is hopeful in reaching a point 'when a new society is crystallized,' a point Frye would rather call novel ('anastrophe') than negative ('catastrophe'), gesturing towards anagogy from a position of structural creativity according to which ritual is not absorbed by comedy but rather resequenced (72-3). Degenerate history may require comic redemption, as in *The Merry Wives* (89), but ritual is always already a structuring of contingency and disorder on the way to 'some postdramatic world where the questions of illusion and of a detached or alienated spectator are no longer raised' (111).

The primacy of structure allows Frye to accommodate the vagaries of style and also alterations of mood to a larger purpose. In the final Bampton lecture, he reaffirms this: 'I said that while structure was the focus of a community, uniformity of mood, which demands uniformity of response, breaks down the community into a mob; the kind of audience appealed to by farce, Grand Guignol melodrama, and extreme didacticism. Sentimentality is the subjective equivalent of the mob's stock response to mood. The sentimental is withdrawn but not detached; it is an egocentric feeling but not an individualized one; it is gregarious but not social' (*Natural* 132). Frye is driven to discriminate here between good and bad social cohesion, good and bad selfhood. That deceptively reassuring term 'community' (Findlay and Findlay 1-3) seems to promise social existence somehow realizable beyond politics, as the effect of a common form of attention or gaze, while the mob represents politics' debasement into dangerously unstructured uniformity. Comedy, as the legitimation of community rather than monarchy (cf. Frye, *Fools* 20-1), runs the risk of being considered sentimental when, in fact, it structures the 'return' of an innocence that we have never known before but have the ability to recognize through our own childhoods, symbolic ordering of experience, and communitarian 'focus.' In best liberal fashion, Frye links the social and the individual in a mutually legitimating structure that can find in comedy 'a genuinely new vision' rather than dangerous or sterile regression. This vision becomes available in the structuring of actions 'not simply cyclical but *dialectical* as well: the renewing power of the final action lifts us into a higher world, and separates that world from the world of the comic action itself' (*Natural* 133). Anagogic elevation is represented in a way that gives a quasi-religious rather than a socio-political resonance to 'dialectic.' The power of sentimental incitement to 'demand' an irrationally unified social response is opposed to comedy's capacity to 'lift us' via our individualized yet collective specular work 'into a higher world.' Politics virtually disappears as the excluded middle of a mythic activity that can awaken us individually and communally from the 'long nightmare of tyranny and injustice which is human history' (133). Perhaps in leaping over or being propelled beyond nationhood in its own change from colony to regionalized, postnational member of the global community (see, for example, Frye, 'Culture as Interpenetration' 15), Canada can achieve in the most serious sense a comic destiny!

It is surely more than happenstance that Frye invests so much in Shakespearean comedy and romance, while his engagement with the tragedies and the histories is less sustained. In the *Anatomy*, tragedy supplements the social emphasis of comedy with the interrogation of the individual in an encounter with natural law (208-9). Reducible neither to fate nor to moral law, tragedy entails rather 'a sense of some far-reaching mystery ... the hero has thrown a switch in a larger machine than his own life, or even his own society' (211). The self-deception of the hero reveals the instability of human power, whether nominally supreme or minimally conditioned. In Shakespeare's versions of the tragic, social disconnection is explored during a 'period of social history in which an aristocracy is fast losing its effective power but still retains a good deal of ideological prestige' (37). As the *Anatomy* avers, tragedy focuses more on the individual, but in a relatively alienated, anomic way that obliquely illuminates the value of integration within a community. Frye's double emphasis on community and structure garners indirect but valuable support from human agents *in extremis* in the tragedies and histories. And in the Alexander Lectures of 1966, subsequently published as *Fools of Time*, there are many socially as well as psychologically telling insights into tragedies of order, passion, and isolation. Here, Frye the taxonomist insists that 'even when a history-play ends on a strong major chord it is never a comedy' but rather a more continuous form of tragedy (15). And tragedy culminates in a post-heroic but 'pre-democratic' 'social contract,' which 'often in Shakespeare ... is merely an exhausted and demoralized huddle' (18, 6). That 'huddle' may not be a mob or quorum for conspiracy, but nor is it the well-mixed makings of a new society. The limits to even a hero's ability to master things as they are leads to a kind of quietism or resignation in which we 'come to terms with irony by reducing our wants' (14). There is a constitutive crisis of authority in historical societies where kings or rulers simulate but do not 'incarnate ... a state of social discipline' (14). The incomplete embodiment of such discipline is also a defective representation of it, which at least indirectly encourages insurgency. The fundamental conflictedness of supreme human authority – the king's two bodies notwithstanding – can be resolved only by comic deferral until the coming of anagogic man, a coming made all the more socially and dramatically necessary by Machiavelli's political solution – 'destroying the integrity of tragedy by obliterating the difference between the order-figure and the rebel-figure' (Frye, *Fools* 20). Shakespeare fends off this threat to 'tragic structure' by ' a subtle combination of *de jure* and *de facto* authority' (20), but this strategy carries dangers of its own, not least of which is the inadvertent authorizing – through more or less 'subtle' recollection and opportunism – of the open-ended economy of revenge.

A little later in this lecture, Frye will claim that in *Hamlet* 'the sanctity of the greater revenge atones for everything: Laertes dies full of remorse for his own treachery and flights of angels sing Hamlet to his rest' (28). However, no sooner is this claim for a complete accounting made than we are back with tragedy's social contract and the instabilities of the composite and conflicted political subject. Where Machiavelli had elided difference, Frye now proposes Heideggerian ecstasy as the key to an 'ordered society' whose 'members are outside themselves, at work in the world, and their being is their function' (29). It is an unsettling claim linked to charismatic followership and to a mimetic order where 'right imitates might' (32) and where social cohesion means either flocking together 'like so many wild-geese' (*2 Henry IV* 5.1.68–71; qtd. in Frye, *Fools* 28) or submission to 'a conservative view of society' such as is contained in 'Ulysses' speech on degree, Canterbury's beehive figure, or Menenius' fable of the belly' (108). Tragic polity, unlike comedic community, seems more carceral than crystalline, more authoritarian than anagogic, but Frye warns us against critical projection and the mistaking of poetic vision for political theory. The critic may be 'almost compelled' to do so but there are stronger compulsions than this available: 'For us, to put a personal loyalty above a loyalty of principle, as the Nazis did, is culturally regressive: it begins in hysteria and ends in psychosis. But Shakespeare has no theory of society: what he has is a vision of society, and that vision is so powerfully convincing that we accept it without question' (33). Tragedy should not be reduced to the history it implicates or seems to explicate. It should be seen in its own terms as a structuring of archetypal settings (passion and power and loyalty and absurdity [33]) whose survival so regularly enriches while endangering our own. As he would insist when teaching *Lear*, Frye is promoting the 'primary power of vision in human consciousness, before it gets congealed into religious or political beliefs or institutions' (Frye, *Northrop Frye on Shakespeare* 120). Poesis offers a version of the (relatively) unconditioned that is best understood by anagogic criticism. It best proclaims the 'priority of mythology to ideology' (143) enacted mythopoetically in Shakespeare's work and critically in Frye's own.

Frye's Canada

Frye's interest in comedy and romance is explicable in part by his commitment to Christianity as a divine comedy (as in *The Great Code* 47ff.), but also by his commitment to Canada as a liberal democracy within which the liberal arts liberate something essential, giving its citizens all the freedom they really need. His is a highly distinctive liberation theology both scrupulous and generous, but we are invited by it to underwrite the impossibility and undesirability of political revolution and urged to prefer mythology to ideology. The implications of this preference may seem reassuring to any Canadian or student of Canada who accepts Frye's linking of revolution to an inaugural violence that then entrenches itself at home and abroad, whether Soviet-style or as the American way. But it is one thing to oppose violence, and quite another to aid unfairness and injustice by hiding ideology within myth. One might conceivably connect patriarchal structures in the comedies and romances to modern analogues in Frye's Canada that patronize and disadvantage many a 'piece of tender air' (*Cymbeline* 5.4.139–40; for the gender implications of the Soothsayer's sexist etymologies, see Findlay, 'Temporality' 125–9.) However, without depreciating the power and problems of the patriarchal dimension of Frye's thought, I wish instead to focus on three other targets of his condescension, markers of the illiberal limits of his arguably Shakespearean liberalism: French Quebec; aboriginal and Metis peoples; and Canadian Marxists (among the last of whom I might myself be numbered).

It is understandable but disappointing to see Frye attempting to confine Quebec separatism to an emancipatory cultural activism defined in its essentials by *Le Refus Global* of 1948 (*Divisions* 62–6). According to Frye, French in North America is a 'beleaguered language' that guarantees its poets and novelists status and a 'social function' (63). Francophone writers and painters particularly have been thriving in this situation, but their achievements ought not to be dubbed 'cultural nationalism.' That label would unduly politicize them, tying them to the quite different pace and direction of economic and political movements. Nationalism is a 'misleading' notion in a country now so strongly aligned with non-aggression, a country whose maturity depends on the vitality of its regions within a stable but permissive confederation. Regionalism in a distinctive register and different language is what should be aspired to and celebrated. Anything more conscripts imaginative vitality once again within an intellectuals' movement, a *trahison des clercs* who have used the academy as a place from which to dominate the 'communications media' and purvey 'a simple emotional construct in which Confederation equals bondage and separation freedom' (64-5). In modern Quebec as in Shakespeare's England, the product of such sentimental incitements is the mob, the very antithesis of a healthy polity. Frye presses home his point in a cultural prophecy both prescriptive and patronizing: 'As an intellectuals' movement, even a revolutionary one, it may settle for a purely symbolic separation; if it goes beyond that, whatever is distinctive in the culture of Quebec will be its first casualty' (65). One may share, as I do, Frye's hope that Quebec remain within Canada, while deploring his anglo-culturalism here and refusing his further defence of what 'may sound like a very English-based view of Canadian history' wherein French Canada shared English Canada's 'Tory opposition to the Whig victory in the American Revolution' and its 'strongly anti-clerical' successor in France (66).

Part of the problem with this analysis of 'dramatic' developments in Quebec is Frye's doctrine of the separation of powers imaginative and intellectual, and spheres symbolic and political. What force, or enforceability, does the adverb have in the expression 'purely symbolic' used above? Behind this and similar usages lies a persistent failure to value adequately power relations in the here and now, an entrenched tendency to overvalue aesthetic transcendence. This becomes clearer and at least as worrying in the case of Canada's native peoples, despite Frye's general and sincere abhorrence of how they have been treated in North America. In talking about Canada's mercantilist presumptions and practices (*Divisions* 29ff.), Frye sees culture as having been employed as the handmaid of an economy in which value is added elsewhere, in the mother country, in the Old World, and then redistributed domestically and in the colonies to maximize profit and reinforce dependency on particular elites. The artificiality of such an arrangement is contrasted with 'a genuinely primitive community, like those of the indigenous peoples, [where] poetry leaps into the foreground as one of the really essential elements of life, along with food and shelter' (29).

Frye's use of the term 'community' here (not to mention 'genuinely primitive') is both honorific and depoliticizing. One consequence of the 'modified mercantilism' that endures into Canada in the 1930s is the 'creative person [determined] to produce the raw material of his [sic] experience as part of an attempt to affect the ownership of production' (29). Frye deplores this as another way of 'reducing literature to rhetoric, and focussing on content.' Yet at the same time, although he does not mention it, 'genuinely primitive' communities continue to be infantilized and/or exoticised by the quasi-scientific rigour of modern linguistics and by the imperialist residues of what the liberal-humanist Frye naively calls 'the humane flexibility of nineteenth-century philology' (but see Olender; and Findlay, 'That liberty'). While openly deploring colonial murder and betrayal of indigenous peoples (see, for example, Frye's comments on Caliban's foreshadowing of further colonial cruelties [*Eternal* 93]), Frye opines that 'the main focus of guilt in Canada seems to fall on the rape of nature' (68). But this literary emphasis has changed, he says in 1977, in the following way:

> Meanwhile, an interest in Indian and Eskimo art, with all their nature-spirits, has grown into a fascination, and many of our younger poets – Susan Musgrave, John Newlove, Gwendolyn MacEwen – write as though Indians and Eskimos were our direct cultural ancestors whose traditions continue in them and in us. In fiction, there are some curious stories, such as Margaret Atwood's *Surfacing* and Marian Engel's *Bear*, of heroines turning away from their civilized heritage toward an identity with nature. It seems clear that for Canadian culture the old imperialist phrase 'going native' has come home to roost. We are no longer an army of occupation, and the natives are ourselves. (69)

While making some allowance for the date when this was written, one can hardly fail to notice the remarkable power Frye attributes to the literary imagination for healing differences. Here this imagination claims to internalize otherness, and effects a transition from military occupation to communal preoccupation with nary a mention of the attendant and still unresolved legal and political battles and the territorial disputes occasioned by cultural kleptomania and the anxiety of authenticity. Postcolonial critical discourse, by virtue of its emphasis on history, politics, 'race,' and the cultural armatures of hegemony, might well have enabled Frye to sound less like an oversanguine Prospero here. The hyphenated Canadianness of 'nature-spirits' may allow Euro-Canadians to push beyond cultural simulation towards cultural identity, but this process is no more complete and fully mutual than Prospero's recognition of Caliban: 'this thing of darkness I / Acknowledge mine' (5.1.275–6). An overdetermined discourse of the *sauvage* combines with Frye's anagogic inclinations and uneasy wit to portray a unitary state seriously skewed in favour of colonizers who will 'repatriat[e]' *their* culture to 'what was an inarticulate space on a map [that is, *terra habitus et nullius*!]'' (70). Continuity and cohesion are achieved, as they had been in *The Critical Path* (38ff.), by de-indigenizing orality and exaggerating the identity across time and cultures of 'the professional oral poet.' The disappointing or disturbing effect of Frye's anachronistic, Eurocentric specification *professional* is intensified rather than dispelled by his further concession regarding oral poets: 'There are of course other kinds.' The fate of the unprofessional Other has been only too predictable in the modern world.

Frye's ongoing investigation of Canadian identity is clearly enriched by his study of Shakespeare, but always to the detriment of what he takes to be 'mere' ideology. Frye consistently values and fiercely defends difference and dissent, but not as fully and unconditionally as some would like. In the Conclusion to the second edition of the *Literary History of Canada* (as reprinted in *Divisions*), his comedic quietism prompts him to suggest that 'perhaps identity only is identity when it becomes, not militant, but a way of defining oneself against something else' (75). He then resorts to 'a different kind of analogy' to illustrate Canadianness:

> in countries where Marxism has not come to power, but where there is a strong Marxist minority, we see what an advantage it is to have a unified conceptual structure that can be applied to practically anything. It may often distort what it is applied to, but that matters less than the tactical advantage of having it. Defenders of more empirical points of view find their battlefronts disintegrating into separate and isolated outposts. They may demonstrate that this or that point is wrong, but such rearguard actions lack glamour. The same principle can be applied to the pragmatic compromising, ad hoc, ramshackle Canadian tradition vis-a-vis the far more integrated and revolutionary American one. The coherence of the 'American way of life' is often underestimated by Americans themselves, because the more thoughtful citizens of any country are likely to be more preoccupied with its anomalies. Hence outsiders, including Canadians, may find the consistency easier to see. (75)

Frye is returning here to the theme of marginality-without-provincialism so important to his sense of his role as a Canadian Shakespearean. This theme requires of him a capacity for discerning structure and complicating uniformity. Marxist critique is useful as well as predictable, so long as it remains a minority discourse in the body politic. But Canadian resistance to American hegemony comes from a different quarter, exemplifying the virtues of unpredictable, non-cohesive, cultural dissent within a polity whose destiny is comedically latent or deferred rather than historically manifest and actual. For Frye, the 'capitalist-socialist controversy is out of date, and ... a detente with nature is what is important now' (70). This move to an ecological 'politics' is informed by Blake's 'Jerusalem,' to be sure, but also by comedy's 'green world' and 'crystalline' new society. As a quasi-Shakespearean construct, Canada seems to have gone from a pastoral to a post-pastoral condition without ever experiencing or desiring a thorough-going, transformative class struggle.

Dramaturge or Demiurge? Towards a Post-liberal *Anatomy*

The separations Frye maintains in the Conclusion to the *Literary History* and in his Shakespearean work in name of autonomy are inescapably hierarchical, and implausibly dialectical. Indeed, they seem in large measure bad ideology, prizing as they do consolation over contestation. And the same can be said for his notion of 'interpenetration,' despite the best efforts of scholars as accomplished as Joseph Adamson and Robert Denham to defend it. I share with these scholars and their distinguished collaborators a sense that Frye has been unfairly neglected and sometimes wilfully misunderstood, and that the current generation of humanities students needs to understand his importance better. However, I cannot accept Adamson's claim that the only truly scholarly options are authoritative imagination and critical disinterestedness (74). Adamson follows Frye in seeing ideology as secondary, mythology as primary, and 'genuine dialectic' as available in ethical criticism that 'involves "the sense of the *real presence* of culture in the community"' ([*Anatomy* 24] 78-9; emphasis added). However, as the phrase I have highlighted indicates, this comes down to an article of (Christian) faith flung defiantly in the face of Jacques Derrida and other debunkers of any metaphysics of presence. Undecidability being what it is, such a difference cannot be resolved; but that does not mean that a deconstructive, Marxist, postcolonial or other hermeneutic of suspicion can simply be trumped by an appeal to Frye's self-identification as 'a liberal' and 'latterly a bourgeois one' (Adamson 96).

Shakespeare and Frye, each a canonical figure in his own right, continue to be claimed for and defended against ideology. To be sure, this struggle will not cease any time soon, nor should it, because it expresses in part the larger agonistic unevennesses of domestic and global 'development.' Accordingly, rather than counter the reductive treatment of ideology with an equally reductive treatment of art – as it is arguably practised by Shakespeare and ably advocated by Frye – I suggest that we recast this performance of difference dramaturgically, as a history play *of* and *for* our time and place, a play in which there is a residue of the optional within the oppositional, in a conjuncture of determinations without determinism.

The need or duty to transcend is arguably less useful, here and now, than the need to oppose massively commodifying trends which impersonate purity, autonomy, and generosity, staging consumption as legitimate escape from the clamour and disfigurements of production. Particularly dangerous among scholars is the attempt to appeal beyond real imperialism to great art's 'imperishable empire' (Macaulay, qtd. in Symonds 294) in order to justify opportunism, diminish the fragility of the dominant, and reinvent 'the human' (see Bloom, *Shakespeare*). Better, then, to do as those working in Marxist traditions today may find themselves doing: namely, taking to heart feminist and postcolonial critique of Marx's work, while refocusing on questions of class, ownership of the means of production, and the production of social relations. This emphasis on production is intended to counter the post-Marxist focus on consumption (see Findlay, 'Valuing') but also Frye's preference of the label 'creative scholar' to 'productive scholar,' with its nineteenth-century industrial overtones (*Eternal* 16). The counter-emphasis I am proposing and performing seems necessary and timely because the contemporary university, with its growing underclass of exploited graduate students, untenured teachers, and unsung research assistants, is rapidly *re-*industrializing itself even as its proclaims itself the harbinger of the *post*industrial. *This* is one of the constitutive contradictions of current capitalism. Political radicalism therefore remains an important option, unembarrassed as it is by its favouring of ideology over mythology, and attentive as it is to the conditions of production of academic knowledge, including knowledge about the literary canon.

In concluding, let me state this another way. Whether one wishes to produce social renewal 'only' dramatically or 'for real,' one is faced with the necessary connections between understanding and action, captured brilliantly but problematically in Marx's formulation 'der Demiurg des Wirklichen' ('the creator [demiurge] of the real world') (*Capital* 102; *Kapital* 23: 27). Marx is stressing that Hegel's version of dialectic is 'ihr direktes Gegenteil' ('the direct opposite of his own'), for Marx is convinced that 'bei mir ist umgekehrt das Ideele nichts andres als das im Menschenkopf umgesetze und ubersetze Materielle' ('the ideal is nothing but the material world reflected in the mind of man, and translated into forms of thought'). But the figure of the demiurge (Greek *demiourgos*) cannot be appropriated exclusively for idealism or materialism, creativity or social production. Since classical antiquity, the demiurge has supported the doubleness of creativity as both the creation of the world from its divine Idea and the human accomplishments of the public servant and the artisanal class (Liddell and Scott). Marx, in defining himself by difference from Hegel, recurs to the anastrophic (some would say catastrophic!) processes of inverting (*umkehren*), transposing (*umsetzen*), and translating (*übersetzen*), hence reinscribing processes of configuration and representation that Marx had just dismissed in Hegel as inadequate and erroneous: 'nur ... bildet' (only ... representing,' and idealistically misrepresenting). Even for Marx, there is no escape from representation, but how we choose to represent that inescapability is crucial to the prospects and accomplishments of knowledge at work in the world. Across languages, cultures, genres, and disciplines, we need to fix our gaze on the challenge of the now while strategically exploiting the prestige of canonical figures. If 'naive induction' is avoided by critics only if they abandon Canada itself to that condition, 'limping along from precedent to precedent' in the 'inductive, Burke tradition' (*World* 252), then perhaps criticism needs a new anatomy for a new body politic. This new anatomy might even be achieved and legitimized in part through reading and teaching Shakespeare and Frye within a more broadly educational and political activism than either of them envisaged. Hitherto, we have ta'en too little care of this.

PART FOUR

Reimagining Shakespeare

It seems fitting to conclude a book devoted to the multiple ways of reimagining Shakespeare in Canada – in institutionalized settings of various kinds, in stage productions, and in debates about interpretation and the functions of tradition – with a section that seeks to theorize and interrogate those forms of reimagining Shakespeare that pull all of these together into what has proved one of the signature elements of our postmodern times: the question of adaptation, appropriation, citation, and recycling of the Shakespearean text and image. Dennis Kennedy identifies this issue as likely to prove most productive in rendering 'the study and performance of Shakespeare fully contemporary and fully international' (300). It has dominated postcolonial and national approaches to Shakespeare, and it has proved perhaps the most challenging for promoters of stable text and author functions in determining the meaning of either Shakespeare or a coherent national culture. Part Four opens with Daniel Fischlin's theorization and illustration of Canadian adaptations of Shakespeare, demonstrating the many ways in which such adaptation has proved productive in Canada. Mark Fortier's chapter continues this examination of the theory and practice of adaptation, analysing further dimensions of Canadian anxiety and creativity in response to the challenge of Shakespeare. After these introductions to the scope and potential of the field come two chapters employing a narrower focus to illuminate specific dimensions of the question. Lois Sherlow attends to problems of translation across linguistic cultures in this bilingual nation and Ric Knowles considers the changing focus of national debates on the interdependence of questions of ethnicity, class, gender, sexual orientation, and race in the last three decades of the twentieth century as dramatized in three notable adaptations of *Othello*.

14
Nation and/as Adaptation: Shakespeare, Canada, and Authenticity[1]

DANIEL FISCHLIN

This chapter examines how Shakespearean theatrical adaptations reinforce, consolidate, and trouble polyphonic, and sometimes extremely dissonant, notions of Canadian national identity. Its thesis is that Canadian adaptations of Shakespeare (from a range of writing positions) puncture the reductive notion of an imagined community, to borrow Benedict Anderson's controversial term, based on the illusion of shared values that authenticate that community's identity. Imagined communities, as elaborated in over a century of Shakespearean adaptation in Canada, are highly variable and elusive: different imaginings produce different communities as mediated through the relationship to Shakespeare. Shakespeare serves multiple identity formations, with differing consequences for how nation is constructed in relation to differing theatrical discourses. Constituted by enormous regional and geographic differences, not to mention significant ethnic and multicultural diversity (at least in its urban centres), tense and complex relations to aboriginal peoples, and the constitutive problems associated with decolonization in the wake of contested relations between two so-called founding peoples, Canada cannot but complicate national identity as an expression of authentic coherence or difference.[2]

Moreover, adaptation, because it implies revision of an 'authentic' source, is one locus where issues surrounding identity are fruitfully pursued.[3] The problem of Shakespeare's iconic centrality to critical thinking generally has particular relevance in a national entity like Canada, still dealing with a colonial legacy and the effects of a less-than-complete decolonization. Instructive in this regard is Linda Hutcheon's summary of Canada's colonial history: 'It took a long time to loosen imperial ties never historically severed by revolution: becoming a nation in 1867 through the British North America Act, a British act of Parliament, Canada achieved full legal independence only in 1931 through another British law, the Statute of Westminster; amendments to the Canadian constitution were the sole preserve of the British Parliament until as late as 1982' ('Academic' 312). Further, Hutcheon notes that, despite the shedding of a legal colonial relation, 'Canada persuaded Britain to legislate it out of one colonial situation (a political and historical one), only to realize that it was already trapped in another (an economic and cultural one)' (312).

Canadian cultural autonomy, in other words, is still very much at issue, all the more so in adaptations of a major canonical figure like Shakespeare, who represents a form of colonial relation even as he is used in (some) adaptations to fracture or productively to reconfigure that relation. Shakespearean adaptation in Canada links colonial heritage with canonical authority, but that authority can then be turned, in what Northrop Frye calls 'interpenetration' (*Divisions* 15-25), to advantage in a revisionary, neo-colonial context. Goldwin Smith's absurd prediction in 1894 that 'no such thing as a literature Canadian in the local sense exists or is ever likely to exist' (qtd. in Findlay, 'Literature') is refuted by Canadian theatrical adaptations that revise canonical texts as a function of a specifically Canadian context, historicity, and territoriality. Frye summarizes, not unproblematically, the general direction this revisionary impetus has taken in Canadian literary culture: 'In proportion as Canada shook off its external and subordinating assumptions about its English and French cultural heritages, the genuine form of cultural development became more obvious. This genuine form is what I mean by interpenetration ... What [the language of the creative imagination] does is to create a vision that becomes a focus for a community' (*Divisions* 24).

In short, the question 'Why Shakespeare as a "focus for a community?"' morphs into 'Why adapted Shakespeare in Canada?': why perpetuate Shakespeare-centrism in the name of complex national signifying practices supposedly seeking a degree of autonomy from their colonial precursors as embodied in the iconicity of Shakespeare, the fraught symbol of colonial cultural dependency?

A simple answer to the question, Stratford aside,[4] is that theatrical and dramaturgical practices in Canada, however divergent and at odds with 'the Shakespeare effect,'[5] are highly invested in Shakespearean configurations. To adapt John Metcalfe's debatable formulation, '*We read what we are*' (104), 'we' (whatever illusory collectivity this pronoun stands in for) are (at times) what 'we' write and perform. And what 'we' write and perform in Canada has at least a partial relation to Shakespearean adaptation. Adaptation is a genre, if one takes the significant increase in adaptations produced in Canada over the last thirty years as any indication, that suits the aesthetics of Canadian self-representation. An ongoing bibliographical and anthology project associated with this chapter has shown that, from the late nineteenth century to the present, there have been a significant number of Shakespearean theatrical adaptations made and produced in Canada. To date, the bibliography comprises over one hundred and sixty entries in little over a century: from McGill University professor Charles Ebenezer Moyse's (Belgrave Titmarsh pseud.) satiric, nineteenth-century reworking of Shakespearean motifs in *Shakespere's* [sic] *Skull and Falstaff's Nose* (1889) to Marjorie Price's reworking, with faint Shakespearean overtones, of the Caesar story in *God Caesar*, which won the 'Sir Barry Jackson prize for the best play by a Canadian presented in the Dominion Drama Festival, 1935' (title page); transplanted Parisian Robert Gurik's adaptation *Hamlet, prince du Québec* (1968), a parody of Canadian politics; and Ken Mitchell and Humphrey and the Dumptrucks's *Cruel Tears* (1977), a 'country opera' adaptation of *Othello* in which the main character is a Ukrainian truck driver from Saskatchewan.[6]

In addition, there is an extensive production practice associated with adapted Shakespeare that attests to the generalized cultural presence of Shakespeare in Canada. Many of the Shakespeare alfresco productions in cities like St John's, Ottawa, Toronto, Winnipeg, Saskatoon, and Vancouver predicate their stagings on innovative and experimental adaptations of source texts, again calling into question the extent to which staged productions are themselves, always necessarily, adaptive. The Saskatchewan Festival, for instance, produced an (in)famous version of *Romeo and Juliet* (1989–90) in which the Montagues and Capulets were divided linguistically into English and French. The feud took on obvious resonances in the Canadian national context, and each group was directed by a person of different linguistic origins in order to emphasize the linguistic differences the production explored (Gordon McCall directed the English Montagues and Robert Lepage the French Capulets). Similarly, 1986 saw the Future Shakespeare Company of Toronto put on a version of *Julius Caesar* with an entirely female cast. Regina's Globe Theatre, founded in 1966 by Ken and Sue Kramer, initially the only professional theatre company in Saskatchewan primarily devoted to educational theatre for younger audiences, had an early repertoire that made use of Shakespearean adaptations 'staged arena-style to encourage audience participation' (Farfan).

In the 1997 adaptive hybrid *MacHomer: The Simpsons Do Macbeth*, an anglophone Montrealer, Rick Miller, toured Canada with a one-man theatrical production that 'features over 60 voices from TV's favorite dysfunctional family, in a performance of Shakespeare's bloodiest tragedy. Over 300 colour slides, handpainted by the author, as well as an original musical score, accompany the 50 minute show. The script (85% of which remains the words of William Shakespeare) is embellished with popular cultural icons, creating that rare jewel: an educational and entertaining show' (qtd. from the publicity poster). The contradictions, cultural displacements, and overlays of Miller's production are significant and worth noting: Shakespeare is conjoined to an epic (the TV character Homer Simpson); the one-man ventriloquism of sixty voices; dysfunctional families and violence, yet an audience favourite, a family show; the cultural value of it all signalled through the three hundred hand-painted slides, original musical score, and the 85 per cent retention of true Shakespearean material in an egregious display of cultural de-formation and adaptation; and the assumption that popular cultural icons are necessary to create an educational and entertaining show. Perhaps most significant is the way in which the show symbolically iterates crucial aspects of the cultural politics of Canada as a nation-state. Miller himself assumes a unique and doubly minoritarian position (of the English minority in a province that is itself a French minority in the larger North American context), hybridizing American and colonial culture so as to produce cultural value in a theatrical context that can tour the country. In short, the production is an exemplary display of adapted Shakespeare in the national context I have been describing, where difference and self-sameness are carpentered together as a function of an identity based upon contradiction, discrepancy, and dissension. Even radical theatrical practices of adaptation that challenge the nation's tolerance of difference are subject to an effect of integration that sustains the difference in the face of its assimilation to the corporate national entity.

Theatrical adaptations reveal the contradictions of national self-fashioning as part of a larger cultural context in which similar disjunctions are evident. This staging occurs in varied contexts, including feminist discourses that examine Black othering, racist anti-indigenous discourses, and Acadian nationalist discourses – all of which are positions, as this essay will demonstrate, that have been taken in the name of a Shakespeare mutated by adaptation. Examples such as these merely foreground the way in which Shakespearean adaptation has taken on a life of its own in Canada, suiting the varied agendas of diverse regional theatres, whether reaching out to younger audiences, commenting on national political issues, addressing issues of identity politics and popular culture, or presenting more broadly based ideological and social critiques. Elizabeth Hanson has cautioned against criticism that makes simplistic assumptions about the Shakespeare effect in relation to a 'reflexive Shakespeare-centrism' (77) that makes of Shakespeare a sort of 'default-mode' (84) for critical pronouncement on the early modern period. The caution is well taken, especially in a critical practice that studies Shakespearean adaptation in relation to Canadian national identity. Neither Shakespearean adaptation nor Canadian national identity are necessarily coherent terms. Both are subject to immense and varying pressures to conform to different ideologies, different sites of national self-identification. Both pose definitional problems that do not necessarily come with stable answers: at what point is a play based on a distinctive Shakespearean character, for example, *not* an adaptation of Shakespeare? What degree of Shakespearean referentiality must a play have in order to qualify as an adaptation?[7] What degree of Canadian referentiality is necessary to qualify as Canadian? At what point is Canadian national identity conceivable only as an illusive essentialism based solely on geography and not on any reductive qualities like 'our' proverbial niceness, tendency to compromise or self-deprecation, capacity for irony, and so on? To what extent does John Metcalfe's skewering of Robin Mathews's assertion that 'Canadian writing in the true tradition ... celebrates collectivity and community' [15]) precisely represent that what it means to be Canadian is to resist such delusory pronouncements in the name of different truths about collectivity and community?

Shakespearean adaptation in Canada, then, fulfils a number of functions, not the least of which is the staging of contestatory sites of interpretation in which interpretation necessarily leads to adaptation. Even as adaptation represents an interpretive consumption of source that may radically change how that source is understood, it is necessarily mediated by its cannibalistic relation to source. In fact, part of the interpretative *frisson* generated by adaptations lies precisely in the extent to which recognizable aspects of the source-text are interwoven into the new contexts, however defamiliarized, of the adaptation. As a genre, then, adaptation pits the supposed normative orthodoxy of the original against its heterodox others, those interpretations that transgress against the expectations of the norm through the revisionary status of the adaptation.

Theatrical Shakespeare, in this last regard, is (and continues to be) the site of ongoing cultural warfare, ongoing transgression, and refashioning. English-born, African-Canadian Djanet Sears's 'rhapsodic-blues' adaptation of *Othello, Harlem Duet* refigures Othello as a Black English professor teaching at Columbia University. Othello lives in Harlem at the corner of Malcolm X and Martin Luther King boulevards with his first wife, Billie, a graduate student, whom he abandons during the play for an unseen white woman. The play's contemporization of *Othello* inverts the story, telling it from within the contexts of African-Canadian and African-American cultures. Sears uses three similar storylines from different historical periods to emphasize the traps of historical amnesia and repetition, all repeating the basic motif of a Black man leaving a Black woman for a white woman. Adaptation in this case calls attention to a particular sense of Black historicity and the need for its revaluation in terms that disallow the forgetting of past errors, past contingencies. The strategy is a radical revisioning of one of the essential factors in the formation of nation, which, as Ernest Renan puts it, is given shape out of 'l'oubli et ... l'erreur historique' ('forgetting and ... historical error') (qtd. in Hobsbawm 12).[8] Obliquely, and despite its setting in Harlem, the play calls into question the silent history of African Canadians by articulating some of the historical contingencies that have contributed to the production of the Canadian nation-state, which has all but effaced, except in the most jejune of ways, Black contributions to its make-up.

Sears's use of background tapes and other archival materials having to do with the history of Black oppression (including Martin Luther King's 'I have a Dream' speech and fragments of speeches and songs from prominent Black figures including Malcolm X, Langston Hughes, Marcus Garvey, Paul Robeson, Louis Farrakhan, Jesse Jackson, Christopher Darden, and Anita Hill) overwrites her Shakespearean source, foregrounding the rich panoply of Black culture and voice that her play animates. Moreover, the play explicitly discusses racism, and especially internalized racism, from within the context of Black culture. Othello leaves Billie because, as a Black male, he has internalized self-hatred to such an extent that the only escape is via the allure of white culture, which then serves only to perpetuate the racist structures in which he is ostensibly trapped. *Harlem Duet*, then, reshapes Shakespeare in the service of a contemporary dialogue about racial issues that has an obvious import for race relations in Canada.

A national theatre critic gave the play two stars, stating, 'The tragedy of Othello and Billie is that they cannot escape their racial consciousness, but it is also the tragedy of this script' (K. Taylor, 'Characters'). The implications of this assessment are clear. Forget difference. Remain colour-blind. Rise above politics. Racial consciousness is racist. In short, become (symbolically) white. Forget about history. The same critic also found the static moments in the play, in which the actors stare directly into the faces of audience members, unappealing and forced, as if all theatre should follow the Stanislavskian convention in which an actor, though knowing she is an actor, 'consciously tries to be unaware of the presence of the audience' (Boal 23), and reject the Brechtian technique in which 'the actor is completely aware of the presence of the audience, which she transforms into genuine ... but mute interlocutors' (23). But having an all-Black cast of actors face into an audience that is predominantly white simply makes explicit the differences the play explores in relation to the Shakespearean original, which would have had an all-white cast performing for predominantly white audiences. Sears's dislocation of Shakespeare into a contemporary discussion of race, then, is a way of transgressing through adaptation, a way of making the margin move to the centre, thus disturbing primarily white notions of national identity.

Harlem Duet's performance history is unique in a Canadian cultural context because it is so closely tied to an emergent Black theatrical aesthetic, one that challenges Eurocentric practices even as it is implicated in mediating and revising them. As Alison Sealy-Smith, the creator of the role of Billie (Sybil), states, 'what was wonderful about working on *Harlem Duet* is that we [Black actors] never get to have all Black people in a room. It doesn't happen. And we weren't working on Shakespeare, we weren't saying to the world, "let's just see what happens when these words come out of Black mouths instead of White ones"' (Sears and Sealy-Smith, 'Nike' 28). Sears herself acknowledges that 'in *Harlem Duet* I wanted a *tension* between European culture and African-American culture' (29), while noting the historical circumstances that make *Harlem Duet* distinctive: 'Before *Harlem Duet*, Canadian Stage [a major Canadian theatre] had never produced a work by an author of ... African descent. And the problem with Canadian Stage is that it's called Canadian Stage, so it represents Canada, and I'm thinking, "I'm Canadian, so it must represent me"' (30). Even as it uses contextual markers that link it to Shakespeare's *Othello* (some names, some thematic materials, and some crucial imagery – the handkerchief, for instance, is a crucial prop in both Shakespeare's and Sears's versions of the Othello story), *Harlem Duet* establishes its revisionary agenda in relation to historic circumstances that have traditionally excluded the representation of Black culture on the Canadian public stage.

Further, the American setting of the play makes problematic the play's Canadianness, if only by its implicit assumption of Harlem as emblematic of Black cultural experience generally. The setting suggests that racial identity transcends political borders even as it contradictorily troubles essentialist notions about national identity in which shared assumptions about what constitutes that identity are in play. (These essentialist notions may include ethnicity, linguistic difference, founding values and myths, and so on as determining factors in the construction of an originary and essential national identity.) Does the play have to be set in Canada to be any more or less Canadian, whatever that may mean? In many ways, the absence of Canada from the play, except for the transitory appearance of Billie's father as a character named Canada, replicates the absence of Black culture from the Canadian stage, a structure of disappearance that makes the play's politics all the more provocative. Sears's adaptation, with its implicit challenge to assumptions of an easily achieved Canadian inter-, trans-, or multiculturalism (its implicit acknowledgment of the existence of other groups who have not achieved cultural presence), exemplifies the use of adapted Shakespeare to address difference and its absence. So, in Canada in 1997, a vestigial, dismembered Shakespeare becomes the site of an identity politics, a transgressive writing of Black culture that challenges those who are its others to reconfigure whom and why they are what they are. And Shakespeare, for better or for worse, becomes one of the chosen sites around which the 'we' (that thinks itself Canadian) engages in the 'authentic struggle to transform' (Freire 29) the very dialogues and interpretations that make us who 'we' are.

Adaptation has also garnered space in the popular press. Brian Mossop, in a 1997 letter to the *Globe and Mail*, calls Shakespeare's plays as obscure as *Beowulf* and *The Canterbury Tales*, both written in different but related languages, provoking a response from Robert Cushman. The latter argues for the so-called original texts and against prefabricated adaptations like the *Compleat Works of Wllm Shkspr (Abridged)* – '37 plays in 97 minutes' (qtd. from the ad campaign). Cushman cites the example of Robert Graves, hired in 1965 to rewrite in prose obscure lines from *Much Ado About Nothing* for the British National Theatre. The production, directed by Franco Zeffirelli, 'proved no more funny, touching or comprehensible than others have done. The National never hired a rewrite man again' ('Modernize'). In making his argument against the 'dumbing down' of Shakespeare via populist abridgments that are also adaptations, Cushman Canadianizes the issue by referring to the Wayne and Shuster 'Masterschtick Theatre' spoof (also, loosely, an adaptation) of *Julius Caesar* that appeared in the 1950s. The spoof is startling because 'it assumes its prime-time audience had a nodding acquaintance with Shakespeare, and it even throws in jokes about Latin. (Wayne orders a m̦rtinus. "You mean martini," says the bartender. "If I want a double," snaps Wayne, "I'll order one."' [Cushman, 'Modernize'].) Here, the issue of Shakespeare as a form of cultural capital, an emblem of contestatory identity politics over which virtually anyone is free to inscribe his or her revisioning, operates in a mode of ironic self-deprecation. The skit assumes the general recognizability of Shakespeare as a cultural referent to a national TV audience even as it lampoons Shakespeare as a synecdoche for academic prolixity. The crucial point is that Shakespeare and adaptations thereof sparked a public debate in a Canadian national newspaper over issues of authenticity, cultural value, and the politics of adaptation, thereby reinscribing Shakespeare's iconicity as a sign of a troubled form of cultural capital. Finally, as a clear indication of the institutional recognition of Canadian theatrical practices involving Shakespearean adaptation, two recent winners of the Governor General's Award for Drama, often seen as the most prestigious award in Canada, have been for radical adaptations of Shakespearean source materials (Ann-Marie MacDonald for *Goodnight Desdemona (Good Morning Juliet)* [1990] and Djanet Sears for *Harlem Duet* [1998]), the former writing from a strongly inflected lesbian and feminist position, the latter, as already discussed, from a feminist, African-Canadian perspective.

It is not the purpose of this essay to detail the numerous theatrical adaptations of Shakespeare written, staged, and produced in Canada over the last century. Suffice it to say that, from the 1880s to the present, and especially in the last thirty years, Shakespearean adaptations have emerged as a distinct subgenre in Canadian theatre. In short, Canada's history of Shakespearean adaptation is coincident with its emergence as a nation-state. Shakespearean adaptation in the modern Canadian context recapitulates a basic configuration associated with the genesis of the nation: it links the iconicity of Shakespeare with the symbolic destiny, however illusory, of nation. At the same time as this general and highly conventional trajectory has been pursued, contrary pursuits under the rubric of different national self-interests in Canada, whether Québécois, Acadian, aboriginal, African-Canadian, immigrant, or otherwise, have come to modify the notion of a monolithic adaptive practice associated with Shakespeare.

In such a context, Shakespeare is no longer 'Shakespeare,' but a discursive instrument whose adaptive suitability is tied to a generalized iconic presence that can be mapped on to a wide range of subjects in the public sphere. An early Canadian adaptation exemplifies this effect. Charles Moyse's 'fancy,' *Shakspere's Skull and Falstaff's Nose* (1889; published under the pseudonym Belgrave Titmarsh), condemns the 'academic fanaticism' promulgated in the name of 'researching the works of Shakespeare' (qtd. in A. Wagner, *Brock* 32). In addition to teaching in the English department at McGill University in Montreal 'for more than forty years,' Moyse served as dean of McGill's faculty of arts and vice-principal of the university from 1903 to 1920 (Fetherstonhaugh 105). Moyse, born in 1852 (Torquay, Devonshire), was appointed Molson Professor of English Literature at McGill in 1879, after graduating from London University in 1874 with a prize in physiology (Morgan 664).

Capitalizing on the late-Victorian taste for farce, *Shakspere's Skull* depicts a pedant, Dryasdustus, under the delusion of being a descendant of Shakespeare, speaking in a take-off on Elizabethan blank verse. Dryasdustus proclaims:

> My brain I'll prove of substance nonpareil;
> My soul, his [Shakespeare's] worthy counterpart: these two
> Beget ten mighty folios of new thoughts ...
>
> The worser sort,
> Although not all mine own, are intermixed
> With others all mine own, tending to this,
> That Shakspere's writ by one called Dryasdust. (19)

Central to the play's thematics is a satire of the Shakespearean authentic: how lunatic scholarship allows the spurious possession of Shakespeare's writings, to the point that Dryasdustus stands convinced of his own authorship of Shakespeare. The attempt to possess Shakespeare is metaphorized in Dryasdustus's attempt to rob Shakespeare's grave of its skull only to discover that the body-snatchers he has employed to do this 'didn't get to the bottom of the grave' (60). As with other moments in the play, the attempt to essentialize Shakespeare, either in scholarly writing or in the materiality of uncertain relics, is exposed as absurd.

When Dryasdustus, now on the lam for the robbery of Shakespeare's grave, encounters another Shakespearean (Second Gentleman), the talk turns to how Shakespeare is transposed and adapted in the name of egomaniacal, literary careerism:

> Then I made the acquaintance of a so-called True Shakperian [*sic*] scholar, who told me I had been utterly misled [about what Shakespeare truly wrote]. He hacked Shakspere in his own style, and presented me with a still bulkier volume of plays [than a preceding critic who has done the same], even more obscure, which *he* had published, and in which he had caused the portions *he* was positive were Shakespeare's to be printed in italics likewise. (57–8)

This Second Gentleman determines to write 'a true Shakespearian book' (58) on two subjects: 'one, to present to the world for the first time the real face of Shakspere by blending, according to a modern process, all the representations of Shakspere in stone or on canvas that have come down to us; the other, to write what my True Shaksperian mind conceived to be the real key to Falstaff's character – his nose. I chose the latter, buried myself in literary rubbish, became disgusted, unlike a True Shaksperian, and resolved to return to mental health' (58). In Moyse's spoof, Shakespeare figures as an endlessly plastic material in the service of ludicrous ends, forever adaptable in the name of truth. That the spoof was published in 1889 in London, ten years after Moyse had become a professor of English at McGill University, hints, however obliquely, at the relations of colonial servitude to, and independence from, Shakespearean authority that the play addresses.[9]

The culminating scenes of the play – in which Dryasdustus assumes a new identity (Mr Robinson) and boards with a mother and her daughter (Janet Fluter), the latter engaged in Elizabethan scholarship with 'keen critical insight into the development and expression of lines of thought peculiar to, and common among, the best exponents of our national literature in the Elizabethan age' (64)[10] – make explicit the relationship between nation and adaptation. Janet, in a speech that invokes Columbus and Cabot, associates her scholarship with a 'New' world (later she will call Drysasdustus/Robinson 'Ferdinand,' figuring herself implicitly as Miranda), and asks why

> ere four centuries are run
> A second world remote, well called the New,
> New in her coyish sweetness and her grace,
> Should teach disdain of antique story, tales
> Worn threadbare by mere iteration, damning
> The judgment or of him who speaks or hears them? (72)

By the end of her exposition to Robinson, which culminates in an apocalyptic vision based on the numerological coincidence of the difference between the appearance of the First Folio (1623) and Shakespeare's death (1616) as the number seven, Janet suggests that the 'import' of her work is to 'illumine all the dark / Professions of a purblind age, of this / My nation' (73).

Though Dryasdustus/Robinson bemusedly asks, 'Is thy bolt shot?' (73), the point Moyse scores is clear enough: Shakespeare is used falsely in the name of illuminating nation. The confrontation between (and questioning of) Old and New World critical values suggests at least one reason for adaptive strategies that recycle 'antique' stories and tales. Recycling tales 'worn threadbare' is to be disdained in favour of 'the storm that 'longs to true discovery,' the latter motif linked by Janet with *The Tempest* (77). Thus, in this very early adaptation of Shakespearean meta-thematics written out of a Canadian context (but not necessarily with any identifying characteristics that would mark it as explicitly Canadian), basic issues of old versus new, colonial versus colonized, scholarly versus artistic, and source versus adaptation are explored in terms that are largely cynical and satirical. This nineteenth-century Canadian adaptation recognizes, derides, and ironizes Shakespeare's iconic centrality to scholarly and national formations. Moreover, the seeking after Shakespearean quintessential truths is shown to be empty, the grave of Shakespearean authenticity, one that yields uncertain fragments of a dismembered and decomposed (original) body.

At the heart of Shakespeare's iconic centrality is an effect having to do with authenticity, a term derived from the Greek for 'one who acts on his own authority, a chief.'[11] Shakespeare, in this context, guarantees and proclaims cultural authenticity, a self-authorizing gesture that, paradoxically enough, is predicated on a writing practice that is itself highly adaptive in relation to so-called source texts.[12] That is, even as Shakespeare is taken to be central to an English canonical literary tradition, the very discursive practice in which he engaged on his way to gaining this role as literary chieftain was itself highly adaptive. Frye captures this sense of independent mastery by saying that the 'place where the greatest fusions of words have occurred in English was in the mind of Shakespeare' (110). Shakespeare's extensive literary borrowings and transformations, what Frye calls his 'fusions,' contribute to his vexed authenticity, his authentic inauthenticity or his inauthentic authenticity. Authentic here is no guarantor of fidelity to a source, nor is it a guarantor of the Oxford English Dictionary's (OED) definition of authentic as meaning 'of undisputed origin,' having to do with the establishment of truth, validity, or genuineness. The complex debates over Shakespearean authorship brought about by highly technical editorial instruments, and by changes in critical ideologies bearing on early modern texts generally, point to Shakespeare as the site of an authenticity in dispute.

The dispute is founded on a misunderstanding of what authenticity signifies: namely, a form of self-authorization that has less to do with 'undisputed origins' than with a form of self-fashioning that seeks autonomy in its relations to originary truth, value, or genuineness. That is, Shakespeare is self-authenticating insofar as he is self-authorizing. In the Greek sense of the authentic, he practices an adaptive revisionism in relation to source texts in the name of self-interest. Yet, at the same time, that self-authorization cannot escape the dialogical contingencies (of source and of immediate performative and historical context) that create the contexts for the revisions – no *Coriolanus* without Plutarch, no *A Midsummer Night's Dream* without Ovid, no *Macbeth* without Holinshed. In short, the authenticity of Shakespeare, his construction as the originary source of English national and literary genius, is, as I am reading it, a form of inauthenticity, precisely because Shakespeare achieves difference in the name of a misperceived monological authenticity. This observation has bearing when transposed into the context of Canadian adaptations. When inauthentic Shakespeare is adapted in the name of authenticating an emergent and troubled sense of nation, critical pathologies flourish, especially when synecdochic Shakespeare (as a sign for all that is culturally good) is realigned with authentic Shakespeare (as a sign of undisputed origins, truth, and genuineness).

Charles Taylor avers that 'the understanding of identity and authenticity has introduced a new dimension into the politics of equal recognition, which now operates with something like its own notion of authenticity, at least so far as the denunciation of other-induced distortions is concerned' (37). In the case of the appropriation of Shakespeare by way of adaptive writing strategies in a Canadian national context, this comment resonates powerfully. Identity and authenticity conspire to produce the trope of nation, even as identity and authenticity come to be used as tropes for identity politics that controvert nation, putting its assumptions of homogeneity and coherence to the question.[13] Shakespearean adaptation is merely one of the sites in which these terms paradoxically align themselves to give shape to an unresolved, dia(poly)logical process, in which multiple contexts and registers of meaning are engaged. Nation assumes assimilation into the authentic bosom of an originary identity, however spurious or illusory such an idea may be. Canada's widely disseminated myth of two founding cultures (English and French), for instance, is counterpointed by indigenous and immigrant histories that make such an 'origin' more than arguable.[14] But, as Taylor points out, 'this assimilation is the cardinal sin against the ideal of authenticity' (38). The authentic, because it is always predicated on a belatedly assimilative effect, signifies an identity crisis by way of a dialectic that presumes and requires the inauthentic (that which is assimilated) in order to give it meaning. Shakespeare's appropriation by state (read 'authentic') culture is used as a bulwark against incursions into state culture by its 'inauthentic,' nomadic margins.

Adaptations work both sides of this coin, whether confirming a myth of authenticity and origin or interrogating such a position through alternative and revisionary definitions of authenticity. Jacques Attali has defined 'Shakespeareanisme' as the 'Théorie de l'Histoire qui attribue un rôle déterminant aux passions, aux luttes, aux bassesses et aux pulsions des puissants. Toujours nécessaire pour comprendre les principales bifurcations géopolitiques' ('Theory of History that attributes a determining role to the passions, the struggles, the baseness, and the drives of the powerful. Always necessary for understanding the principal geopolitical divergences') (294). That is, Shakespeare signifies history, power, geopolitical difference, and, by extension, nation. For Alan Filewod, speaking to the question of a specifically Canadian national theatre, 'the rhetorical proposal of a national theatre in effect means the canonization of a theatre and drama that reflects the national ideals of the governing élite' ('National' 23). Filewod traces the 'obsession with a Canadian identity' (16) to the nineteenth century, which 'fuelled the movement of romantic poetic drama that produced the ponderous pseudo-Shakespearean tragedies which plague today's students of CanLit' (16).

It is no accident that Filewod associates national identity with 'pseudo-Shakespearean tragedies.' The pattern of constructing national identity in a colonial context, as the example of India forcefully shows, was facilitated by the use of Shakespeare, if only as the easily imported sign of a transcendental civilized excellence and cultural identity (in the supposed absence of the latter). As Filewod argues, 'the idea that Canadian national drama was an appropriation of British cultural models gathered strength in the years after the Great War, and led directly to the model of public regional theatres advocated by the Canada Council in the 1960s' (18). Under the direction of anglophile culture czar Vincent Massey, the mark of 'civilization' was understood as an 'extension' of English culture adapted to the Canadian context. Here, nation, the politics of literary canons, the aesthetic proclivities of those in power, and the specific historical contingencies that underlie a colonial past conjoin under the name of that inauthentically authentic guarantor of difference and self-sameness that is Shakespeare. Shakespearean theatrical adaptations in Canada represent a particular formation of this larger trope.

Elizabeth Hanson proposes reading plays 'as traces of complex interactions between literary resources and the social fantasies of particular groups' (84). I take this to be an effective strategy for discussing the notion of Shakespearean adaptation in Canada as a literary and social practice with implications for how the nation gets 'worried,' to borrow Jonathan Kertzer's term. Just as adaptation presupposes a transformational process whose revisionary politics serve the particular self-authorizing ends of the adapter, so nation, when conjoined with adaptation, operates under the sign of what Michel Seymour calls the 'perpetuelle transformation de l'identité civique commune' ('the perpetual transformation of the shared civic identity'). Adaptations, like other cultural artefacts, work to produce a range of possible responses to national identity, including its very thinkability. National identity is an imaginary entity, an ideality based on the simultaneous production and eradication of difference through the filter of communal values, in this case, putatively embedded in Shakespeare and the Shakespeare effect. The latter are both guarantors of a dubious authenticity linked to literary and state cultures.

Adaptations, then, as they attempt to efface in the name of a national singularity, consolidate, assimilate, and produce difference, effectively showing such assimilated difference(s) to be inauthentic. Radical adaptive practices, such as those evident in previously discussed plays like *Harlem Duet* and *Shakspere's Skull and Falstaff's Nose,* challenge simplistic national configurations strung together in the name of tradition, homogeneity, and genuinely shared cultural values that are not. And, as we have seen, one of the earliest known examples of Shakespearean adaptation in Canada, *Shakspere's Skull*, effectively burlesques Shakespearean scholarship in pursuit of an authentic, true Shakespeare that will never be found. And Sears's more recent adaptation explicitly addresses issues pertaining to the presence of ethnic difference on the national stage. Adaptation exposes the sham of nation as a sign of meaningful coherence, for Canada is, as Filewod explains, 'without a consensual recognition of a national drama, and without ... a specifically defined national theatre' ('National' 16). Similarly, adaptation questions the essentialist qualities associated with Shakespearean authority, canonicity, and cultural value. In short, adaptations serve multiple positionings with regard to national self-identity as mediated by a cultural icon like Shakespeare.

To be sure, the way in which national identity gets 'worried' by Shakespearean adaptation in Canada is not necessarily always particularly enlightened, politically sensitive, or without controversy. In English-born, western-Canadian Warren Graves's play *Chief Shaking Spear Rides Again (or the Taming of the Sioux)*, 'commissioned by Walterdale Theatre Associates for their 10th annual Klondike Days Melodrama at the Citadel Theatre, Edmonton, 1974' (Graves),[15] the Corn Exchange Theatre is threatened at the turn of the century by a rapacious land developer, Cramden Twinge. The theatre is run by a hodgepodge of English expatriates, an 'alien group' (23). Their only recourse to save the theatre is through 'the old Cultural Identity Preservation Clause,' which states that if the group can find someone '"whose residence in the area commenced at birth and continues to be extant"' then Twinge will be unable to 'foreclose' on the contract (22). To the rescue comes an 'authentic' chief, literally a literary chieftain, Shaking Spear, who has had a vision: 'The spirit tell me that my name from that day will be Shaking Spear ... And he tell me that I shall write the stories that he will tell me and that these stories will tell of my people and their ways' (26). The chief then goes on to name, in a series of painfully bad puns, the plays he has written: 'First, there was "A Midsummer Night's Sweatlodge" – a comedy. After that, the words came quickly and I wrote "Two Gentlemen from Kelowna," "The Factor of Venice," "Henry Hudson Parts One and Two," "Troilus and Kalynchuck" ... then I got into the story of my people on the reserves applying for municipal status' (26). Walter Dale, the manager of the Corn Exchange, asks, 'What did you call that?' Shaking Spear responds, 'Hamlet' (27). In a final series of increasingly offensive jokes,

Walter asks Shaking Spear what inspired him to write *The Taming of the Sioux*. Shaking Spear first invokes 'the story of my people and Sitting Bull when he fled from the longknives south of the Medicine line' before leading into the following exchange:

> *Chief.* Then there was this girl I met once in Winnipeg. She was a Sue when I met her, but a Gros Ventres [Big Belly] when I left. (Laughs) That's what we call an Indian joke.
> *Walter.* Oh I see.
> *Chief.* Ethnic.
> *Walter.* Yes, of course.
> *Chief.* Like, 'Hi, there Chief. What do you think of bilingualism'? Do you know what the Chief says?
> *Walter.* I can't imagine.
> *Chief.* (Folds arms) 'White Man speak with forked tongue.' (27)

The passage puts racist, white dialogue into aboriginal mouths. Ethnic jokes here are the domain of Native culture even as offensive stereotypes are implicitly promulgated by white, settler culture. Shakespeare is refigured in aboriginal terms precisely as a means of diminishing the threat of alterity through racist belittlement. Furthermore, the smug irony is that Graves has the aboriginal saviour of the colonial theatre being told the stories 'of my people' by a spirit who has him writing take-offs of Shakespeare put into an explicitly Canadian context. So, a neo-colonial, English-expatriate (Albertan) Canadian usurps the cultural authority of Shakespeare to foreground racist stereotypes of aboriginal culture in the name of a language not its own. The dynamic is exemplary of the sort of inauthentic striving after authenticity that gives shape to some aspects of Canadian identity formations.

The dream of eradicating aboriginals' special status by way of a strategy of assimilation is one context for understanding the Graves play. In 1969, five years before the first production of Graves's play, a federal government White Paper that raised the possibility of eliminating natives' special status became the focal point of bitter opposition which led to the government's repudiation of its proposed policy change. *The Taming of the Sioux* trope, in this context, reminds the white audience of its own material dominance in relation to Native culture. Moreover, the play shows Shaking Spear to have internalized the lessons of Sitting Bull's defeat (read 'taming') by conforming to the stereotype of the randy Native, impregnating Sue in Winnipeg and making light of western Canada's other national fixation, official bilingualism. Shaking Spear voices the regional anxieties of English-Canadian, western culture with regard to its own capacity to deal with difference, whether aboriginal or French. Aboriginal culture is shown to allow itself willingly to be co-opted to colonial purposes (in this case, the saving of the Corn Exchange Theatre as a metonym for settler culture), thus perpetuating long-standing falsehoods about Native cultures' complicity in their own demise. The precise point of all this is to expose, in a western Canadian regional context, the difference between a presumed Shakespearean authenticity and aboriginal inauthenticity, thus validating the former at the expense of the latter.

Inauthentic difference, then, is a function of the very fissures that underlie Canada's national imaginary based on supposedly multicultural and bilingual values, the essentialist myth of a constitution grounded in two founding peoples. At the core of relations between nation and adaptation in Canada is the desire to conform to an unsundered affiliation (*A mari usque ad mare*)[16] even as that myth is haunted by the realities of racism, linguistic intolerance, and the dream of a domesticated (assimilationist) difference, at the service of hegemonic culture. In this scenario, Shakespeare serves as the symbolic capital that consolidates difference, even as that difference and its consolidation are shown to be inauthentic, forever under the sign of a scepticism that destabilizes notions of origin (and thus of tradition), truth, and genuineness. In the community that is no community (other than as shorthand for a recognizable structure of power), Shakespeare mediates the illusion of nation that serves various interests, from those at the margins of Canadian culture to those at its imagined core. Shakespearean adaptation is one of the discourses by which a '*cultural construction of colonialism,* the ways in which colonialism was helped by and in turn produced images of both the Self and Other' (Pennycook 15), is achieved.

In his discussion of how Shakespearean tropologies are useful in understanding the relations between literatures of alterity and their canonical counterparts, Max Dorsinville notes that

> one does not have to go beyond the Shakespearean meaning to find in the Prospero-Caliban set of symbols an appropriate metaphorical application for the dilemma brought about by the sprouting of a number of minor, regional, national or ethnic literatures. African, Antillean, French-Canadian and Black American writers need not hurl abuse at their French or

English/American Prosperos, but they do claim a metaphorical or actual land of their own, and an experience of the world differentiating them from linguistic or geographic congeners. (15)

Or, as François Paré puts it:

Les ecrivains et leurs personnages y sont particulièrement susceptibles à la métamorphose et ultimement à la perte de l'identité formelle. Tout le discours du colonisé semble intérioriser les modes de comportement du colonisateur, semble épouser les rôles du dominant; ce discours devient ainsi le théâtre d'une aliénation, d'une présence en soi de l'alterité. (188)

(Writers and their characters are particularly susceptible to metamorphosis and ultimately to the loss of formal identity. The entire discourse of the colonized seems to interiorize the modes of comportment of the colonizer, seems to wed the roles of the dominant culture; this discourse thus becomes a theatre of alienation, of the presence in oneself of alterity.)

Shakespearean adaptation locates one site of this interiorization that threatens identity, that takes alterity and makes it over in the name of dominant culture, thus producing a theatre of alienation.

But this is hardly the whole story. Alterity can and does write back. Shakespearean adaptation can signal a productive interiorization that challenges and remakes dominant culture in the name of alterity, threatening dominant culture with the 'spectres d'alterité' ('spectres of alterity') (188) discussed by Paré. A good example of this 'writing back' occurs in Acadian writer Antonine Maillet's theatrical adaptation of Shakespearean motifs, *William S*, first staged in 1991 at the Théâtre du Rideau Vert in Montreal. The play poses the problem of what Shakespeare's characters might ask him if he were given a chance to respond 'aux craintes, plaintes et récriminations ... des créatures incomplètes, inachevées, condamnées comme vous et moi à un destin trop petit pour elles' ('to the fears, complaints, recriminations ... of incomplete, unfinished characters condemned, like you and me, to too limited a destiny') (7). The play stages a meeting between Shakespeare and eight Shakespearean characters, including Lady Macbeth, Falstaff, the Shrew (La Mégère), King Lear, Hamlet, Juliet, Shylock, and Juliet's nanny (Nounou). In its basic structure and premise, then, the play sets itself up as an interrogation of the relationship between authorial source and his creations.

The characters enunciate a litany of complaints against Shakespeare in the early stages of the play, with Shakespeare present in his disguised role as fool. Lady Macbeth and Shylock, in a crucial passage, articulate one of the play's central concerns:

> *Lady Macbeth.* Nous sommes tous sortis de lui. Et pourtant, lui-même est né de nous. Qu'il ne se trompe pas: sans Prospero, Othello, Richard III, Antoine et Cléopâtre et Lady Macbeth, Shakespeare ... n'est rien.
> *Fou* [Shakespeare]. Shakespeare ... n'est rien.
> *Shylock.* Rien du tout, c'est un Anglais mesquin, médiocre et anti-sémite, comme la plupart des chrétiens de son espèce. Sans nous, personne aujourd'hui ne se souviendrait même du prénom de ce scribouilleur dramatique. (39)

> (*Lady Macbeth.* We all come from him. And yet, he's born of us. Let him not be mistaken. Without Prospero, Othello, Richard III, Antony and Cleopatra and Lady Macbeth, Shakespeare ... is nothing.
> *Fou.* [Shakespeare]. Shakespeare ... is nothing.
> *Shylock.* Nothing at all. He's a mean-spirited Englishman, mediocre and anti-Semitic, like most Christians of his kind. Without us, nobody today would even remember the Christian name of this dramatic scribbler.)

Shakespeare's dependence on the characters he has created reveals a profound split between the authoritative source and the way in which source is mutated by adaptation. Maillet's adaptation thus shows how necessary adaptation is to the ongoing memorialization of Shakespearean cultural presence, in this case in an Acadian and French-Canadian theatrical context. The gesture is significant in this latter context because it subverts a basic colonial relation, using the very instrumentality of Shakespearean cultural and colonial presence as its primary tool. Thus, source culture is shown to be reliant on its colonial adaptations, deserving of critique from a perspective that recognizes the interdependence of the particular cultural, social, and national identities that emerge from the colonial enterprise.

Shylock's attack on English national identity as mean-spirited, anti-Semitic, degraded Christianity cannot be detached from the larger context of Acadian nationalist sentiment. This is especially the case in relation to the massive deportation and diaspora of Acadians effected from 1755 to 1762 by the English under Governor Charles Lawrence. An estimated three-quarters of the Acadian population was displaced along the east coast of Canadian and American territories (to make room for

English and American settlers) and was stripped of basic civil and legal rights (to own property or to vote). A climactic moment in *William S* has Shakespeare's hands and feet being chained by his characters, whereupon the Shrew states: 'À ton tour, misérable, de goûter à la douceur des chaînes et de l'asservissement' ('Your turn, miserable one, to taste the sweetness of chains and of slavery') (75). The symbolic import of this moment is significant in the Acadian colonial context for obvious reasons, not the least of which involve the transgressive repositioning, by way of adaptation, of Shakespeare's cultural presence as slave – not master. The play ends with Shakespeare acknowledging that his characters have good reason to complain about him: 'Au fond, vous n'êtes pas tellement réussis. Je crains de vous avoir ratés' ('Basically, you weren't that much of a success. I'm afraid I failed with you') (104). Shakespeare goes on to recognize that what his characters desire is 'l'éternel recommencement. Une nouvelle chance, une autre vie ...' ('eternal renewal. A new chance, another life ...') (107).

Maillet literally has Shakespeare authorizing the liberation of his characters from their confined destinies in the plays, suggesting that alternative modes of their being given life in adaptations is one way of instituting the renewal they seek. Enslaved Shakespeare thus stands trial for his creations and is forced to recognize both his failure and the need to release his characters from *their* enslavement in/as Shakespearean texts. The move symbolically recapitulates the examination and condemnation of colonial relations that underlie the play's seemingly universalist thematics having to do with creator and created. And it refigures the notion of authentic Shakespeare as radically dependent on creations that are inauthentic and incomplete, yearning for an unpredictable renewal that remakes their experience as authentic while de-authenticating Shakespearean monumentality. Maillet's general importance to the Acadian literary revival is not to be underestimated. Nor is her decision to write a play that radically appropriates a major icon of English colonial culture (Shakespeare) in the name of a parodic attack on that icon's self-authorizing influence and power.

Adaptive to both authoritative discourse and transgressive counter-discourse, Shakespeare's use-value is exploited in a symbolic economy of literary and theatrical values that give shape to the national imaginary. Shakespeare is the potentiality of ideology, form, and identity that pits the 'heterological discoveries of self and other' (Siemerling 212) against the inauthentic singularity of his authority. The inauthenticity of Shakespeare as a cultural force capable of effacing the differences that form the imagined singularity of Canada is exposed, as is the impossibility of the 'authentic' (more generally) as it relates to notions of state provenance and historical veracity. This is not to neutralize the general project(s) of Shakespearean adaptations in Canada. A certain kind of power is at stake, one that has to do with who has access to modes of cultural representation and dissemination, who gets to realize aspirations of difference or similitude in the public arena of the theatre: in short, who gets to have a public at all, who gets to do what, where, and why. As Frank Davey states in his discussion of Canadian literary power, the 'imbrication [or overlapped arrangement] of literary "power" within the texts of generalized social aspiration and conflict means that, while literary "power" may seem limited and unspecifiable, it is also neither illusionary or trivial ... How we map literary power is itself one of the discursive means by which power is constructed, disputed, contained, and allocated' (6–7).

Shakespearean adaptations in Canada cannibalize Shakespearean authenticity in the name of the inauthentic upon which any adaptation is predicated – they exemplify a form of literary and theatrical expression in which various contingencies, personal, historical, economic, and otherwise, combine to produce a text or a performance that 'fits' its moment. In Shakespearean adaptations particular to the Canadian context, this process of being made 'fit' puts to the question issues of national self-identification and self-formation. Why, in Canada, has there been a sustained body of theatrical work that maps itself onto the Shakespearean 'authentic' in ways that consistently deform that authentic, reveal it to be inauthentic? If anything, the answer lies in Shakespeare's phantasmal capacity for permutation. Permutation occurs both as a function of canonical authority and identity and as an index against which differential registers of that authority and identity are measured. In this phantasmal guise – dismembered, cannibalized, spectral, consumed, and consuming – the Shakespeare that is no Shakespeare in Canada (or elsewhere) gives shape to the fraught imaginary of nation and/as adaptation.

Notes

1 I am indebted to a number of people for help in writing this essay. Jennifer Ailles provided much needed research support, as did Ric Knowles, Harry Lane, Alan Filewod, Leanore Lieblein, and Leslie Lester. A small portion of this essay reproduces (in modified form) materials published in *Adaptations of*

Shakespeare. Finally, I am grateful to the Department of English at the University of Manitoba, on whose invitation I had the opportunity to present these ideas in their earliest form, and to the Shakespeare Association of America, at whose April 2000 annual conference a truncated version of this paper was given in the plenary session on 'Theorizing Adaptation: Shakespeare in Canada.'

2 Competing theories of how to address ethnic, racial, and class difference in Canada have further complicated the scenario: on the one hand, the vertical-mosaic model, with its assumption of a static hierarchy divided along class and ethnic lines, and, on the other, the melting-pot model, with its assimilationist dream of the erasure of all such differences into a national whole. Lest we forget, in 1971, when Pierre Elliot Trudeau 'officially declared Canada a bilingual and multicultural nation ... only 5% of Canadians were non-white' (Driedger). From the early 1970s to the 1990s, 'visible minorities in Canada doubled from 5% to 10%' (Driedger). Jean Burnet notes that 'diversity, heterogeneity and multiculturalism has [*sic*] increasingly been recognized by Census Canada, when in the 1981 census they allowed multiple ethnic designations which 1.2 million chose. By 1996, 10.2 million respondents reported multiple ethnic group heritages.'

3 For the purposes of this chapter, I distinguish two forms of Shakespearean adaptation: the first based on the Shakespeare effect that is a function of Shakespeare's cultural pervasiveness, in which echoes, resonances, and direct integration of that effect are in evidence in a given play; the second based on thematic and formal adaptations of specific playtexts in which the adapted play retropes the Shakespearean original(s). For further discussion of the different senses of adaptation, see Fischlin and Fortier 2–7.

4 Frye argues that 'the beginning of the Shakespeare Festival at Stratford turned out to be a very important event in the history of *Canadian* drama' and that 'Shakespeare at Stratford does not stand alone, because Molière played a very similar role in the development of French Canadian drama, at roughly the same time' (*Divisions* 23–4).

5 For more on the Shakespeare effect, see Fischlin and Fortier 8–19.

6 Entries continue to be made to this bibliography as research progresses (see *CTR* III, *Adapting Shakespeare in Canada*, co-edited by Daniel Fishlin and Ric Knowles, for the most recent version of this bibliographical work). The bibliography does not include non-theatrical adaptations, like those of Charles Heavysege, the Victorian poet born in England who emigrated to Montreal in 1853 and published a series of bombastic religious poems heavily influenced by Shakespeare (among others), or, more recently, musician and actress Loreena McKennitt, whose 1994 album *The Mask and Mirror* uses a

range of musical styles and texts from Shakespeare and the Spanish mystic John of the Cross.
7 For instance, would American-born John Murrell's *Farther West, New World* (1985), with its island setting, its title's oblique reference to Miranda's phrase 'brave new world' from *The Tempest* (5.1.183), its examination of characters whose experience is shaped by the colonial frontier in which they have gathered, its depiction of otherness and border-crossing within a Canadian national context, and its various thematic motifs (like the intrusion of technology into personal relations à la Prospero), be considered an adaptation, however distanced, of Shakespeare's *The Tempest*? Or would the seven-play cycle *La Vie et mort du roi boiteux* (1981–2), loosely based on Shakespeare's *The Tragedy of Richard the Third* and written by French-born Jean-Pierre Ronfard, who came to Canada in 1960 as director of the French section of the National Theatre School in Montreal, be considered a Canadian adaptation? Would Normand Chaurette's *Les Reines* (1991), about the women affected by Richard III's accession to power, with its distinctive Shakespearean echoes, constitute a specifically Canadian adaptation, especially within the nationalist contexts of Québécois theatre? Would a French-language production of *Hamlet* (1999; the Geordie Space and La Licorne) by Alexandre (Sasha) Marine, a Québécois with Russian roots and theatrical training, in which Yorick makes an actual onstage appearance (as opposed to the Shakespearean original, in which he is absent), be considered an adaptation, especially when that director's aesthetic is marked by 'intervention' and an aversion to the 'respect timide des textes' (R. Lévesque, *Hamlet*)? Further definitional problems exist with regard to both adaptation and national identity. Anton Wagner notes some of these in relation to Canada's long history of immigration: 'The frequent migration of writers to and from Canada makes it very difficult to determine Canadian nationality. To define what constitutes a Canadian play, we have maintained the definition set out in the 1972 edition of the *Brock Bibliography* [*of Published Canadian Stage Plays in English 1900–1972*], "plays written by Canadians, native, naturalized or landed immigrant." Therefore, plays written by an immigrant before he or she came to Canada are not Canadian, and presumably plays written by a native Canadian after he or she becomes a citizen of another country are not Canadian either' (Introduction v). These definitions, though workable, are hardly unproblematic.
8 All French translations are mine.
9 Stanley Brice Frost notes that 'in the 1920's, a new sense of national identity began to emerge in anglophone Canada which expressed itself first in literary activities, particularly the writing of poetry, and a little later in social and political activism. In literature the movement took the form of a rejection of

Victorian models and canons of judgement, and particularly of colonial dependence on British traditions in poetry and creative writing' (9–10). Moyse's play anticipates this larger literary 'movement,' its anti-colonialism figured implicitly in its anti-Shakespeareanism.

10 'Her first contribution to literature,' we are told in her imaginary description of a biographical entry that will be written as a result of her scholarly fame, 'is entitled *Shakspere Settled*, in which she has proved, with great ingenuity, that the Swan of Avon must give place to the philosopher of Gray's Inn' (65).

11 Lionel Trilling traces the etymology of 'authentic' in greater detail: '*Authenteo*: to have full power over; also, to commit a murder. *Authentes*: not only a master and a doer, but also a perpetrator, a murderer, even a self-murderer, a suicide' (131). Murderous Shakespeare, then, would signify Shakespeare's capacity to overwrite his sources, to murder them in the richness of his own fashionings. Suicidal Shakespeare would signify the energy thereby released as a model for further adaptive fashionings of Shakespeare, the creative energy (falsely thought to originate in Shakespeare) that effectively gives others the means to do away with him through adaptive revisions. That is, the underlying problem of the authentic in relation to adaptation is one of violence and mastery over source and self and their respective fashionings and erasures. Even as Shakespeare is symbolically murdered through adaptation, his ongoing cultural presence is acknowledged and resurrected within the Shakespearean adaptive tradition.

12 For a more complete discussion of this, see the section of the general introduction entitled 'Virtual Shakespeares' in Fischlin and Fortier.

13 Kertzer discusses this dialectic in relation to Canadian critical models that attempt some form of national self-definition: 'Earlier literary historians, who were anxious that English Canada find its literary voice, listened for what is most authentic in that voice: the call of the wild, the colonial compromise, the ironic tone. By the mid-twentieth century, several critics were claiming that only a tentative/unending/fruitless quest for authenticity defines our literature. The questing itself grants authenticity, even when it is unsuccessful. Today's critics, always vigilant against essentialist thinking, characterize our literature by the way it studiously/playfully/sensuously renounces all claims to authenticity. Although these views differ drastically in their faith in authenticity, they all assume that a literary community, however combative, will produce "our" literature, however conflicted' (22–3). See Kertzer 22–5 for a more complete discussion of this issue. See also Adorno's discussion of fascism in relation to Germany. His linkage of national self-identification with the 'jargon of authenticity,' whose 'language is a trade-

mark of societalized chosenness, noble and homey at once – sub-language as superior language' (5–6), speaks to the significance of the authentic as a signifier of national self-interest. In such a context, the political side-effects of a de-authenticated Shakespeare are not to be underestimated.

14 As Peter Dickinson argues, 'the challenge to Canadian literary nationalism is perhaps nowhere more evident than in the work of contemporary First Nations writers. The term "First Nations" itself – in daring to posit prior origins, nationalities, *and* pluralisms – thoroughly destabilizes the bicultural model of Canadian literature at the same time that it raises problematic questions of cultural authenticity' (9).

15 Graves was the former artistic director of the Walterdale Playhouse at the time of the play's publication, and later its membership chairman. Walterdale Theatre Associates, Western Canada's longest-running amateur theatre group, runs the Walterdale Playhouse. Walterdale Theatre Associates is located in the heart of Old Strathcona in Strathcona's old Firehall No. 1 (later Edmonton No. 6), which the WTA converted into Walterdale Playhouse, its third location since 1958.

16 The Canadian motto, derived from Psalm 72:8, literally means 'from sea to sea,' a trope of dominion that technically applied to Canada only in 1871, after British Columbia became a province. The motto came to be an official part of the Arms of Canada in 1921 only after it had been approved by King George V of England in May of that year (almost twenty-eight years before Newfoundland entered the confederation).

15

Undead and Unsafe: Adapting Shakespeare (in Canada)

MARK FORTIER

In this chapter, I want to explore certain aspects, theoretical/situational and ethical/political, of adapting Shakespeare in light of a specific set of Canadian adaptations that are part of a larger theoretical and political pattern. In undertaking this exploration, I have been spurred on by my fellow Canadian academic and Shakespeare scholar Denis Salter, specifically by two passages in his writings on contemporary dealings with Shakespeare.

The first passage is from his essay 'Acting Shakespeare in Postcolonial Space,' in James Bulman's *Shakespeare, Theory, and Performance.* Speaking of 'tradaptations,' translation-adaptations of Shakespeare, Salter writes:

> I would argue that tradaptations, like postcolonial acting, should never be granted timeless status, for to do so would inadvertently reinforce the mystifying assumption that Shakespeare, and the values that he has been made to represent, can never be changed. Rather, tradaptations should be exercises in radical contingency, responsible only for the particular historical moment in which they attempt to decolonize and reinterrogate the Shakespearean text. They should vanish once their particular historical moment has passed and new tradaptations should take their place. (126)

The second passage is from *Shakespeare and Postcolonial Conditions*, a special issue of *Essays in Theatre* edited by Salter. He begins his introduction: 'At times I wonder if there's anyone left who wants to create and defend traditional interpretations of "Shakespeare." It's beginning to seem as if everyone wants to give him a bloody nose or, at the very least, a good talking to' (3).

Salter's two statements are in different registers, one more prescriptive, the other more descriptive – although the registers are intertwined. Together, they could be taken to imply a number of propositions specifically about the adaptation of Shakespeare and more generally about the relations between the cultural past and present: that Shakespeare and the culture of the past are definable, limitable, and graspable; that it is possible and advisable to work in the present and momentary independent of the past; and that the appropriate relation in the present to works of the past such as Shakespeare's is confrontation and hostility. There is also, however, an opening up, in what these passages say and leave unsaid, of other ways of seeing the issues: as I am going to argue in this chapter, Shakespeare, like other cultural entities, is sublimely unknowable; the past haunts the present inescapably; and if our relationship with works of the past is often one of confrontation, it is often confrontation bound to collaboration.

First, I want to rethink the situation of adaptation, and to do this I turn to some notions from Slavoj Žižek's *Tarrying with the Negative*. Žižek begins his book with a discussion of a recent political image: during the fall of communism in Romania, the national flag was carried around with the red star cut from its centre (1–2). For Žižek, this image reveals the moment when the master signifier has been lost and not yet replaced, but it also reveals something about the master signifier at all times: that it covers over an absence or lack, or a sublimely unknowable object, the 'sublime object of ideology.' In the photograph of this hollowed-out flag on the cover of Žižek's book, we see, in black and white, two dark vertical strips on either side of a white central section missing its centre. If one did not know better, one could think it a Canadian flag with its maple leaf missing. One could think this not only because the physical form of this flag resembles Canada's, but because this sublime image speaks to a Canadian sense of identity, or its lack.

Following Kant, Žižek differentiates between two forms of the sublime: the noumenal and the phenomenal (53–6). The noumenal sublime is the unrepresentability of what is in essence unrepresentable: his examples are God and the soul. The phenomenal sublime is the unrepresentability of infinite or complex phenomena: for example, the universe as a whole. Canadian identity, exemplary, perhaps, of (national) identity in general (although the specifics will vary widely), partakes of both forms of the sublime. What would be missing from Žižek's flag, if it were Canadian, would be the maple leaf, which is the representation of Canada's identity as noumenon. The maple leaf, that is, stands for something unrepresentable in essence: nation, state, nationality. Moreover, historically, the current Canadian flag was put forward only after an earlier version was rejected by parliament. This earlier flag, more representational, had blue edges, representing the oceans, and three maple leafs, representing English, French, and other Canadians. This earlier flag was a more phenomenal than noumenal representation. What is clear, however, is that three maple leafs are simply not enough: to represent the complexity of Canadian identity as a multicultural, multidimensional phenomenon would call for an indefinite number of maple leafs. Therefore, what the flag with the hole in it captures, as Canadian flag, is the sublime double unrepresentability of Canada, as both noumenon and phenomenon. There cannot be, in this light, a unified, or even representable, Canada, or, it follows, a graspably Canadian response to Shakespeare or to anything else.

But posit this image: the Droeshout portrait of Shakespeare from the First Folio with the face cut out. Does not such an image open up the sublime unrepresentability of Shakespeare? As noumenon, Shakespeare is a thing in essence unrepresentable, not text, person, intention, but the name for something ineffable: genius, spirit, creativity. As phenomenon, Shakespeare is, as Graham Holderness has said, 'here, now, always, what is currently being made of him' ('Preface' xvi) – and, I would add, what has been and will be made of him. The unavoidable confusion is there in the second of the quotations I began with: is it Shakespeare who is to be punched, or is it traditional interpretations of Shakespeare? Are they the same thing? In Salter's terms, if we try to give him/it a bloody nose, there is no thing – or too much – there to punch. To say, in this light, 'I hate Shakespeare' or 'I love Shakespeare' becomes inevitably a statement about the hole in the picture, about our personal or culturally limited Shakespearean imaginary rather than about the unlimited complexities of the phenomenon itself.

Adapting Shakespeare (in Canada), therefore, is a confrontation between two complexly sublime unrepresentables: one phantom of identity and an indefinitely complex actuality facing another. On this general level, Canada and Shakespeare are much like other sublime objects of ideology, other nations, for instance, or other complex and ongoing cultural formations.

Two other notions from Žižek are helpful to understand specifically how the relationship of past and present is played out – in a way that I hope to show is relevant to understanding particular Canadian adaptations of Shakespeare. Žižek discusses what he calls the *noir* subject (9–12), as in *film noir* and, especially, its recent manifestations – his examples are drawn from the films *Angel Heart, Blade Runner,* and *Total Recall,* but also from literary works such as *Paradise Lost* and *Frankenstein* (40). The *noir* subject is one who does not know what he or she is and who comes to an awareness of a forgotten or hidden identity that is irreconcilable with and radically undermines his or her sense of the self. The *noir* subject faces the sublime other as the otherness of his or her own identity. The second notion from Žižek, also taken from popular film, is that of the 'living dead' or 'undead' (113). The undead is that sublime thing, neither living nor dead, from the past but haunting the here and now, the past that refuses to vanish. Shakespeare (in Canada) is, I would argue, the undead in this sense. It is interesting to note that Jacques Derrida, drawing upon the image of the ghost in *Hamlet,* has argued that we should see Karl Marx in a similar fashion – actually, not as a spectre but as *Specters of Marx,* not singular, but plural. The plural in two senses – as not one unified thing and as widespread – is as true of the spectres of Shakespeare as of Marx. To resort to reference to another popular film, as the little boy in *The Sixth Sense* says of the ghosts he sees, 'They're everywhere.' There is no escaping them. *The Sixth Sense* is a film Žižek, one would think, must inevitably write about, concerning, as it does, the *noir subject,* the one who is undead without knowing it. The point I wish to extrapolate from these notions is that there is always something un-Canadian about being Canadian, that the from-elsewhere is part of the being here. Shakespeare, therefore, is one manifestation of the from elsewhere at work in Canada. As such, Canadians confront Shakespeare as the cultural undead, neither dead nor living, not a person but an other forming part of living personalities, if only as part of the sublime personality I have been outlining, the otherness of the past the remains of which reside here. Canadians too, in their specific ways, are the undead, although as *noir* subjects they may not always realize this. I think it important to put something along these lines inside the simple opposition between timelessness and radical contingency. Only by opening up in this way the place of the present as irreducibly the place of the past, rather than as a 'particular historical moment' in any isolated sense, will we see the possibilities in the complex situation of adaptation.

There is a long and wide-ranging history of Shakespeare in Canada and within that a substantial tradition of adapting Shakespeare. The arguments in the first part of this chapter suggest that it would be futile to attempt to know fully or to represent adequately this tradition. There is no single Canadian approach that would distinguish the Canadian situation from others and hence no simply representative Canadian adaptations. I have chosen to focus on a handful of works from the 1980s and 1990s. These works tell only the smallest part of the story. Nevertheless, what I want to point out in these particular pieces are echoes, in theme and event, of the condition I have been suggesting. Specifically, the notions of the *noir* subject and the undead seem helpful in elucidating these particular Canadian adaptations, which present the return of the undead amid *noir* confusions.

In early 1987 an interesting adaptation of Shakespeare debuted in Toronto. It was by Québécois playwright René-Daniel Dubois and coincided with an English-language production of his better known *Being at Home with Claude*. The adaptation of Shakespeare was called *Pericles, Prince of Tyre, by William Shakespeare*, and it was Dubois's first English-language play and the first of his plays to premiere in English Canada – a situation that evokes one of the many alterities of Canadian identity. The premise of the play is that on 8 April a production of Shakespeare's *Pericles* opened. That opening was catastrophically disrupted by strange forces, and those involved were sent into a dreamland full of danger, death, and a hoped-for but deferred salvation. On 9 April and nights following, what the audience witnesses is Dubois's *Pericles*, which is the shambles left behind by the catastrophic disruption of Shakespeare's version.

The director of the play-within-a-play – although it is not quite that – had set out to 'make a statement about today using very old means' (19) and also 'to fight death' (14) by bringing the poet back to life. Rather than fighting death, however, opening night brings about the deaths of everyone involved: the living dead now wander the stage. What happened is that not Shakespeare but the much more ancient and primal Gower returned to walk the stage, not Shakespeare's domesticated Gower but a wild and uncontrollable force. Witworth, the actor playing Gower, is possessed by the spirit of the long-dead poet. 'I was a spectre,' Witworth says, 'but not even my own spectre' (34). The invocation of Shakespeare here calls forth another, older spirit, so that to produce Shakespeare is to produce something else: the dead return but not as we expected them to be. The ancient spirit of Gower is both apart from the sterility of a big modern city like Toronto and something that lingers behind the urban façade, a force for great destruction and, at the same time, a drive for poetic rebirth. Gower is something not us, yet waiting in us to erupt. Similarly, the play is set both in contemporary Toronto and in a strange dreamland, a dreamland not Canada yet happening here nonetheless. Rather than Shakespeare's *Pericles*, therefore, it is 'an old, very very old play' (3) that is invoked. Shakespeare, like Witworth, is here a *noir* subject, haunted by an ancient otherness, as *Pericles* is a kind of *noir* play, revealing at its heart something other and darker than itself.

An 'old, very very old play' is invoked, but there is also in Dubois's play a spectre, intentional or not, of a relatively more recent work: Federico García Lorca's *The Public*, which enacts what happens after an attempted production of *Romeo and Juliet* is catastrophically disrupted by the spirit of the dead. What we begin to see are the multiple forces that haunt the production of Shakespeare on a stage in 'contemporary' Toronto. The present is ancient, Canada is Toronto, dreamland, Europe, French and English, and its people are possessed, the living dead, overcome by forces they did not know existed.

While *Pericles* haunted a contemporary Canadian location with Shakespearean and pre-Shakespearean presences, another recent Canadian adaptation of Shakespeare has little or no ties to Canada in its content and setting, which goes another direction in complicating the notion of a 'particular historical moment.' Michael O'Brien's *Mad Boy Chronicle*, which was first produced at the Alberta Theatre Projects playRITES Festival in Calgary in 1995, is an adaptation of *Hamlet*, but it works by turning back to the thirteenth-century *Gesta Danorum* by Saxo Grammaticus – again, Shakespeare is a *noir* subject, more than himself, harbouring within an older presence. The play is set in Helsingor, Denmark, in the winter of 999 AD. *Mad Boy Chronicle* is the story of Horvendal, the Hamlet character, who finds Christianity and turns away from revenge. However, monks arrive in Denmark and see politically in Fengo, the marauding Claudius character, 'God's Gateway to the Danes' (132). They convert Fengo and submit their Christian ethics to his self-interests. Horvendal encounters the ghost of Christ (the undead *par excellence*), who tells him to save his 'Strangled Gospel' (135) by returning to murder Fengo. Horvendal attacks Fengo, but he is killed by a monk who comes to Fengo's defence.

O'Brien claims that he set out originally 'to debase the greatest play of all time' (8) – to punch Shakespeare in the nose, so to speak – and the tone of his presentation has been compared to that of Monty Python (152). However, in the long tradition of adaptations of Shakespeare, I think more apt comparisons could be made to Alfred Jarry, as in *Ubu Roi*, and Bertolt Brecht. The tone of *Mad Boy Chronicle* owes much to the grotesqueries of expression and action of Alfred Jarry and features a fractured, obscene, comic-book English in touch with the stupidity and libidinousness of the major characters. In its thematic approach, however, the play echoes (as Dubois's echoes Lorca) Bertolt Brecht's reading of *Hamlet*: 'It is an age of warriors ... [The events of the play] show the young man ... making the most ineffective use of the new approach to Reason which he has picked up at the University of Wittenberg. In the feudal business to which he returns it simply hampers him. Faced with irrational practices, his reason is utterly unpractical. He falls a tragic victim to the discrepancy between such reason and such action' (201–2). Heiner Müller, Brecht's follower and author of *Hamletmachine*, writes that he sees Hamlet 'quite as Brecht once defined him: The man between the ages who knows that the old age is obsolete, yet the new age has barbarian features he simply cannot stomach' (Weber 137). But here Müller follows Brecht only by reversing him: for Brecht, Hamlet is the new man of reason who fails to negotiate the transition from the old feudal barbarism to the new enlightenment; Müller's Hamlet is a man of the old reason who cannot deal with the necessary new barbarism. What *Mad Boy Chronicle* does is draw a complex complicity in the change from one age to another. Christianity is bureaucratic reason in service of irrational desire on the one hand, and a spirit of forgiveness driven to righteous yet impractical vengeance on the other – here the play also echoes the conflict between Christ and the institutional church in the 'Grand Inquisitor' section of Dostoevsky's *The Brothers Karamazov*: Christ, in that *noir* work, discovers that he is not a Christian. Thus, O'Brien's play takes up a place in a high European intellectual debate, the from elsewhere that inhabits the Canadian; yet, in the lingo of the play, he states, 'Only in Canada could such a play get writ' (9).

For my third example, I move to Winnipeg, and, in this text, outside theatre to children's fiction, one of many other modes – opera, comic books, t-shirts, education, film, and so forth – in which Shakespeares continue to proliferate. *Cloning Miranda* is a 1999 novel by Winnipeg children's writer Carol Matas. Its title, as well as its originally intended name, *Rough Magic*, points to its connection with *The Tempest*. The novel, Canadian as it is, is set in a wealthy enclave of the southern California desert. Miranda is a beautiful and accomplished adolescent suddenly struck with a seemingly incurable disease. Her parents, being so very un-Canadian (unless they were from Alberta), are the owners of a chain of private, technologically cutting-edge health clinics. Miranda is admitted to one of her parents' clinics, but not before she discovers strange photo albums featuring pictures of her and her parents on vacations she has never taken. At the clinic, Miranda happens upon a sequestered young girl who seems to be a younger version of herself. To give little more away than the title does, Miranda, it turns out, is a clone of an earlier daughter, Jessica, who died of the same disease Miranda has acquired – Jessica is the girl in the photo album; the young girl hidden away is a clone of Miranda, Ariel, who is to be sacrificed so that her organs can save Miranda. Miranda discovers the plan and forces her parents to adopt another course of action, whereby Miranda and Ariel are both saved and Ariel is admitted into family life as a full member.

Cloning suggests a number of significant connections with the acts of adaptation under discussion. The clone is the supposed perfect copy, the perfect reproduction, much as a certain critical stance, dated but haunting, demands or expects the faithful transmission, the traditional production, of Shakespeare and his works. But Shakespeare, like Miranda's sister Jessica, is dead, and the supposed perfect reproduction is a new being, even if it is one haunted in its very essence by the past. Miranda is, in this way, a model *noir* subject: she does not know who she really is; she is someone else in her very DNA. And yet, although Jessica is in Miranda and lives through Miranda an undead existence, Miranda is not simply Jessica, any more than Ariel is simply a subordinated entity of spare parts for Miranda. Miranda is a multiple being: clone of the dead, dutiful daughter, monster, self, other. Cloning functions in the parents' plan as an insurance policy against death, a way of armouring their offspring against corruption. This armouring, however, produces something inevitably other than its original, an Other that takes on a disruptive life of its own.

Although the novel is not closely based on the plot, characters, or language of *The Tempest*, there are significant echoes: in the names Miranda and Ariel; in Miranda's school project comparing Ariel and Caliban in *The Tempest*; and in the themes of technology, power, and ethics, nature and nurture, the dutiful daughter, and the monster. Like many contemporary readings of Shakespeare's play, the novel's sympathies lie against the power-wielding parental figures of authority and with the child, the other, the monster, those intended only as 'spare parts.' In the end, the two daughters have moved beyond the fate intended for them, and Ariel, 'thrilled about everything,' cannot wait to enjoy 'new situations' (137). In this way, the novel moves toward the openness suggested in Shakespearean romance, while looking to difficult reconciliations between the daughters and their parents. Miranda writes: 'My parents, who I thought were so reasonable, who I never argued with because there was no need, who stressed honesty over all else – they were honest in every little detail and lied about the biggest thing, my life. Suddenly Prospero from *The Tempest* pops into my mind. He used magic to make his daughter happy. It's what Mom and Dad have done. But their magic means someone must be killed. They'll be *murderers!*' (103). And later: 'I'm still trying to figure out how to forgive my parents. I'm very angry with them. They did it out of love, but that's no excuse, is it? I don't think their reasons excuse what they did. It was wrong. I spend a lot of time over at [a friend's] now. Her parents seem to know the difference between right and wrong' (137–8).

In *Cloning Miranda*, therefore, we begin to be confronted by ethical questions of the *noir* undead. To understand the situation of adaptation is to impinge on understanding the politics and ethics of adaptation. To want to give Shakespeare a bloody nose, when Shakespeare is not, noumenally or phenomenally, one thing to which we could give a bloody nose, is to replace the face in the empty portrait with something hittable, thereby inevitably limiting Shakespeare in order to have something to hit. There is nothing wrong in doing so – indeed to engage with Shakespeare is always to engage with some limitation of Shakespeare. And confronting the hegemonic imaginary is often a necessary and useful political strategy. But it is important to understand the complexities of this confrontation and to realize that the Shakespeare we wish to bloody is not the only story. Moreover, within a *noir* subjectivity, it is important to realize that it may be part of ourselves that we assault.

To elaborate further the ethics and politics of adaptation, I want to turn to two famous dicta from Walter Benjamin's 'Theses on the Philosophy of History.' The first is: 'There is no document of civilization which is not at the same time a document of barbarism' (256). This assertion has served quite justifiably as a kind of mantra for politically oppositional cultural critique. Its force lies in part in the removal of the thought-restricting aura that traditionally attaches to works of art. Adaptation of Shakespeare often entails seeing the barbarism in Shakespeare. What I want to emphasize here, however, is the phrase 'at the same time.' What Benjamin asserts is that the documents of civilization are *at the same time* documents of barbarism, not that they are simply one or the other. 'At the same time' complicates our relationship to these works and opens a space where the giving of a bloody nose or a hope for the past simply to vanish is a one-sided reaction that does not constitute the full range of possible and appropriate responses.

The other dictum from Benjamin is a more mysterious, indeed haunting, one: 'Only that historian will have the gift of fanning the spark of hope in the past who is firmly convinced that *even the dead* will not be safe from the enemy if he wins' (255). Just before this, Benjamin writes, 'In every era the attempt must be made anew to wrest tradition away from a conformism that is about to overpower it.' Tradition and conformism are not the same thing; the past hangs in the balance between the two. But the past is not, we are told, 'the way it really was.' Rather the past is something we seize hold of as it exists in the present, in a present moment of danger, Benjamin writes. The past is, dare we say, 'not safe.' An ambiguity hangs over this phrase: the dead are in danger; they are dangerous. The past cultural object is both an object in our care and a threat to us. Benjamin's regard for the past does not come out of an unthinking respect for the documents of civilization nor out of a sentimental desire to do justice to the dead. To turn one more time to *The Sixth Sense*, the boy in the film learns not to hide his head from spectres, nor to expect them to vanish, nor even to give them a good talking to, but rather to listen to their traumas in order to discover the ways in which the dead and the living are still not safe. The past is a danger and an opportunity because it lives on as part of the present.

Some of this dynamic of confrontation and collaboration, of danger and vulnerability, is at work in Dubois's *Pericles*. In this play, Dubois engages with Shakespearean romance, not only in the return of the past in the present, but also in the workings of destruction and renewal. There is in the play catastrophic loss, and recovery and resurrection are cast into an uncertain future. The play leaves us in the space of danger where nothing is yet safe, a place of 'Awful stories. Gentle endings' (48), an 'infinite land of never ending hope and despair' (89). Just as Shakespeare is not simply Shakespeare and his *Pericles* not simply his *Pericles*, the effect of the past on the present and future is not simply good or bad but complex and open.

I want to explore more acutely, however, this politics of adaptation as confrontation and collaboration in two feminist Canadian adaptations of Shakespeare. The first is Ann-Marie MacDonald's *Goodnight Desdemona (Good Morning Juliet)*, which premiered at the Annex Theatre in Toronto early in 1988. MacDonald's play is an adaptation, as its title suggests, of both *Othello* and *Romeo and Juliet*. In the play, Constance Ledbelly is a victimized Canadian academic who pursues the quirky theory that behind both of Shakespeare's plays lies the 'Gustav manuscript,' which contains earlier versions of both stories, versions truer to the strength of the feminine character and versions that Shakespeare distorted. Constance finds herself magically transported into the two Shakespearean scenarios, where she realizes that she, partaking of a feminine archetypal power, is the author of the Gustav manuscript.

Once again we are in the realm of *noir* subjectivity. Constance comes to realize that she herself is the author she is seeking. Indeed, the three female heroes (Constance, Desdemona, and Juliet) are not three individuals at all, but aspects of one larger female psyche. Shakespeare's plays turn out to have an older, hidden identity. Genre itself is a *noir* categorization, and *Othello* and *Romeo and Juliet* are really comedies. Moreover, if Shakespeare is a kind of *noir* villain in the play, distorting and covering over, for his own sinister, masculinist purposes, the way things really are, his works nonetheless serve as a conduit to a more sympathetic reality of which they are the corrupted image.

In its original production, *Goodnight Desdemona* was called 'a comical Shakespearean romance' (qtd. from the publicity poster), a generic label that has since been discarded. What this designation captures is the movement from the Shakespearean tragedy of *Othello* and *Romeo and Juliet* through comic disruption to the romantic rearrangements of *Goodnight Desdemona* itself. As romance, the play finds a complex reconciliation with Shakespeare. It begins with Constance's dissatisfaction with and rejection of Shakespeare's weak tragic women. But the new-made women of the Gustav manuscript are made from aspects of character found, if unstressed, in Shakespeare's version. In this way, as well as through the appropriation of romance itself, *Goodnight Desdemona* aligns itself with Shakespeare. Ultimately, however, it is something other than Shakespeare that is being unearthed in this play: the name of the Gustav manuscript echoes Carl Gustav Jung, whose ideas work their way through this and other works by MacDonald. As universal archetypes (dare we say in this case, timeless representations of the feminine character), the old truths of the pre-Shakespearean manuscript are also the truths that emanate from Constance in the present. Here, as in Dubois's *Pericles*, the play looks past but within Shakespeare to a romantic resurrection of much older, yet ever-present, forces – forces that, consequently, are, and are not, Canadian. There appears, most sublimely, near the end of the play, a ghost. The ghost evades answering the question 'Who are you?' (73). In costume drawings we see only a white, featureless skull, a hole in the flag of identity. It seems to be in part an echo of two of the dead in *Hamlet*: Yorick and Hamlet's father. But it seems to be many others as well, including Shakespeare and Jung. The closest it comes to identifying itself is to say 'You're it': the spectre is Constance, the archetypal everywoman of the play, or the audience, or Canadians, or everyone.

Gertrude and Ophelia is a play by Margaret Clarke, first performed by the Black Hole Theatre Company in Winnipeg in 1987. The play *Gertrude and Ophelia* consists of rehearsals for the play *Gertrude and Ophelia*, which tells the story of these two women from Shakespeare's *Hamlet* while keeping Hamlet himself offstage. By focusing on these two women and keeping Hamlet from taking centre stage, the play explores the complex dynamics of alliance and opposition that bind women in a male-dominated society. The playwright is a woman who also acts the part of Gertrude in scenes with Ophelia. These rehearsals are troubled by a male actor and an unseen male director who work intentionally and unintentionally to undermine the playwright's feminist vision. In part, they disrupt this vision by working to bring Hamlet back on the stage, by bringing more of Shakespeare's play back into the production. The playwright argues against this strategy:

> *Playwright.* We cannot have your scene, because your scene is Prince Hamlet's scene and I will not have him in my play.
> *Actor.* But you already have him; he permeates your play. These two women are obsessed with him.
> *Playwright.* Yes, they are, but it is *their* obsession that I want to present on the stage, not his, not his body on the stage, his flesh invading my play.
> *Actor.* You make it sound like a rape!
> *Playwright.* The words of the play are of my body; they come out of my body. They are my flesh made words ... You must stop writing inside other people's plays.
> *Actor.* But that's exactly what you are doing? Writing inside Shakespeare's play.
> *Playwright.* Yes, but I'm doing it to write myself out of the world that Shakespeare had to write in. The world we still live in because of the power of his plays.
> (S14)

The playwright here adopts a somewhat uncompromising and purist rejection of the invasion of her work by Hamlet or Shakespeare. At another point she rejects the director's attempts to bring Tom Stoppard to bear on her work:

> He wants word-play, he wants pastiche, he wants ... Stoppard! Damn that man. He's been reading his Stoppard as well as his Shakespeare. Tell him if

he wants Stoppard, he can pay the royalties for *Rosencrantz and Guildenstern Are Dead.* (S9)

What the Playwright does not admit here is the degree to which the very premise of her work – a play about two characters from *Hamlet* other than Hamlet in which Hamlet makes little or no appearance – resembles the work of Stoppard. Indeed, one must also note that Clarke's *Gertrude and Ophelia* is a different play from the playwright's *Gertrude and Ophelia*. Certainly, there is some degree of identification between Clarke, a feminist writing a play based on *Hamlet* called *Gertrude and Ophelia*, and the Playwright, a feminist writing a play based on *Hamlet* called *Gertrude and Ophelia*, but it is a *noir* identification. Clarke's play, after all, unlike the Playwright's, includes a scene from *Hamlet*, even if it is to be played suspiciously or ironically. Clarke's play follows a politics similar to that in the play-within-the-play, but it does so by a different relation with other texts. The Playwright admits to writing inside Shakespeare's play, but what Clarke's structure also does is to have Shakespeare write within hers. Even Clarke's understanding of Hamlet is neo-Brechtian with a feminist twist:

> He is one of those representatives of a man on the cusp of history between the medieval world and the Renaissance world, a man who's called upon to act and to forget scruples, and a man who has had an education and wishes to live as a moral human being. And what I discovered in writing my script is that such a man when he's frustrated, put down in his public life, takes out that frustration and that anger in his private life. (qtd. in Burnett 19–20)

The tensions between the two plays called *Gertrude and Ophelia* and the interplay in Clarke's play of elements from Shakespeare, Stoppard, and Brecht indicate that the purist assumptions of 'my play' and 'my words' from which the Playwright works are not supported by the play in which she is character rather than author. *Gertrude and Ophelia* works, rather, by both confrontation and collaboration, guarding borders and incorporating others at once.

Looking back over these texts in an attempt to conclude, I find it impossible to draw from them a simple representation, or clone, of Shakespeare, of Canada, or of the relation of past and present between them. They do not as a whole work from the notion of a particular historical moment separated from the past or of Shakespeare as someone who should be given a bloody nose. They engage with the relation of Shakespeare and the past to Canada and the present in ways that indicate a complex vision and a more entwined politics. But the theory I have outlined implies that that should not be very surprising. The undead and the unsafe demand a careful negotiation, not based on a simple and mystifying assumption of unchanging timelessness, certainly, but rather on a sense that the radical contingency of the particular historical moment is formed by things not wholly of that moment.

Finally, three of the five texts I have discussed have had something to do with Shakespearean romance, and I want to suggest that the spectres of romance bear thinking about. Romance deals with the relationship with the past, not, as I argue elsewhere about *The Winter's Tale* ('Married'), with the past as the way it really was, but with the past as it returns in the present, we could say as it arises in the present moment of danger. Often, romance entails a restoration, reconciliation, saving of this past, but again only as a past that is not anything that has happened before. But that is not the only relation to the past in romance. Elsewhere I have also argued, using Northrop Frye against his own readings of Shakespearean romance, that struggle is basic to romance ('Two-Voiced'). The past is a danger as well as something to be protected and restored. Ultimately, within romance the space of the unknown future opens up – Ariel free to the four elements, or *The Winter's Tale*'s 'unpath'd waters, undream'd shores' (4.4.567), which offers the promise of something completely different. All of these trajectories are at work, for instance, in Phillip Osment's British adaptation of *The Tempest*, *This Island's Mine*. Susan Bennett, in her discussion of this play, traces the complex dynamics of past, present, and future possibilities that the play enacts. She captures the complexities of danger and possibility we have seen through Benjamin when she writes, 'We can best salvage the Shakespearean text when we savage it, when we plunder it for its gaps and blind spots' (*Performing* 149), when we look into those gaps and blind spots to see what lurks there for us.

What I want to suggest, to conclude this discussion, is that adapting Shakespeare – in Canada or anywhere else – is a romantic activity, no matter what specific generic conventions are at work in any particular production. Adaptation is a process of savaging and salvaging the undead who reside in the present – although, to call adaptations romance is to try to represent an unrepresentable complexity.

Normand Chaurette's *Les Reines*: Shakespeare and the Modern in the Alchemical Oven

LOIS SHERLOW

R udenesse itselfe she doth refine
E ven like an Alchymist divine,
G rosse times of iron turning
I nto the purest forme of gold
N ot to corrupt till heaven waxe old,
A nd be refin'd with burning.

– Sir John Davies (qtd. in Nicholl 17)

Normand Chaurette's *Les Reines* (1991) is a verse play derived primarily from Shakespeare's *Richard III*. Its characters are six royal women who, in 1483, are awaiting the death of King Edward IV, the assassination of George, Duke of Clarence, and the accession of Richard to the throne. To the four women, Elizabeth, Margaret, Anne Warwick, and the Duchess of York, appropriated from Shakespeare's play, Chaurette has added two more Plantagenet women, Isabelle Warwick, sister of Anne and wife of Clarence, and Anne Dexter (named for the historical Countess of Exeter), daughter of the Duchess of York and sister of George, Richard, and Edward. The play was first produced at the Théâtre d'Aujourd'hui, Montreal, under André Brassard's direction. In November 1992 Linda Gaboriau's English translation was directed by Peter Hinton for the Canadian Stage Company, and in the same year the play earned Chaurette the Chalmers Award for best play produced in Canada. A revival of *Les Reines* by Théâtre Blanc, Quebec (1997, directed by Gill Champagne) afforded a very different interpretation of the script from Brassard's. In 1997 *Les Reines* was also performed at the Théâtre du Vieux

Colombier, Paris, with Joël Joanneau directing: it was the first Québécois play ever to be performed by the Comédie Française.

Amid the wide array of translations, adaptations, parodies, and performance texts generated from Shakespearean origins in Quebec since the late 1970s, *Les Reines* is particularly resistant to classification. Neither adaptation nor parody, it is a play in its own right, which nevertheless originated from a translation of *Richard III* abandoned by Chaurette in 1987 (Riendeau 19). Chaurette absorbs the world of *Richard III* while dispensing with most of the plot and the conventional dimensions of the few characters he retains. Apparently taking as his starting point that clear opposition in Shakespeare's text between the domain of aggressive, power-seeking males and that of endlessly talking women, who, as wives, widows, and mothers, are passive commodities in the symbolic order, the playwright invents a parallel world 'somewhere offstage in the play of history, in a domestic-yet-regal women's antechamber to the playing out of "great events"' (Knowles, Rev.). Rather as Tom Stoppard does in *Rosencrantz and Guildenstern Are Dead* (1966), Chaurette negates the Aristotelian framework of the source tragedy while at the same time alluding to its key structural developments. In some ways like Stoppard's courtiers or Beckett's tramps, Chaurette's queens pass the time while waiting for the inevitable. In *Les Reines*, however, the relationship between tragedy and the absurd is more than a matter of negated structure: it is also densely figured throughout the text in multiple allusions to both classical and twentieth-century texts.

Paul Lefebvre's preface to *Les Reines* merely hints at the extent of the figuration of the modern in Chaurette's text: 'Il y a surtout notre siècle chez ces reines. Les énumérations d'Élisabeth nous rappellent qu'il est vain de faire semblant d'écrire du Shakespeare à l'époque de Ionesco' ('These queens belong first and foremost to our century. Elizabeth's lists remind us that it is pointless to try to write Shakespeare in the era of Ionesco') (5).[1] (Here Lefebvre refers to a pastiche of Ionesco's own pastiche of English phrasebook sentences in *La Cantatrice chauve* [1954].) Ionesco's presence in *Les Reines* is more than stylistic: in the key scenes in which King Edward and the Duchess of York meet their deaths, there are strong echoes of *Le Roi se meurt* (1962), itself a parody of classical tragedy. *Les Reines* enacts no simple opposition of Shakespearean tragedy to the absurdist comedy of Ionesco, however. Chaurette's text is also extensively marked by stylistic references to French classical tragedy, on the one hand, and, on the other, echoes of the language of surrealist as well as absurdist texts of the modern French theatre; that is, classical textuality may be accessed in *Les Reines* only through the alienations of a twentieth-century textuality, whose subversive, parodic, imagist, and firmly anti-realist activity Chaurette espouses and extends.

Chaurette's textual mingling of elements of classical tragedy and medieval history with twentieth-century surreal and absurd references figures its own transformative process in alchemical symbolism. As a playwright noted for his hermeticism, Chaurette is in his element in this text, playing the alchemist. The scenes of the play bear titles (only available to the reader, as is typical of Chaurette) that allude to some of the major arcana of the Tarot (the Moon, the World, the Chariot); the play also features important images based on other major arcana, the Tower, the Sun, the Lovers, the Empress, and the Star. Titles of some scenes – 'Effigie d'Edouard' ('Effigy of Edward'), 'La fournaise' ('The Furnace'), 'Le déluge' ('The Deluge'), 'La Chine' ('China') – allude to stages of the alchemical transformation of *prima materia*, or base matter, into the final product, the self.

The title of Chaurette's play is the device under which the allegory of dissolution and decay, and, ultimately, transcendence of matter proceeds. The drama of the queens is the drama of the 'feminine unconscious' of which C.G. Jung writes extensively in his works on alchemy and psychoanalysis. Charles. J. Nicholl finds that tragedy and the alchemical process are closely allied in their purpose, that is, to enact the cycle of destruction and renewal: 'This is the underlying pattern, the classical model of tragedy: purgatorial and redemptive. It is also the underlying pattern of alchemy ... alchemical parables ... allegorize the alchemical process [and also] *dramatize* it – to present the *magnum opus* as a symbolic drama of purgation and redemption. As such, we find in them stringent echoes of tragic heroism and destiny' (142). The queens of Chaurette's play expose the alchemy of the unconscious that underlies classical tragedy. Chaurette himself describes them as powerful forces in the individual, more enduring than the specifics of history:

> Elles ont existé. Fabuleuses, visionnaires, profondément ancrées dans le déroulement de l'histoire ... menées par les aléas de guerre ... parsemées de sang, de noblesse, de déchirements. Mais au-delà des références historiques, les reines existent encore, elles existent toujours ... [elles] vivent en chacun de nous, qui somnolent, mélancoliques, et qui parfois s'éveillent en sursaut, réclamant l'impossible, l'infini. Elles sont à la base de nos pires souffrances, mais par elles il nous arrive d'atteindre des instants de

grandeur où le monde, ne serait-ce que dix secondes, devient une facette de nous-même appelée à disparaître avec nous. (qtd. in R. Lévesque, 'Des farces')

(They were there. Fabulous, visionary, deeply anchored in the unfolding of history ... entangled in the ups and downs of history ... sprinkled with the blood of nobility and divisions. But the queens existed beyond history; they are still there ... they live in each of us, dormant and melancholy, and they sometimes awaken suddenly, demanding the impossible, the infinite. They are there in our worst sufferings, but through them we can attain moments of grandeur, in which the world, if only for ten seconds, becomes an aspect of ourselves, summoned to disappear with us.)

Chaurette's account of the queens suggests that they are the forces that both animate the creative moment and dissolve the given version of history. They are not in any sense realistic characters: if they were, they might still belong to the classical tragic text from which they are derived. Rather, they are presented as personifications of the elements of alchemical allegory. Nicholl's account of the symbolic persons of alchemical narrative may aptly be applied to *Les Reines*: 'On the surface are people. Symbolic, two-dimensional people, moving across an emblematic landscape, but "characters" nevertheless: kings and queens, princes and princesses ... and, of course, the ubiquitous alchemist, part onlooker, part hero. They are characters in both senses; persons and ciphers' (141). The alchemical 'drama' is remarkably similar not only to tragedy but also to the contents of Chaurette's play: 'The beginning is grossness, infertility, poverty, incompleteness. The middle, or "action," of the narrative entails a submission to some drastic, mysterious and overwhelming process; the torment of dismemberment, the perils of a sea journey, the incestuous marriage which leads to imprisonment or death. The end, as a result of this purgatorial process, is exultant. The qualities which prevailed ... are each healed, transformed into spirituality, abundance ... and wholeness' (Nicholl 141).

Chaurette begins his play in a storm ('winter of discontent') with rumours of disease and dearth; among his most significant narrative passages are a grotesquely literal description of the disintegration of the king's body at death, Margaret's account of a perilous sea journey to China with the infant princes, and Anne Dexter's retelling of the incestuous love between herself and her brother George, for which she has been mutilated, he imprisoned, and both silenced. The end of the play is the death of the Duchess of York, on whose final breath are exhaled all the elements of the text of her life and times.

Chaurette's texts tend to defy theatrical convention, to the chagrin of some directors, and to obstruct the construction of any single meaning. Chaurette himself, however, has expressed strong respect for and knowledge of theatrical convention, which is borne out in his writing (Loffrée 62). The necessary presence of theatrical tradition in his work is often indicated, for instance, by a firm statement of time and place: in *Les Reines*, 'la scène est à Londres en 1483' ('the action takes place in London in 1483') (12). Once the anchor to tradition is thrown, however, Chaurette's texts usually turn out to be fictions full of allegorical meaning and dream logic. Undecidability and ambiguity prevail. To critics who suggest that his hermeticism makes his plays too difficult for their audience, Chaurette is unapologetic: 'Hermétique? Ça ne me gène pas du tout. Je crois beaucoup dans l'art hermétique ... au théâtre, on aime rejoindre le plus possible, mais pas à n'importe quelle condition' ('Hermetic? That doesn't bother me. I believe strongly in hermetic art ... in the theatre, one wants to reach as many people as possible, but not at any cost') (qtd. in Loffrée 60). Chaurette expects his audiences to adjust their receptive capacities.

Hermeticism implies, in the words of Éliphas Lévi, that 'one is one ... all is in all' (qtd. in Orenstein 10). This alchemical view of text can be equated with the Jamesian 'figure dans le tapis' ('figure in the carpet'), an image used by Stéphane Lépine to define the way in which Chaurette's indirection always works to conceal a secret, which, once revealed, totalizes the meaning of all that has been said and remains to be said ('*Le Sceau*'). In Chaurette, the 'barred scene' is crucial: in *Les Reines*, Anne Dexter tells at length of the incestuous love between herself and her brother George, which led to their apparent muteness, her banishment, and his incarceration (59–68). The secret itself is singular in meaning: it opposes the overt sense of the text and defies the speculations of all other characters who are engaged in worldly or intellectual pursuits: 'Ce secret est bien au contraire d'ordre uniquement mentale; ce secret est un véritable secret ... une configuration mystérieuse de l'esprit, un détour caché de l'intelligence, un refuge presque inabordable de l'âme ... parfois toute un amour, parfois toute la vie d'un être' ('This secret completely contradicts any strictly mental order; the secret is truly a secret ... a mysterious configuration of the spirit, a detour concealed from the intellect, an almost inaccessible refuge of the soul ... sometimes an entire love, or the entire life of a person') (10).

To mark further the queens' identity as unconscious, alchemical elements, or, taken together, the anima (the property of a male, according to Jung, not a female), Chaurette incorporates a double significance in the title, which alludes to both royal females and male homosexuals. This device alienates the characters of the play from the realm of realistic representation of gender. In psychological terms, the play may properly be located in the male unconscious. There, the queens function collectively – not as individuals – both to negate the tragic hero's sacrifice and the kinship patterns it must preserve and, at the same time, to double the tragic pattern in their own underworld. Taken in alchemical terms, however, the play need not be restricted to the masculine realm of the tragic subject.

As an 'alchemical' text, *Les Reines* is heavily allegorical: it may be read at both personal and historical levels as a narrative of dissolution and purification. It is, of course, only one of many Québécois scripts of the 1980s and 1990s that appropriated Shakespeare's plays for their transformative, allegorical potential. The Elizabethan stage and late medieval history had attracted, before Chaurette, several Québécois writers and directors – among, them Jean-Pierre Ronfard, Jean Asselin, and Robert Claing – to create their own allegories, all thoroughly and irreverently debased by anachronism.[2] Chaurette's drama of the mourning, squabbling, distracted queens, confined in their crumbling tower as kings die and the usurper prowls, should be viewed, then, as belonging to that post-nationalist trend to allegorize the darker side of political hubris by reference to the Middle Ages and the Renaissance stage. Although *Les Reines* is structured on a symbolic matrix that is comparable with those found in earlier Québécois versions of English history, it differs from Ronfard's and Asselin's works in that its hermetic self-referentiality excludes references to the contemporary political world (as do all of Chaurette's plays). This is not to say, however, that Chaurette's theatre bears no relation to the spectator's world.

Chaurette's historical allegory (like those of Ronfard, Asselin, and Claing) clearly follows a modernist pattern of interpretation and appropriation of Renaissance drama that Richard Halpern has identified in European and American works from the late nineteenth century to the present, including critical, theoretical, fictional, and dramatic works by T.S. Eliot, Walter Benjamin, James Joyce, Bertolt Brecht, Antonin Artaud, Jean Cocteau, Northrop Frye, Jacques Lacan, Heiner Müller, and Stephen Greenblatt. Halpern argues that the modernist tendency, exemplified in Eliot's allegorical reading of early modern English drama and Benjamin's allegorical linking of baroque German drama with modern expressionism, is identifiable even in works usually termed postmodern and postcolonial: 'The modernists' reading of Shakespeare has not vanished, because the world that gave birth to it has not' (2). Among contemporary Québécois interpreters of Shakespeare, however, only Chaurette seems to sense his own alliance with twentieth-century modernist predecessors as he amalgamates allusions to Ionesco and language that mirrors surrealist poetics with Renaissance tragedy. Chaurette's exploitation of the difference between classical and modernist texts is undoubtedly the result of his being the most literary of Québécois playwrights, and one who always refers his own dramaturgy to a broader field of textuality, both dramatic and non-dramatic.

Eliot's reading of the past informs Halpern's conception of modernist historical allegory: 'He allowed the past to be reconfigured in conformity with current needs and preoccupations ... [and] constructed an image of Elizabethan drama largely in response to what he sees as a crisis in contemporary theater' (3). Modernists have favoured the Renaissance as a source of allegory, because there they find a 'unified sensibility' breaking down 'into component parts' under the pressure of 'an accelerated transition to modernity' (26). Halpern argues that 'a spirit of decline' and of decay is found in Eliot and Benjamin that still informs historical allegory in the late twentieth century:

> For Eliot, 'even the philosophical basis, the general attitude toward life of the Elizabethans, is one of anarchism, of dissolution, of decay.' 'It seemed as if, at that time, the world was filled with broken fragments of systems, and that a man like Donne merely picked up, like a magpie, various shining fragments of ideas as they struck his eye, and stuck them about in his verse.' For Eliot, as for Benjamin, early modern culture, is marked by the predominance of the fragment or ruin. (9)

If modernist allegory is marked by this sense of 'anarchism ... dissolution ... decay,' then Chaurette is a certainly a modernist: he triply enriches his own allegory of transformation by incorporating shards of twentieth-century texts, late medieval and Renaissance images, and some neoclassicist diction, and then subjects them all to the overall rubric of alchemical dissolution, decay, and purification.

Halpern explores in depth the production of primitivism in modernist readings of Shakespeare from Artaud and Brecht to Greenblatt and other new historicists. 'Modernism,' he points out, 'succeeded in inventing a "primitive" Shakespeare' (17). Chaurette himself (like Ronfard before him) has elevated the primitive above history and cultural tradition in his play. In *Les Reines*, an allegory of the dissolution and ruin of a culture, his 'feminization' of Shakespearean tragedy figures primitive forces that work to undermine the political hubris that Richard III and his contemporaries represent in Shakespeare. In Chaurette's own account of the queens, they are unconscious agents of both destruction and transcendence (qtd. in R. Lévesque, 'Des farces').

In postmodern allegory (in contrast to the more colonial allegories of earlier interpreters such as Eliot), Halpern observes, Shakespeare often becomes a '"Caliban" ... the poet-as-native-informant ... both guide and quarry, leading us through a cultural landscape which, as in a dream, seems both alien and our own' (50). Richard Paul Knowles responds to Halpern's assertion by noting that, when Shakespeare is used by contemporary writers or directors as a '"third-position" cultural translator and native informant about our "primitive," essential selves,' the results may be assimilationist: 'My formalist, inscrutable, unchanging work of art includes – *comprend* – your messy, corporal, feminized, social, and otherwise threatening life: my shaping understanding kills you into art' ('From Dream' 194, 190). Chaurette, although he does use Shakespeare as a figurative 'native informant' in a dreamlike, alien landscape, escapes the accusation of imperialist intentions towards otherness. His text specifically repudiates masculine 'understanding' of the feminine. The queens are only symbolically gendered female, as is *prima materia* in alchemy: these women are 'symbolic, two-dimensional people ... [in] an emblematic landscape' and are firmly isolated from the conventional realism that would be necessary to enforce their political status as the colonized (Nicholl 141).

Les Reines, like most surrealist plays, works by banishing all real external political and historical referents, so that the allegorical and symbolic can work at their own ceremonial, ritual level.[3] As somewhat inscrutable as this quasi-surrealistic purification of the writer's base matter (including source texts both classical and modern) may be, it can still be said to work as what Gloria Orenstein calls 'an alchemical stage in the psychic evolution of the spectator,' an affirmation that the 'final transmutation' of the alchemical process takes place with the return of the spectator to the social world (287). In the reading, Chaurette's allusive, dense text does evoke a sense of such an affirmation. On the other hand, as a review of the play's critical reception will underline, the hermetic qualities of the text render it difficult to translate into the medium of the contemporary theatre and susceptible to reductive *mises en scène*. The subversion of the audience's expectations in the face of a version of a classical text seems to be the primary theatrical intention of the author. Not only does Chaurette remind his audience that it is impossible to write Shakespeare in the age of Ionesco (Lefebvre, 'Dans'), but that modernist theatre such as that of Ionesco is now itself also of the past and as subject to pastiche as Renaissance and neoclassical drama.

In *Les Reines*, the secret is represented by the mystery surrounding Anne Dexter's identity. When Anne Dexter repeatedly asks her mother, the Duchess of York, 'Qui est Anne?' ('Who is Anne?'), she is told, 'Elle n'est rien. Nothing' ('She is nothing. Nothing') and 'Dis-toi qu'elle est à notre langue / Ce que zéro est à nos nombres' ('Accept that she is to language / What zero is to numbers') (*Les Reines* 66; Gaboriau 67–9). These responses identify Anne Dexter as The Fool, an important figure in the major arcana of the Tarot. (She is as well one of the Lovers of the Tarot.) The Fool, variously characterized as a child and a madman, is 'blind to the trivial concerns of everyday life' (Cavendish 62). In the Tarot, the Fool is 'bisexual or neuter' and 'combines or transcends ... all opposites.' He is 'Spirit ... the one omnipresent reality' (64). In relation to the presence of Anne Dexter (the Fool), all of the preoccupations of the queens – possessions, power, love, past and future glories, time itself – are rendered insignificant. The speeches of the queens often burst with frenetic series of imaginary objects of passing interest, or else they coagulate in grandiose, but emptied, style. Anne Dexter's confrontation with her mother, the oldest of the Plantagenet women, is the prerequisite for the termination of the agitations of language. When the Duchess expires (in 1483, the end of the Plantagenet history and the start of a new era), her final breath exhales all of the imagery that embodied the world of the play:

> *La Duchesse de York.* Ma vie s'achève et l'Occident commence
> L'univers était prisonnier de mon souffle
> J'expire à présent
> Et je le libère
> Les lévriers, les cerfs
> Les oiseaux et les biches
> La lune ô la merveille
> de luire!
>   (92)

> (*Duchess of York.* My life is ending and the New World begins
> The universe was imprisoned on my breath
> Now I exhale at last

> And I release it all
> The hounds, the stags
> The birds and the does
> The moon oh the marvel
> The glow!) (Gaboriau 94–5)

If the Fool is an airy spirit – breath – that spirit has been contained in the mother's body. The separation from the mother's body is at the same time the end of signification, the end of history, and the end of the alchemical process.

The passing of the Duchess beyond material and historical existence is a fitting end to a play imbued with alchemical symbolism and the surreal. Orenstein argues that, as André Breton is the surrealist prophet of transformation through the word, Antonin Artaud is the surrealist prophet of transformation through the flesh. Chaurette's ending is consistent not only with Breton's project to transform language but also with Artaud's project to transform material and bodily reality. Artaud's alchemical theatre, as he defined it, 'would be analogous to a laboratory in which the human spirit would be liberated from the matter in which it was imprisoned' (qtd. in Orenstein 26). For Artaud, theatrical alchemy was 'the passionate and decisive transfusion of matter by mind [spirit]' (qtd. in Orenstein 26). *Les Reines*, like other plays by Chaurette, most notably *Provincetown Playhouse*, often recalls Artaud in its poetical, and often grotesque, rendering of the mysticism of the flesh.

In *Les Reines*, Chaurette develops a theme that had also been central to his previous play, *Fragments d'un lettre d'adieu lus par les géologues* (1988): the sanctity of the dissolution of the flesh in the infinite and of the spirit that pre-exists and survives time. Anne Dexter and her brother George are first united at the mouth of a river (the Thames): 'ISABELLE WARWICK. Ils avaient faim ce jour-là / Sur le rivage à marée basse / Et ils ont dévoré le silence' ('ISABEL WARWICK. They were hungry that day / On the shore at low tide / And they devoured silence') (20; Gaboriau 26–7). Anne reminds her mother how impossible it was for the Duchess, wedded as she was to the world and to history, to visit that same estuary and penetrate the mysteries of the speechless union of brother and sister (the alchemical androgyne):

> *Anne Dexter.* Tu les voyais tous
> Jean sans terre, Jean sans Chagrin ...
> Mais pas de trace d'Anne ni de George

C'était avant le temps
Tu as compris que nous avions été là d'abord
Et que le monde était venu ensuite
Tu n'étais que motre mère
Mais engendrée après nous.   (61)

(*Anne Dexter.* You could see them all
Jean Sans Terre Jean Sans Chagin ...
But not a trace of Anne nor George
It was too ancient
It was before time immemorial
You understood that we had been there first
And the world arrived afterwards
You were only our mother
But born after us.)   (Gaboriau 62)

As in *Fragments*, however, in *Les Reines*, Chaurette's rejoicing in the infinite silence of the soul must be expressed in conjunction with the mystical sense of the transformation of the body through disintegration and decay. In both of these plays, a pivotal feature is a vivid and detailed description of the physical breakdown of a corpse.[4] In *Les Reines*, the corpse is that of King Edward.

In alchemical symbolism, the king is equated with both the sun (as in *Richard III*, in which Edward is the 'sun of York') and consciousness. In Jung's account of alchemy, 'the King represents the domineering conscious mind which, in the course of coming to terms with the unconscious, is swallowed up by it. This brings about the *nigredo*, a state of darkness that eventually leads to the renewal and rebirth of the King' (415–17). In the refinement of matter and spirit, the *nigredo* is the stage of putrefaction, 'the nadir of matter's journey through formlessness' (Nicholl 39). This stage follows directly after the alchemical marriage of the king and queen, and, as Jung indicates, it is necessary to rebirth. In *Les Reines*, Queen Elizabeth has given birth to the two princes at the same time as her husband, Edward, lies on his deathbed; thus, Chaurette transforms history and tragedy into alchemical symbolism. The *nigredo* of the play is a scene titled 'Effigie d'Edouard' ('Effigy of Edward') in which there is one speech, a pastiche of neo-classical narration of offstage events, spoken by Queen Margaret. Her account of Edward's death – or rather his (alchemical) putrefaction, since he returns to life – is visceral and grotesque. It is as if the language of both

Shakespeare and Racine is modulated into the black, funereal humour of Ionesco in *Le Roi se meurt* (which *Les Reines* often parallels) or *Amédée, ou Comment s'en débarrasser* (1954):

> *La Reine Marguerite.* Edouard en suprématie
> Morcelé par la roue de son mal
> Edouard notre souverain ...
> Le jour à peine levé
> Ses pieds sont morts en premier lieu
> Tandis qu'au milieu de sa poitrine
> Le coeur était proie d'invisibles animaux
> En quête de son sang pour la nourriture
> Peu avant sept heures le roi
> A perdu l'une de ses deux mains
> Laquelle s'est détachée
> De son bras le plus faible
> Pour rouler jusqu'au pied du lit ;
> Quinze ou vingt minutes plus tard
> L'oeil gauche se répandait
> En éclats de glace
> Sur sa joue grise
> Se hâtant vers une fin
> Encore incertaine à la reine
> Vers qui les lèvres
> Asséchées du mourant remuaient:
> 'Pourquoi quitter le temps
> Pourquoi quitter le temps?' ... (25)

> (*Queen Margaret.* Edward in supremacy
> Rent by the wheel of his pain
> Edward our sovereign ...
> The day had barely risen
> First his feet were overcome
> While in the center of his chest
> His heart was prey to invisible animals
> Seeking to feed off his blood
> Just before the stroke of seven
> The king lost one of his hands
> Which fell from the weaker
> Of his arms
> And rolled to the foot of his bed

> Some fifteen twenty minutes later
> His left eye spattered
> In icy trickles
> Down his ashen cheek
> Hurrying towards an end
> Still uncertain for the queen
> To whom the dying man's
> Cracked lips mouthed:
> 'Why leave time
> Why leave time?') (30)

Queen Margaret's speech functions not only to dramatize a crucial stage in the alchemical process but also to synthesize neo-classicism and the absurd in a double pastiche.[5]

As Julia Kristeva points out, the fantastic 'never appears in epic or tragedy' (*Desire* 83). But in the surrealist text – and *Les Reines* belongs to that genre – the fantastic, or preconscious, disrupts all of the rules of linearity and subjectivity that belong to tragedy. According to Orenstein, the common attributes of surrealist theatre, derived from Breton's Manifesto, are:

1. Simultaneity, or the negation of chronology and of linear temporal sequence.
2. The dislocation of language from its usual function of communication to one of simultaneous, discrete, and interwoven monologues.
3. The juxtaposition of new and unexpected elements in a single image or conversation, obliterating the dictates of logic, reason, or chronological time sequence.
4. The spiritual climate of rite, ritual, or ceremony. (21)

The relationship between modern surrealism and early alchemical literature is evident here. The alchemical characters ('symbolic, two-dimensional people, moving across an emblematic landscape') move through 'darkness and ruin' to 'wholeness' (Nicholl 141). In the alchemical process, whether represented in traditional works or in modernist texts, all of the substantial reality of personality, language, and time is destabilized to reconstitute itself moment by moment, not only in new emblematic images, but in agitated and ever-shifting emotional states that give rise to those 'discrete ... monologues' that refuse communication.

Margaret Owens rightly notes that the queens' is a 'decentred realm.' Instead of the centre with which tragic – and political – subjectivity would endow the text, here there is an enclosing vessel, external to but defining the linguistic content and transformational action of the text. Wladimir Krysinski likens the queens' space to a waxwork museum 'qu'on visite rarement' ('rarely visited') (121). This suggests an interior place concealed from the gaze of the social being, which must be viewed with unaccustomed eyes. Chaurette has turned the world of *Richard III* inside out by the simple device of locating the queens and all of the action in the Tower of London. In Shakespeare, and in popular history, the Tower is the prison and place of execution of Clarence and the two young princes (as well as Hastings). Chaurette adopts the Tower as the link between history and Shakespeare on the one side and his own alchemical text on the other. The 'Tower Struck by Lightning' is the seventeenth major arcanum of the Tarot.[6] Orenstein notes, 'The tower is generally a symbol for spiritual elevation and can be related to the alchemist's oven in shape' (62). Chaurette does indeed make this symbolic connection to the oven: one of his scenes is titled 'La fournaise' ('The Furnace'). The unseen Richard – an alchemist-hero, not a politician-hero – is master of both the Tower and the furnace. The Tarot tower is traditionally related to the Tower of Babel, the original site of the confusion of tongues. Chaurette acknowledges the association in his Prologue, which is titled 'Babil des reines' ('Babble of the Queens') and consists of fragmented whispers alluding to the text that follows. According to Cavendish, 'the bolt of lightning is a sudden flash of illumination which reveals and demolishes mistaken values' (123–4). The Tower is the site of the deconstruction of materialist assumptions. Peter Hinton, who directed Linda Gaboriau's English translation, *The Queens*, defines the Tower thus: 'a place of ambition built on false premises ... with the stones of tradition and the wrongful use of personal will ... the crown of materialist thought falls ... Cosmic consciousness struggling to break through material ambitions, to bring them down in order to build again: *change, catastrophe, overthrow of existing ways of life ...*' ('Foreword'). Since the date of the action of *Les Reines* is 1483, which marks the end of the Plantagenets and the symbolic beginning of the modern world, Chaurette, as he does with the Tower itself, deliberately aligns a specific historical moment with 'alchemical' time.

The Tower contains the furnace, or oven. In Chaurette's Tower, or furnace, the drama of the alchemical process does not recognizably follow a traditional pattern in every detail. We have noted only some crucial stages in the process of refinement: the putrefaction of the flesh, the reconciliation of body and spirit, and the final release of the spirit from the material world. To view the alchemical process as a whole in *Les Reines* is to identify a complex and dynamic chain of doubling (characteristic of Chaurettian dramaturgy) and a rich pattern of linguistic transformation. Characters – insofar as they are characters – run into their doubles at every turn: Anne Warwick and her sister Isabel are doubles, as are Queen Elizabeth and Queen Margaret; Anne Dexter and her mother, the Duchess (a sort of female version of Lear), though opponents, are also doubles; the invisible alchemist Richard and his brother King Edward, are doubles in that one seems to be the spirit and the other the body. As signifiers shift rapidly, the dictions of early modern and twentieth-century sources seem to collapse into each other. There is no peace in this text until the final moment of the Duchess's life: speech is always either agitated or declamatory and grandiose.

More than most plays, *Les Reines* seems to offer divergent experiences to its reader and its spectator. In the reading, what is striking is the intricate weaving of intertexts with alchemical and Tarot symbolism. The emotional quality of the text is hard to grasp on the page. On the stage, on the other hand, as the reviews generally indicate, the predominant impression is of an emotionally destabilized subversion of elevated diction, ceremony, and ritual, in which farce, clowning, and hysteria displace tragedy. The exaggerated pastiche of classical diction is experienced as 'heavy,' or empty, and the juxtaposition of the domestic and the tragic, so reminiscent of Ionesco, is experienced as trivialization (Abarca 36; Léonardini). Only one character, Anne Dexter, is permitted to counterpoise the extreme spatialization of language with her intense rejection of all signification that does not express her own primordial experience. Her revelation of her incestuous secret gains its shock value by contrast with the mechanistic, automatic qualities of the rest of the 'cirque existentiel' ('existential circus') (Krysinski 123).

To comprehend the effect of this play in performance, it is helpful to return to Halpern's account of Shakespearean tragedy as it is rewritten by modernists. His analysis of an eclectic selection of 'Hamlet machine' texts (among them, Müller's *Hamletmachine*, Cocteau's *La Machine infernale* [*The Infernal Machine*], and Lacan's seminars on *Hamlet*) throws light on the purpose behind Chaurette's retelling of *Richard III*. *Hamlet* has been characterized as the prototype of a modernist text: in it the tragedy of Oedipus already fails to work as it did for Sophocles' audience, because of a breakdown of ritual. It has been described as an

'Oedipal *Trauerspiel*, a mournful and decadent repetition of its Sophoclean original' (Halpern 247). After Freud, however, the reproduction of the impact of Oedipal tragedy becomes all the more problematic: '"The scandal ... resides in *the loss of scandal*, in the fact that the analytic shock has itself become a cliché, that the tragedy has become a farce"' (Shoshana Felman, qtd. in Halpern 247). Clearly, it is a similar recognition that causes Chaurette to fail to reproduce *Richard III* in a translation, and to write *Les Reines* instead ('Il est vain de faire semblant d'écrire Shakespeare à l'époque de Ionesco' ('It is pointless to try to write Shakespeare in the era of Ionesco'). Modernism's predicament is that it must find a way to deal with its own decadence. If *Hamlet* provides one allegory for this decadence, then *Richard III*, which dramatizes extreme decadence at the beginning of the modern period, offers another. If Chaurette (like Ronfard before him) finds absurdity in the tragedy of Richard, and uses Shakespeare's play to allegorize the impossibility of tragedy, it is because he can come close to expressing the tragic only by acknowledging the absurdity of the attempt.

The acceptance that tragedy can no longer function in the modern era as it once did permits the dramatist to create a new form of ritual, in which the repetition of the texts of the past represents a process of mourning. *Les Reines* is a rite of mourning: the distracted, hysterical, fugal expressions of the queens and their formal, ceremonious speeches and rituals are all symptomatic of the process. For Lacan, mourning is a 'mobilization of the entire system of signifiers in an (impossible) attempt to fill the "hole in the real" produced by the absence of the mourned individual' (Halpern 265). The object of mourning, though it may be symbolized as the corpse of a king, is cultural tradition. As in *Hamlet*, in modernist texts some form of interiorized signification must be substituted for external rituals that no longer work. Halpern points out that Lacan's seminar is itself 'an elaborate apparatus of cultural repetition and remembrance ... that attempts to sustain modernity's sense of the tragic ... a machinery for mourning and a mournful machine' (268). The hermetic text of *Les Reines*, too, with its intricate web of references to archaic, early modern, and late modern texts drawn together into a ritual of signification, can also be viewed as a work of mourning – one that 'exhausts rather than renews' (Halpern 267). The mourning ritual is at the same time the allegory of Eliot's 'dissolution and decay.' Beneath the ruin, however, there remains the secret that lies at the heart of the text, Anne Dexter's hidden and culpable love for her brother, which opposes not only intellectual sense but the entire fabric of cultural history that is broken down in the rest of the process of signification. That secret represents the playwright's belief in the persistent presence of the tragic, concealed though it may be, despite the intellectual and material encroachments of modern culture. In the end, the work of discursive subversion is undertaken in order to affirm the existence of a mythic pretext.

Notes

1 Translations are mine, except in the case of the primary text: translations for *Les Reines* are taken from Linda Gaboriau's translation.
2 Jean Pierre Ronfard's epic *Vie et mort du roi boiteux* (Nouveau Théâtre Expérimental, Montreal, 1982) signalled the end of the nationalist theatre and the predominance of Québécois language on the stage with its monumentally intertextual version of *Richard III*, grounded in the actual quarter of Montreal (the Arsenal) in which it was performed. Ronfard explores an intricate web of kinship, both endogamous and exogamous, amid references to ancient and modern texts, to create 'au mépris de toute convention réaliste, de toute vraisemblance historique ou linéaire, un monde brutale et baroque, une sorte d'univers barbare et grandiose' ('without regard for realistic convention or historical and linear plausibility, a brutal and baroque world, a sort of barbarous and grandiose universe') (Lapointe 224). Jean Asselin of the Théâtre de l'Omnibus, a mime-based group, created *Le Cycle des rois* (1988) by marrying *Richard II* and both parts of *Henry IV* and *Henry V* with anachronistic theatrical devices – clowning, electronic sound, costumes made from cast-off clothing – to produce a contemporary script located neither in 'historical' England nor in the Montreal of the audience: 'l'Angleterre médiévale ... est citée d'une façon qui la rapproche radicalement de l'expérience contemporaine ... jouées sans distance historique, sans cette sorte de respect hieratique pour la tradition culturelle ... les jeux de pouvoir ... shakespeariens ont une humanité de tous les instants' ('medieval England is cited in a way that brings it radically close to contemporary experience ... played without historical distance nor that sort of hieratic respect for cultural tradition ... the Shakespearean power games have a timeless humanity' (Pavlovic 19). In the same year, Théâtre de l'Omnibus also produced an expressionistic allegory by Robert Claing, *La Mort des rois*, in which Eleanor of Aquitaine 'isolated in a throne room waiting for death ... bemoans the brutality of loss,' and her son, King John, 'hides in a damp dungeon fearing life and death ... recall[ing] torture and murder and his deep resentment of more illustrious siblings' (Nashman 39–40).
3 The play is, however, cryptically signed as the work of a homosexual play-

wright. As Margaret Owens has noted, the date on which the play takes place (in 1483) is 20 January, the feast of Saint Sebastian (11). Such a use of significant dates is characteristic of Chaurette's writing.

4 Chaurette has alluded to a text in progress, *Magnificat*, which he calls 'une pièce sur les cadavres' ('a play about corpses') (Chaurette, qtd. in Loffrée 62). It has yet to appear.

5 One cannot help but be reminded by Margaret's narration of Edward's death of reports of the offstage corpse of Rosaire Baril in Michel Tremblay's *Les Belles-soeurs* (1972).

6 The Tower may also allude to Breton's surrealist work *Arcane 17*, written while Breton was in the Gaspésie in 1944, a cryptic detail of which Chaurette would likely be aware (Lamy). It is also the central symbol in *Le Roi Gordogane* (1968), a surrealist play by Radovan Ivšić.

17

Othello in Three Times[1]

RIC KNOWLES

'The Shakespeare's mine, but you can have it.'

– Djanet Sears, *Harlem Duet* 52

Among Shakespeare's best-known plays, *Othello* has been of relatively little interest to Canadian theatres in the last half of the twentieth century, and, when it has been staged, it has not been notably successful.[2] This may be so because, as Edward Pechter says, the play is 'unpleasant' (Address),[3] perhaps because of its treatment of gender, race, and class in ways that cannot comfortably be subsumed under the general wash of universalist humanism that still dominates the discourses of most Canadian theatre companies and reviewers. Its central role, moreover, has proven difficult to cast, a difficulty that uncomfortably exposes systemic racism in a mainstream theatre industry that lags behind those of Britain and the United States in the representation (and casting) of difference.

In each of the last three decades, however, there has been one significant and widely successful Canadian dramatic adaptation of the play that has presented itself as revisionist: the regionalist and populist *Cruel Tears*, by Ken Mitchell and Humphrey and the Dumptrucks, first produced at Persephone Theatre in Saskatchewan in 1975, which subsequently toured the country to some acclaim; the feminist *Goodnight Desdemona (Good Morning Juliet)*, by Ann-Marie MacDonald, first produced by Nightwood Theatre in Toronto in 1988, which also toured the country in a revised version and won the Governor-General's Award for Drama in 1990; and the Black feminist *Harlem Duet*, by Djanet Sears, first produced by Nightwood Theatre in 1997 and subsequently remounted by Canadian Stage Company, which won the Governor General's Award in 1997. An examination of these adaptations, each a product of its time, suggests a shifting relationship over three decades between 'Shakespeare' and the construction of gender, race, ethnicity, and class in Canada. Such an analysis may elucidate the different ways in which, and the degrees to which, adapting Shakespeare has served as cultural intervention (resisting gendered, classed, and raced constructions of dominant, normative subjectivities), or as cultural affirmation (at once renewing 'Shakespeare,' validating by association the adaptation itself and the cultural position from which it emerges, and consolidating dominant social norms).

Cruel Tears: Populism, Regionalism, and Ethnicity

'There was Stratford. But I'm talking about Canadian theatre.'
– Ken Mitchell, 'Ken Mitchell' 153

Cruel Tears, billed as a 'country opera,' is very much a product of its mid-1970s moment, a time when counter- (versus anti-) hegemonic nationalism and anti-centric regionalisms were the alternative movements of choice, often leaving little room for other kinds of resistance. Canadian cultural nationalism was at its peak in 1975, when *Cruel Tears* was first produced, spurred by the residue of the Canadian centennial in 1967 and the founding of the passionately nationalist *Canadian Theatre Review* in 1974. The top prize for a new Canadian play, the Chalmers Award, was won in 1977 (the year that *Cruel Tears* was runner-up) by the stereotypically 'Canadian' hockey play, *Les Canadiens*, by Rick Salutin (with an 'assist' from hockey legend Ken Dryden). Militant regionalism was everywhere manifest, not only in cultural revivals in Newfoundland, Acadie, the Maritime and prairie provinces, 'Souwesto,' and elsewhere, but in a proliferation of separatist rhetoric in reaction to the Trudeau government's centralist federalism: there was, with varying degrees of seriousness, talk of nationalist movements in Newfoundland, Cape Breton, and British Columbia as well as Quebec. In theatres across the country, regional content sold tickets, while in theatre criticism regionalism emerged as an analytical tool, as the Massey Commission's model of taking 'Culture' from the centre to the uncivilized regions was replaced by theorizings of cultural production as home-grown, ground-up activity less interested in civilizing the masses than in cultural and physical geography and local forms of work and social activity.[4] In 1985, in a survey article, 'Writing the Land Alive,' Robert Wallace grouped

Cruel Tears with a variety of populist 'regional plays that ... successfully toured the country' (77) in the mid-1970s, bringing 'culture' from the regions to the urban centres. Most of these, not surprisingly, were folk, country, or rock musicals, including *Paper Wheat* (Saskatchewan), *Rock and Roll* (Nova Scotia), and *They Club Seals, Don't They?* (Newfoundland).

Novelist, playwright, poet, and polemicist Ken Mitchell, editor of the *Prairie Anthology*, was, at the time, a leader among the regionalists, so much so that his contribution to a 1981 book of interviews is called, simply, 'Prairies,' and his biography there lists him as a 'former pig farmer' (163). The interview stresses 'the so-called search for identity': 'I believe prairie people know their identity,' claims Mitchell. 'I believe a natural writer or poet is really somebody who is only a voice for a people or region' (165). 'History is slowly realizing that the art which originates in the prairies is stronger, on a per capita basis let's say, than art which originates elsewhere' (166). *Cruel Tears* establishes its regionalist credentials early. It opens with a 'bright prairie sun,' the trilling of a meadowlark, and 'a mime suggest[ing] a prairie environment.' Its first line is, 'Well we got a song about the West' (13), and it builds on this through the careful use of localist detail ranging from prairie slang ('Holy Hannah' [94]) to pan-national rural customs (the drinking of 'Five-Star' Canadian rye whisky [109]). It ends as it began, with a song about 'a lady of the prairie' (144-5).

As a regionalist revisioning of a canonical play, taking 'Shakespeare' down a peg or two, *Cruel Tears* is wittily effective, its co-authorship with a country and western (C&W) band making clear its populist appeal. A 'country opera' (Littler 281) set in a truckers' culture, the play makes loose use of the *Othello* plot, most notably its melodrama: a Ukrainian-Canadian trucker in Saskatoon, Johnny Roychuk (Othello), falls in love with and marries the boss's daughter, Kathy (Desdemona), and, after much weeping and country-music wailing, is promoted to a supervisory position by her father, Earl (Brabantio). A worker's representative, union-buster, and covert company stooge, Jack Deal (Iago), whose wife, Flora (Emilia), has befriended Kathy, turns against Johnny and plots to make him jealous of a fellow trucker, Ricky (Cassio). In the end, Johnny strangles Kathy with the embroidered scarf given to her by his Ukrainian mother. When he learns of his mistake, he kills Jack. As Johnny says, it is a play about 'the big bohunk and the boss's daughter' (38), and as such it presents itself as a populist revisioning of Shakespeare, well positioned to undertake localist interrogation, not only of centrist notions of High Culture, but also of gender, race, and class on the 1970s prairie. But counter-hegemonic nationalist or regionalist movements have not always been sensitive to other forms of difference, and it is worth taking a closer look at the play's construction of gendered, raced, and classed subjectivities.

Ken Mitchell claims in a number of interviews that 'I'm trying to jab at some sore spots of sexual politics' in *Cruel Tears* ('Ken Mitchell's progress' 40), but the play seems more to reinforce than undermine traditional gender relationships in society, *Othello*, and country music. It includes a politically soft song, 'Liberated Lady,' by the 'waitress' character, Debbie Lou, 'heavily made up, still looking for her man' (20), who slings beer and sexist banter with the truckers. But the song is more about wanting 'a dude/That isn't rude/To spread butter on my bread' (92) than about independent subjectivity. In fact, the play's representation of gender is depressingly familiar: 'The men drive trucks and the girls keep house' (17). Social change is figured more-or-less exclusively as upward mobility within the dominant sex-gender system:

> Johnny's a foreman, climbin' real fast.
> He wears a tie and his pants get pressed.
> Kathy's in the kitchen cookin' up a storm
> Sewin' all the curtains for their cozy little home. (59)

In the bar and the workplace, the talk is all of women as 'used goods' (46) and of 'coppin' feels for free' (109). Jokes about 'shaggin'' and penis size (18), moreover, seem to be endorsed by the play. Even the script's list of characters identifies Kathy only as '[Johnny's] sweetheart and wife' (12). What gestures are made towards heightened consciousness are classed: when Flora says to Kathy, 'I just didden think you'd be the type to take up cookin' and cleaning and all that,' Kathy replies, conscious that she has 'married down' but unconsious of insulting her new friend, 'Neither did I. Just no *way* Kathy Jenson was going to be trapped into a traditional housewife role.' But it doesn't matter, because 'I *do* like cooking. Isn't that weird?' (65).

The play seems, then, to relocate rather than interrogate the gender hierarchies of *Othello*: Debbie Lou in her miniskirt, titillating the truckers, is a fair approximation of Shakespeare's Bianca; Flora, abused by her brutish husband and deflating Kathy's idealism, stands in comfortably for Emilia; and Kathy, if anything, is less adventuresome than Desdemona, who at least 'goes on the road' with her partner. Kathy's passive last words before joining Johnny in a romantic death song (hers) are, 'I'm so scared when you're not here. I need you – to put me to bed ... Promise me you'll always be here to put me to bed' (136–7).

Oddly, for an adaptation of *Othello*, the only things 'black' in *Cruel Tears* are 'the stage' (13) and the setting at 'the Blacktop bar' (17). Although all the characters are white, however, the racism that drives *Othello* is reproduced in *Cruel Tears* as 'prejudice' on the bases of ethnicity and class. Jack/Iago's jealousy of Johnny/Othello and Earl/Brabantio's resistance to Kathy's marriage with his Ukrainian-Canadian employee are rooted in racist revulsion to ethnic miscegenation. Jack tortures Earl, Iago-like ('an old black ram/Is tupping your white ewe' [1.1.89–90]), with images of 'a sweet little girl from the suburbs involved in some pretty funny business on the other side of town ... you know – animal acts – like the kinda stuff you were tellin' us *you* saw down in Vegas ... I know you don't get to that part of town much, Mr. Jensen – lotta DPs, yuh know, Indians. But there's this big dumb bohunk over there ... and this sweet little chick from the suburbs gets the blocks put to her by the bohunk – every night ... (41–2). Elsewhere, ethnic slurs and stereotypes – 'Just like a Uke' (66), 'Kin smell the garlic from here!' (57), and 'Tell her how the bohunks beat their women' (50) – are used to motivate the characters against 'the big Yewkeranian' (101) in a way that is clearly condemned by the play.

At the same time, the play's attempt to portray Saskatchewan's Ukrainian community in a positive way is uncomfortably aligned with a Trudeau brand of liberalism that produced official multiculturalism in Canada, positioning French and English as founding, institutionalized, and evolving 'cultures' against a variety of static and exoticized 'ethnicities' to be preserved through folkloric activities (see Gomez 29, Hawkins 11). In *Cruel Tears,* Johnny is indistinguishable in lived experience from the rest of the play's truckers – a fact that is used to represent the prejudice against him as particularly heinous – while his family appears as ethnic 'DANCERS,' with no individual identities or even familial roles, dressed in 'traditional Ukrainian costumes' (57) and unrepresented, in person or textual reference, except at the wedding. And finally there is the scarf, which retains many of the exoticizing overtones of its source in *Othello*'s handkerchief: made of expensive silk, colourfully embroidered (in ethnic Ukrainian patterns), and given to Kathy at her wedding by Johnny's mother (61, 86), the scarf is here a kerchief, the traditional Ukrainian symbol of a married woman's status, or possibly an embroidered 'towel,' which is placed over icons in the home and taken down during the wedding ceremony literally to bind the young couple's hands together. It serves to reinforce Mitchell's reinscription of traditional gender roles – particularly in its resurfacing as 'evidence' of Kathy's infidelity and, in a significant deviation from the source, as the weapon used to strangle her: she is killed by the index of his ethnicity.[5]

But ethnicity is only partly the issue. Another deviation from the source sees the problematics of class elevated from one root cause of Iago's envy of Cassio to a central factor in the main plot and in the play's cultural intervention. Part of the central conflict is that Johnny (from 'across the tracks') and Kathy ('the boss's daughter,' 'the sweet little girl from the suburbs') are from different social classes, a fact that his Ukrainian origins seem to naturalize, conflating ethnic with class difference: *all* Ukrainians, 'Indians,' and 'DPs' are, 'naturally,' from across the class divide. In fact, much of the action feels like a cross-class *Romeo and Juliet*, as the young lovers fight to overcome her family's (30), or father's, problems with *his* class:

> You listen to me, you worthless bum,
> It cost me a fortune to bring her up.
> She's used to having everything –
> Brand spanking new! (51)

Once the father is won over and Johnny is promoted, Johnny's fellow workers resent his new rank, together with his class disloyalty and his feminized desertion of the bar for the boudoir and a 'stuck-up bitch' (75–8, 103) who 'isn't going to lower herself to take in a truck driver party!' (85). Kathy herself has trouble reconciling herself to the tastes, world-view, and resignation of her new friend Flora and her world of 'Korman's Cut-Rate House of Bargains' (63). The young lovers are left, *West Side Story*-style, to dream of how 'together we'll find a way' (31).

But class plays itself out in *Cruel Tears* in more significant ways than simply as an engine of the plot. The play makes a conscious assault on class in Canada, on the construction of Canadian theatre audiences, and of theatre itself as a High Culture. In interviews, Mitchell indicates his intention 'to bring an audience into the theatre that's normally not attracted at all' ('Ken Mitchell' 147): 'I'm a populist by nature,' he says (148), and in his use of popular culture from C&W to K-Tel ('Kar-Tel' in *Cruel Tears* [94]),[6] together with his replacement of 'Venice's noble senators and patricians' with 'Knights of the Road' (Redfern 28), he validates the popular. Mitchell also articulates his use of country-opera and Shakespearean sources as reclamations of Shakespeare and opera as popular forms ('Ken Mitchell' 149–50): 'I wanted to write a political play ... to break down some of the barriers between art and politics; I wanted to reach a different kind of audience. We haven't broken through yet to this audience, a different audience than the university-educated, regular, theatre-going audience – the 'elite,' if you want to call it that' ('Prairies' 40).

Cruel Tears, then, is a complex blend of interventionist critique, High cultural aspiration, and reification of traditional gender, class, and ethnic positionings. And among its most interesting and unusual features is its ambivalent treatment of its Shakespearean source. Mitchell and the Dumptrucks seem to want to have their cultural authority and eat it too: the play seems to avoid deliberately explicit citations of Shakespeare that might alienate the populist 'crowd' – to the degree that at least one review does not mention Shakespeare (McIlroy); but, at the same time, it allows the hegemonic operation of unconscious influence and provides self-congratulatory rewards for the cognoscenti who recognize parallels and revisions. These include such moments as Kathy's remarkably faithful (to the lyrics) country version of the Willow song (133) and Othello's otherwise inexplicable 'Now snuff out the candles' (137). Mitchell talks in an interview about 'evoking and parodying [*Othello*] in a contemporary setting' ('Ken Mitchell' 150), but in many ways his attempt to recuperate the play for populism reifies, renews, and revitalizes Shakespeare while making High Culture claims for *Cruel Tears* itself. It is telling that two of the three dedicatees in the script are 'Geraldi Cinthio' (Shakespeare's source) and 'William Shakespear' [*sic*] (the third is Brian Sklar), positioning Shakespeare himself as a revisionist and Mitchell and the Dumptrucks as inheritors of a noble tradition of renewing classic texts.

Goodnight Desdemona (Good Morning Juliet): Gender and Genre

'It's like opening up a trunk that used to be full of instruments of torture and now everything has turned into toys.'
– Ann-Marie MacDonald, 'Ann-Marie MacDonald' 142

If *Cruel Tears* filters its revisionism through mid-1970s regionalism, ethnicity, and class, Ann-Marie MacDonald's *Goodnight Desdemona (Good Morning Juliet)* – which also draws directly on popular culture, and more explicitly brings together *Othello* and *Romeo and Juliet* – works through a second-wave feminist focus on gender and genre that was very much of its 1980s context at Toronto's Nightwood Theatre near the end of its second mandate.[7] According to its director, Baṇuta Rubess, the original idea for *Goodnight Desdemona* emerged as a joke on a 1985 tour of *This Is for You, Anna*: 'Ann-Marie MacDonald crammed a pillow on my face and with great hilarity pronounced: "Goodnight, Desdemona!"' (Rubess 7). There is no sign of regionalism in the play, except insofar as references to Queen's University mark it as Ontario-based. Nor is there much nationalism, though, as Joanne Tompkins argues (15–16, 20–1), the play *does* operate as 'canonical counter-discourse' (22), and it does assert postcolonialist resistance to the imported authority of 'British cultural achievement,' represented by the canonical 'Shakespeare' and the despicable Claude Night (A. Wilson 3). (The latter is a British-born male academic with a job in the colonies, 'dignified and irritated' [MacDonald, *Goodnight* 70], 'perfectly groomed and brogued,' who 'speaks with an Oxford accent' [22] in a 'cultivated voice' [71] and exploits his female graduate students.)[8] As Mark Fortier notes, moreover, 'there is little in this play about class' ('Shakespeare' 51) beyond 'pok[ing] fun at the Bard' (Crew) and some acute commentary on the classed and gendered system of graduate student labour, tenure, and promotion in the academy (see Dvorak 132). Fortier also notes that the play 'completely elides the issue of race' (51); in fact, when its central character, Constance Ledbelly, first sees Othello, the whole issue is sidestepped in a throwaway pun: 'He's not a Moor!' Constance marvels, in response to which Iago says, 'Amour? Ah-ha! C'est ça! Et pourquoi pas?'

What *Goodnight Desdemona* does provide is an acute dramatic interrogation of the gender politics of genre that is characteristic of 1980s feminist work, and a theoretically sophisticated enactment of resistant reading in a play in which, unlike in *Cruel Tears*, the metadramatic context and the overt revisioning of Shakespeare provide the opportunity 'for a hybrid form' and the possibility 'of *performatively* altering the power structures embedded in the original text' (Tompkins 16). 'What if a Fool were to enter the worlds of both "Othello" and "Romeo and Juliet?"', the play asks, noting the 'flimsy mistakes' on which their tragic actions turn. 'Would our fool defuse the tragedies by assuming centre stage as comic hero?' (21). MacDonald proceeds from this to stage the literal entry of Constance into the worlds of *Othello* and *Romeo and Juliet* as part of her research for her doctoral dissertation, an attempt to prove that these plays consist of Shakespeare's own colonizing of his source texts. The originals, she determines, were comedies, turned tragic through Shakespeare's appropriative expurgation of their wise fools.

Transported into the action of the plays at their crises, Constance summarily intervenes, instantly deflects their ersatz tragic inevitability, and proceeds to search through clues in her alchemical source text, the 'Gustav Manuscript' (written, as is her own dissertation, on 'foolscap'), for evidence of the (original) Author and the Fool that is the agent of the plot. Not surprisingly, she discovers that the 'fo-o-ol's cap' (73) is her own red toque, and that 'the Fool and the Author are one and the same' – 'a lass' (86). 'You're it,' as the ghost (imported from *Hamlet*) tells her (73–4, 86). Along the way, Constance encounters revisionist versions of the major characters in *Othello* and *Romeo and Juliet*. Much has been made of the play's representation of Desdemona and Juliet as strong, independent women, its appropriation of the male characters' best lines by women who are agents of the action rather than objects of the gaze, its (muted) representation of polymorphous sexuality and lesbian eroticism, and its deployment of a resistant feminist comedy (Hengen). All of this is true, but perhaps the single most important contribution is the play's representation and enactment of female readerly agency in the production of meaning: 'It's not a man you seek,' the ghost tells Constance, but 'the Manuscript' (the man you script, yourself) (73). The entry of Constance into the worlds of Desdemona and Juliet, like the trope of ongoing rehearsal discussed by Tompkins, 'creates a site for the negotiation and re-negotiation of the Shakespearean text's cultural centrality' (16). It renders Shakespearean meaning negotiable, and reconstructs the texts as writerly rather than readerly, or interrogative rather than declarative (Barthes, *passim*; Belsey 91).

Like *Cruel Tears*, however, *Goodnight Desdemona* blends intervention and complicity, and, like Mitchell, MacDonald positions herself with Shakespeare as revisionist: 'I was being mischievous by using Shakespeare as a source in the same way he used everyone else as a source' ('Ann-Marie MacDonald' 141). In any case, depending as it does on the audience's recognition of its revisionism, *Goodnight Desdemona* can be read as pop-cultural slumming for an 'educated audience' (Dvorak 131). 'A farce for "highbrows"' (130), the play is 'delightfully literate and engagingly lowbrow' (Johnston, Rev. 86), and it can be read, therefore, less as cultural intervention than mainstream literary interpretation, as when Dvorak sees its Desdemona less as a feminist reappraisal than as 'quite a sensitive reading' of 'what we actually find in Shakespeare's text' (131).[9] Like *Cruel Tears*, too, the play rewards the cognoscenti with the pleasures of recognition, as when Constance deciphers the words on Shakespeare's grave (82), when the revisionist point rests on audience recognition of lines taken out of context, or when the audience is able to decipher the difference between Shakespeare's blank verse and that of MacDonald.[10]

MacDonald has made explicit her intention to reach as wide an audience as possible and has resisted a feminist label for her play. As Fortier says, 'she prefers to think of it as humanism through a woman's point of view' ('Shakespeare' 50), a rewriting of the plays 'as they would be if Shakespeare were a woman, with a woman's experience' (51). Indeed, the play circulates around, in addition to its enactment of resistant reading, a Jungian version of unitary humanism that sees Constance's search for identity fulfilled in a coming together of three archetypes: Desdemona (Courage), Juliet (Passion), and Constance (Intellect). The play ends on the birthday of all three characters, when 'two plus one adds up to one, not three' (86), and represents the rebirth of a central character who subsumes all three. It is this aspect of *Goodnight Desdemona* that has made it subject to mainstream cultural appropriation in its afterlife, when it has transferred or toured to mainstream venues (see Knowles, 'Reading' 276–83). But the Jung is not just Jung. It is an explicitly feminist Jung (see MacDonald, 'Ann-Marie MacDonald' 142). The deference to Shakespeare is in part a recognition of what MacDonald cherishes about his 'multivalency and ability to challenge a heterogenous audience' (Fortier, 'Shakespeare' 51). And the flip side of the play's openness to appropriation is a refusal to settle into unitary meanings, an acknowledgment of multiple discursive, cultural, and theatrical contexts together with the shifting meanings that attend them, and an invitation, as Dvorak says, 'to dip into competing discourses' (133). Ultimately, what *Goodnight Desdemona* performed in Toronto in 1989 was the feminist work of 'marginalizing the mainstream,' a 'strategy for replacing a theatre which celebrates the objectifying gaze with a theatre which seeks the political and the popular in a performance/audience relationship' that is (inter)active (Bennett, 'Politics' 13).

Harlem Duet: Race, Sex, Gender, and (Black) History

'Canada, where did you get these ideas of Harlem from?'

– Djanet Sears, *Harlem Duet* 79

Also in 1989, between its first production of *Goodnight Desdemona* and the national tour, Nightwood Theatre adopted a new anti-racist mandate and turned its attention to women of colour. Within and beyond Nightwood, by the time Djanet Sears's *Harlem Duet* premiered at the Tarragon Extra Space, Toronto, in April 1997, an adaptation of *Othello* that did not address race would be unthinkable. Not only had Sears herself written and performed *Afrika Solo* in the intervening years, the script of which in 1990 became the first play published by a Canadian of African descent; not only had Black directors, playwrights, and actors emerged to play prominent roles in the cultural life of the city; and not only had *Canadian Theatre Review* published a special issue in 1995 on African-Canadian theatre; but Toronto had experienced well-publicized incidents of police racism and a significant incidence of rioting and looting on Yonge Street (the subject of Andrew Moodie's first play, *Riot*) in the wake of the Rodney King verdict in Los Angeles.[11] It was no longer possible to pretend that Black people were not a presence or race an issue in Canada. So, as Vit Wagner wrote in a review of the production that noticed the connection with *Goodnight Desdemona*, 'this time, *Othello* is glimpsed through the prism of race rather than gender.' In fact, *Harlem Duet* is *all* about race: race and nation, race and class, (especially) race and (Black) history, and (above all) race and gender.

Harlem Duet is neither populist comic opera nor revisionist comedy but 'rhapsodic blues tragedy' (14), a self-consciously hybrid form that links tragedy with jazz, high-Western with Black culture even as its musical bridges perform blues on orchestral strings.[12] It tells the story, set in 1860, 1928, and, most substantially, the present, of Billie, Othello's Black first wife, before he met Desdemona. According to Sears's introduction to the published text, the play takes on Shakespeare's Othello, 'the first African portrayed in the annals of western dramatic literature,' in 'an effort to exorcize this ghost' (14). The 1860s action focuses on 'Him' and 'Her,' slaves planning an escape up the underground railroad, a plan that is aborted when he announces his love for the (white) woman who owns him. The 1928 action focuses on 'He,' a Black, blackface minstrel with aspirations to play the classics, who is in love with a white woman; and 'She,' his jealous wife, who is in possession of a razor. The present-tense action, set in Harlem, concerns Billie's deteriorating mental state as Othello packs and prepares for his wedding to 'Mona.' It is punctuated by flashbacks to the better days of their arrival in Harlem, and by visits from Billie's landlady, Magi, her sister-in-law, Amah, and her father, Canada.

But *Harlem Duet* is not centrally concerned with Canada, although it does insist on there being a Black history in this country. Canada (the character) arrives on the scene from Dartmouth, Nova Scotia, to which the family had fled after Billie's mother died, and Sears seems compelled to include the somewhat awkward line, 'I love that Nova Scotia was a haven for slaves way before the underground railroad. I love that ...' (45). The 1860s scenes cite Canada as the final destination of the underground railroad, 'a white house on an emerald hill' (35), but if Canada is romanticized by some of the characters – 'What's that them old slaves used to say? "I can't take it no more, I moving to Nova Scotia"' (82) – it is no Harlem: Billie and her brother have relocated, and the one who stayed in Canada – 'My Dad, the drunk of Dartmouth' (45) – seems to have found little haven there. He remains in Harlem, recovering, at the end of the play.

Neither is class a significant issue, though the play does make clear the middle-class status of its central characters, avoiding the type of elision caused by the merging of class and ethnicity in *Cruel Tears*, and allowing a focus on the specifically racial quality of what George Lamming calls 'specific punishments' for which Black Americans, rich or poor, are targets (33).[13] Othello teaches at 'Harlumbia, those ten square blocks of Whitedom, owned by Columbia University, set smack dab in the middle of Harlem' (67). He and Billie drink cognac (50), read Shakespeare, and dream of the day when there will be 'Black boutiques./Black bookstores./Black groceries./Filled with Black doctors and dentists. Black banks' (106). There are moments, fed by a 'sit-com' quality to some of the writing (K. Taylor, 'Characters'), when this insistence on the characters' class status lends the action a 'Cosby-show' combination of privilege and flippancy that threatens its seriousness. What redeems the choice, in addition to its avoidance of stereotypes and its enabling of a focus on race, *tout court*, is the clarity it brings to the conflict, particularly around the central issue of African-American identity, history, and culture. At one point Othello says, 'I am a middle class educated man. I mean, what does Africa have to do with me?' (72). 'My culture is Wordsworth, Shaw, *Leave it to Beaver*, *Dirty Harry*. I drink the same water, read the same books. You're the problem if you don't see beyond my skin. If you don't hear my educated English ... We struttin' around professing some imaginary connection for a land we don't know ... Some of us are beyond that now. Spiritually beyond this race bullshit now. I am an American' (73-4). This debate permeates the action, which is framed by voice-overs from Black history in America and by the literal intersection (of views) at which the action is set. 'Sears describes Harlem as "both a place and a symbol ... There is an actual intersection that serves as the theoretical axis of the arguments in the play." Billie and Othello's apartment is set ... at the corner of Martin Luther King and Malcolm X boulevards. Omnipresent are the themes of self-esteem and race in concert with the contrasting black/white schism advocated by Malcolm X and the integration of Martin Luther King's "dream."' (Lingerfelt and Kershaw).

It is the thickness of the play's sense of 'the baggage of contemporary North American black experience' (Lingerfelt and Kershaw) and history – from the 1860s action and the legacy of slavery (33–6, 62–3, 74) through the evocation of minstrelsy (99–100, 113), the references to the historic Apollo theatre (57), Paul Robeson's *Othello* (113), Langston Hughes and the Harlem Renaissance (114), Jesse Jackson's oratory (72), the Clarence Thomas/Anita Hill hearings,[14] the Rodney King riots, and the O.J. Simpson trial (92) – that undermines Othello's argument that 'I am not my skin' (74). As Billie says, 'a history is trapped in me' (101): 'Did you ever consider what hundreds of years of slavery did to the African American psyche?' (103).

The play's present consists of a world in which that psyche, when damaged, is treated, even in Harlem, by white doctors and nurses who can see their patients' questions only through 'flashing blue eyes' (114–15); a world in which cosmeticians' certificates, even in Harlem, are awarded for courses on 'how to do White people's hair' but not dreadlocks (26); a world in which 'if you spend too much time among white people, you start believing what they think of you' (97). Staging debates about affirmative action (53), ethnocentrism (52), assimilation and segregation, equality and difference, the play is deeply resistant to an inherited world in which Laurence Olivier in blackface can serve even for Black people as a cultural marker (14), and where, as Billie says to Othello, 'White people are always the line ... [t]he rule ... the margin ... the variable of control' (55). Othello argues that 'liberation has no colour' (55), and Billie teaches her young niece that 'colour's only skin deep' (44), but both Billie and the play know that 'progress is ... proving we're as good as Whites ... like some holy grail ... Our success is Whiteness.' 'That's economics,' argues Othello. 'White economics,' Billie replies (55).

Othello's only recourse – 'God! Black women always –' (at which point Billie cuts him off) – brings us to the play's central concern: the intersection of race and gender, where, in Sears's view, the *most* damage has been done to the African-American psyche. In each of its actions, characters, and relationships, both depicted and recounted (and framed by voice-overs, among others, from the trial of O.J. Simpson, a Black man, for the murder of his white wife, and around which *Othello* was often invoked), *Harlem Duet* is permeated by stories of Black men in relationships with white women – the central fact of *Othello* that seems to have been ignored in previous adaptations of the play. Here the present-tense action concerns itself with Othello's leaving his Black partner for a white colleague; the 1860 story concerns itself with the Black slave's betrayal of *his* Billie's plans to flee to Canada because of his perverse love – fascinating, in its construction of gender roles – for the white woman who is his master ('She respects me ... When I'm with her I feel like ... a man' [63]), and the 1928 story focuses on the actor/minstrel, 'of Ira Aldridge stock' (99), and his longing for the 'Skin as smooth as monumental alabaster' (Shakespeare, *Othello* 5.2.5; Sears 99) of the very woman who casts him only in Black Shakespearean and Black minstrel roles. We learn from Billie, moreover, in the main plot, that her father had also dated a white woman, Debbie – 'that hairdresser ... the one with the mini skirts' – after her mother died (82). We also hear snippets of the Michael Jackson/Lisa Marie Presley interview on ABC's *Dateline* (79).[15] Finally, in a reversal of the general pattern, we also hear that Magi's Black great-grandmother gave birth to two children by her white boss (95).

The historical relationships turn out badly, but they serve to illuminate the main plot. The 1928 action ends with 'She' cutting the throat of 'He' as he removes his blackface (99–100, 73). The 1860s plot ends with a *pietà* of 'Him' lying motionless in 'Her' arms with a noose around his neck, while '*a presidential voice reads from the Emancipation Proclamation.*' She speaks: 'Once upon a time, there was a man who wanted to find a magic spell in order to become White. After much research and investigation, he came across an ancient ritual from the caverns of knowledge of a psychic. "The only way to become White," the psychic said, "was to enter the Whiteness." And when he found his ice queen, his alabaster goddess, he fucked her. Her on his dick. He one with her, for a single shivering moment became ... her. Her and her Whiteness' (91).

The allegory underscores the main action. Billie's 'dream' – articulated in a scene framed by a voice-over of Martin Luther King (47), in which parts of King's 'I have a dream' speech are shared between Billie and Othello (54) – is that 'one day a Black man and a Black woman might find ...' (56), but the sentence is never completed. Billie is reduced early on to having 'nothing to say to him. What could I say? Othello, how is the fairer sexed one you love to dangle from your arm the one you love for herself and preferred to the deeper sexed one is she softer does she smell of tea roses and baby powder does she sweat white musk from between her toes do her thighs touch I am not curious just want to know do her breasts fill the cup of your hand the lips of your tongue not too dark you like a little milk with your nipple don't you no I'm not curious just want to know' (43).

But she determines that it is not about sex or sensuality for Othello, who ends up in bed with Billie even as he returns with Mona to pack his things. Billie and Magi postulate in one uproarious scene that Othello simply wants to 'White wash his life.' 'Corporeal malediction,' Billie calls it. 'A black man afflicted with Negrophobia,' 'a crumbled racial epidermal schema ... causing predilections to coitus denegrification' (66). But the real reason Othello leaves Billie for Mona seems to be that 'now he won't have to worry that a White woman will emotionally mistake him for the father that abandoned her' (though Magi wonders if 'she might mistake him for the butler' [67]). Othello himself seems to concur:

> Yes, I prefer White women. They are easier – before and after sex. They wanted me and I wanted them ... We'd make love and I'd fall asleep not having to beware being mistaken for someone's inattentive father. I'd explain that I wasn't interested in a committed relationship right now, and not be confused with every lousy lover, or husband that had ever left them lying in a gutter of unresolved emotions ... I am a very single, very intelligent, very employed Black man. And with White women it's good. It's nice. Anyhow, we're all equal in the eyes of God, aren't we? Aren't we? (71)

We do not hear how the Othello-Mona relationship works out, but we do hear a warning: 'You young-uns don't know the sweetness of molasses,' Canada tells Othello. 'Better watch out for that refined shit. It'll kill ya' (111).

What is the cultural work performed by this 'brittle exploration of race and gender' (Chapman, 'brittle')? How does it function as an adaptation, or exorcism, of *Othello*? To begin, it does take full part in a 1990s attempt to redress the imbalances of a feminist movement that to many seemed problematically to elide race within a gender-based solidarity among women. When Othello tells Billie of his plans to marry Mona – 'I wanted to tell you ... Mona wanted me to tell you' – they enter an exchange that is central to the cultural work performed by the play:

> *Billie.* Yes. Yes. Being a feminist and everything – a woman's right to know– since we're all in the struggle ... I thought you hated feminists.

Othello. Well ... I didn't mean that. I mean ... the White women's movement is different.
Billie. Just Black feminists.
Othello. No, no ... White men have maintained a firm grasp of the pants. I mean, White men have economic and political pants that White women have been demanding to share.
Billie. White wisdom from the mouth of the mythical Negro.
Othello. Don't you see! That's exactly my point! You ... The Black feminist position as I experience it in this relationship, leaves me feeling unrecognized as a man ... There was a time when women felt satisfied, no, honoured being a balance to their spouse, at home, supporting the family, playing her role –
Billie. Which women? I mean, which women are you referring to? Your mother worked all her life. My mother worked, her mother worked ... Most Black women have been working like mules since we arrived on this continent ... When White women were burning their bras, we were hired to hold their tits up. (70–1)

Like *Cruel Tears* and *Goodnight Desdemona*, then, *Harlem Duet* has its own areas of revisionist intervention, helping to shift the construction of Canadian subjectivities to include Black women's experience. Like those plays, too, *Harlem Duet* has its blind spots, notably in the narrowness of its recuperative focus on middle-class heterosexual Black life. And also like *Cruel Tears* and *Goodnight Desdemona*, Sears's play has a vexed relationship to Shakespeare, to *Othello*, and to High Culture generally. In her introduction, 'NOTES OF A COLOURED GIRL: 32 SHORT REASONS WHY I WRITE FOR THE THEATRE,' Sears positions her play in the (counter)canonical tradition of black women's playwriting in America, invoking in her typeface and text the work of Ntozake Shange, together with that of Lorraine Hansberry. Citing Hansberry's *A Raisin in the Sun* and a production of Shange's *For Coloured Girls Who Have Considered Suicide When the Rainbow is Enuf* that she saw at the age of eighteen, Sears claims a place in that tradition and articulates her responsibility to see to it that her newborn niece will not have to wait until she is eighteen for this experience: 'She must have access to a choir of African voices, chanting a multiplicity of African experiences ... And I will not wait. I harbour deep within me tales that I've never seen told. I too must become an organ and add my perspective, my lens, my stories, to the ever growing body of work by and about people of African descent' (12).[16]

But contributing to a counter-canon also has its perils, and, if Sears places her work within a counterhegemonic canon of work by African-American women, she also carves a place within more problematic canons and traditions, both African-American and white. The framing device of inter-scene voice-overs that locate the action within Black history, for example, quotes men exclusively – Martin Luther King, Malcolm X, Marcus Garvey, Langston Hughes, Paul Robeson, Jesse Jackson, Louis Farrakhan, and Christopher Darden (the Black prosecution lawyer at the Simpson trial). To a certain extent, this makes the fundamentally resistant point of the play itself, since we hear Billie only through the filter of a Black history that tends to erase her. But the barrage of male voices also threatens to contain the play's Black feminist interventions within a normalization of the male voice as that of History and Culture, just as the use of Shakespeare, in spite of Sears's attempts to 'exorcise' *Othello*, serves to reinscribe its (white) canonical authority.

Harlem Duet neither depends upon nor rewards a knowledge of Shakespeare to the same degree as the other plays under consideration, but it does rely on some familiarity with the story, and it does reward the audience's recognition of 'Mona,' 'Chris Yago,' and the planned trip to Cypress (53) as Shakespearean echoes. At one point it even inserts a gratuitous echo, when Othello confides to Canada, 'I do confess the vices of my blood' (Shakespeare, *Othello* 1.3.123; Sears 111).[17] And the play seems to use the artefacts of High Culture, including knowledge of Shakespeare, to claim cultural authority for itself and for Black culture generally – to claim a place at the table rather than to overturn it. It is perhaps this evocation of Shakespeare and the European humanist tradition that makes it possible for one reviewer to read the play as partaking in the generic history of Western tragedy and the realist tradition of individualist psychology – as one in which 'the central issue ... is self-esteem': 'Much of the drama depends on the ability of [actors Alison] Sealy-Smith and [Nigel Shawn] Williams to find the tragic flaws in their characters ... Sealy-Smith and Williams reveal that Billie and Othello are victims, not merely of culture and history, but to a certain extent by choice' (V. Wagner, 'Theatre').

But the echoes of Shakespeare and High Culture are perhaps evoked with (critical) difference.[18] If, for example, the play's reference to '*The Great Chain of Being*' cites E.M.W. Tillyard's *The Elizabethan World Picture*, it does not pass without criticism, grouped as it is with *African Mythology* and *Black Psychology* as 'the scientific foundation for why we're not human' – and why 'an African can't really be a woman' (51).[19] Perhaps audiences need to recognize Sears's reclamatory voice in Billie's throw-away line, 'the Shakespeare's mine, but you can have it' (52).

The play's invocations of African and female histories, traditions, and cultures are themselves not without problematic aspects. Of the plays under consideration, *Harlem Duet* makes the most extensive use of the handkerchief motif from Shakespeare, which the main line of Shakespeare criticism, like *Goodnight Desdemona*, has until recently taken as a (too) simple plot device.[20] Sears prints as an epigraph lines from Shakespeare's play that are echoed throughout *Harlem Duet* and that trace the handkerchief to an African and female source:

> That handkerchief
> Did an Egyptian to my mother give
> She was a charmer ...
> There's magic in the web of it
> A sybil ... in her prophetic fury sewed the work.
> (Shakespeare 3.4.51–68; Sears 19)[21]

The exoticism of the story is not shirked by Sears but reinforced and contextualized, both historically and culturally, to an unusual degree, invoking an alternative African tradition of spirituality. Throughout the play, Billie is busy preparing for Othello's wedding 'a potion ... A plague of sorts' (102) – 'Saracen's Compound ... Woad ... Hart's tongue ... Prunella vulgaris' (40) – in which she soaks the handkerchief: 'Anyone who touches it – the handkerchief, will come to harm' (102). It is eventually revealed that Billie's real name is Sybil: 'prophetess. Sorceress. Seer of the future' (81). Sears frames her story of Billie's revenge both within popular women's folklore, which has its own resistant valences, and as an evocation of more formal Black history. On the one hand, Billie's enchantments are grouped with comic, tabloid-style charms – if you want to keep a man 'rub his backside with margarine' (28), or 'boil down some greens in panty stock' (29). On the other hand, they are linked to the solemn marriage vow of jumping over a broom, practised by slaves who had no access to official rituals (56, 107) – a vow broken by Billie's Othello, to his disgrace. Finally, the handkerchief itself and Billie's practices upon it are linked in the play with history, particularly Black women's history:

> Othello? I am preparing ... [a] gift for you, and your new bride. Once you gave me a handkerchief. An heirloom. This handkerchief, your mother's ...

given by your father. From his mother before that. So far back ... It is fixed in the emotions of all your ancestors. The one who laid the foundation for the road in Herndon, Virginia, and was lashed for laziness as he stopped to wipe the sweat from his brow with this kerchief. Or your great, great grandmother, who covered her face with it, and then covered it with her hands as she rocked and silently wailed, when told that her girl child, barely thirteen, would be sent 'cross the state for breeding purposes. Or the one who leapt for joy on hearing of the Emancipation Proclamation, fifteen years late mind you, only to watch it fall in slow motion from his hand and onto the ground when told that the only job he could now get, was the same one he'd done for free all those years, and now he's forced to take it, for not enough money to buy the food to fill even one man's belly. (76)

In this treatment of the handkerchief – which also permeates the historical plots – Sears risks exoticizing Black culture in ways complicit with Western orientalism. But she also uses the device to question Western rationalisms and perhaps the canonical *Othello* through her own magic, even as Billie exorcizes *her* Othello through her exotic blending of ingredients.

The most significant cultural intervention made by *Harlem Duet*, as by *Cruel Tears* and *Goodnight Desdemona*, may, in fact, be generic. Where Mitchell's play recuperates the popular as art and MacDonald's recuperates feminist comedy from a masculinist tragic tradition, Sears invents a new, hybrid genre that incorporates the comic and tragic within 'rhapsodic blues tragedy' (14). In an interview, Sears speculates on the possibility of forging a 'black aesthetic' out of blues, jazz, and improvization in ways that resonate with regionalist efforts to develop dramaturgical forms out of local landscapes and histories, and also out of feminist efforts to forge women's forms of expression (Sears and Sealy Smith 28–9). *Harlem Duet* frames its action not only within excerpts from recorded Black history but also within forms of (live) Black musical expression that play against their Western orchestral instrumentation even as the action of the play resonates against Shakespearean tragedy. Scenes are introduced by 'heaving melancholic blues' (21), 'blues/jazz riff[s]' (32), 'blues from deep in the Mississippi delta' (33), and so on throughout a play that makes a virtue of its hybridity but resists any confident settling in to generic, racial, or ideological purities. This, together with the placing of the intersection of contemporary and historical Black experience, the intersection of Malcolm X and Martin Luther King (boulevards), and the intersection of gender and race at centre stage in

Toronto theatre in the late 1990s, may constitute the play's most significant cultural intervention.

Conclusion

In 'Re-Citing Shakespeare in Post-Colonial Drama,' Joanne Tompkins argues that 'post-colonial revisions of Shakespeare's plays displace an inherited tradition in order to accommodate other cultural traditions that ... have developed in quite different social, literary, and political directions' (21). Each of the revisionings that she examines 'counter-discursively resituates the cultural weight of Shakespeare to establish cultural specificities that destabilize important, unquestioned reiterations of imperial paradigms that are no longer relevant' (21). Tompkins is focusing on the cultural specificities of different national sites of resistance, but her argument also applies intra-nationally within Canada. An examination of adaptations and re(-)citations over time and region of a play such as *Othello*, with its different valences of Otherness, is suggestive within Canada of a cultural negotiation over the corpus of Shakespeare, not only with 'imperial paradigms' – the colonizing Other – but also with internal negotiations of power and cultural colonisation over time. Each of *Cruel Tears*, *Goodnight Desdemona*, and *Harlem Duet* is very much a product of its place and moment and, at the same time, productive of its own and subsequent moments as a marker of, and site for, the negotiation of social change around specific issues. Each in its way and to its own degree invokes 'Shakespeare,' 'Culture,' and universalist discourse to make its particular claims, and each elides other issues – sexual preference in *Cruel Tears* and *Harlem Duet*, race in *Goodnight Desdemona*, class in *Goodnight Desdemona* and *Harlem Duet*. But each also represents genuine intervention, shifting the cultural ground and changing what it is possible to think about Canadian subjectivities as produced through the interrelationships among (counter-)discourses of nation, region, gender, class, race, and ethnicity.

It would have been unthinkable in Saskatchewan in 1975 to have set *Cruel Tears* outside Canada, as Sears set *Harlem Duet* in the American heart of North American Black culture. In the Toronto of 1997, however, that play's relevance could be assumed; its status as 'Canadian' was not an issue. Indeed, in 1975 to set *Cruel Tears* in Saskatoon was an act of regionalist resistance, a claim that historical and cultural events of significance do not just happen to Canadians elsewhere. Similarly, the model of resistant reading enacted by *Goodnight Desdemona* – for whom the reproductive economy of recycling Shakespeare was no longer sufficiently resistant – was not available to Mitchell and the Dumptrucks, who, in any case, felt the need to claim rather than debunk the cultural authority of Shakespeare. And such an enactment was unnecessary for Sears as an explicit gesture in a play that was free to cite its Shakespeare less directly, or less directly confrontationally, because by the late 1990s, at least within a Toronto theatre community that had witnessed a great many resistant revisionings, Shakespeare was legible as a site for the negotiation of values rather than simply as a marker of imperialist High Culture.

Perhaps the major contribution of these plays to the ongoing reinvention of Canadian subjectivities, however, is that they provide models for ongoing generic in(ter)vention and a recurrent trope of self-rebirth. Mitchell's 'country opera' is an invented form that asserts through its hybridity the existence and value of rural, regional, and populist cultures; MacDonald's feminist comedy asserts its productive generic revisioning ('I've had it with all the tragic tunnel vision around here' [85]); and Sears's 'rhapsodic blues tragedy' inscribes a High Culture hybridity that at once asserts, reclaims, and undermines canonical cultural authority, staging raids and making claims on Shakespeare, African-American history, and Black women's culture, and using whatever intersections work at its particular historical cultural moment to stake claims for itself and the place of its subject(ivity) on Canadian (centre) Stage(s).

Sears talks in her 'NOTES OF A COLOURED GIRL' about 'giving birth to myself' in *Harlem Duet* (15) in ways that echo the staging of a social/communal (re)birth of the feminist, Jungian Self in *Goodnight Desdemona* (and less explicitly of the regional, populist self in *Cruel Tears*), and it is perhaps this continual and ongoing auto-rebirthing (rebirthing of the self) of national, regional, gendered (and genre-ed), racial, ethnic, sexual and social selves, through the inevitable mixed blessing of Shakespeare, which characterizes the reinscriptions under consideration here. It may be that adapting Shakespeare risks reinscribing his cultural Author-ity, but that authority permeates Canadian culture Will-y-nilly. It may also be that challenging, appropriating, and deconstructing the discursive bases of that authority – with all the complex negotiations that doing so entails at any given moment – has been important as a way in which Canadian cultural values and Canadian gendered, racial, ethnic, and classed subjectivities have been productively renegotiated in works such as *Cruel Tears, Goodnight Desdemona*, and *Harlem Duet* in the last three decades of the twentieth century.

Notes

1 I would like to thank Diana Brydon and Irena Makaryk for suggestions and comments that have significantly improved this essay, as I would like to thank Christine Bold for her always helpful contributions.
2 J. Alan B. Somerset, in his 1991 catalogue index to the Festival's archives, lists only four productions at Stratford between 1953 and 1990, as opposed to seven of *Hamlet*, eight of *Lear*, and seven of *Macbeth*, among the 'major tragedies.' The most popular comedies, *Twelfth Night* (9), *A Midsummer Night's Dream* (8), *As You Like It* (10), *Much Ado About Nothing* (8), *The Taming of the Shrew* (8), and *Love's Labour's Lost* (7), significantly outstrip *Othello* at Stratford, where even *The Merry Wives of Windsor* (5), *Julius Caesar* (5), and *Measure for Measure* (5) have been produced more often than *Othello*. None of the four productions, and no other Canadian productions with which I am familiar, received favourable reviews. Pettigrew and Portman describe the 1959 production as being 'something of a shambles' by the end of the run (1: 141), the 1973 production as that season's 'major disaster' (2: 35), and the 1979 production as a mixed success let down by Alan Scarfe's Othello, which one reviewer felt was less a character than a 'loud, tedious vacancy' (2: 163). The 1987 production, with an unhealthy Howard Rollins in the title role, was even less successful. Even before Rollins took ill, opening-night reviews were less than favourable, and more than one critic found it, as Bob Pennington did, 'a major disappointment.' Since Somerset's book, there has been one more production, in 1994, which again received mixed reviews, though H.J. Kirchhoff, in the *Globe and Mail*, found it 'a superb piece of theatre' ('Tapping').
3 See also Pechter, *Endless*.
4 The Massey Commission was a royal commission initiated by Prime Minister Louis St Laurent in 1949 and chaired by Vincent Massey, which issued its report in 1951. See Rubin 153–5 and 176–83 for a reprinting of the sections of the report related to theatre. The report led directly to the founding of the Canada Council for the Arts.

The key piece in the regionalist theorizing of Canadian drama and theatre, Diane Bessai's 'The Regionalism of Canadian Drama,' was not published until 1980, but it cites many of the major playwrights and theatre companies across the country in the 1970s development of Canadian regionalist drama and theatre. Bessai defends 'regional' (as opposed to 'provincial') as a theoretical term that 'in its positive sense ... means rooted, indigenous, shaped by a specific social, cultural and physical milieu. It reflects the past as well as the present and at its best absorbs innumerable influences from beyond its

borders, particularly as these have bearing on the informing regional perspective' (7).
5 I am grateful to Irena Makaryk for information about the traditional role of the kerchief.
6 K-Tel is a mail-order company producing cut-rate compilations of pop-music hits from earlier decades and marketing them on television using short clips from long lists of song titles.
7 Nightwood's first mandate, in 1979, was not, in fact, feminist – or was so only in the sense that Nightwood was a company of women creating work for themselves. It focused on the creation of theatre based on the visual arts. What I am calling the second mandate, which seems to have begun informally in the early 1980s, concentrated on the creation of women-centred work and shifted from feminist collective creations early in the mandate to individually authored plays by the late 1980s. In 1989, between the first production of *Goodnight Desdemona* and its remount, the company's third-mandate focus on women of colour came into effect.
8 In the 1988 version there was more focus on Claude Night, who returned at the end to attempt further exploitations and begin his own quest for self-knowledge.
9 Dvorak makes a similar argument about the play's reading of *Romeo and Juliet* (132).
10 In the published script, all direct appropriations of Shakespeare are signalled by italics, though the original sources of or contexts for these lines or scenes are never given.
11 Four white members of the Los Angeles Police Department were notoriously found not guilty in 1992 on state charges of beating a Black man, Rodney King, after he was arrested for speeding on 3 March 1991, in spite of amateur videotape of the incident having been widely broadcast. The acquittal prompted riots in Los Angeles and widespread protests across North America. Two of the officers were subsequently found guilty on federal charges.
12 Sears says, 'I asked Allan [Booth] to create blues music for cello and double bass. But double bass and cello says chamber music. So the blues creates that tension [between European and African American culture], it's beautiful and it has that drama implicit in it' (Sears and Sealy-Smith 29).
13 Lamming writes that 'to be black, in the West Indies, is to be poor; whereas to be black (rich or poor) in an American context is to be a traditional target for specific punishments' (33). I am indebted to Diana Brydon for bringing this passage to my attention.
14 Clarence Thomas is a conservative Black Republican lawyer nominated to the Supreme Court by then-President George Bush in July 1991, in spite of a

record of opposing women's rights. The appointment was challenged when Thomas was charged by Anita Hill, a Black law professor at the University of Oklahoma, with sexual harassment. In spite of significant evidence, the Judiciary Committee approved his appointment, and he subsequently aligned himself with the most reactionary, anti-woman, anti-civil rights wing of the court.

15 The interview, with ABC's Diane Sawyer, was broadcast live around the world on 14 June 1995. It may not be stretching things to argue that the world's fascination with the troubled relationship between Jackson and Presley had less to do with the intersection of celebrity musical families than with its complex intersections of race and sexuality, as Jackson, a Black man with an effeminate manner, a reputed affinity for boys, and a history of plastic surgery that increasingly diminished stereotypically racialized characteristics, married the (white) daughter ('tupped the white ewe,' in Iago's terms) of the man most directly responsible for the appropriation of American Black music by the (white) music industry.

16 I have omitted from this quotation the bold-faced numberings **7, 8,** and **9** of the '32 SHORT REASONS WHY I WRITE FOR THE THEATRE.'

17 Other Shakespearean citations include 'If virtue no delighted beauty lack,/ Your son-in-law is far more fair than black' (*Othello* 1.3.285–6; Sears 99), as well as lines from *Hamlet* and references to *Pericles* in the same scene, and the fractured rehearsal of parts of the speeches Shakespeare's Othello addresses to the Senators in 1.3.79–94, 128–62 (Sears 113).

18 See Hutcheon, *Theory* 5–16 and *passim* for her first formulation of parody as repetition with a critical difference, 'a method of inscribing continuity while permitting critical distance' (20).

19 Interestingly, when Amah tries to evoke sympathy for Othello from the institutionalized Billie at the end of the play, Billie replies, 'I'm not that evolved' (115).

20 Thomas Rymer initiated this tradition when he (in)famously dismissed the play by determining its morals: 'First, this may be a caution to all Maidens of Quality how, without their parents consent, they run away with Blackamoors'; and 'Secondly, this may be a warning to all good Wives, that they look well to their linen' (89). In the last two decades, feminist criticism, in particular, has productively revisited the role of the handkerchief.

21 I have quoted this passage as Sears excerpts and punctuates it, but have cited the Shakespearean source as listed in the References. The edition I am using punctuates it slightly differently.

Afterword

Relocating Shakespeare, Redefining Canada

DIANA BRYDON

> While Shakespeare dreamed of Caliban Snow-Owl
> Coyote and Glooskap gathered at Red River's edge
> dreaming of Shakespeare
> – Tom Marshall, 'Out There: Objects Disposed,
> Fragmenting, In Our Own Space' 155

How does one read a culturally different text? The question implicitly raised by Gayatri Spivak in her article 'How to Teach a "Culturally Different" Book' resonates in different ways within the fields of Canadian, postcolonial, and Renaissance studies, as the individual chapters that form this book suggest. In this afterward, I am deliberately turning Spivak's venture into exploring the dynamics of 'international cultural exchange' (239) away from her attempt to explain a text that seems obviously culturally unfamiliar to a North American audience back towards two texts ('Shakespeare' and 'Canada') that are too often deemed readily familiar to Canadians. Part of the purpose of this book has been to interrogate each through the medium of the other. To ask what is culturally different about Shakespeare-in-Canada is to notice what Mark Fortier terms in this collection 'the from elsewhere that inhabits the Canadian.' This 'from elsewhere' is not just the undead past, the colonial legacy, or indigenous, immigrant, or cosmopolitan traditions, including the English literary tradition with its special claim to Shakespeare, but also increasingly the imbrications of 'Canada' and 'Shakespeare' within the circuits of transnational capital. With Spivak, the authors of the chapters within this collection believe that questions about how international cultural exchanges operate need 'to be kept alive, not answered too quickly' (Spivak 239).

This openness is crucial because, as Dennis Kennedy suggests in his Afterword to *Foreign Shakespeare*, 'we have not even begun to develop a theory of cultural exchange that might help us understand what happens when Shakespeare travels abroad, and so far there has been little interest among Shakespeareans in such an enterprise' (300). Since Kennedy published this statement in 1993, considerably more work in this vein has appeared, yet its function has been to open up further areas of inquiry rather than to create any satisfactory theory of explanation for this travelling concept. The substantial body of work completed on this topic by postcolonial writers well before the appearance of Kennedy's book is now, belatedly, being integrated within mainstream Shakespearean studies. As Peter Hulme argues, 'the institution of Shakespeare studies has too easily been able to sidetrack "anti-colonial" readings of *The Tempest* by putting them in the category of "appropriations" or "allegories" (in effect saying "very interesting, but not actually speaking to the *real* Shakespearean text").' Like us, he argues that there must be a place for such critique within Shakespearean criticism itself and that such an integrationist approach has 'significant pedagogical and political advantages' (233).

Thus, although Shakespeare is extremely mobile, the nature and functions of that mobility are difficult to assess and continue to be queried, primarily through the insights brought to questions of cultural transmission and transformation developed through postcolonial and transnational studies. This book has situated itself at the crossroads where work in literary, theatre, and cultural studies meet to track 'the movement of a cultural object across different cultural sites' (Palumbo-Liu 10). Such work necessarily complicates received understandings of national cultures and of a world culture 'understood simply as an amplified version of a national cultural model' (Palumbo-Liu 8). Attention to Shakespeare in Canada, as demonstrated here, tends to shift the emphasis of Canadian literary studies away from attempts to pin down some recognizable forms of an essential Canadian identity towards consideration of uneven cross-cultural flows and the localized production of meaning within the nation-state. Yet 'Shakespeare' is not just any cultural object.

If one accepts, with the narrator of John Moss's story 'Understanding Shakespeare,' that 'Shakespeare transformed a concatenation of medieval words into the stable and eloquent language we now live within,' then it is possible for one Canadian, at least, to suggest that 'I am molecules of air expanding, and Shakespeare is the membrane, the balloon holding it all together. Can the contained know its container?' (73). He continues: 'Reaching to Shakespeare is not reaching back but reaching out all around us' (74).

In making such an effort, we can see that Shakespeare is both Canadian and 'from elsewhere,' as the cover image of the June 2000 issue of the *Canadian Forum* makes clear. Shakespeare, that familiar goateed icon, here clothed in a red shirt emblazoned with a white maple leaf and white collar, looks out at the reader. The reversal of the Canadian flag (red maple leaf on white background) suggests repetition with a difference. He is holding a skull in his left hand and a quill pen in his right hand, conflating actor and writer, repeating the classic pose assumed by Hamlet, with a difference. In the background, the circular Canadian Stratford theatre, topped with the Canadian flag, lurks at a vertiginous angle beneath the enormous heading 'I AM CANADIAN: STRATFORD HAS A NEW ACCENT.' The implied allusion to a popular series of Molson beer commercials, which successfully linked Canadian nationalism to consumer capitalism, here links both to the implied decolonization of a Canadian stage built on the veneration of an imperial author and another country's accent.[1] As the chapters discussing Stratford in this volume attest, Stratford's imbrication in such processes requires careful unpacking.

Keith Garebian's article inside the *Canadian Forum* issue with this striking cover bears an equally intriguing title: 'Bringing Hamlet Home.' Home to whom? Home for whom? In what sense is Canada Hamlet's home? Together, Leanore Lieblein's chapter discussing Québécois interpretations of Hamlet and Jessica Schagerl's on anglophone Hamlets demonstrate just how complicated this question may be, further reinforcing Homi K. Bhabha's insights into the 'unhomely' or *unheimlich* ambivalence of 'the civil State as it draws its rather paradoxical boundary between the private and the public spheres' (10). Garebian's article (like Moss's story) shows that Shakespeare crosses that paradoxical boundary between private and public spheres in unsettling ways, that Canadians still care about such questions linking nation, culture, and the public sphere, and that there is little consensus about their resolution. In his posing of alternatives for the naming of an authentically Canadian Shakespeare, he provides further fuel for the arguments made by C.E. McGee and Jessica Schagerl in this volume. Garebian quotes Richard Monette, Stratford's artistic director, and Douglas Paraschuk, Stratford's head of design, and he discusses current productions of Shakespeare's plays, but he ignores what our collection poses as a third alternative, that of appropriation, recycling, or reimagining Shakespeare, as demonstrated, for example, in Timothy Findley's play, *Elizabeth Rex*, a complex Canadian engagement with Shakespeare the author, his plays and their period, which opened for the first time in the 2000 Canadian Stratford summer season. Findley's play locates Bhabha's unhomely within what he terms 'a contradiction of genders,' staged through 'a glorious theatrical confrontation' (9) between Shakespeare and Queen Elizabeth, through which they explore the entanglements of public and private, court and stage, art and life, male and female.

In *Shakespeare in Canada*, we locate the variety of cultural work performed by revisionings, such as Findley's play, and by journalistic surveys, such as Garebian's piece, within the kinds of cultural, historical, and theoretical contexts that can help to explain and connect them. Why do these questions matter to (some) Canadians? Why are they so often posed in terms of the search for an authenticating Canadian identity and the authority of a fetishized author? How do these works function in shaping communities of Canadians? Or do they? What is their relation (if any) to Shakespeare's plays? How is the Shakespeare featured on the cover of the *Canadian Forum* related to the Shakespeare dramatized in Findley's *Elizabeth Rex*? And how do these Shakespeares relate to those taught in the classroom, staged in the theatre, and recycled in various other adaptations and revisions, including the poetry sequence that heads this Afterword?

To address these questions, this collection has been organized around several permeable and interlinking contexts. There are the national (and, because this is Canada, the regional and Quebec national) cultural contexts of engagements with Shakespeare. The historical narrative of Shakespeare in Canada provided by Irena Makaryk's Introduction maps the general terrain, preparing the ground for chronologically based discussion of the various modes of institutionalizing Shakespearean studies in Canada from the late nineteenth century through to the mid-twentieth century, with the establishment of Stratford as Canada's national theatre and its most controversial, institutional site for Shakespearean production. The following chapters trace the narrative through to the end of the twentieth century, demonstrating – through the histories of Shakespeare on stage, critical debates and traditions, and adaptations – the continuing tensions negotiated among national, regional, and local uses of Shakespeare.

Jonathan Kertzer begins his study *Worrying the Nation: Imagining a*

National Literature in English Canada with the statement, 'The object of theoretical inquiry in Canadian literary studies – Canada – no longer functions as it once did' (3). True enough, but how did 'Canada' once function? We still do not know enough about how the national, the local, and the international worked together in earlier periods. Kertzer's focus falls almost entirely on the creation of a narrow university-determined national literary canon and the increasing theoretical challenges to that model since the 1980s. (He makes no mention of Shakespeare.) Yet English-Canadian literature, as Paul Hjartarson points out, still 'lacks many of the basic research tools' (18) for understanding the formation of Canadian literary traditions. We have sought to remedy some of that lack here.

The benefits of an approach such as ours for Canadian literary studies are outlined by Heather Murray in her contribution to a panel discussion on literary histories:

> Focus on the Canadian reception of non-Canadian works may expose 'the mutual interplays of literary reception and production.' It can span the anachronistic distinction between 'high' and 'low' cultures that has been the by-product of certain processes of *post hoc* academicization. ('Canadian literature' reconfigured on these terms is less the expression of an emergent set of national cultural drives and identities, more a series of complex intertextualities in a multidiscursive and polycultural situation.) ... Such examinations can help us to further locate English-Canadian literature in the framework of colonial and post-colonial studies, by showing, in all its messy, local and immediate detail, the primary process of the making – and taking – of cultures. ('Institutions' 6)

In taking on these tasks, this collection contributes to current rethinking of what the global and the local, the universal and the particular actually mean in literary study, and how they have been, and continue to be, intertwined in Canada. It is not enough simply to assert, with Harold Bloom, that 'the enigma of Shakespeare is his universalism' (*Western* 524), without also asking how universalism means, and interrogating if it does indeed mean, universally. Or as Arnold Harrichand Itwaru and Natasha Ksonzek insist: 'It is the *universalizing* of Shakespeare rather than the spurious claim that he is "universal" that needs to be looked into' (36).

At the same time, it is also important to investigate opposing claims that Shakespeare is merely a tool of imperialism. A.H. Itwaru and

Natasha Ksonzek query the ideological function of Shakespeare in educational institutions (an institutional site we wish we could have investigated more thoroughly in this collection), arguing that in their educational experience of Shakespeare 'our appropriate appreciation of this Great Writer was required, not our criticism' (37). For them, 'the high regard there is for Shakespeare in anglophone Canada has also the affirmation of the perspectives in relation to power over people celebrated in this writer's work' (40). They conclude: 'When he is annually resurrected in Canada through huge sums of money from the Canada Council, it is more than "theatre" that is taking place. An insidious imperialism is reproduced as Great Theatre' (44). In this book, we have sought to contextualize such claims, investigating how Shakespeare has been appreciated and analysed, nationalized and universalized, through a range of Canadian cultural practices.

Shakespeare in Canada thus presents the harmonies and dissonances created when dialogue across the normally separate spheres devoted to the study of Canada and Shakespeare takes place across the divisions constituted by the various fields of inherited disciplinary formations (English, Drama) and their emergent, inherently interdisciplinary challenges (cultural, performance, and postcolonial studies). When Canada and Shakespeare are viewed not as givens but as social texts constantly under production, the boundaries between their disciplinary constructions shift and new configurations emerge. The book initiates an interlocking series of reciprocal dialogues across the various boundaries drawn by such disciplinary specialization and by regional and linguistic location. We think that this structure, and its revisionist methodology, is crucial, if we are to avoid the danger identified by Thomas Healy: 'Part of the problem with Shakespeare is that his protean qualities across histories, cultures and languages are still critically conceived as possessing a type of homogeneity' (213). In avoiding the Scylla of that homogeneity, we risk the Charybdis of what Michael Bristol deems (in *Big-Time Shakespeare*) one of the limitations of a purely local focus: 'Overly strict attention to the local utilities served by particular works does not provide an adequate account of that work's larger social history. The danger inherent in particularist research of this kind is that it may promote an unnecessarily fragmented picture of Shakespeare as a random aggregate of local practices and partisan ideological appropriation' (26). In constructing this collection we have sought continuously to test the theoretical against the specific and to contextualize the local detail through attention to broader contexts.

As implied by Tom Marshall's poetic account (cited in my epigraph) of the roles played by Snow-Owl, Glooskap, and Coyote in shaping 'Will's' dream of *The Tempest*, of the shaman's role in dreaming Snow-Owl, and of a large man (the poet himself?) dreaming Glooscap, Canadian encounters with Shakespeare are necessarily multifaceted and may prove surprising, but they are always, already enmeshed in the global. Marshall's poem asks forgiveness 'of earth and Indian ghosts ...' (146) for the shipwreck on Turtle Island that initiated America's history and Shakespeare's play, imagining that, with Will's decision, through Native intervention, 'to break his staff' (156), the world may yet be free to be 'born again' (157). Such utopian hopes, however, are balanced by Glooskap's prescient doubt that this intervention will be successful and by Coyote's move from laughter to chagrin and finally derision. For Marshall, as for Walter Mignolo, there is a 'darker side of the Renaissance [that] underlines ... the rebirth of the classical tradition as a justification of colonial expansion and the emergence of a genealogy (the early colonial period) that announces the colonial and the postcolonial' (Mignolo vii), and Canada is a participant in these processes. Eerily echoing Mignolo, Himani Bannerji explains that 'if one stands on the dark side of the nation in Canada everything looks different' (104). Perhaps few of the chapters in this collection completely share her view that '"Canada," as a national imaginary, its multiculturalism and its lip service to Quebec's Canadianness notwithstanding, is actually an anglo-white male idea that blurs the class lines' (79), yet our investigations into the cultural work in which 'Shakespeare' has been employed by Canadians over the years suggests that her analysis must be taken seriously.

What Marshall poses through imagery and story, we seek to investigate through the protocols of academic research and theory. Like him, we posit a reciprocal relation between the animating questions of Shakespearean, Canadian, and postcolonial study, and, more specifically, we ask what issues seem to be at stake when Shakespeare is analysed, appropriated, produced, and reproduced in Canada. These issues are likely to be simultaneously local, national, and global in their provenance, and multiple in their intersecting pasts. Untangling their cross-purposes demands new kinds of flexible and nuanced critical practices and the communal effort of the multi–voiced collection.

Marshall's poem reverses the traditional definitions of influence as unidirectional from imperial centre to colony, repositing them as a reciprocal two-way flow of interaction. Shakespeare and Glooskap dream each other and shape each other's dreams (and nightmares). Michael Bristol's *Shakespeare's America, America's Shakespeare* performs the critical equivalent of this gesture, balancing a section on 'Shakespearizing America' against another on 'Americanizing Shakespeare,' although his focus throughout is in identifying the nature of Shakespeare as 'an American institution' (1) rather than in explicitly contrasting the specific history of Shakespeare in Britain with that of the United States. Instead, he argues that 'the interpretation of Shakespeare and the interpretation of American political culture are mutually determining practices' (3). Richard Burt, in *Unspeakable ShaXXXspeares*, extends Bristol's argument to 'maintain that Shakespeare's citation in American popular culture registers the way his "classic" texts resonate with deep, unconscious elements of the United States's cultural self-legitimation' (xi). This book arose from our desire to understand where Canada fits within, or beyond, such trajectories. Is it possible to speak of Shakespeare as a Canadian institution, or are Canadian Shakespeares just a small part of the American Shakespeares described by Bristol and expanded upon by Burt? Our title, 'Shakespeare in Canada,' implies that this question remains open.

In considering the Canadian construction, preservation, and transmission of literary and theatrical history, as embodied in Shakespeare, we participate in the contemporary shift in focus from Shakespeare studies to 'Shakespeare' studies, a shift that relocates meaning from a stable lodging within a literary text to a new space constituted by the interplay of author, text, and reader and their various places of production and reception. As K.K. Ruthven puts it, 'central to "Shakespeare" studies is the question of why these plays have been taken to mean different things at different times' (560). He might have added, and in different places, to different cultures. To write 'Shakespeare' instead of Shakespeare is to recognize, in Terry Eagleton's words, that 'Shakespeare is today less an author than an apparatus – that his name ... is merely metonymic of an entire politico-cultural formation, and thus more akin to "Disney" or "Rockefeller" than to "Jane Smith"' (204). Less an author, no longer just an author, but still an author, too, which is why this Afterword oscillates in its use of quotation marks to indicate the instability of reference in the Shakespearean enterprises of cultural, literary, and theatrical criticism.

When I first studied Shakespeare in a Hamilton, Ontario, high school in the 1960s, I knew that I was reading a culturally different text, but I thought that the difference I faced was primarily one of linguistic difference, caused by temporal more than by national shifts in register. As a Canadian growing up in Ontario, I was taught that English literature was my heritage, and I embraced it eagerly. Studying Commonwealth literature at university, especially George Lamming's brilliant revisionary readings of *The Tempest* in *The Pleasures of Exile*, first opened my eyes to the centrality of cultural, and gendered, difference in shaping reading experience, but it was not until I was studying and teaching English in Australia that I began to realize how national differences could influence reader response from one settler colony to another.

What in 2000 seems obvious, in the early 1980s still appeared to be radically adventurous, even somewhat sacrilegious and faintly comical: reading Shakespeare against the bardolatry grain, not just as culturally specific in production, but also as amenable to variously situated interpretative readings in different places and times, each of which might carry specific consequences in its wake. As a critic working on Canadian and postcolonial literatures, I returned to Shakespeare through Lamming, Edward Kamau Brathwaite, Aimé Césaire, and Max Dorsinville, and welcomed the shift marked by the appearance of the first volume of *Alternative Shakespeares*, edited by John Drakakis, as a convergent venture between the interests and questions of Shakespearean studies and the currents of the postcolonial field. Together with feminist revisions of Shakespeare, those convergences have tended to focus on the specific roles of reception, mediated through its multiply-situated locations (for example, in gender, race, class, and nation) in creating meaning. Within this framework, even production and reproduction are understood as initially filtered through mediated reception. Responding to Trinh T. Minh-ha, Canadian critic Susan Bennett describes this shift in Shakespeare studies as 'the struggle to bring Shakespeare into a different arena where other questions might be asked of his dissemination and power' (*Performing* 153). In this collection, that different arena is not just Canada but a different way of understanding cultural tradition, transmission, and transculturation at the beginning of the twenty-first century.

Contemporary criticism reminds us that, although, as Terence Hawkes puts it, 'the phenomenon called "Shakespeare"' is almost universally recognized, it 'operates simultaneously on a number of levels' (Introduction 1). For Eagleton, it has become a brand name or logo. For others, it is a very special kind of brand, evoking universal recognition and erasing cultural differences. In *Shakespeare Reproduced: The Text in History and Ideology*, Jean E. Howard and Marion F. O'Connor suggest that Shakespeare 'functions, in many quarters, as a kind of cultural Esperanto, a medium through which the differences of material existence – differences of race, gender, class, history, and culture – are supposedly cancelled' (4). Their book contests that assumption, revealing instead 'ways in which historically specific features determine the "Shakespeare" produced in criticism, in the classroom, and on the stage' (4). To what extent these determinations are absolute, and to what extent they may be negotiated, remains an issue of debate among contemporary critics and a question left open by the arguments of this volume. Yet, whatever degree of agency we may theorize around the production of various 'Shakespeares,' when Shakespeare is cited as a universally transparent language, these local specificities may go unrecognized but they do not disappear. As Edward Kamau Brathwaite notes, there is often a terrible cost meted out for universality, when universality is constructed by a Eurocentrism intent on denying cultural difference (20). Whereas in the past, this universal Shakespeare may have simultaneously served both British imperial interests and English nationalism, to many observers, contemporary Shakespeare's apparent universality seems firmly lodged in the service of consolidating American cultural dominance and its redefinition of culture as an industry like any other.

Given such limitations in theorizing 'Shakespeare' as a form of universal language, it seems more helpful to identify 'Shakespeare,' in Terence Hawkes's terms, as forming 'part of the ideological landscape of national life in Europe, North America and beyond' (Introduction 2). In other words, even when 'Shakespeare' may appear most transparently universal, it becomes most necessary to understand the conditions creating that impression and the interests it serves. Often, as Tom Healy suggests, and John Drakakis reiterates, this global 'Shakespeare' may be substituting the fantasy of cross-cultural understanding for a reality much more difficult to achieve (Healy 213; Drakakis, Afterword 331, 335). Xiaomei Chen's analysis of the cultural functions of Shakespearean productions in post-Mao China bears witness to the potential complexity of such transactions. She argues that what could easily be seen as cultural imperialism might also plausibly be understood as 'a powerful antiofficial discourse' in the local conditions of that time and place (156–7). Certainly, if Shakespeare can be seen as a 'medium of textual exchange,' it is, in Thomas Cartelli's words, 'unusually charged' (23).

In Canadian cultural history, as this volume demonstrates, the contradictions set up among imperial, global, national, and regional Shakespeares are charged with the ambivalences of a particular experience of colonialism. Simon Gikandi locates the genesis of his study, *Maps of Englishness*, in his effort to understand why formerly colonized people, who had often fought against colonial domination, 'seem to invest so much in cultural institutions – such as the school, Shakespeare, and cricket – that were closely associated with imperial conquest and rule' (ix). I have often puzzled over a similar contradiction in Canada, focusing on Canadian reinscriptions of the figure of Miranda in an effort to unravel the cultural compacts she seemed to embody and negotiate (see Brydon, 'Sister' and 'Tempest'). While Shakespeare as colonial cultural institution is part of the ideological landscape of Canada, such questions have seldom been asked in the Canadian context. Maria Tippett's *Making Culture: English-Canadian Institutions and the Arts before the Massey Commission*, for example, makes just one passing reference to 'the Shakespeare Reading Class (1906) in Charlottetown' as an example of the many groups in this period with the objective of adhering to primarily British forms of culture (7). Neither the record of Shakespeare in Canada nor the problematic determination of whether or not there is or can be or ought to be a Canadian Shakespeare has yet been subjected to the kind of sustained analysis the subject requires. This volume begins to redress the balance.

Certainly, the Shakespeare that is part of the ideological landscape of English and theatre studies has been quite thoroughly studied from a variety of theoretical perspectives since the 1980s, although such an enterprise by its very nature can never be completed. Various national Shakespeares have also received increased attention as critics consider the ways in which Shakespeare has been employed, not only to signify Englishness, but also to refashion and articulate 'a vast range of other cultures and identities too' (Joughin, Introduction 1). The dialogue between postcolonial and Shakespearean studies, ongoing since the 1960s, first achieved Canadian consolidation in Denis Salter's guest-edited special issue of *Essays in Theatre/Études Théâtrales*, *Shakespeare and Postcolonial Conditions*, in 1996. As Salter points out, this issue 'offers a Canadian perspective on the subject, though in widely dispersed locations of meaning' ('Introduction' 9). Salter calls for 'more investigations, from a clearly marked out postcolonial theoretical and empirical approach, of the stage, film, television, and video histories of individual Shakespeare texts, and of what happens not only to Shakespeare but to local performance traditions and innovations – *and* to moral and ideological orthodoxies – when Shakespeare undergoes an inter- or intra-cultural sea change' (7–8). In this collection we have begun to compile such an inventory of the reciprocal relations between Canadians and these differently mediated versions of Shakespeare, an inventory that may shed fresh light on how to describe what it means to be Canadian as well as how Shakespeare has been understood in various Canadian contexts.

Salter's special issue was followed by Ania Loomba and Martin Orkin's co-edited collection, *Post-colonial Shakespeares*, in 1998. In their Introduction, Loomba and Orkin argue that one area of 'sharp controversy' between postcolonial and Shakespearean criticism 'is the question of the location' (11). They explain that 'various critics have complained that not enough attention is paid within post-colonial studies and theories to specific locations and institutions' (11). Canada receives only passing mention in this collection of papers from a conference held in South Africa. In contrast, *Shakespeare in Canada* brings focused attention to specific locations and institutions within the history of Shakespeare in Canada, while attending to the kinds of cultural function that Shakespeare (as author, icon, and text) has performed for Canadians in various regional locations at different times, and for this once-colonial nation as a whole. Although not every chapter is written from a specifically postcolonial perspective, an awareness of postcolonial questions and methodologies, and of the need to revise these to deal with the particularities of Canada's colonial inheritance, informs the project as a whole.

Loomba and Orkin conclude with the belief that 'the Shakespearean text, which for so long helped anchor a disciplinary formation called "English studies," can become a means for discussing the nature of our diverse post-colonialities' (19). Others are less sure that Shakespeare's texts can continue to play such a role within contemporary multicultural constituencies (Erickson) or within cultures seeking radical alternatives to accepted cultural norms (Bennett; Drakakis; Sinfield). Bennett concludes *Performing Nostalgia* with the caution, 'I cannot help but wonder if Shakespeare is bound inextricably and persistently to exercise a colonial will that its performance might not often resist. The transnational, high and low cultural performances which form the focus of this book offer some suggestions of where and how that will is made visible' (155). Even Loomba herself warns elsewhere against the resilience of 'the myth of an endlessly pliable bard who has said it all, and through whom we can say everything' ('Shakespeare' 165).

The chapters in this volume demonstrate the potential and limitations of such a continued reliance on the infinite adaptability of the

Shakespearean text. Certainly the nature of Canada's own colonial experience appears to impose its own limits on the postcolonial uses to which Shakespeare has most often been put in this country. Cartelli's wide-ranging *Repositioning Shakespeare* sets itself an expansive postcolonial agenda: 'to explore how Shakespeare is repositioned, as emerging or residually postcolonial cultures seek either to respond critically to the depredations and misrepresentations of colonialism, or to renegotiate Shakespeare's standing as a privileged site of authority within their own national formation' (1). From the research included in this book, the second part of Cartelli's agenda appears to have been the more extensively explored within Canada. Given Canada's ambivalent position as a settler-invader colony, its conservative traditions, and the continued marginalization of indigenous peoples, such a focus may seem predictable. Certainly it corresponds to the scope of the roughly parallel Australian study, *Shakespeare's Books: Contemporary Cultural Politics and the Persistence of Empire*.

With an agenda similar to ours, that collection considers 'the historical processes of the institutionalisation of Shakespeare in Australia, and the contemporary uses of his "name" and "books" in current cultural and political debates, particularly those centring on education and theatre' (Campbell 1). But unlike *Shakespeare's Books*, our study is not a collection of conference proceedings. We are therefore able to provide a more continuous historical record, often supplemented by original archival research, and to maintain a tighter focus on the particularity of the Canadian location and the specific questions to which it gives rise.

In focusing on the centrality of location, Loomba and Orkin's *Postcolonial Shakespeare* seeks to initiate a closer dialogue between postcolonial critics working primarily on contemporary cultures and Renaissance scholars immersed in the history of their period. In *Rewriting Shakespeare, Rewriting Ourselves*, Peter Erickson demonstrates how one critic might engage in such a dialogue. Taking his impetus from the shared insistence of both 'the new historicism as practiced in English Renaissance scholarship' and 'contemporary feminist criticism' on the centrality of location, he addresses the importance of locating the critic in his or her own historical moment (1), concluding that 'the contemporary renaissance of minority literatures allows us to resituate Shakespeare's Renaissance in a wider field. The relation between the two renaissances is then figured as a triangulation, the two points providing a powerful resource for articulating crucial issues in our own historical period' (175–6). A decade after the publication of Erickson's book, we focus our study on how Canadians have shaped our own identities through rewriting and restaging Shakespeare, demonstrating how Canadian critics bring the special inflections of their Canadian preoccupations and experiences to their scholarship on Shakespeare.

Like Michael Bristol in *Big-Time Shakespeare*, we have hoped 'to set out a way of reading that will help to bridge the gap between the conservative demand for unreflective affirmation of the ideals and achievements of Western civilisation and the equally unhelpful oppositional programs of compulsive resistance and critique' (146). But negotiations within this terrain of the middle ground need not take a single route, and our collection is the stronger for the genuine dialogue and disagreements that emerge across our approaches to these questions. In general, the experience of invoking Shakespeare in Canada tends to confirm the judgment of W.B. Worthen that, although 'legitimating the Author *is* a way of authorizing ourselves,' this excessive veneration of the Shakespearean author-function may backfire, in that it tends to 'reify Shakespearean drama – and the past, the tradition it represents – as sacred text, as silent hieroglyphics we can only scan, interpret, struggle to decode ...' The result is that we may impoverish 'the work of our own performances, and the work of the plays in our making of the world' ('Staging' 25). The work in this collection provides ample proof, were proof required, of Dennis Salter's assertion that Canadian anglophilia has 'sought to authorize Shakespeare himself as a natural – that is, stable, lasting, and pervasive – symbol of imperial/colonial relations. English-Canadian actors' attitudes towards Shakespeare ... have therefore tended to be ... predicated on the assumption that it is they who must adapt themselves to Shakespeare, not Shakespeare who must adapt himself to them ('Acting' 118–19).

But our work also concludes that anglophilia is only part of the Canadian story. Other historical forces and compelling social issues countered (and continue to counter) these tendencies, hegemonic as they once were. Appropriation, and other forms of Shakespearean interpretation, are complex and contingent processes, whose motivations, enactments, and receptions are seldom predicable. As Paik Nak-chung argues in an essay on 'Nations and Literatures in the Age of Globalization,' Shakespeare's mobilization within 'the cause of cultural imperialism demands constant watchfulness; for all that, we do not wish – indeed cannot afford – to do without the emancipatory potentials we may find in him' (220). Ultimately, it is this emancipatory potential, within writing, reading, and performance traditions developed and recalibrated to meet the needs of specific communities within diverse Canadian localities, that this volume celebrates, interrogates, and seeks to renew.

Note

1 For an article describing this ad, see Aniko Bodroghkozy, '"I ... Am ... Canadian!" Examining Popular Culture in Canada: Recent Books.' *Topia* 5 (2001): 109-18. In a further ironic twist on nationalism's uneasy alliance with globalization, the *Canadian Forum*, one of Canada's most influential cultural journals over the last half-century, ceased publication shortly after the appearance of this issue, although plans are, as I write, currently under way to revive it again.

Appendix

Research Opportunities in Canadian Shakespeare

JESSICA SCHAGERL

Now as to Shakespeare's influence on our ideas and our language – the last point on which I wish to touch – it is not easy to exaggerate its past extent, or its still growing increase.

– Thomas D'Arcy McGee, 'Tercentenary' 58

Shakespeare's appearance in 1876 outside Mrs Morrison's Grand Opera House and the Royal Opera House in Toronto, as depicted in the cartoon below, encapsulates both the easy familiarity and the fascination of (some) nineteenth-century Canadians with the Bard. While drawn here by the most famous of Canada's caricaturists from the second half of the nineteenth century, John Wilson Bengough, who frequently employed references to the Bard in his cartoons, Shakespeare, at least since the mid-nineteenth century, also figures in an extremely wide range of material including memoirs, scrapbooks, program notes, parodies, allusions, caricatures, and adaptations. The National Archives of Canada and the National Library of Canada house a treasure trove of material on Shakespeare reception in English-speaking Canada. The records of politicians, writers, actors, scholars, suffragettes, 'ordinary' theatregoers – hitherto the exclusive purview of Canadian historians and literature specialists – offer Shakespeareans a still little explored source for a study both of Shakespearean reception and of Canadian intellectual life and the place of the classic in it.

Bengough's caricature also brings together the twin themes of moral instruction and anti-theatrical prejudice that are found in many of the literary discourses of the period and that may be an inheritance of English-Canadian puritanism. 'The Pulpit and the Stage' has William

Appendix 411

John William Bengough, 'The Pulpit and the Stage,' *Grip* (Toronto), vol. 8, no. 4, 1876, p. 3, reproduced with permission from the National Library of Canada.

Shakespeare, standing outside the theatres in early modern dress, speaking Hamlet's advice to the players. This casual, passing reference to Shakespeare in Canada, made as a visually recognizable caricature of the Droeshout engraving from the First Folio (1623), represents Shakespeare holding his own tome, labelled 'Shakspere.' Captioned with a quotation from *Hamlet*, the caricature both invokes Shakespeare's cultural authority and subverts it, much like the general use made of 'Shakespeare' in the print culture. There, the travesty of select Shakespearean passages or scenes frequently responds to immediate contemporary concerns, such as on the severe weather conditions in Toronto ('Once more into the coats, dear friends'), and suggests the thoroughness with which Shakespeare has been assimilated into Canadian culture.

'The Pulpit and the Stage,' as I have suggested, holds in balance two opposing views of the theatre in nineteenth-century Canada: one view, represented by Shakespeare, shows the theatre's capacity to instruct the population. Thus, Joseph Howe, one of Canada's Fathers of Confederation, for instance, claims that the plays provide 'infinite instruction and delight' (24). The other view stresses the opposite, emphasizing, as in the cartoon, the potential for the theatre to be not only libellous and the cause of social disruption but also a magnet drawing people away from the church – as the broadsheet announcement held by one of Shakespeare's antagonists reads: 'The stage is utterly bad and should be shunned by all Christians.' It is testimony to Shakespeare's prominence – and currency – as a visual icon that his depiction is intended to balance the four figures to the left of the image. Thus, the image of Shakespeare serves a dual effect, in that it both implicitly authorizes theatrical production and damns the figures who seek to close the theatres. By highlighting the contemporaneity of Shakespeare and the applicability of various plays to Canada, these nineteenth-century examples show that twentieth-century commentators are not the only ones able 'to update and resituate the Shakespearean text' (Salter, 'Acting' 127).

Apart from chronicling general attitudes towards the theatre and Shakespearean stage history, primary source material can prove useful in other ways, for instance, in providing an index of the popularity of certain plays and certain touring companies. Thus, the Agnes Baskerville Sherry Collection (MG 30–D131),[1] an album consisting mainly of programs from theatres in Ottawa, contains, among other things, details of an amateur production of the trial scene of *The Merchant of Venice* in which Agnes Baskerville played Portia, 'with much dignity and simplicity,' and programs for *Romeo and Juliet* (1902), *Macbeth* (1902), *Cymbeline* (1907), and *As You Like It* (1907). Likewise, the Elizabeth M. Coffin collection (MG 30–D138), a scrapbook collection of professional and amateur theatre programs dating from 1910 to 1960, contains programs for Sir John Martin-Harvey's tour performing *Richard III* (1926) and programs for Shakespearean productions at the Canadian Repertory Theatre and the Ottawa Little Theatre.

The involvement of women in the production of Shakespeare is another area where archival material could be richly drawn upon. For instance, Julia Wales Grace (MG 30–C238) – born in the Eastern Townships, educated at McGill University (BA 1903) and Radcliffe College (MA 1904) – made a name for herself as both a peace activist and a Shakespeare scholar at the University of Wisconsin (where she accepted her PhD in 1926). Most relevant for Canadian Shakespeare are her writings and publications as a Shakespeare scholar, but the collection also has excerpts of an unpublished memoir, correspondence, and materials related to her participation in the peace movement during and after the First World War. During the time of the war (and before, looking back to the nineteenth century), women also played a chief role in drama guilds, like the Ottawa Women's University Club (which later became the Ottawa Drama League) and Shakespeare clubs (like those founded in Montreal and Toronto).

For both amateur and professional theatre history in the early twentieth century, in fact, the collection Theatre Canada (MG 28–I50) is of much interest. It contains material related to the Dominion Drama Festival, including correspondence with the Earl of Bessborough, then governor general of Canada. This collection also includes nominal files, programs, scrapbooks, microfilm accounts, and sound recordings of varying quality. The Ottawa Little Theatre's collection (MG 28–I 30) reaches back to its inception as the Ottawa Dramatic League and contains material that complements the Theatre Canada holdings, particularly related to the formation of the Dominion Drama Festival. The Ottawa Little Theatre Collection chronicles in vivid detail the hardships suffered by Canadian theatres, recording a fire, declining attendance, management crises; however, it also documents the use of the theatre to raise morale during the war and efforts to encourage children to make theatre a part of their lives.

Robertson Davies, whose interest in the theatre and Shakespeare is well known, fits into a discussion of touring companies and the beginnings of a national theatre. The Robertson Davies Fonds (MG 30–D362) has an archival collection related to Sir John Martin-Harvey, who toured Canada and the United States with popular productions of Shakespeare and who occasionally lectured on the theatre at the Empire and Canadian clubs. The collection necessarily contains Davies's own work, including his winning entry in the Dominion Drama Festival play-writing contest. But Davies was certainly not the only Canadian literary figure to engage with Shakespeare on a creative and critical level. The National Archives has several other collections of potential interest, at least one of which intersects with above-mentioned collections. Wilfred Eggleston participated in a reading circle with Duncan Campbell Scott (who at one time headed the Ottawa Little Theatre); his collection contains portions of his memoir *Literary Friends* and his edited version of the correspondence between Ephraim Weber (his former English teacher) and Lucy Maud Montgomery, among other items (MG 30–D282). Another head of the Ottawa Little Theatre, the writer and journalist Madge Macbeth (MG 30–D52), was president of the Canadian Author's Association. Wilson Pugsley MacDonald (MG 30–D279) and George Johnson (MG 30–D11) also both wrote on Shakespeare: MacDonald's collection includes an unpublished history of William Shakespeare and his works, and Johnson wrote notes and essays on Shakespeare, among other topics.

In addition to the Stratford Festival Archives (found in Stratford, Ontario), researchers chronicling the stage history of the Stratford Festival may be interested in director John Hirsch Fonds (MG 31–D81), the Amelia Hall Fonds (MG 30–D324), and the Leo Ciceri Fonds (MG 31–D205). Beginning with his career at the Winnipeg Little Theatre, Hirsch's collection contains personal papers, clippings, programs, and production and subject files related to the Stratford Festival. The Amelia Hall Fonds contains a wide range of documentary evidence about Hall's career (including the Ottawa Drama League, the Junior Theatre in Ottawa, the Montreal Repertory Theatre, the Canadian Repertory Theatre, and the Stratford Festival) and events and organizations related to theatre in Canada (c. 1890–1984). The Ciceri collection includes personal correspondence, diaries, scrapbooks, programs, clippings, and photographs spanning his career from his start at McGill University to the Open Air Playhouse, the Montreal Drama Guild, the Shakespeare Society of Montreal, and the Montreal Repertory Theatre, with which he was affiliated for a large part of his career. The archival holdings of another Montrealer renowned for his Shakespeare, Charles Burket Rittenhouse (MG 30–D315), also hold promise: this collection shows the work of the actor, director, producer, and teacher, through personal material, teaching notes, playscripts, manuscripts, music scores, and theatre programs. Among other notable directors and actors whose papers are at the National Archives, the Fonds Gilles Provost (MG 31–D93) is a microfilm collection of material related to the Canadian Repertory Theatre, including clippings, programs, and photographs; the Fonds Gratien Gélinas (MG 30–D406) chronicles the more than fifty years spent in the theatre by the director, writer, actor, and cultural administrator; the John Michael Meiklejohn Fonds contains a manuscript memoir by Michael Meiklejohn about his experiences with the Dominion Drama Festival and theatre in Canada (Reference #119-0201 10-0); and lastly, the Andrew Allan Fonds (MG 31–D56) and Lister Sinclair Fonds (MG 31–D44) both relate to the *Stage* series created for CBC Productions (discussed in more detail by Marta Straznicky in this volume).

While a large part of these fonds is necessarily centred on the theatre in Ottawa, the National Archives and National Library also house material relevant to other regions. London (Ontario's) Grand Theatre is a good example. The Grand Theatre Poster Collection is part of the Documentary Art collections of the National Archives; one of the striking visual images in this collection is a photomechanical print entitled 'Educating Rita,' with the description: 'Rita's hair is dried in a beauty salon while she reads Shakespeare hidden behind a tabloid paper' (DAP/ADP: 1993–394–73). In another collection of photographs (DAP/ADP: 1982–153, box 4727), Kate Reid and Barbara Hamilton are shown in a 1959–60 London, Ontario, production of *The Taming of the Shrew*.

In addition to these varied and eclectic sources, complementary material is held in local archives and in private collections throughout Canada. Nearly all major centres and quite a few smaller towns – in English-speaking Canada especially – have had a prolonged engagement with Shakespeare, chiefly through performance. Shakespeare, thus, *can* have a Canadian accent (see Loomba and Orkin 7). Despite this continued fascination, many questions still remain unanswered and unexplored: the nature and composition of the reading and theatrical audiences; the origins and identity of many of the anonymous writers and satirists who employed Shakespearean allusions; and, most broadly, the Canadian role in the complex processes of larger issues of cultural transmission, appropriation, and transformation.

Note

1 All files referred to in this Appendix are in the National Archives of Canada.

References

1892 Programme for Canada's Great Industrial Fair ... Sept 5 to 17th ..., File C3–0–1–00. Canadian National Exhibition Archives, Toronto.

1969 Stratford Festival Programme. National Library of Canada, Ottawa.

Abarca, Pauline D. Rev. of *Les Reines*, dir. André Brassard. Théâtre d'Aujourd'hui, Montreal. *Theatrum* 23 (1991): 35–6.

Adamson, Joseph. 'The Treason of the Clerks: Frye, Ideology, and the Authority of Imaginative Culture.' Boyd and Salusinszky 72–102.

Adorno, Theodor W. *The Jargon of Authenticity*. Trans. by Knut Tarnowski and Frederic Will. Evanston, Ill.: Northwestern UP, 1973.

Allan, Andrew. 'Andrew Allan Says.' Interview with Fred Davies. *The Performing Arts in Canada*. Summer 1963: 4+. Andrew Allan.

– 'Andrew Allan Talks about Canadian Talent.' *Radio World* 28 Sept. 1946. Andrew Allan.

– 'Broadcast Drama.' *CFRB Tenth Anniversary Year Book*. Andrew Allan.

– 'Cheers and Jeers.' *Radio World* 2 Aug. 1947. CBC Correspondence 1944–57. 31 D56, vol. 21. Andrew Allan Papers.

– 'An Exciting Episode of English History.' *CBC Times* 21 Feb. 1954: 3.

– Internal memo, CBC Radio, Toronto. 19 April 1951. CBC Correspondence and Memos. MG 31–D56, vol. 21. Andrew Allan Papers.

– Letter to General Supervisor of Programs. 20 March 1946. RG 41, vol. 210, file 11–19 part 1. National Archives, Ottawa.

– *Self-Portrait*. Toronto: Macmillan 1974.

– 'Shakespeare.' *CBC Times* 18 Oct. 1953: 2+.

– 'Shakespeare's Histories: A Talk by Allan Andrew.' Shakespeare. 31 D56, vol. 18. Andrew Allan Papers.

– 'The Sound of Shakespeare.' Address to the Toronto Shakespeare Society, 1964. Shakespeare.

- 'A Stage in "The Stages."' *CBC Times* 23 Jan. 1949: 2+.
- Untitled. Shakespeare. Ts. 31 D56, vol. 18. Andrew Allan Papers.
- Untitled typescript for a radio talk. Shakespeare. Ts. 31 D56, vol. 18. Andrew Allan Papers.

Allen, Graham. Radio talk on 'Critically Speaking.' 19 June 1949. Wednesday Night.

Allibone, S. Austin. *A Critical Dictionary of English Literature and British and American Authors ...*, 3 vols. Philadelphia: J.B. Lippincott, 1897.

Anderson, Benedict. *Imagined Communities: Reflections on the Origin and Spread of Nationalism.* London: Verso, 1991.

Andrès, Bernard, and Paul Lefèbvre. '"Macbeth"/théâtre de la manufacture.' *Cahiers de théâtre Jeu* 11 (1979): 80–8.

Andrew Allan [file]. CBC Reference Library, Toronto.

Andrew Allan Papers. National Archives, Ottawa.

Annual Birthday Dinner, 1943–1969. File 13. Papers of the Shakespeare Society.

Anon. 'Halifax troupe does "lost play" by Shakespeare.' Ottawa *Citizen*, 5 October 1998, Arts Section 2.

'Another Successful Day at the Great National Exhibition.' *Empire* [Toronto] 8 Sept. 1892: 2.

An Appeal to Pride. Administration/Fund Raising Literature (Campaign) 1956–. Stratford Festival Archives, Stratford, Ont.

Appleton, Elizabeth. *Edward de Vere and the War of Words.* Toronto: Elizabethan P, 1985.

- *Supplementary Appendices to Edward de Vere and the War of Words.* Toronto: Elizabethan P, 1985.

Arnold, Matthew. *Culture and Anarchy.* 1869. Ed. J. Dover Wilson. Cambridge: Cambridge UP, 1955.

Ashley, Audrey M. '*As You Like It* set in Quebec is full of mischief.' Rev. of *As You Like It,* dir. Richard Monette. Stratford Festival. Festival Theatre, Stratford, Ont. *Beacon Herald* [Stratford, Ont.] 31 May 1990: 1.

- 'Feore makes Hamlet's familiar words his own.' Rev. of *Hamlet,* dir. David William. Stratford Festival. Festival Theatre, Stratford, Ont. *Stratford Beacon Herald* 28 May 1991: 1+.

Assmann, Aleida. 'The Curse and Blessing of Babel; or, Looking Back on Universalisms.' *The Translatability of Cultures: Figurations of the Space Between.* Ed. Sanford Budick and Wolfgang Iser. Stanford, Calif.: Stanford UP, 1996. 85–100.

As You Like It. By William Shakespeare. Dir. Richard Monette. Stratford Festival. Festival Theatre, Stratford, Ont. 1990.

Attali, Jacques. *Dictionnaire du XXIe siècle.* Paris: Fayard 1998.

Avigdor, Jeanine C. 'John Scadding's Cabin.' *York Pioneer* 13 (1988): 2–11.
- 'The Scadding Cabin 1794. Toronto's Oldest House.' *York Pioneer* 89 (1994), spec. insert: 1–27.

Ayre, John. *Northrop Frye: A Biography*. Toronto: Random House, 1989.

Bacon, Delia. *The Philosophy of the Plays of Shakspere [sic] Unfolded*. London: Broombridge, 1857.
- 'William Shakespeare and His Plays: An Inquiry concerning Them.' *Putnam's Monthly* 7.37 (1856): 1–19.

Bacon, Theodore. *Delia Bacon: A Biographical Sketch*. Boston: Houghton, Mifflin, 1888.

Bains, Yashdip S. *English Canadian Theatre, 1765–1826*. Bern: Peter Lang, 1998.

Bannerji, Himani. *The Dark Side of the Nation: Essays on Multiculturalism, Nationalism and Gender*. Toronto: Canadian Scholars' P, 2000.

Barish, Jonas. *The Antitheatrical Prejudice*. Berkeley: U of California P, 1981.

Barthes, Roland. *S/Z*. Trans. Richard Miller. London: Jonathan Cape, 1974.

Bate, Jonathan. 'Golden Lads and Chimney-Sweepers.' In 'The Ghost of Shakespeare.' *Harper's Magazine* April 1999: 60–2.
- 'Shakespearean nationhoods.' Hattaway, Sokolova, and Roper 112–29.

Baylis, Samuel Mathewson. *'Shake-Speare': An Inquiry*. Toronto: William Briggs, 1910.
- *At the Sign of the Beaver*. Toronto: William Briggs, 1907.

Baxter, Arthur Beverly. 'The Birth of the National Theatre.' Rubin 38–43.

'Beat nerves, 17 rivals/won Shakespeare Cup.' *Telegram* [Toronto] 8 Feb. 1956: 29.

Beauchamp, Hélène. 'The Repère Cycles: From Basic to Continuous Education.' *Canadian Theatre Review (CTR)* 78 (1994): 26–31.

Beckett, Samuel. *Waiting for Godot*. London: Faber and Faber, 1956.

Bélair, Michel. *Le nouveau théâtre québécois*. Ottawa: Leméac, 1973.

Belsey, Catherine. *Critical Practice*. London: Routledge, 1980.

Bemrose, John. 'Emasculated Lear Loses Its Potency.' Rev. of *The Tragedie of King Lear*, dir. Richard Rose. Necessary Angel Theatre Co. Canadian Stage, Berkeley Street Theatre Upstairs, Toronto. *Maclean's* 3 April 1995: 65.

Bengough, J.W. 'The Pulpit and the Stage.' Cartoon. *Grip* [Toronto] 16 Dec. 1876: 2.

Benjamin, Walter. 'Theses on the Philosophy of History.' *Illuminations*. Ed. Hannah Arendt. Trans. Harry Zohn. New York: Schocken, 1969. 253–64.

Bennett, Susan. *Performing Nostalgia: Shifting Shakespeare and the Contemporary Past*. London: Routledge, 1996.
- 'Politics of the Gaze: Challenges in Canadian Women's Theatre.' *Canadian Theatre Review* 59 (1989): 11–14.

Benson, Eugene, and L.W. Conolly. *English-Canadian Theatre.* Toronto: Oxford UP, 1987.

Béraud, Jean. *350 ans de théâtre au Canada Français.* Ottawa: Le Cercle du Livre de France, 1958.

Berger, Carl. *The Sense of Power: Studies in the Ideas of Canadian Imperialism, 1867–1914.* Toronto: U of Toronto P, 1970.

Berger, Harry. *Imaginary Audition.* Berkeley: U of California P, 1989.

– 'Text against Performance in Shakespeare: The Example of *Macbeth.*' *The Power of Forms.* Ed. Stephen Greenblatt. Norman, Okla.: Pilgrim, 1982. 49–81.

Berger, John. *Ways of Seeing.* 1972. Harmondsworth, U.K.: Penguin, 1976.

Berry, Ralph. *On Directing Shakespeare: Interviews with Contemporary Directors.* London: Hamish Hamilton, 1989.

Bertoldi, Andreas. 'Shakespeare, Psychoanalysis and the Colonial Encounter: The Case of Wulf Sachs's *Black Hamlet,*' Loomba and Orkin, *Post-Colonial* 235–58.

Berton, Pierre. 'Everybody Boos the CBC.' *Maclean's* 1 Dec. 1950: 7+.

Bessai, Diane. 'The Regionalism of Canadian Theatre.' *Canadian Literature* 85 (1980): 7–20.

Bhabha, Homi K. *The Location of Culture.* New York: Routledge, 1994.

Birthday Dinner Programs. Annual Birthday Dinner.

'Birthday of Shakespeare Being Commemorated Here.' Toronto *Daily Star* 22 April 1933: 22.

Black, Hugh. 'Bacon's Claim and Shakespeare's "Aye."' *North American Review* 145 (1887): 422–6.

Blais, Marie-Christine. 'Un songe qui brasse et retrousse.' Rev. of *Le Songe d'une nuit d'été,* adapt. and dir. Oleg Kisseliov. Théâtre Espace La Veillée, Montreal. *La Presse* [Montreal] 3 Oct. 1998: D12.

Bloom, Harold. *Shakespeare: The Invention of the Human.* New York: Riverhead Books, 1998.

– *The Western Canon: The Books and School of the Ages.* New York: Harcourt Brace, 1994.

Boal, Augusto. *The Rainbow of Desire: The Boal Method of Theatre and Therapy.* Trans. Adrian Jackson. London: Routledge, 1995.

Boling, Ronald. Untitled. Shakespeare Association of America. Renaissance Cleveland Hotel, Cleveland. 21 March 1998.

Bolster, Charles Gordon. 'Shakespeare in French Canada.' MA thesis. U of New Brunswick, 1970.

Bono, Norman de. 'Monette's direction not intentionally political.' Rev. of *As You Like It,* dir. Richard Monette. Stratford Festival. Festival Theatre, Stratford, Ont. *Beacon Herald* [Stratford, Ont.] 26 May 1990, Festival ed.: 86.

Boulanger, Luc. 'La Mégère apprivoisée: Détournement majeur.' Rev. of *La Mégère apprivoisée*, adapt. Marco Micone, dir. Martine Beaulne. Théâtre du Nouveau Monde, Montreal. *Voir* [Montreal] 23–29 March 1995: 34.
Brady, Owen E. '*Twelfth Night, Hamlet, Much Ado About Nothing.*' *Theatre Journal* 44.2 (1992): 237–43.
Brathwaite, Edward Kamau. *History of the Voice*. London: New Beacon, 1984.
Brecht, Bertolt. *Brecht on Theatre*. Trans. John Willett. New York: Hill and Wang, 1964.
Brisset, Annie. *Sociocritique de la traduction: Théâtre et altérité au Québec (1968–1988)*. Longueuil: Préambule, 1990.
Bristol, Michael. *Big-Time Shakespeare*. London: Routledge, 1996.
– *Shakespeare's America. America's Shakespeare*. London: Routledge, 1990.
Brook, Peter. *The Empty Space*. Harmondsworth, U.K.: Penguin, 1972.
Brookes, Chris. *A Public Nuisance: A History of the Mummers Troupe*. Social and Economic Studies 36. St John's: Institute of Social and Economic Research, Memorial U of Newfoundland (ISER), 1998.
Brotton, Jerry. '"This Tunis, sir, was Carthage": Contesting Colonialism in *The Tempest*.' Loomba and Orkin, *Post-Colonial* 23–42.
Brown, Paul. '"This Thing of Darkness I Acknowledge Mine": *The Tempest* and the Discourse of Colonialism.' Dollimore and Sinfield 48–71.
Brown, Stewart. '*As You Like It*, Or how the Bard met Johnny Canuck.' Rev. of *As You Like It*, dir. Richard Monette. Stratford Festival. Festival Theatre, Stratford, Ont. Hamilton *Spectator* 31 May 1990: B1.
Brydon, Diana. 'Sister Letters: Miranda's Tempest in Canada.' Novy 165–84.
– 'Tempest Plainsong: Retuning Caliban's Curse.' *Transforming Shakespeare: Contemporary Women's Re-visions in Literature and Performance*. Ed. Marianne Novy. New York: St Martin's P, 1999. 199–216.
Bucke, R.M. [Richard Maurice]. 'Bacon's Cipher on Shakespeare's Tombstone.' *Canadian Magazine* Jan. 1900: 272–5.
– *Richard Maurice Bucke, Medical Mystic: Letters of Dr. Bucke to Walt Whitman and His Friends*. Ed. Artem Lozynsky. Detroit: Wayne State UP, 1977.
– 'Shakespeare or Bacon?' *Canadian Magazine* September 1897: 363–78. Published simultaneously in England as 'Shakespeare Dethroned.' *Pearson's Magazine* 4 (1897): 642–54.
– *Walt Whitman*. Philadelphia: David McKay, 1883.
Bulman, James C., ed. *Shakespeare, Theory, and Performance*. New York: Routledge, 1996.
Burdett, Lois, and Christine Coburn. *Twelfth Night for Kids*. Windsor: Black Moss P, 1994.
Burnet, Jean. 'Multiculturalism.' *Canadian Encyclopedia*.

Burnett, Linda. 'Margaret Clarke's *Gertrude and Ophelia*: Writing Revisionist Culture, Writing a Feminist "New Poetics."' *Essays in Theatre* 16.1 (1997): 15–32.

Burnside Reading Group: Financial Record, 1956–8. File 24. Papers of the Shakespeare Society.

Burt, Richard. *Unspeakable ShaXXXspeares: Queer Theory and American Kiddie Culture.* New York: St Martin's P, 1998.

Caillou, Allan [Alan Lyle-Smith]. 'Short History of the Festival.' Caillou, Walter, and Chappell.

– Arnold M. Walter and Frank Chappell. *The Shakespeare Festival: A Short History of the Initial Five Years of Canada's First Shakespeare Festival 1949–1954*. Toronto: Ryerson P, 1954.

Campbell, Marion. Introduction. *Shakespeare's Books* 1–5.

Canada. House of Commons. Special Committee on Reconstruction and Reestablishment. *Minutes of Proceedings and Evidence.* No. 10. June 1944.

– Royal Commission on National Development in the Arts, Letters and Sciences [Massey Commission]. *Report: Royal Commission on National Development in the Arts, Letters and Sciences, 1949–1951* [Massey Report]. Ottawa: Edmond Cloutier, 1951.

– *Royal Commission Studies: A Selection of Essays Prepared for the Royal Commission on National Development in the Arts, Letters and Sciences.* Ottawa: Edmond Cloutier, 1951.

'Canadian citizen aptly portrayed by Judge Riddell.' *Globe* [Toronto] 26 April 1929: 16.

The Canadian Encyclopedia 2000: World Edition. CD-ROM. Toronto: McClelland and Stewart, 1999.

Canadian Press. 'Employment equity drawing vocal critics (Ontario).' Canadian Press Newswire 8 Sept. 1994.

The Canadian Who's Who. 35 vols. Toronto: U of Toronto P, 1910–2000.

Cappel, Manuel. Letter. 'Full fathom five.' *Globe and Mail* 10 Aug. 1996: D7.

Cartelli, Thomas. *Repositioning Shakespeare: National Formations, Postcolonial Appropriations.* New York: Routledge, 1999.

Cavendish, Richard. *The Tarot.* New York: Harper and Row, 1975.

CBC Annual Report. Toronto: CBC, 1939, 1948.

CBC Drama and Features: Five Years of Achievement, 1936–1941. Toronto: CBC, n.d. RG 41, vol. 210, file 11–19 part 1. National Archives, Ottawa.

CBC Press Release. 21 Nov. 1947. Wednesday Night.

Césaire, Aimé. *Une Tempête: d'après 'La Tempête' de Shakespeare: adaptation pour un théâtre nègre.* Paris: Du Seuil, 1969.

Chapman, Geoff. 'A brittle exploration of race and gender.' Rev. of *Harlem Duet*, dir. Djanet Sears. Tarragon Extra Space, Nightwood Theatre; Canadian Stage, Berkeley Street Theatre, Toronto. Toronto *Star* 2 Nov. 1997: C6.
- 'Cross-casting makes us Leery of this *King Lear*.' Toronto *Star* 26 March 1995: C4.
- '*Hamlet* a dazzling start for Stratford Season.' Rev. of *Hamlet*, dir. David William. Stratford Festival. Festival Theatre, Stratford, Ont. Toronto *Star* 28 May 1991: D1.
- 'Ouimette's Hamlet vivid and accessible.' Rev. of *Hamlet*, dir. Richard Monette. Stratford Festival. Tom Patterson Theatre, Stratford, Ont. Toronto *Star* 3 June 1994: F8.

Charney, Maurice, and Hanna Charney. 'The Language of Shakespeare's Madwomen.' *Signs* 3.2 (1977): 451–60.

Chaurette, Normand. *The Queens*. 1992. Trans. Linda Gaboriau. Vancouver: Talonbooks, 1998.
- *Fragments d'un lettre d'adieu lus par les géologues*. Montreal: Éditions Leméac, 1988.
- *Provincetown Playhouse, juillet 1919, j'avais 19 ans*. Montreal: Éditions Leméac, 1982.
- *Les Reines*. Montréal: Editions Actes-Sud/Leméac, 1991.

Chen, Xiaomei. 'Occidentalist Theatre in Post-Mao China: Shakespeare, Ibsen, and Brecht as Counter-Others.' Palumbo-Liu and Gumbrecht 155–78.

Choquette, Dominique. Rev. of *Le Songe d'une nuit d'été*, adapt. and dir. Oleg Kiseliov. Théâtre de la Veillée, Montreal. *Mag Plus Ultra* CIBL, Montreal. 5 Oct. 1998.

Clarke, Cecil. 'The Stratford Festival Theatre.' *Stratford Festival Souvenir Program 1953*.
- 'Stratford Ontario (Canada).' *World Theatre* 5 (1955–6): 42–50.

Clarke, Margaret. 'Gertrude and Ophelia.' *Theatrum* 33 (1993): S1–S15.

Clarke, Mary Cowden. Letter to Rev. Henry Scadding. 6 Sept. 1864. The letter is pasted to the flyleaf of Scadding's copy of Clarke's *Complete Concordance to Shakespeare*. Thomas Fisher Rare Book Library, U of Toronto.

Cohen, Nathan. 'Across the Footlights.' CJBC Radio Broadcast, Toronto. 10 Jan. 1951.
- Editorial. *The Critic* 1.10 (1951): 1. Nathan Cohen Papers. National Archives, Ottawa.
- 'Stratford after Fifteen Years.' *Queen's Quarterly* 75 (1968): 35–61. Rpt. in Rubin 259–77.
- 'Stratford So Far.' *Saturday Night* August 1963: 7–9.

- 'Theatre Notes: Tyrone Guthrie – A Minority Report.' *Queen's Quarterly* 62 (1955): 423–6.
- 'Theatre Today: English Canada.' *Tamarack Review* 13 (1959): 24–37. Rpt. in Rubin 228–37.
- *Views the Shows*. CJBC, Toronto. 11 July 1954, 24 July 1955, 1 Jan. 1956.

'A Company of Fools: History.' *A Company of Fools dot com*. Online. 20 March 2000. <www.cyberus.ca/~fools/history.html>.

Connerton, Paul. *How Societies Remember*. Cambridge, U.K.: Cambridge UP, 1989.

Constitution and By-Laws [of the Shakespeare Society of Toronto] (undated). N. Horn Papers. File 9. Papers of the Shakespeare Society.

Cotnoir, Diane. 'Directing in Quebec.' Trans. Mark Czarnecki. A. Wagner, *Contemporary* 300–10.

Coulbourn, John. 'Fit for a King: Janet Wright Proves She's Woman Enough for her Role as *King Lear*.' Rev. of *The Tragedie of King Lear*, dir. Richard Rose. Necessary Angel Theatre Co. Canadian Stage, Berkeley Street Theatre Upstairs, Toronto. *Sunday Sun* [Toronto] 19 March 1995: 14.

- 'Her Majesty the King.' Rev. of *The Tragedie of King Lear*, dir. Richard Rose. Necessary Angel Theatre Co. Canadian Stage, Berkeley Street Theatre Upstairs, Toronto. *Saturday Sun* [Toronto] 25 March 1995: 47.

Coulson, Herbert. Letter to *Wednesday Night*. 'Wednesday Night – Audience.'

Coulter, John. 'Some Festival Visions of a National Theatre.' *Saturday Night* 17 May 1947: 20–1.

Coursen, H.R. 'Two Productions of Hamlet: Stratford and Ashland.' Rev. of *Hamlet*, dir. Richard Monette. Stratford Festival. Tom Patterson Theatre, Stratford, Ont. (1994). Rev. of *Hamlet*, dir. Henry Woronicz. Oregon Shakespeare Festival. Angus Bowmer Theatre, Ashland, Oreg. (1994). *Shakespeare Quarterly* 47.1 (1996): 61–72.

Cowan, Jennifer. 'Take Two: The Play's the Thing in Toronto and Stratford Where 2 Different Hamlets Unfold.' *Toronto Life Fashion* Summer 1991: 48.

Coyne, James H. *Richard Maurice Bucke: A Sketch*. Transactions of the Royal Society of Canada. 2nd ser. 1906–7, vol. 12, sec. 2. Toronto: Royal Society of Canada, 1906. 159–96.

Craig, Joanne. 'Hamlet at the Festival Theatre in Stratford, Ontario, Canada.' *Hamlet Studies* 14.1–2 (1992): 88–90.

Craig, Thelma. 'Little-known tragedy of Shakespeare staged.' Rev. of *Timon of Athens*. Shakespeare Society of Toronto. Hart House, Toronto. *Globe and Mail* 1 March 1940: 4.

Crawford, Alexander W. *Hamlet, an Ideal Prince*. Boston, Toronto: R.G. Badger, Copp Clark, 1916.

Crew, Robert. 'Desdemona delicious fun.' Rev. of *Goodnight Desdemona (Good*

Morning Juliet), dir. Baṇuta Rubess. Stage Downstairs, Nightwood Theatre, Toronto. Toronto *Star* 29 March 1990. C3.

Critically Speaking. CBC Radio, Toronto. 9 Jan. 1949. Wednesday Night.

Crowley, D.J. *Understanding Communication: The Signifying Web.* Ed. Lee Thayer. Communication and the Human Condition 2. New York: Gordon and Breach, 1982.

Cushman, Robert. 'Modernize the Bard? No Way!' *Globe and Mail* 2 Dec. 1997: D6.

– 'Shakespeare as it was meant to be performed.' *National Post* 2 March 1999: B9.

Dafoe, Chris. 'Duke of Darkness.' Rev. of *Richard III*, dir. Robin Phillips. Citadel Theatre, Edmonton. *Globe and Mail* 7 Feb. 1995: D2.

– 'Stylish Hamlet short on substance.' Rev. of *Hamlet*, dir. Henry Woolf. Shakespeare on the Saskatchewan, Saskatoon, Sask. *Globe and Mail* 12 July 1996: A11.

Davey, Frank. *Canadian Literary Power.* Edmonton: NeWest, 1994.

David, Gilbert. 'Le dernier-né de Paula de Vasconcelos.' Rev. of *Le Making of de Macbeth*, by Jean-Frédéric Messier, based on an original idea by Paula de Vasconcelos, dir. Paula de Vasconcelos. Pigeons International. Salle Beverly Webster Rolph, Musée d'Art Contemporain, Montreal. *Le Devoir* [Montreal] 6–7 April 1996: B3.

– 'Shakespeare au Québec: théâtrographie des productions francophones (1945–1998).' *L'Annuaire théâtral* 24 (1998): 117–38.

Davies, Robertson. 'The Director.' Guthrie, Davies, and Macdonald, *Renown* 35–40.

– Foreword. Pettigrew and Portman I: xiii–xv. (Foreword)

– 'Future of the Festival.' *The Stratford Festival Souvenir Program 1954.*

– 'The Genius of Dr. Guthrie.' *Theatre Arts* March 1956: 28–30+.

– 'Shakespeare Living and Dead.' *Saturday Night* 11 June 1955: 21–2.

– 'The Theatre.' Canada, *Report* 192–200. Rpt. in Rubin 175–83.

– 'The Theatre: A Dialogue on the State of the Theatre in Canada.' Canada, *Royal* 369–92. Rpt. in Rubin 155–75.

– 'Through Ritual to Romance.' *Saturday Night* 1 August 1953: 7–8.

Dawson, Anthony B. *Hamlet: Shakespeare in Performance.* Manchester: Manchester UP, 1997.

– 'The Impasse over the Stage.' *English Literary Renaissance* 21.3 (1991): 309–27.

Dawson, Anthony B., and Paul Yachnin. *The Culture of Playgoing in Shakespeare's England: A Collaborative Debate.* Cambridge: Cambridge UP, 2001.

Day, Moira. 'Shakespeare on the Saskatchewan 1985–1990: "The Stratford of the West" (NOT).' *Essays in Theatre/Études théâtrales* 15.1 (1996): 69–90.

Debord, Guy. *The Society of the Spectacle.* Trans. Donald Nicholson-Smith. New York: Zone Books, 1994.

Denham, Robert D. 'Interpenetration as a Key Concept in Frye's Critical Vision.' Boyd and Salusinszky 140–63.

– *Northrop Frye: An Annotated Bibliography of Primary and Secondary Sources.* Toronto: U of Toronto P, 1987.

Derrida, Jacques. *Specters of Marx: The State of the Debt, the Work of Mourning, and the New International.* Trans. Peggy Kamuf. New York: Routledge, 1994.

Dickinson, Peter. *Here Is Queer: Nationalisms, Sexualities, and the Literatures of Canada.* Toronto: U of Toronto P, 1999.

Dobson, Teresa. '"High-Engender'd Battles": Gender and Power in *Queen Lear.*' *New Theatre Quarterly* 54 (1998): 139–45.

Dollimore, Jonathan, and Alan Sinfield. 'Foreword: Cultural Materialism.' Dollimore and Sinfield, *Political* vii–viii.

– eds. *Political Shakespeare: New Essays in Cultural Materialism.* Manchester: Manchester UP, 1985.

Donnelly, Pat. 'Absurd tilt at the Bard proves his durability.' Rev. of *Le Songe d'une nuit d'été*, adapt. and dir. By Oleg Kisseliov. Théâtre Espace La Veillée, Montreal. *Gazette* [Montreal] 10 Oct. 1998: D11.

– '"Hath not a Jew eyes?"' *Gazette* [Montréal] 2 Oct. 1993: E1+.

Donohue, Joseph W. *Dramatic Character in the English Romantic Age.* Princeton, N.J.: Princeton UP, 1970.

Doran, Terry. '*As You Like It* saves the day at Stratford.' Rev. of *As You Like It*, dir. Richard Monette. Stratford Festival. Festival Theatre, Stratford, Ont. *Buffalo News* 31 May 1990: B4.

Dorsinville, Max. *Caliban without Prospero: Essay on Quebec and Black Literature.* Erin, Ont.: P Porcépic, 1974.

Dorval, Patricia. E-mail to Leanore Lieblein. 12 May 2000.

Doucette, Leonard E. *Theatre in French Canada: Laying the Foundation, 1606–1867.* Toronto: U of Toronto P, 1984.

Drakakis, John. Afterword. Joughin, *Shakespeare* 326–37.

– ed. *Alternative Shakespeares.* Vol 1. London: Methuen 1985.

Driedger, Leo. 'Prejudice and Discrimination.' *Canadian Encyclopedia.*

Dubois, René-Daniel. *Pericles, Prince of Tyre, by William Shakespeare.* Unpublished playscript.

Dufett, Marilyn. Rev. of *The Tempest*, dir. Stephen Bush. LSPU Hall, St John's. *Newfoundland TV Topics* 20 Feb. 1982: 9.

Dvorak, Marta. 'Goodnight William Shakespeare (Good Morning Ann-Marie MacDonald).' *Canadian Theatre Review* 79/80 (1994): 128–33.

Eagleton, Terry. Afterword. *The Shakespeare Myth.* Ed. Graham Holderness. Manchester, U.K.: Manchester UP, 1988. 203–8.

'Eaton Club girls delight audience at May festival.' *Globe* [Toronto] 27 May 1929: 20.

Edinborough, Arnold. 'Canada's Permanent Elizabethan Theatre.' *Shakespeare Quarterly* 8.4 (1957): 511–14.

– 'The Director's Role at Canada's Stratford.' *Shakespeare Quarterly* 20.4 (1969): 443–6.

– 'Large Life with High Jinks.' Rev. of *A Life in the Theatre*, by Tyrone Guthrie. *Saturday Night* 16 April 1960: 35.

– 'Stratford, Ontario – 1968.' *Shakespeare Quarterly* 19.4 (1968): 381–4.

Edmonstone, Wayne E. *Nathan Cohen: The Making of a Critic.* Toronto: Lester and Orpen, 1977.

Edwards, Murray D. *A Stage in Our Past: English-language Theatre in Eastern Canada from the 1790s to 1914.* Toronto: U of Toronto P, 1968.

Egervari, Tibor. *Le Marchand de Venise de Shakespeare à Auschwitz.* Typescript, 1998.

– *Shakespeare's The Merchant of Venice in Auschwitz.* Trans. Annick Léger. Typescript, 1999.

Elliott, J.L. 'Canadian Immigration: A Historical Perspective.' *Two Nations, Many Cultures.* Ed. J.L. Elliott. Scarborough, Ont.: Prentice-Hall, 1979. 160–72.

'Empire's democracy lauded at Hamilton by Canon Shatford: British ideals discussed at [IODE] Provincial Chapter's annual meeting.' *Globe* [Toronto] 12 April 1929: 24.

Engle, Ron, Felicia Hardison Londré, and Daniel J. Watermeier, eds. *Shakespeare Companies and Festivals: An International Guide.* Westport, Conn.: Greenwood P, 1995.

Erickson, Peter. Afterword. 'Trying Not to Forget.' Novy 251–64.

– *Rewriting Shakespeare, Rewriting Ourselves.* Berkeley, Calif.: U of California P, 1991.

Evans, G. Blakemore, et al., eds. *The Riverside Shakespeare.* 2nd ed. Boston: Houghton-Mifflin, 1997.

Farfan, Penny. 'Globe Theatre.' *Canadian Encyclopedia.*

Feder, Alison. Rev. of *Macbeth*, dir. Michael Cook. Little [Reid] Theatre, St John's. *The Muse* [Memorial University, St John's] 4 Nov. 1961: 6.

Fetherstonhaugh, R.C. *McGill University at War, 1914–1918, 1939–1945.* Montreal: McGill U, 1947.

Filewod, Alan. 'National Theatre/National Obsession.' *Canadian Theatre Review* 62 (1990): 5–10. Rpt. in Heble, Pennee, and Struthers 15–23.

Finding Aid. Shakespeare Society of Toronto Records, 1940–69. Archives of Ontario, Toronto.

Findlay, L.M. [Len, Leonard M.]. 'Literature in English: Theory and Criticism.' *Canadian Encyclopedia*.

– 'Temporality Puts on Airs: Process, Purpose, and Poetry in Shakespeare's Histories.' *Analecta Husserliana* 23 (1988): 123–38.

– '[T]he Liberty of Writing.' A special issue on 'The Containment and Redeployment of English India.' Ed. Daniel O'Quinn. http://www.rc.umd.ed.u/praxis/containment/findlay/findlay.html. Published by U of Maryland.

– 'Valuing Culture, Interdiscipining the Economic.' Aldritch Interdisciplinary Lecture and Conference for Graduate Students. Memorial University, St John's. February 1998.

Findlay, L.M., and Isobel M. Findlay. Introduction. *Realizing Community: Multidisciplinary Perspectives*. Ed. L.M. Findlay and Isobel M. Findlay. Saskatoon: Humanities Research Unit and Center for the Study of Co-operatives, U of Saskatchewan, 1995. 1–18.

Findley, Timothy. *Elizabeth Rex*. Winnipeg: Blizzard, 2000.

– 'Making the Leap.' Green and Moore 263.

Fink, Howard. *Canadian National Theatre on the Air. 1925–1961: CBC-CRBC-CNR Radio Drama in English. A Descriptive Bibliography and Union List*. Toronto: U of Toronto P, 1983.

Fink, Howard, and John Jackson. 'Andrew Allan's Role in the History of Canadian Radio Drama.' *All the Bright Company: Radio Drama Produced by Andrew Allan*. Ed. Howard Fink and John Jackson. Kingston, Ont.: Quarry P, 1987. v–xvi.

Firth, Edith G., and Curtis Fahey. 'Henry Scadding.' *Dictionary of Canadian Biography*. Vol. 13. Toronto: U Toronto P, 1994. 927–9.

Fischlin, Daniel, and Mark Fortier, eds. *Adaptations of Shakespeare: A Critical Anthology of Plays from the 17th Century to the Present*. London: Routledge, 2000.

Fishkin, James F. *Justice, Equal Opportunity, and the Family*. New Haven, Conn.: Yale UP, 1983.

'The flag issue again.' Editorial. *Sentinel* [Toronto] 9 June 1927: 2.

Foakes, R.A. *Hamlet versus Lear: Cultural Politics and Shakespeare's Art*. Cambridge, U.K.: Cambridge UP, 1993.

Fortier, Mark. 'Married with Children: *The Winter's Tale* and Social History; or, Infacticide in Earlier Seventeenth-Century England.' *Modern Language Quarterly* 57.4 (1996): 579–603.

– 'Shakespeare with a Difference: Genderbending and Genrebending in *Goodnight Desdemona*.' *Canadian Theatre Review* 59 (1989): 47–51.

– 'Two-Voiced, Delicate Monster: *The Tempest*, Romance, and Post-colonialism.' *Essays in Theatre* 15.1 (1996): 91–101.

Fournier, Hannah. 'Lescarbot's Théâtre de Neptune: New World Pageant, Old World Polemic.' *Canadian Drama* 7.1 (1981): 3–11.
- ed. *Le Théâtre de Neptune.* By Marc Lescarbot. *Canadian Drama* 7.1 (1981): 44–50.
Freeman, Neil. *Introduction to the Folio Scripts.* Agincourt, Ont.: privately printed, 1990.
- Personal interview with Anthony B. Dawson. February 1992.
Freire, Paolo. *Pedagogy of the Oppressed.* Trans. Myra Bergman Ramos. New York: Continuum, 1995.
Frick, N. Alice. *Image in the Mind: CBC Radio Drama 1944 to 1954.* Toronto: Canadian Stage and Arts, 1987.
- adapt. *Richard II.* By William Shakespeare. Prod. Andrew Allan. 30 min. Readings from Shakespeare. CBC Radio, Toronto. Trans-Canada Network. 22 March 1945. Ts. E–436–18. CBC Radio Drama Archives, Centre for Broadcasting Studies, Concordia U, Montreal.
Frisby, Walter G. Letter to the Shakespeare Society of Toronto. 10 June 1950. President's Papers.
- Letter to the Shakespeare Society of Toronto. 19 Oct. 1954. Papers of Mrs R. Glassford.
'The Front Page: A Towering Figure.' *Saturday Night* 11 July 1953: 4.
Frost, Stanley Brice. *The History of McGill in Relation to Montreal and Quebec.* Montreal: Commission d'étude sur les universités 1979.
Frye, Northrop. *Anatomy of Criticism: Four Essays.* Princeton, N.J.: Princeton UP, 1957.
- *Collected Works of Northrop Frye.* 7 vols. to date. Ed. John M. Robson and Alvin A. Lee. Toronto: U of Toronto P, 1996– .
- *The Critical Path: An Essay on the Social Context of Literary Criticism.* Bloomington: Indiana UP, 1971.
- 'Culture as Interpenetration.' Frye, *Divisions* 15–25.
- *Culture and the National Will.* Convocation Address at Carleton University. Carleton Institute for Canadian Studies, Ottawa. 17 May 1957.
- *Divisions on a Ground: Essays on Canadian Culture.* Ed. James Polk. Toronto: Anansi P, 1982.
- *The Eternal Act of Creation: Essays, 1979–1990.* Ed. Robert D. Denham. Bloomington: Indiana UP, 1993.
- *Fables of Identity.* New York: Harcourt, Brace, and World, 1963.
- *Fools of Time: Studies in Shakespearean Tragedy.* Toronto: U of Toronto P, 1967.
- 'The Function of Criticism at the Present Time.' *University of Toronto Quarterly* 19 (1949): 1–16.
- *The Great Code: The Bible and Literature.* Toronto: Academic P, 1982.

- *A Natural Perspective: The Development of Shakespearean Comedy and Romance.* New York: Columbia UP, 1965.
- *Northrop Frye in Conversation.* Ed. David Cayley. Concord, Ont.: Anansi, 1992.
- *Northrop Frye on Shakespeare.* Ed. Robert Sandier. Markham, Ont.: Fitzhenry and Whiteside, 1986.
- *A World in a Grain of Sand: Twenty-Two Interviews with Northrop Frye.* Ed. Robert D. Denham. New York: Peter Lang, 1991.

Fuchs, Elinor. *The Death of Character: Perspectives on Theater after Modernism.* Bloomington: Indiana UP, 1996.

Gaboriau, Linda, trans. *The Queens.* By Normand Chaurette. Vancouver: Talonbooks, 1998.

Gallant, Mavis. 'CBC's Wednesday Night programs bring new listeners to the radio audience.' *Standard* [Regina] 8 Oct. 1949: 7.

Gard, Peter. Rev. of *Hamlet,* dir. Ken Livingstone. Arts and Culture Centre, St John's. *Newfoundland Herald* 18 April 1992: 8.

- Rev. of *As You Like It,* dir. Gordon Jones. Little [Reid] Theatre, St John's. *Newfoundland Herald* 14 Aug. 1993: 13.

Gardner, David. 'My Favourite Review.' Green and Moore 62.

Garebian, Keith. 'Bringing Hamlet Home.' *Canadian Forum* June 2000: 16–19.

- *William Hutt: A Theatre Portrait.* Oakville, Ont.: Mosaic, 1988.

Garneau, Michel, trans. *Macbeth de William Shakespeare: Traduit en québécois.* Montreal: VLB Editeur, 1978.

Germain, Jean-Claude. *Rodéo et Juliette.* 1970; rev. 1971. Typescript 1971.

Gikandi, Simon. *Maps of Englishness: Writing Identity in the Culture of Colonialism.* New York: Columbia UP, 1996.

Gilbert, David. 'Shakespeare au Québec: théâtrographie des productions francophones (1945–1998).' *L'Annuaire théâtral* 24 Traversées de Shakespeare, Centre de recherche de littérature (CRELIQ), L'Université Laval, 1998: 117–38.

Gilbert, Helen, and Joanne Tompkins. *Post-colonial Drama: Theory, Practice, Politics.* London: Routledge, 1996.

Gillson, A.H. Letter of 10 Dec. 1947. 'Wednesday Night – Audience.'

Glastra, Folke, et al. 'Employment Equity Policies in Canada and the Netherlands: Enhancing Minority Employment between Public Controversy and Market Initiative.' *Policy and Politics* 26.2 (1998): 163–76.

Godin, Jean-Cléo, and Laurent Mailhot. *Théâtre québécois II.* Ville Lasalle, Que: Hurtubise HMH, 1980.

Godin, Jean-Cléo, and Pierre Lavoie. Introduction. *Vie et mort du roi boiteux.* Vol.1. By Jean-Pierre Ronfard. Ottawa: Leméac, 1981. 9–24.

Gomez, Mayte. 'Healing the Border Wound: *Fronteras Americanas* and the Future of Canadian Multiculturalism.' *Theatre Research in Canada/Recherches théâtrales au Canada* 16.1–2 (1995): 26–39.

Goodwin, Jill Tomasson. 'Andrew Allan and the *Stage* Series.' *Canadian Drama/ L'Art dramatique canadien* 15.1 (1989): 1–24.
Gould, Jack. 'Words in Behalf of Canadian Drama.' New York *Times* 1 Sept. 1946: X7.
Graham, Roger. *Arthur Meighen*. 3 vols. Toronto: Clarke, Irwin, 1965.
Granatstein, J.L. 'Staring into the Abyss.' *Readings in Canadian History Post-Confederation*. Ed. R. Douglas Francis and Donald B. Smith. 5th ed. Toronto: Harcourt Brace, 1998. 362–76.
'Grand Lodge plea for the retention of British ideals.' *Globe* [Toronto] 14 March 1929: 3.
Grant, George. *Lament for a Nation*. 1965. Carleton Library No. 50. Toronto: McClelland and Stewart, 1970.
Granville-Barker, Harley. *Prefaces to Shakespeare*. First series. London: Sidgwick and Jackson, 1927.
Graves, Warren. *Chief Shaking Spear Rides Again, (or The Taming of the Sioux)*. Toronto: Playwrights Co-op, 1975.
Green, Lynda Mason, and Tedde Moore, eds. *Standing Naked in the Wings: Anecdotes from Canadian Actors*. Toronto: Oxford UP, 1997.
Greenberg, Joel. '*The Two Gentlemen of Verona*.' Rev. of *The Two Gentlemen of Verona*, dir. Richard Rose. Stratford Festival. Festival Theatre, Stratford, Ont. AISLE SAY: *Toronto, Ontario (Canada) Index* 6 Aug. 1998. Online. 8 Sept. 1998 <http://www.escape.com/-theanet/ONT-VERONA>
Grey, Earle. 'Shakespeare Festival, Toronto, Canada.' *Shakespeare Survey* 10 (1957): 111–14.
Groberman, Michael. 'This "Merchant" hits anti-Semitism.' *Gazette* [Montreal] 2 Oct. 1993: E1+.
Groome, Margaret. 'Affirmative Shakespeare at Canada's Stratford Festival.' *Essays in Theatre* 17.2 (May 1999): 139–63.
– 'Canada's Stratford Festival 1953–67: Hegemony, Commodity, Institution.' PhD thesis. McGill University, 1988.
Gurik, Robert. *Hamlet, prince du Québec: Pièce en deux actes*. Adapt. of *Hamlet*, by William Shakespeare. Montreal: Les Éditions de l'Homme, 1968; Ottawa: Leméac, 1977.
Gushue, John. '*Hamlet* really icky.' Rev. of *Hamlet*, dir. Michael Wade. LSPU Hall, St John's. *The Muse* [Memorial U, St John's] 14 May 1984: 14.
Guthrie, Tyrone. 'The Development of Live Drama in Canada.' *Saturday Night* 6 June 1953: 7–8.
– 'First Shakespeare Festival at Stratford, Ontario.' Guthrie, Davies, and MacDonald, *Renown* 1–33.
– 'Is Canada Ready for Big-time Theatre?' *Mayfair* October 1953: 27–9.
– *A Life in the Theatre*. New York: McGraw-Hill, 1959.

- 'A Long View of the Stratford Festival.' Guthrie, Davies, and MacDonald, *Twice* 143–93. Rpt. in Rubin 204–15.
- 'Problems of the Next Stratford Festival.' *Saturday Night* 12 Dec. 1953: 7–8.
- 'Shakespeare Finds a New Stratford.' *Theatre Arts* 37 (1953): 76–7.
- 'Shakespeare at Stratford, Ontario.' *Shakespeare Survey* 8 (1955): 127–31.

Guthrie, Tyrone, Robertson Davies, and Grant MacDonald. *Renown at Stratford: A Record of the Shakespeare Festival in Canada 1953*. Toronto: Clarke, Irwin, 1953.
- *Twice Have the Trumpets Sounded: A Record of the Stratford Shakespearean Festival in Canada 1954*. Toronto: Clarke, Irwin, 1954.

Habicht, Werner. 'Shakespeare and Theatre Politics in the Third Reich.' *The Play Out of Context: Transferring Plays from Culture to Culture*. Ed. Hanna Sčolnicov and Peter Holland. Cambridge, U.K.: Cambridge UP, 1989. 110–20.

'Halifax troupe does "lost play" by Shakespeare.' Ottawa *Citizen* 5 Oct. 1998: Arts 2.

Halpern, Richard. *Shakespeare among the Moderns*. Ithaca, N.Y.: Cornell UP, 1997.

Hamlet. By William Shakespeare. Dir. Alexandre Marine. Théâtre Deuxième Réalité. Espace Geordie, Montreal. 11–12 March 1999; La Licorne, Montreal. 3–27 Nov. 1999.

Hamlet. By William Shakespeare. Trans. Antonine Maillet. Dir. Guillermo de Andrea. Théâtre du Rideau Vert, Montreal. 26 Jan.–29 Feb. 1999.

Hamlet, prince du Québec. By Robert Gurik. Dir. Roland Laroche. Théâtre de l'Escale, Montreal. 17 Jan. 1968.

Hanson, Elizabeth. 'Against a Synecdochic Shakespeare.' *Discontinuities: New Essays on Renaissance Literature and Criticism*. Ed. Viviana Comensoli and Paul Stevens. Toronto: U of Toronto P, 1998. 75–95.

'The Hart House Travelling Players ...' *Curtain Call* 26 Jan. 1931: 4–5.

Hattaway, Michael, Boika Sokolova, and Derek Roper, eds. *Shakespeare in the New Europe*. Sheffield, U.K.: Sheffield Academic P, 1994.

Hawkes, Terence. Introduction. Hawkes, *Alternative* 1–16.
- ed. *Alternative Shakespeares*. Vol. 2. New York: Routledge, 1996.

Hawkins, Freda. 'Canadian Multiculturalism: The Policy Explained.' *Canadian Mosaic: Essays on Multiculturalism*. Ed. A.J. Fry and C. Forceville. Canada Cahiers. 3. Amsterdam: Free UP, 1988. 9–24.

Healy, Thomas. 'Past and Present Shakespeares: Shakespearian Appropriations in Europe.' Joughin, *Shakespeare* 206–32.

Heble, Ajay, Donna Palmateer Pennee, and J.R. (Tim) Struthers, eds. *New Contexts of Canadian Criticism*. Peterborough, Ont.: Broadview P, 1997.

Hengen, Shannon. 'Towards a Feminist Comedy.' *Canadian Literature* 146 (1995): 97–109.

Henry V. By William Shakespeare. Dir. Michael Langham. Perf. Christopher

Plummer. Stratford Festival. Stratford Festival Theatre, Stratford, Ont. 1956.

Hinton, Peter. Foreword. *The Queens*. By Normand Chaurette. 1992. Trans. Linda Gaboriau. Vancouver: Talonbooks, 1998. 9–10.

'His Honor to address Shakespeare Society.' Toronto *Daily Star* 5 Dec. 1962: 65.

Hjartarson, Paul. 'Of Literary Historians and Other Storytellers.' *Editorial Round Table on Reading and Writing Literary Histories*. Spec. issue of *Textual Studies in Canada* 3 (1993): 12–20.

Hobsbawm, Eric J. *Nations and Nationalism since 1789: Programme, Myth, Reality*. Cambridge: Cambridge UP, 1997.

Hodgdon, Barbara. 'Katherina Bound: or Play(K)ating the Strictures of Everyday Life.' *PMLA* 107 (1992): 538–53.

– 'Looking for Mr. Shakespeare after "The Revolution": Robert Lepage's Intercultural *Dream* Machine.' Bulman 68–91.

Holderness, Graham. 'Preface: "All This."' *The Shakespeare Myth*. Ed. Graham Holderness. Manchester: Manchester UP, 1988. xi–xvi.

Holmer, Joan Ozark. 'Runnawayes Eyes: A Fugitive Meaning.' *Shakespeare Quarterly* 33.1 (1982): 97–99.

Holmes, Jeffrey. *Shakespeare Was a Computer Programmer*. Fredericton: Brunswick P, 1975.

Holmes, John. Rev. of *A Midsummer Night's Dream*, dir. Michael Wade. LSPU Hall, St John's. *Evening Telegram* [St. John's] 3 Aug. 1984: 21.

– Rev. of *Richard III*, dir. Michael Wade. LSPU Hall, St John's. *Evening Telegram* [St John's] 31 Oct. 1985: 2.

Hope-Simpson, John, Sir. *White Tie and Decorations: Sir John and Lady Hope-Simpson in Newfoundland 1934–1936*. Ed. Peter Neary. Toronto: U of Toronto P, 1996.

Hopkins, Vivian C. *Prodigal Puritan: A Life of Delia Bacon*. Cambridge, Mass.: Belknap P, 1959.

Hortmann, Wilhelm. *Shakespeare on the German Stage: The Twentieth Century*. Cambridge: Cambridge UP, 1998.

House, A.W. 'The Miracle of Stratford.' *Industrial Canada* 54.5 (1953): 60–5.

Howard, Jean E., and Marion F. O'Connor. Introduction. *Shakespeare Reproduced: The Text in History and Ideology*. Ed. Jean E. Howard and Marion F. O'Connor. New York: Methuen, 1987. 1–17.

Howe, Joseph. *Shakspeare [sic]. Oration Delivered by the Honourable Joseph Howe [...]*. Halifax, N.S.: 'Citizen' Printing and Publishing Office 1864.

Hubert, Henry A. *Harmonious Perfection: The Development of English Studies in 19th Century Anglo-Canadian Colleges*. East Lansing: Michigan State UP, 1994.

Hulme, Peter. 'Reading from Elsewhere: George Lamming and the Paradox of

Exile.' *'The Tempest' and Its Travels.* Ed. Peter Hulme and William H. Sherman. London: Reaktion, 2000. 220–35.

Humphreys, Chris. 'Bard on the Beach.' Green and Moore 308–9.

Humphreys, W. Eason. Letter of 17 Dec. 1947. 'Wednesday Night – Audience.'

Hutcheon, Linda. 'Academic Free Trade? One Canadian's View of the MLA.' *PMLA* 114.3 (1999): 311–17.

– *A Poetics of Postmodernism: History, Theory, Fiction.* Toronto: U of Toronto P, 1988.

– *A Theory of Parody: The Teachings of Twentieth-Century Art Forms.* London: Methuen 1985.

Iacovetta, Franca. *Such Hardworking People.* Montreal: McGill-Queen's UP, 1992.

Industrial Exhibition Association of Toronto. Reports for 1895. Toronto: Mail Job Printing 1896. CNE Archives, Toronto.

Ingram, Neil. Appendum to 'Message from the Artistic Director.' *1991 Stratford Festival Programme.* 5.

'The Intellectual Capital of Canada.' *Canadian Forum* March 1931: 210–12.

Ionesco, Eugene. 'Amédée, ou Comment s'en débarrasser.' *Théâtre I.* Paris: Éditions Gallimard, 1954.

– 'La Cantatrice chauve.' *Théâtre I.* Paris: Éditions Gallimard, 1954.

– *Le Roi se meurt.* Paris: Éditions Gallimard, 1963.

Isajiw, Wsevolod W. *Understanding Diversity.* Toronto: Thompson, 1999.

Itwaru, Arnold Harrichand, and Natasha Ksonzek. *Closed Entrances: Canadian Culture and Imperalism.* Toronto: TSAR, 1994.

Ivšić, Radovan. *Le Roi Gordogane.* Paris: Éditions Surréalistes, 1968.

Jackson, B.W. Foreword. Jackson, *Stratford* vi–vii.

– ed. *Stratford Papers on Shakespeare 1964.* Toronto: Gage, 1965.

Jackson, Berners A.W. 'Stratford Festival, Canada.' *Shakespeare Quarterly* 28.2 (1977): 197–206.

Jansen, David. 'Thoughts on Playing Proteus.' *Stratford for Students* 41 (1998): 3–7.

Jennings, Charles, comp. 'Wednesday Night – Audience.'

John Hancock Insurance Company. Advertisement. *The Stratford Festival Souvenir Program 1953.*

Johnson, Samuel. *Samuel Johnson on Shakespeare.* Ed. H.R. Woodhuysen. London: Penguin, 1989.

Johnston, Denis [W.]. Rev. of *Bag Babies,* by Allan Stratton, *Goodnight Desdemona (Good Morning Juliet),* by Ann-Marie MacDonald, and *The Half of It,* by John Krizanc. *Canadian Theatre Review* 74 (1993): 85–6.

– *Up the Mainstream: The Rise of Toronto's Alternative Theatres, 1968–1975.* Toronto: U of Toronto P, 1991.

Jones, Emrys. 'Stuart *Cymbeline.*' *Essays in Criticism* 11 (1961): 84–99.
Jones, Gordon. Rev. of *A Midsummer Night's Dream*, dir. Jillian Keilly. Mine Shaft No. 3, Bell Island, Nfld. *Evening Telegram* [St John's] 3 Aug. 1999: 19.
– Rev. of *Timon of Athens*, dir. Michael Wade. LSPU Hall, St John's. Morning Show. CBC Radio One. 24 April 1986.
Joughin, John J. Introduction. Joughin, *Shakespeare* 1–15.
– ed. *Shakespeare and National Culture.* Manchester: Manchester UP, 1997.
Jung, C.G. *Psychology and Alchemy. The Collected Works.* Ed. Herbert Read, et al. 2nd ed. Vol. 12. Princeton, N.J.: Princeton UP, 1968.
Kahn, Coppélia. 'The Absent Mother in *King Lear.*' *Rewriting the Renaissance: The Discourses of Sexual Difference in Early Modern Europe.* Ed. Margaret W. Ferguson et al. Chicago: U of Chicago P, 1986.
Keats, John. 'To George and Thomas Keats.' 21 Dec. 1817. *Letters of John Keats.* Ed. Hugh l'Anson Fausset. London: Thomas Nelson and Sons, n.d. 79–82.
Keefer, Elsie. Letter to the Shakespeare Society of Toronto. 3 May 1955. Papers of Mrs R. Glassford.
– Report of the Women's Committee, 22 May 1951. Reports, 1952–55.
'Keep Canada British is dominant note at Ward 5 dinner.' *Globe* [Toronto] 7 May 1929: 2.
Kennedy, Dennis. 'Afterword: Shakespearean Orientalism.' Kennedy, *Foreign* 290–303.
– 'Introduction: Shakespeare without His language.' Kennedy, *Foreign* 1–18.
– ed. *Foreign Shakespeare: Contemporary Performance.* Cambridge: Cambridge UP, 1993.
Kertzer, Jonathan. *Worrying the Nation: Imagining a National Literature in English Canada.* Toronto: U of Toronto P, 1998.
Kesterton, Michael. 'Social Studies: A Daily Miscellany of Information.' *Globe and Mail* 26 March 1994: B5.
King, Thomas. 'Borders.' *One Good Story, That One.* Toronto: HarperCollins 1993. 129–45.
Kirchhoff, H.J. 'Hamlet cut to the bone.' Rev. of *Hamlet*, dir. Richard Monette. Stratford Festival. Tom Patterson Theatre, Stratford, Ont. *Globe and Mail* 4 June 1994: C10.
– 'Tapping into the primal.' Rev. of *Othello*, dir. Brian Bedford. Stratford Festival. Avon Theatre, Stratford, Ontario. *Globe and Mail* 29 June 1994: E3.
Kishi, Tetsuo, Roger Pringle, and Stanley Wells, eds. *Shakespeare and Cultural Traditions.* Newark, N.J.: U of Delaware P, 1991.
Knight, G. Wilson. *The Crown of Life.* 1947. London: Methuen, 1965.
– *The Imperial Theme.* London: Methuen, 1954.
– *Shakespeare and Religion.* London: Routledge and Kegan Paul, 1967.

- *Shakespeare's Dramatic Challenge.* London: Croom Helm, 1977.
- 'St. George and the Dragon.' Knight, *Shakespeare and Religion* 91–111.
- *The Wheel of Fire.* London: Methuen, 1949.

Knowles, Richard Paul [Ric, R.]. 'From Dream to Machine: Peter Brook, Robert Lepage, and the Contemporary Shakespearean Director as (Post)Modernist.' *Theatre Journal* 50 (1998): 189–206.
- 'From Nationalist to Multinational: The Stratford Festival, Free Trade, and the Discourses of Intercultural Tourism.' *Theatre Journal* 47 (1995): 19–41.
- 'Focus, Faithfulness, Shakespeare, and *The Shrew.* Directing as Translation as Resistance.' *Essays in Theatre/Etudes théâtrales* 16 (1997): 33–52.
- 'Reading Material: Transfers, Remounts, and the Production of Meaning in Contemporary Toronto Drama and Theatre.' *Essays on Canadian Writing* 51–2 (1993–4): 258–95.
- Rev. of *The Queens,* by Normand Chaurette. Trans. Linda Gaboriau. *Canadian Theatre Review* 78 (1994): 61.
- 'Shakespeare, 1993, and the Discourses of the Stratford Festival, Ontario.' *Shakespeare Quarterly* 45.2 (1994): 211–25.
- 'Shakespeare, Voice, and Ideology: Interrogating the Natural Voice.' Bulman 92–112.

Koltai, Judith. 'Authentic Movement: The Embodied Experience of Text.' *Canadian Theatre Review* 78 (1994): 21–5.

Kristeva, Julia. *Desire in Language: A Semiotic Approach to Literature and Art.* Trans. Thomas Gora, Alice Jardine, and Leon S. Roudiez. Ed. Leon S. Roudiez. New York: Columbia UP, 1980.
- *Nations without Nationalism.* Trans. Leon S. Roudiez. New York: Columbia UP, 1993.

Krysinski, Wladimir. Rev. of *Les Reines,* dir. André Brassard. Théâtre d'Aujourd'hui, Montreal, 18 Jan.–10 Feb. 1991. *Jeu* 60 (1991): 121–4.

Lafon, Dominique. 'Shakespeare à l'Arsenal ou Comment une filiale rompte avec la société mère.' *L'Annuaire théâtral* 13 (1998): 85–99.

Lamming, George. *The Pleasures of Exile.* 1960. Ann Arbor: U of Michigan P, 1992.

Lamy, Suzanne. 'André Breton, hermétisme et poésie dans Arcane 17.' Montreal: Les Presses de l'Université de Montréal, 1977. 23 Aug. 1999. <http://mistral.ere.umontreal.ca/pum/livres/catalog/10118.html>.

Langham, Michael. 'Twelve Years at Stratford.' Introduction. *The Stratford Scene 1958–1968.* Comp. and ed. Peter Raby. Toronto: Clarke, Irwin 1968. 6–12.

Lapointe, Gilles. '*Vie et mort du roi boiteux* de Jean-Pierre Ronfard.' *Canadian Drama/L'Art dramatique canadienne* 9.2 (1983): 220–5.

Lawless, Jill. 'Necessary Angel gives King Lear a gender twist.' Rev. of *The Tragedie of King Lear,* dir. Richard Rose. Necessary Angel Theatre Co. Canadian

Stage, Berkeley Street Theatre Upstairs, Toronto. *NOW* 16–22 March 1995: 69.
Laws of the Shakespeare Club. Montreal: Lovell and Gibson, 1845.
Laycock, John. 'Monette's *As You Like It* mimics Meech.' Rev. of *As You Like It*, dir. Richard Monette. Stratford Festival. Festival Theatre, Stratford, Ont. Windsor *Star* 31 May 1990: E2.
Lear. by Jean-Pierre Ronfard. Collective creation. Théâtre Expérimental de Montréal. 15 Jan.–6 Feb. 1977.
Lee, Betty. 'Stratford's Michael Langham.' *Globe Magazine* 29 June 1957.
Lefebvre, Paul. 'Dans l'anarchie des ombrages.' Preface. *Les Reines.* By Normand Chaurette. Montreal; Éditions Actes-Sud/Leméac, 1991. 5–6.
– 'Playwrighting in Quebec.' Trans. Barbara A. Kerslake. A. Wagner, *Contemporary* 60–8.
The Legacy of Northrop Frye. Ed. Alvin Lee and Robert D. Denham. Toronto: U of Toronto P, 1994.
Leggatt, Alexander. *English Stage Comedy 1490–1990: Five Centuries of a Genre.* London: Routledge, 1998.
Léonardini, Jean-Pierre. 'Six reines en queue de poisson: Shakespeare avait des poches immenses.' Rev. of *Les Reines*, dir. Joël Joanneau. Comédie Française. Théâtre Vieux Colombier, Paris. *L'Huma Quotidien.* Le Web de l'Humanité. 26 mai 1997. On-line. 27 July 1999. <http://www.humanite.presse.fr/journal/1997/1997-05/1997-05-26/1997-05-26-052.html>.
Lepage, Robert. Program Notes for *Elsinore/Elsineur.* Ex Machina and National Arts Centre Production, Ottawa. 9–13 Sept., 1997.
Lépine, Stéphane, ed. 'Le Sceau du secret.' Lépine, *Société* 9–22.
– *La Société de Normand Chaurette: Figures et manières.* Montreal: Théâtre UBU, 1996.
Lévesque, Robert. 'Des farces des reines.' Rev. of *Les Reines*, dir. André Brassard. Théâtre d'Aujourd'hui, Montreal. *Le Devoir.* 24 Jan. 1991: D4.
– 'La gentille Mégère de monsieur Micone.' Rev. of *La Mégère apprivoisée*, adapt. Marco Micone, dir. Martine Beaulne. Théâtre du Nouveau Monde, Montreal. *Le Devoir* [Montreal] 21 March 1995: B7.
– '*Hamlet* ou le carnaval de Yorick.' *Ici.* 28 Oct.–4 Nov. 1999: 10.
– 'La semaine des deux Shylock.' *Le Devoir* [Montreal] 28 Sept. 1993: B8.
Lévesque, Solange. Interview with Francine Moreau. Midi-Culture. S[ociété] R[adio] C[anada], Montreal. 9 Oct. 1998.
– 'Traduire, c'est émigrer: Entretien avec Marco Micone.' *Cahiers de théâtre Jeu* 70 (1994): 17–30.
Levine, Lawrence W. *Highbrow/Lowbrow: The Emergence of Cultural Hierarchy in America.* Cambridge, Mass.: Harvard UP, 1988.

Liddell, Henry George, and Robert Scott. *A Greek-English Lexicon: Revised and Augmented.* Oxford: Clarendon P, 1977.
Lieblein, Leanore. 'Shakespeare and the Québec Nation.' *The Elizabethan Theatre 15/16.* Ed. L. Magnusson and C. Edward McGee. Port Credit, Ont.: P.D. Meany. Forthcoming.
– 'Taming Shrews in Quebec.' *Le Shakespeare français: sa langue.* Special issue of *Alfa* 10/11 (1997/98): 19–32.
– 'Theatre Archives at the Intersection of Production and Reception: The Example of Québécois Shakespeare.' *Textual and Theatrical Shakespeare: Questions of Evidence.* Ed. Edward Pechter. Iowa City: U of Iowa P, 1996. 164–80.
Lieblein, Leanore, and Patrick Neilson. 'Alfred Pellan, *Twelfth Night*, and the Modernist Shakespeare.' *Shakespeare Yearbook* 11 (2000): 389–422.
Lingerfelt, Jim, and Roger Kershaw. 'Harlem's Two Solitudes.' Rev. of *Harlem Duet*, by Djanet Sears. Tarragon Extra Space, Nightwood Theatre, Toronto. 20 Apr.–18 May 1997. *Stage Door*. Online. 16 Feb. 1999. <http://www.stage-door.org/all.htm>.
Liston, William T. 'Hamlet.' Rev. of *Hamlet*, dir. Richard Monette. Stratford Festival. Tom Patterson Theatre, Stratford, Ont. *Cahiers Elisabethians* 47 (1995): 95–6.
Litt, Paul. 'The Battle for the Airwaves.' Litt, *Muses* 123–45.
– *The Muses, the Masses and the Massey Commission.* Toronto: U of Toronto P, 1992.
Littler, William. 'Developing Opera and Musical Theatre.' A. Wagner, *Contemporary* 274–82.
Lloyd, David. *Nationalism and Minor Literature: James Clarence Mangan and the Emergence of Irish Cultural Nationalism.* Berkeley, Calif.: U of California P, 1987.
Loffrée, Carrie. 'Normand Chaurette: Pour mieux saisir l'insaisissable.' *Nuit blanche* 55 (1994): 59–62.
Loomba, Ania. '*Hamlet* in Mizoram.' Novy, *Cross-cultural Performances* 227–50.
– 'Shakespeare and Cultural Difference.' Hawkes, *Alternative* 164–91.
Loomba, Ania, and Martin Orkin. 'Introduction: Shakespeare and the Post-Colonial Question.' Loomba and Orkin, *Post-Colonial* 1–19.
– eds. *Post-Colonial Shakespeares.* London: Routledge, 1998.
Loranger, Françoise, and Claude Levac. *Le chemin du roy: Comédie patriotique.* Ottawa: Leméac, 1969.
Lorca, Federico García. *The Public and Play without a Title: Two Posthumous Plays.* Trans. Carlos Bauer. New York: New Directions, 1983.
Lynde, D., H. Peters, and R. Buehler, eds. *Newfoundland Theatre Research: Proceedings.* St John's: Memorial U, 1993.

Lyons, Bridget Gellert. 'The Iconography of Ophelia.' *English Literary History* 44 (1977): 60–74.
McCall, Gordon. 'A Bilingual *Romeo and Juliette* in Saskatoon.' *Canadian Theatre Review* 62 (1990): 35–41.
MacDonald, Ann-Marie. 'Ann-Marie MacDonald.' Interview with Rita Much. *Fair Play: 12 Women Speak: Conversations with Canadian Playwrights*. By Judith Rudakoff and Rita Much. Toronto: Simon and Pierre, 1990. 128–43.
MacDonald, Ann-Marie. *Goodnight Desdemona (Good Morning Juliet)*. Toronto: Coach House Press, 1990; Playwrights Canada P, 1990.
Macdonald, Rose. 'Acting marks fine performance at Hart House.' Rev. of *Antony and Cleopatra*, dir. G. Wilson Knight. Shakespeare Society of Toronto. Hart House, Toronto. *Evening Telegram* [Toronto] 11 Nov. 1937: 20.
– 'The Lieutenant-Governor speaks on Shakespeare – Feat of memory and knowledge.' *Telegram* [Toronto] 6 Dec. 1962: 40.
– 'Unveil silver trophy for reading contest.' *Telegram* [Toronto] 25 April 1955: 30.
McIlroy, Randal. 'Truckers' tale delivers light load.' Rev. of *Cruel Tears*, dir. Kim McCaw. Prairie Theatre Exchange, Winnipeg, Man. Winnipeg *Free Press* 16 Feb. 1990: 34.
MacKay, J. Keiller. Letter to the Shakespeare Society of Toronto. 24 Oct. 1958. President's Papers.
McKim, Mary. '*Colour the Flesh the Colour of Dust*: Worthwhile Experience says adjudicator.' *Evening Telegram* [St John's] 19 Feb. 1971: 43.
McLuhan, Marshall. 'Canada: The Borderline Case.' *The Canadian Imagination: Dimensions of a Literary Culture*. Ed. David Staines. Cambridge, Mass.: Harvard UP, 1977. 226–48.
McLuskie, Kathleen E. 'The Shopping Complex: Materiality and the Renaissance Theatre.' Pechter 86–101.
McVicar, Leonard H. 'From Little Acorns ... Stratford's Shakespearean Festival.' *Recreation* 48 (1955): 110–11.
Maillet, Antonine. *William S*. Ottawa: Leméac, 1991.
Makaryk, Irena. E-mail to Margaret Groome. 30 Jan. 2000.
Le Making of de Macbeth. By Jean-Frédéric Messier, based on an original idea by Paula de Vasconcelos. Dir. Paula de Vasconcelos. Pigeons International. Salle Beverly Webster Rolph, Musée d'Art Contemporain, Montréal. 9–21 Apr. 1996.
Le Marchand de Venise de Shakespeare à Auschwitz. By and dir. Tibor Egervari. Théâtre Distinct (Ottawa). Les Salles de Gesù, Montreal. 7, 8, 14, 15 Oct. 1993.
Marder, Louis. *His Exits and His Entrances: The Story of Shakespeare's Reputation*. London: John Murray, 1963.

Margolies, David. 'Teaching the Handsaw to Fly: Shakespeare as a Hegemonic Instrument.' *The Shakespeare Myth.* Ed. Graham Holderness. Manchester: Manchester UP, 1988. 42–53.
Marshall, Tom. 'Out There: Objects Disposed, Fragmenting, in Our Own Space.' *The Elements.* Toronto: Oberon, 1980. 146–67.
Marx, Karl. *Capital: A critique of political economy.* Trans. Ben Fowkes. 2nd ed. Vol. 1. Harmondsworth: Penguin, 1976.
– *Kapital.* Marx-Engels Gesamtausgabe. Vol. 23. Berlin: Dietz Verlag, 1974.
Mason, Lawrence. 'Shakespeare week.' *Globe* [Toronto] 27 April 1929: 22.
Massey, Raymond. 'Theatregoing, Christmas 1913.' Rubin 21–4.
Massey, Vincent. *On Being Canadian.* Toronto: J. M. Dent, 1948.
– 'The Prospects of a Canadian Drama.' Rubin 50–63.
Matas, Carol. *Cloning Miranda.* Toronto: Scholastic Canada, 1999.
La Mégère apprivoisée. By William Shakespeare. Adapt. Frank Varon. CBFT, Montreal. 15 March 1953.
Meighen, Sir Arthur. *Unrevised and Unrepented.* Toronto: Clarke, Irwin, 1949.
Messier, Jean-Frédéric. *Le Making de Macbeth/De Pigeons International/d'après une idée originale de Paula de Vasconcelos.* Typescript, Version 04/03/96.
'"Me swear, me drink, me a Canadian," declares newcomer.' *Globe* 9 May 1929: 15.
Metcalf, John. *What Is A Canadian Literature?* Guelph, Ont.: Red Kite P, 1988.
Micone, Marco. *La Mégère de Padova d'après* La Mégère apprivoisée *de William Shakespeare.* Typescript, 1995.
– Telephone interview with Leanore Lieblein. 15 June 1995.
Middleton, J.E. [Jesse Edgar]. 'The Theatre in Canada (1750–1880).' Rubin 2–10.
– *Toronto's One Hundred Years.* Toronto: Centennial Committee, 1934.
Mignolo, Walter D. *The Darker Side of the Renaissance: Literacy, Territoriality, and Colonization.* Ann Arbor: U of Michigan P, 1995.
Mikalachki, Jodi. *The Legacy of Boadicea: Gender and Nation in Early Modern England.* London: Routledge, 1998.
Minutebook 1940–6. File 1. Papers of the Shakespeare Society.
Minutes: 1945–55. File 2. Papers of the Shakespeare Society.
Minutes, 3 Feb. 1941. Minutebook.
– 3 March 1941. Minutebook.
– 23 Dec. 1947. Minutes: 1945–55.
– 25 June 1947. Minutes: 1945–55.
– April 1952. Minutes: 1945–55.
Minutes, Executive and General Committee Meeting, 3 Feb. 1941. Minutebook.

Minutes, Executive Committee, 1951–53. File 3. Papers of the Shakespeare Society.

Mitchell, Ken. 'Ken Mitchell.' Interview with Robert Wallace. *The Work: Conversations with English-Canadian Playwrights*. By Robert Wallace and Cynthia Zimmerman. Toronto: Coach House P. 1982. 142–55.

– 'Ken Mitchell's progress as a writer, from *Cruel Tears* to thoughts on Booze.' Interview with M.T. Kelly. *Books in Canada* 7.5 (1978): 40.

– 'Prairies.' Interview with Alan Twigg. *For Openers: Conversations with 24 Canadian Writers*. By Alan Twigg. Madeira Park, B.C.: Harbour Publishing, 1981. 163–73.

Mitchell, Ken, and Humphrey and the Dumptrucks. *Cruel Tears*. Vancouver: Talonbooks, 1977.

Moon, Barbara. 'Why Guthrie Outdraws Shakespeare.' *Maclean's* 6 Aug. 1955: 18+.

Moore, Dora Mavor. Toronto Shakespearean Society Founded by DMM Dec. 2, 1931. Box 75, file 7. Ms. 207. Dora Mavor Moore Papers. U of Toronto Archives, Toronto.

Moore, Mavor. 'An Approach to Our Beginnings: Transplant, Native Plant or Mutation?' Rubin 293–9.

– 'A Theatre for Canada.' Rubin 238–50.

Morgan, Henry James, ed. *The Canadian Men and Women of the Time: A Hand-book of Canadian Biography*. Toronto: William Briggs, 1898.

Morgan-Powell, S. 'Margaret Anglin: Star of Canada.' Rubin 30–5.

Moss, John. 'Understanding Shakespeare.' *Being Fiction: Short Stories*. Ottawa: Tecumseh P, 2001. 69–81.

Mossop, Brian. 'Shakespeare in the vernacular.' Letter. *Globe and Mail* 1 Nov. 1997: D7.

Moyse, Charles Ebeneezer. [Belgrave Titmarsh]. *Shakspere's [sic] Skull and Falstaff's Nose: A Fancy in Three Acts*. London: Elliot Stock, 1889.

Mullens, Raymond. Rev. of *Henry VIII*, dir. G. Wilson Knight. Shakespeare Society of Toronto. Hart House, Toronto. *Saturday Night* 28 April 1934: 10.

– Rev. of *Henry VIII*, dir. G. Wilson Knight. Shakespeare Society of Toronto. Hart House, Toronto. *Saturday Night* 20 Oct. 1934: 22.

Murray, Heather. *'Come, Bright Improvement!': The Literary Societies of Nineteenth-Century Ontario*. Toronto: U of Toronto P, 2002.

– 'Daniel Wilson as Littérateur: Poet, Professor and Critic.' *Thinking with Both Hands: Sir Daniel Wilson in the Old World and the New*. Ed. Elizabeth Hulse. Toronto: U Toronto P, 1999. 211–33.

– 'Frozen Pen, Fiery Print, and Fothergill's Folly: Cultural Organization in Toronto, Winter 1836–38.' *Essays on Canadian Writing* 61 (1997): 41–70.

- 'Great Works and Good Works: The Toronto Women's Literary Club 1877–1883.' *Historical Studies in Education/Revue d'histoire de l'éducation* 11.1 (1999): 75–95.
- 'Institutions of Reading: New Directions in English-Canadian Literary History.' Editorial Round Table on Reading and Writing Literary Histories. Spec. issue of *Textual Studies in Canada* 3 (1993): 2–7.
- *Working in English: History, Institution, Resources.* Toronto: U of Toronto P, 1996.

Murrell, John. *Farther West, New World.* Toronto: Coach House P, 1985.

Nardocchio, Elaine F. *Theatre and Politics in Modern Quebec.* Edmonton: U of Alberta P, 1986.

Nashman, Alan. Rev. of *La Mort des rois*, dir. Jean Asselin. Théâtre de l'Omnibus, Montreal. *Theatrum* 19 (1990): 39–40.

National Council of Women of Canada. *Year Book 1928.* Toronto: 1928.

Necessary Angel Theatre Company. 'Necessary Angel Presents William Shakespeare's Epic *The Tragedie of King Lear* with Janet Wright as Lear.' Media Release. 20 Feb. 1995.

The Need for a Permanent Theatre at Stratford. Campaign brochure. Stratford Festival Archives, Stratford, Ont.

Neely, Carol Thomas. '"Documents in Madness": Reading Madness and Gender in Shakespeare's Tragedies and Early Modern Culture.' *Shakespearean Tragedy and Gender.* Ed. Shirley Nelson Garner and Madelon Sprengnether. Indianapolis: Indiana UP, 1996. 75–104.

New, William. *Borderlands: How We Talk about Canada.* Vancouver: UBC P, 1998.

Newman, Fred C. *The First Fifty Years: A Brief History of the St. James Literary Society.* Montreal: 1948.

Nicholl, Charles J. *The Chemical Theatre.* London: Routledge and Kegan Paul, 1980.

'The Non-Professional Stage.' *Curtain Call* February 1938: 20.

Norwood, Gilbert. 'Woman's Clubs.' *Spoken in Jest.* Toronto: Macmillan, 1938. 149–51.

Novy, Marianne, ed. *Cross-cultural Performances: Differences in Women's Re-Visions of Shakespeare.* Chicago: U of Illinois P, 1993.

'Now let the crowds come: Lieut. Gov. Kirkpatrick opens the fair.' *Empire* [Toronto] 7 Sept. 1892: 3.

O'Brien, Michael. *Mad Boy Chronicle.* Toronto: Playwrights Canada P, 1995.

'Old England Recreated by 12th Night Revelers.' Scrapbook.

Olender, Maurice. *The Languages of Paradise: Race, Religion, and Philology in the Nineteenth Century.* Trans. Arthur Goldhammer. Cambridge, Mass.: Harvard UP, 1992.

O'Neill, Paul. 'Theatre in Newfoundland: The Beginning.' Lynde, Peters, and Buehler 73–80.
Orenstein, Gloria Feman. *The Theater of the Marvelous: Surrealism and the Contemporary Stage.* New York: New York UP, 1975.
Orgel, Stephen, and Roy Strong. *The Theatre of the Stuart Court.* ... 2 vols. London: Sotheby Parke Bernet; Berkeley: U of California P, 1973.
Orkin, Martin. 'Whose Things of Darkness? Reading/representing *The Tempest* in South Africa after April 1994.' Joughin 142–69.
Osborne, W.F. *The Genius of Shakespeare and Other Essays.* Toronto: Briggs, 1908.
Owens, Margaret E. 'The Effigeal Body in Normand Chaurette's *Les Reines (The Queens).*' Unpublished conference paper. Association for Canadian Theatre Research (ACTR). Congress of the Social Sciences and Humanities, University of Ottawa, June 1998.
Paglia, Camille. *Sexual Personae: Art and Decadence from Nefertiti to Emily Dickinson.* New York: Vintage, 1991.
Paik Nak-chung. 'Nations and Literatures in the Age of Globalization.' *The Cultures of Globalization.* Ed. Fredric Jameson and Masao Miyoshi. Durham, N.C.: Duke UP, 1998. 218–29.
Palumbo-Liu, David. 'Introduction: Unhabituated Habituses.' Palumbo-Liu and Gumbrecht 1–22.
Palumbo-Liu, David, and Hans Ulrich Gumbrecht, eds. *Streams of Cultural Capital.* Stanford, Calif.: Stanford UP, 1993.
Pancheva, Eva. 'Nothings, Merchants, Tempests: Trimming Shakespeare for the 1992 Bulgarian Stage.' Hattaway, Sokolova, and Roper 247–60.
Papers of Mrs R. Glassford, Secretary, 1945, 1952–5. File 7. Papers of the Shakespeare Society.
Papers of the Shakespeare Society of Toronto. MU 2660–3. Archives of Ontario, Toronto.
Paré, François. 'Me voici, c'est moi, la femme qui pleure.' Heble, Pennee, and Struthers 188–201.
'Parliaments of Ontario: The first met in a log house at Newark.' *Empire* 19 Sept. 1892: 3.
Patmore, Coventry. 'The Modern British Drama.' *North British Review* (1858): 68–80.
Patterson, Tom. 'The Festival in Retrospect.' *Saskatchewan Community* 5.6 (1954): 1–2.
– Interview. *Stratford under Cover: Memories on Tape.* Comp. Grace Lydiatt Shaw. Toronto: New Canada Publications, 1977. 45+.
Patterson, Tom, and Allan Gould. *First Stage: The Making of the Stratford Festival.* Toronto: McClelland and Stewart 1987. Rev. ed. Willowdale, Ont.: Firefly, 1999.

Pavlovic, Diane. 'Comme un somptueux manège.' *Jeu* 48 (1988): 18–35.
Pechter, Edward. Address. Association for Canadian College and University Teachers of English and the Association for Canadian Theatre Research at the Congress of the Humanities and Social Sciences Federation of Canada. Arts Building, U of Ottawa, Ottawa. June 1998.
– *The Endless Controversy of* Othello: *A Performance History of Shakespeare's Most Disturbing Play*. Iowa City: U of Iowa P, 1999.
Pelletier, Gérard. 'La Mégère apprivoisée à CBFT.' Rev. of *La Mégère apprivoisée*, adapt. Frank Varon. CBFT, Montreal. *Le Devoir* [Montreal] 21 March 1953: 6.
Penfield, Wilder. 'Into the Woods with Monsieur Shakespeare.' Rev. of *As You Like It*, dir. Richard Monette. Stratford Festival. Festival Theatre, Stratford, Ont. Toronto *Sun* 1 June 1990: 92.
Pennington, Bob. 'Rollins' Othello falters.' Rev. of *Othello*, dir. John Neville. Stratford Festival. Festival Theatre, Stratford, Ontario. Toronto *Star* 3 Aug. 1987: E3.
Pennycook, Alastair. *English and the Discourses of Colonialism*. London: Routledge, 1998.
Pettigrew, John, and Jamie Portman. *Stratford: The First Thirty Years*. 2 vols. Toronto: Macmillan, 1985.
Phrenological Developement [sic] *of Henry Scadding*. Chart. Scadding Scrapbooks. Baldwin Room, Toronto Reference Library.
Pilditch, James. 'The Stratford Shakespearean Festival.' *Canadian Geographical Journal* December 1953: 242–7.
Pilon, Stéphane. 'Le Songe d'une nuit d'été: Rêve éveillé.' Rev. of *Le Songe d'une nuit d'été*, adapt. and dir. Oleg Kisseliov. Théâtre Espace La Veillée, Montreal. *Voir* [Montreal] 24–30 Sept. 1998: 51.
Pioneers' Cabin, Industrial Exhibition Park, 1896. Baldwin Room, Toronto Reference Library.
Plant, Richard. 'Chronology: Theatre in Ontario to 1914.' *Early Stages: Theatre in Ontario 1800–1914*. Ed. Ann Saddlemyer. Ontario Historical Studies Series. Toronto: U of Toronto P, 1990. 288–346.
Players of Shakespeare: [Further] Essays in Shakespearean Performance. Ed. Philip Brockbank, Russell Jackson, and Robert Smallwood. 4 vols. Cambridge: Cambridge UP, 1985–98.
Plays – notices, programmes, 1943–61. File 12. Papers of the Shakespeare Society.
Plummer, Christopher. 'Memories of Sir John.' Green and Moore 201–3.
Pope, Karl Theodore. Interview with Tom Patterson, 29 July 1965. 'An Historical Study of the Stratford Ontario Festival Theatre.' PhD thesis, Wayne State U, 1966. 25.

Porter, John. *Canadian Social Structure.* Carleton Library no. 32. Toronto: McClelland and Stewart, 1967.
- *The Vertical Mosaic: An Analysis of Social Class and Power in Canada.* Studies in the Structure of Power: Decision-Making in Canada 2. Toronto: U of Toronto P, 1965.

Porter, McKenzie. 'Inside Toronto: Black Tie Protocol.' *Telegram* [Toronto] 23 April 1964: 9.

Portman, Jamie. 'There's little to redeem Stratford's Gentlemen.' Rev. of *The Two Gentlemen of Verona*, dir. Richard Rose. Stratford Festival. Festival Theatre, Stratford, Ont. Ottawa *Citizen* 13 Aug. 1998: F8.

Posner, Michael. 'Time to bury Shakespeare, or to praise him?' *Globe and Mail* 18 Oct. 1997: C13.

Potter, Christopher. 'Hectic staging upsets serenity of *As You Like It*.' Rev. of *As You Like It*, dir. Richard Monette. Stratford Festival. Festival Theatre, Stratford, Ont. Ann Arbor *News* 9 June 1990: F6.

President's Papers, 1942-68. File 6. Papers of the Shakespeare Society.

Price, Marjorie. *God Caesar.* Toronto: Samuel French, 1935.

Program for *This Sceptred Isle.* G. Wilson Knight. Ms. 41. Trinity College Archives, Toronto.

Prospectus of an Institution To Be Called 'The Athenaeum,' A General Association for the Advancement of Literature and Science. Toronto?: 1843?

'Queen Bess Holds Court Again ...' *Telegram* [Toronto] 12 Jan. 1950: 7.

Rama, Ángel. *Transculturación narrativa en América Latina.* Mexico: Siglo Veintiuno editores, 1982.

Rea, Stephen. Interview. 'Irish actor pulls no punches.' *Globe and Mail* 30 Aug. 1999: A18.

Reaney, James. 'The Stratford Festival.' *Canadian Forum* August 1953: 112-13.

Redfern, Jon. 'Tribal Brecht and a wail of an Othello.' Rev. of *The Great Wave of Civilization*, by Herschel Hardin, *Cruel Tears*, by Ken Mitchell and Humphrey and the Dumptrucks, and *Have*, by Julius Hay. *Books in Canada* 6.10 (1977): 27-8.

Reed, Carole Ann. 'Contradictions and Assumptions: A Report on Employment Equity in Canada.' *Resources for Feminist Research/Documentation sur la Recherche Feministe* 24.3-4 (1995-96): 46-8.

Reed. T.A. 'An Explanatory Comment.' *York Pioneer* (1955): 12.
- 'The Scaddings, a Pioneer Family in York.' *Ontario Historical Society Papers and Records* 36 (1944): 6-20.

Reid, Robert. 'Courtship comedy: *As You Like It* ignores romance, approaches farce.' Rev. of *As You Like It*, dir. Richard Monette. Stratford Festival. Festival Theatre, Stratford, Ont. Kitchener-Waterloo *Record* 31 May 1990: C6.

Report of the General Secretary, 1954–5. Reports, 1952–5.
Reports, 1952–5. File 4. Papers of the Shakespeare Society.
Rereading Frye. The Published and Unpublished Works. Ed. David Boyd and Imre Salusinszky. Toronto: U of Toronto P, 1999.
'Revive English spirit at St. George's night.' *Telegram* [Toronto] 24 April 1953: 3.
Richmond, Anthony A. *Post-war Immigrants in Canada.* Canadian Studies in Sociology. Toronto: U of Toronto P, 1967.
Riendeau, Pascal. 'Normand Chaurette face a Shakespeare ou traduisez *Comme il vous plaira* ...' *L'Annuaire théâtrale* 24 (1998): 17–33.
Robbins, Bruce. 'Introduction Part I: Actually Existing Cosmopolitanism.' *Cosmopolitics: Thinking and Feeling beyond the Nation.* Ed. Pheng Cheah and Bruce Robbins. Minneapolis: U of Minnesota P, 1998. 1–19.
Roberts, Charles G.D., and Arthur L. Tunnell, eds. *A Standard Dictionary of Canadian Biography: The Canadian Who Was Who.* Vol. 1. Toronto: Trans-Canada P, 1934.
Roberts, Leslie. *A Report from Stratford.* Woodstock, Ont.: Commercial Print Craft, [c. 1955].
Robertson, N.A. 'The Order in Council.' Canada, *Report* xi–xiii. Rpt. in Rubin 153–5.
Robson, Frederic. 'The Drama in Canada.' Rubin 11–15.
Rodéo et Juliette. By and dir. Jean-Claude Germain. Théâtre du Même Nom. Théâtre du Canada à la Terre des Hommes, Montreal. 30 June 1970.
Romeo and Juliet. By William Shakespeare. Dir. Douglas Campbell. Perf. Louise Marleau and Christopher Walken. Stratford Festival. Stratford Festival Theatre, Stratford, Ont. 1968.
– Dir. Michael Langham. Stratford Festival. Stratford Festival Theatre, Stratford, Ont. 1960.
Roméo et Juliette. By William Shakespeare. Trans. Normand Chaurette. Dir. Martine Beaulne. Théâtre du Nouveau Monde, Montreal. 12 Jan.–6 Feb. 1999.
Ronfard, Jean-Pierre. *Lear. Cahier Trac.* Montreal: Théâtre expérimental de Montreal, 1977.
– *Vie et mort du roi boiteux.* 2 vols. Ottawa: Leméac, 1981.
Ronk, Martha C. 'Representations of Ophelia.' *Criticism* 36.1 (1994) 21–43.
Rooke, Leon. *Shakespeare's Dog.* Toronto: General, 1984.
Rose, Richard, and D.D. Kugler, eds. *The Tragedie of King Lear,* by William Shakespeare. Production Script. Toronto: Necessary Angel Theatre Company, 1995.
Ross, Malcolm, ed. *Our Sense of Identity: A Book of Canadian Essays.* Toronto: Ryerson P, 1954.

Roux, Jean-Louis. 'Shakespeare ... en québécois?' Interview by Jean-Luc Denis and Pierre Lavoie. *Cahiers de théâtre Jeu* 56 (1990): 38–43.
Rowe-Sleeman, Alice. 'A National Theatre for Canada.' *Canadians All* 3 (1945): 24+.
Rubess, Baṇuta. Introduction. MacDonald, *Goodnight Desdemona* 7–9.
Rubin, Don, ed. *Canadian Theatre History: Selected Readings.* Toronto: Copp Clark, 1996.
Ruthven, K.K. 'Bardbiz in Australia.' *Meanjin* 3 (1993): 559–71.
Rutter, Carol. *Clamourous Voices: Shakespeare's Women Today.* London: Routledge, 1989.
Rymer, Thomas. *A Short View of Tragedy: It's Original, Excellency, and Corruption.* Facsimile of original 1693 edition. London: Frank Cass, 1971.
Saddlemyer, Ann, and Richard Plant, eds. *Later Stages: Essays in Ontario Theatre from the First World War to the 1970s.* Ontario Historical Studies Series. Toronto: Government of Ontario, U of Toronto P, 1997.
Salter, Denis. 'Acting Shakespeare in Postcolonial Space.' Bulman 13–32.
– 'Between Wor(l)ds: Lepage's *Shakespeare Cycle.*' *Theater* 24.3 (1993): 61–70.
– 'The Idea of a National Theatre.' *Canadian Canons: Essays in Literary Value.* Ed. Robert Lecker. Toronto: U of Toronto P, 1991. 71–90.
– 'Introduction: The End(s) of Shakespeare?' Salter, *Shakespeare* 3–14.
– ed. *Shakespeare and Postcolonial Conditions.* Spec. issue of *Essays in Theatre/Études Théâtrales* 5.1 (1996).
Sandwell, Bernard K. [B.K.]. 'The Annexation of Our Stage.' Rubin 16–20.
– 'On the Appointment of Governor-General Vincent Massey, 1952.' Scott and Smith 59.
Scadding, Henry. *An Address to the Pioneer and Historical Society of the County of York on the Exhibition Grounds. Toronto June 18, 1891.* Toronto: Office of *The Week*, 1891.
– *Address Spoken by Master Henry Scadding, on the 9th April, 1829. At the Royal Grammar School, York, Upper Canada.* York: *U.C. Gazette* Office, [1829].
– *Catalogue of the Contents of A Log Shanty Book-Shelf ... 1887.* Toronto: Copp Clark, 1887.
– *Catalogue of the Log Shanty Book-Shelf for 1888 ... The Collection of a Not-Forgetful Devonshire Man.* Toronto: Copp Clark, 1888.
– *Centennial of Upper Canada Now the Province of Ontario. The Hundredth Anniversary of the Establishment of the Representative System, July 16, 1792.* Toronto: Office of *The Week*, 1892.
– *After Gleanings for the Log-Shanty Book Shelf of 1896 [...].* Toronto: Copp, Clark 1896.

- 'On Errata Recepta, Writen and Spoken. Read before the Canadian Institute, April 2nd, 1864.' *Canadian Journal* New series. Vol. 9. Offprint. May 1864.
- *Horace Canadianizing. Early Pioneer Life in Canada Recalled by Sayings of the Latin Poet Horace, Being the Log Shanty Book-Shelf Pamphlet for 1894*. Toronto: Copp Clark, 1894.
- Letter to the Legislative Assembly. N.d. File: York Pioneers. Scadding Scrapbooks, Printed Matter. Baldwin Room, Toronto Reference Library.
- 'Mrs. Jameson on Shakespeare and the Collier Emendations.' *The Week* 9.13 (1892): 200–1.
- *Mrs. Jameson on Shakespeare and the Collier Emendations*. Toronto: Office of *The Week*, 1892.
- 'Pioneer Literary Endeavours in Western Canada.' *Canadian Magazine of Politics, Science, Art and Literature* 2.4 (1894): 395–8.
- *Pioneer Shakespeare Culture in Canada, Collection of Shakespeare Literature ...* Toronto: Copp Clark, 1892.
- 'The Prize Poem: Emigration.' *Canadian Literary Magazine* 1.1 (1833): 12–15.
- *The Prize Poem. As Recited on the 14th of January, 1832 . ...* York: Robert Stanton, [1832].
- *Relics of a Pioneer Anti-Obscurantist Erasmus of Rotterdam. ... The Log Shanty Book-Shelf for 1891*. Toronto: Copp Clark, 1891.
- *Seneca's Prophecy and Its Fulfillment . ...* Toronto: Copp Clark, 1897. Scadding Papers. Urban Affairs Library, Metro Hall, Toronto.
- *Shakespeare, The Seer – The Interpreter . ...* 1864. Toronto: Copp Clark, 1897.
- *Toronto's First Germ (Fort Toronto): Some Explanatory Notes in Relation Thereto*. Toronto: *The Guardian* Book and Job Office, 1878. Baldwin Room, Toronto Reference Library.
- *The Valedictory Address Delivered before the Athenaeum of Toronto, at the Close of Their Annual Session, on Thursday, April 30. 1846*. Toronto: H. and W. Rowsell, 1846.

Scheff, Aimee. 'Shakespeare Arrives in Canada.' *Theatre Arts* July 1953: 83.
Schoenbaum, S. [Samuel]. *Shakespeare's Lives*. Rev. ed. Oxford: Clarendon P, 1991.
Scott, F.R. 'Communists, Senators, and All That.' *Canadian Forum* January 1932: 127–9.
- 'W.L.M.K.' *The Blasted Pine*. Ed. F.R. Scott and A.J.M. Smith. Toronto: Macmillan, 1960. 27–8.

Scrapbook. File 25. Papers of the Shakespeare Society.
Sears, Djanet. *Harlem Duet*. Winnipeg: Scirocco Drama, 1998, c. 1996.
Sears, Djanet, and Alison Sealy-Smith. 'The Nike Method: A Wide-ranging Con-

versation between Djanet Sears and Alison Sealy-Smith ...' Ed. R. Knowles. *Canadian Theatre Review* 97 (1998): 24–30.
Second Annual Competition. File H4–35. MG 30–D321. The Shakespeare Society of Toronto. National Archives of Canada, Ottawa.
Seeley, R.S.K. Foreword. Caillou, Walter, and Chappell.
Seymour, Michel. 'Le problème de la nation québéoise n'est pas son existence mais sa (non) reconnaissance.' *Le Devoir* 11–12 Sept. 1999: A11.
'The Shakespeare Festivals in Canada: The Earle Grey Players.' *Food for Thought* May–June 1953: 8–12.
'Shakespeare is compared with rivals: Prof. E.A. Dale assesses works of Jonson and Massinger but finds them in second rank.' *Evening Telegram* [Toronto] 8 Dec. 1948: 16.
Shakespeare, William. *Cymbeline*. Ed. Roger Warren. Oxford Shakespeare. Oxford, U.K.: Clarendon P, 1998; Evans et al. 1565–1611.
– *Othello*. New Cambridge Shakespeare. Ed. Norman Sanders. Cambridge: Cambridge UP, 1984.
– *Richard III*. New York: Signet, 1988.
– *The Second Part of Henry the Fourth* [*2 Henry IV*]. Evans et al. 928–73.
– *The Tempest*. Evans et al. 1656–88.
– *The Tragedy of Coriolanus*. Evans et al. 1440–8.
– *The Tragedy of Hamlet, Prince of Denmark*. Evans et al. 1183–245.
– *Two Gentlemen of Verona*. Evans et al. 177–207.
– *The Winter's Tale*. Evans et al. 1612–55.
Shakespeare's Books: Contemporary Cultural Politics and the Persistence of Empire. Ed. Philip Mead and Marion Campbell. Melbourne U Literary and Cultural Studies Ser. 1. Parkville, Victoria, Australia: Dept. of English, U of Melbourne, 1993.
Shakespeare's Merchant of Venice *in Auschwitz*. By and dir. Tibor Egervari. Théâtre Distinct (Ottawa). Les Salles du Gesù, Montreal. 9, 16, 17 Oct. 1993.
'Shakespeare's Message.' *Herald and Express* [Torquay, U.K.] 17 Jan. 1941. G. Wilson Knight. Ms. 41. Trinity College Archives, Toronto.
Sheppard, Nancy. 'Fine acting, timeless quality make *As You Like It* work.' Rev. of *As You Like It*, dir. Richard Monette. Stratford Festival. Festival Theatre, Stratford, Ont. *Times-Journal* [St. Thomas, Ont.] 31 May 1990: 5.
Sherlow, Lois. 'Shakespearean Dramaturgies in Quebec.' *Ilha do Desterro: A Journal of English Language, Literatures in English and Cultural Studies* 36 (1999): 185–218.
Shewring, Margaret. *Shakespeare in Performance: Richard II*. Manchester: Manchester UP, 1996.
Showalter, Elaine. 'Representing Ophelia: Women, Madness, and the Responsi-

bilities of Feminist Criticism.' *Shakespeare and the Question of Theory.* Ed. Patricia Parker and Geoffrey Hartman. New York: Methuen, 1985. 1–36.

Showalter, Harrison. Fund-raising letter. 6 April 1953. Ref. Book 9. Stratford Festival Archives.

– Fund-raising letter. 5 May 1953. Ref. Book 9. Stratford Festival Archives.

Sidnell, Michael J. 'Following the Arts: Adventures in the Culture Trade: The Stratford Festival 1991.' *Journal of Canadian Studies* 26.4 (1991–2):146–57.

Siemerling, Winfried. *Discoveries of the Other: Alterity in the Work of Leonard Cohen, Hubert Aquin, Michael Ondaatje, and Nicole Brossard.* Toronto: U of Toronto P, 1994.

Siemon, James R. 'Perplex'd Beyond Self-explication: *Cymbeline* and Early Modern/postmodern Europe.' Hattaway, Sokolova, and Roper 294–309.

'Silence safe, if not golden: Canon Cody emphatic in support of Governor-General's "Indies Speech."' *Evening Telegram* [Toronto] 24 April 1930: 5.

Simpson's. Advertisement. *Globe* [Toronto] 7 April 1929: 14.

Sinclair, Lister, adapt. *Richard II.* By William Shakespeare. Prod. Andrew Allan. 60 min. CBC Wednesday Night. CBC Radio, Toronto. Trans-Canada Network. 21 April 1948. King Richard the Second. Ts. E–1137–143. CBC Radio Drama Archives, Centre for Broadcasting Studies, Concordia U, Montreal.

– adapt. *Richard II.* By William Shakespeare. Prod. Andrew Allan. 150 min. CBC Wednesday Night. CBC Radio, Toronto. Trans-Canada Network. 21 May 1953. King Richard the Second. Ts. E–1137–145. CBC Radio Drama Archives, Centre for Broadcasting Studies, Concordia U, Montreal.

Sinfield, Alan. 'Reproductions, Interventions.' Dollimore and Sinfield, *Political* 130–3.

– 'Royal Shakespeare: Theatre and the Making of Ideology.' Dollimore and Sinfield, *Political* 158–81.

Six Dividends in Perpetuity: Why You Should Invest in a Great Canadian Enterprise, the Stratford Permanent Theatre Fund. Campaign brochure. Stratford Festival Archives, Stratford, Ont.

The Sixth Sense. Dir. M. Night Shyamalan. Perf. Bruce Willis and Haley Joel Osment. Buena Vista, 1999.

Skinner, Alan. 'Drama.' *Food for Thought* 10.8 (1950): 25–8.

Skinner, Ches. 'Newfoundland Amateur Theatre – Historical Sources.' Lynde, Peters, and Buehler 88–93.

Smith, Mary Elizabeth. 'Shakespeare in Atlantic Canada during the Nineteenth Century.' *Theatre History in Canada* 3.2 (1982): 126–36.

Solomon, Alisa. *Re-dressing the Canon: Essays on Theater and Gender.* London: Routledge, 1997.

Somerset, J. Alan B. *The Stratford Festival Story: A Catalogue Index to the Stratford Ontario Festival.* New York: Greenwood P, 1991.

Le Songe d'une nuit d'été d'après William Shakespeare. Adapt. and dir. Oleg Kisseliov. Théâtre Espace la Veillée, Montreal. 19 Sept.–18 Oct. 1998.

Speeches, 1936–63. File 10. Papers of the Shakespeare Society. 'Spirit of Merrie England recreated in home at Simpson's.' *Globe* [Toronto] 17 April 1929: 20.

Spivak, Gayatri Chakravorty. 'How to Teach a "Culturally Different" Book.' *The Spivak Reader: Selected Works of Gayatri Chakravorty Spivak.* Ed. Donna Landry and Gerald MacLean. New York: Routledge, 1996. 237–66.

Statistics: CBC 'Stage' Series. 14 Feb. 1949. Stage Series. CBC Reference Library, Toronto.

Steele, Kenneth B. 'The Stratford, Ontario, Festival 1992: A Canadian's Overview.' *Shakespeare Bulletin* 10.4 (1992): 13–17.

Stepan, Alfred. 'Modern Multinational Democracies: Transcending a Gellnerian Oxymoron.' *The State of the Nation: Ernest Gellner and the Theory of Nationalism.* Ed. John A. Hall. Cambridge: Cambridge UP, 1998. 219–42.

'St. George's Day.' Editorial. *Evening Telegram* [Toronto] 23 April 1930: 6.

'St. George's Society holds 95th service in traditional way.' *Globe* [Toronto] 22 April 1929: 16.

Stoppard, Tom. *Rosenkrantz and Guildenstern Are Dead.* London: Faber and Faber, 1967.

Stříbrný, Zdeněk. *Shakespeare and Eastern Europe.* Oxford: Oxford UP, 2000.

Stuart, Ross E. *The History of the Prairie Theatre.* Toronto: Simon and Pierre, 1984.

Suczek, Alex. '*Two Gents* gets clever interpretation at Stratford.' Rev. of *The Two Gentlemen of Verona*, dir. Richard Rose. Stratford Festival. Festival Theatre, Stratford, Ont. *Grosse Pointe News* 20 Aug. 1998: B6.

'Swamping of Canada by Non-Britishers now to be stopped.' *Globe* [Toronto] 9 Jan. 1929: 1.

Swanson, Cecil. Letter to the Shakespeare Society of Toronto. 6 Jan. 1955. Papers of Mrs R. Glassford.

Symonds, Richard. *Oxford and Empire: The Last Lost Cause?* Oxford: Clarendon P, 1986.

The Taming of the Shrew. By William Shakespeare. Dir. Richard Rose. Stratford Festival. Festival Theatre, Stratford, Ont. 1997.

Taylor, Charles. *Multiculturalism and 'The Politics of Recognition.'* Princeton, N.J.: Princeton UP, 1992.

Taylor, Kate. 'Characters lost in political lessons.' Rev. of *Harlem Duet*, by Djanet Sears. Tarragon Extra Space. Nightwood Theatre, Toronto. *Globe and Mail* 28 April 1997: C3.

– Rev. of the 1998 Halifax Shakespeare by the Sea Festival. Point Pleasant, Halifax. *Globe and Mail* 30 June 1998: A14.

– 'Saving Stratford from the excesses of success.' *Globe and Mail* 18 July 1998: C1+.

- 'A sprightly take on *Twelfth Night*.' Rev. of *Twelfth Night*, dir. Michael Langham. Atlantic Theatre Festival, Wolfville, N.S. *Globe and Mail* 2 July 1996: A10.
Tepper, Bill. 'The Forties and Beyond: The New Play Society.' *Canadian Theatre Review* 28 (1980): 18–33.
Thomas, David M. *Whistling Past the Graveyard: Constitutional Abeyances: Quebec and the Future of Canada*. Toronto: Oxford UP, 1997.
Tillyard, E.M.W. *The Elizabethan World Picture*. London: Chatto and Windus, 1943.
Tippett, Maria. *Making Culture: English Canadian Institutions and the Arts before the Massey Commission*. Toronto: U of Toronto P, 1990.
'Told in the Foyer.' *Curtain Call* 25 April 1931: 5. ('Told')
Tompkins, Joanne. 'Re-citing Shakespeare in Post-colonial Drama.' *Essays in Theatre* 15.1 (1996): 15–22.
Toronto Athenaeum, Instituted May 1, 1845. ... Toronto: H. and W. Rowsell, 1845.
Townsend, Aurelian. 'Antemasques for *Florimène*.' Orgel and Strong 2: 631, 636–7.
The Tragedie of King Lear. By William Shakespeare. Dir. Richard Rose. Perf. Janet Wright. Necessary Angel Theatre Co. Canadian Stage, Berkeley Street Theatre Upstairs, Toronto. 21 Mar.–15 Apr. 1995.
Tremblay, Michel. *Les Belles-soeurs*. Montreal: Éditions Leméac, 1972.
Trilling, Lionel. *Sincerity and Authenticity*. Cambridge, Mass.: Harvard UP, 1973.
Twain, Mark. *Is Shakespeare Dead?* New York: Harper and Brothers, 1909.
Two Gentlemen of Verona. By William Shakespeare. Dir. Richard Rose. Perf. David Jansen. Stratford Festival. Festival Theatre, Stratford, Ont. 1998. 12 Aug.–7 Nov. 1998.
Vaïs, Michel. 'Montréal russophone.' *Cahiers de théâtre Jeu* 90 (1999): 82–6.
Victory Bonds. Advertisement. *Evening Telegram* [Toronto] 24 April 1943: 11; 26 April 1943: 7.
Vincent, Thomas, comp. *Index to Pre 1900 English Language Canadian Cultural and Literary Magazines*. CD-ROM. Ottawa: Opticom.
Voaden, Herman. 'The Theatre in Canada: I. A National Theatre?' *Theatre Arts* July 1946: 389–91.
- 'Theatre Record 1945.' *Canadian Forum* November 1945: 184–7.
Wade, Michael. Rev. of *Twelfth Night*, dir. Gordon Jones. Little [Reid] Theatre, St John's. Morning Show. CBC Radio One. 23 July 1987.
Wagner, Anton, ed. *The Brock Bibliography of Published Canadian Plays in English 1766–1978*. Comp. Bonita J. Orosz Bryan et al. Toronto: Playwrights P, 1980.
- ed. *Contemporary Canadian Theatre: New World Visions: A Collection of Essays Prepared by the Canadian Theatre Critics Association*. Toronto: Simon and Pierre, 1985.
- Introduction. A. Wagner, *Brock* i–xi.

Wagner, Vit. 'No gender rules for Rose's *King Lear*.' Rev. of *The Tragedie of King Lear*, dir. Richard Rose. Necessary Angel Theatre Co. Canadian Stage, Berkeley Street Theatre Upstairs, Toronto. Toronto *Star* 19 March 1995: C11.
- 'Stratford's young veteran, Colm Feore: This Hamlet is ready to act.' Toronto *Star* 25 May 1991: H4.
- 'Theatre as it should be.' Rev. of *Harlem Duet*, by Djanet Sears. Tarragon Extra Space. Nightwood Theatre, Toronto. *Globe and Mail* 27 April 1997: B3.
Walcott, Derek. 'Prelude.' *In a Green Night: Poems 1948–1960*. London: Cape, 1969. 11.
Walden, Keith. *Becoming Modern in Toronto: The Industrial Exhibition and the Shaping of Late Victorian Culture*. Toronto: U Toronto P, 1997.
Wallace, Malcolm W. 'The Humanities.' Canada, *Royal* 99–118.
Wallace, Robert. 'Writing the Land Alive: The Playwrights' Vision in English Canada.' A. Wagner, *Contemporary* 69–81.
Wanger, E.G. 'Bard's tragedies perfect, Professor tells followers.' *Globe and Mail* 8 Dec. 1948: 25.
Weber, Carl. 'Heiner Müller: The Despair and the Hope.' *Performing Arts Journal* 12 (1980): 135–40.
Wednesday Night. CBC Reference Library, Toronto.
'Wednesday Night – Audience Mail: Dec. 1947–Mar. 1948.' Comp. Charles Jennings. CBS 003–008. CBC Radio Drama Archives. Centre for Broadcasting Studies, Concordia U, Montreal.
Weil, Herbert S., Jr, E-mail to Irena R. Makaryk. 29 March 2000.
- 'Shakespeare Festival, Canada, 1986.' *Shakespeare Quarterly* 38.2 (1987): 227–40.
Weimann, Robert. 'A Divided Heritage: Conflicting Appropriations of Shakespeare in (East) Germany.' Joughin 175–205.
Whiteway, Louise. 'History of the Arts in Newfoundland.' *Newfoundland Government Bulletin* March 1953: 7–9.
'Whither Now.' Caillou, Walter, and Chappell.
Whitman, Walt. 'What Lurks behind Shakespeare's Historical Plays?' *The Complete Poetry and Prose of Walt Whitman*. Ed. Malcolm Cowley. Vol. 2. New York: Pellegrini and Cudahy 1948. 404–6.
Whittaker, Herbert. 'New theatre, play will open Friday.' *Globe and Mail* 1 April 1964: 14.
- 'Shakespeare in Canada before 1953.' B.W. Jackson, *Stratford* 71–89.
- *Whittaker's Theatre: A Critic Looks at Stages in Canada and Thereabouts 1944–1975*. Ed. Ronald Bryden with Boyd Neil. Toronto: U of Toronto P, 1985.
Wigh, Sylvia. 'One woman's opinion: "MacBeth" technical triumph for Palmer.' Rev. of *Macbeth*, dir. George Palmer. Little [Reid] Theatre, St John's. *Evening Telegram* [St John's] 14 Oct. 1961: 11.

William, David. 'The 1990 Stratford, Ontario, Festival: An Interview with Artistic Director David William.' *Shakespeare Bulletin* 8.4 (1990): 5–8.

Wilson, Ann. 'Critical Revisions: Ann-Marie MacDonald's *Goodnight Desdemona (Good Morning Juliet).*' *Women on the Canadian Stage: The Legacy of Hrotsvit.* Ed. Rita Much. Winnipeg: Blizzard 1992. 1–12.

Wilson, Daniel. *Caliban: The Missing Link.* London: Macmillan, 1873.

Wilson, Mary Floyd. 'Ophelia and Femininity in the Eighteenth-century: "Dangerous Conjectures in Ill-Breeding Minds."' *Women's Studies* 21 (1992): 397–409.

Winsor, Christopher. 'Only Their Dressers Know for Sure: Maggie Huculak and David Jansen Switch Sexes for *King Lear*.' Rev. of *The Tragedie of King Lear*, dir. Richard Rose. Necessary Angel Theatre Co. Canadian Stage, Berkeley Street Theatre Upstairs, Toronto. *eye* 16 March 1995: 31.

Woodcock, George. *Strange Bedfellows: The State and the Arts in Canada.* Vancouver: Douglas and McIntyre, 1985.

'World peace British hope, society told: Sir Willmot Lewis is speaker before 500 who celebrate memory of St. George.' *Evening Telegram* [Toronto] 24 April 1935: 17.

Worthen, W.B. *Modern Drama and the Rhetoric of Theater.* Berkeley: U of California P, 1992.

– *Shakespeare and the Authority of Performance.* Cambridge: Cambridge UP, 1997.

– 'Staging "Shakespeare": Acting, Authority, and the Rhetoric of Performance.' Bulman 12–28.

'Wright, Don [Donald John Alexander].' *The Canadian Who's Who 1996.* Ed. Elizabeth Lumley. Vol. 31. Toronto: U of T Press, 1996. 1315.

Yeo, Leslie. *A Thousand and One First Nights.* Canadian Theatre History Ser. 2. Academy of the Shaw Festival. Oakville, Ont.: Mosaic P, 1998.

York Pioneer and Historical Society Annual Report ... 1921. Archives of Ontario, Toronto.

Zeffirelli, Franco, dir. *Hamlet.* Perf. Mel Gibson, Glenn Close, Alan Bates, Ian Holm, and Helena Bonham Carter. Warner Bros., 1990.

Žižek, Slavoj. *Tarrying with the Negative: Kant, Hegel, and the Critique of Ideology.* Durham, N.C.: Duke UP, 1993.

Zola, Émile. *Naturalism in the Theatre.* Trans. Albert Bermel. *The Theory of the Modern Stage.* Ed. Eric Bentley. London: Penguin, 1990. 351–72.

Contributors

Peter Ayers is an associate professor at Memorial University of Newfoundland. He has taught in Africa, the Middle East, England, and Canada, and has published a variety of articles on medieval and early modern drama. He is also the co-editor of an anthology of West African literature and another on early West Indian writing.

Karen Bamford is associate professor at Mount Allison University in New Brunswick. The author of *Sexual Violence on the Jacobean Stage* (St Martin's, 2000) and co-editor, with Alexander Leggatt, of *Approaches to Teaching English Renaissance Drama* (forthcoming), she is currently researching the Shakespeare Society of Vancouver (1916–1979).

Diana Brydon, Robert and Ruth Lumsden Professor of English, teaches Canadian and postcolonial literatures at the University of Western Ontario. She is the author of *Christina Stead* (Macmillan/Barnes Noble 1987), *Timothy Findley's 'Famous Last Words'* (ECW 1995), and *Timothy Findley* (Twayne 1998), the co-author of *Decolonising Fictions* (Dangaroo 1992), and the editor of the five-volume anthology *Postcolonialism: Critical Concepts in Literary and Cultural Studies* (Routledge 2000). She guest-edited the postcolonial issue of *Essays on Canadian Writing* (1995) and is currently working on globalization, autonomy, and postcolonial studies.

Anthony B. Dawson is professor of English at the University of British Columbia and the former president of the Shakespeare Association of America (2001–2). His books include *Indirections: Shakespeare and the Art of Illusion* (University of Toronto Press, 1978), *Watching Shakespeare* (Macmillan 1988), *Hamlet* (Shakespeare in Performance, Manchester

University Press, 1995), and, with Paul Yachnin, *The Culture of Playgoing in Shakespeare's England* (Cambridge University Press, 2001). He is at present completing the forthcoming edition of *Troilus and Cressida* for the Cambridge Shakespeare series.

L.M. (Len) Findlay is a graduate of Aberdeen and Oxford and professor of English and director of the Humanities Research Unit at the University of Saskatchewan. He has published extensively on nineteenth-century European literature and more recently on Canadian/aboriginal topics and the cultural politics of globalization. His current publications include the co-edited *Pursuing Academic Freedom: 'Free and Fearless?'* (Purich Press, 2001) and a new edition of *The Communist Manifesto* (Broadview Press, forthcoming). Projects well advanced include a book on public intellectuals and English Studies in Canada and a study of intellectual and artistic freedom based on his Frye lectures of 2001.

Daniel Fischlin is professor in the School of Literatures and Performance Studies in English at the University of Guelph and director of the joint PhD program in Literary Studies/Theatre Studies in English offered by the University of Guelph and Wilfrid Laurier University. He holds an Ontario Premier's Research Excellence Award for a project entitled 'Canadian Adaptations of Shakespeare' and is co-editor of *Adaptations of Shakespeare: A Critical Anthology of Plays from the Seventeenth Century to the Present* (Routledge, 2000).

Mark Fortier is associate professor of English at the University of Winnipeg. He is author of *Theory/Theatre: An Introduction* (2nd ed. Routledge, 2002) and co-editor of *Adaptations of Shakespeare: A Critical Anthology of Plays from the Seventeenth Century to the Present* (Routledge, 2000).

Margaret Groome is assistant professor of English, theatre, and drama at the University of Manitoba. Her research interests are mainly in Shakespeare studies and feminist theatre work. At present, she is concluding work on a book on Canada's Stratford Festival and is mid-way through a major project on women directors of Shakespeare in Britain, from 1879 to the present day. Margaret received the Richard Plant Award from the Association for Canadian Theatre Research for the best essay in English published in 2000 for 'Affirmative Shakespeare at Canada's Stratford Festival.' The essay appears in *Essays in Theatre* 17.2

(1999): 139–64. Margaret also directs for the theatre: recent directing projects include *Tartuffe* and *As You Like It* for the University of Manitoba's Black Hole Theatre.

Ric Knowles teaches drama and is a member of the Centre for Cultural Studies at the University of Guelph as well as a faculty member of the Graduate Centre for the Study of Drama at the University of Toronto. He is editor of *Modern Drama* and co-editor of *Canadian Theatre Review*. He publishes on Shakespeare and on Canadian theatre, and his recent book, *The Theatre of Form and the Production of Meaning*, won the 2001 Ann Saddlemyer Prize for Outstanding Book on Canadian Drama and Theatre.

Alexander Leggatt is professor of English at University College, University of Toronto. His publications include *Shakespeare's Comedy of Love* (1974), *Shakespeare's Political Drama* (1988), *English Stage Comedy 1490–1990* (1998) and *Introduction to English Renaissance Comedy* (1999).

Leanore Lieblein is a member of the McGill Shakespeare in Performance Research Group. She has published articles on early modern theatre, theatre archives, theatre criticism, and theatrical translation, and is working on a study of Shakespeare in francophone Quebec. She has also directed medieval, Renaissance and modern plays.

Irena R. Makaryk is professor of English at the University of Ottawa, where she has been teaching since 1981. Her teaching and research interests embrace Shakespeare, Renaissance, comparative, and Slavic drama. She is the author of numerous articles and author, editor, or co-editor of eight books, including the general editor and compiler of *The Encyclopedia of Contemporary Literary Theory* (University of Toronto Press, 1993). Her special interest is Shakespeare reception studies and issues of nationalism and national identity. She has just completed *The Undiscovered Bourne: Shakespeare, Modernism, Kurbas*.

C.E. McGee, associate professor of English at St Jerome's College, University of Waterloo, co-edited with Rosalind Hays the *Records of Early English Drama: Dorset* (University of Toronto Press, 1999). He is currently working on the New Variorum *Othello*, canoeing the Canadian wilderness in the summer, and playing for the Waterloo Worriers in the winter.

Michael McKinnie teaches in the Department of Drama and Theatre Arts at the University of Birmingham. His research focuses on theatre and urban development, cultural theory and arts policy, and Canadian theatre. Publications include articles and reviews in *Theatre Journal, Essays on Canadian Writing, Theatre Research in Canada, Essays in Theatre,* and *Canadian Theatre Review.* He is the recipient of the 1999–2001 Distinguished Dissertation Award from the Association for Canadian Studies in the United States.

Heather Murray teaches in the Department of English at the University of Toronto. She is the author of *Working in English: History, Institution, Resources* (University of Toronto Press 1996), and *'Come, Bright Improvement!' The Literary Societies of Nineteenth-Century Ontario* (University of Toronto Press, 2002). Her current research interests are early Canadian cultural history and book history.

Jessica Schagerl is a doctoral student at the University of Western Ontario. Her MA thesis, '"A Shakespearian View Of It": Shakespeare in Canada, 1848–1891' (University of Ottawa 2001), examined the prevalence of Shakespeare in Canada's nineteenth-century comic press.

Lois Sherlow teaches dramatic literature at Sir Wilfred Grenfell College, Memorial University of Newfoundland, in Corner Brook. She obtained her doctorate at the University of Ottawa. She has recently published articles on the theatre of Robertson Davies and Shakespearean dramaturgies in Quebec.

Marta Straznicky is associate professor of English at Queen's University. She has published on Shakespeare, Renaissance comedy, and closet drama of the sixteenth and seventeenth centuries. She is completing a book entitled *Privacy, Playreading, and Early Modern Women's Closet Drama,* and beginning a second book on the history of playreading.

Brent E. Whitted is a teacher of English literature at the Marlborough School in Los Angeles. His research interests include relations between the early modern English theatre and the market, connections between literature and other art forms, and modernist literature.

Paul Yachnin is Tomlinson professor of Shakespeare Studies at McGill University. His first book was *Stage-Wrights: Shakespeare, Jonson, Middleton,* *and the Making of Theatrical Value* (University of Pennsylvania Press, 1996); his second, co-authored with Anthony Dawson, was *The Culture of Playgoing in Shakespeare's England: A Collaborative Debate* (Cambridge University Press, 2001). He is an editor of the forthcoming Oxford edition of *The Works of Thomas Middleton*, and editor of *Richard II*, also under contract with Oxford. His book-in-progress is *Shakespeare and the Dimension of Literature*, which will argue that literature's political consequentiality is an effect of the long rather than the short term.

Index

Abbey, Graham, 152
aboriginal people. *See* First Nations
Ackerman, Marianne, 12
actors, 72, 242–3, 247, 339; adaptations for, 13, 98, 201; bodies of, 223, 225–7, 248–9; Canadian, 14–15, 142–3, 156n6; at CBC, 92, 93–4, 101–2, 103; and characters, 217–19, 237–8, 245, 249, 252n6; and cultural colonialism, 13–14, 408; and gender, 31, 193, 214, 215–19, 223–9; and race, 223, 319; training of, 218, 236–42, 245–7, 249–51, 252n3–4. *See also* touring companies
Actors Colony Theatre (Toronto), 133n11
Adamson, Joseph, 306
adaptation, 35–8, 315, 398; for actors, 13, 98, 201; and authenticity, 313, 326, 337n11; and Canadian identity, 313, 321–2, 323–4; as collaboration, 340, 347, 351; as confrontation, 339–40, 341, 344, 347, 351; definition of, 317, 335n3, 336n7; and difference, 327–8; as genre, 315, 317–18, 321; politics of, 318–20, 343–4, 347–8, 352, 372; radio, 93–4, 96–103; and source, 317–18, 324–5, 332, 354, 376–7, 378–80, 386–7. *See also* titles of plays
Adorno, Theodor W., 337n13
Afrika Solo (Sears), 381
agency, 379, 404
Aird Report (1929), 22
Albany Club (Toronto), 66, 67, 69
Alberta Theatre Projects (Calgary), 344
Alchemist, The (Jonson), 203
alchemy, 355–68
Alexander, W.J., 17
Alexandra Players, 195, 210n4
Alexandra Repertory Theatre (England), 195
Allan, Andrew, 415; adaptations by, 94, 96, 98–9, 105n7–9, 106n12; directorial style of, 101, 103; Shakespearean interpretations by, 97–8, 99–103, 106n13, 107n17; use of broadcast drama by, 95, 98, 100–2, 104
allegory, 369n2, 396; and alchemy, 355–7, 358; and modernism, 358–9, 368; postmodern, 360
Allen, Graham, 103

All's Well That Ends Well (Shakespeare), 70, 296
Alternative Shakespeares (Drakakis, ed.), 403
alternative theatres, 30–2, 83, 182, 199
Amateurs Canadiens, Les, 32
amateur theatre, 72, 114, 196, 412; and elitism, 19–20, 74; function of, 69, 193–4, 195, 202–3; types of, 73, 197
Amédée, ou Comment s'en débarrasser (Chaurette), 364
amnesia, historical, 318–19
anagogic criticism, 296–7, 301
Anatomy of Criticism (Frye), 18, 294, 296, 300
Anderson, Benedict, 313
Andrès, Bernard, 190n12
Anglin, Anne, 162
Anglin, Margaret, 14–15
Annand, James, 66, 69, 73, 77, 84n6
Anne of Green Gables (Montgomery), 157n6
Annex Theatre (Toronto), 348
Another Shakespeare (Ottawa), 131n2
Antony and Cleopatra (Shakespeare), 274; adaptations of, 96, 105n7; productions listed, 194; productions reviewed, 72
Appeal to Pride, An (Stratford Festival), 129–30
Applebaum, Louis, 166
Appleton, Elizabeth, 255, 265
Aquin, Hubert, 37
Arcane 17 (Breton), 370n6
Arnold, Matthew, 74, 86n18, 295–6, 298
Art Gallery of Ontario, 16
Artaud, Antonin, 358, 359, 362
Arthur, Julia, 14
Arts and Letters Club (Toronto), 112
Arts and Letters Club Players (Toronto), 20
Ashley, Audrey, 148
Asselin, Jean, 358, 369n2
Assiniboine Theatre, 28
Assmann, Aleida, 253n14
Aster Place riot (1849), 258, 267
As You Like It (Shakespeare), 285; adaptations of, 99; Canadianized, 146, 148–51, 156; productions described, 24, 158n10; productions listed, 14, 27, 28, 70, 134n13, 392n2, 413; reviews of, 148–51, 208
At the Sign of the Beaver (Bayliss), 262
Atienza, Edward, 166
Atkinson, Brooks, 26
Atlantic Theatre Festival (Wolfville, N.S.), 28, 131n2
Attali, Jacques, 326
Atwood, Margaret, 37
Audet, André, 177
audience, 98, 199, 283; address to, 220, 223, 228, 319; assumed, 177, 222–3, 299, 379–80; CBC radio 93–6, 97–8, 100–3, 105n11, 106nn15–16; communication with, 189n3, 215–16, 218, 240–1, 243–4; contemporary, 101–3, 239, 243–4, 247, 369n2; creation of, 198, 201, 202; education of, 157n6, 161, 165; elitist, 376–7; expectation, 357, 360; identification, 248; participation, 316; positioning of, 221–2, 228, 329, 388; reactions of, 9–10, 12, 155; university, 14; younger, 315, 317
authenticity: and identity, 325–7, 329–30, 333–4, 337n13, 398; myth

of, 37, 327; problematized, 324–5, 333–4, 337n11, 338n14
author, 244; controversy over, 18, 51, 58; 255–71, 272n2, 325; of culture, 71–2, 271; function, 311, 398, 402, 408; identity of, 257, 322, 349–50; intentions of, 118–19, 361; relationship to characters, 331–3
Ayer, John, 294
Ayers, Peter, 13

Bacon, Delia, 256–9, 271; and elitism, 266, 267; prose style of, 261, 262–4, 265
Bacon, Francis, 51, 58, 255–7, 261, 264, 268, 271
Bahktin, Mikhail, 209
Bains, Yashdip, 9
Bamford, Karen, 16, 21
Bannerji, Himani, 401
barbarism, 345, 347
Bard on the Beach (Vancouver), 28, 29–30, 31, 131n2
Barish, Jonas, 8
Barrymore, John, 13
Bartholomew Fair (Jonson), 203
Barton, John, 240
Baskerville, Agnes, 412
Bate, Jonathan, 276
Bates, Alan, 24
Baumander, Lewis, 160
Bawtree, Michael, 135n25
Baxter, Arthur Beverly, 19
Bayliss, Samuel, 255, 262–4, 265, 266
Beaulne, Martine, 34, 191n21
Beaver-Instinct, 60
Beckett, Samuel, 354
Being at Home with Claude (Dubois), 343
Beissel, Henry, 135n25

Belke, David, 37
Bell, Alf, 156n2
Belles-soeurs, Les (Tremblay), 180, 370n5
Belshaw, Diana, 218, 219, 225
Bemrose, John, 225, 228
Bengough, John Wilson, 410–12
Benjamin, Walter, 347–8, 352, 358–9
Bennett, Susan, 174, 248, 352; on *King Lear*, 212, 214; on Shakespeare studies, 403, 406
Benson, Eugene, 6
Benson, Frank, 100
Bentley-Fisher, Patricia, 163
Béraud, Jean, 6, 36
Beresford-Howe, Constance, 37
Berger, Carl, 45
Berger, Harry, 243, 247, 249, 253n10
Berkeley Street Theatre (Toronto), 220
Bernhardt, Sarah, 12–13, 162, 223
Bertoldi, Andreas, 161
Berton, Pierre, 106n14
Bessai, Diane, 392n4
Bessborough, Earl of, 21, 117, 413
Best, Wayne, 166
Bhabha, Homi K., 109, 397–8
Bienvenue, Yvan, 34
Big-Time Shakespeare (Bristol), 400, 408
bilingualism, 184, 330
Black, Hugh, 272n6
Black Hole Theatre Company (Winnipeg), 350
Blake, Mervyn, 165–6
Blatchley, John, 27
Blendick, James, 163
Blind Man's Buff (Euringer), 135n25
Bloom, Harold, 399
body: of actor, 223, 225–7; transformation of, 362–5, 367

Boland, Rick, 199
Boling, Ronald, 291n6
Boll, Sidonie, 164
Bolster, Charles, 177
Bonham-Carter, Helena, 172
Booth, Agnes, 14
Booth, Allan, 393n12
Booth, Edwin, 13
Booth, John Wilkes, 13
borders, 290
Bouchard, Lucien, 185
Boulet, Marcel, 29
Bowring, Sir Eric, 210n4
Brady, Owen E., 173n8
Branagh, Kenneth, 160, 171
Brassard, André, 353
Brathwaite, Edward Kamau, 403, 404
Bread, Françoise, 30
Brecht, Bertolt, 344–5, 351, 358, 359
Breton, André, 362, 365, 370n6
Breuer, Lee, 229n2
Brewster, Elizabeth, 37
Brind'Amour, Yvette, 34
Brisset, Annie, 180, 182
Bristol, Michael, 131n3, 400, 408; on culture industry, 208, 209, 402
British National Theatre, 320–1
Bromley, Patricia, 211n16
Brook, Peter, 207, 242, 244
Brookes, Chris, 192, 193, 209; on theatre and community, 195, 198–9, 210n12
Brothers Karamazov, The (Dostoevsky), 345
Brown, Frederick, 12
Brown, Stewart, 148
Bucke, Richard Maurice, 255, 259–62, 263, 265, 266, 268
Bulman, James, 339
Burbage, Richard, 241

Burdett, Lois, 38
Burnet, Jean, 335n2
Burnside, Ruby, 74
Burnside Reading Group, 74, 75
Burt, Richard, 402
Bush, Stephen, 200
Butt, Donna, 199, 201
Byrne, Barbara, 210n5

Caliban: The Missing Link (Wilson), 54, 57
Cambridge Companion to Shakespeare in the Theatre (Wells and Stanton), 253n9
Campbell, Douglas, 145, 155–6, 161
Campbell, Ken, 206–7, 208
Campbell, Mrs Patrick, 173n4
Canada, 90n38, 284, 338n16; Atlantic, 9–11, 13; Black history in, 318, 381–2; central, 157n8; as comedy, 299–300, 302, 306; cultural position of, 23, 259, 264, 268–9; dialectic in, 251, 276–7; diversity of, 143, 335n2; English-French politics in, 144–6, 150, 157nn7–8, 167–8, 180–1, 302–3, 315; founding cultures of, 326, 330, 375; immigration to, 81, 83, 91n42–5, 121, 336n7; national politics in, 150, 156, 166, 170–1; as New France, 146, 148, 158n9, 182; prairie, 373; relationship to United States, 261–2, 275, 280, 305; Western, 16–17, 20–1, 157n8, 328–30. *See also* colonialism: in Canada; national identity; national theatre; Newfoundland; Ontario; Quebec
Canada Council for the Arts, 199, 202, 211n13; creation of, 23, 392n4; and cultural imperialism, 327, 400
Canada First Movement, 12

Canadian Arts Council, 132n7
Canadian Broadcasting Corporation (formerly Canadian Radio Broadcasting Corporation), 22, 37; *Critically Speaking* (CBC), 97; mandate of, 92–4, 104; productions by, 93–4, 98–9; programming by, 92–6, 105n2, 106n14; *Stage*, 95–8, 415. See also *Wednesday Night*
Canadian Forum, 397, 398, 409n1
Canadian National Theatre (Ottawa), 19
Canadian National Theatre on the Air: 1925–1961 (Fink), 105n2
Canadian Players, 25, 158n11
Canadian Repertory Theatre (Ottawa), 27, 413, 414, 415
Canadian Stage Company (Toronto), 319, 353, 371
Canadian Theatre Review, 372, 381
Canadiens, Les (Salutin), 372
canon, 294; authority of, 314, 334, 387; creation of, 39, 109–10, 307, 399; opposition to, 35, 180, 330–1, 336n9, 386–7, 391; politics of, 36, 293, 326–7; Shakespeare in, 40, 306, 314, 378
Cantatrice chauve, La (Ionesco), 354
Canvas Barricade, The (Jack), 135n25
Cappel, Manuel, 39–40
Card, Raymond, 66, 74, 76–7, 83n2
Card, Mrs Raymond, 66
Carlyle, Thomas, 256, 258
Carrier, Roch, 135n25
Cartelli, Thomas, 404, 407
Carver, Brent, 163
casting: and gender, 31–2, 163, 212, 214, 215–19, 223–9, 230n8; on merit, 212, 214–17, 219, 224–5; and politics, 145–6, 156; and race, 230n8, 371
Catherine and Petruchio (Garrick), 8, 9, 12, 14
censorship, 9
Centaur Theatre (Montreal), 25
Césaire, Aimé, 403
Chalmers Award, 353, 372
Champagne, Gill, 353
Chancellor, Sir Christopher, 210n7
Chapman, Geoff, 224
character: creation of, 237–41, 245, 251, 252n4; naturalized, 217–19, 241, 252n7; stability of, 247, 249
Characteristics of Women (Jameson), 52, 57
Charlottetown Conference, 277
Charlottetown Theatre, 25
Chaurette, Normand, 35, 37, 336n7, 353–69, 370n3
Chautauqua Literary and Scientific Circle, 51
Chen, Xiaomei, 404
Chief Shaking Spear Rides Again (or the Taming of the Sioux) (Graves), 328–30
Christianity, 302, 344, 345
Cibber, Colley, 14
Ciceri, Leo, 16, 162, 414
Cid maghané (Ducharme), 180
Citadel Theatre (Edmonton), 25, 328
civilization, 284–5, 327; and theatre, 110–11, 116–17
Claing, Robert, 358, 369n2
Clamorous Voices (Rutter), 242
Clark, Stanley K., 67, 75
Clarke, Margaret, 37, 350–1
class: in Canada, 87n25, 306, 335n2, 376; construction of, 372, 373; and ethnicity, 375–7, 382; and gender,

374, 377; and race, 382, 393n13; and Shakespeare, 75–6, 271
classics, 111, 120; and Canadian theatre, 126, 141–2; value of, 117, 120–2
Cloning Miranda (Matas), 345–7
CNRV Players, 92
Coburn, Christine, 38
Cocteau, Jean, 358, 367
Codco (St John's), 198–9
Coffey, Denise, 25
Cohen, Nathan, 25–6; on Stratford Festival, 115, 133n10, 135n21, 142, 156n5
Coleman, Beau, 212
Colicos, John, 16
Collected Works of Billy the Kid, The (Ondaatje), 135n25
Collier, J. Payne, 51, 52, 57, 64n10
Collins, Patricia, 164, 165
colonialism: anti-, 337n9; in Canada, 35, 81, 192, 275, 292, 313–14, 404–5, 407; dynamics of, 161, 263–4, 332–3, 401–2; and literature, 330–1, 336n9; and national identity, 326–7, 330; reverse, 24; Shakespeare as, 4, 22, 59–60; and theatre, 30, 35, 159, 175–6; and transculturation, 36; Yankee, 158n11. *See also* colonialism, cultural; imperialism; postcolonialism
colonialism, cultural, 76–8, 323, 333, 390, 399; opposition to, 182, 314; and Stratford Festival, 25, 132n6, 192, 213, 397
Colours in the Dark (Reaney), 135n25
Colour the Flesh the Colour of Dust (Cook), 210n12
Columbus, Christopher, 56, 58, 59, 60, 61

Comédie Française, 354
comedy, 296–300, 302, 389. *See also titles of plays*
Comedy of Errors (Shakespeare), 14, 29
commodification, 29, 38–40, 307
community, 303–4, 398; and culture, 306, 314; and drama, 299–300; global, 300; imagined, 313, 317, 330
Community Stage Theatre, 199
community theatre, 195
Compagnons de Saint-Laurent, Les, 33, 175, 176, 177, 178
Company of Comedians, 8
Company of Fools (Ottawa), 28, 31
Compleat Works of Wllm Shkspr, 320
Conlogue, Ray, 200
Conolly, L.W., 6
Cook, Michael, 198, 210n12
Copeau, Jacques, 176, 178
Copeman, Elizabeth, 153, 154
Coquelin, 13
Corbeil, Carole, 37
Coriolanus (Shakespeare), 3, 325; adaptations of, 99; productions listed, 12, 14; in translation, 183–4
Cosmic Consciousness (Bucke), 259
cosmopolitanism, 45
costumes: in *As You Like It*, 148–9; and gender, 207, 227; in *Hamlet*, 162, 164, 166, 168–9; in *Two Gentlemen of Verona*, 151–4, 156
Coulbourn, John, 216
Coulter, John, 111, 112, 113, 133n8
country opera, 373, 376, 391
Coursen, H.R., 170
Cowden Clarke, Mary, 51, 52, 64n8
Cox, Dudley, 210n11
Crainford, Leonard, 74, 80
Crawford, A.W., 18
Crean, Patrick, 135n25

Creation 2, 30
Critical Path, The (Frye), 305
cross-casting. *See* casting: and gender
Crown of Life, The (Knight), 18
Cruel Tears (Mitchell et al.), 37, 315, 371, 372–7, 378, 379, 382, 386; context of, 390–1; genre in, 391; populism in, 389
Crying Game, The, 238
cultural authority, 67, 119, 243, 249; affirmation of, 121, 126–7, 198, 242; appropriation of, 82–3, 181, 244, 266, 329, 377, 387, 391; invocation of, 91n42, 412; subversion of, 179, 391, 412
culture, 22, 119, 316, 340; authorship of, 71–2, 271; and autonomy, 314; Black, 318–20; Canadian dependence for, 13–15, 35, 110; critics of, 47, 61, 297–8; defined, 74, 86n18–19; development of, 73, 74, 93–4, 104, 399; elitist, 11–12, 16, 159–60, 258, 264, 267, 327; globalization of, 5, 13; and imperialism, 192, 213; industry, 25, 134n15, 208, 209, 404; and language, 182, 184, 190n12, 302, 314; and maturity, 22, 110–11, 124–5, 128, 141–2, 213; and nationalism, 4–5, 24, 108, 266; popular, 266, 316, 317, 377, 379, 402; reading, 56–7, 61, 65n16; transmission of, 63, 395–6, 403, 415; university, 264–5, 307, 378
culture, high, 266, 373, 387; desirability of, 122, 198; relationship to, 298, 377, 386; resistance to, 258–9, 182; Shakespeare as, 200, 208, 391; theatre as, 110, 376
Culture and Anarchy (Arnold), 86n18
Cumyn, Steve, 228

Curnock, Richard, 163
Curzon, Sarah Anne, 59
Cushman, Charlotte, 223
Cushman, Robert, 238, 320–1
Cycle des rois, Le (Asselin), 369n2
Cymbeline (Shakespeare), 277–89; productions described, 134n13; productions listed, 20, 413; scholarship on, 290n2, 302; variant texts for, 290n3

Dafoe, Chris, 28
Dagenais, Pierre, 33, 175
Dale, Ernest A., 70–1, 75, 85n9, 86n16
Darden, Christopher, 318, 387
Davenport, Jean, 13, 193
Davey, Frank, 334
David, Gilbert, 175
Davidson, Kerry, 252n2
Davies, Brenda, 21
Davies, Emlyn, 77
Davies, Robertson, 21, 37, 413–14; 'Special Study' by, 120–2; and SST, 78, 85n10; on Stratford Festival, 25, 127–8; on theatres, 10–11, 22
Davis, Donald, 20
Davis, Jim, 204
Dawson, Anthony B., 28
Day, Moira, 157n7
Day-Lewis, Daniel, 160
Dean, Charlotte, 152, 154, 227
deconstruction, 250, 251
de Gaulle, Charles, 181
demiurge, 307–8
democracy, 18, 93
Denham, Robert D., 294, 306
de Poutrincourt, Sieur, 144
Derrida, Jacques, 306, 342
design: for *Hamlet*, 166, 168–9; and politics, 145–6, 156; representing

Canada in, 146, 148; for *Twelfth Night*, 178
de Vasconcelos, Paula, 184
de Vere, Edward. *See* Oxford, Earl of
dialectic, 299
Dick's Kids (St John's), 131n2
Dickinson, Peter, 338n14
Diltz, Bert, 85n10
Dinicol, Keith, 163
Doat, Jan, 33, 176
Dodd, John, 85n10
Dollimore, Jonathan, 131n3
Dominion Drama Festival, 21, 195, 413, 414, 415; purpose of, 114; reaction to, 198, 199
Donaldson, Peter, 169
Donne, John, 359
Donnelly, Ignatius, 257, 261
Donnelly, Pat, 185
Doran, Terry, 150
Dorsinville, Max, 330–1, 403
Dostoevsky, Fyodor, 345
Doucette, Leonard, 6
Drakakis, John, 403, 404, 406
drama, 37, 198; academic programs for, 18, 112–13, 201, 203–4, 205, 235; Canadian dependence for, 19, 35; development of Canadian, 83, 91n44, 95, 113, 116, 141, 335n4, 392n4; student, 202–4
Dramatic Club (Queen's University, Ontario), 20
Dramatic Society (University of Alberta), 20
Dramatic Society (University of Manitoba), 20
Dream in High Park (Toronto), 28, 29, 131n2
dreams, 279
Dryden, Ken, 372

Dubois, René-Daniel, 343–4, 348, 349
Ducharme, Réjean, 180
Duchess of Malfi, The (Webster), 203
Due South, 160
Duncan, Sara Jeannette, 45
Duncannon, Viscount, 21
Dunlop, W.J., 86n20
Dunlop, William, 163
Dvorak, Marta, 379, 380, 393n9
Dyde, W.S., 20
Dykstra, Ted, 37

Eagleton, Terry, 402, 403
Earl Grey Music and Dramatic Trophy Competition, 20
Earle Grey Shakespeare Festival, 73, 117–18
Eaton's Girls Club, 82
economy: and culture, 303, 333; of labour, 222–3, 224–5; liberal, 216, 228; of reproduction, 391; of revenge, 301; of theatre, 222–3
Edinborough, Arnold, 145, 162
Edinburgh Festival, 128
education: elementary, 38–9; self-, 50–1; Shakespeare in, 17, 38, 50–1, 93–4, 106n14, 400, 402–3
Edward III (Shakespeare), 38
Edward de Vere and the War of Words (Appleton), 265
Edwards, Murray, 6, 10
Egervari, Tibor, 37, 185–6, 191n17
Eggleston, Wilfred, 414
Eliot, T.S., 103, 358–60, 368
Elizabeth II, 77
Elizabeth Rex (Findley), 398
Elizabethan era. *See* Renaissance
Elizabethan World Picture, The (Tillyard), 387

Ellesmere, Lord, 264
Elsinor/Elsineur (Lepage), 34
Emerson, Ralph Waldo, 256, 257
Enfants de Chénier dans un autre grand spectacle d'adieu, Les, 180
English Players, 14
English Speaking Union of Canada, 38–9
Équipe, L', 33, 175
Erasmus, 48
Erickson, Peter, 406, 407
essentialism: and national identity, 317, 320, 330; and selfhood, 242, 249; of Shakespearean, 119, 323, 328
ethnicity, 372, 375–7
Euringer, Alfred, 135n25
Eve (Fineberg), 136n25
Événement 38, 34

Fables of Identity (Frye), 18
Fairbanks Wharf Theatre (Halifax), 12
fantastic, 365
farce, 322
Farrakhan, Louis, 318, 387
Farther West, New World (Murrell), 336n7
fascism, 337n13
Fechter, Charles, 12
Feder, Alison, 196–7
Fellowship (Tait), 135n25
feminine unconscious, 355
feminism, 316; anti-, 85n15; gender and genre in, 377–8, 389, 391; gender and race in, 385–6; in productions, 242–3, 348–50; and Shakespeare, 379, 403; and theory, 307, 394n20, 407
Fenwick, Gillie, 210n5

Fenwick, Moya, 210n5
Feore, Colm, 164, 165
Festival de théâtre des Amériques, 34, 183, 190n15
Figgy Duff, 200
Filewod, Alan, 131nn5–6, 326–7, 328
Findlay, L.M., 18
Findley, Timothy, 23, 37, 398
Fineberg, Larry, 136n25
Fink, Howard, 105n2
First Canadian Shakespeare Festival, 21–2
First Nations, 303–4; position in Canada, 144, 313, 329–30, 338n14; and racism, 316, 328–30; and Shakespeare, 31–2, 213, 401
First Stage: The Making of the Stratford Festival (Patterson), 122
First World War, 19, 154–5, 167, 413; and Canadian identity, 275, 283, 327
Fischlin, Daniel, 37
Fishkin, James, 216–17
folk songs, 146, 158n9
Follows, Megan Porter, 25, 157n6
Follows, Ted, 20
Fool, 361–2, 378–9
Fools of Time (Frye), 18, 300
For Coloured Girls Who Have Considered Suicide When the Rainbow is Enuf (Shange), 386
Foreign Shakespeare (Kennedy), 396
Forrest, Edwin, 13
Fortier, Mark, 37, 378, 380, 395
Foucault, Michel, 243
Fragments d'un lettre d'adieu lus par les geologies (Chaurette), 362–3
Fraser, John, 159
Frederic Douglass Self-Improvement Club (Amherstburg), 50

Freeman, Neil, 236, 245–7, 252n2, 253nn15–16
Frehner, Harry, 166
Freud, Sigmund, 368
Frick, Nora Alice, 94, 96, 97
Friedman, Milton, 216
Frisby, Walter G., 74
Frost, Stanley Brice, 336–7n9
Frye, Northrop, 85n10, 314, 358; on Canadian culture, 302–5, 335n4; critical development of, 293–6; on cultural location, 3, 274, 285; importance of, 18, 292–3, 306, 307; liberalism of, 293, 304, 306; on Shakespeare, 296–301, 325, 352
Fuchs, Elinor, 220
Furness, H.H., 51–2
Future Shakespeare Company (Toronto), 315

G.K.C. (van Bridge), 135n25
Gaboriau, Linda, 353, 366
Gallant, Mavis, 106n16
Galloway, Pat, 163
Gard, Peter, 204, 208
Gardner, David, 27, 158n11
Garebian, Keith, 158n11, 397–8
Garneau, Michel, 37, 184; tradaptation by, 182; translations by, 33, 183, 190n12, 190n15
Garnier, John Hutchinson, 35
Garrick, David, 14, 241, 252n7
Garvey, Marcus, 318, 387
Gascon, Jean, 34, 177, 178
Gass, Ken, 37
Gélinas, Gratien, 24, 415
gender, 268, 271, 302; and actor, 31–2, 193, 214, 215–19, 223–9; and casting, 163, 212, 230n8; and character, 171, 215; and class, 374, 377;
construction of, 373–6, 377; and genre, 377–9, 389, 391; and identity, 226, 358, 372; performance of, 218, 219, 227; and power, 226; and race, 383–7, 389–90; representation of, 358; and tragedy, 358, 360, 389
genre, 349; adaptation as, 315, 317–18, 321; and gender, 377–9, 389, 391; of *Harlem Duet*, 318–19, 381, 387, 389–90; and nationalism, 100, 293
Geordie Space (Montreal), 336n7
Germain, Jean-Claude, 37, 181
Gertrude and Ophelia (Clarke), 350–1
Gesta Danorum (Grammaticus), 344
Gibson, Mel, 160, 204
Gielgud, Sir John, 162, 241
Gikandi, Simon, 405
Gilbert, Helen, 159–60
Gilbert, Sir Humphrey, 7, 27
Gilbert, John, 227
Gillmore, Jack, 92
Gillson, A.H., 107n18
Globe Theatre (Regina), 315–16
Glossop-Harris Company, 194
God Caesar (Price), 315
Godwin, Mary, 21
Goodnight Desdemona (Good Morning Juliet) (Macdonald), 37, 255–6, 321, 371; context of, 390–1; gender and genre in, 377–9, 381, 389, 391; identity in, 267–9, 271, 348–50; language in, 269–71; source in, 386, 388, 393n10
Gottler, Mara, 252n2
government: arts support by, 74–5, 104, 116, 122; theatre funding from, 110–11, 115, 199, 202, 211n13
Governor General's Award for Drama, 267, 321, 371–2

Grace, Julia Wales, 413
Grammaticus, Saxo, 344
Grand Opera House (Toronto), 12
Grand Theatre (London), 415
Grandmont, Éloi de, 180
Granville-Barker, Harley, 19, 21, 132n6, 178, 243
Graves, Robert, 320
Graves, Warren, 328–30, 338n15
Gray, John, 31, 135n25
Grdevich, Sabrina, 169, 171–2
Great Cryptogram, The (Donnelly), 257
Green, Nina, 255, 265, 272n9
Greenblatt, Stephen, 358, 359
Greet, Ben, 14
Grein, J.T., 21
Grey, Earl, 20
Grey, Earle, 21, 73, 80, 112; artistic principles of, 118–19
Groome, Margaret, 23–4
Gross, Paul, 160
Grotowski, Jerzy, 31
Groulx, George, 34
Group of Seven, 276
Guerre, Yes Sir!, La (Carrier), 135n25
Guinness, Alec, 24
Gurik, Robert, 37, 167, 180–1, 182, 184, 315
Gushue, John, 202
Guthrie, Tyrone, 23, 116, 121, 161; on Canadian Shakespeare, 24, 126, 141–3; production style of, 123–5, 134n19, 143; on Stratford Festival, 26, 156n2

Hall, Allan, 200
Hall, Amelia, 414
Halpern, Richard, 358–60, 367–8
Hamilton, Barbara, 415
Hamlet (Shakespeare), 159, 378, 394n17, 412; adaptations of, 31, 34, 94, 99, 100, 106n14, 344–5, 349–51; Canadian, 33, 159, 160, 161, 164, 172; criticism on, 294–5, 301, 342, 345, 367–8; first production of, 32, 161; history of, 162, 253n22; politics in, 166–8, 173n7; productions described, 11, 21, 28, 29, 31, 203–4, 235–6, 249–50, 251n1, 336n7; productions listed, 9, 12, 14, 16, 20, 30, 33, 70, 84n7, 85n8, 160, 183, 194, 198, 201, 211n14, 392n2; psychology in, 170–1; reviews of, 117, 161–6, 168–71, 173nn7–9, 202, 204; sexuality in, 167, 168–9, 171–2; at Stratford, 159–72; in translation, 187–8, 189n6, 190n11; variant texts of, 164–5, 170, 173n5, 235
Hamlet, prince du Québec (Gurik), 167–8, 180–1, 315
Hamletmachine (Müller), 345, 367
Hansberry, Lorraine, 386
Hanson, Debra, 146, 166, 168–9
Hanson, Elizabeth, 317, 327
Harlem Duet (Sears), 37, 327–8; allegory in, 383–4; awards for, 321, 371; Black culture constructed in, 318–20; Black history in, 381–3, 386–9; class in, 382; context of, 390–1; gender and race in, 383–7, 389–90; genre of, 318–19, 381, 387, 389–90; music in, 381, 389–90, 393n12; Shakespeare in, 387, 394n17
Harris, Lawren, 20
Harris, Mike, 216, 230n7
Harrison, G.B., 20, 106n14
Hart House Theatre (Toronto), 20, 70, 115
Hart House Touring Players, 82, 84n6

Harvey, Gabriel, 265
Hausvater, Alexandre, 34
Hawkes, Terence, 403, 404
Hawthorne, Nathaniel, 256
Healy, Thomas, 400, 404
Heavysege, Charles, 35, 36–7, 335n6
Hébert, Paul, 176
Hegel, G.W.F., 307–8
Heliconian Club (Toronto), 71, 85n11
Hendry, Tom, 135n25
Hennig, Kate, 173n5
I Henry IV (Shakespeare): adaptations of, 94, 96, 106n14, 369n2; productions listed, 9, 16, 198
II Henry IV (Shakespeare): adaptations of, 96, 105n10, 369n2; productions listed, 9
Henry V (Shakespeare), 283; adaptations of, 94, 105n10, 369n2; Canadianized, 144–5, 155; productions described, 128–9; productions listed, 24, 70, 78; as war propaganda, 89n34
I Henry VI (Shakespeare): adaptations of, 105n9, 106n12
II Henry VI (Shakespeare): adaptations of, 105n9, 105n10, 106n12
Henry VIII (Shakespeare), 274; and imperialism, 76, 77; productions listed, 16, 70, 78, 194; productions reviewed, 72
Herbert, John, 37
hermeneutics, 63
hermetics, 357, 358, 368
Hermitage Gardens (Montreal), 33
Heyme, Hansgunther, 251n1
Hibbard, George, 18
Hicks, R. Keith, 76, 85n10
Hill, Anita, 318, 383, 394n14

Hinton, Peter, 353, 366
Hirsch, John, 162, 414
historicism, 99–100, 243, 390; new, 192, 197, 359, 407; and temporality, 212–15, 339, 347–8, 351–2; and universalism, 236, 241–2, 244–7, 249
history plays, 99–103, 105n10, 300, 307. *See also titles of plays*
Hjartarson, Paul, 399
Hockey Night in Canada, 95
Hodder, Morris, 200
Hodgdon, Barbara, 248–9
Hoeniger, F.D., 18
Hoffman, Guy, 34
Holden, John, 133n11
Holderness, Graham, 341
Holinshed, Raphael, 325
Holman, William, 70–1
Holmes, John, 202, 210n5
Horace, 48, 60–1
House, Eric, 20
Howard, Jean E., 403–4
Howe, Joseph, 412
Huculak, Maggie, 226
Hughes, Langston, 318, 383, 387
Hulme, Peter, 396
humanism: aspirations to, 213, 214–15, 380; and character, 238, 242–3; liberal, 243, 293, 304; and theatre, 111, 116–17, 120, 371; transcends difference, 178, 185–6, 189
Humphrey and the Dump Trucks, 37, 315, 371, 377, 391
Humphreys, Chris, 29–30
Hutcheon, Linda, 36, 313–14, 394n18
Hutt, William, 20, 161; and *Hamlet*, 163, 168, 169
Hyland, Frances, 157n6
Hysterica (Rose), 31

identity, 159; and authenticity, 325–7, 329–30, 333–4, 337n13, 398; coherence of, 184, 217–18, 238, 285–7, 380; and community, 313, 373; cultural, 3–4, 209n1, 266, 304; and gender, 226, 358, 372; loss of, 287, 331; narratives of, 36, 220; and other, 342; phantom, 341, 349, 361; politics of, 317, 320, 326. *See also* national identity

ideology, 301–2, 305–7, 340–1

I Hate Hamlet (Rudnick), 204

Iliffe-Ean, Douglas, 77

Imperial Theme, The (Knight), 18

imperialism, 45, 89n33; and art, 307, 400; cultural, 192, 280, 391, 404, 408; embodied, 291n4; and gender, 360; and language, 278–80, 281–2, 292, 304, 329; resistance to, 280–3, 390. *See also* colonialism; postcolonialism

Imperialist, The (Duncan), 45

indigene. *See* First Nations

Ingram, Neil, 161

Inook and the Sun (Beissel), 135n25

interculturalism, 320

interpenetration, 306, 314

Ionesco, Eugène, 354, 359, 364, 367

Irving, Henry, 11, 13, 241

Irving, Washington, 61

Itwaru, Arnold Harrichand, 399–400

Ivšić, Radovan, 370n6

Jack, Donald Lamont, 135n25

Jackson, A.Y., 20

Jackson, B.W., 18

Jackson, Jesse, 318, 383, 387

Jackson, Michael, 384, 394n15

Jacques, Stephane F., 34

Jameson, Anna, 49, 52, 57

Jameson, Robert, 50

Jansen, David, 155, 218, 226, 227–8

Jarry, Alfred, 344–5

Jennings, Charles, 105n11

Joanneau, Joël, 354

Johnson, George, 414

Johnson, Samuel, 277

Jones, Andy, 199, 200, 202

Jones, Cliff, 38

Jones, Emrys, 285

Jones, Gordon, 200, 202–3, 206, 211n15

Jones, Sandra, 135n25

Jonson, Ben, 71

Joyce, James, 358

Julius Caesar (Shakespeare): adaptations of, 94, 99, 106n14, 321; productions described, 207, 211n16, 315; productions listed, 14, 194, 392n2; in translation, 190n11, 197

Jung, Carl Gustav: on alchemy, 355, 358, 363; in *Goodnight Desdemona, Good Morning Juliet*, 269, 349, 380, 391

Junior Theatre (Ottawa), 414

Kahn, Coppélia, 226

Kean, Charles, 12

Kean, Edmund, 12

Keats, John, 277

Keefer, Elsie, 71–2

Keilly, Jillian, 207–8, 209

Kemble, Charles, 12

Kemble, Fanny, 12

Kennedy, Dennis, 311, 396

Kennedy, Lorne, 163

Kertzer, Jonathan, 327, 337–8n13, 398–9

King, Charmion, 20

King, Mackenzie, 21, 81, 277, 280
King, Martin Luther, 318, 383, 384, 387, 389
King, Rodney, 381, 383, 393n11
King, Thomas, 289–90
King John (Shakespeare), 26; adaptations of, 31, 105n10
King Lear (Shakespeare), 277, 285, 367; adaptations of, 14, 31, 34, 99, 229n2; Canadianized, 158n11; canonicity of, 212–13; cross-casting in, 212, 215–19, 223–9, 229n2, 229n4; liberal humanism in, 215, 219–20, 222, 225, 229n4, 301; marketing for, 216; patriarchy in, 226; productions described, 25, 31; productions listed, 12, 14, 16, 31, 183, 201, 204, 392n2; reviews of, 225, 227–8; staging of, 214–15, 220–2, 227, 229n2; variant texts for, 229n6
King Lear (Tate), 14
Kirchhoff, H.J., 169, 392n2
Kisseliov, Oleg, 187–8
Kline, Kevin, 160
Knight, G. Wilson, 16, 18, 20; academic affiliation of, 75–6, 85n10; as director, 72, 73, 84n7; and imperialism, 88n29; on Shakespeare and religion, 75, 79–80, 86n21
Knight of the Burning Pestle, The (Beaumont), 203
Knowles, Richard Paul (Ric), 37; on actor training, 248, 252n4; on political Shakespeare, 157n7, 214, 228, 229n4; on postcolonialism, 360; on Stratford, 131n4, 132n6, 213, 229n3
Koenig, Josephine Anna, 85n14
Koltai, Judith, 252n3
Komisarjevsky, Theodor, 133n13
Kramer, Ken, 315

Kramer, Sue, 315
Kristeva, Julia, 40–1, 365
Krysinski, Wladimir, 366
Ksonzek, Natasha, 399–400
Kugler, D.D., 229n6

Lacan, Jacques, 358, 367, 368
Lafleur, Joy, 161
Lamming, George, 382, 393n13, 403
Langham, Michael, 24, 28, 134n17; directs *Hamlet*, 161–2; directs *Henry V*, 128–9, 144–5, 155, 157n7; directs *The Merchant of Venice*, 26; directs *Othello*, 25; *Romeo & Juliet* by, 145, 157n8
language: and class, 269–71; and culture, 182, 184, 190n12, 302, 314; end of, 361–3, 365, 367, 396–7; and imperialism, 278–80, 281–2, 292, 304, 329; and nationalism, 337n13; and postcolonialism, 206–7; and translation, 180, 206–7; universal, 239–42, 404
Laroche Roland, 30
Last of the Tsars, The (Bawtree), 135n25
Lawrence, Charles, 332
Lawrenchuk, Michael, 31
Laycock, John, 148
Lear (Ronfard), 182
Leaves of Grass (Whitman), 259–61
Leech, Clifford, 18, 85n10
Lefèbvre, Paul, 190n12, 354
Legault, Father Émile, 33, 176
Legend, The, 235
Léger, Annick, 191n19
Leggatt, Alexander, 18, 20, 293
Leonowens, Anna Harriette, 15
Lepage, Gaston, 185
Lepage, Monique, 33

Lepage, Robert, 12, 30, 33–4, 183–4; production of *A Midsummer Night's Dream* by, 188, 267; production of *Roméo & Juliette* by, 157n8, 315
Lépine, Stéphane, 357
Lescarbot, Marc, 7, 27
Lessard, Jacques, 252n3
Létourneau, Jacques, 33
Levac, Claude, 179
Lévesque, René, 167, 181
Lévesque, Robert, 185, 191n18
Lévi, Éliphas, 357
Levy, Barry, 252n2
Lewis, Amanda, 38
liberalism, 215, 229, 375
Licorne, La (Montreal), 336n7
Lieblein, Leanore, 33, 164, 397
Life of Columbus (Irving), 61
Liscinsky, Michael, 163
Lismer, Arthur, 20
Liston, William T., 173n9
Literary History of Canada (Frye), 305, 306
literary societies. *See* Shakespeare clubs
literature, 38; Canadian, 398–9; minor, 35–6; Shakespeare's works as, 15, 28, 96, 107n17
literatureism, 62
Little Theatre movement, 20–1, 78, 83, 196
Livingstone, Ken, 201
Lloyd, David, 35–6
Locandiera, La, 191n21
Logos, 297
Log Shanty Book-Shelf, 47, 48; *After Gleanings* (1896 catalogue), 51; context of, 58–9; exhibits, 55–7, 60, 61–2, 63; *Horace Canadianizing* (1894 catalogue), 60; *Pioneer Shakespeare Culture in Canada* (1892 catalogue), 47–8, 54, 57, 61; *Seneca's Prophecy and Its Fulfilment* (1897 catalogue), 61
London Shakespeare Group, 210n10
London Theatre Company, 195–6, 199, 211n13
Longshoremen's Protective Union (LSPU) Hall, 199, 202, 206, 211n16
Loomba, Ania, 160, 406–7
Lorca, Federico García, 344
Love's Labour's Lost (Shakespeare), 261; adaptations of, 96; Canadian premiere of, 20; productions described, 29, 211n16; productions listed, 392n2
Loyalism, 81, 90nn38–40
Lundrigan, Art, 210n7
Luscombe, George, 30, 83
Lyceum Players, 194

Mabou Mines, 212, 229n2
McAfee, Heather, 291n8
McArthur, W., 11
Macbeth (Shakespeare), 325; adaptations of, 94, 96, 99, 105n7, 106n14, 206–7; productions described, 33, 205–6; productions listed, 12, 13, 14, 20, 29, 34, 85n8, 134n13, 194, 201, 204, 206, 211n14, 392n2, 413; reviews of, 196–7; in translation, 182, 183, 190n15
Macbeth, Madge, 414
McCall, Gordon, 28, 157n8, 249–51, 315
McCamus, Tom, 170
McCowen, Alec, 210n4
MacDonald, Ann-Marie, 37, 255; awards for, 321, 371; and feminism, 377–80; on identity, 266, 267–71, 348–50

MacDonald, J.H., 20
Macdonald, Rose, 66, 69, 84n5
McDonald, Tim, 166
MacDonald, Wilson Pugsley, 414
McDougall, Robert, 97
McGee, C.E., 24, 397
Machiavelli, *Prince*, 300–1
Machine infernale, La (Cocteau), 367
MacHomer: The Simpsons Do Macbeth (Miller), 37, 316
MacKay, J. Keiller, 66–7, 69, 75, 80, 84n4, 86n20
McKennitt, Loreena, 37, 335–6n6
McKinnie, Michael, 31
McLeay, Franklin, 15
McLuhan, Marshall, 40
McLuskie, Kathleen E., 166
MacRare, Farqhuar J., 80
Macready, William Charles, 12
Mad Boy Chronicle (O'Brien), 344–5
Magnificat (Chaurette), 370n4
Maillet, Antonine, 37, 177, 189n6, 331–3
Makarov, Vitaly, 188
Makaryk, Irena, 398
MakBed (Campbell), 206–7, 208
Making Culture: English-Canadian Institutions and the Arts before the Massey Commission (Tippett), 405
Making of de Macbeth, *Le* (Pigeons International), 183–5
Malcolm X, 318, 383, 387, 389
Man's Moral Nature (Bucke), 259
Manitoba Theatre Centre (Winnipeg), 25, 160
maps, 56, 285
Maps of England (Gikandi), 405
Maraden, Marti, 26, 163
Marchand de Venise, Le. See *Merchant of Venise, The*

Marchand de Venise *de Shakespeare à Auschwitz*, Le (Egervari), 185–6, 191n16–18
Margolies, David, 124–5
Marine, Alexandre, 187–8, 336n7
Mark (Wylie), 135n25
marketing: of productions, 191n20, 216; and promotional materials, 29, 202; use of Shakespeare in, 82, 91n42
Marleau, Louise, 145
Marshall, Tom, 395, 401
Martin-Harvey, Sir John, 132n6, 413, 414
Marx, Karl, 342
Marxism, 198, 305–8
Mason, Lawrence, 82–3
Mason, Libby, 31
Massey, Raymond, 14
Massey, Vincent, 392n4; class of, 75, 87n24, 90n41; cultural colonialism of, 327; on national theatre, 22–3, 110, 132n6
Massey Commission (1949–51), 22, 120, 122, 372, 392n4
Massey Commission report (1951), 73, 111; on amateur groups, 69, 72; on Americans, 90n41; and arts funding, 75, 104, 392n4; defines culture, 74, 86n19, 119; 'Special Study' with, 120–2; on theatre, 23, 117, 119–20
Massinger, Philip, 71
master signifier, 340
Matas, Carol, 345–7
materialist criticism, 25, 134n15; cultural, 31–2, 131n3, 192, 197; and cultural discourse, 248–9; Frankfurt School of, 134n15; and subjectivity, 237–9, 242–3

Mathews, Robin, 317
Mawson, Michael, 238, 241
Mazumdar, Maxim, 136n25
Measure by Measure; or, the Coalition in Secret Session (anon.), 37
Measure for Measure (Shakespeare), 243; adaptations of, 34; productions listed, 392n2; reviews of, 162–3
Mechanics' Institutes, 51
Meech Lake Accord, 150, 171, 277
Mégère apprivoisée, La. See *Taming of the Shrew, The*
Mégère de Padova, La, d'après La Mégère apprivoisée *de William Shakespeare* (Micone), 186
Meighen, Arthur, 76, 87n28
Meiklejohn, John Michael, 415
Memorial University Drama Society. See MUN Drama
Mennonites, 158n10
Merchant of Venice, The (Shakespeare), 7; adaptations of, 94, 106n14, 183–6; and anti-Semitism, 185–6; and postcolonialism, 160; productions described, 412; productions listed, 9, 12, 14, 26, 183, 194, 195, 198; in translation, 180, 185–6, 191n16, 191n18
Merry Wives of Windsor, The (Shakespeare), 299; productions listed, 69, 73, 85n7, 85n8, 392n2
Messier, Jean-Frédéric, 37
Metcalfe, John, 314, 317
Micone, Marco, 37, 186–7, 188, 191n21–2
Middleton, J.E., 14
Midsummer Night's Dream, A (Shakespeare), 325; adaptations of, 31, 94, 96, 105n7; productions described, 27, 28–30, 33, 34, 207, 267; productions listed, 14, 20, 78, 201, 392n2; reviews of, 188, 202, 206; in translation, 175, 180, 187–8, 190n13
Mignolo, Walter, 401
Mikalachki, Jodi, 290n2, 291n4
Millais, John Everett, 173n8
Miller, Paul, 166
Miller, Rick, 37, 316
Minh-ha, Trinh T., 403
Mitchell, Ken, 37, 315, 371, 379, 391
Mnouchkine, Ariane, 242
Modern Times Stage Company, 31
modernism, 354, 358–60; and tragedy, 359, 367–9
Modjeska, Helen, 13
Moiseiwitsch, Tanya, 24, 145, 161
Molière, 335n4
Monette, Richard, 24, 397; directs *As You Like It*, 146, 148–51, 156; and *Hamlet*, 163, 168, 170–2, 173n7
Montreal Drama Guild, 414
Montreal Repertory Theatre, 21, 117, 414
Monty Python, 344
Moodie, Andrew, 381
Moore, Dora Mavor, 23, 84n6, 134n13
Moore, Mavor, 3, 23, 111, 133n8
Morgan-Powell, S., 14–15
Morley, Malcolm, 27, 134n13
Mort des rois, La (Claing), 369n2
Moss, John, 396–7
Mossop, Brian, 320
mourning, 368
Moyse, Charles Ebenezer (Belgrave Titmarsh), 37, 315, 322–4, 337n9
Mrs Jameson and the Collier Emendations (Scadding), 49, 52
Much Ado about a Midsummer's Shrew (Smallwood et al.), 200

Much Ado About Nothing (Shakespeare): productions described, 211n16, 274; productions listed, 16, 70, 85n7, 85n14, 210n10, 392n2; variant texts of, 320–1
Mullens, Raymond, 72
Müller, Heiner, 345, 358, 367
multiculturalism, 313, 320; official, 335n2, 375; representation of, 275–6, 341; and Shakespeare, 31, 286
Mummer's Troupe, 192, 198–9
mummering, 193, 198
MUN Drama (formerly Memorial University Drama Society) (St John's), 131n2, 196, 202–4
Murphy, Sarah, 37
Murray, Heather, 17, 64n7, 399
Murrell, John, 336n7
music, 101–2, 374, 394n15; rhapsodic blues, 381, 389–90, 393n12
mythology, 279, 301–2, 306

Namjoshi, Suniti, 37
Nanabush, 31
Nanaimo Festival, 131n2
Nardocchio, Elaine, 11
narration, 101–2
Nashe, Thomas, 265
National Arts Centre (Ottawa), 25, 190n15
National Film Board, 122
national identity: and authenticity, 327, 329–30, 333–4, 337n13, 398; construction of, 267, 318, 326–7; and difference, 305, 316–17, 320, 342, 343, 395; essential, 320, 396; exclusions in, 264, 272n8, 319, 401; jokes about, 275, 291n5; and literature, 36, 292, 336n9, 337n13, 338n14; multiplicity in, 33, 40–1, 275–6, 313, 322, 341; representation of, 275–6; 315, 340–1; Shakespeare as basis of, 271, 326, 328–30, 408; and Stratford Festival, 129, 172; and war, 141, 275, 283–4
National Radio Drama Contest (CBC), 95
National School Broadcasts, 94, 106n14
national theatre, 131n6, 328; and DDF, 114; models for, 112–16, 117, 121, 127; need for, 19, 22–4, 108–11, 131nn5–6; purpose of, 111–12, 116–17, 119–20, 326; Stratford as, 127–9, 213, 398
National Theatre School of Canada, 176
nationalism, 168, 378; Acadian, 316, 332–3; construction of, 45, 397; cultural, 4–5, 100; and genre, 100, 293; and globalization, 290; and hegemony, 372, 374; literary, 338n14; and Loyalism, 81, 90n38; post-, 25; process of, 4, 83, 90nn39–41, 107n18, 131n4, 277–8; Québécois, 190n13, 302–3, 369n2; and theatre, 141, 143, 179–80; and tyranny, 132n6, 337n13; and universalism, 213, 409n1. *See also* national identity
Nationalism and Minor Literature (Lloyd), 35
Natural Perspective, A (Frye), 18
naturalism, 217–19, 225
Naturalism in the Theatre (Zola), 225
NDWT Theatre Company (Toronto), 30
Necessary Angel Theatre (Toronto), 212, 214–29
Need for a Permanent Theatre at Stratford, The (Stratford Festival), 130

negative capability, 277
Neville, John, 163
New Criticism, 103, 106n13
Newfoundland, 338n16; Arts and Culture Centres in, 197–8, 199, 203, 210n7, 210nn9–10; colonialism in, 192; indigenous drama in, 198–9; 210n12; Shakespeare in, 9–10, 13, 194, 198–1, 203, 205; theatre history in, 192–5, 208
Newfoundland and Labrador Arts Council, 202
Newfoundland Broadcasting Company, 37
Newfoundland Shakespeare Company, 201–2
Newfoundland Tempest (Resource Centre for the Arts), 199–200
Newfoundland Travelling Theatre, 210n11
Newman, Fred C., 272n7
New Play Society, 23, 116, 133n11, 134n13
New Shakspere [sic] Society, 57, 58
Nicholl, Charles J., 355
Nielsen, Dorise, 132n7
Nightwood Theatre (Toronto), 371, 378, 380–1, 393n7
Norwood, Gilbert, 85n15
Notes and Emendations to the Text of Shakespeare (Collier), 52, 57
Nouveau Théâtre Expérimental (Montreal), 190n13, 369n2
Nouvelle Compagnie Théâtrale, 33
Nyland, Frances, 161–2

O'Brien, Michael, 37, 344–5
O'Connor, Marion F., 403–4
O'Donnell, Mike, 252n2
Oedipus, 367–8

Official Languages Act (1969), 184
Old Vic Theatre Company (England), 121, 134n13, 134n17, 176
Olivier, Sir Laurence, 162, 172, 383
On Being a Canadian (Massey), 90n41
Ondaatje, Michael, 135n25
O'Neill, James, 14
O'Neill, Paul, 193
Ontario, 72, 214–15; employment-equity legislation in, 214, 223–5, 229n5, 230nn7–8
Open-Air Playhouse (Montreal), 27, 117, 134n13, 414
oral tradition, 298, 305
Orenstein, Gloria Ferman, 360, 362, 365
orientalism, 389
Orkin, Martin, 274, 406–7
Osborne, W.F., 18
Oscar Remembered (Mazumdar), 136n25
Osment, Phillip, 352
Othello (Shakespeare): adaptations of, 37, 99, 315, 318–20, 348–50, 371–94; criticism on, 294, 394n20; handkerchief in, 375–6, 388–9, 394n20; and postcolonialism, 160; productions described, 25; productions listed, 9, 12, 13, 14, 16, 32; reviews of, 392n2; variant texts of, 394n21
Other, 316, 346; and identity, 304–5, 342; and imperialism, 360, 390; and universalism, 174–5, 178
Ottawa Briefs, 110–11
Ottawa Drama League, 413, 414
Ottawa Dramatic League, 20, 413
Ottawa Little Theatre, 21, 117, 413, 414
Ottawa Shakespeare Festival, 28

Ottawa Women's University Club, 413
Ouimette, Stephen, 169
outdoor productions. *See* productions, outdoor
Ovid, 325
Owens, Margaret, 366, 370n3
Oxford, Earl of, 255, 264

Paglia, Camille, 274
Paik Nak-chung, 408
Palomino, Mercedes, 34
Pancheva, Evgenia, 274
Panet, Brigid, 28
Paper Wheat, 373
Paraschuk, Douglas, 397
Paré, François, 331
Parker, Carolyn, 145
parody, 228, 265; in adaptation, 35, 333, 377; and postmodernism, 36, 394n18
Parsa, Soheil, 31
Pater, Walter, 39
Patmore, Coventry, 35
Patterson, Tom, 23, 39, 116, 121, 122-3, 142
Peacock, Lucy, 163
Pearson, Lester B., 181
Pechter, Edward, 371
Pellan, Alfred, 178
Pelletier, Gérard, 177
Penfield, Wilder, 148
Pennell, Nicholas, 163
Pennington, Bob, 392n2
performance. *See* production
Performing Nostalgia (Bennett), 174, 406
Pericles, Prince of Tyre (Shakespeare), 278, 296, 298, 394n17; adaptations of, 343-4, 348, 349
Pericles, Prince of Tyre, by William Shakespeare (Dubois), 343-4, 348, 349
Perlin, John, 197-8, 210n8, 210n10
Persephone Theatre (Saskatoon), 371
Pettigrew, John, 392n2
Phillips, Nathan, 86n20
Phillips, Robin, 24, 26, 129; directs *As You Like It*, 148; directs *Hamlet*, 163
Philosophy of the Plays of Shakspere Unfolded, The (Bacon), 256
photographs, 67-9, 340
Pickthall, Marjorie, 37
Pigeons International, 183-4
Pioneer Shakespeare Culture in Canada. *See* Log Shanty Book-Shelf
Plant, Richard, 6
Playing Shakespeare (Barton), 240
playRITES Festival (Calgary), 344
Pleasures of Exile, The (Lamming), 403
Plummer, Christopher, 16, 24, 27, 39, 145, 161-2
Plutarch, 325
poesis, 301
Pollock, Sharon, 135n25
populism, 258, 266-7, 320-1, 373, 376-7
Porter, John, 75-6, 79, 87n25
Portman, Jamie, 392n2
Postcolonial Drama: Theory, Practice, Politics (Gilbert and Tompkins), 159-60
Post-Colonial Shakespeares (Loomba and Orkin, ed.), 406-7
postcolonialism, 4, 304, 307, 359; and *Hamlet*, 159, 164, 167; and language, 206-7; and Shakespeare, 271, 378, 390, 396, 403; and *The Tempest*, 31, 160, 172n2, 304, 330-1, 396

postmodernism, 244, 359; characteristics of, 36, 311; and fragmentation, 278; and *Hamlet*, 159, 166; and parody, 36, 394n18
Potter, Christopher, 148
power relations, 242, 250, 303, 334
Pownall, Leon, 164
Prairie Anthology, 373
Pratt, E.J., 85n10
Presley, Lisa Marie, 384, 394n15
Price, Addison B., 12
Price, Marjorie, 315
Prigmore, Seth, 12
Prince Pedro (Garnier), 35
productions: Canadianized, 144, 151; context of, 174–6, 184–5, 187–8, 189n3; failure of, 201–2; funding for, 199, 202; history of, 4–5, 14, 212; in Newfoundland, 193, 195, 197, 199, 204–5, 208; outdoor, 7, 14, 131n2, 175, 204–6, 315; power relations in, 242, 250; and pragmatism, 248; radio, 92; student, 200–1, 235–6; success of, 176–7, 204, 215; touring, 158n11, 371; underground, 207–8; women in, 413
professional theatre, 114–16, 120, 133n11
Provincetown Playhouse, July 1919 (Chaurette), 362
Provost, Gilles, 415
Prud'homme, Firmin, 32
psychoanalysis, 103, 106n13, 161, 355
Public, The (Lorca), 344
'Pulpit and the Stage, The' (Bengough), 410–12
Pygmalion (Shaw), 180

Quayle, Anthony, 100
Quebec: culture in, 179, 182, 187, 190n7; effect of Second World War in, 175, 178; nationalism in, 190n13, 302–3, 336n7, 369n2; Shakespeare production in, 32–5, 157n8, 174–7, 180, 354, 358–9; theatre in, 174–6, 183, 190n13, 369n2; universalism in, 174, 177–9, 181, 185, 187, 190n13, 369n2
Queens, The. See *Reines, Les*
Queen's Arctic Theatre, 11

race, 372, 373–4, 381
Racine, Jean, 364
racism, 316, 381, 401; in *Othello*, 318–19, 375; in Canadian theatre, 319–20, 329, 371
radio drama, 92–4, 96–8, 104–5; audience response to, 97–8, 100, 103; production style of, 98–9, 101
Radio Guild (NBC), 93
Rain, Douglas, 26, 169
Raisin in the Sun, A (Hansberry), 386
Rama, Angel, 36
Rawls, John, 216
Rea, Stephen, 238, 242
reading, 379; context of, 274, 280, 283; culture, 56–7, 61, 65n16; and identity, 314, 403; versus performance, 248, 355, 367; resistant, 378, 380, 390–1; theories of, 60–3, 395, 408
Ready Steady Go (Jones), 135n25
realism, 356, 358, 360, 387
Reaney, James, 30, 135n25
reception, 157n8, 183, 403, 410; context of, 149–50, 156, 214–15, 223–5, 229. *See also* audience
Redgrave, Sir Michael, 162
Reed, Carole Ann, 224
Reeves, Keanu, 160

regionalism, 302, 372–3, 378, 389, 390, 392n4
regional theatres, 25, 30, 317, 327
Reid, Kate, 20, 415
Reid, Robert, 150
Reines, Les (Chaurette), 35, 336n7, 353–70
Renaissance, 61, 63, 267; interiority in, 241, 252n6; new, 77, 407; theatre, 244, 358–9; world-view, 100, 387, 401
Renan, Ernest, 318
Repercussion Theatre (Montreal), 27, 28, 131n2
Repositioning Shakespeare (Cartelli), 407
representation, 308, 315, 358; cultural, 275–6, 334, 341; and race, 319, 371; and unrepresentability, 340–1, 351–2
reproduction, 242–3, 345–6
Republic of Vanuatu (formerly New Hebrides), 206
Resource Centre for the Arts (formerly Resource Foundation for the Arts) (St John's), 199
reviews, 72. *See also titles of plays*
Rewriting Shakespeare, Rewriting Ourselves (Erickson), 407
Richard II (Shakespeare): adaptations of, 94, 96–7, 99, 101–2, 105n10, 369n2; productions listed, 100; in translation, 175, 180
Richard III (Cibber), 14
Richard III (Shakespeare): adaptations of, 14, 105n10, 336n7, 353–69, 369n2; productions described, 24, 25, 30, 193, 211n16; productions listed, 9, 12, 13, 70, 201, 206, 413; reviews of, 202; translations of, 354, 368

Richards, G.H., 11
Richards, Gladys, 210n5
Riot (Moodie), 381
Rising Tide Theatre (St John's), 199, 201, 203–4, 205–6
Rittenhouse, Charles Burket, 414
ritual, 368
Robbins, Bruce, 45
Robeson, Paul, 318, 383, 387
Robinson, John Beverley, 59
Robinson, Lady, 67, 86n20
Robson, Frederic, 16–17, 19
Rock and Roll, 373
Rocking Horse Theatre (Victoria), 28
Rodéo et Juliette (Germain), 182
Roi Gordogane, Le (Ivšić), 370n6
Roi se meurt, Le (Ionesco), 354, 364
Rollins, Howard, 392n2
romance, 302, 346, 348–9, 352. *See also titles of plays*
Romeo and Juliet (Garrick), 14
Romeo and Juliet (Shakespeare): adaptations of, 910, 14, 96, 105n7, 344, 348–50, 376, 377–80; Canadianized, 145, 156, 157n8, 274, 315; language in, 239–40, 241–2; productions described, 29, 235–6; productions listed, 12, 14, 16, 21, 70, 84n7, 85n8, 183, 194, 201, 413; reviews of, 145; in translation, 175, 180; variant texts of, 52
Ronfard, Jean-Pierre, 35, 37, 182, 184, 190n13, 336n7, 358, 359, 368, 369n2
Rooke, Leon, 37, 255, 266–7
Rose, Richard, 211n16; on casting, 214, 218–19; production of *King Lear* by, 31, 212, 214–29, 229n2; production of *Taming of the Shrew* by, 151; production of *Two Gentlemen of Verona* by, 24, 151–5, 156, 158nn12–13

Rosencrantz and Guildenstern Are Dead (Stoppard), 163–4, 204, 235, 351, 354
Rosie Backstage (Lewis and Wynne-Jones), 38
Ross, David, 199
Ross, Donna, 199
Rossi, Ernesto, 13
Rough Magic. See *Cloning Miranda*
Roux, Jean-Louis, 34, 177, 180, 189n6, 190n11
Royal Alexandra Theatre (Toronto), 82
Royal Shakespeare Company (formerly Stratford-upon-Avon Festival Company), 82, 122
Rubess, Baṇuta, 378
Rubin, Don, 6
Ruby, Bradley C., 166
Ruskin, John, 294–6
Ruthven, K.K., 402
Rutter, Carol, 242
Rymer, Thomas, 394n20

Saddlemyer, Ann, 6
Sadiq, Laara, 252n2
Saint-Denis, Michel, 176
St George's Society (Toronto), 53, 79, 88n32, 89n33, 89n35
St James Literary Society (Montreal), 262, 264, 272n7
St Laurent, Louis, 392n4
St Lawrence Centre (Toronto), 25
Salle Gesù, 185
Salter, Denis, 182; on adaptation, 339–40, 341, 408; on national theatre, 109–10, 131n5–6; on postcolonialism, 167, 172, 339, 405
Salutin, Rick, 372
Salvini, Tomasso, 13

Sandwell, Bernard K., 15, 19, 36, 75, 110
satire, 322
Satyricon, The (Hendry), 135n25
Saul (Heavysege), 35
Scadding, John, 48, 61
Scadding, Rev. Henry, 15, 17–18; biographical information, 48–9, 65n15; historical work of, 48, 58–9; and literature, 56–7, 60–3; as pioneer, 47, 50, 57; scholarship of, 49–53, 58, 64n8, 64n10
Scadding Cabin, 54–5
Scarfe, Alan, 392n2
Schagerl, Jessica, 33, 397
Schoenbaum, Samuel, 255
scholarship: amateur, 51, 264–5; dramatic, 18, 102; interdisciplinary, 400–1; postcolonial, 396, 405–6; professional, 5, 17–18, 151, 265–6, 272n1; satirized, 322–4, 328
Scholte, Tom, 252n2
Scott, Duncan Campbell, 414
Scott, F.R., 277
Sealy-Smith, Alison, 319, 387
Sears, Djanet, 37, 318–20, 321, 327–8, 371, 380–90
Second World War, 21, 79, 211n16; effect on culture, 108–9, 111, 116, 132n6, 134n15, 141; and Quebec, 175, 178
secret, 357, 368–9
selfhood. *See* subjectivity
Seneca, 61, 63
Seneca Indians, 63
Sense of Power, The: Studies in the Idea of Canadian Imperialism, 1867–1914 (Berger), 45
Seymour, Michel, 327
Shakespeare, the Seer – the Interpreter (Scadding), 51, 52, 53, 57, 61

Shakespeare, Theory, and Performance (Bulman, ed.), 339
Shakespeare, William, 32, 236–7, 256; appropriation of, 174, 181, 213, 325; and Canadian playwrights, 98, 105n8, 117; Canadianized, 20, 54, 100, 118, 142–4, 235–6, 397, 402, 406, 412; as commodity, 38–9, 82, 118–19, 124, 134n15, 209; compared with St George, 79–80, 89n34; and context, 48, 50, 59–60, 102–3; and cultural capital, 214, 321; cultural presence of, 104, 337n11, 410; and cultural value, 202, 208–9, 328; exceeds representation, 340–1, 342–3, 344, 347, 352; as foundation, 121, 125–6, 141, 324–5; grave of, 256, 271, 322–3, 379; hidden meaning of, 256, 257, 268, 272n6, 324, 328, 349; and historicism, 118–19, 228–9, 246; images of, 341, 412; mobility of, 396–7, 403–4, 405–9; relevance of, 53–4, 87n28, 207–8; variant texts of, 51–2, 158n13; and war propaganda, 21, 79–80, 88n29, 89n34, 100; works as drama, 28, 96, 121; works as literature, 15, 28, 96, 107n17. *See also titles of plays*
Shakespeare Association of America, 265
Shakespeare and Postcolonial Conditions (Salter, ed.), 339, 405
Shakespeare Can Be Fun! series, 38
Shakespeare Club (Montreal), 264, 272n7
Shakespeare clubs, 15–16, 50, 64n7, 405, 413
'Shakespeare Cycle,' 93–4
Shakespeare effect, 253n11, 314, 327, 335n3; contextualized, 39–40, 243–4, 317
Shakespeare for Fun and Profit, 30–1
Shakespeare in the Park (Winnipeg), 28, 29, 131n2
Shakespeare in the Red (Winnipeg), 31–2
Shakespeare in the Ruins (Winnipeg), 29, 131n2
Shakespeare Memorial Theatre (Stratford-upon-Avon), 80, 100
Shakespeare on the Platform (Ottawa-Carleton), 38
Shakespeare Quarterly, 265
Shakespeare Reproduced: The Text in History and Ideology (Howard and O'Connor), 403–4
Shakespeare on the Saskatchewan (Saskatoon), 28–9, 157n8, 160, 315
Shakespeare by the Sea (Halifax), 27, 29, 38, 205
Shakespeare by the Sea (Logy Bay, Nfld.), 27, 204–5, 206, 208, 211n16
Shakespeare Society (Halifax), 16
Shakespeare Society (Montreal), 16, 117, 414
Shakespeare Society of Toronto, 16, 20, 75, 83n2; Annual Dramatic Contest of, 74, 86nn20–1; elitism in, 67, 69, 75–6, 81; fundraising by, 71–2, 73, 86n17; gender imbalance in, 67–9, 70, 71–2, 85n8; imperialism in, 76–7, 80, 88n30, 89n35; meetings of, 66–7, 69–71, 88n31; membership in, 69, 73; origins of, 83, 84n6; and patronage, 69, 84n4, 86n20; philanthropy of, 73, 86n16; productions by, 69–70, 72–3, 84n7, 85n8, 85n14; purpose of, 16, 69, 73–4; and religion; Shakespeare's

birthday celebrations by, 78–81, 89n35, 90n36; venues used by, 66, 67, 69–70, 71, 78, 85n11, 88n30
Shakespeare's America. America's Shakespeare (Bristol), 131n3, 402
Shakespeare's Books: Contemporary Cultural Politics and the Persistence of Empire (Campbell), 407
Shakespeare's Dog (Rooke), 255, 266–7
Shakspere's Skull and Falstaff's Nose (Moyse), 37, 315, 322–4, 327–8, 337n9–10
Shand, Skip, 229n6
Shange, Ntozake, 386
Shannon, Sean, 38
Shaw, George Bernard, 180
Shaw, Joseph, 210n5
Shaw Festival (Niagara-on-the-Lake), 210n5, 241
Shepherd, Elizabeth, 163
Sheppard, Nancy, 148
Sherlow, Lois, 35
Showalter, Harrison, 135n24
Shuster, Frank, 38, 321
Siemon, James R., 278
Simcoe, Elizabeth Posthuma, 48
Simcoe, John Graves, 48, 59–60, 65n1
Simpson, O.J., 383
Sinclair, Lister, 96, 97, 99, 105nn7–8
Sinfield, Alan, 122, 131n3, 136n27, 406
Sipes, John, 37
Sixth Sense, The, 342, 348
Skog, Troy, 252n2
Skylight Theatre (Toronto), 131n2, 213
Smallwood, Joey, 197, 210n7
Smallwood, Wendi, 200
Smith, Goldwin, 314
Smith, Maggie, 24

Smith, Marion B., 18
Smith, William H., 264
Sobiesky, Leon, 202
Société Française Shakespeare, 179
Soir des rois, Le. See *Twelfth Night*
Somerset, J. Alan B., 392n2
Songe d'une nuit d'été, Un. See *Midsummer Night's Dream, A*
sonnets, 31
Sophocles, 367–8
Spanish Tragedy, The (Kyd), 203
Speaight, Robert, 176
Specters of Marx (Derrida), 342
Spedding, James, 258
Spence, Denny, 210n5
Spivak, Gayatri Chakravorty, 395–6
Sprung, Guy, 30
staging, 16, 123–4, 164
Staveley, Annette, 210n6
Stead, John, 169
Stephenville Festival, 211n14
Stoppard, Tom, 163–4, 204, 235, 350–1, 354
Strachan, John, 48
Stratford Festival (Stratford Theatre Festival), 80, 119, 128–9; Canadian plays at, 129, 135n25, 398; Canadianized Shakespeare at, 144–56; as commodity, 129–30, 133n10; cultural authority of, 30, 108, 121, 128–30, 133n10, 182; and cultural colonialism, 25, 192, 213, 397; cultural importance of, 19, 26, 123–30, 134n17, 142, 335n4; design of, 112, 127–8, 143; effect of, 22, 73, 104; founding of, 23–4, 92, 122–4, 141, 156n2; marketing material for, 115, 123, 126–30, 135n23; as national theatre, 127–9, 131n4, 213, 398; objectives of, 123, 125–6; opening

night at, 128, 142; production style at, 16, 25–6, 31, 115, 117, 123–5, 166, 168, 241; productions by, 159–72, 197, 229n3, 392n2, 414; training at, 127, 143, 238
Stratford Festival Young Company: production of *Hamlet*, 161, 163–4
Straw Hat Players, 27
Straznicky, Marta, 22, 415
structure, 299–301, 320, 351, 354
subjectivity, 36, 301: construction of, 237–8, 372, 374, 386, 390–1; and essentialism, 242, 249; liberal-humanist, 215, 220; *noir*, 341–2, 343, 344, 346–7, 349; and tragedy, 365, 366. *See also* identity
sublime, 340, 349
Sullivan, Barry, 12
Summer on the Bight (Trinity, Nfld.), 205, 211n14
summer theatre, 131n2; cultural value of, 7, 29, 208, 211n16; as entertainment, 27–30, 204–6; production style in, 28–9, 108
Sun Never Sets, The (Crean), 135n25
surrealism, 359, 360, 362, 365, 370n6
Swanson, Cecil, 77–8, 80, 86n20, 89n35

Tait, Michael, 135n25
Tamahnous Theatre Workshop (Vancouver), 31
Tamburlaine the Great (Shakespeare), 128
Taming of the Shrew, The (Shakespeare): adaptations of, 8, 9, 12, 14, 34, 177; Canadianized, 151; criticism on, 248–9, 253n21; first production of, 10; productions described, 25; productions listed, 9, 13, 20, 21, 27, 85n8, 134n13, 183, 195, 392n2, 415; reviews of, 176, 177, 187; in translation, 34, 180, 186–7, 188
Tarragon Extra Space (Toronto), 381
Tarrying with the Negative (Žižek), 340–2
Tate, Nahum, 14
Taylor, Charles, 325–6
Taylor, Kate, 26, 205, 206, 207, 211n16, 382
Teacher, The (Gray), 135n25
Tempest, The (Davenant and Dryden), 14
Tempest, The (Shakespeare), 39–40, 54, 209, 274, 324; adaptations of, 14, 34, 99, 199–200, 336n7, 345–7, 352, 401, 403; and postcolonialism, 31, 160, 172n2, 304, 330–1, 396; productions described, 204, 213; productions listed, 12, 16, 20, 28, 34, 85n14, 183; reviews of, 211n15; in translation, 183, 190n13
Tempest, The/tempête (Lepage), 34
Terry, Ellen, 13, 173n4
Têtes Heureuses, Les (Chicoutimi), 190n15
text, 311, 351; authority of, 242, 251, 336n7, 408; as construct, 246–8, 249, 251, 253n17, 379; culturally different, 395–6; historicity of, 243–4, 246; and performance, 357, 360–1, 378; power in, 246, 378; relationship to actor, 240–1, 253n20; as source of character, 238–9, 245; sub-, 238, 241–2; universal truth in, 239, 245–7
theatre, 249, 380; civilizing influence

of, 110–11, 116–17; and colonialism, 30, 109, 110, 331–3; criticism, 136n27; and cultural identity, 4, 180, 331; and economics, 194, 195, 201, 203, 211n13, 248; entertainment value of, 113–14, 116, 198, 210n8, 316; morality of, 8–9, 410, 412; nature of, 189n3, 359; as production facility, 10–12, 112, 115, 182; Québécois, 174–7, 183, 190n13; and society, 121–2, 125, 179, 196, 198, 214–15, 358, 360; in Toronto, 390–1; training in, 176. *See also* Little Theatre movement; national theatre; nationalism: and theatre; regional theatres, summer theatre
Theatre 1774 (Montreal), 34
Theatre Arts Club, 210n5
Theatre Arts Guild (St John's), 196
Théâtre d'Aujourd'hui (Montreal), 34, 353
Théâtre Blanc (Quebec City), 353
Théâtre-Club, 33, 175
Theatre Columbus (Toronto), 213
Théâtre Deuxième Réalité, 188
Théâtre Distinct (Ottawa), 185, 191n18
Théâtre de l'Egrégore, 30
Théâtre Espace la Veillée, 188
Théâtre Haut Parleur (Ô Parleur) (Montreal), 190n15
theatre history, 144, 192–3; military productions in, 7, 11; scholarship on, 6, 413
Théâtre de Neptune en la Nouvelle-France (Lescarbot), 7
Theatre New Brunswick, 197
Théâtre du Nouveau Monde (Montreal), 34, 183, 190n11, 191n21; co-productions by, 145; *Hamlet* at, 33; *The Merchant of Venice* at, 185–6, 191n18; *A Midsummer Night's Dream* at, 188; *The Taming of the Shrew* at, 175, 176, 177, 186–7
Théâtre de l'Omnibus (Montreal), 369n2
Theatre Passe Muraille (Toronto), 30, 31
Théâtre du Rideau Vert (Montreal), 34, 183, 188, 189n6, 331
Theatre Royal (Montreal), 12, 32
Theatre Royal (Winnipeg), 10
Théâtre du Trident (Quebec City), 188, 190n15
Théâtre Urbi et Orbi (Montreal), 34
Théâtre du Vieux Colombier (Paris), 353–4
They Club Seals, Don't They? 373
This Is for You, Anna, 378
This Island's Mine (Osment), 352
This Sceptred Isle (Knight), 88n29
Thomas, Audrey, 37
Thomas, Clarence, 383, 393n14
Thomey, Greg, 202
Thomlinson, Charles, 202
Thompson, Judith, 37
Tillyard, E.M.W., 387
Timon of Athens (Shakespeare): productions listed, 84n7, 201; reviews of, 72, 166, 202
Tindale, William, 76, 85n10
Tippett, Maria, 73, 132n7, 405
Titmarsh, Belgrave. *See* Moyse, Charles Ebenezer
Titus Andronicus (Shakespeare): productions listed, 29
Tocilescu, Alexandru, 252n1

Tom Patterson Theatre, 168
Tompkins, Joanne, 159–60, 390
Toronto Central Library, 16
Toronto Civic Theatre Association, 113
Toronto Free Theatre, 131n2
Toronto Industrial Exhibition, 47, 56, 62
Toronto Literary Club, 50
Toronto of Old (Scadding), 49, 50
Toronto Shakspeare Club, 50
Toronto Women's Literary Club, 50
Toronto Workshop Productions, 30, 83
To Thine Own Self Be True, 31
touring companies, 8, 9, 19, 412–14; cultural impact of, 13–14, 110; in Newfoundland, 193–5, 197, 206, 210n11
Tovell, Vincent, 111, 133n8
Townshend, Aurelian, 144
tradaptation, 182, 339
tragedy, 270, 301, 319, 354–6; and gender, 358, 360, 389; and modernism, 359, 367–9; personal, 96–7, 99, 300–1, 387; 'rhapsodic blues,' 381, 391; and subjectivity, 358, 365
transcendence, 303, 307, 320
transculturalism, 36, 320
translation, 177, 180, 189n6, 191n22, 206–7
Tree, Sir Herbert Beerbohm, 15
Tremblay, Michel, 180, 370n5
Trilling, Lionel, 337n11
Troilus and Cressida (Shakespeare), 70; adaptations of, 99; productions listed, 20
Trudeau, Pierre Elliott, 181, 335n2, 372, 375
Tudor Myth, 99–100

Turgeon, James Grey, 132n7
Turnbull, Winnifred, 85n14
Twain, Mark (Samuel Clemens), 272n4
Twelfth Night (Shakespeare): adaptations of, 38, 99, 100; productions described, 33, 178, 213; productions listed, 28, 84n6, 183, 194, 197, 210n10, 392n2; reviews of, 162, 203; in translation, 175, 177, 180, 190n11
Twelfth Night for Kids (Burdett and Coburn), 38
Twelfth Night Revels (SST), 78, 81
Two Gentlemen of Verona (Shakespeare): Canadianized, 151, 153–5, 156; productions listed, 24; reviews of, 158n12; variant texts for, 158n13

Ubu Roi (Jarry), 344
Ukrainians, 375–6
United Empire Loyalist House (Toronto), 66, 67, 69, 88n30
United Empire Loyalists, 78
United States of America: Black history in, 382–3, 393n14; and British culture, 258, 267, 402; cultural dominance of, 81, 90n41, 93, 132n6, 275, 404; and economic imperialism, 280; frontier in, 259–60, 262; identity in, 305; and manifest destiny, 259, 262; touring companies from, 14, 110
universalism, 161, 260–1; critiqued, 4, 236, 253n14, 399, 403–4; and drama, 111, 236, 251, 333; and feminism, 349; and particularism, 236, 241–2, 244–7, 249; and Québécois Shakespeare, 174, 177–9, 181, 185, 187, 190n13; in Shakespeare, 28, 31–2, 40, 70, 132n6, 160, 212–15,

228–9; and textual meaning, 239–40, 243–4
Unspeakable ShaXXXspeares (Burt), 402
Ustinov, Peter, 24

van Bridge, Tony, 135n25
Vancouver East Cultural Centre, 31
Vancouver Shakespeare Society, 80
Vernon, Hilary, 210n5
Vertical Mosaic, The (Porter), 75–6, 79, 87n25
Victoria Shakespeare Festival, 28
Vie et mort du roi boiteux, La (Ronfard), 35, 190n13, 336n7, 369n2
Vincent, Thomas, 51
Voaden, Herman, 110–11, 133n9
voice, 337n13; Black, 318, 387; homogeneous, 175, 181–3, 185; and multiplicity, 183, 184, 189, 290; and performance, 174–5, 188, 252n4; universal, 179, 189, 190n13

Wade, Michael, 201, 203
Wagner, Anton, 6, 336n7
Wagner, Vit, 216, 381, 387
Waines, Lisa, 252n2
Walcott, Derek, 209n1
Walken, Christopher, 145
Walkley, A.V., 217
Wallace, Malcolm, 86n19
Wallace, Robert, 372–3
Walsh (Pollock), 135n25
Walsh, Edel, 252n2
Walsh, Kenneth, 162
Walsh, Norman, 210n5
Walterdale Playhouse, 338n15
Walterdale Theatre Associates, 328
Warburton, Charles, 93
Warren, Roger, 290n3
Wayne, Johnny, 37, 321

Wednesday Night (CBC), 92; audience response to, 100, 103, 105n11, 106nn15–16; elitism of, 98, 103–4; programming on, 96, 98, 106n14; significance of, 107n18
Weil, Herbert S., Jr, 163
Weimann, Robert, 277
Weiss, Peter Eliot, 37
Western Theatre Conference, 113
Wheel of Fire, The (Knight), 18
Whitman, Walt, 259–61
Whittaker, Herbert, 6, 11, 111; on Canadian drama, 4–5, 80, 91n44; as director, 25, 133n8; on production designs, 145; on Stratford Festival, 19, 142
Whitted, Brent, 18
Wigh, Sylvia, 196–7
wilderness, 284–5
Willful Pursuits (Deon), 204
William, David, 150, 161, 164–8, 170
William S (Maillet), 331–3
Williams, Nigel Shawn, 387
Wilson, Sir Daniel, 17, 18, 54, 57
Wilson, Harold, 85n10
Winnipeg Little Theatre, 414
Winnipeg Shakespeare Company, 131n2
Winsor, Chris, 216, 219
Winter Studies and Summer Rambles (Jameson), 49
Winter's Tale, The (Shakespeare), 278, 296; adaptations of, 99; criticism on, 352; productions described, 211n16; productions listed, 201; reviews of, 211n15
women: cultural role of, 71–2, 85n13, 85n15; in productions, 413
Women's Art Association (Toronto), 71, 78, 85n11

Wood, Angela, 162
Wood, John, 163
World Wide Web, 40
Worrying the Nation: Imagining a National Literature in English Canada (Kertzer), 398–9
Worthen, W.B., 221; on acting, 217–18, 252n4, 253n16; on authority, 242, 243, 244, 408
Wright, Donald, 66, 67, 84n3
Wright, Janet, 169; as Lear, 212, 215, 217–18, 226, 227
Wylie, Betty Jane, 135n25
Wynne-Jones, Tim, 38

Yachnin, Paul, 18
Yeo, Leslie, 13, 195, 210n5, 211n13
York Pioneers (later Pioneer and Historical Society), 47–9, 55–6, 58, 60, 65n15
Young, Roly, 113–14
Young Vic (England), 166

Zeffirelli, Franco, 160, 171, 172, 320
Zitner, Sheldon P., 18
Žižek, Slavoj, 340–2
Zola, Émile, 225